# Twenty years around

John Guy Vassar

**Alpha Editions**

This edition published in 2024

ISBN : 9789362519801

Design and Setting By
**Alpha Editions**
www.alphaedis.com
Email - info@alphaedis.com

As per information held with us this book is in Public Domain.
This book is a reproduction of an important historical work. Alpha Editions uses the best technology to reproduce historical work in the same manner it was first published to preserve its original nature. Any marks or number seen are left intentionally to preserve its true form.

# PREFACE.

Early in life the author of these letters suffered from ill-health, and necessity obliged him to seek more genial climes in order to escape the rigors of our northern winters. Duty towards his only brother and a beloved uncle induced him to sketch his travels, and keep them advised of his movements. His letters passing into the hands of kind friends, for perusal, led to further inquiries; and demands for publication in a weekly paper in his native city, were the result.

He has always hesitated to come before the Public, although constantly solicited and urged by his friends to do so, as a duty he owed to society; at length, through constant importuning, and to avoid the clamors of those he loves and esteems, he has concluded to accede to their wishes. This book is the result.

Travelling becomes a passion with some, and in this instance, a decided one. Necessity at first, with improvement in health, and finding himself better on the move than when quiet, sight-seeing and obtaining general information became more and more desirable.

After having seen every State and Capital in his own country, his desire was to visit every Capital in Europe. After having seen the antiquities and works of art of Italy, Greece, and Turkey, his ambition led him to see the older objects of Egypt and Asia Minor. Then came the desire to visit the Celestial Empire, and the East Indian world.

The West Indian Islands brought a disposition to see those of the Pacific, and those of the Mediterranean, the Levant, and the Polynesian, Canary, Cape de Verde, Azores. North America, including the Canadas, having been seen, South America in all parts could not be neglected. Northern Africa, Egypt, Syria, Algeria, and Morocco had been visited; but the western and south-western coast of Africa, the Gulf of Guinea, demanded their share of effort and exposure. When in China, he desired to visit Japan, but Commodore Perry had not yet made a treaty. While at Singapore, he wished to embark for Australia; but no opportunity offering during the typhoon season, he was obliged to renounce the idea. Last Spring he made an attempt to get around from the south coast of Africa, but without success. Had he succeeded, his twenty-one years of travel would have probably closed his extended wanderings, as the whole world would have been seen, large portions of it having been repeatedly visited.

He has great reason to be thankful to the Almighty for his preservation of life and health. Surrounded by dangers of every name and nature, while scores of his companions have been swept off by shipwreck, cholera, fever, assassins, and barbarous tribes of savages, or Indians, he has passed unscathed and unharmed.

J. G. V.

# 1839.
# I.

HAVANA, *February 10, 1839.*

By the advice of my physicians my second sea voyage was by the ship Norma, which sailed from the port of New York on the 20th of January. After a passage of fourteen days, with alternate gales and calms, we sighted Abaco, and the Hole in the Wall. We crossed the Bahama Banks; the water was of a bright blue color, with a clay bottom, which was distinctly seen. The thermometer went up to 72°, so we threw, off our winter-garments, and put ourselves in summer apparel.

A cheerful sight was the old Moro Castle, at the entrance of the harbor. It has three hundred guns, and is built upon a rock. Opposite stands a new fort called the Punta, and three hundred yards from the Moro Castle is a gigantic work called the Cabana. These defences are on an immense scale, with heavy rock excavations, and are said to have cost eighteen millions of dollars. When the bill was presented to the Court of Madrid, the old King Ferdinand asked if they were made of silver. The passport system is onerous and rigorous here; but time and progress will produce a change.

The landing, or shipping-port, is a stout, well-planked wharf, of great length, sufficient for the landing of cargoes: vessels lie head on, and discharge and receive over their bows. Our ship anchored in the stream, and boats took our baggage to the Custom-house. We were struck by the novel sights on landing. A large number of negroes was employed in unloading ships, and transporting merchandize, singing the while their merry sailor songs. Mules with heavy saddles, and small trucks on two wheels, were waiting for our effects. Huge carts for heavy goods were drawn by oxen, with rings in their noses, and yokes resting on their horns. Next comes the Volante, or pleasure carriage, which is universally adopted, and, although odd-looking at first, it is extremely comfortable, and is adapted to the climate. Figure to yourself a pair of wheels from seven to eight feet high, and shafts eighteen feet long. Upon these shafts a chaise body suspended with leather-straps. At the extreme end of the shaft the horse or mule, with his braided tail tied up to a large Mameluke saddle. Upon that saddle a shiny, black negro, with leather leggings strapped up to his knees; shoes and spurs, and coat and hat of livery. The hacks, which are rather rusty, stand about the squares for customers; but the equipages of the nobility and wealthy citizens are really magnificent, and the sight of the fair sex, in full dress, on a gala-day when hundreds are seen on the Paseo, is one of the most pleasing and beautiful to be found in any country.

I have just witnessed a display of the kind; some three hundred Volantes were present with a band of music. The vehicles go up on one side of the Paseo and return by the other, driving through a paradise of garden. An accident occurred; the lancers on horseback were instantly on hand to preserve order. The police is numerous and efficient; the men carry spears, and a lantern in the night. The military force is large, and belongs to the regular troops from Old Spain.

The style of building strikes a stranger with surprise as he enters the city. The houses are generally of stone, one or two stories high, and are covered with fluted tiles, or flat roofs of cement. Many of the residences of the wealthy are commodious and magnificent. The building material is a yellow, calcareous stone, which is easily shaped by an axe to any form, and being porous it receives cement readily. The fronts of the houses are painted with gay colors, yellow, pink, or blue. They have low windows, with iron bars for shutters, and curtains supply the place of glass, which is yet almost unknown here. No chimneys are needed, as the cooking is mostly done with earthen furnaces.

Havana is well supplied with market buildings of a quadrangular form: the outer structure is for the butchers, and the interior for venders of fruits and vegetables. The fish-market is tastefully ornamented with marble and porcelain slab counters, and the various kinds of fish thereon have all the hues of the rainbow. The fish market is in the hands of a monopoly, who employ many vessels along the Florida coast for supplies.

A grand masquerade-charity ball has just taken place at the Tacon Theatre, outside the city walls, and it is computed that seven thousand tickets were sold. The great variety of costumes, within and without, representing all the characters that could be suggested to one's mind, the multitude of the dances, and the different strains of music, the five tiers of boxes of open bronze-work, displaying the rich robes and dazzling gems of the lady spectators, gave it additional charms.

I have just returned from the plantation of a fellow passenger, and am much pleased with the rack or gait of my horse, which is peculiar to the island of Cuba. The road, which was rough, was of calcareous stone. The shell, which is easily discovered in the rock, can be cut in any shape; it hardens with age. The house which I visited was comfortable, and pleasantly situated, with negro-houses among groves of oranges, citron and lemon trees, and fields of sugar-cane in the background. The reception was a warm one, for the mistress of the place, an affectionate old lady, was delighted at the return of her son; I witnessed her kindness towards her negroes. The Bishop's Garden gave me an opportunity of seeing tropical plants and fruits in their perfection. It seemed neglected, however, while the Tacon Garden is a splendid affair.

## II.

MATANZAS, *March 1, 1839.*

This is a considerable shipping port. Large quantities of lumber are brought hither by New England vessels, which in return take cargoes of sugar, molasses, and coffee. I saw a drove of mules and horses with pack-saddles, fifty in number, all laden with these articles, coming to market. Twenty-eight of them were laden with four kegs, each containing five gallons of molasses, and were tied head and tail together. One man had charge of that number. In this warm climate they stop and wash or swim their animals in the streams to refresh them; the drivers drink the fresh milk from the cocoa. The number of game-cocks owned here attracted my attention; cock-fighting takes place frequently. I noticed, in passing an inclosure, an arena for practising, and stakes were driven for forty of them, to which they were attached by the leg; some are even valued as high as six ounces, or a hundred dollars; two negroes were cracking corn with their teeth to feed them, and others were sprinkling aguardiente or Cuba rum over their heads and bodies; it gives them a reddish color after the feathers are plucked out. If game, they fight until they die. In the pit they take them up and blow in their mouths, lick their heads, raise their wings, run their bills together, and then put them down to see who will conquer.

In the vicinity are found very extensive caves, inhabited by bats, which are well worth a visit. Myself and a fellow-traveller hired a Volante to visit a coffee estate on the banks of the little Canaimar river. The weather was warm; the rays of the sun were oppressive like one of our July days; it was dry and dusty. We met with droves of muzzled mules laden with products; we crossed the river in scow boats, drawn by a rope. The coffee-tree grows about three or five feet high, and is lopped to make the branches expand, otherwise it grows seven or eight feet in height. The blossom is white, the leaf resembles the laurel of our country, only larger; there is a fragrant but insipid flavor to the blossom; the berry is red, and tastes sweet. On opening it you discover two grains of coffee. It is gathered in baskets, and carried to the yard where they have large earthen floors with descents both ways to carry off the rain; here it remains until perfectly dry, then it passes through a machine which completes it. It is then put up in sacks for market. They commence picking about the 1st of November, and continue until they have finished, often as late as February. The tree lasts fifteen or twenty years, if well attended to.

The Canaimar is a beautiful stream, with high banks covered with trees, and is from fifty to eighty yards wide; it is navigable some fifteen or twenty miles, for schooners up to Barcadero. For pretty scenery it reminds me of the Hudson, but decidedly in miniature.

We saw several fine coffee plantations, and others exhausted, devoted to the production of sugar. Our Calesero with his droll costume wore his sword, which he flattered himself was a great protection after nightfall. The roads were rough, and little travelled by carriages; but it was amusing the way we rattled over the hills with three horses attached to our odd-looking vehicle. We have followed up our visits to sugar and coffee plantations in other directions. Some of the latter are most beautiful with avenues of palms, interspersed with orange and myrtle trees. One sugar estate of three hundred acres turned off three hundred hogsheads of sugar. The owner had one hundred and fifty negroes, one hundred of whom were working hands; we visited their cabins and the sugar-works. He had seventy yoke of oxen, thirty on the grinding mill; they work night and day, five pair at a time, cracking the cane with three large rollers. The juice is insipid but healthful; it soon becomes acid when exposed to the sun. It runs direct from the mill in reservoirs, and in the iron boilers with sides of brick-work. It is dipped from one pot to the other, and boiled until the guarappa or syrup passes into reservoirs or granulators, after which it is put into hogsheads, and stands over vats to allow the escape of the treacle or molasses, which is pumped up and forwarded to market. The crushed stalk is dried and used for fuel, when engines are in vogue as they now are. The cane may be used up entirely. In the cutting the cattle follow and consume the tops; the balance decays and enriches the soil. The negroes cut the cane systematically with long knives in the fields. The cane here springs up again without replanting, and lasts from five to seven years.

In the gardens were guava trees, from which the delicious jelly is made, and pomegranates, oranges, and other fruits. The most graceful tree is the palm: it grows straight to a great height, with rings from the root, and looks like a column of marble of greyish blue color until within fifteen feet of the top, when it lessens in size, and is of a bright green color, with an offshoot or thread that grows up like the winding-sheet of a candle, about four feet to the top, from which spread the branches, like an umbrella. From the green spot spring bunches of berries which are green, but ripen red, and are used by the negroes to feed their hogs. The mango, shaddocks, sweet oranges, and forbidden-fruit, are interesting to the stranger. We have just paid the sad rites to one of our Northern invalids; only four of us followed him to the grave. The funeral of a child three years old has just passed; this beautiful infant lies in a half coffin, with face and hands exposed, a wreath of flowers about its head, and a bouquet in its little hand. One half of the coffin is supported by four boys in fashionably cut garments, and bright coat-buttons; the other half is supported by other boys. The friends of the dead do not go to the grave.

The manner of burial being so different from ours, one is struck with every peculiarity. Some distinguished person who died recently had ten negro bearers dressed in military apparel, red and grey livery trimmed with lace, with black chapeaux and feathers. Ten Volantes followed. The bodies are buried in trenches, with all their clothing on, which is cut before interment. They are put in the ground without the coffin, quick-lime is thrown upon them with a little earth; others are buried over them. When room is required, the ground is dug over, and the fragments are burned.

The convicts here are employed upon the public works, and in the streets, pounding stone and regulating the thoroughfares; they are guarded by soldiers, and wear chains on one side from the waist to the ankle. I recently accompanied a planter who wanted to add to his stock of negroes. A cargo of two hundred and eighty-five had just arrived from Africa. They were in the Barracoons, men, women, and children. I had some oranges, which I cut up and gave them; they did not know what they were at first, but soon found out, and flocked around me and drove me to the door, with their hands all up, clamoring for more. It was amusing to see the scampering and jubilee when the fruit was thrown among them. They were fond of snuff, tobacco, and pipes. The planter made a selection of twenty, at twenty-four ounces, or four hundred and eight dollars each, and they seemed happy to get out of the barracks.

# III.

SOUTH-WEST PASS, BALIZE, *April 1, 1839.*

The steamer Tacon brought me down from Matanzas to Havana. The renowned Ravels were drawing immense houses at the Tacon theatre. I took the railway for Guines, a small town, towards the south side of the island, much resorted to by invalids. We made many excursions on horseback, visiting different cafetals and sugar plantations, passing through orange groves, the eye resting upon acres of pineapples. I attended high mass at the Cathedral in Havana, where rest the ashes of Columbus, which are said to have been brought from St. Domingo. Our passengers returning to the States have converted our brig into a sort of Noah's ark; it has twenty poodle dogs, quantities of pigeons, doves, Guinea pigs, game cocks, etc., and about ninety thousand oranges on deck. No steamer offering, we were obliged to take this brig. We should have made the passage in five days, but a norther came on within twelve hours' sail of the Balize, and we were among the Chandeleur Islands at one time without a chronometer, and the officers could not tell our course. The first appearance of two rival tug-boats, the Lion and Mohican, in the distance, running for us, was a grateful sight. We are now rapidly ascending the river, whose water is charged with alluvial deposit, and is very muddy. The low banks, covered with grass and cane-brakes, arrest the floating logs from the undermined forests of the upper rivers, brought down by the freshets; alligators are seen crawling upon them, and basking in the sun's rays. Further up, we come in sight of sugar plantations, with the whitewashed huts of the negroes. The appearance of a high-pressure steamer, with hurricane deck, is very striking at first sight; and the eternal puff of the escaping steam, may be heard distinctly for miles. Towing on the Mississippi, against a current six miles per hour, requires enormous power. The shipping at New Orleans is immense, extending for six miles along the Levee, which is of a semicircular form, and gives New Orleans the name of the Crescent City. The cotton warehouses and presses are of gigantic size, to meet the demands of the trade. Many of the public buildings are substantial, and in good architectural taste. The St. Charles and St. Louis hotels are of a superior order, and are among the largest in the United States. The exhibition of merchandize on the levees, consisting of cotton, sugar, molasses, tobacco, lard, flour, grain, and all the products of the Western and Southern states bordering on the rivers, is immense, and connecting here from a hundred steamers with a fleet of shipping for most of the ports in the world, gives a faint idea of the trade of this commercial city.

A drive over the shell road, along the banks of the canal, to the Lake House, and the return by rail from Lake Pontchartrain—a peep at the French opera in the second municipality—a drive to Carrolton, the new and upper portion of the city—a walk over the battle-field below the city, where General Jackson defeated the British—will suffice for this visit, as I return again. I now take the steamer for the *new Republic of Texas*!

# IV.

MOBILE, ALABAMA, *April 27, 1839.*

The steamship New York carried us to Galveston in fifty-six hours. The fine weather promised us a shorter passage, but our ship grounded for several hours at the south-west Mississippi pass. When we sighted the few masts in the distance from the harbor of Galveston, a gay wag pointed them out to a verdant passenger as the steeples of the city. Only a limited number of buildings are yet erected. A wrecked steamer on the beach with upper cabins answered the purposes of a hotel. Levees will be made for the protection of the city from inundation; the city lies on Galveston island at the foot of Galveston Bay, which situation, with an energetic and increasing population, will render it in time a place of great trade and commerce. A small high-pressure steamer took us up to the Capital of the Republic, Houston, named in honor of the late president and hero of San Jacinto.

We had a fair number of cabin passengers, and a goodly number in the steerage, migrating to the new settlements.

One of those amusing mock criminal cases which help to beguile the tedious hours at sea, came off on the charge of a slight indiscretion against a New Orleans merchant. Counsel in behalf of the state and defence of the prisoner was procured; the judge took his seat; the sheriff arrested the prisoner; witnesses were subpœnaed; special-pleading began, and the examination of defence before the jury, half of them ladies, being the entire number of our fair passengers, contributed not a little to the amusements, in which Finn, the renowned punster and comedian, took part. The jury retired to the ladies' cabin, dropped the curtains upon the court, rendered a champagne verdict, which resulted in a similar sentence upon the judge, advocates, and sheriff, the consequence of which was no want of exhilarating material for the voyage.

A beautiful sail up the bay; a view of the battle-ground of San Jacinto; a description of the positions occupied by the Mexican forces of Santa Anna, and the Texans in hot pursuit; the perfect slaughter of the former; the finding of the Mexican leader up a tree, and many other details from an old Texan who was engaged in the combat, passed the time agreeably, and we were in the narrow Buffalo Bayou, the branches of the trees grazing our wheel-houses. The little town of Harrisburg, fifteen miles below Houston, was burnt by the Mexicans. It should have been the head of navigation, it was remarked, but the Allens founded the city as it now is, and built a capital and engaged the settlers to occupy it. There are some thirty frame houses being erected per month. I visited the log cabin still standing, occupied formerly by Sam Houston. Took a ride on the seven-mile prairie; visited General Hunt,

Secretary of the Navy, President Lamar, and was presented to Sam Houston, Ex-President, at New Orleans, on my return to that city. The accommodations, of course, in a new country just opened, cannot be expected to equal those of old settled cities. Carriages are not yet introduced; stumps still stand in the streets. Time has scarcely permitted to make foundation walls, but the buildings are set up on blocks, giving the pigs and chickens free ingress underneath.

My luggage was taken on a wheelbarrow, and at the first hotel I stopped at I verdantly called for a single room; the landlord smiled, and said that he had only a single one, which was a fifty-bedded room, and all occupied. My curiosity induced me to see it. There were rows of bunks, not unlike coffins in size, a little raised from the floor. I then proceeded to another hotel, which was also full, the rush of emigrants, land-purchasers, and speculators, being great.

I found a private house, but did not ask for a single room; there were three apartments for three beds each, with two and three in a bed. My Mississippi companion and myself were obliged to double up; we could lie upon our backs and study astronomy through the roof, and in case of rain put our clothes under the bed.

Our single rough pine table was well covered with arms, which travellers use largely for safety and shooting. Deer are found in great abundance, consequently venison, as well as fish and oysters, in the vicinity of Galveston, is abundant.

After some few excursions I returned to New Orleans, much gratified with my trip, and the exhibition of American energy in adapting itself to the settlement of a new country.

I asked a Mississippi land speculator what he thought of Houston. He unhesitatingly replied: "It is the largest three-year-old I ever saw."

The steamer Merchant brought me through Lake Pontchartrain, sighting Fort Pike in the pass to Lake Bourgne, passing the mouth of Pearl river and the Dauphin Island, into the Gulf of Mexico, and up Mobile Bay to the city. The shipping lies thirty miles below; light draught ships and brigs come up to the city; heavy vessels load by lighters; large numbers of steamers are at the wharves from the Upper Tombigbee and Alabama rivers. It is an agreeable city, with hospitable inhabitants, and an extensive cotton trade; many broad fine avenues and streets are studded with the Pride of India, a tree filling the air with fragrance.

My friends have driven me out to Spring Hill in the suburbs, with its pretty private residences, the race-course, Choctaw point, and other localities. The hotel is comfortable; the markets and restaurants are well supplied, and lunches at the saloons supply the inner man with game, Barataria Bay oysters, and all their accompaniments. The South prides itself upon its choice imported liquors, and the genuine leaf Havana cigars. The sabbath is well observed here; attendance at church is general. The negro population is well dressed and happy.

---

N. B. Some years since the writer visited Galveston, Houston, and many other portions of Texas in the interior, and was highly gratified at the great growth of the cities named, the style of brick dwellings which had replaced frame buildings, the march of civilization, and the general comfort. In the interim of time since his first visit he had seen the early settlement of California and Oregon, as well as the new states of Iowa, Minnesota, Missouri, Illinois, and watched the progress of American advancement.

# V.
## TRIP FROM ALABAMA THROUGH FLORIDA AND GEORGIA.

The steamer Champion brought us in nine hours to Pensacola, well known as a United States' Naval Station. We took the steamer Leroy for Lagrange, with three passengers, passing through Santa Rosa sound; the island of the same name rose in the distance, by moonlight, like a walled city, with some verdure and shrub trees, and the beach of white sand appeared like snow; the main land, covered with live oak, has been purchased by Government, for ship building. We left Pensacola at five P.M. and arrived at Lagrange in time for breakfast, and took stage for Choctahatchie, Dead Lake, where we left the conveyance and went a mile and a half in small boats to connect with another stage coach. This Dead Lake is surrounded with cypress trees, and abounds with alligators; a huge fellow, with distended jaws, showed himself beside our little canoe; we fired a musket shot and he sank. We crossed the Choctahatchie, a rapid stream, in a small boat, walked up the hill to a barn, and found a stage to proceed. Magnolias of immense height were found in the everglades in abundance, and in full bloom. A day's ride from Lagrange brought us to the village of Mariana; we stopped at Holmes' Village, P. O., and dined by the road in a log-house, in a wilderness of pines; we could look through the sides and roof of this dwelling. The woman said she had nothing in the house for dinner, which was true: salt bacon, corn bread, and buttermilk, were the prominent articles. At Mariana, twenty-seven miles from the Chattahoochie, we found supper and the first signs of a town since we left Pensacola. Leaving Mariana, the stage had seven passengers inside and three outside, with heavy luggage; coming down Chipola hill, the equilibrium was almost lost; we were going over when the driver let the horses go to save an upset, and they ran away. A refractory horse has given us a good fright. We crossed the Apalachicola river in a flat, poled up the stream, and took the current to the opposite bank; negroes lay by a camp fire waiting for the boat. Walked a mile to Mount Vernon, and stopped at Scott's new Arsenal and Magazine; the steamer coming in view, we heard the puff of steam fifteen miles. I took the steamer Commerce for Apalachicola; we had undertaken to haul a raft of timber, when we saw the Irvington coming. Come on, boys, says the Irvington. Don't be alarmed, says the Capt. of the Commerce. Firemen all anxious, passengers hurried on board. Cut the hawser, cries the Capt.; now go it. The vibration of the boat was excessive; we could scarcely raise a cup to the lips at table; boilers and flues almost red hot, the upper deck grew so hot that my clothing in the trunk was heated through. The scenery is pretty, the trees and growth of underbrush and cane-brake, down to river bank of this serpentine river, are picturesque.

We beat our enemy, and he was obliged to round to, as a make-believe, for wood.

I found Apalachicola a small place, with some good brick stores; the shipping lies below, brigs and schooners only get over the bar. They are trying to make St. Joseph a rival, with a railway from Iola to the junction of the Chattahoochie and Flint rivers, but it is not probable that the river trade can be diverted from its natural channel. I visited cotton plantations to see the young plant growing, and the gins for dressing; saw the poisonous moccasin snakes, five feet long, and alligators in abundance. Visited Quincy, a county seat, in Florida; the stage had eleven passengers, nine inside, among the rest a gentleman's black servant; in the night I found him fast asleep, quietly resting on my shoulder. I supped at Bainbridge, and tolerably well, and one man offered a Watumpka bill, to which the woman objected, and he said he could pay when he came along again. He left his card to the amusement of all concerned. We halted at a place in the piny woods, where the man had his wife and a dozen white-headed, flaxy children, dirty as pigs; he said he was from North Carolina, and could give us corn bread and molasses, fat bacon, and three cups of coffee, for the whole party.

At twelve at night coming to a station, I found a part of my baggage and valise missing; I put a negro on the track and went myself in search through the woods; detached one of the lead horses and sent another negro in hot pursuit. I heard or saw some wild animals in the brush, and hurried up and found the boys who had found my baggage by the road-side, where it had fallen. Arrived at Macon, on the Ocmulgee river; it is a pretty city, with several churches, a young ladies' seminary, one of the largest in the Union, besides several banks. Rode from thence to Milledgeville, the capital of Georgia, thirty-six miles; a rough country, scenery different from that of Florida. A State Convention was being held to reduce the number of representatives in the Legislature. The public-houses were crowded. The Government House and States Prison are prominent buildings.

The heat and dust were overpowering. I took supper at Sparta at twelve at night, arrived at Warrenton at four A.M.; went to bed and slept for the first time in three days. I was rejoiced to find the first railroad since I left New Orleans; rode fifty-one miles to Augusta, on the Savannah river. The yellow nankeen cotton is produced in this section. They are now raising 20,000 bales of staple annually. The city has ten thousand population. There are many northern people among the residents; the markets, wharfs, public buildings, and society give evidence of thrift and progress. The Morus multicaulis speculation is now the rage. This reminds me of meeting a northern man in Matanzas, who proposes taking out plants to get the winter growth and profit by the advance of the cuttings. The bubble will soon burst. Hamburg, in South Carolina, lies on the opposite bank of the Savannah, connecting with a bridge, where are seen the fortifications of nullification days.

# VI.
## TRIP FROM AUGUSTA, GEORGIA, TO NEW YORK.

I left Augusta by the South Carolina Railroad for Charleston, stopping at Aiken, a dining station on the road, where a hurried dinner was taken, and the bell rung when the party was half through, which induced one of the number to snatch a roasted fowl, to the amusement of the passengers and chagrin of the landlord. The distance was one hundred and thirty-six miles, mostly in light soil and pine wood region. There were some good plantations. When in sight of the Four Mile House I recognised the spot which I had visited some years previous. The great oak trees were still standing as if clad in mourning, with the moss three or four feet in length hanging from the branches.

In the low humid regions of Texas, and upon the banks of rivers, are found large quantities of this material, which is dried and used for mattresses, cushions, etc., and is quite an article of commerce. My mind was carried back to my former retreat on Sullivan's Island, upon which is situated Fort Moultrie, and which is the resort and residence of many who fly thither to enjoy the sea air, and to escape the fevers produced from the low banks of the Ashley and Cooper rivers, and the marshes in the neighborhood.

I tarried six days enjoying the hospitalities of numerous friends whom I had known there, and in Cuba. My health had suffered some from exposure, and I was happy to repose myself. The steamer Gov. Dudley took me to Wilmington, N.C., upon Cape Fear river.

The great quantity of saw-dust from the steam mills and bark from the tannery, filled up the low places. The trade of the place is in pitch, tar, and turpentine. I crossed over the river to look at the rice fields, which at will are flooded from the river. Gangs of negroes were engaged in hoeing and pulling out weeds.

Our landlord gave us the best the place afforded. But he was a wag, and had placed the sharpest-breasted turkey I had ever met with on the table. Standing at the head, he disarmed all complaint by saying: "Now, gentlemen, I wish to call your attention to this bird. He was kept for the races, and could outrun any turkey in all Wilmington." A burst of laughter ensued, and all were delighted with the dinner. We proceeded from Wilmington to Waynesburg on the Neuse river, eighty miles, and were obliged to take stage over a corduroy road, the railway not being yet constructed within seventy miles of Abbeville.

Such a horrible jolting I had never experienced, except in the low grounds along the Bay of Quinte in Canada. Rails and logs were thrown across marshy soil with but little earth upon them, and from time to time one found himself with his hat over his eyes, striking the top of the stage. At three in the morning we found ourselves at the point where the railway was progressing. The little tavern had only one bed left. What was to be done? I had made application and secured it. We were all exhausted with the ride, and six passengers had equal claims for a portion.

The bed was taken off, placed upon the floor, and occupied by three. Two took the bed cords, with some of the covering, and I reconnoitred the house. I found a country doctor's room with his pharmacy and some anatomical remains; as good luck would have it for once, his services had been required elsewhere, so the doctor's room was occupied, and Morpheus's subject lost sight of dry bones. Twenty miles by rail brought us to Weldon, and from thence to Petersburgh, Virginia, on the Appomatox river. Here I visited some friends whom I had formerly known at Tappahanock, on the Rappahannock river, when I first visited the Old Dominion.

The writer of these Letters, finding his health, which had improved from his last winter's trip to Cuba, again suffering in a northern climate, left the cold weather behind him, and proceeded south, via Philadelphia, Baltimore, Washington, Richmond, and thence to Charleston. He made the outside passage to Savannah by steamer, and thence proceeded by steamboats to Brunswick, in Georgia, passing through the Florida wilds to Tallahassee, at imminent risk from the Seminole Indians. From Tallahassee he proceeded to St. Joseph, and embarked for Mobile and New Orleans, which cities he had left the spring before. He revisited the island of Cuba during the winter, and returned in the spring to the Crescent City. He took steamer bound up the Red river to Natchitoches and Alexandria; returned and visited Natchez, Mississippi, a few days after the great tornado, which destroyed a large portion of the city under the hill, and did immense damage in the city on the bluff. Many lives were lost, and a fleet of flat-boats and steamers sunk. He then proceeded up the Mississippi to Memphis, Tennessee, and St. Louis, Missouri; from the latter place he embarked for Louisville, Kentucky, and Cincinnati. His next route was via Wheeling, Virginia, over the beautiful Cumberland pass of the Alleghany mountains to Hagerstown and Frederick, Maryland; thence to Baltimore; up to Philadelphia, and so home.

To avoid repetition, and inasmuch as the cities and countries of our Union are so generally known, and, not to tax the reader, he has avoided the recounting of the thousand incidents of travel which would require too much space in this limited work. Suffice it to say, he returned in improved health, with a superficial knowledge, at least, of the products and resources of our country.

# 1840.
## VII.
## A TRIP TO EUROPE.

*Dec. 7, 1840.*

I left by the British Queen, in bad health, on Tuesday, upon two days' notice, as I had intended to go to Santa Cruz. The weather was cool but pleasant, until Friday, which was stormy; it continued blowing a gale until Sunday, which was very rough and boisterous. I was very sea-sick, and was afraid of raising blood. We had a cold, disagreeable passage, and were on the ocean three Sundays; we reached Southampton on the twenty-first of December. The ship arrived at London on the twenty-third. Our coal was exhausted, and we burned up all the spare wood we could find to carry us to Southampton.

I was rejoiced to get ashore in a comfortable English hotel, with kind and attentive servants. I left for London the following day, and was struck with the style of the English farm-houses and cottages—stacks of grain—thatched roofs—hedge fences—the straight furrows in ploughing—draining of lands—the old style of brick buildings with pot chimneys, and the dense smoke from the bituminous coal.

Our captain had promised us to land at Plymouth, if could not work up to Cowes; the ship was out of trim, and short of water. A little tug-boat came alongside for passengers and luggage; a heavy sea was on, and it was difficult to get transferred. I took cold, and was fearful I could not proceed south, but soon improved.

On approaching London, it appeared as if a cloud of smoke enveloped it as from a great conflagration. I remained in London ten days, visiting all the great works of art and public buildings; St. Paul's Church—four hundred steps to the cupola—occupying one square—forty years in building, and said to have cost seventy million dollars, our money—remarkable echo in dome, the closing of a door producing a report like the discharge of cannon. The statues of Lord Nelson and scores of others are contained therein. The tunnel under the Thames is one thousand one hundred and forty feet through; thirty-eight feet wide, for two carriage ways. Looked in at Drury Lane, Covent Garden, and Haymarket Theatre. Visited St. James's Park, Waterloo Barracks, Regent's Park, Houses of Lords and Commons, and Westminster Abbey. Made an excursion to Windsor Castle, Virginia Water, and drove through the extensive Park ground. Visited the West India Docks, with basins of immense extent, and massive stone wharfs, solid as rocks. Returned from Southwark by railway, three and one-half miles, upon arches over the tops of houses. Visited the armory rooms in the old Tower, and saw the crown jewels, of great value. The spot was pointed out where Lady Jane Grey and Anne Boleyn were beheaded. Was in the cell where Walter Raleigh was confined and wrote his history.

Newgate Prison and St. Giles's were not neglected—the latter dirty and filthy to a degree—low buildings, black as night—streets ten to twelve feet wide—carts blocking up the way—no living animal inside except pigs—shavings for fuel—men cutting up old wood in little bundles to sell to the poor wretches. Decent-looking men hurried rapidly through. I was almost afraid some wretch would sally out upon me—signs in the windows "Shaving half-penny—hair-cutting one penny"—"Travellers' lodgings, and rooms for single persons"—rooms like so many hog-sties—looked in at Goldsmiths' Hall, and saw statues of Gog and Magog. The sights of London would demand a volume itself for description.

I left London for Dover by the mail coach, which is comfortable and fast when railways are not spoken of. Rode alone to Gravesend, twenty miles; it is much resorted to by the Londoners in summer. Passed through Stroud, Rochester, and Chatham; the three towns almost join; the latter has dockyards on the river Mersey. Passed Canterbury, and many other towns, and came in sight of the chalk hills of Dover. At every change the coachman presents himself, "I leave you here, sir," which means a fee. The servants in hotels, if not taxed in the bill, array themselves in line at the door, "Remember the chambermaid, sir." "Boots, sir, if you please." "I am the waiter, sir, if you will be so kind." The guineas vanish rapidly in England. A little iron mail steamer carried us over the British Channel in three hours to Calais in France. Sea so rough, we could not land for some hours. Passengers very sick. When the tide rose we run in harbor. At next day's low tide I saw brigs, schooners, and steamers floundering in the mud all aground; good substantial docks. Walled city; population, ten thousand inside, seven or eight thousand outside; garrisoned by a regiment of soldiery; luggage taken to custom-house, and examined closely. Visited Notre Dame Church; no pews; chairs all around upon the paved floor, with tops to lean upon; payment is exacted for use of them. The streets are narrow; the women wear caps, few bonnets, and perform all the menial service of men. Coming from America and England it strikes one's attention. Left with the diligence in the coupé or front part, with glass windows, and a good look-out; pleasant ride to Boulogne. We were overtaken by the phenomena of a violent storm, thunder and lightning, hail and snow. We passed through Montreuil and Abbeville, prominent towns. The roads were in bad order, and it took thirty-three hours for the one hundred and sixty miles to Paris. To cross some of the hills we were obliged to put on nine horses, and look like a caravan. As soon as I got settled in the French capital I found constant occupation in sight-seeing, all being new to me. The remains of Napoleon, brought back from the island of St. Helena, by order of Louis Philippe, have just been deposited with extraordinary pomp at the Hotel des Invalides. I am not prepared to describe the sights of Paris in detail on this occasion. My health had suffered from cold, and I found it necessary to push off south. My passport being prepared at the Prefecture de Police, and all the necessary visés of ministers from the different countries which I may visit, obtained, I took the lumbering diligence en route for Marseilles, a distance of some five hundred miles. We reached Chalon on the Saône, where I had hoped to get a steamer, but the freshet prevented our passing the bridges. Proceeded to Lyons, the great manufacturing city of France, and rejoiced to get in quarters with a good fire and comfortable bed. The ravages of the flood and inundation of the country were distressing to behold. Left Lyons, in a little steamer, for Avignon upon the Rhone, not much wider than a canal boat, but very long in proportion, say one hundred and fifty feet. It was cold and blustering, blowing a hard gale. We descended rapidly. The steamer had no wheel, but four men at the rudder; it was hard to keep her straight. Passed the bridges and stone arches over the river with lightning speed, the inundation and current being tremendous. Struck an arch, and came near being dashed to pieces; all hands frightened; the engineer said that he had been on the river for years, but never had seen such a blow. Dust flew so, we could scarcely see the shore; clouds of it covered rigging and deck. Passed Vienne, Valence, Tournon, and arrived at St. Esprit. Great doubt expressed if we could pass through the arches of the stone bridge, but it was done safely and splendidly. There being no sleeping accommodation, we went ashore to get the best lodgings we could. We found an old castle of a hotel; arched entrance, stone steps worn by time, and replaced in part with wood; heavy, massive doors and windows; large chimney and fire-places; grape-vines and green wood for fuel; violent wind, and cold. In the morning looked around the ancient town, around the fort, and crossed the narrow stone bridge, with solid, heavy abutments, the work of the monks in the middle ages. The steamer started at two P.M., much to our relief, for our wants were better supplied in her than ashore. The gale was over, and we arrived at Avignon, and thence proceeded to Aix and Marseilles, where I was obliged to rest myself for a few days. A funeral service next door attracted my attention. First came the Catholic clergy, in full robes; next sisters of charity and little girls; then charity boys; the bearers, all sturdy, clod-hoofed fellows, covered with coarse cloth, and sacks over their heads, with holes only for the eyes; candles and torches burning in their hands.

Passing through the south of France, I was struck with the immense resources of the country in the vine. Millions of acres are cultivated with it as the products of the cereals are in our own country. The refuse and dried branches are sold for fuel and lighting fires. The beauty of the Rhone, with its old towers and castles, high peaks and mountain scenery, amphitheatred walls, and hanging gardens, covered with the vine, is remarkable. The limestone country approaching Marseilles produces the olive and fig in great abundance. The houses in southern France generally have tile or porcelain floors, and are very cold at this season. At Marseilles, I saw the column of Napoleon; it is at the head of the promenade, with a fine view of the harbor.

A great variety of character and costume is found in this seaport, and all the different dialects are spoken; Arabs, Italians, Greeks, Germans, and Swiss abound; and it is quite amusing, to stroll upon the quays.

I looked about the city, and saw all there was of interest. I stopped at the Hotel d'Orient, recently opened, and was glad to get where comfort was to be found. The floors are all of hexagonal tile, glazed or polished, and slippery; the stairs of the same, except the projecting part of wood. Good table-d'hôte; a dozen dishes of meat and vegetables come on in succession, all hot. The cuisine in the south of France will not compare with that of Paris. Dessert of native fruits, prunes, olives, pears, apples, raisins, figs. Visited the theatre; large house, but poorly supported; no style in fitting up; the outside presents a fine front, but miserable inside. Opera-glasses in general use. On entering, you see women with stands for coats, hats, sticks, etc., and a table filled with opera-glasses for hire, all of which gives a small emolument to these honest people. The civility and politeness of the French are proverbial: a glove or a handkerchief left on your seat is sure to be respected, and your right of place maintained. In comedy the French excel. With two American gentlemen, with whom I crossed the Atlantic, and whom I now met here, I dined at the house of our Consul, Mr. Fitch, who entertained us handsomely.

The steamer Maria Antoinette takes me to Genoa.

# 1841.
# VIII.

NAPLES, *February 22, 1841.*

After landing at Marseilles I proceeded by steamer to Genoa. On approaching the city from the sea it shows to great advantage. Its numerous and stately edifices resemble the seats of a vast amphitheatre placed on the declivity of the Apennines. It is termed the City of Palaces, and deservedly so, as its palaces are very numerous, and composed of beautiful marble, splendidly adorned with noble entrances and elegant staircases, with floors of marble. Among the most prominent sights of the city are the palaces and churches. The cathedral of St. Lorenzo is an ancient Gothic structure, built of marble, and paved with the same material. The sacristy contains an emerald vase, found at Cesarea when the Genoese captured that town, and they chose it in preference to any other tribute offered. (A.D. 1101.) This vase is said to have been presented by the Queen of Sheba to Solomon, and deposited by him in the temple at Jerusalem. Napoleon carried it to Paris when he conquered the Genoese, but it was afterwards returned. I was shown the mortal remains of St. John the Baptist, brought from Lycia and placed in the cathedral, inclosed in a silver sarcophagus. The plate of beautiful agate and gold which held the head of the saint, when presented to Herod, is also exhibited. The cross of gold worn by Constantine was also shown. It is two feet long, one foot wide, and weighs almost ten pounds, and is filled with precious stones, and contains a small fragment of the *true cross*. I visited the palace of the king of Sardinia, which is a large and magnificent edifice, and contains a large collection of paintings, among the most remarkable of which is one representing Mary Magdalen at the feet of our Saviour in the house of the Pharisee, by Paul Veronese; also one of Titian's, representing Christ bearing his cross. I visited several other palaces where are to be seen beautiful collections of paintings. The rooms are gorgeous. One saloon in the palazzo Serra is lined with the most costly materials, white marble, large mirrors, etc., with ornaments of precious stones and the richest gilding; in short, it combines taste with splendor in its gorgeous decorations, and is considered equal to any single saloon in Europe.

From Genoa I, with two travelling companions, took private carriage to Pisa, a distance of one hundred and thirty miles, passing through several interesting towns, visiting the marble mines of Carrara, where are eighty-five workshops, preparing statuary and various kinds of work for foreign markets.

The scenery on this route is enchanting. Genoa is left in the distance as you wind along the coast of the Mediterranean, at the base of the Apennines. Villages are continually presenting themselves; the walled hills and mountains are filled with olives and the vine, and cultivated to their tops. The valleys, beautified with gardens, produce an abundance of the orange, lemon, &c. On arriving at Pisa, which is situated on the banks of the Arno, fourteen miles from Leghorn, I visited all the objects worthy of notice. One of the most remarkable is the Leaning Tower. It is of a circular form, one hundred and ninety feet high, and declines thirteen feet from perpendicular. This beautiful structure was commenced in the year 1174, and consists of eight stories, adorned with two hundred and seven columns of granite and marble, many of which have evidently been taken from other buildings. The stairs leading up are easy of ascent, and the view extensive.

The Campo Santo, or ancient burial ground, a beautiful edifice, is a vast rectangle, surrounded by sixty-two light and elegant Gothic arcades of the Greco-Arabic school, built of white marble, and paved with the same. It is founded on a part of the earth brought from Mount Calvary, by two warriors from the Holy Land, and was commenced in the year 1200. The interior walls are decorated with ancient fresco-paintings, statues, and monuments of the best artists, bearing testimony of the most distinguished characters.

From Pisa I went to Leghorn, a fine commercial city, with a population of sixty thousand, and took steamer for this city.

On entering the harbor of Naples, the city presents itself beautifully to view, rising in the form of an amphitheatre, and crowned by the castle of St. Elmo; with its noble bay, thirty miles in diameter; and the island of Capri, rising in the centre. The towns of Sorento, Portici, Castellamare, Pozzuoli, and others, stretching along the promontory right and left, with Mount Vesuvius "eternally smoking in the distance," at the base of which lie the ill fated cities of Pompeii and Herculaneum, all of which I shall visit in a few days, and describe in my next. Naples is nine miles in circumference, and contains a population of three hundred and fifty thousand, but with the towns in the suburbs is said to contain five hundred thousand. On the summit of the hill, which is difficult of ascent, and adjoining the castle of St. Elmo, is a convent, and the church of San Martino, which is more magnificent than any other sacred edifice in Naples, being rich in gilding, paintings, precious marbles and jewels. The view from this spot is enchanting. The flat-roofed city, whose streets appear like narrow footpaths; the buzz of the inhabitants who seem like pigmies; carriages appearing no larger than children's toys, and with difficulty distinguished; on one side the rich Neapolitan country, on another the majestic Apennines, with Vesuvius in front, and on the other side the bay covered with boats, and its shores lined with villages—the whole produces a rich and beautiful sight.

## IX.

MESSINA (Sicily), *March, 10, 1841.*

In my last, from Naples, I promised, after having visited Mount Vesuvius and the entombed cities of Pompeii and Herculaneum, to describe them. On arriving at Resina, about five miles distant from Naples, our party took mules and donkeys and ascended to the hermitage by a good mule path, occupying about two hours time. Here we were compelled to leave our animals, and ascend slowly and cautiously through masses of lava for about an hour—an exceedingly fatiguing task. At times we were almost suffocated with the sulphurous smoke which seemed to burst forth in different directions. The most difficult task was in returning from the mouth of the crater after having descended about twelve hundred feet. It is rare that persons descend to the verge or the mouth of the crater, and our guide was quite unwilling to attempt it, but our party persisted, and it was accomplished with great labor. The top of the crater is computed at two and a half miles in circumference, and at the bottom the opening is about thirty feet in diameter, and ejects forth sulphurous smoke, with a loud rumbling noise, resembling the escape of steam of a Mississippi steamer.

The distance from Naples to Pompeii is about twelve miles. The city of Pompeii was buried under ashes and pumice stones, and deluged with showers of boiling water, in the year 79 of the Christian era, and accidentally discovered in 1775 by a peasant while planting a vineyard.

On arriving at the gate we were conducted by a guide through part of the town, already excavated. The streets are straight and well paved with lava, which prove an eruption previous to the destruction of the city. Traces of carriage wheels still remain in the pave. The houses were generally two stories high, and had flat roofs. The walls of most of the rooms were stuccoed, painted and polished; many of the paintings and frescoes are in a good state of preservation. The apartments were paved with mosaic, some very magnificently executed. On many houses are seen the name and occupation of the owner, written in deep red; on the walls of some public buildings advertisements of gladiatorial shows, festivals, &c.

Here are seen remnants of public baths, theatres, amphitheatres, the Basilica, the houses of Sallust, Diomede, the temples of Isis, Hercules, and other gods.

We also visited Herculaneum, which lies about five miles from Naples. Some portions of the city were buried six feet deep, others one hundred feet. The towers of Resina and Portici are built over the city, which prevents much excavation. We descended by torchlight a narrow and winding staircase a considerable depth below the surface, where part of the theatre is exhibited.

It is said that it was capable of containing ten thousand persons. After having visited most of the objects of antiquity in the city, I made an excursion along the coast, visiting the tomb of Virgil, and passing through the grotto of Posilippo, which is two thousand three hundred and sixty feet long, twenty-three feet broad, and eighty-nine feet high, to the small town of Pozzuoli, where St. Paul landed and remained seven days before commencing his journey to Rome. I also visited the ruins of the ancient city of Baiæ, near which are the ruins of Nero's villa, and the hot vapor baths, which will boil an egg in two minutes. One of my most interesting excursions was to the ruins of Pæstum, about forty miles from Naples. The disease called malaria, which exists to an alarming extent in the vicinity of this ruined city, prevents travellers from visiting it at all seasons of the year. Persons should not sleep there, nor approach until an hour after sunrise. We took our supplies with us, as nothing can be obtained in this land of solitude and silence. Our sympathies were excited and charity exercised by seeing many squalid and wretched objects of malaria lying in huts upon the bare ground. This city was supposed to have been built seven hundred and twenty years before Christ, and to have been destroyed in the tenth century by the Saracens. Here are some of the finest ruins of temples in Europe. One, called the temple of Neptune, is very majestic. Its shape is quadrilateral, length one hundred and ninety-four feet, and breadth seventy-eight feet; and it has two fronts, with six minute fluted columns of the Grecian Doric order. The exterior columns, thirty-six in number, are twenty-seven feet high, and there is a Doric frieze and cornice all round the building. The situation of the high altar, and those on which victims were sacrificed and offerings made, is still visible. Fragments of sea-green and dark blue mosaic are still found on the spot. The temple of Ceres and the Basilica are still quite perfect and very beautiful. On our return through this gloomy tract of country and pestilent swamps we saw herds of buffalo, which are the only animals that inhabit it. I next visited the towns of Salerno and Amalfi, situated along the shores of the Mediterranean. The latter is bounded by lofty mountains on three sides, with beautiful cascades running through the town. The front opens on the sea. On the summit of a lofty wall is the Capuchin convent, which we visited, and then crossed the mountain of St. Angelo, over a height of four or five thousand feet. The route was difficult, but we were compensated for the fatigue by the many picturesque scenes constantly presented. At times the ascent was so rough among the craggy rocks I was compelled to dismount my donkey; at other times he would wind his course along the brink of a frightful precipice, where one mis-step would launch me into eternity. He proved as sure-footed as the herds of goats we frequently passed, jumping from one crag to another on the verge of a precipice.

I left Naples by steamer, stopping at Tropea, in Calabria, for a short time; then, passing down through the straits of Messina, we saw Scylla and

Charybdis, which have been the dread of mariners so long, and about which so much has been said and sung. It is said that during tempestuous gales, the noise of the waves dashing violently against Scylla, and then precipitating themselves in the cavern, still resembles the howl of dogs and beasts of prey. The rapidity of the current here is very great, and the boiling eddies very strong. On passing the mountain of Stromboli, not far distant from Scylla, situated in the sea, I was struck with the beautiful eruption and ejection of fire, smoke, and red-hot stones, thrown up at intervals of fifteen minutes—a beautiful sight in the night.

## X.

CATANIA, SICILY, *March 27, 1841.*

I wrote you at Messina on the 10th inst. That city is delightfully situated, partly on an eminence and partly on a plain, surrounded by a luxuriant country, abounding with oranges, lemons, and many other tropical fruits. The population was, at one time, eighty thousand, but it is now somewhat reduced. It is said that the plague of 1743 carried off fifty thousand of its inhabitants, and the earthquake of 1783 nearly destroyed its beautiful quays in a few minutes, levelled its finest buildings, and killed one thousand persons. The city, as now rebuilt, has magnificent quays and a very pretty harbor. The walls of the present buildings are very massive, and usually from two to three stories high, to resist the shocks of earthquakes, which they are still subject to. I omitted to state in my last that I had experienced one slight shock since I had been in this latitude.

After remaining a sufficiently long time at Messina to see all the objects of interest, and its beautiful sunrises, I took a steamer for the city of Palermo, a distance of one hundred and fifty miles. The approach to the city presents fine scenery. The mountains which form the background, the deep blue sea, whence rise the most picturesque rocks imaginable, the luxuriant plains immediately surrounding the city, altogether, are peculiarly striking. The city has a gay and Asiatic appearance, and the architecture is of the Saracenic, Greek, and Roman styles. It is one of the most regular built cities I have yet seen, and has a population of two hundred thousand. The Strada Toledo, which is about a mile in length, wide, clean, and well paved, intersects another street of the same character at right angles, and leads into a handsome octangular piazza called Quatro Cantori, from the centre of which both parts of each street and the four principal gates of the city, are visible. The number of nunneries is immense. The basements of these—many of them in the principal streets—are occupied as shops, while the upper stories are the apartments of the nuns, as may be discovered by the long, grated, projecting galleries.

The church of the Capuchins, about a mile distant from the city, attracts the attention of travellers. Here we descended into an immense vault, about one hundred and fifty feet in length, and probably sixty in width, which is used as a depository for the defunct brethren. They are dried, dressed, and placed upright in railings against the wall, that their friends may visit and pray by them annually, on the second of November. These catacombs also contain the vaults with iron doors where the body is placed and dried for six months; at the end of which time it is clad in its usual habiliments, and placed with the general assembly. The floors are covered with coffins inclosing the remains of persons not in holy orders. In one coffin I saw the late viceroy, who had been embalmed seven months, and was in good preservation. In one apartment are shelves devoted to females, who are disposed of in glass cases, and are richly dressed, and decorated with ornaments. This apartment must contain several thousands. The atmosphere is not altogether agreeable, and the grim-visaged defunct monks contribute not a little to make the sight appalling and disgusting.

Having finished our observations with the dead, we next visited the palace of the king, which is rich in marbles, mosaics, fresco paintings, tapestry, &c., and then made an excursion to the Chinese villa, called "*La Favorita,*" the summer residence of the king of Naples and Sicily, while at Palermo. The grounds are beautiful, inclosing splendid drives, four miles in extent, embellished with fountains, thickets, labyrinths, all varieties of tropical fruits, &c. The palace is purely Chinese in construction, in furniture, and in decorations.

After having examined most of the prominent sights of the city, we chartered a private carriage, to take the route from Palermo to Catania, a distance of one hundred and sixty-eight miles. The tour of Sicily is not generally made by travelling about the island, as it is attended with great fatigue and exposure, and want of accommodation; the usual mode of travel being on mules and donkeys.

In the principal cities all the comforts required by a traveller can be obtained, but in the interior the estates are large and owned by few, the peasants poor and living mostly in villages, going for miles to perform the labors of the day, instead of having farm-houses scattered along the road. The accommodations to be found are of the worst character. But we passed through a delightful country, with all the variety of mountain scenery. Sicily was once denominated the granary of Rome, and some writers say that hounds lost their scent in hunting over Sicilian heaths, on account of the odoriferous flowers which perfumed the air. This is the most delightful season of the year for travelling here, as the green almond trees are in blossom, the weather delightfully warm, and the flowers abundant. On our route we saw immense pasturages and herds of sheep on the mountains, attended by faithful shepherds with their crooks and watch-dogs. At sunset the sheep are all gathered to the folds.

The city of Catania was greatly injured by an eruption of Mount Etna in 1669, and almost destroyed by the earthquake of 1693, when most of the inhabitants were buried under the ruins of their houses and churches. But it rose rapidly, and now has a population of seventy thousand. It is regularly and handsomely built, and the streets are paved with the lava of Mount Etna.

So terrible have been the eruptions that parts of the city have been buried sixty feet deep with the burning lava. Excavations have been made in many places, and one of the number I visited, and descended sixty-three steps, when I came to the original earth and a spring of water. In another place the excavation exhibits the ancient Greek Theatre with its corridors, rows of seats, and other fixtures. In another place may be seen the remains of an amphitheatre, with its dens for wild beasts, and aqueducts for water, far below the surface on which the present city is built. It is necessary to descend with torches. All these things render it probable, if not certain, that Catania shared the fate of Herculaneum and Pompeii, in ancient times as well as in modern.

Since our party arrived here we have made an excursion up Mount Etna. Having each provided ourselves with a mule, and one extra to carry supplies, we set out on a lovely morning for Nicholosi, a small settlement, twelve miles up the mountain from Catania. The first part of the route presented a luxuriant and beautiful country abounding with vineyards, olives, figs, oranges, limes, and almonds. Vegetation was far advanced; the soil was very rich from the vast quantity of lava, cinders, and ashes which covered this extensive tract of country at the time of the eruption, and the destruction of Catania. On starting the weather appeared highly favorable for the entire ascent, but on arriving at Nicholosi the guide declined going up to the summit, as the sky indicated a snow-storm, in which, if caught, we could not possibly be saved at this season of the year. We therefore only ascended to the top of what is called Monte Rossi, the volcano that destroyed Catania in 1669, and covered the country with lava for thirty or forty miles.

The summit of Mount Etna is always covered with snows. Before we returned we found that the snow-storm had commenced, and rejoiced that we had escaped. At the height we attained we lost sight of all vegetation, nothing being visible but lava, cinders, and ashes.

## XI.

ROME, *April, 1841.*

I wrote you last from Catania, Sicily. On leaving that city for Messina we passed through a fine country bordering on the Mediterranean, and stopped at Gardina, a small fishing town, prettily situated, with a fine view of the Straits of Messina and the shores of Calabria. The following morning we took donkeys, which were simply provided with rope halters and sheepskins for saddles, and proceeded to Taormina, an ancient Roman city, celebrated for its antiquities. It is situated on the top of a high rock, crowned with an ancient Saracenic castle. Pre-eminent among the antiquities is the theatre, a colossal edifice located in a singular hollow in the upper part of the rock. The ascent to the top is about two miles, and is very steep.

We next arrived at Messina, passing through a luxuriant country abounding in all the tropical fruits, and from Messina came by steamboat to Naples. On the route from Naples to Rome the first object of particular interest was in diverging from the present town of Capua to the ruins of the ancient city, where are the remains of one of the largest amphitheatres I have yet seen, and a part of it is quite perfect. It is said to have contained four hundred gladiators, and the school of gladiators amounted to four thousand in number. Cicero described it as holding one hundred thousand spectators. It was one thousand seven hundred and eighty feet in circuit, one hundred and forty feet high; length of arena two hundred and ninety-four feet, width one hundred and seventy-six. On the road we saw the cenotaph of Cicero, placed on the spot where he was murdered while endeavoring to escape from his enemies.

On entering the Pope's dominions we had our baggage rigorously examined. We halted at the town of Albano, fourteen miles from Rome. Here are several subjects worthy of attention. A large monument supposed to have been erected by Pompey, to inclose the ashes of his wife Julia, daughter of Cæsar; the lake of Albano, an extinct volcano, six miles in circumference, and four hundred and eighty feet in depth; castle Gandolfo, a village built in the lava, stands on the top of the hill, and here the Pope has a summer residence. It is a beautiful location, and the walks through the avenues of shady trees are delightful. From this point I first caught sight of St. Peter's, the first view of Rome. On arriving in the truly wonderful city my first desire was to see the great Basilica, St. Peter's, far surpassing any other in the world, in size, splendor, and magnificence. The length of the church in the interior is six hundred and fourteen feet; the front is three hundred and seventy feet, and one hundred and forty-nine feet high, ornamented with columns of the Corinthian order, each column eight feet in diameter and eighty-eight feet in height. The front terminates with a balustrade surmounted by thirteen colossal statues, seventeen feet high, representing our Saviour and his Apostles. The width of the nave is two hundred and seven feet; diameter of cupola one hundred and thirty-nine; height from the pavement to first gallery one hundred and seventy-four; to second gallery two hundred and forty; to the representation of the Deity in the Lantern three hundred and ninety-three; and to the summit of the eastern cross four hundred and thirty-eight feet.

The interior is adorned with rare marble, columns, statuary, gilding, and solid bronze, gold and silver, the sacred Confessional with one hundred superb and elegant lamps, always burning. In the year 1694 this edifice was supposed to have cost forty-seven millions dollars, since which time immense amounts have been expended in mosaics, statuary, &c.

Under St. Peter's is a subterranean church built by Constantine. Here are many tombs of the Popes, and that of Charlotte, Queen of Jerusalem. The height of this subterranean church is twelve feet, and the pavement the same as in the days of Constantine. The ascent to the top of St. Peter's is not difficult, and there may be had a magnificent view of the city and country.

The Vatican, which is a city of itself, contiguous to St. Peter's, contains some thousands of rooms, variously estimated. It is seventy thousand feet in circumstances. Some writers suppose it was erected by Nero, others are of opinion that it was built by Constantine; but every sovereign extended it. It is the residence of the Popes, in which are the Latin Chapel, the Pauline Chapel, also occupied with the most extensive collection of statuary, paintings, bronzes, &c., in the world; and here we saw the master-pieces of the world, as Rome may justly be called the mistress of the globe in the arts. Here are rooms twelve hundred feet long used as libraries, and for the collections of the museums.

Rome contains such a vast variety of antiquities that one is compelled to be very industrious to accomplish much in seeing the objects of interest unless two or three months are spent in the work. It is impossible to give an adequate description of the manifold objects of curiosity in this wonderful city.

I visited the Coliseum first by moonlight, which gives a very pretty effect; the pale light throws a beautiful shadow, and leaves the imagination to cover the defects. It is an immense edifice. Titus at the consecration exhibited gladiatorial shows ten days, and five thousand wild beasts with some thousands of gladiators are said to have been sacrificed at the horrid festival. It was opened in the year 80. It is of an oval form, one thousand six hundred and forty-one feet in circumference, and one hundred and fifty-seven feet high; the arena is four hundred and eighty-five feet long, and one hundred and eighty-two wide. It was four years in building. The benches held eighty-seven thousand, and the gallery twenty thousand spectators.

The Pantheon is a beautiful structure, and has so well resisted the ravages of time that it is in quite a perfect state. The front and sides of the portico contain sixteen Corinthian columns of red ornamented granite, each fourteen feet in circumference and thirty-nine feet high, with bases and capitals of white marble. The portico is surmounted by an entablature and pediment finely proportioned. The inside is circular, one hundred and thirty-four feet in diameter; the walls are nineteen feet thick, with an opening in the top twenty-six feet wide. Verde-antique, porphyry, and other valuable marbles are everywhere prominent. The dome was originally lined with bronze, but it was taken by Pope Urban Eighth to make the great canopy over the high altar of St. Peter's.

Among the many other objects of interest the most conspicuous are the ancient Forum, the arch of Constantine, the arch of Titus, temples of various heathen gods, the tombs of Scipio, the palaces of the Cæsars, the baths of Titus and Caracalla, Trajan's column, the Mausoleum of Augustus, and the Mausoleum of Adrian. The latter was erected by the Emperor Adrian to be a deposit for his remains; it is now converted into the Castle of San Angelo, and occupied by the military on the banks of the Tiber. The bridge that leads to it is surmounted by the figures of many angels, bearing in their hands the instruments of torture said to have been used at the crucifixion of our Savior. Near the Campidolio, which contains a vast collection of antiquities, is the Tarpeian Rock, celebrated as the place from which the ancient Romans executed their criminals by throwing them headlong down the precipice.

Near the Temples of Concord, Jupiter, and Fortune, is situated the prison in which St. Peter and St. Paul were confined with forty-seven other prisoners. A light is kept burning continually in one of the cells, in which are an altar, and figures of the saints on a side screen. You descend by torchlight into a vault or prison, on one side of which in passing down you see the grated iron window through which the prisoners looked, and near it is the iron frame to which they were bound. Here also, far below the surface of the ground, is the living stream which gushed up for the baptism of the convicts after their conversion, and which now in case of severe droughts never fails to flow.

In visiting the immense ruins of the palace of Cæsar we descended by torchlight to the baths of Livia, where are seen the remains of stucco and fresco work in the wall, arabesques, medallions, &c. Near this place on the hill, we had a view of the seven hills of Rome, and looked down upon the Forum, Senate House, and on the other side the Circus Maximus, which extended for miles, and held in the time of Constantine three hundred and eighty thousand persons. It was used for horse and chariot races, as well as feats of wrestling, boxing, combats with wild beasts, and other exercises to improve the Roman youth.

Rome, according to the published statistics, contains six hundred and thirty-five palaces, three hundred and twenty-eight churches, fifty public fountains, one hundred small fountains, thirty-four bishops, one thousand four hundred and sixty-eight priests, two thousand one hundred and eighteen monks, one thousand four hundred and seventeen young monks, one hundred and fourteen convents, thirteen obelisks, and sixteen city gates. The ancient Romans had aqueducts to convey to the city eight hundred tons of water daily. Three of them still remain, one of which supplies the Vatican and the fountains in front of St. Peter's, and is thirty miles in length. Another is twenty-two miles long. The ancient mistress of the world, reduced as she now is in size, population, wealth, and power, still has her stately palaces, noble churches, splendid fountains, stupendous obelisks of Egyptian character, matchless amphitheatres, and almost innumerable antiquities, with their classical associations, which can never fail to attract strangers from all enlightened quarters of the globe, to say nothing of the finest modern works of art, to be found almost everywhere, and in which she is unrivalled.

## XII.

VIENNA, AUSTRIA, *June 25, 1841.*

I promised to give you some account of this beautiful city and the characteristics of the government and people. The registers kept at the police are so accurate and full that the history of a person from his birth, his changes of abode, his journeyings, in fact all his movements, are ascertained with perfect precision, so arbitrary and jealous is the government. No Austrian is allowed to leave the empire unless by making a deposit of five hundred florins, or giving security to that amount, to indemnify his return. The consequence is that we seldom see them in America. I find no Americans here at present. It is a fine country for a stranger to reside in, but he must not meddle with affairs of state—if he does so he must not be surprised if an officer hands him his passport with orders to leave the empire instantly.

The expenses of living are one third higher here than in Paris. You find no *table d'hôte* at the hotels, but merely take a lodging room, and then have your meals at the *restaurant* connected with the hotel, or where you please. The city abounds with *cafés*, which are resorted to by all classes. In these establishments you are almost constantly enveloped in smoke, as every one uses a pipe or cigars. There are some *cafés* in which smoking is not allowed.

At this season of the year, to escape the heat, a general resort is had to the different gardens, where you find innumerable tables spread in the open air under the trees, in the hearing of bands of music, and occupied by well dressed, orderly people of both sexes. The city is highly favored with shade trees.

Vienna has been pronounced by travellers the most dissolute capital in Europe. But in this I should think there was much exaggeration. There is, at all events, none of that open display of vice that disgraces Paris and London. Violations of the peace are said to be rare, and you seldom see a drunken man. No public gambling is allowed. In the public walks and gardens all seem to be alike merry and happy—feasting, dancing, and amusements being the order of the day. London is celebrated for its wealth, Paris for its beauty and gaiety, but Vienna for all these characteristics.

In a former letter I stated that I had visited the vault of a Capuchin convent, where the remains of the royal family are deposited. There are in all seventy metal coffins; the oldest is of the Emperor Matthias; the most splendid is that of Margaret of Spain, being of pure silver; the most interesting is that of young Napoleon, Duke of Reichstadt. A singular custom they have here in disposing of the remains of the royal family. The body is deposited in one place, the bowels in the cathedral, and the heart in a silver urn in the church of the Augustins. I visited the latter, and had the urn containing the young Napoleon's heart in my hand, and also that having the heart of his grandfather, the late Emperor.

The imperial jewel office surpasses all sights of that kind I have ever witnessed. Here are riches unbounded. Among the prominent objects is the crown of Charlemagne, consisting of gold, diamonds, and precious stones, taken from his grave at Aix-la-Chapelle. It was used at the coronation of many Roman Emperors. There are also the crown worn by Napoleon at his coronation at Milan as King of Lombardy, the entire Austrian crown, necklaces, and jewels of all kinds. Six large rooms are used to display them, with many other articles, including robes, sceptres, orbs, and shelves filled with precious stones—the largest diamond in the world, weighing one hundred and thirty-three carats, gold vases, basins, the gold and silver cradle of young Napoleon, &c. Here is also preserved a variety of sacred relics, a piece of the holy cross, the spear and nails of the cross used at the coronation of the Roman Emperor, a piece of the table-cloth spread for the Lord's Supper, three links of the chain of St. Peter, Paul, and John, and so many other objects displaying the superstitions of the people and the extravagance of the government, that a mere enumeration of them is out of the question.

The Imperial Arsenal is the finest I ever saw, far surpassing anything of the kind in London or Paris. It is an immense building, the court of which is filled with cannon of all sizes, the largest being twenty-four feet long, and carrying one hundred and twenty-four pound balls. A chain goes round the entire square where the building stands, hung in festoons of immense size; it contains eight thousand links, and was taken from the Turks, who had thrown it across the Danube.

In the upper rooms of the building are tastefully displayed one hundred and fifty thousand stand of arms, in all forms and figures, so as to present a beautiful decoration, while at the same time they are ready for use. Columns which to appearance support the halls, are all of warlike instruments. You see the large double-headed eagle, the arms of Austria, from twelve to fifteen feet long, with out-stretched wings, all composed of instruments of warfare beautifully arranged.

The coach establishment of the royal family is scarcely less magnificent than the great arsenal. I thought the coaches and equipages of the Pope of Rome must be superior to those of any other potentate, but those of the Emperor of Austria surpass them. There are about thirty large and small coaches, all glittering with gold. The largest of the number corresponds in size with an American stage coach; the wheels, pole, and all but the body, being covered with plated gold, the driver's and footmen's seats covered with scarlet velvet, the inside lined with the same material, and the body painted after the design of Rubens, with beautiful characters and emblematic figures, and finished in a style that cannot be excelled in beauty. On the top is an immense crown of gold, which serves as a grand finish of the efforts for grandeur. The painting alone cost thirty thousand dollars, the whole vehicle ninety thousand dollars! It is used but twice a year, and is one hundred and twenty years old. Such is some of the pomp and pageantry of crowned heads, and, after all, what wretched governments, compared with our enlightened republic, do they give the people!

The Emperor is, however, a plain man, beloved by his people. He gives audience one day in the week to all who choose to make application beforehand in writing. He usually sets the example of dining at one o'clock, and, as a consequence, that is the fashionable dinner hour in the city. He is a regular attendant on Divine service in his own chapel connected with the palace. But any citizen can go and see, at certain times, what is called his private side-box, where he does no business and observes few ceremonies.

Since my arrival here I have tested the qualities of the mineral baths, which are the resort of thousands at this season of the year. The warm springs contain large portions of sulphur, are strongly impregnated with carbonic acid gas, and are very extensive.

Among other curiosities worthy of attention, in a public square near the centre of the city, is the trunk of an old tree, the only one remaining of an ancient forest, which occupied half the ground now covered with buildings. It has several iron hoops to aid in preserving it, and as it has been the custom of apprentices on setting out on a journey to drive a nail in it by way of memorial, it has become so filled with nails that there is no place left to drive another. It has the appearance of, and is called, "the tree of iron," and gives its name to the square in which it stands.

With regard to apprentices, Austria has some peculiar regulations. The law compels them to travel in the empire two years in search of employment, and to gain information. They can enter any city and apply to the head of a committee for employment. If none can be obtained they are provided for, but can remain only two days, before they must travel again. They are required to keep a journal of all the places visited and bring back testimonials of character. When their time has expired they return home and pass an examination; if pronounced worthy, they are then allowed to open a shop. In consequence of this regulation it is not uncommon to see fine-looking young men, with packs on their backs, come up to a coach door and beg for any trifle of money, which their necessities drive them to solicit, and it is a rule with the Austrians always to aid them liberally.

# XIII.

PEST, HUNGARY, *July 2, 1841.*

My last letter was from Vienna, which city we left a few days since for the capital of Hungary. We took a steamer on the Danube, about three miles from Vienna, and descended to Presburg, about fifty miles. The navigation of this part of the Danube is difficult, owing to the shoals and rapidity of the currents. On the route we passed the memorable battle-ground of Wagram. Traces of the works of Napoleon's fortified camp on the island of Lobau, still remain. This narrow island—two and one-third miles long, and three-quarters of a mile broad—it is said contained one hundred and fifty thousand foot and thirty thousand horse, and seven hundred pieces of cannon, concentrated from all parts of Europe. We also passed the villages of Aspern and Essling, the scene of a memorable engagement in 1809, when the Austrians, under the Archduke Charles, gained a temporary but important advantage over Napoleon. Aspern was reduced to ruins; and scarcely any traces now remain of it; save the marks of cannon and shot in the walls of the churchyard.

We soon arrived at Presburg, the place of coronation of the king of Hungary, with a population of forty thousand, pleasantly situated on the Danube. The most conspicuous edifice to be seen here is the royal palace on the hill above the city. It was here that Maria Theresa, the youthful queen, at the commencement of her reign, when attacked on all sides, appeared in deep mourning, with the cross of St. Stephen in her hand, and girt with his sword, and delivered a speech, stating the disastrous condition of her affairs, and throwing herself on the fidelity of her people. The Hungarians could not resist the appeal, but in the excitement of feeling voted supplies to carry on the war, and summoned the wild tribes from the remote quarters of Hungary, to carry terror to all parts of the continent. Near the city an artificial mound is pointed out, about forty feet high, called Konigsburgh, to which every new king of Hungary has heretofore repaired on horseback, after his coronation, and from its summit made the sign of the cross in the air with the sword of St. Stephen, and waved it towards the four points of the compass, signifying thus his intention to protect the land on all sides.

We visited the Jews' quarter, where, to the number of seven thousand, they are inclosed along the slope of the castle hill. They are restricted to that part of the city. The shores here are connected by a bridge of boats which rise and fall with the tide. Along the river may be seen, constantly, barges rudely constructed, mostly flat bottoms, with produce destined for the Black Sea, and descending rapidly with a current very like the Mississippi; others ascending, with supplies for the cities, or with merchandize, and towed by twenty to thirty horses, which traverse the banks, or up to the middle in water. We repeatedly passed fleets of water-mills, driven by the current, stretching obliquely in long lines from the shore into the middle of the river. They consist of a water-wheel suspended between two large boats moored in the line of the current; one boat, with a temporary dwelling, used by the miller. Heretofore, about the only use this mighty river was applied to, was propelling the mills. Steamers, to a limited extent, have been introduced within the last twelve years. The scenery along its banks is rather monotonous until you arrive at the town of Gran, numbering a population of twelve thousand: here is seen a chain of hills, the sides of which are planted with vineyards, producing some of the finest Hungarian wines. The town is celebrated as being the birthplace of St. Stephen, and for a long time the residence of the Hungarian monarchs, and was the finest city in Turkey until it was nearly annihilated by the Turks.

After passing many towers and battlemented walls, all full of interest as connected with the history of the country, we arrived at this city, one hundred and eighty-two miles from Vienna.

Buda, the old town on the right bank of the Danube, is the residence of the Palatine, and seat of government; and Pest on the left, connected by a bridge of boats one thousand two hundred feet long—both places containing a population of one hundred and twenty thousand. In 1838, a sudden rise of the Danube destroyed three thousand eight hundred dwellings. Since that time the city has improved rapidly, and I was agreeably surprised to see here, in almost the extreme Eastern part of Europe, a city that would compare with, and remind me of a new American city in many respects. The chief languages are the Hungarian and German, but I find the people in the cities of Hungary apt in the acquirement of languages. Many of them speak five languages. Their own is of an oriental character, differing from all European ones, and most difficult to acquire.

On crossing the bridge of boats, we passed without any demand being made; but observed that others were stopped, and toll demanded. On inquiry, the reply from a traveller was, that all persons who had good coats to their backs were allowed to pass free; while those who, from their costume, appeared to belong to the class of peasants of the poorer and lower orders, especially *beggars in rags*, are compelled to pay. The nobleman in every part of Hungary is free from all taxes. This is the Hungarian constitution! All the taxes of Hungary, which contains five millions of people, are wrung from the hard earnings of the peasants. The nobleman may have millions of acres, and immense revenues, and does not contribute a dollar. The excuse offered for this monstrous abuse is, that the peasant has a right in the land in consequence of his paying taxes, and that the tax is a part of the rent paid to government instead of to the lord.

# XIV.

PRAGUE, BOHEMIA, *July 12, 1841.*

I will give you some idea of the mode of travel in Hungary. Between Vienna and Pest there is a separate posting establishment, set on foot by peasants, who drive their own horses, and travel twice as expeditiously as an ordinary post. Their only carriage is a light wagon, which is furnished with an abundance of straw or hay to make it comfortable, with a rude temporary cover of matting thrown over it, to protect from the rays of the sun, and rain. The pace at which these conveyances travel is absolutely wonderful, especially some of the stages. One of these stages, of forty miles, was performed within four hours, with a stop of fifteen minutes to water. Most of the time they went at the most rapid speed, keeping the horses, of which there were four, at a full gallop.

It is a curious, but attractive sight, to see the wild looking driver, with his long black hair floating in the breeze, his broad-brimmed hat and feather, as he turns around to ask for your admiration when his four, little, clean-limbed nags are rattling away over hills and through hollows, at a rate absolutely frightful. Go slow he will not; and if you escape being overturned, and left by the road-side, you are fortunate.

Hungary is a rich agricultural country, producing immense quantities of grain of different kinds. In the opinion of some, it is not uncommon for travellers to exaggerate; and when I say that we passed through fields ten miles in extent, with wheat on both sides as far as the eye could reach, it will scarcely appear credible. The small Hungarian towns present a singular appearance, having mostly one long and very broad street. The houses all stand with their gables to the street, are one story high, and about eighteen feet wide, with but one front window, but extending very deep to the rear. In towns of three or four hundred houses, you will scarcely discover two with any other covering than a thatched straw roof, but they are all well whitewashed, and have a greater appearance of comfort and neatness than one would suppose.

The estates are very large, and most of the peasants are mere slaves. It is amusing to see them on Sunday, or a holiday, with their gay attire; their round-topped broad-brimmed hats filled with feathers and gay flowers, and the rest of their peculiar dresses decked in corresponding style, with gaudy finery, remind one of our American Indians.

On our route to this city from Vienna, we stopped at Brunn, the capital of Moravia, a city with a population of forty thousand. The sect called Moravians originated in this country. It is a manufacturing city, and may be regarded as the Austrian Leeds for its cloths and woollen stuffs. Baron

Trenck, the savage leader of the Pandours, the wild vanguard of the Austrian army, died here, and is buried in the church of the Capuchins. About ten miles from Brunn lies the famous battle-field of Austerlitz.

This city stands in a basin-shaped valley, cut in two by the river Moldau. It is surrounded on all sides by rocks or eminences, upon which slope the buildings of the city, rising tier above tier as they recede from the water's edge. There is something of Asiatic splendor in the aspect and form of the domes, turrets, spires, and minarets, which rise up without number on all sides. The most imposing building is the ancient palace of the Bohemian kings, which stands upon the crest of an eminence, and overlooks all the other buildings of the city. The population is one hundred and twenty thousand.

The city contains much to interest strangers. The Aldstadt, as its name imports, is connected with the new part of the town by a bridge of massive stone, which was begun in the year 1356, by the emperor Charles IV., and finished in 1507; it is one thousand seven hundred and ninety feet long, and is ornamented with fifty-six statues of saints, twenty-eight on each side,— one of them a bronze statue of St. Nepomuck, who, according to the Popish legend, was thrown from this bridge into the river and drowned, in 1383, by king Wenceslaus, because he refused to betray the secrets confided to him by his queen in the holy rite of confession. The spot is now marked by five stars and a cross, in imitation of the miraculous flames which for three days after he was drowned, were seen flickering over the place where his body lay under water. The river was dragged, his body found and encased in a gorgeous silver shrine, and placed in the cathedral. From this circumstance, he became the patron saint of bridges; and wherever I have travelled in Catholic countries, I find the statue of St. John Nepomuck occupying the same situation by the bridges. The shrine and chapel in the cathedral are among the most richly finished in the world. The body is contained in a crystal coffin, inclosed in one of silver, and held aloft by angels as large as life, also of silver. The candelabra which stand around, the ever-burning lamps which hang above, are of the same precious metal, weighing altogether two thousand five hundred pounds. About three miles from the city is the field of the famous battle of Prague, won by Frederick the Great, in the celebrated Seven Years' War. The cathedral is still standing at which Frederick aimed his cannon when he attacked the city, and is now a perfect museum of antiquities. Two hundred and fifteen balls passed through the roof. It is an interesting place to visit. The Jews quarter here, and occupy a part of the city by themselves, but are not locked up at night as in Rome and some other places that I have visited. It is recorded that in 1290 they were almost exterminated here by the fanaticism of the ignorant part of the people, who charged them with insulting the Host.

The most ancient synagogue here, the Jews assert, is nine hundred years old; the dust of ages remains undisturbed in it, and brooms, water, or whitewash would be considered sacrilege. It is a small apartment, supported on arches by three pillars, dingy with age and smoke. In some of their festivals they bear torches and lamps for days and nights, which accounts for the smoky and gloomy walls. The burial-ground, not far from the synagogue, is a singular spot. It is a large inclosure in the centre of the Jewish city, filled with the dead of centuries. One old headstone was pointed out which bears the date of the twelfth century. Many of them bear symbols of the tribes to which the departed belonged; a pitcher marks Levi, and so on.

We visited the palace of the Bohemian Kings. It is said to contain one thousand four hundred and forty apartments, and some are very splendid in size and decorations. The window is shown where three nobles were thrown out and fell eighty feet, having issued tyrannical edicts against the Protestants, which gave rise to the Thirty Years' War that ended in 1640. We next visited the palace of the great chieftain Wallenstein. It is stated that one hundred houses were purchased and pulled down to make room for building the palace and clearing the grounds around it. It is now occupied by the descendants of Wallenstein. Those who visited the palace in his lifetime have left behind a surprising account of its splendor, and the regal style kept up by the proprietor. His stables contained three hundred saddle and carriage horses, fed out of marble mangers. Sixty pages, of noble families, were kept in the establishment to wait upon him, and when he went from home fifty carriages each drawn by four or six horses conveyed himself and suite, and fifty wagons carried his baggage, while the whole train was followed by fifty extra horses. His fortune was enormous, and yet during the wars he was often at a loss for means to raise a few thousand florins, so terribly did the country suffer.

The monastery of Straliew, whose library contains fifty thousand volumes, has scarcely its equal in this part of the world for its splendor, being lined throughout with walnut wood, and richly ornamented with gilding. It contains, among other things of interest, the autograph of Tycho Brahe, the great astronomer, and a portrait of the famous Ziska, who, it is said, bequeathed his skin to his followers with directions that it should be tanned and stretched upon a drum, in order that its sound might inflict upon his enemies a portion of that terror which his presence while living had invariably produced among them.

# XV.

DRESDEN, SAXONY, *July 18, 1841.*

It was one day's ride from Prague to Töplitz, celebrated above all other watering places in Austria for its baths. It is pleasantly located on a small stream, and contains two thousand seven hundred and fifty inhabitants, and four hundred houses, sixty of which are inns. There is hardly a house in the town that is not used at times as a lodging-house. A great part of the place belongs to Prince Clary, who has such very extensive possessions in this part of the Austrian empire that he is put down as the proprietor of sixty villages! On the way from Vienna to Prague we passed for fifty or sixty miles through the estate of Prince Lichtenstein, whose entire possessions extend two hundred miles, the land being nearly all of the choicest quality.

Attached to the palace of Prince Clary in Töplitz are parks and gardens abounding with tall groves of fruit trees, and long promenades, fountains of water, lakes with beautiful flocks of swans gliding over the surface, and within the circuit lie the theatre, reading, dining, and ball rooms, which are thrown open for the use of visitors who wish to patronize the baths. The hot springs are seventeen in number, their temperature one hundred and twenty degrees Fah. During the summer there are thousands of persons at these baths. Being one of the most fashionable watering places, it is frequented not only by the nobility of Russia, Prussia, and Austria, but by the sovereigns of those countries, dukes, and princes of smaller estate, &c. There are six public baths and eighty private ones, which are in requisition from four o'clock in the morning until late at night. Each bathing establishment is placed under the direction of a "Badmeister" and his wife, and at the entrance hangs a list, where the hours at which every bath is engaged are noted down.

The visitor must be punctual in occupying only three quarters of an hour, and before the time is up he is notified by the ringing of a bell to prepare to dress.

On the route from Töplitz leading to Aussig, on the banks of the Elbe, at which place the steamer starts for Dresden, we passed through the battleground of Kulin, near the Nollendorf pass, which will always be famous in history. The French forces under Vandamme, and the allied forces under Count Colleredo Mansfield, fought a battle here that had a vast influence upon the fortunes of Napoleon. He had despatched Vandamme, with forty thousand men, under strict orders not to descend into the plain; but, contrary to those orders, he attacked Count Ostermann, who had with him eight thousand guards, chiefly Russians, and the Prussian and Austrian forces came up in time to rout the entire French force before any aid could reach them, killing and making prisoners all except a few thousands who threw away their arms and fled across the mountain. The Prussian, Russian, and Austrian governments have each erected a monument in the field. The Prussian is inclosed within an iron railing, and is of cast iron, with the inscription in German—"*A grateful King and country honor the heroes that fell;*" the Austrian is dedicated to Prince Colleredo Mansfield, who was wounded in the battle; the Russian was placed by the Emperor Nicholas in the centre of the field. It is an obelisk, surmounted by a figure of Fame, with a lion reposing at its base.

From Aussig, a small town on the Elbe, we descended rapidly, touching at Teschen, a small village most romantically situated, where commences the country called "Saxon Switzerland." The village lies at the foot of a high rock, on which stands the castle of Teschen, owned by Count Thurn, who is also the proprietor of the village and a district of country around occupied by eighteen thousand inhabitants.

The Elbe here seems pent up between bold cliffs and huge rocks, clothed in rich foliage wherever it is possible for a tree to hang; but it finds its way through them into a most romantic and picturesque country. In passing along we had a view of the Bartec, a rock that rises near the margin of the river to the height of eight hundred feet, and commands an extensive view of the surrounding country. The Konigstein rock, which is a fortress seven hundred and seventy-nine feet above the river, is deemed impregnable, and has never yet been taken. It is surrounded on all sides by perpendicular rocks, and so isolated that it cannot be commanded by artillery from any point. Napoleon tried to batter it from Lilienstein, the nearest eminence, but the shot fell short. The treasures of the Saxon government were fortunately placed here, and were thus kept secure. A space of two miles in circumference on the top of the rock, is laid out in fields and gardens, and is finely cultivated. The present garrison numbers only six hundred men.

The scenery on the banks of the Elbe, until within a few miles of Dresden, is of the most enchanting character. Dresden has a population of seventy thousand. It is delightfully situated on the bank of the river, and ranks high among European cities for its attractions, and the number and objects calculated to gratify the intelligent traveller. It is the residence of the king, and has consequently all the accompaniments of a national capital. Its picture gallery has the finest collection of paintings to be found north of the Alps. When Frederic the Great bombarded Dresden, battered down its churches, and laid its streets in ruins, he commanded his troops to keep clear of the picture gallery. Napoleon treated Dresden well, and respected its pictures. The collection is very extensive, consisting of many thousands, one of which, by Raphael, cost forty thousand dollars. It represents the Virgin soaring up to Heaven, bearing in her arms the Divine Child, while Pope Sixtus is represented as gazing upon the scene and trembling with pious awe; opposite to him kneels St. Barbara, and below the group stand two angelic children, their countenances beaming with innocence and intelligence. It is considered the best picture out of Italy.

The Green Vaults, so styled, are a range of vaulted apartments on the ground floor of the royal palace, containing a vast and rich collection of valuables. The Saxon princes in former times were among the richest sovereigns in Europe. This collection is probably the richest in Europe, amounting to many millions in value. The treasures are contained in eight apartments, each surpassing the other, as you reach them successively, in richness and splendor. The objects are so numerous that it is quite impossible to allude to more than a few of the most prominent: A large quantity of gold and silver plate which adorn the banquets of the Saxon palace; vessels formed of agates, precious stones, &c.; goblets composed entirely of cut gems, valued at six hundred dollars each; vessels cut out of solid rock crystal. Among the wonders of the cabinet are the works of Durglinger, an artist formerly employed exclusively by the Electors of Saxony. One piece is called the Court of the Great Mogul, and represents the Emperor Aurungzebe upon his throne, surrounded by his guards and courtiers in the most appropriate costume, in all one hundred and thirty figures of pure gold enamelled. It employed three persons eight years to complete it, and cost eighty-five thousand dollars. Last of all comes the eighth room, in which is one case containing valuables sufficient to pay off the national debt of Saxony, amounting to many millions; comprising the most precious jewels, sapphires, rubies, pearls, diamonds, &c. The diamond decorations of the gala dress of the Elector consist of buttons, collar, sword hilt and scabbard, *all of diamonds*. The most remarkable in the mass of chains, bracelets, orders of the Golden Fleece, and so on, is a green brilliant, weighing forty carats, and of great value.

The Historical Museum of Dresden contains all the weapons, offensive and defensive, of chivalrous warfare, all the trappings and accoutrements of tournaments, and other wild sports of feudal times. Here are whole suits of armor for man and horse, ornamented in great profusion with gold and silver. The entire armory occupies nine long galleries, and excels that of the Tower of London. One suit of armor is covered with reliefs representing the labors of Hercules, and other subjects, in gold and steel.

Among the historical relics in the last apartment are the robes worn by Augustus the Strong at his coronation as King of Poland; the little cocked hat of Peter the Great, and a wooden bowl turned by his own hand; the saddle of red velvet upon which Napoleon rode, the boots he wore in the battle of Dresden, and the satin shoes worn at his coronation.

The bridge over the Elbe here is considered one of the finest of stone in Germany. It is very solid, in order to resist the ice in the spring. There is a bronze crucifix on one of the arches, denoting the part blown up by the

French Marshal Davoust in 1813, to cover his retreat to Leipsic. One church here is composed of solid stone to the top of the dome, and is of such solid construction that cannon balls directed against it by Frederic the Great rebounded from its surface without doing the least injury.

# XVI.

WITTEMBERG, PRUSSIA, *July 23, 1841.*

We this morning arrived in this interesting town. I say interesting, from historical association only, as the town itself is dull and lifeless, with a population of seven thousand. It has been termed the Protestant Mecca; it was the cradle of the Reformation, as Martin Luther openly engaged here in opposition to the Church of Rome.

After procuring a valet-de-place, we proceeded to the market-place, where, beneath a Gothic canopy of cast iron, is a bronze statue of Luther, inscribed with these words in German: "If it be the work of God, it will endure; if of man, it will perish."

We next visited the town hall, where are preserved several paintings, among the number one of Luther and one of Melancthon; also the drinking cup of Luther, and several other relics. On passing up the street to visit the ancient Augustine convent, where Luther meditated the change of the religion of Europe, we passed the house of Melancthon, on which are inscribed these words, "*Hier wohnte, lehrte, und starb Melancthon.*"—(Here lived, taught, and died Melancthon.) On arriving at Luther's cell, we found the old chair and table at which he wrote, and the jug from which he drank. The wall bears the name of Peter the Great, written with his own hand. Outside of the gate of the town is an oak tree surrounded by a railing, marking the spot where Luther burnt publicly the Papal bull, by which Pope Leo X. condemned his doctrines and excommunicated him as an obstinate heretic, in Dec. 1520. Luther and his friend Melancthon are both buried in one church here. Two tablets of bronze inserted in the pavement mark their graves. Here are also the tombs of Frederic the Wise and John the Steadfast, Electors of Saxony, who were great friends of Luther and the Reformation. Against the doors of this church Luther hung up his ninety-five arguments, which condemned the doctrine of Papal indulgence, and which he offered to defend against all comers.

We leave here to-morrow morning for Berlin, the capital of Prussia. I wrote you last from Dresden, and next visited Leipsig, interesting as a commercial place, and celebrated for its memorable battle—the battle of the nations—one of the longest, sternest, and bloodiest actions of the war, and one of the largest battles recorded in history; the number of troops on the side of Bonaparte being one hundred and thirty-six thousand, and on the part of the allies two hundred and thirty thousand—two thousand cannon and eighty thousand horse. It is said that after the battle had raged three days in the vicinity of the city, on the 19th of Oct. 1813, it reached up to the walls, and cannon shot fell in showers in the streets. The castle of Plazenburg, the ancient citadel, is lofty, and from the observatory the guide gave us an accurate description of the position of all the armies. I visited the spot where the bridge was, unfortunately for the French, blown up, whereby twenty-five thousand soldiers were lost or taken. The river Elster runs through the city, and by this mistake many thousands of French, on the retreat, were precipitated, with wagons, cannon, and horses, into the stream. The gallant Pole, Poniatowski, whose tomb I found near the bank of the river, lost his life here. Leipsig contains a population of forty-seven thousand five hundred, and its sale of books forms one of the chief branches of commerce, said to amount to twenty million francs yearly. Three fairs are held here during the year, and while they continue Leipsig is said to be the mart of central Europe, and is visited by foreigners from all quarters, sometimes to the extent of thirty thousand. Then every hotel and lodging-house is filled to overflowing, and temporary booths occupy the streets. The old walls of the city have long since been demolished, and instead of them the city is now encircled with a belt of trees, forming delightful promenades bordered with flowers. It is said that in the year 1834, eighty thousand names of strangers were enrolled on the police books, and during the fair the streets were thronged with Jews, Tyrolese, Persians, Armenians, Turks, and Greeks, mingled together in a masquerade. Our valet took us to a cellar for refreshments, where, according to tradition, the famous magician Dr. Faustus performed his feats, which are represented by rude daubs upon the wall. Goethe has laid in the cellar a scene of the tragedy of Faust. It is said that the poet, as well as his hero, not unfrequently caroused here, while a student.

On leaving Leipsig we took passage for Dessau, the residence of Prince Anhalt Dessau, a separate and distinct principality. There is nothing remarkable on this route except the palace of gardens, at Worlitz, belonging to this prince. The grounds are very extensive and beautifully laid out, as is usually the case with those of the titled nobility—adorned with artificial caves and grottoes, miniature Gothic castles, a temple of Venus, an imitation in miniature of the Pantheon at Rome, lakes, labyrinths, &c. The church and chapel are very pretty; the palace is magnificently arranged, and filled with statuary, paintings, antiquities, &c.; it is only used as a summer retreat. While attending service recently we were struck with the fine vocal music produced by about thirty young boys. On inquiry, I found that singing is a part of Prussian education, and in no country, perhaps, is the system of general knowledge so extended as in Prussia. By law every child, at the age of eight years, must attend school.

In most states, although every man is obliged to serve in the army, a substitute may be had; not so in Prussia; every able-bodied man, from prince to peasant, must serve in person. Three years is the usual time, but as an encouragement for superior education, on the meeting of the board of military examination, young men showing proof of superior education may claim the right of serving only one year. All are liable to duty in case of war. By this system it is said that Prussia can, in a short period, furnish over half a million of men for the defence of its wide-spread frontier.

# XVII.

BERLIN, PRUSSIA, *July 30, 1841.*

I arrived in this city the day following my last letter from Wittemberg. Our approach to the capital of Prussia was through a dreary plain of sand, destitute of either beauty or fertility, and differing widely from the rich agricultural country through which I had been travelling. It is surprising that the foundation of a city should have been laid in so uninteresting a spot, and still more surprising that it should have grown to be the capital of a great kingdom.

Frederic the Great, ambitious to have a capital in proportion to his extended dominions, inclosed a vast space with walls, and ordered it to be filled with houses; the consequence is that the streets are very broad, and regularly laid out. One street, called Friedrichstrasse, is two miles long, and has not a foot of descent from one end to the other. Berlin has been termed a city built for effect, all that is exceedingly beautiful being concentrated in one focus. The palaces, museum, arsenal, opera-houses, some of the finest churches, and other magnificent buildings, are quite contiguous. The street on which they stand is at least two hundred feet wide, with four rows of linden trees running the entire length of it. The central grand promenade for pedestrians has rows of trees on each side, then comes the equestrian road on the right and left, with one row of trees on each side, after which are the carriage roads and side walks, on both sides of this great avenue. The river Spree, a small stream which runs through the city, communicates with the Elbe, and by means of canals with the Oder, the Baltic, and the German Sea, and is navigated by boats.

The population of Berlin is three hundred thousand. Owing to the scarcity of stone the city is mostly built of brick, stuccoed and painted, or colored in a variety of ways, which gives it a light and beautiful appearance. Notwithstanding all its disadvantages of situation Berlin is one of the most splendid cities in Europe. Few can show so much architectural splendor as is seen in the colossal palace, the beautiful colonnade of the new museum, and many other buildings. The Brandenburg Gate, one of the principal ornaments of the city, is probably the most splendid portal in Europe, built after the model of the Propylæum at Athens, but larger. The Car of Victory on the top, drawn by three horses, with the goddess in a standing position, was taken to Paris by Napoleon, but the Prussians recovered it after the battle of Waterloo.

The royal palace is of vast size, and gorgeously furnished. One apartment, which is very splendid, and called the Knights' Hall, has a throne and sideboard covered with massive old plate of gold and silver, large collections of paintings, one large chandelier of solid crystal, the ball suspended from the bottom of which cost twenty-four thousand dollars, and is larger than the crown of my hat. In the attic story of the palace is the Cabinet of Art, occupying several rooms. Among the most prominent objects of the large collection are Japanese and Australian weapons, Chinese collections, cloaks of feathers from the Sandwich Islands, works of art in ivory and gold, vast collections of jewels, a model of a windmill made by Peter the Great with his own hands while working as a ship carpenter in Holland, the robes of the Order of the Garter, given by George IV., and those of the Order of the Holy Ghost, given by Louis XVIII., to the late Prussian king. Some of the relics are entirely national. The bullet that wounded Frederic the Great in the battle of Rossbach in 1760; a wax figure, said to resemble him, as a cast was taken after his death; he is clothed in the same rusty and tarnished uniform he wore on the day of his death; the scabbard of his sword is mended with sealing-wax by his own hand; his books, flute, and cane lay before him on the table, also his pocket-handkerchief, which is ragged and patched, and which he used to the last.

Frederic the Great was certainly a singular character. Dr. Moore says his whole wardrobe consisted of two blue coats faced with red, the lining of one a little torn; two yellow waistcoats, considerably soiled with snuff, and three pairs of yellow breeches. Here is also a glass case containing the stars, orders, and decorations presented to Napoleon by the different sovereigns of Europe, except England. They were taken by the Prussians after the battle of Waterloo, in his carriage, from which he escaped so narrowly that he left his cap behind him, which is also preserved here.

The new museum is liberally thrown open to the public. It contains a very extensive picture gallery; some of the paintings are good originals, but most of them are copies, and in this branch of the arts Berlin bears no comparison to the Italian cities. There are also sculpture galleries, galleries of antiquities, collections of vases, bronzes, &c. The vases amount to one thousand six hundred in number. The ornithological collection in the University is one of the richest and most extensive in Europe, comprising all classes of birds from every quarter of the globe, the collections of Baron von Humboldt and others. The Egyptian museum ranks very high, and is said to be the most curious in Europe. Among the figures are those of various Egyptian deities, with the symbols belonging to each, and worn on the image. Among the mummies are not only those of human beings, but of the animals worshipped by the Egyptians, such as cats, young crocodiles, frogs, and lizards, all embalmed and wrapped in fine cloths. The most interesting object is the contents of the tomb of an Egyptian High Priest, discovered and opened in the Necropolis of Thebes. The body was inclosed in a triple coffin, the work of which is most intricate and extraordinary. All the specimens shown here of the produce of different trades are calculated to give a good idea of the extent of civilization and progress of the arts three thousand years ago in that country.

The Arsenal here is well worthy of a visit, as specimens of the arms and accoutrements used in all parts of Europe are seen in great abundance. Fire-arms used from the first invention of gunpowder to the present time; two leather cannons used by the great Gustavus in the Thirty Years' War, are shown; many ancient weapons and suits of armor; and against the walls hang upwards of one thousand standards taken during the campaigns that overthrew Napoleon. About five miles from the city is Charlottenburg, a small village on the Spree, made mostly of villas, for the summer residence of the rich, and taverns to accommodate others who resort there from Berlin.

At Charlottenburg is a palace built by Frederic the Great, the grounds about which are exceedingly beautiful, and open to the public, being finely laid out and constantly thronged. Arms of the Spree run through them, and the waters abound with carp as large as shad, which come up to the surface on the ringing of a bell, and are so tame that any one may feed them. The interior of the palace, which may be seen by feeing the Castellan, as he is called, is very interesting, and gorgeous in silver and gold decorations, Gobelin and Prussian tapestry, statuary and paintings. The length of the entire building, furnished complete, is six hundred feet. We were shown the room that Napoleon occupied during his stay here. It had been previously occupied by the queen, but she never would stay there afterwards, but took another apartment. One of the most attractive objects is the beautiful statue of Queen Louisa, said to have been one of the most beautiful and amiable princesses of her day. She is buried within a small Doric temple, at the extremity of a shady walk, in a retired part of the garden. The work is by Rauch, of Berlin, and is not surpassed by any modern work of art. The figure of the queen reposes on a sarcophagus of beautiful white marble, and as Russell describes it, "it is a form and face of the most exquisite beauty, but at the same time a most perfect resemblance." The expression is not that of cold death, but of undisturbed repose, the hands being modestly folded on the breast, and the attitude easy, graceful, and natural. Only the countenance and part of the neck are bare, the rest of the figure is shrouded in drapery beautifully wrought. There is no inscription, or catalogue of titles, but simply the Prussian eagle at the head and foot of the sarcophagus, with four lions at the corners to support it.

# XVIII.

FRANKFORT-ON-THE-MAINE, *Aug. 6, 1841.*

On leaving Berlin our party proceeded to Potsdam, denominated the Prussian Versailles, lying on the bank of the river Havel, about twenty miles from Berlin. It may be called a town of palaces, not only from the four royal residences in and about it, but because the private residences are copied from celebrated edifices. It has a population of thirty-three thousand, including a large garrison. The principal objects that attract travellers are the grounds and extensive palaces; also, Peacock Island, in German, "Pfauen Insel." This island was the late king's hobby, and he made it an enchanting spot. The distance of four or five miles from Potsdam is soon accomplished, where the island is reached by a boat. It is beautifully situated in the centre of a lake, and is about three miles in circumference, and what was a wilderness of sand and fir trees, is now converted into the most delightful pleasure grounds, adorned with rare plants, shrubbery, and groves of trees of all varieties. Here is every variety of building which enlivens English or French gardens; fancy Gothic buildings, pavilions, menageries, and animals of all kinds, from the noble lion to the innocent lama, the deer and the elk, running at large. A great variety of birds, from the vulture, eagle, and ostrich, to the owl and parrot, may be seen in their different habitations. The king was engaged twenty years in bringing it to perfection, and it was his favorite retreat during summer. The mounted frigate, presented by William IV. of England to the king, is stationed here in the lake, and its proportions suit well the scenery by which it is surrounded.

We visited Sans Souci, the residence of the king, beautifully situated on the top of a flight of steps like terraces. The terraces are fronted with glass, beneath which grow vines, olives, and orange trees. Frederic the Great, who took great pride in his grounds as well as in his faithful dogs and horses, had a favorite spot of resort at the extremity of the terrace, and just before his death was brought out to bask in the sun. He desired to be buried in this spot, with his favorite animals, but this request was not granted, although the graves of his favorites were shown to us. We saw the remains of this great man in the garrison church, beneath the pulpit, in a plain metal sarcophagus above ground. His sword, which originally lay upon it, was taken by Napoleon; but in place of that there hung on each side the pulpit the standards taken by the Prussian armies from Napoleon.

The new palace, about two miles from Potsdam, was built at enormous cost by Frederic the Great at the end of the Seven Years' War, by way of bravado, to show that his funds were not exhausted. It contains two hundred apartments. One large room is floored with marble and entirely lined with shells and minerals of all kinds—a very peculiar taste. As usual with these stately palaces, a vast amount of money was lavished in marble, gold and silver, gilding, &c.

On leaving Potsdam we took extra post to Magdeburgh, a distance of seventy miles. It is situated on the Elbe, with a population of fifty-two thousand. It has a fortress of the first class, and owing to its vast extent would require from fifty to seventy-five thousand men. The citadel on the island serves as a state prison. Gen. Lafayette was confined in it. The famous Baron Trenck was also confined in one of the prisons here. In 1552 Magdeburgh was besieged and taken by Maurice, king of Saxony. During the Thirty Years' War it resisted the army of Wallenstein seven months, but was afterwards taken by the ferocious Tilly, who murdered thirty thousand inhabitants without distinction of sex, and left only one hundred and thirty-nine houses standing. In his despatch he says, "never was victory so complete since the destruction of Jerusalem and Troy."

The cathedral, one of the noblest Gothic buildings in Germany, built in 1211, and recently repaired by the Prussian government at a cost of *three hundred thousand dollars*, was saved by one Bake, a schoolmate of Tilly. It contains many curiosities of art. At this city we regretted parting with one of our travelling companions, who took a steamer for Hamburgh, to go from thence to London or Amsterdam. My present American companion and myself next proceeded to Cassel, the capital of the Electorate of Hesse-Cassel, one hundred and forty miles from Magdeburgh. In passing through this rich agricultural country I observed, in addition to all the products of our northern country, vast quantities of poppies for the manufacture of oil, and large fields of beets to be made into sugar.

Fences in the interior of this country are unknown. The same may be said of most parts of Austria and Prussia. The farmers cultivate large tracts of land, but live in villages. All the varieties of the products are seen from the road in passing, as the width or front of each growing crop is ordinarily quite narrow on the road, and so arranged in most instances as to extend back in strips as far as the eye can reach.

Cassel, for a town with a population of thirty thousand, contains much to attract the attention of a traveller for a few days. In the Frederic Platz, a very large square, is placed a statue of the Elector Frederic, who was one of the number that elected the Emperor of Germany in former times. To that prince Cassel owes its embellishments and extravagant works. He disgraced himself and his people by trafficking in the lives of his subjects, when he hired them out to the King of Great Britain to fight his battle in America. It is said also that five thousand Hessian troops were hired in England, with the consent of Parliament, to fight against the Pretender in Scotland.

Some of the Hessians are still living who went to America in our revolution. I have seen two of the old veterans passing along the road, with ancient chapeaux that reminded me of prints I had seen many years since. Among the extravagances of the Elector, was the construction of the cascade of Carlsburgh, about three miles from the town, in the rear of the palace and grounds, and on the top of a high hill. You ascend a flight of nine hundred and two steps from the base to the top of the hill. A carriage road leads by the side of this gigantic staircase, in zigzags, to the summit. To the left of the steps, ascending, are flat stones laid one above another, very like a huge stairs, but with a greater acclivity, from the top of which the water is permitted to fall whenever it is desired, forming a beautiful cascade. The summit is surmounted by an octagon temple, called the Temple of the Winds, on which is raised an obelisk, serving as a pedestal for a colossal Hercules, thirty-one feet high, of beaten copper. It is possible to get up into the figure, and eight persons can stand in the hollow of the club, and out of a little window is one of the most extended views imaginable. The aquatic staircase, octagon temple and statue, altogether, employed two thousand men twenty-four years. When finished, the expenses were found to be so enormous that the accounts were burned to destroy all record of them.

Attached to the palace is a theatre, which was built by Joseph Bonaparte, in which he himself used to act. The grounds and walks are very beautiful, and once a week the principal fountain plays. It is the highest in Europe, and throws up a jet of water two hundred feet perpendicular, and twelve inches in diameter. It is supplied from reservoirs three hundred feet higher up the hill. Here are also artificial waterfalls, bridges, aqueducts, &c., finished at great cost.

From Cassel to Frankfort we travelled by Lohnkutch, which is a private conveyance, making the distance, one hundred and six miles, in two days, stopping to dine and lodge. We had also an opportunity to examine any remarkable church, manufacturing establishment, or other curiosity that might be attractive. Through Austria, Hungary, Saxony, and Prussia, we had all the varieties of travelling conveyances, known by such titles as Eilwagen, Schnellpost, Stellwagen, Bauernpost, Eisenbahnen, Railroad, Extra post, Zugkutcher, &c.

On the route from Cassel to Frankfort, we stopped over night at the town of Marburg. Its only object of curiosity is the church of St. Elizabeth, a beautiful specimen of the early Gothic pointed style of architecture, and in most perfect preservation, begun in the year 1231, and completed in forty-eight years. In one part of the church is the richly ornamented Gothic chapel dedicated to St. Elizabeth, the Landgravine of Hesse, who was canonized for the sanctity of her life in 1231. The carved tablet represents the saint lying on her coffin, surrounded by cripples and sick persons, the objects of her bounty Her soul is seen hovering above, on its way to Heaven, whence Christ extends his hands to receive her. The stone steps around it are worn hollow by the knees of pilgrims, who have resorted here for ages. There is now a partition through the church, for the accommodation of Catholics and Lutherans, who will never meet together.

In some parts of Bavaria and Austria, the pilgrimages are still kept up. Thousands and tens of thousands every year make a journey to the shrine of some favorite saint, to kiss some precious relic, or worship, in all but pagan idolatry, before some miracle-working picture or statue of the Virgin. At one place I saw as many as a thousand men, women, and girls, who were setting out on a journey to Maria Zella, a celebrated pilgrimage place in the Styrian Alps. They entered the cathedral from which they started, in procession, kissed the cross, made their prayers, and then marched forth on their pious tour on foot, many with scanty clothing to protect them from the storms, and with miserable supplies of food, carried in sacks or baskets, to sustain them on their fatiguing march. But such are the severe burdens that superstition, ignorance, and bigotry impose upon their wretched subjects.

# XIX.

COLOGNE, PRUSSIA, *Aug. 16, 1841.*

Frankfort, from which I wrote last, is one of the free towns of Europe, being governed by a senate of its own; but it is considerably influenced by Austria and Prussia. Its territory is limited, not exceeding ten square miles, and the city and environs contain a population of fifty-two thousand—five thousand of whom are Jews. It is quite a lively city, the walls of which were levelled many years since and planted with trees, which now afford a delightful shade and promenade, being interspersed with a variety of plants and flowers. The desire for shade and fine promenades is an admirable feature in the European character, and in almost all cities I have yet visited on the Continent, I find the taste for agreeable and shady public walks to be prevalent; and I regret that their utility is so little considered in our own beautiful country, especially as they are greatly conducive to health, as well as comfort and pleasure.

Frankfort is the seat of the German diet, and the deliberations of the Confederation of the German States are held there. It is the residence of many foreign ambassadors and wealthy merchants, and from the extent of its monied transactions, may be called the city of bankers; the most prominent of them is Baron Rothschild, who lives in princely style, having a magnificent villa and pleasure grounds in the suburbs of the city. Frankfort was the cradle of the Rothschild family; the house in which they were born is in the Judenstrasse, or Jews' street, which is narrow, with gaunt old buildings and gable ends to the street. The houses never having been cleaned or painted, the dust and smoke of centuries are upon them. I was directed to the house, which the mother of the Rothschilds still occupies, and which, since it is the old homestead of the family, narrow and confined as it is, she refuses to leave for the palace of her son, not far distant.

The condition of the Jews here is much ameliorated. Formerly, the part of the city they occupy was closed by gates at an early hour; and another tyrannical law restricted the number of marriages among them to thirteen yearly. Both of those oppressions are now removed.

There are many objects of interest to occupy the attention at Frankfort. The banker to whom my letter was addressed, had a gallery of works of art. Among the sculpture, a piece representing Ariadne is the most prominent, and considered the lion of Frankfort; it is the figure of a female resting gracefully on the back of a tiger, beautifully executed, of pure Carrara marble. The gallery is liberally thrown open to the public. Before leaving the city, I thought it would not be unprofitable or uninteresting to visit the new cemetery, and take a melancholy but impressive walk among the abodes of the dead, as I had done while at Leipsig and some other German cities, as the cemeteries are places of public resort at all hours, and the gates always stand open during the day. One of the peculiarities of the German character is their veneration for the abodes of the dead. The grounds are beautifully and tastefully laid out, with walks adorned with shade trees and every variety of flowers. At one end of the inclosure is a long and beautiful arcade, under which repose, beneath pompous monuments, the rich and noble. Other parts of the ground are thickly studded with crosses, gravestones, and monuments, among which may be seen groups of young and old, entwining wreaths of flowers and evergreens around the monuments of those they loved, or perhaps placing a basin of holy water, or arranging a little border of flowers, by the side of some new-made grave. I saw many new graves strewed over with strips of lace, with tassels of gold and silver attached, on many of which the name and age of the deceased were imprinted.

A police regulation here requires that all bodies for interment shall be placed in the dead-house for a certain length of time, to guard against accidents by burial in cases of suspended animation. The building contains ten rooms for the bodies, and a room in the centre for a watchman; also a room provided with beds, medicines, and all other necessary articles, in case of the reviving of a subject. The fingers of the prostrate corpses are placed in the loops of a string attached to an alarm clock; and on the slightest motion or pulsation of the body, it gives the alarm to the watchman, who immediately summons assistance. But I will dwell no longer in the places of the dead, but return to the ways of the living.

On leaving Frankfort I visited Wiesbaden, which is the capital of the Duchy of Nassau, and has a population of ten thousand. Thousands resort thither for health and pleasure, and the efficacy of its baths; it being favorably situated, and connected with Mayence on the Rhine, and Frankfort, by railroad, it is more frequented than any of the German watering-places. My stay at this place of bustle and high life was short, but to give an idea of it, I will state that on our arrival at the junction of the railroad, we pursued our way to the Kursaal, the prominent hotel of the town, through a long line of beautiful sycamore trees. Having arrived at the usual dinner hour (one o'clock), we found a magnificent saloon, with three hundred guests at table, and a band of music playing in the same room. As there were no vacancies, we ordered dinner at a later hour, and in the meantime visited the springs, and strolled through the beautiful grounds by the side of a lake, on which white swans were seen gliding gracefully over the surface; the banks were lined with dahlias and other flowers. One spring has the appearance of a boiling cauldron, with a temperature of one hundred and fifty-six degrees Fahrenheit. Its waters are used for drinking, and taste very much like weak chicken broth. It supplies many baths, and the quantity that runs to waste is very considerable. In addition to this principal one, there are thirteen other springs.

On returning from our interesting walk, we saw many groups descending the hill on donkeys, which are always ready to convey visitors to the heights about Wiesbaden, to enjoy the fine view up and down the Rhine. To my surprise, on returning to the hotel, I found the grand saloon converted to a use which is not tolerated publicly at any of the Austrian and Prussian watering-places that I have yet visited. Here they have a special privilege from the government to gamble in public. Among the many hundreds of visitors, some were occupied in promenading, or in sipping coffee and ices under the shade of the trees; others were engaged in play at the different games, and among them were many well dressed ladies taking part with all the coolness and gravity possible. Such are the customs, and such is life, among the gentry who collect here. The grand saloon of the hotel I found to be occupied regularly for four distinct purposes; that of a dining, a ball, an assembly, and a gambling room.

I next visited Mayence on the Rhine, a town with a population of thirty-one thousand. It is strongly garrisoned with Austrian and Prussian troops, being the chief fortress of the German confederation. The troops stationed here vary from eight thousand to sixteen thousand. Every town or city has something peculiar, or some attractive sights command the attention of the visitor; but there are few remarkable things about Mayence. Its cathedral, which was built in the tenth century, is noted for its antiquity. Europe is indebted to Mayence for two things, which have had the greatest influence in effecting human improvement—free trade and the printing-press. The art of printing was first known in Mayence, and it was the birthplace of John Gutenberg, one of the associates of the celebrated Faust in the invention and early promotion of the art. The town is connected with the opposite side of the river by a bridge of boats one thousand six hundred and sixty-six feet long.

At Mayence I took the steamer for Coblentz, and visited Ehrenbreitstein, the Gibraltar of the Rhine, an immense fortification on the opposite side, about eight hundred feet high, on a rock with steep slopes. It has cost the Prussian government four millions of dollars. Capable of holding fourteen thousand men, the magazines are large enough to contain provisions for eight thousand men ten years. The view from the heights is splendid, the banks of the "Blue Moselle," with the bridge of boats, and other interesting sights, being directly opposite.

But the scenery along the Rhine, so celebrated throughout Europe, and so worthy of admiration, no pen can justly describe. It is of such a varied, delightful, and interesting character that it is impossible to convey an adequate idea of its beauties. No river in the world combines so many picturesque and magnificent views with so many historical associations. Its variety of wild and precipitous rocks, thick and gloomy forests, ruined castles, strongholds of the robber knights of former times, ruins of all descriptions, monuments, fortresses frowning from the lofty summits of the rocky elevations, with fertile plains, wide-spreading vineyards, towns and villages almost line the banks between Mayence and Coblentz. But this is the most interesting part of the river.

The vine is very extensively cultivated along the Rhine, producing some of the most celebrated wines. In some places the vineyards are nothing more than a succession of terraces, extending from five hundred to one thousand feet high, up the face of a hill, and frequently comprising from fifteen to twenty, each supported by a front wall from five to eight feet high.

## XX.

AMSTERDAM, HOLLAND, *Aug. 24, 1841.*

In my last from Cologne I promised to say something descriptive of its attractions, and its being termed the Rome of the north. For its origin and antiquity it is deserving of notice; besides, it is a commercial city, and the largest on the Rhine. History says Cologne was founded by the Romans, and that Agrippina, the mother of Nero, was born here. The cathedral, which was commenced in the year 1248, by the Elector and Archbishop of Cologne, has remained up to the present between a fragment and a ruin. If it had been finished, it would have been one of the prettiest Gothic edifices existing. The choir is the only part completed. It is one hundred and eighty feet high, and internally, from its height, size, and disposition of arches, chapels, and beautifully colored windows, strikes one with awe and astonishment. The entire length of the cathedral is four hundred feet, its breadth one hundred and sixty. The towers, which were only partly finished, were to have been five hundred feet high. In a small chapel is the celebrated shrine of the three kings of Cologne, or the Magi, who came from the East with rich gifts for the infant Jesus. The bones were obtained by the Emperor Barbarossa and presented to the Bishop of Cologne. By a payment to the sacristan we entered the inclosure, which is under double locks. The case, or coffin, in which they are deposited, is of solid silver gilt, about six feet long, three high, and three wide, and is curiously wrought—surrounded by small arcades, supported by silver pillars, and by figures of the apostles. The case is enriched with cameos, enamels, antique gems, diamonds, rubies, and other precious stones in abundance. The skulls of the three kings, inserted with their names, Gaspar, Melchior, and Balthazar, written in rubies, are exhibited to view through an opening in the shrine, crowned with diadems. The sacristan says the treasures are worth six million francs. There are many other relics of saints, church plate, &c., exhibited.

The church of St. Ursula and of the eleven thousand virgins is too singular to be forgotten. As the legend goes, St. Ursula, with eleven thousand virgins, set sail, in the second or third century, I think, from Britain for Armenia, and was carried by tempest up the Rhine, where the whole party were slaughtered by the barbarian Huns because they refused to break their vows of chastity. In the church, which is large and commodious, in cases beneath and around the altars, inclosed and built in the walls, are these hideous bones. They are displayed in gaunt array, in glass cases, about the choir and the altar. In the golden chamber, encased in silver, a select few of the number are deposited, while St. Ursula reposes in a coffin behind the altar. The walls in this church are decorated with bones, fashioned in all fantastic shapes. One of the stone vessels is here shown which Christ used at the marriage supper, and in which he converted water into wine.

On leaving Cologne, by steamer, we descended to Nymwegen, the first frontier fortress of Holland, which we entered without a very strict examination of luggage. On sallying forth the morning following my arrival, I was forcibly struck with the unusual cleanliness and neatness of the Dutch, particularly as the day previous I had left Cologne, which is not only celebrated for Eau de Cologne, but for its filth. We left Nymwegen for Utrecht by diligence, and it being Saturday, the general "schoonmaking," or cleaning day, I had a fine opportunity of witnessing what may be termed an excess of cleanliness, in passing through several small villages before arriving at Utrecht. Almost every house presented a scene of the utmost activity. The brushing, scrubbing, and mopping are not confined to the inside of the house, the steps, and door-ways, but the windows, walls, and sidewalks must undergo a course of ablution. Scarcely a domestic is seen without a water-pail and broom, or a small engine pump for throwing water to wash the windows, and a traveller stands a small chance of avoiding a shower bath, if he walks carelessly along the sidewalks. The drawing-room is a sort of sanctum, and is said to be rarely entered oftener than once a week, and then only by the housewife and her maid, with list shoes, to avoid scratching the polished floors. After having finished washing and dusting, the door is closed, and windows fastened for another week. Sabots, or wooden shoes, are generally worn during the purification, and after the work is finished they must undergo a regular wash as well as the brooms and other articles used in cleaning.

One of the peculiarities of the Dutch towns is the little mirrors projecting in front of the windows of almost all the houses. Ordinarily they are two pieces of looking-glass framed at an angle of forty-five degrees from each other, the one reflecting up the street and the other down, whereby the Dutch ladies may sit ensconced behind the blinds or curtains, and see all that is passing in the street, and not expose themselves to the gaze of the public.

At Utrecht, a city with a population of forty-four thousand, we found sufficient to entertain us for a day. On ascending the steeple of the cathedral, three hundred and eighty-eight feet high, we obtained a view of the surrounding country, which is a perfect flat, watered by canals in different directions, and avenues of trees, all planted by the rule, with an occasional windmill and steeple in the distance, to break the monotony of a Dutch landscape. Half way up to the top we were introduced into a room where refreshments are furnished, and found the family of the sexton, who had lived there thirty years and reared a family. While resting we enjoyed the merry chime of thirty or forty bells in the steeple, which is repeated every hour.

On leaving Utrecht we took the national conveyance, the treckschuite, or canal boat, which does not differ very materially in size from our Erie canal boats, with the exception of having separate apartments for the accommodation of different classes of passengers. The towing horse is ridden by a lad, who is very dexterous, in passing bridges and other vessels, in disengaging the tow rope without impeding the progress of the boat. The canals in Holland run in all directions through the country and through the towns and cities, and are the great high-road for the transportation of goods and passengers. The consequence is, that in the vicinity of large towns and cities, on the principal canals, which are about sixty feet wide and six feet deep, are located many beautiful villas, country seats, and pleasure gardens.

On the entire route to this city, since I have entered Holland, either along the highway or along the canal, especially in the vicinity of populous cities, I have discovered the abodes of those who seemed to study cleanliness and comfort. In the suburbs of the cities you will find those country-seats where great wealth is expended. At the end of the gardens overlooking the canal, or main road, is always placed a small temple, pagoda, or snug, comfortable building, where you will see the men smoking their pipes and sipping their beer, or the ladies their tea and coffee, engaged in knitting, or criticising the passers-by. Perhaps there is no country in the world where flowers grow to such perfection as in Holland, and nowhere have I seen such an array of plants and flowers as these gardens contain. The roads for wagons and diligences run along the line of the canal, or upon the dykes which are thrown up to protect the influx of the sea. The soil is of such a nature that roads are constructed with difficulty, and at an expense of seven thousand dollars per mile, all of hard burned brick placed edgeways. In traversing the canals in many instances, you look down upon the "polders" (so called) on both sides, with the cattle grazing far below the surface of the water you are navigating. Those polders are frequently liable to inundation during the winter season. You observe hundreds of windmills employed in sawing timber, grinding wheat, and other occupations, and among the number, in passing along, you discover many pumping the water from low grounds, or polders, that lie below you, and throwing it into the canal. It may well be said that the Hollander has made the wind his slave, for not a puff of air is suffered to escape without turning a windmill.

Amsterdam is a large commercial city, with a population of over two hundred thousand, and is one of the most remarkable cities in Europe for its peculiar location, being intersected by various small canals, which divide it into ninety-five islands with two hundred and ninety bridges. Had I not seen Venice, which is still more remarkable, I should have considered it very extraordinary. The entire city, quays and sluices, are all founded on piles, which are driven through the upper stratum of mud and loose sand until they reach the firm sand below. The palace of the king is a large and imposing building of stone, standing upon thirteen thousand six hundred and ninety-five piles. The second day after my arrival a grand fête took place, and towards evening I strolled up the main street, crossing many bridges, to the suburbs of the city, passing through an immense crowd of persons, and among the number I should think there were all of ten thousand females, most of them without bonnets. I seldom attempt a description of costume, but I must here observe that the females in Holland are particularly distinguished for neatness and gracefulness of costume, as well as clearness of complexion. To see such an immense group, very many of whom were domestics, all in tastefully arranged caps and head-dresses, was a novel sight. Numbers have the back of the head encircled by a broad fillet of gold, shaped like the letter U, which confines the hair and terminates on each side of the temple with two long rosettes, also of gold. Over this is worn a cap, or veil, of finest lace, hanging down the neck, with a pair of enormous gold ear-rings. Among the group I discovered many orphan children, who have their particular dresses to distinguish them.

The people of Amsterdam are celebrated for their charitable institutions. One particular costume, for male and female, I observed, was red and black cloth, extending from the shoulders to the feet, which reminded me of the dress of a clown, red one side and black the other; and I could not but pity the wearers, especially young females, who were thus made so conspicuous in the eyes of strangers.

# XXI.

ROTTERDAM, *August 30, 1841.*

Well, at last I am in Rotterdam, and I assure you I was heartily glad to reach this city, as one may rest quietly for a few days without seeing extraordinary sights. Rotterdam is a fine commercial city, with a population of seventy-four thousand, and exceedingly novel and interesting to a stranger who has just arrived in the country; but to one who has made the tour of Holland it possesses none of those extraordinary sights which a traveller is in duty bound to see. The remark may appear strange that one becomes tired and exhausted with sights; but in a long line of travel, in visiting cities in rapid succession, where a sort of obligation is imposed upon every good traveller to see all that is remarkable, it becomes laborious.

During the time we tarried at Amsterdam, we made an excursion to Broeck, celebrated as the cleanest village in the world. It has a population of eight hundred persons. In making this excursion we passed through a part of the great ship canal, which is one hundred and twenty-five feet wide, twenty-one feet deep, and fifty miles long. Two ships can enter side by side. After leaving this we took a conveyance which runs by the side of a lateral canal, on which are seen men and women, harnessed like horses, trailing the canal boats to market. On arriving at this extraordinary village our carriage was left outside, as neither horse nor wheel is permitted within the precincts. Our valet leading the way, we proceeded, in pattens, through the various passages or lanes, which are paved with brick or little stones, the paths being composed of shells. I had formed an idea of the extraordinary neatness of the place from the accounts I had heard of it, but the fantastical arrangement and construction of the houses exceeded my expectation. The houses are mostly wood with tile roofs, painted and varnished, which glitter in the sun. The buildings are most scrupulously painted with different colors, many representing different temples, and all sorts of architecture. We were taken to the garden of the rich clergyman of the village, and the guide-book describes it as surpassing all the others in its absurdities, and in the miscellaneous nature of its contents, beating the "groves of Blarney" all to nothing. Here are pavilions, arbors, summer-houses, pagodas, temples, bridges, &c., the small canals running through the garden, and indeed through every part of the village. Most of the front doors are closed during the week until the housewife opens the door, takes down the shutters, dusts the china and the furniture, and arranges everything, then closes it for another week, unless in case of a marriage, a funeral, or christening. The residents are mostly retired merchants, landed proprietors, stockbrokers, or other persons who have made fortunes. In one part of the village are made many Dutch cheeses. We went into the apartments of the cows in one house, the animals being absent from home in the fields. The pavement was of Dutch tiles, the walls and partitions of boards, scrubbed as clean as a dining table. We were permitted to enter the front door of one of the sanctums after having placed our feet in list slippers to avoid soiling the floor, and it is said that the Emperor Alexander, on visiting Broeck, was compelled to comply with this usage!

Having finished our excursion, we next went to Saardam, a place with a population of nine thousand, and remarkable for its four hundred windmills, which are applied to all uses. Some of them are of immense size, with wings eighty feet in diameter, and have houses attached to them. One street of windmills is five miles in length. The next remarkable object for a stranger is the hut of Peter the Great, in which he lived while working as a ship-carpenter, in 1696. The building is of rough plank, and consists of two rooms; in one is a cupboard, used as his sleeping-place, above a loft entered by a ladder. The property was bought by the sister of the Emperor Alexander, and is now inclosed in a case of brick-work, with shutters to close in bad weather. Here you find registers filled with names, and the walls of the hut are so completely covered that it is almost impossible to register another name.

On quitting Amsterdam we took the railroad to Haarlem, which route is accomplished in thirty minutes. It has a population of twenty-four thousand, and its environs are very pretty. The main attraction here is the great organ, which is celebrated over the world. Its size is immense, filling up the whole end of the Cathedral; it has five thousand pipes, the largest fifteen inches in diameter; two of them are thirty-two feet, and eight sixteen feet long. Its power is wonderful when played on by the organist in private, with all the variety of mutations which it is capable of. The charge for a private performance is thirteen guilders, for one person or a party, equal to five dollars and fifty cents. An English gentleman had just employed the organist and finished when our party applied for his services. The imitation of the flute, fife, and piano, followed by the loud charge of the trumpet, was an admirable performance; after which came the tinkling of bells, which one could scarce believe came from the pipes, and then came "the storm," grand and terrific beyond description, the mimic thunder roared frightfully, and the walls of the building fairly seemed to tremble. The great diapason produced a sound like the whizzing of the machinery of a cotton factory. All these efforts are to show the strength and power of the instrument. An ordinary performance is of the most rich and melodious character.

Our next city to visit on the route was Leyden, celebrated in the annals of Holland as having resisted the siege of the Spanish army in 1573–4 for four months, and displayed the most resolute patriotism. At a period of extreme exhaustion, when bread had not been seen for seven weeks, and pestilence had followed famine and carried off six thousand inhabitants, and when the people were subsisting on horses, dogs, cats, and other foul animals, then it was they came to the resolution to open the dykes and inundate their country to overwhelm the cruel enemy, sooner than submit. History records that the expedient had not an immediate effect, but as if Providence soon and directly interfered, the wind suddenly changed and brought in the sea to the walls of the city, drowning thousands of the Spaniards; and when that was accomplished, veered as suddenly about and carried most of the flood back again so as to enable them to repair the dykes. Among all the collections of Dutch paintings are some portraying the horrors of that dreadful siege.

Leyden has a population of thirty-five thousand, and differs but little from other Dutch cities, being intersected by canals in every direction, most of them bordered by rows of trees; the suburbs are beautiful, with many pretty villas and flower gardens. There are several collections of Chinese and Japanese articles, as the Dutch carry on a great trade with the East. I cannot enumerate the objects of interest further in Leyden, as I must bear in mind the Hague, the next city which we visited, and which is the residence of the Court.

The population of the Hague is about fifty-five thousand. It is situated about three miles from the sea-shore, intersected by canals in every direction, the waters of which present less activity that those of any other city in Holland. We visited Scheveningen, a small fishing town near the sea shore, riding through an avenue of fine shade trees. The bathing establishments are much resorted to by the nobility and persons of distinction on the Continent, who take up their residence here during the summer. The "Dunes," so called here, are immense banks of sand, thrown up by the wind, and forming a natural barrier against the encroachments of the sea. The sand being very light is scattered by the wind, but in order to preserve the ridges or embankments from injury they are secured by being planted with rushes, or matted over with straw and reeds. Here are also windmills which pump up the water from the ocean, which runs down the Hague, and displaces the stagnant water from the canals, forcing it into another canal which leads it to the river Meuse. The Hague possesses the finest picture gallery in Holland, and the Royal Cabinet is highly interesting and instructive. The Japanese collection is the largest in Europe. Among a thousand other relics I saw the armor of Admiral Von Tromp, bearing marks of several bullets. He was engaged in no less than thirty-two sea fights, conquered the English under Blake in 1652, and afterwards sailed through the British Channel with a broom at his masthead, signifying that he would sweep the ocean of all foes.

Since our arrival at the Hague we have made an excursion to Schiedam, famous for its fine gin, of which there are one hundred and seventy-two distilleries in that small town. Thirty thousand pigs are fed on the refuse grain.

It is a neat, pretty village, surrounded by comfort and cheerfulness. Throughout Holland I find the people are more moral, cleanly, temperate, industrious, and strict in their observance of the Sabbath, than in any other part of the Continent that I have visited. It is a country of comfort and extortion—the latter because the taxes are high and the necessaries of life dear.

# XXII.

MILAN, ITALY, *Nov. 7, 1841.*

The mail post, the mode of conveyance from Paris to Strasburg, is the most rapid in France. The number of passengers is limited to three persons, with a stipulated allowance of baggage. The horses are changed frequently and with expedition, scarcely giving the passengers time for refreshment on the road. But on this route, where there is little of interest to be seen, it is far more agreeable than the Diligence. The distance is nearly three hundred miles, which were accomplished in thirty-six hours and a half.

Strasburg, the frontier fortress of France, is situated very near the banks of the Rhine, and contains a population of sixty thousand, and a garrison of six thousand men in time of peace. It is the strongest fortification in France. It has the appearance of a German city, and that language is much spoken, and altogether it appears quite unlike France. The principal curiosity here is the cathedral, one of the noblest Gothic edifices in Europe, and celebrated for its spire, which is the highest in the world: it is four hundred and seventy-four feet above the pavement. The cathedral was commenced in the eleventh century. It is the most remarkable piece of open airy stonework imaginable. It was not finished until the fifteenth century, over four hundred years after it was commenced. To ascend the steeple it is now necessary to apply to the magistrates of the city for permission, as several persons have fallen or thrown themselves off the top. There is no difficulty for one with firm nerves to make the ascent, but the stonework of the steeple is so completely open, and the pillars which support it so wide apart, and cut so thin, that they nearly resemble bars of iron or wood, so that at such a height one might imagine himself suspended in a cage over the city, and if the foot were to slip the body might easily drop through the open fretwork. At the same time the elaborate work, and the shapings of the angles and ornaments, are proofs of the skill of the architect and the excellent materials he had chosen. The interior of the building is rich, but what strikes the eye most is one window of painted glass, of a circumference of fifty feet diameter, and rising to the height of two hundred and fifty feet, at the west end of the nave.

After leaving Strasburg I took the railroad which connects that city with Basle in Switzerland, running through an interesting country, nearly one hundred miles. Railroad travel is rather a novelty for the French and Swiss, being quite a new enterprise with them.

From Basle I proceeded to Berne, a city with a population of twenty thousand, beautifully situated and much resorted to during the summer by strangers. The scenery of this part of Switzerland is not so grand and majestic as the mountain views, but the country is undulating and productive. The varied costumes of the peasantry in the different Swiss cantons (of which there are twenty-four comprising the Republic), strike the eye of the stranger as being singular and beautiful.

From Berne I took diligence for Friburg, which, in addition to its magnificent and lofty situation, is celebrated for its suspension iron bridges; the length of the two over which our diligence passed is nine hundred and three feet, their height one hundred and sixty-three feet above the river. It appears frightful in the extreme the first time you pass the bridge, but it is considered perfectly safe. The other bridge, over which I passed subsequently, while examining the work, is seven hundred feet long and two hundred and eighty-five feet above the valley over which it is suspended. During heavy gales they are said to vibrate considerably.

The route from Friburg to Vevay, situated upon the lake of Geneva, is very beautiful, passing through immense vineyards loaded with fruit, and the peasantry, male and female, are busily employed in gathering and pressing the juice of the grape; nothing can exceed the beauty of the snow-capped mountains in the distance, while the blue and limpid Lake of Geneva bathes the shore of Vevay. From Vevay I took the steamer on the lake, visiting Lausanne, a city of some importance, and beautifully situated on an eminence commanding extensive views of the country around. I next took the steamer and traversed the extent of the lake to Geneva, which is the principal and largest city in Switzerland. Here are generally to be found strangers from all quarters, good hotels, reading rooms, and all the comforts and necessaries of life for those who choose to make it a residence. It is the resort of many wealthy English. The situation upon the lake at the outlet—the beautiful and magnificent scenery—its public promenades—its interesting suburbs and adjacent country—altogether lend many charms to Geneva for a permanent residence.

About six miles from Geneva is the château and villa of Voltaire, to which most strangers pay a visit. Here are shown many relics—his garments, cane, books, correspondence, &c.; also the room in which he lodged, which contains his bed, furniture, pictures, &c. Among the latter I discovered a portrait of Dr. Franklin, who once paid Voltaire a visit.

On quitting Geneva for Milan, to pass over the Simplon, which traverses the Alps, ten thousand feet above the level of the sea, I was compelled to take the diligence, the only conveyance which left, just towards night, and on entering Savoy, in the middle of the night, was obliged to submit to the abominable practice of police authority, the examination of luggage and delivery of passport, and in the entire route to Milan had my baggage examined four times. After riding all night and the following day, passing through the most wild and romantic scenery imaginable, with occasional cascades from the mountains, we arrived at a little village called Brieg. In order to appropriate an entire day to the passage of the Simplon, travellers usually sleep at Brieg and set out with the dawn next morning. The journey across the mountain is about forty miles, and generally occupies about twelve hours. We started at three o'clock in the morning in the ascent. The weather, which in the valley was warm and agreeable, began to change sensibly; as we proceeded the cold increased; finally we found snow, and much to my surprise, at length were compelled to leave the diligence and take wooden sledges, upon which was lashed the luggage, while the passengers rode upon rudely constructed sledges with wooden runners. We soon found the cold intense, and the snow from two to four feet deep. Fortunately for me, when we arrived at the foot of the mountain, we were told that the mountain was almost impassable; the passengers had been detained five days, the roads being blocked up, a thing almost unprecedented even on the Simplon in the month of October. We provided ourselves with the requisite comforts and clothing for the passage. This passage of the Alps, planned by Napoleon in 1801, was finished in 1805 by the governments of France and Italy. Its breadth is twenty feet; the number of the bridges thrown across the rocks is fifty, and the number of grottoes hewn through the solid rocks is six. There are placed several rude buildings of stone, at different intervals, for the shelter of the traveller when threatened by the avalanches, with the marks "Refuge" No. 1, 2, 3, 4, &c. On the summit of the pass stands the new hospice, a good establishment for the passengers, begun by Napoleon, but only recently completed. It is occupied by the hospitable monks of St. Bernard, who showed us their famous dogs for dragging benighted travellers out of the snow. At the point where vegetation ceases, and where the avalanche has swept everything before it, is a dreary tunnel about one hundred and fifty feet long, through which we passed, which is cut through the rock over which the avalanches tumble. After emerging you pass along the brink of a precipice of immense depth. We started early in order to avoid the avalanches which commence about mid-day. We were forced in some places to pass over beds of snow twenty feet deep, the avalanches having blocked up the road. A large number of the hardy pioneers of the mountain were employed with their shovels in clearing the way. At about three P.M. we arrived over the side of the mountain at the little village of Simplon, where we were able to take wagons, as the snow was melting fast, and when we had got down in the valley, or gorge of the rocks, another grand scene presented itself. The snow melting rapidly formed cascades in every direction, which were coursing down the ragged and perpendicular rocks, sometimes exhibiting all the colors of the rainbow, and at others foaming in torrents. Altogether the passage of the Simplon, under the circumstances in which I crossed it, is one of the most wild, frightful, and yet grand and majestic scenes I have witnessed. In the early part of the evening we found ourselves at

Domo d'Osola, where we lodged, and the next day went to Bavano, upon the Lago Maggiore, where we stopped to visit the beautiful and enchanting islands called Isola Bella and Isola Madre, which I will speak of in my next.

# XXIII.

TRIESTE, AUSTRIA, *Nov. 16, 1841.*

In my last communication from Milan, I promised to speak of the charming lake called in Italian Lago Maggiore, and of the enchanting islands, Isola Madre and Isola Bella. The lake is about forty or fifty miles in length, and from four to six in breadth. Its shores are lined with forest trees, olives, and vineyards, and here and there are scattered villages and hamlets, some of which are remarkable for elegance of construction. The two islands above named contain palaces and gardens belonging to the family of San Carlo Boromeo. On visiting the Isola Madre, which is about one and a half miles from the shore, we were delighted on seeing, on the south side, four gardens, or rather terraces, rising one above the other, embellished with luxuriant flowers, shrubs, forest trees, all the tropical fruits, &c., in great abundance, and crowned with a palace. But we were still more gratified on visiting Isola Bella, about a mile distant, which is certainly the most remarkable work of the kind I ever saw—it being a small island, occupied entirely with gardens and the palace. It is said a great proportion of the earth was originally carried there. The southern exposure consists of eight terraces, rising one above the other, carpeted with flowers, oranges, lemons, and other fruits in profusion, and adorned with an immense number of statues. This great work is supported by stone arches, which, together with the basement or lower story of an immense palace, front a series of grottoes tastefully fitted up, and for a summer abode delightful. The palace in itself is magnificent, and loaded with all the valuables that wealth can bestow, in sculpture, paintings, &c. The king of Sardinia has passed some time at this agreeable spot. What is most remarkable is in the position of the island, for during the winter, while the mountains in the vicinity are covered with snow, here may be found all the tropical fruits and rare plants from all parts of the world.

After leaving Lago Maggiore, we proceeded by diligence to Milan, which is the capital of Lombardy, and the largest city in northern Italy, its population being one hundred and fifty thousand. There are many attractions in it calculated to detain a traveller, among the principal of which is the Duomo, or cathedral, which is the largest in Italy, excepting St. Peter's at Rome. It is four hundred and forty-nine feet long, two hundred and seventy-five broad, and the height two hundred and thirty-six feet to the top of the cupola. It is divided into five parts by one hundred and sixty columns of marble, and paved with the same material. Under the cathedral is a sumptuously decorated chapel, which was open while I was there, it being an anniversary, and thousands during the day passed into the subterranean chapel to see the remains of San Carlo Boromeo, which are inclosed in a crystal sarcophagus, adorned with gold and silver gilt. His figure is encased with superb robes, while his crosier and mitre rest by his side. His countenance, with the exception of the nose, is pretty well preserved. The interior of the chapel is also covered with marble, and gold and silver gilding, extremely rich. In order to appreciate this immense Gothic edifice, it is necessary to mount to the top of the cathedral, four hundred and sixty-eight steps, where you can view the spires, turrets, and exterior decorations, in white marble.

The triumphal arch of Napoleon, at the termination of the grand Simplon road, is another great ornament to Milan. It is an immense work, and crowned with a car, bearing the figure of Victory, drawn by six colossal horses in bronze; there are also four other horses, of the same material, standing on the four corners.

During the time I remained at Milan I made an excursion to the lake of Como. At the village of Como I took a small steamer, which plies upon the lake, and had an opportunity of seeing the beautiful gardens, pleasure grounds, and orangeries which line the shores. Nothing can be more delightful to the lover of fine scenery than an excursion upon this lake.

While in Rome, last spring, I saw an original cast in plaster, ordered by Napoleon, from the great sculptor Canova. It represented the triumph of Alexander the Great, and was said to have been purchased at a sum equal to fourteen thousand dollars, and was in a village upon the lake of Como. I landed at the villa Sonimorira, and visited the grounds and interior of this villa, or more properly speaking, palace, where I had an opportunity of seeing this admirable piece of sculpture in bas-relief, in white marble. It is attached to the wall. I made another excursion to Monza, about twelve miles from Milan, which contains a royal residence, well worth visiting; also a cathedral, where is deposited the crown of the Lombard kings, called the "Iron Crown," because it is lined with an iron hoop, but of small size, and, as the story goes, is composed of the nails with which our Saviour was fastened to the cross. The outside of the crown of gold is studded with precious stones. Charlemagne was crowned king of Lombardy with it in the cathedral where it is deposited. The sacristy also abounds with ornaments of gold, silver, diamonds, and other precious stones, belonging to the church. There was an unusual degree of form and ceremony before we could get to see this celebrated relic. After we had obtained permission from the highest functionary, I was not a little surprised to find that this relic was placed in the wall behind the altar, making it necessary to ascend by ladder to unlock the double doors, one of which was a part of the front of the altar; after which many candles were lighted and two priests put on their robes and made a short service, when an enormous cross of gold was produced, in the centre of which was inclosed in crystal the crown already described; for all of which our party paid five francs. I was rather credulous in the belief of the story that the interior of the crown was made from the nails of the cross, as I have already seen, in different parts of Europe, more relics of the kind than were necessary for the crucifixion of our Saviour.

After I left Milan I came to Verona, on the route to Venice, where I tarried one day. Verona has its objects of curiosity, but not sufficient to detain one who has seen the cities of southern Italy. The ancient amphitheatre here is one of the most remarkable; it is more perfect than any other in Italy. It accommodated twenty-three thousand four hundred and eighty-four persons seated, according to report, and is composed of large blocks of marble without cement. It is of an oval form, four hundred and sixty-seven feet long and three hundred and sixty-seven feet wide. The arena is two hundred and twenty-five feet in length, and one hundred and thirty-three feet wide. There are forty-five rows of seats encircling the arena. The exterior wall is destroyed, but the other parts of this immense work of antiquity are quite perfect. In the suburbs of Verona, in a building near the former cemetery of a Franciscan convent, is a sarcophagus called the tomb of Juliet, and made of Verona marble, with a place for her head, a socket for a candle, and two holes for the admission of air. This sarcophagus is nothing in itself, but associated with Shakespeare, and the history of Romeo and Juliet, it is full of interest.

On arriving at Venice, I visited the palace of the Doges, the Basilica of San Marco, the Bridge of Sighs, the Giant Stairs, the Rialto, and several other parts of the city. Venice is about seven miles in circumference, with a population of one hundred thousand. It is situated in the midst of shallows called Lagunes, and stands mostly on piles. It is entered in all directions by canals, which amount to some hundreds, and bridges of stone without number. The streets are narrow, frequently not exceeding six feet in width, but having shops on each side, and then again many passages not exceeding four feet wide. There are, however, many squares, but they are not generally large. The Place of St. Mark, upon which is situated many of the principal buildings, is magnificent, and presents a lively scene. The only conveyance is in gondolas, which traverse all parts of the city, and are a necessary appendage to every family. One is induced to pronounce it a singular and beautiful city, because no other is like it.

It is surprising that the city should be supplied with all the necessaries, comforts, and luxuries of life without any apparent difficulty. Here are to be found thousands of persons who never saw the bubbling of a fountain or the growth of the vegetables upon which they subsist, who know not the use of a horse, and never saw such an animal, who perhaps have never seen a tree.

On approaching Venice in a gondola it has the appearance of a city submerged, while the steeples in the distance resemble the masts of vessels. The silence is profound, and at first it appears dull. The canals in general being the streets, the only noise to disturb the tranquillity is that made by the oars and the cries of the gondoliers. On leaving Venice I took the steamer for Trieste, the passage being accomplished across the head of the Adriatic in from ten to twelve hours ordinarily. As I depart to-morrow for Greece you may not expect to hear from me again until after my arrival at Patras, or the Ionian Islands.

# XXIV.

ATHENS, GREECE, *Nov. 28, 1841.*

When I wrote you last, from Trieste, I was on the point of embarking by one of the Austrian steamers for this city, with the additional advantage of stopping at three ports on the route, which gives the passenger an opportunity of seeing some interesting sights. Soon after leaving Trieste we were visited with one of those violent gales of wind which so frequently occur on the Adriatic, against which the steamer struggled with difficulty, and all the passengers, except one, experiencing the horrors of sea-sickness, were snugly stowed away in their berths. This man solitary and alone, I noticed in his enviable position, seated at the supper table, whilst the sea was making a complete breach over the deck of the steamer, and the chairs and plates were secured by straps and braces. Within twenty-four hours we made the harbor of Ancona, the principal commercial port of the Pope of Rome, whose dominions extend from the Mediterranean on the west to the Adriatic on the east, and where we remained nearly a day, giving us an opportunity of seeing all that was most remarkable in the town. We next departed for Corfu, one of the most important of the Ionian islands, and the seat of government, and where we arrived after two days. The approach to the island is beautiful, with a fine harbor or bay for vessels. The opposite coast of Albania, the fortifications of the island of Vido, and the citadel of Corfu, built on two precipitous rocks running out into the sea, with the town and the mountains in the distance, form a splendid panoramic view.

The island is in the possession of the British, who have many troops stationed here. Its circumference is said to be one hundred and twelve miles, and the population sixty thousand, that of the city being twenty thousand. We have found the weather delightfully warm and pleasant, and observed many plants and fruits peculiar to the West India climate. On landing I was struck with the gay and picturesque costume of the male population, who mostly wear the Albanian dress, which is the gayest, and in some cases the most fantastic, of any I have seen in Europe. It consists of a red cap of beautiful material, of the form of a hat without the rim, with a large tassel of blue silk suspended from the top; a round jacket and vest, of cloth of various colors, beautifully embroidered with cord, and sometimes with gold and silver lace, which fits to the figure; from the waist is suspended a white frock with heavy folds which hang gracefully, barely covering the knees, with leggings of the same colored cloth as the jacket, embroidered in the same manner, and covering the shoes. The waist is encircled with a sash of red or blue silk, the ends hanging negligently by the side. We remained at Corfu only one day, but long enough to give us time to visit the villa of the governor, beautifully situated on a cliff overhanging the sea; also to visit the esplanade or parade ground, and some of the Greek churches, in one of which rest the remains of Capo d'Istria, the late governor of Greece, who was assassinated in Nauplia.

After leaving Corfu we proceeded to Patras, in Greece, passing the island of Santa Maura, where Sappho made her famous leap, and next the island of Ithaca, the birthplace of Ulysses, which is only eighteen miles long, and presents an air of ruggedness and barrenness, but is said to produce fruit, wine, and honey, of good quality. On arriving at Patras, where we remained part of a day, we found it had the appearance of a new town, and to my surprise I learned that during the last revolution every house was demolished by the Turks, as well as the orange groves, the woods of olives and vineyards; in fact everything was laid waste by fire and sword. There are not many remains of antiquity here. The new streets are well laid out, but the houses are mostly one story high, the country being subject to earthquakes.

On the opposite side of the gulf lies Missolonghi, celebrated for its battles with the Turks, as also for being the spot where Marco Bozzaris fell during an engagement in 1823. It was also the place where Lord Byron ended his career.

On leaving Patras we coasted along with the islands of Cephalonia and Zante in view, afterwards passing Navarino, so memorable for the battle of the allied forces against the Turks in 1827, which in its effects ended the war in Greece. After passing Cape Matapan, the most southern point of Greece, nothing occurred of interest until we arrived at the Piræus the morning of the eighth day from Trieste.

In order to convey an idea of the variety of character one meets on a voyage in this part of the world, I will mention that we had in the main saloon of the steamer sixteen persons, and that the ordinary conversation at table was in six different languages. Among the number a Turk from Smyrna, who had been interpreter to the English embassy in the East, conversed in eight languages. He was dressed in full costume, and wore his turban at meals and on all occasions. His long rich robes of satin, and yellow morocco slippers, presented a novel appearance, his favorite position being a seated one with his legs crossed. On entering the harbor of the Piræus the remains of the tomb of Themistocles were pointed out, looking down on the Gulf of Salamis, the scene of his glory. The modern town has been entirely built up since 1834. The distance to Athens is five or six miles. We took a carriage, and in approaching that celebrated city the ruins of the Parthenon struck our view, rising in all its majesty, one of the finest edifices formerly, and on one of the finest sites in the world.

During the last revolution Athens was entirely destroyed by the Turks, but it has again risen, and now has the appearance of a new city, with a population of twenty thousand. Since it became the seat of government, and king Otho made his public entry in 1834, it is said to have advanced rapidly. Although many houses are of very rude construction, and in some sections of one story high, with tile roofs, still in general the style of building is very good and substantial, and I am only surprised that in such a short space of time they could have advanced so far. Many of the public buildings are well constructed. The palace of the king, now in progress of erection, is of white Pentelic marble, three hundred feet long and two hundred and eighty feet in depth. It will cost an immense sum of money, which might have been better employed in other improvements than in building a palace, while the new government is in its infancy.

As soon as I had located myself at a hotel, I procured a guide to obtain a permission to mount the Acropolis and visit all the antiquities of the city. It is necessary to apply to one of the officers of the city for this, and to pay a small sum, to ascend this celebrated Cecropian Rock, which has been a fortress from the earliest ages down to the last day of the war. The walls form a circuit of two thousand five hundred and thirty yards, and are built on the edge of the perpendicular rock, which rises one hundred and fifty feet above the plain in which stands the city. The area inclosed is about fifteen hundred feet long, and the greatest breadth five hundred feet. On entering the only gate, after winding round the hill, the first subject is the ruins of the Propylæa, which was built during the most brilliant days of Athens. There is little remaining except six fluted marble columns in front, and six in the rear, of the Doric order, with frieze, entablature, &c.; to the right is a high tower, rudely constructed. The Temple of Victory is the next ruin presented to view, with some fine Ionic fluted columns still standing, and quite perfect. Next comes the Parthenon, which stands in the centre of the Acropolis. When perfect the length was two hundred and twenty feet, the breadth one hundred. The front and rear are still standing, and many of the columns on the sides (in all thirty-two) still remain. The columns are sixty-four feet in diameter at the base, and thirty-four feet high, standing on a pavement to which there was an ascent of three steps. The height of the temple was sixty-five feet; parts of the frieze on the exterior still remain; they represent the procession to the Parthenon at one of the grand festivals. The Parthenon was constructed of white Pentelic marble. Within the Acropolis is an immense collection of ruins and antiquities too numerous to detail. The Temple of Theseus, not far distant from the Acropolis, is quite perfect, and the interior is occupied as a museum—all the fragments of marble which have been discovered by the government being placed there. It was built four hundred and sixty-five years before Christ. Thirty-four Doric columns, with the walls, remain entire, all of Pentelic marble.

On ascending the Areopagus, or Hill of Mars, where the council of the Areopagus sat, one finds sixteen steps cut in the rock; above the steps, on the level of the hill, is a bench of stone excavated in the rock. It was here that the judges sat, in the open air and in the dark, that they might not be influenced by seeing and knowing the accuser or the accused. It was here that St. Paul preached, that Orestes was tried for matricide, and Socrates for theism. The prisons of Socrates are four dungeons, cut in the rock at the base of a hill, and there he drank the poisoned cup. The temple of Jupiter Olympus was the largest in Athens. It was begun five hundred and thirty years before Christ, and completed by the emperor Hadrian, A.D. one hundred and forty-five. The only remains of that immense edifice are sixteen Corinthian columns, six and a half feet diameter and sixty feet high. It is supposed the entire circuit was two thousand three hundred feet; the length being three hundred and fifty-four feet, and breadth one hundred and seventy-one; the whole number of columns was one hundred and twenty.

Since I have been in Athens I have made acquaintance with Mr. Perdicaris, the American consul, Mr. King and Mr. Benjamin, the American missionaries stationed here, as also Mrs. Hill, whose husband is now absent in America. The judgment, talent, and perseverance of this lady and her husband have contributed much to the advancement of the children of Athens. The gentlemen named have been very polite and communicative, and from them I have derived much valuable information in reference to Greece. I had an opportunity of seeing the young king Otho and his queen at a concert soon after my arrival. He was clad in rich Albanian costume, such as I have described as being worn at Corfu, and which is in general use here also. I judge he is about twenty-five years of age. The queen is young and beautiful; she was handsomely clad in Frank costume.

After having finished the sights at Athens I shall make a tour in the interior, in company with one of the American missionaries from the southern parts of Greece, who desires to visit Nauplia, Argos, ancient Tergus, Mycenæ, &c.; but in addition I desire to see Corinth, where St. Paul lived one year and a half, and wrote his Epistle to the Corinthians. The weather being delightfully warm, and my companion speaking modern Greek perfectly, I anticipate great pleasure in making an excursion of six or eight days.

# XXV.

ATHENS, *December 7, 1841.*

I have just returned from my tour, after an absence of seven days, during which time we were favored with delightful weather, but our journey was attended with all the fatigue and want of comfort appertaining to travelling on horseback in the interior of Greece. But we were more than fully compensated with the incidents of travel and the remarkable objects of antiquity and curiosity presented to our view. I must first inform you that there are only six or eight carriage roads in Greece, and those only for a short distance. All travel is performed on mules or horses, and all manner of burdens carried in the same manner. In the interior hotels are almost unknown, there being but few guests to encourage them, as during the desolating wars with the Turks almost all the towns and cities were laid waste, and the Greeks sought refuge in the mountains.

The first object of my missionary companion and myself was to procure a Greek servant, a supply of provisions, with bed and bedding, when we started for the Piræus, a distance of five miles, in search of a boat to carry us to Epidaurus, upon the Gulf of Salamis, where our land travel commenced. On arriving, at five o'clock in the afternoon, we were fortunate in finding a caique ready for departure. There is an immense number of these vessels employed along the coast; they are from twenty to thirty feet in length, the only shelter being in the hold, the flooring of which is pebble-stones. The passengers numbered about twenty, who were stretched upon the deck, or on the gravelly floor, with nothing but a Greek coat, or a blanket under them, my companion among the group. By special favor I had the cabin to myself, for the reason that there was only room for one person. It was a small partition astern, with a board floor, say three feet broad, and scarcely long enough to lie at full length. Here I spread my bed and passed a tolerable night. The next morning we passed the island of Egina, and at noon arrived at Epidaurus, a place which formerly sent eight hundred fighting men to battle, now a miserable village of eighty inhabitants. But the town has recently acquired a celebrity from having given its name to the Greek constitution, adopted by the Greek Congress of Deputies from all parts of the nation, on the 15th of January, 1832.

We procured horses and a guide for Nauplia, making a *detour* of two hours to visit the ruins of the ancient city of Yero. Part of the road was through a fertile plain, producing tobacco and corn; then passing through a romantic defile by the side of a rocky hill, with a mountain torrent tumbling beneath. The path in some places is a mere shelf, only broad enough for one to pass, with a steep precipice above and below; while in others it winds through beautiful shrubbery where the myrtle and arbutus joined over our heads in festoons, and scarcely permitted the horse and rider to pass. The most remarkable remains of antiquity in this sequestered region are the ruins of a theatre. It was of white marble, and thirty-two rows of seats still appear above ground. The orchestra was ninety feet long, and the theatre, when entire, three hundred and seventy feet in diameter, and capable of containing twelve thousand spectators. There are also remains of several temples.

Night overtook us at Lygouno, where we found a Khan to spread our beds, and fire to cook our provisions. The next morning we made Nauplia, a distance of five hours (which is the only mode of reckoning in Greece, not being able to calculate by miles, as the roads are mostly paths winding in different directions). The city, with a population of nine thousand, was once the seat of government, and is a commercial place, with a magnificent harbor. It is strongly fortified. The fortress of the Palamedi, on the summit of a lofty and precipitous rock, seven hundred and twenty feet above the sea, is almost inaccessible, and has been called the Gibraltar of Greece. The view of the country and the Gulf of Nauplia from the summit is beautiful. I noticed many brass cannons of 1650, 1662, with the Venetian stamp, the lion of St. Mark. There are cisterns hewn in the top of the rock, large enough to hold rain water to supply the garrison three years. In visiting one of the Greek churches here, we were shown the spot where Capo d'Istria, the governor of Greece, was assassinated when leaving the church. We remained here one day, and proceeded for Argos, seven miles from Nauplia, an ancient city, which contains some antiquities—a ruined Acropolis upon the summit of a rocky hill. In 1825 the modern town was entirely destroyed by the Turks, but is partly rebuilt. The plains are productive with good cultivation, but the manner of cultivation in this country is quite primitive.

On our way to Argos we turned aside to visit the ancient city of Tiryns, built thirteen hundred and seventy-nine years before Christ. The Cyclopean walls of the fortress, which was one-third of a mile in circumference, are immense, and in remarkable preservation; some are twenty-five feet thick. The city was destroyed four hundred and sixty-six years before Christ, and it is most remarkable that some of the galleries, in the form of a Gothic arch, still exist, almost perfect. It was the birthplace and frequently the residence of Hercules. The Lernean lake, not far distant, is the spot celebrated for being the place where Hercules destroyed the Lernean hydra.

At Argos, there were no accommodations to be had, and we were thrown upon the hospitality of an English gentleman, a friend of my compagnon de voyage. We were informed here that it would not be safe to travel without a guard across the country, as two travellers had recently been robbed. We accordingly applied to the authorities, and procured a mounted horseman, armed to the teeth with musket, sword, and pistols. Altogether, our party presented a novel appearance. Our guard in full regimentals, our guide in Greek costume, running or walking beside the horses, making a distance of thirty or forty miles a day without fatigue, but singing gaily even till night approached; our servant, with the Hydriote costume, which differs from the Albanian—the pantaloons being not unlike a great sack secured to the waist, and below the knees of a blue color—with his red sash and cap, mounted on a pack-horse carrying supplies and bedding, with our horses in advance; altogether we formed a novel and formidable appearance. There is a law in Greece prohibiting the carrying of fire-arms without license. We met several suspicious characters with pistols and muskets, in the mountain passes, who were interrogated by our guide, and compelled to produce their permits; but it is not difficult to obtain a permit, under pretence of protecting the flocks of sheep and goats. On the route to Corinth, we passed through a wild and mountainous country, sometimes winding along a narrow path on the brink of a precipice, and then again following the course of a ravine. We visited the ancient city of Mycenæ, built by Perseus one thousand three hundred years before Christ. It was built on a rugged height, situated in a recess between two commanding mountains, of the range which bounds the Argolic plain. The entire circuit of the citadel still exists, and is very large. The gate of the lions is quite perfect; upon it are represented two lions, standing upon their hind legs, on either side of a pillar, or altar, on which they rest their fore paws. The tomb of Agamemnon is still perfect, as it was, perhaps, when the city was destroyed, four hundred and sixty-six years before Christ. The entrance is twenty feet broad; the diameter of the dome is forty-seven feet, and the height fifty feet. In the middle of the great doorway the holes for the bolts and hinges of the door are observed. We visited, also, the ancient city of Nemæa, which has only three columns standing of the temple of Jupiter, some remains of the Nemæan theatre, and in the vicinity, several caves, supposed to be those of the Nemæan lion. It was situated on a beautiful plain; and where once existed a large population, now nothing is heard but the cry of the shepherd, or the barking of his dog.

In some sections of the country, we would travel many miles without discovering a habitation of any kind, occasionally meeting a solitary Greek, with his heavily laden mule or donkey, going to market; or, perhaps, upon the mountain's ridge, would find a regular encampment of itinerant shepherds, with their flocks of goats and sheep. It was an amusing and novel sight, to see these people emigrating to another section of the country, or taking up their winter quarters in the valleys. I observed several of these parties, composed of three or four families together. They not only have considerable flocks, but raise horses for sale. On making a move, their tents are lashed on pack-saddles, with all their supplies of clothing, cooking utensils, &c. The small children are lashed upon the backs of the horses in the same manner, while the girls and boys, in their picturesque costumes, are leading and driving the horses and colts, sometimes to the number of seventy or eighty. The men are employed in driving the flocks of sheep and goats, while the women are driving the horses which carry different kinds of poultry on their backs, and, at the same time, are engaged in spinning cotton with a portable distaff, which they carry in one hand, and twist the thread upon a spool with the other, with great dexterity.

On arriving at Corinth, situated on the gulf of Lepanto, we visited the remaining antiquities of that city, which once ranked first among the states of Greece. During the last revolution it was reduced to ashes. It is now being rebuilt, but in a very different manner. Seven Doric columns of a temple still exist, amidst modern desolation. There are also the remains of an amphitheatre, and excavated in the rock, at one end, is seen a subterranean entrance for the wild beasts and gladiators. In this city St. Paul resided and wrote his Epistles to the Corinthians. Back of the city rises a mountain, upon the summit of which, one thousand eight hundred feet high, stands an immense fortress, considered the strongest in Greece, next to Nauplia. A steep ascent, winding through rocks, leads up to the gate, which requires an hour's walk, and where one of the most magnificent views imaginable is to be seen, comprising six of the most celebrated states of ancient Greece.

On leaving Corinth, we crossed the Isthmus and struck Cenchrea, mentioned in the Acts of the Apostles as the spot whence St. Paul departed for Syria. We arrived at Megara the same night, and our guide conducted us to the only house of entertainment in the town, which contains a population of one thousand persons. But this modern village is in a ruinous state. We found the landlord had only one room, and that was occupied. Accordingly, our gend'arme conducted us to the house of the Demarch, or mayor of the town, where we had an opportunity of partaking of Greek hospitalities, which is not unusual for strangers to accept in the interior. Suffice it to say, we were made very comfortable, and felt ourselves under many obligations for comforts that money could not procure.

Soon after leaving Megara we dispensed with the services of our gend'arme, as we struck upon the road to Eleusis, which is considerably frequented. In passing along the coast of the Saronic Gulf we had the island of Salamis in full view, half a mile distant, where three hundred and eighty Greek ships defeated two thousand ships of Xerxes. At Eleusis are many antiquities about the modern town, and the piece of ground is here pointed out where, according to tradition, the first corn was sown.

On the way to Athens may be seen the old causeway, called Via Sacra, along which the ancient processions moved to that city. During our last day's march we found the sun's rays rather oppressive, and I was rejoiced when we entered the olive groves of the academy, which afforded a fine shade in our approach to Athens.

# XXVI.

CONSTANTINOPLE, *Dec. 22, 1841.*

I took the steamer for this city, stopping at the island of Syra, which is the concentrating point for passengers changing steamers for Egypt, Constantinople, Malta, &c. The town is built upon the summit of a lofty hill, so remarkable for its conical form that it may be compared to a vast sugar-loaf covered with houses. In the distance it looks well enough, but in the interior everything is dirty and filthy.

From Syra we came to Smyrna, which is prettily situated upon the Asiatic shore, and on entering the city were struck with the Oriental costume of Turks, Armenians, Jews, and Greeks; the women, with their faces covered with a sort of white veil, disclosing only their sparkling black eyes, appeared singular enough. The streets are ranges of houses constructed of wood, mostly one story high, and without chimneys. The population is about one hundred and fifty thousand. The bazaars are crowded with buyers and sellers, while trains of camels with loads upon their backs are passing through the narrow streets, scarcely admitting the foot passenger to pass.

On the 14th I left Smyrna for this city, making the passage in less than two days, passing the ruins of ancient Troy by daylight, the island of Tenedos, stopping at Chesme, where the Turkish fleet was burned in the harbor. On entering the Dardanelles we had a magnificent view of the old forts and villages scattered along the coast. I should think the width of the Hellespont about equal to the Hudson river at Poughkeepsie. Our steamer received and discharged some Turkish passengers at Gallipoli, a city of considerable importance, just before we left the Sea of Marmora, which was the last point touched until our arrival at Constantinople. We arrived about mid-day, having an opportunity of seeing, under favorable circumstances, the most beautiful port in the world. Nothing can exceed the magnificent view that is before you on entering the Golden Horn, the eye resting upon scenery one half in Europe and the other half in Asia, the painted and gilded minarets of the mosques, the swelling cupolas, and immense cypress trees towering above the houses—the forest of masts, the thousands of caiques which cover the waters, all combined, render it perhaps the most remarkable sight of the kind in the world.

On entering the city one finds the scene much changed, although there is a vast deal of magnificence still; the streets are narrow and dirty, thronged by immense crowds of people, and it is impossible to form an idea of the extremes of grandeur and wretchedness that are exhibited. Nothing can be more striking than the contrast in the character and customs of the Turks and the other nations of Europe, and I hardly know where to commence a description.

We procured a dragoman to accompany us, and speak the language, and started to see the sights of the city. After visiting some of the mosques and viewing the exterior—no one except "the faithful" being permitted to enter until a firman is obtained from the Sultan—we strolled along, and I was struck with the sight of an immense cemetery, almost in the middle of the city, the tombstones being in the shape of a turban on the top, with gilded letters, and tastefully decorated; the grounds were filled with stately cypresses, as it is the custom to plant one of these trees at the birth and burial of each person. Singular as it may appear, the cemetery is the grand promenade, and here the Turk sips his coffee and smokes his pipe under the shade of trees when the weather is warm. On passing you observe the coffee-houses, occupied also with groups squatted round the room on a counter, which is raised from the floor and carpeted, and it is amusing to see the attendants glide about through the long pipes and the winding smokes of nargilhès supplying their customers with coffee, without deranging the peculiar apparatuses for smoking.

The next day after our arrival was Friday, the Turkish Sabbath, and it was announced that the Sultan would visit the mosque near the arsenal. We were there in good time, and at mid-day precisely we heard the thundering of cannon from the vessels of the port. Soon after we discovered approaching four gorgeous state barges about fifty feet in length, propelled by twenty-four oarsmen, the canopies glittering with gold. An immense array of officers and military to escort him were in attendance from the barges to the mosque. He walked on a carpet which was laid for the occasion. I observed many prisoners carrying baskets of gravel, and on inquiry learned that it was scattered for the Sultan to walk on after he came from the mosque.

We next went to the place of worship of the Whirling Dervishes. We entered with slippers, according to their custom, and found many Turks squatted on the floor, in their usual position. In the centre was a ring about thirty feet in diameter, where were thirteen priests, dressed in cloth frocks, with a white cloth cap, almost of a conical form, without rim, passing round the circle, and going through many strange evolutions. At length, to the music of the fife and drum, they commenced whirling slowly, and then more rapidly, until the motion was like a top; continuing this and other strange exercises for about an hour, finishing by a tremendous howl, which is intended to make the Christians, or the infidels, as they call them, tremble. The Turks consider all Christians as dogs, of which animals they have thousands upon thousands in Constantinople. They subsist in the streets, without masters, and seem to despise Christians and Turks alike. The people, however, are very kind to animals, that being a part of their religion. Their litters are never destroyed, and they are the only scavengers of the city. They feed upon the offal of the butchers' shops and private houses, and carcasses of animals. They are never domesticated within private dwellings. The mosques are guarded to prevent their polluting them, as they are very susceptible of the plague. One not unfrequently hears the cry of "*Giaour*" from the lips of the Turks, in passing, and the growling and barking of hundreds of dogs testify their hatred.

It is unsafe for a stranger to appear in the streets after dark, and never practicable to do so without a lantern. It is a strange sight, on a clear, starlight night, to see perhaps one hundred lanterns at once, flitting about the streets, which are so narrow and dark that all who move about in them are compelled to carry lights. No strangers are permitted to reside in Constantinople; the gates are closed at an early hour, and all foreigners live at Pera, on the opposite side of the harbor.

On visiting the slave-market, we found perhaps one hundred and fifty slaves, all females, the largest proportion black. The blacks are sold for servants, the whites for wives. The latter are mostly Circassians or Georgians, belonging to good families in those provinces, who entrust their daughters to the commissioner, who is responsible for any insult or affront, while the female has the right of refusal to be sold to any whom she may dislike. The female blacks are bought to be the slaves of the mistress, not of the master. He is bound to support them through life. The male slaves rise with the condition of the master.

The population of Constantinople is variously estimated from five hundred thousand to seven hundred thousand, with the environs of Scutari on the Asiatic shore, and Pera and Galata on the opposite side of the Golden Horn, which is an arm of the Bosphorus running up and forming the harbor. The city is well supplied with baths and fountains, and nothing can exceed the luxury of the Turkish bath. It is amusing for a stranger merely to enter one of these establishments. The rooms, of which there are a number, of a circular form and lighted from the top, have different gradations of heat, the last or warmest of which is excessive. The first room entered, which is about sixty feet in diameter, with a dome, is supplied with galleries, upon which are seen, lying on different couches, the bathers reposing after their ablutions, each with a pipe from four to six feet in length in his hand, the servants supplying coffee and other refreshments.

Beautiful fountains are found near the mosques, as well as in other parts of the city. You may see the Turks at all hours of the day, bathing their faces, hands, and feet at the fountains attached to the mosques, ablution being compulsory, under the Mahometan religion, before entering the mosques. We enter a place of worship with our heads uncovered; they shave their heads, upon which they wear a turban, at all times, and enter their mosques with their feet uncovered. Some of their fountains are of a quadrangular form, the roofs of which bend out like a pagoda whose corners are cut off. On all sides are gold inscriptions and Arabic characters.

The covered bazaars have more the appearance of a row of booths, than a street of shops. Here may be found the jewelers, occupying one quarter, the silk merchants another; one alley glitters for hundreds of yards with yellow and red morocco boots and shoes, which are worn by Turkish and Armenian ladies, all classes being distinguished by their costume. The arrangement of the different trades, and the exposure of their gaudy and rich articles, surprise even those who are acquainted with London and Paris.

On Sunday last I found the little Episcopal church which is supported here, and tolerably well attended. The service was all in English, and the scene and associations presented by such a worship, so far from England, were of the most pleasant and interesting character. Generally the Americans attend this church, there being no other Christian church here.

To-morrow we make an excursion upon the Bosphorus as far as the mouth of the Black Sea, and the next day are to visit the seraglio of the Sultan, the mosques, the tombs of the late Sultans, the Mint, and other objects of interest, from which all strangers are excluded, except by the special firman of the Sultan. The Austrian admiral, who is now here, has obtained a firman, and my travelling companion, a young Prussian, and myself, are invited to join the party.

# XXVII.

SMYRNA, *December 30, 1841.*

My last was from Constantinople, in which I mentioned my intention of making an excursion along the Bosphorus to the mouth of the Black Sea. Having procured a Kislangist, or swallow boat, with twenty-six oarsmen, we started—our party, with the dragoman, consisting of four in number. These boats are built of light beech wood, neatly finished and elaborately furnished. They go over the water with amazing rapidity. They are so extremely light that great caution is necessary in getting into them, as from their nature they are easily upset; but once in, all seated themselves in the cradle of the caique, upon carpets, like the Turks, there being no seats. It is difficult to convey any idea of the beauties of the scenery along the banks of the Bosphorus. The eye is constantly attracted by new and beautiful objects, both on the European and Asiatic shores; rapidly passing palaces, summer villas, fortifications, villages, &c., as the boat glides along from bay to bay, of which the Bosphorus forms itself into seven. The currents at the narrowest points in some places are extremely rapid. At one point, called the Dents current, which is the narrowest, the boatmen were obliged to give up the oars and seize a rope which was thrown them to draw the boat up stream. It was a beautiful sight to see the fleet of vessels coming from the Black Sea, availing themselves of the north wind and the rapid current, and going with great velocity. After visiting Stenia, Therapia, and other places along the coast, each being celebrated for some particular event, we visited the Giant's Mountain, the highest point on the Asiatic side, which affords a magnificent view of the windings of the Bosphorus and the coast of the Black Sea. Here in this great height we found two of the Dervish priests, who remain there to guard the grave of the giant. It is called the Mountain and Grave of Joshua by the Turks, who say that Joshua, during the battle of the Israelites, stood upon a mountain to pray that the sun might stand still and victory attend his arms. The grave is about twenty feet long and five feet wide, and is inclosed with a framework of stone, and planted with flowers and bushes. Here are also pieces of cloths and votive offerings hung up on the bushes, against fevers and other diseases, their owners believing that if they hang a remnant there the disease will leave their persons. On descending we visited the valley of the Heavenly Water, one of the most delightful scenes in the East.

But I must try to give an idea of the Seraglio of the Sultan, though I cannot speak of the beauty of his forty or fifty wives, who were screened from the gaze of all our party. This splendid work is inclosed with walls for nearly three miles in circuit, the longest side situated upon the coast and harbor. It is filled up with palaces, houses, and gardens. Some of the rooms are very rich in gilding and ornaments, but I have seen other palaces in Europe far surpassing it in splendor. I must except the magnitude of the inclosure, and the magnificence of the baths and spouting fountains of marble, which, according to oriental custom, are placed over the first floor. Nothing can be more luxurious for the women of the harem than those marble basins and bath rooms, magnificently furnished, and always of the proper temperature. The principal entrance to the Seraglio is an immense guarded gate, which looks more like a guard-house than the entrance to a palace of one of the most remarkable princes in the world. Fifty porters, it is said, keep this gate. After entering the first court may be found the slaves of the Bashas, who await their masters and attend their horses. Passing through another guarded gate you discover many eunuchs, both white and black, performing the different services of the palace. After visiting the interior of the palace, the gardens, the stable of Arabian horses, the exhibition of ancient armory, all of which is so extensive that it is really fatiguing, we proceeded to the mosque of St. Sophia, which has undergone so many changes for the last fifteen hundred years, and now stands in such magnificent grandeur. The interior is extremely rich in marble and mosaics. Three of its sides are surrounded by vaulted colonnades covered with cupolas. The length of the interior is one hundred and forty-three feet, the breadth two hundred and sixty-nine feet. The centre of the great dome is one hundred and eighty feet above ground, and is so flatly vaulted that its height is only a sixth of its diameter, which is one hundred and fifteen feet. Here are eight porphyry columns from the Roman Temple of the Sun, and four of green granite from the temple of Diana at Ephesus. It would occupy too much time and space to describe this magnificent structure. The floors are well paved with large flag-stones, covered with matting, and then carpeted, and here may be seen groups of Turks, both men and women, the latter veiled in long caftans, all squatted on the floor, with feet bare or in slippers, paying their devotions. Overhead are suspended in every direction, immense rows of lamps, with ostrich eggs and artificial flowers, which, when lighted, must produce a magical effect. Among other objects of curiosity here is the sweating column, visited by pilgrims as miraculous. The dampness which it emits is considered a marvellous cure. There are holes worn into the column by the constant touching of fingers. The tops of the minarets of some of the mosques glitter with highly gilded crescents, the ancient arms of Byzantium; the one on the top of St. Sophia is of immense size, the gilding alone costing fifty thousand ducats. It is said to be visible fifty miles at sea, glittering in the sunshine.

Notwithstanding the Turks differ so widely in their manners and religion, still they possess many good traits of character. They are more honest than some other nations, and not so much addicted to lying. The Greeks say sometimes that the Mahometans dare not lie or steal, as their religion forbids it. They are exceedingly devotional, and generally hospitable to the stranger in distress, which is a part of their duty as laid down by the false prophet, but they still hold infidels in detestation. On visiting the house of a Turk the other day we found the proprietor, with his legs crossed, smoking his pipe, seated upon a sofa which extended round three sides of the room; the sofa was about four feet wide, and was raised a foot and a half from the floor, with deep fringe hanging down to the floor. There was not a chair in the room. After being introduced and seated, pipes were ordered, and as many servants as there were visitors appeared, with pipes five or six feet in length, placing the bowl on the floor, and with a great deal of accuracy presenting the mouth-piece of amber to each guest within an inch or two of the mouth. They then knelt down and put a brass plate under the bowl of the pipe; after which coffee was presented in small cups with small silver holders, the servants retiring to the bottom of the room with hands crossed, each watching the cup he has presented and has to carry away.

At Scutari, on the Asiatic side, we visited the largest and most beautiful cemetery in the Ottoman dominions. The extensive groves of dark cypress, through which one may ride for miles, interspersed with white turbaned stones of marble, are remarkable. As no grave is opened a second time, and as it is the custom to plant trees at a birth or funeral, these graveyards have become forests, extending for miles and miles. The aromatic odor of the trees is supposed to destroy all pestilential exhalations. It is said the Turks suppose the soul to be in torment from the time of death until the burial of the body, therefore the funeral succeeds death as soon as possible. The only occasion on which a Turk is seen to walk with a quick step is when conveying a body to the cemetery, as the Koran declares that he who carries a body forty paces procures for himself the expiation of a great sin.

# 1842.
# XXVIII.

ALEXANDRIA, EGYPT, *January 10, 1842.*

A few days since, at an early hour in the morning, all hands were on deck looking anxiously for the land of Egypt. At length we discovered in the distance the minarets of the mosques, Pompey's Pillar and other objects, and soon found ourselves in the harbor of Alexandria. Our steamer was immediately surrounded by about sixty boats, filled with half naked Arabs and Egyptians, of all colors and complexions, whose yells and cries for luggage would surpass those of savages. Having heard that the plague still existed, none were permitted to board us, but our fears in getting ashore were soon dispelled on learning that few cases existed. After procuring camels to carry our luggage, we were beset by another swarm in the shape of donkeys and drivers, and in self-defence our party all mounted, and soon found ourselves going at a fearful gallop through crowded streets, amongst loaded camels and yelping dogs, with our half-naked, sore-eyed Arabs chasing alongside and applying the stick in a lively manner. The Egyptian donkey is peculiar to this country, and superior in point of speed to any I have found in Europe. They are the omnibuses of the city, and it is surprising to see how rapidly and easily they pass through crowded streets.

I must first give you a better idea of Alexandria as it now is under Mehemet Ali, and not as it once was under Alexander the Great, when it only yielded to imperial Rome in wealth and magnificence. Formerly it was fifteen miles in circumference, with a population of three hundred thousand citizens and as many slaves, with four thousand palaces, four thousand baths, and four hundred theatres and public edifices. In different directions may be seen the ruins of ancient days. The Frank quarter of Alexandria reminded me more of a new American city than anything that I have seen since I left Trieste. The Pasha is doing everything in his power to resuscitate the city and increase its commercial importance, at the expense of Damietta, Rosetta, and Cairo. The population, notwithstanding the fearful ravages of the plague, is said to be fifty or sixty thousand. I must here mention that the interior of the town is, in most places, a succession of narrow, dirty, unpaved lanes, filled with camels, asses, lizards, and dogs, and I only wonder the plague does not exist all the year.

My first excursion was to Pompey's Pillar. My friend and myself mounted on donkeys, and away we galloped through the suburbs of the city, passing occasionally groups of Egyptian women with their heads and faces covered with a sort of blue cotton cloth, concealing all except their eyes, the lids of which are singularly colored with India ink. They are particularly fond of ornaments, which are suspended from the ears and from the forehead over the veil. On passing several groves of palm, date, and banana trees, and feeling the powerful rays of the sun at mid-day, I was reminded of the West India climate, from which this does not materially differ. After passing through a long line of Arab huts we came to this magnificent column, erected by Pompeius, governor of Lower Egypt, in honor of the Emperor Diocletian. Standing on a gentle elevation it rises nearly one hundred feet in height. The shaft is of red granite, ten feet in diameter, with a clumsy Corinthian capital on the top to crown the summit. Notwithstanding it is more than two thousand years old, it still remains almost perfect.

We next directed our attention to the beautiful Obelisks, one of which is commonly called Cleopatra's Needle, and still stands erect in all its grandeur and beauty, covered with hieroglyphics on every side. It is sixty-four feet high and eighty-eight feet square, and was brought from the city of Memphis to adorn the palace of the Ptolemies. The hieroglyphics are as clear on one side as if but recently sculptured, but the sirocco blowing from the desert two thousand years has effaced the marks on one side considerably, and worn away the solid granite. The other obelisk, which lies beside it, is said to have been taken down by the English many years ago; but Mehemet Ali prevented them from taking it away, and there it lies half covered with sand, a magnificent piece of work.

On entering the harbor of Alexandria I was surprised at the extent of the Egyptian fleet, and had a strong desire to visit some of the naval vessels, the arsenal, &c. On visiting the latter we were accompanied through every department by the commandant, a French gentleman, who was exceedingly polite; and here we found about four thousand persons, which is only a portion of those employed during the war. I was also surprised at finding shipbuilding, casting furnaces, ropemaking, in a word all that is necessary for fitting out a navy. Among the number of officers there were some young Arabs who had been sent to England to acquire knowledge in the arts. I observed among the workmen that many had lost an eye, and others had the two first fingers of the right hand cut off. I concluded that the cause of the first was ophthalmia, which is very general in Egypt, being caused by the burning rays of the sun upon the desert, but found on inquiry that during the war, when conscriptions were made for soldiers in the army, hundreds and thousands, to prevent being liable to military service, preferred destroying the pupil of the right eye with a small rod of hot iron, or by cutting off the forefingers of the right hand, thus preventing the use of it in pulling the trigger; but the Pasha was not to be thwarted in his designs, and actually formed left-handed regiments, and also employed those conscripts in the public service.

The next day, after visiting the public works, our party visited the palace of the Pasha, which is extensive and fitted up with taste, in the oriental style, with high ceilings and divans extending on three sides of the grand saloons; also the great luxury of the East, splendid marble bathing rooms. The palace is beautifully situated, with a view of the harbor in front, and picturesque and rich gardens in the rear.

On leaving the palace on the water side by arrangement with the Swedish consul, under whose patronage we were, we found the captain of an Egyptian cutter, with fourteen oarsmen, in attendance to convey us on board of one of the one hundred gun frigates, which carries seven hundred men. After having satisfied our curiosity in the examination of a beautiful frigate in fine order, we repaired to the cabin and accepted the universal civilities of the East, a pipe six feet in length, well charged with Egyptian tobacco, and a small cup of coffee, all of which must be submitted to, or you give offence.

My two travelling Companions and myself, who purpose visiting Upper Egypt in going to the cataract of the Nile, taking Grand Cairo, the Pyramids, Memphis, and the ruins of Thebes in the route, are now busily employed in procuring a suitable boat, with supplies of all provisions necessary for six weeks or two months.

We intend leaving to-morrow if our servants succeed in getting beds, furniture, provisions, and all the paraphernalia of housekeeping which are necessary for such a voyage. Therefore you may expect to hear from me next at Grand Cairo.

# XXIX.

GRAND CAIRO, EGYPT, *Jan. 20, 1842.*

We started off all our boat furniture, supplies of cooking utensils, provisions, &c., on camels, ourselves and Arab servants on horses and donkeys, making quite a formidable party, bringing up the rear. On arriving at the Mahmoudie Canal, which connects Alexandria with the Nile, we took our boat for Atfe, a small town at the junction of the canal with the river. We soon commenced our journey, towed by four Arab boatmen, with ropes across their breasts; and when the wind favored, made use of sails. This canal is considered one of the greatest works of the age, being sixty miles in length, ninety feet in breadth, and eighteen in depth, through a perfectly flat country. It is certainly a remarkable work, and could only be made in a country like Egypt, where the will of Mehemet Ali is law. Every village was ordered to furnish a certain quota, in proportion to its population, and thus one hundred and fifty thousand workmen were secured at once; and in one year from its commencement, the whole excavation was completed. As a grand stride in public improvement it was a great work, and does honor to the energies of the Pacha; but the wanton disregard of human life that attended it was shocking to humanity, as it proved the grave of thirty thousand of the laborers.

On arriving at Atfe, we discharged our canal boat, and went in search of a suitable river boat for the Upper Nile. Having succeeded in finding one, of the class called "canziah," and made our contract with the reis, or captain, we were prepared to depart; but as the north wind, which usually blows the same way for eight or nine months in the year, making it easy to ascend the Nile, was contrary, we employed our time in visiting an Arab village near by.

These villages are, in most instances, mere huts, built of mud, or unburnt bricks, and so low that the inmates cannot stand erect in them, but have a hole in front to crawl in. The Delta, stretching out from the banks of the river, and inundated annually by the Nile, is remarkably rich and productive. The town called Atfe, at the junction of the canal, concentrates all the products of the upper country, and presents a lively scene, of vessels unloading cotton and various kinds of grain, with hundreds of men and women employed in discharging them.

The Nile here is about a mile wide, and the current tolerably strong. After a stay of one day, the wind having changed, we started up the river. Our boat was about fifty feet in length, manned with ten stout Arabs, who were stretched upon the deck, or gathered around a pail of rice, proving conclusively that fingers were made before forks; whilst the two immense lateen sails, in the form of a triangle, were spread to the breeze, and we went with great velocity. As the wind slackened at night, where the banks permitted, the Arabs would twist the huge ropes around them, wade ashore, and commence pulling the vessel against the stream.

On the third day of our voyage to Cairo, the wind being strong against us, my two companions having taken their guns in hand, to go in pursuit of pigeons and other kinds of game, that are found in abundance, I strolled along the banks of this mighty and most extraordinary and interesting river, which rolls its waters more than a thousand miles through a sandy desert, fertilizing a narrow strip by its inundations, and could not be surprised that the Arabs loved, and the Egyptians worshipped, that which produced fertility in a soil where every species of fruit and grain grows almost spontaneously. I soon discovered an Arab village, to which I directed my steps, through beautiful fields of grain and groves of palm trees, which present a splendid view in the distance; but on entering them the illusion vanishes. On gazing at the men and women—many of whom were almost in a primitive state, with scarcely clothing enough to cover their nakedness—I could only wonder whether the effects of climate, or bad government, reduced them to their abject state, in such a fruitful country.

On the morning of the fourth day, we arrived at Boulac, a populous town by the river's side, and in another half hour found ourselves within the walls of Cairo; and here, several novel scenes presented themselves. Many loaded dromedaries and camels; the dashing Arab steed, with the Turk and glittering sabre; the Jews and Armenians, in costume; the haughty Janizary, dashing through the crowd; the harem of some rich Turk, the women robed in black, riding on donkeys, with two or three black eunuchs for a guard; the swarthy Bedouin of the desert; in fact, all characters forming a perfect masquerade, or miniature representation of the oriental world.

Cairo has a population of two hundred thousand; its appearance from a distance is pleasant, with its minarets, domes, and cupolas, and it has a much cleaner and more comfortable interior than other Mahomedan cities. The streets are narrow and dark, producing a shade which is necessary in this climate; although they appear warmer than they are, because of the projection of the first floors, or second stories, which advance so far that in some of the narrowest streets they are only a few inches distant from the houses opposite.

Among our many excursions was one to the "Valley of the Wanderings," or forest of Agate in the Desert, on the route to the Red Sea. After quitting Cairo, and passing through the great Mameluke Cemetery, we entered into the desert for about five miles, where we found immense quantities of petrifactions of trees, in which are seen the grain of the wood; in some places trunks from twenty to fifty feet in length lie prostrate. Reeds and roots are also found, and quantities of shells. It appears as if a forest had been petrified, and then thrown down by a hurricane, or some other convulsion, and shattered to fragments in the fall. All is conjecture as to the origin and cause of these forests.

On visiting the citadel of Cairo we were shown the place where the unfortunate Mamelukes were slaughtered by the present Pasha, while smoking their pipes of peace, having been invited on a visit of friendship, and were pent up and murdered, only one escaping by leaping his horse over the citadel walls and down an immense precipice. Here was also the Mint, and Joseph's Well, or the well of Saladin, forty-five feet wide, and cut two hundred and seventy-four feet through solid rock, to a level with the Nile.

On visiting the slave market I found perhaps five or six hundred slaves for sale, most of them naked, except a slight covering across the loins, and some covered with blankets. A large proportion were from Dongola and Sennaar, and exceedingly black and ugly. The Abyssinians have yellow complexions and good teeth; and some quite pretty are kept separate from the mass, among whom were some well dressed, wearing ornaments of gold and chains; two particularly good-looking caught hold of my hand as I passed, smiling and coquetting, and seemed to express by their gestures a desire that I would buy them, and pouted when I left. Prices vary from one hundred dollars to two hundred and fifty dollars; but some who were sick were offered at almost nothing, as so much perishable goods, which the seller wanted to dispose of before it was entirely lost.

Yesterday we went to the Pyramids, passing through a succession of beautiful gardens of Ibrahim Pacha. We reached Old Cairo, occupying the site of the Egyptian Babylon, on the Nile, and celebrated in sacred history as the spot where Pharaoh's daughter found the infant Moses in his cradle of bulrushes. Further on we stopped to examine the ovens for hatching chickens, in general use in Egypt. It was a large establishment, and capable of hatching by the wholesale. The entrances were so narrow and low as to be difficult, leading into small vaulted chambers, connected with each other, on one side of which are ovens. The eggs remain seventeen days, and on the eighteenth the chickens quit the shell. Out of two thousand eggs the manager counts on one thousand chickens. The general heat is one hundred degrees Fahrenheit during the process.

On crossing the Nile I discovered the Pyramids in the distance, near the margin of the desert, but they did not appear what I had imagined, and it was only until I approached and beheld the four that I could realize them, and not until I approached and commenced ascending, that I could appreciate this mammoth work. The Great Pyramid, the largest of the four, is a gigantic work, being a square of seven hundred and forty-six feet, and its perpendicular height four hundred and sixty-one feet, being higher than St.

Peter's at Rome, or the Cathedral at Strasburg, and one hundred and seventeen feet higher than St. Paul's of London, all of which I have ascended. The quantity of stone used in this single pyramid is estimated at six million tons, and a hundred thousand men are said to have been employed ninety years in raising it. The top is about thirty feet square. There are two hundred and six layers of stone, the average height from two to four feet. They are so arranged as to form a series of steps, so that any person may mount with the assistance of two Arabs on the outside to aid in stepping up. We were aided by two Arabs each, and others carrying the supplies of provisions and water, of which we made a repast on the top. The prospect from the summit, the rich valley of the Nile covered with verdure, with herds of buffalo quietly feeding, caravans of camels winding their way along the margin of the river, is very beautiful. On the other side it is dreary and gloomy indeed, the surface only broken by the tracks of the caravans, and no signs of vegetation. It is estimated that this great pyramid covers eleven acres of ground. The next largest pyramid is six hundred and eighty-four feet square, and four hundred and fifty-six feet high. Besides the four great pyramids there are smaller ones that appear in the distance, and also ruins of mausoleums about the grand pyramid, which, seen from the top, look like tombstones round a church. On entering the pyramid, knowing that it was difficult of access and almost insufferable on account of dust, we sent in three Arabs with candles, forbidding the others who swarmed around to enter, but they were determined to go in, thereby hoping to get a few *paras* more for services. It was not until our dragoman placed himself at the narrow passage, three and a half feet square, with his musket in hand, and threatened to shoot the first man who attempted to enter, that we could pass alone. We descended about ninety feet from the opening, which is the one hundred and sixty-third step of the pyramid, at an angle of twenty-seven degrees, then turned and mounted several steps into a passage one hundred feet long and five feet high. At the end is found the queen's chamber, seventeen feet long, fourteen wide, and twelve high, of polished granite. Above this, ascending an inclined plane one hundred and twenty feet long, of granite, highly wrought, is the king's chamber, thirty-seven feet long, seventeen wide, and twenty feet high. The slabs of stone which form the ceiling, consisting of nine, extend from side to side. The walls are highly polished, of red granite, and here is a sarcophagus seven feet six inches long, three and a half feet deep, and three and a half broad, supposed to have been the tomb of one of the greatest rulers of the south. It was very hot and suffocating, with the glare of the light and the abundance of dust, and I was rejoiced when I came out.

On our arrival at Cairo we discharged our boat, having suffered considerably from fleas and other vermin, while our baggage was injured by rats. We, however, procured another boat, with a comfortable little cabin astern on deck, just large enough for three persons. The first move was to sink her in the Nile, thereby destroying all the vermin. After she was hauled out her owner, according to contract, painted our little cabin, furnished us with glass windows, which were a novelty, thereby making our habitation for six weeks as comfortable as possible. She is furnished with new sails, and a crew consisting of the reis and twelve stout Arabs. She is almost seventy feet long, with a sharp bow, and two enormous sails, triangular in form, and attached to two tall spars eighty or ninety feet long, heavy at the end, and tapering to a point. These rest upon two short masts, changing their position with the wind, playing upon pivots. Having again furnished ourselves with supplies of provisions, this being the last place for purchasing many articles in use by Europeans, we shall start for the upper country to-morrow or next day, and you may not hear from me again in some time, there being no communication by mail.

# XXX.

THEBES, UPPER EGYPT, *February 13, 1842.*

We left Cairo on the 24th of January, and arrived here after a passage of twenty days. I must now recur to my journal to recount some of the adventures of the voyage.

The first day we made but little progress against a strong current, although we had all our Arab crew ashore, with ropes across their breasts, pulling, and at night found ourselves moored among the reeds of the island of Rhoda, where it is recorded that Moses was found by the daughter of Pharaoh. While here, we were boarded by a Nubian, of a dark, tall, and fine figure, bearing his orders in diamonds and sabre by his side. Not knowing his designs, we desired him to be seated, and following the custom of the country presented coffee and a pipe, when he produced a paper in Arabic for the arrest of our reis, or captain, who owed a certain sum of money. High words ensued, in which the captain, crew, and domestics took part, and we, being determined not to be detained, produced the firmans of the Sultan and Mehemet Ali, stating that we could not be stopped, when he very politely concluded to defer the arrest until the return of the barge. The second day the scene had changed; with a fine wind and our tall sails spread to the breeze, we were dashing against the rapid current, and making fine progress, and leaving Cairo in the distance, when we suddenly found ourselves upon a sand bank, which, as we have since found, is a thing of frequent occurrence. Instantly ten or eleven naked Arabs and Barbary negroes plunged into the river, and we soon found the boat lightened and again under way. At night the wind ceased, and we drew up to the bank, alongside of an Arab village, while the rays of the setting sun gilded beautifully the mountains and the desert in the distance. The village, surrounded with palm trees gently waving, and the rich verdure of the plain, seemed to me more beautiful than ever. The morning of the 26th, to our surprise, found the wind dead ahead and strong; I started along the bank with my two companions shooting pigeons, which are found in great abundance, and saw about two hundred Egyptians, a large proportion half naked, employed in making dyes. Our appearance and guns created a sensation. We frequently encountered groups of women and girls with massive jugs, which, after having filled them with Nile water, they put upon their heads and march off in line. Their appearance differs from those in large cities, from their not having a veil to cover their faces; but on our approach they endeavored to cover them with a blue cotton shawl which is worn on the head and shoulders. They are swarthy, with feet and ankles bare, their faces and hands marked with a blue color resembling India ink; they wear many ornaments about the neck, wrists, and even ankles, and not unfrequently rings in the nose.

27th.—Wind still contrary, which is rare, as it usually blows from the north during the winter months. Although our men tugged heavily all day, we made very little progress. At night we halted at a small village, where we found a caravan of men, women, and children, with their camels, all reposing upon their mats and straw for the night, whilst our Arab crew were gathered around a fire on the bank. Had an eclipse of the full moon this evening, which has created an excitement among the superstitious Arabs, causing many invocations to the prophet.

28th.—This is the most horrible and disagreeable day we have had upon the Nile. The wind ahead, and blows a perfect gale; cannot change our position. Yesterday was warm and delightful, but to-day extremely cold. Our men are wrapped up in all the covering they can find, and we are glad to confine ourselves to the cabin.

29th and 30th.—The wind still being against us, we were almost discouraged with the prospect; but the ruins of immortal Thebes, which had her hundred gates, were before us, and beckoned us on.

31st.—We made some progress to-day in towing, but no wind. Discovering a mud village in the distance, I took an Arab servant with me, to bring a supply of poultry, eggs, and mutton, which can be procured at almost all places along the Nile. These articles, with a species of cake called bread, are about all that can be procured, excepting in the largest towns. On returning to the boat, I saw several mounted horsemen, who were cautioning my companions not to go alone into the villages, as four soldiers had just been killed by the villagers.

Feb. 4th.—I made my appearance again on deck, having been confined to my bed for the last three days with cold and fever, from the effect of checked perspiration. Fortunately, I had a medicine chest, to which I am indebted for my quick recovery. In a country like Egypt, where no medical attendance can be procured, it is all-important to be provided with the necessary remedies; besides which, among the Arabs, who have a great passion for medicine, one soon acquires distinction in the title of "hakim." Before our arrival at Thebes, three of our crew fell sick, but a strong dose to each was sufficient to effect a cure, and they seemed to feel under many obligations.

After the 4th, our prospects changed; the wind veered round to the north, and we found our bark gliding along with great velocity, passing some important towns and villages, with the determination to stop on our return, not wishing to lose such a fine wind, which we held most of the way to Thebes. In ascending the Nile new sights are continually rising to view. In one place may be seen a herd of buffalo and camels, quietly grazing upon the rich plain; while near at hand are discovered half-a-dozen Egyptians, in a state of nature, raising water to irrigate the soil, by buckets fastened to a pole, like our old-fashioned well-poles. The next moment, perhaps, you discover fifteen or twenty crocodiles, from ten to fourteen feet long, and as numerous as in the days when the Egyptians worshipped them. As they lay basking in the sun, we would give them a passing shot, which would shake their scaly sides and send them tumbling in the water. Upon the Nile, one who is fond of shooting, finds plenty of amusement, as pelicans, wild ducks, geese, and eagles abound, and in many places are found the hyena, gazelle, foxes, wolves, and other animals. The slave trade is still continued from Dongola and Senaar. We saw one large boat descending with upwards of one hundred on board, who were bought for a small sum, or some article of necessity, from their parents, and were now wending their way to the slave market at Cairo, or perhaps to Siout, where the abominable traffic in eunuchs for the harems is still carried on. It is to be hoped, under the enlightened government of Mehemet Ali, that the latter detestable practice will be abandoned.

On arriving at Dendera, within a day's sail of Thebes, we visited the ruins of the temple, &c., which stands about a mile and a half from the river, on the side of the desert, and occupies an area of three and a half miles in circumference. It is the first temple one sees on coming up the Nile, and is decidedly the best preserved one in Egypt. It is impossible to describe this superb building, which I found much more beautiful than I had expected, although considerably choked up with sand and stones, and forming the centre of an Arab village, which was abandoned from some cause or other. Their huts not only surrounded it, but crowned the summit of the temple itself. Nothing can exceed its magnificence. It is as rich in sculpture, hieroglyphics, and mythological paintings, as the greatest lover of antiquity could desire. Its dimensions are enormous. The vestibule, or porch, has twenty-one figures along the ceiling, ending with the vulture, the guardian genius of the kings and heroes of Egypt. On each hand are three rows of columns, with three columns in each row—making eighteen—which occupy the body of the vestibule. The exterior walls, as well as the interior, and columns, are covered with sculptured devices of the most remarkable execution: the winged globe, vulture, hawk, ibis, Isis, Osiris, gods, goddesses, priests, and women, sacred boats, with the sacred bulls which were formerly exhibited to the admiring multitude. What is most remarkable is, that after the lapse of two thousand years, the painting should appear, in many instances, as if executed but a month ago. There are several other smaller temples and gates of the city still standing, which are also full of interest. Dendera, which was anciently called Tentyra, is situated near the west bank of the Nile, about two hundred and sixty miles south by east of Cairo, and its ruins bespeak its former greatness.

In my next I shall endeavor to give you some idea of the gigantic ruins of Thebes, with Luxor and Karnak, which are said to have extended twenty-three miles in circumference; and the valley of the Nile not being able to contain them, their extremities rested upon the bases of the mountains of Arabia and Africa.

# XXXI.

DJIRJEH, UPPER EGYPT, *February 20, 1842.*

My last was from Thebes, after having made the ancient port of Luxor and found ourselves some seven or eight hundred miles from the sea, secured to the old quay where the Egyptian boatmen tied their boats three thousand years ago. On the eastern or Arabian side of the Nile are the immense ruins of Luxor and Karnak. The temple of Luxor is a mere skeleton; the greater part of the columns stand yet, but the outside walls have been thrown down, and the materials carried away. It stands very near the river bank, and was supposed to be for the use of the boatmen. The temple was six hundred feet in length; the interior court was three hundred feet long and one hundred and sixty feet wide, and the double row of columns, twelve feet diameter and one hundred and forty feet high, were covered with sculpture. Before a magnificent gateway of the temple stands the survivor of the beautiful obelisks which have withstood the hand of time for three thousand years. It is a single block of red granite, eighty or ninety feet high, covered with sculpture and hieroglyphics beautifully executed. Its fellow was taken by the French, and now stands in the Place de la Concorde at Paris. The refinement of civilization has dared to remove what the grossness of barbarism feared to touch. The obelisks were among the few objects spared by the Persians on entering Egypt, probably from the fact that they were the symbols of the sacred element, *fire*, which the Persians worshipped.

The gateway of this magnificent ruin is two hundred feet long and sixty feet high; the front of the interior wall is covered with sculpture, representing the battle scenes of an Egyptian warrior in different attitudes, advancing at the head of his army, breaking through the ranks of the enemy; sometimes in a chariot drawn by fiery steeds, with plumes waving over their heads, the bow bent, the arrow drawn to its extremity, whilst the dead and wounded are falling under the wheels of his car; with a great variety of other devices.

Leaving Luxor we proceeded to Karnak, a distance of about two miles, and in approaching the ruins of the immense temples which occupy a mile in diameter, we passed through the avenue of sphinxes, each a solid block of granite, lining the whole length of the road, which was sixty feet wide, regularly formed, and shaded by rows of poplar trees. Many are broken, but some are quite perfect, and solemn as when the ancient Egyptians passed to worship in the great temple of Ammon. Here we saw several rows of sphinxes. The grand temple of Karnak, which was twelve hundred feet in length, and four hundred and twenty feet in breadth, stood in the centre of a series of smaller temples, with avenues of sphinxes and colossal statues radiating from it. The principal entrances, of which there were twelve, were so contrived as exactly to front the corresponding temples on the other side of the river at Thebes, which must have added much to the effect produced by the annual processions of the priests and gods of Egypt, when they were carried in solemn triumph from the Arabian to the Lybian side of the Nile. Some of the smaller temples surrounding this gigantic structure are larger than many other temples elsewhere. Here are seen many colossal statues, twenty or thirty feet high, some sitting, others erect. In front of the body of the temple is a large court, with an immense colonnade on each side, of thirty columns in length, and through the middle two rows of columns fifty feet high; then comes an immense portico, the roof supported originally by one hundred and thirty-four columns; I counted one hundred and twenty-six still standing, which measured from thirty to thirty-six feet in circumference. Here are three beautiful obelisks, seventy feet high, the sanctuary of highly polished granite, the walls of which are covered with sculpture representing offerings to the gods. The walls inside and out, as also the columns in every part, are covered with every variety of device, representing the acts of their kings, the worship of their gods, &c. Here are immense walls and gates and ruins, with cemeteries, in which are still standing colossal figures of rams, and those of men with the heads of animals. In fact, it is impossible to form any correct estimate of these gigantic remains. One is struck with wonder and confusion, and, to use the language of Dr. Richardson, who, looking from one of the gateways, exclaims, "the vast scene of havoc and destruction presents itself in all the extent of this immense temple, with its columns, and walls, and immense propylons, all prostrate in one heap of ruins, looking as if the thunders of heaven had smitten it at the command of an insulted God."

I have visited all the ruins of Thebes, on the other side of the river, which occupied several days, but it is useless to attempt to describe them, as what I have already spoken of is not half of the ruins of this once magnificent city. Many are prostrate and nearly buried in the sand, but the traces are still visible. The temples of Goorneh, Northern Dair, Memnonium and Medinet Abou, with their columns and colossal figures, still raise their giant skeletons above the sands, and, as Mr. Stevens has said, "volumes have been written upon them, and volumes may yet be written, and he that reads all will have but an imperfect view of Thebes—that all the temples were connected by long avenues of sphinxes, statues, propylons, and colossal figures, and the reader's imagination will work out the imposing scene that was presented in the crowded streets of the now desolate city, when, with all the gorgeous ceremonies of pagan idolatry, the priests, bearing the sacred image of their god, and followed by thousands of the citizens, made their annual procession from temple to temple, and, 'with harps, and cymbals, and songs of rejoicing,' brought back their idol, and replaced him in his shrine in the grand temple at Karnak."

The tombs of the kings are by far the most ancient and interesting of all the antiquities of Thebes. There is nothing in the world like them, and he who has not seen them can scarcely believe in their existence. The whole mountain range is one vast cemetery, and it is supposed that some millions of bodies were deposited there. On passing through an Arab village, one half of which was composed of excavations for mummies, in which the Arab finds a better resting-place than his mud cottage, we were almost suffocated with the dust and scorching rays of the sun, and were also surrounded by scores of men, women, and children, with various relics of antiquity, such as heads, hands, and feet of mummies, also remnants of sarcophagi, beautifully painted. The road is through a dreary waste of sand after leaving the fertile valley of the Nile, and the tombs show their dark and gloomy openings in one of the most desolate spots imaginable. There are very many of these tombs, but the principal one, which is called Belzoni's, having been discovered by him, is three hundred and nine feet long, and contains fourteen chambers of different sizes. A flight of thirty steps descends to the entrance, where the doorway, wide and lofty, is without sculpture. Here is a hall, extremely beautiful, twenty-seven feet long and twenty-five feet broad, having at the end an open door leading into a chamber twenty-eight feet long by twenty-five feet broad, the walls covered with painted figures as perfect as if only a month old. Another flight of steps here descends to a chamber twenty-four feet by thirteen. The walls are covered with figures, marching in solemn procession to the regions of the dead. This flight of steps leads to another doorway, over which is seen the sign of the goddess of darkness. Advancing to the next corridor, the walls are covered with figures of boats, rams, mystic emblems of the gods of Egypt, &c. Another apartment is adorned by massive square pillars, which, like the others, are covered with hieroglyphics. Returning into the great chamber, and descending a flight of eighteen steps, we follow a continuation of the corridor, the walls of which are covered with paintings representing the actions of the monarch, perhaps the tomb of Pharaoh. In passing from hall to hall, we saw a lofty arched saloon, thirty-two feet long and twenty-seven feet broad. One of those chambers is forty-three feet long and eighteen wide. One apartment is adorned with two columns and a raised stone bench, hollowed out, in recesses extending all around the chamber. In the centre of the grand saloon was found a sarcophagus, of the finest oriental alabaster, only two inches thick, minutely sculptured within and without with several hundred figures, and, it is said, perfectly transparent when a light is placed upon it. The walls of these chambers and other tombs are generally covered with intaglio and relief, representing funeral processions, the serpent, and many other emblems of eternity—sarcophagi, religious processions, a great variety of animals and birds, agricultural scenes and implements, sacrifices, sacred boats, gods, goddesses, priests, chained captives, the cutting off hands from the arms by way of punishment, &c. &c. These magnificent halls, by the light of our torches, produced a magic effect in going from the dreary desert without.

After having visited many of the tombs of the kings and others, we took the statues of Shamy and Damay on our route. These two sitting statues, of enormous size, are in the centre of a vast cultivated plain, and are of equal size, being fifty-two feet high and forty feet apart. The thrones on which they sit, are thirty feet long, eighteen broad, and eight feet high. Both have suffered considerably from violence, particularly the vocal Memnon. These figures were formerly part of a grand avenue of sphinxes.

While at Thebes we had a mutiny among our crew. We were unfortunate in having Arabs and half Barbary negroes, who could not agree. Our only recourse was to present ourselves before the governor or sheik of the little village of Luxor, with the all-powerful firman of the Sultan and Mehemet Ali in hand, and make known our grievances. The usual form of justice was administered with the calash, or piece of rhinoceros' hide, to one of the worst by way of example, and the sheik finding the barbarians still obstinate, imprisoned them until we were ready to start, while he and his associate, the governor of the Nile, came down to our boat, sipped our coffee, smoked our long pipes with the dignity of a grand seignor, received the "backsheesh" of eight piastres each, equal to three-fourths of a dollar, and went off perfectly happy.

Our next place of debarkation was at Belianach, where we mounted donkeys, without saddle or bridle, and rode to the ruins of Abydos, the capital of the great Osymandias or Osmendes, who is supposed to have lived 2276 years B.C. There are some remarkable ruins there. Among the number the Memnonium and small temple of Osiris, remarkable for having had a sanctuary made of alabaster, and for containing the famous tablet of the kings, which, next to the Rosetta stone, has been of the greatest assistance to the students of hieroglyphics. The valley of the Nile at this point, I should think, is six miles broad, and abounding in vegetation. The wheat is in blossom, beans and peas are ripened, and it was a rich sight to see the herds of goats and sheep, camels and buffalo, grazing upon the plain.

We were obliged to stop here for want of wind, and to replenish our crew, the barbarians having taken the liberty of making off, sans ceremonie. I have therefore been obliged to have another interview with the two governors at this place, who have promised to furnish us with men. The past two days my two companions have had plenty of amusement in shooting at crocodiles, as we had no wind, and the weather was warm. They are prepared for the heat of the climate, being dressed in Turkish costume, with heads shaved. It being a sin to shave the beard in this country, we have all a great profusion of hair upon the visage.

# XXXII.

AFRICAN DESERT, *March 8, 1842.*

The governor sent us four men, called sailors, to supply the place of six who had absconded; but such a crew I never saw. One was blind of an eye, another lame, the third too old for service. The instructions of the governor, who had forced them on board, were, to continue with us to Siout, the capital of Upper Egypt, where plenty of men could be found. To cap the climax, the next day, while detained by a strong head wind, the lame, blind, and halt took leg bail, unperceived. We made a further application at another village, and succeeded in getting men to go as far as Siout, at which place we wished to stop, to visit Caves, about four miles distant from the river, in the mountains.

Having mounted donkeys, we started for the city, which is situated about a mile and a half from the river; and the road being studded with rows of trees on each side, it was an agreeable excursion.

On arriving within the walls, we presented ourselves before the Effendi, who occupied a handsome house, with a grove of palm trees in the rear. We found him squatted with his officers upon carpets, on a low divan, each enjoying the luxury of a long pipe, with an amber mouth-piece. He desired us to be seated, when coffee and pipes were presented; and, after the usual etiquette had been passed through, our credentials were presented, and our wants made known to the dragoman. He immediately sent his janizary to the governor of the Nile, with instructions to procure us a complement of good sailors, which was effected; and on paying them all they demanded, we succeeded remarkably well.

The streets of Siout are unpaved, narrow, and irregular; the houses are built of unburnt brick, and differ in no respect from the generality of those usually met with on the Nile. During the inundations the whole country is overflowed, and boats of the largest size anchor under the wall of the city, at which time it communicates with the river by an artificial causeway of immense size. The country about is rich and fertile in the extreme, owing to the annual inundations of the Nile. The palace and gardens of Ibrahim Pacha were well worthy of a visit. The tombs and immense chambers which are found in the mountain in the vicinity, are very interesting, but bear no comparison with those of the tombs of the kings at Thebes. On entering some of those gloomy chambers, with our torches, we were beset by bats of enormous size, that literally swarmed there, and afforded much amusement in the chase. On firing a gun in one of the dark recesses, we killed two, and found them to be the most extraordinary animals of the kind I had ever seen, being the size of a full-grown rat, and with much the same appearance, with the exception of the mouth, which was like that of a wolf, and the extended wings. On coming out of the tombs, covered with dust, and fatigued, we proceeded to the city to enjoy the luxury of a Turkish bath. The Orientals enjoy the vapor and hot baths to such an extent, that in almost all their towns and villages they are to be found; but I had no idea of finding such perfection here, and must, for the novelty of the thing, describe it. After passing two chambers, one hotter than the other, we arrived at the third, where the heat and vapor were almost suffocating, and there found half-a-dozen naked Arabs waiting for their three customers; when such a scene of confusion commenced as I cannot describe, to decide who should have the "white skins." After they had fought it out, and our servants had settled it by agreeing to divide the backsheesh, or gift, they commenced with burning musk and perfume. While the perspiration rolled out from every pore, I was rubbed from head to foot with a camel's hair glove, and then laid on the hot marble floor, while my arms were crossed upon my back and breast, and almost the weight of the Arab's body thrown upon me. All my joints were drawn and cracked, while showers of hot water were thrown upon me; and, almost in an exhausted state, myself and my two companions were led into an adjoining room, with white turbans on our heads, wrapped in sheets, where we reposed upon divans for an hour, partaking of coffee, lemonade, and pipes. After this fatiguing, but refreshing, bath, one feels like a new man, particularly when the heat of the day is intense.

On descending the Nile, we stopped at several towns and villages to see the bazaars, and study further the manners and customs of the people, but I cannot attempt a description for want of space. I will, however, mention that we visited the pyramids of Sakkara, and the site of ancient Memphis; but as nothing of interest now exists at the latter, and having described in a former letter the immense pyramids of Ghizeh, I shall not speak of Sakkara, which is smaller, and of less consequence. Near the same site is Abousir, a small, miserable village, situated upon the edge of the desert, where are three pyramids of large size, and many tumuli. Near this place, after an excursion of four or five miles from the verdant banks of the Nile, we found the mountain which contains the famous Catacomb of Birds. With torches, we entered the narrow hole, on our hands and knees, to see places formerly occupied by the mummies. We found passages leading in every direction through the mountain, many fragments of mummies, and many a sarcophagus entire. The entrance to the Catacomb of Birds is by a pit, twenty-two feet deep, at the bottom of which is a horizontal passage, sixty feet long, nearly choked up with sand, dirt, and broken jars, along which one has to creep; but after some distance, the passage is high enough to stand erect, and there are large rooms in which are deposited the jars containing the sacred birds.

We arrived at Cairo on the 28th of February, having had fine winds and a rapid current in descending the Nile, for several days. My great anxiety to visit the Holy Land had been increasing upon me, although it was attended with great fatigue and risk, but my travelling companion, a Prussian nobleman, whom I met in Greece, concluded to accompany me. I took our dragoman, called upon the sheik of the Bedouin tribe, who could furnish us with camels, and with whom I made a contract before the Consul, in Arabic, to cross the desert to Jerusalem in fifteen days, he attending us. No danger was to be apprehended from the tribe, but some alarming events have already taken place, which I will recount in my next letter.

On leaving Cairo our caravan presented quite a formidable appearance, consisting of three dromedaries for ourselves and dragoman, four camels for our tent, water, luggage, and two servants, with five Arabs to drive the camels. For the greater security I had forwarded the most valuable part of my luggage to Alexandria, and myself and companion had an ample supply of fire-arms, and we were also disguised in the Turkish costume, which does not attract so much attention as a European dress. On the second day after leaving Cairo we encamped at Tanta, on the borders of the Delta and the Desert, where we understood Mehemet Ali had retired to his country-seat, and having made the acquaintance of Artim Bey, the first dragoman to his Highness, we were promised a presentation in the evening, our letters of introduction being satisfactory. On arriving at the gate of the wall which surrounds the country palace we were escorted by a number of the body guards, a corps which comprises a select body of one hundred men, to the portico, where were several sentinels with presented arms. Artim Bey here presented himself and invited us in, when we were delighted in seeing the extraordinary man who has figured so largely in Egypt for the past forty or forty-five years. On entering the saloon we discovered Mehemet Ali seated upon a divan which extended around three sides of the apartment. He was dressed in full Turkish costume, with his feet drawn up under him. He saluted us, and beckoned us to be seated, when our conversation commenced on different topics, and continued for half an hour. The subject of agriculture upon the Nile, the necessity of great exertion and labor to prevent the encroachment of the sands of the desert, the introduction of foreign trees and plants into Egypt, in which he has effected much, seemed particularly to interest him. He has yet the appearance of vivacity, is a man of strong constitution, short in stature, with a venerable long beard as white as snow. His age is now seventy-five. His leaning couch or pillow was of crimson, richly embroidered with gold, with long tassels suspended. In front of us on the floor stood two large chandeliers, elegantly wrought; his nephew sat upon the opposite divan, while the interpreter stood at his side, and some fifteen or twenty beys and officers, forming a separate group in a semicircle, following the laws of etiquette, remained standing during our visit.

In all private houses in Turkey and Egypt the pipe and coffee are almost immediately presented on being seated, but at the palace of the Pasha the pipe is dispensed with, and coffee only is presented in small gold and silver cups.

We are now in the solitude of the desert, and feel somewhat relieved from our apprehensions of robbers, with whom we have had an adventure, the particulars of which I must defer till my next. Our little hut in which I now write is about ten feet in diameter, sufficiently large for my companion and myself to spread our mattresses, arrange our private luggage and table, while outside of the tent the camels lie crouched upon all fours, forming a semicircle around a small charcoal fire, around which lie the Arabs stretched upon the sand. Our servants, having furnished us our evening's repast, and satisfied their own appetites after a hard day's ride upon the camels, have stretched their mats upon the sand by the side of the interpreter, and all is quiet except an occasional groan from a camel, or the half conscious song of an Arab. Really this travelling in the desert is of the most novel and extraordinary character, and, although attended with great fatigue, one is somewhat compensated by the peculiarity of the voyage, independent of the strong desire to see Palestine.

# XXXIII.

QUARANTINE, GAZA, *March 18, 1842.*

My last was written in the desert, since which time we have been en route, and were quarantined yesterday on entering this place, it being represented that the plague existed in Egypt. On this voyage by the desert we have had adventure after adventure, and I must here relate the incidents alluded to in my last. The fourth day of our departure from Cairo we had travelled most of the time through a desert country, occasionally striking in the palm groves. At four o'clock P.M. we found ourselves near an Arab village, and our camels were discharged and tent struck, while the Count and myself started in pursuit of some wild ducks, but were followed by one of our Arabs, who, by signs and gestures, insisted that we should not pass by the village. We, however, persisted, and on returning I made the remark that I would not trust myself there without arms. In the evening one of our servants, an Armenian, to our surprise told us not to hang any clothes or loose luggage on the side of the tent opposite to where the camels and their drivers were stationed, saying there were many robbers who would steal our things in the night. We rather ridiculed the idea, not believing they dared approach the tent, knowing us to be armed. Our camel drivers pretended to watch through the night, and at one o'clock in the morning we were awaked with the report of a musket and the whizzing of a ball alongside of our tent, and the cries of our men to sally forth with our arms. In an instant with muskets and pistols we were outside the tent, while the bustle and excitement showed the brigands that we were ready for them if they came. It was the most fearful night I ever passed. The idea of being shot like a dog under cover of night, was not only exciting but provoking. In a state of anxiety we watched until four o'clock in the morning, during which time we had two pistol shots, but none taking effect. At this hour the men rose; we heard the cry of the Musselmans for the morning prayer in the village, and considered ourselves exceedingly fortunate in escaping unhurt.

At an early hour we left this place which was so full of danger, and which gave rather fearful apprehensions for the future. Our guns and pistols were kept charged and ready for use, and this evening we encamped some distance in the desert, away from the trees which form a cover for the robbers. In the evening one of our servants entered the tent, and I observed he drew a heavy sigh, and on demanding the cause he said nothing, but pressing him still further for an explanation, he said he had great anxiety for our safety; that in the village they were all Musselmans, and did not like the Christian pilgrims who go to Jerusalem, and would kill us—which was not very agreeable information, but this part of his story we could not credit. That evening after I had extinguished the candle and laid myself upon my mattress for a half hour, I heard the report of a gun not far distant. It was really extremely exciting after the events of the past night. Our men were watching, and we had resolved, if we were compelled to sell our lives, it should be at a dear rate. We passed the night under great apprehension, and in the morning passed through the village and found the walls of many mud-houses destroyed and deserted, and the inhabitants who remained appeared fit subjects for robbery.

The next night, after a hot and fatiguing journey, we found ourselves upon the borders of the vast desert which we were about to enter for several days. Not having slept for two nights, and there still being danger, we presented ourselves before the sheik of this village, which was of some importance, and with the firman of Mehemet Ali demanded a guard of eight armed men for the night, who surrounded our tent while we enjoyed the repose which we so much needed.

Here we were obliged to fill our vessels with water, and buy fresh supplies for six or seven days in crossing the desert. After quitting this village and getting into the desert we felt ourselves more safe, and encamped with much less anxiety. Occasionally we would see some Bedouin Arabs with their swarthy features and long black beards, with a carbine swung over their shoulders and a brace of pistols in their belt, having every appearance of the bandit, but of them we had no fear, as our camel drivers belonged to the same tribe, and our contract was made with the sheik.

In many parts of the desert we found the sand exceedingly light and the travelling difficult, the sand forming itself into mountains with the drifting of the wind, and resembling in the distance fields and mountains covered with snow. In other parts, particularly as we approached the sea towards Gaza, we found immense salt marshes, which were filled with the wild boar, and on the sand hills adjoining we would see large numbers of gazelles scampering away from us. Some of those salt water lakes which we passed are very beautiful indeed, and, with the crystallization of the salt, have the appearance of new-made ice all along the edges, and in some instances half skimmed over, while the banks are covered with stunted bushes of a grey color, and one imagines for an instant that it is the season of winter. Near one of these salt marshes we discovered a small pool of brackish water, from which the Arabs who had joined our caravan replenished their sacks, which they carry on their backs, and which are made of hog-skin. I could not help remarking the facility with which those travelling Arabs prepared their supplies. One of them, after filling his sack with water, took a sheepskin which covered his shoulders, and, placing it on the sand, poured on the inside some flour from another small sack, and with the water made his bread; then gathering some brush together, he instantly had a fire, and in a very short time all his wants were satisfied. The Arab of the desert is contented with bread and water; he looks upon what we consider necessaries as luxuries, and if he had them perhaps would not use them.

The gait of the camel is awkward and very fatiguing to the rider. He kneels and rises at pleasure, is very patient, subsists upon what he can gather from plants and shrubs, like the goat, goes many days without water, and seems in every way adapted for the desert. At night, in striking our tent, a scene of life and bustle presented itself in discharging our beasts; the mats are laid, the mattresses brought and spread, the luggage looked after and stowed away for the night; the camel-drivers are searching for wood and sticks, the camels stroll and graze; the cook makes a fire on the sand and prepares the dinner, after which comes the refreshing sleep, until the bustle of loading in the morning, which must be repeated every day.

After having passed the desert we arrived at El Arish, a miserable village on the frontier of Palestine, where we were told that at Gaza we would have to perform a quarantine of five or eight days, as we were supposed in coming from Egypt to bring the plague with us.

On approaching Scheik Inde, which is distant twenty miles, the soil is light, and grass and sand dispute possession with each other. Here we were stopped and tribute-money demanded. We wished to know the reason, to which one of the four persons who stopped us replied that they had been placed there by the Sultan to demand tribute of all strangers. This we doubted, and wanted to see their authority. Two of them were armed, and refused to let us pass without compliance, and threatened to hold our luggage. Really it was an act of daring impudence to be attacked thus on the high-road, and in the name of the Sultan too. We finally dared them to stop us, threatening not only with weapons but the vengeance of the Sultan, whose firman we had at command, when they concluded to let us pass. We have since understood that several persons through fear had paid the scoundrels heavy tribute.

The next day we came to the village of Khan Yunes, the environs of which were beautiful; the gardens filled with fruit trees and flowers, the hedges of cactus indicus or prickly pear, and the fields clothed with verdure, presented a lovely sight after having been in the desert country so long time. On approaching the gate of the village we were stopped and notified that we were to perform quarantine, which we believed they had no right to demand, and therefore we had no disposition to be thus delayed. We demanded an audience of the governor, but found he was absent. We insisted on passing, but they stopped our camels. We said we would perform quarantine at Gaza, but they would not allow us to pass through the village, and ordered us to pitch our tent on the commons, there to serve out our quarantine. High words ensued, the Count took up his gun and threatened to shoot the officer if he stopped his dromedary. We passed around the village on the road to Gaza, when I discovered some half-dozen armed men coming up, who were determined we should stop. Our next move was to show them that we had the firman of the Sultan and could not be arrested. Fortunately for us they could not read Turkish, and on our promise to be quarantined at Gaza, they permitted us to pass. We saw many others less fortunate, who were quarantined in the open field without a covering to their heads.

Yesterday we arrived at Gaza, the approach to which is beautiful indeed, the road winding through a series of gardens fenced with the cactus indicus, reminding me of Mount Etna at the base and of other parts of Sicily. The groves of olives with the sycamore tree form an agreeable shelter from the rays of the sun, and the country is exceedingly fertile. Before reaching the city we discovered a tent by the road side, from which approached an armed guard, and keeping at a respectful distance informed us we were to be quarantined from five to fifteen days at the direction of the Nazro, or chief officer of the quarantine. We found resistance would be fruitless, and were marched off to the ground, a mile from the city, where we pitched our tent upon the grass, and where I now write you. It is ludicrous, but at the same time disagreeable, to observe the guards keeping us off at the length of a stick to prevent our coming in contact with them, the plague being a contagious disease, and much to be dreaded. We desired an audience of the governor on arriving, that we might endeavor to lessen our quarantine, which of course could not be granted, as all persons coming from Egypt at this season of the year are suspected of having the plague with them. We then desired a visit from the Nazro, who this morning came to see us. Turkish rugs were sent outside the tent and spread upon the grass; coffee, pipes, and lemonade ordered for his reception. The first he had no occasion for, being squatted upon his own carpet, and indeed he dared not touch ours, as it was supposed to be pestiferous. The coffee and lemonade being in non-conductors were first placed upon the ground by our servant, at the distance of six or seven feet, when his attendant presented them to him. After having explained through our dragoman the time we had been in the desert, that the plague did not exist in Cairo when we left, and expressed great anxiety to arrive at Jerusalem, we then exhibited a firman from the Sultan, which was held at the distance of three feet with a sort of tongs and read; but he also discovered a small bit of paper which enveloped something *curious*, and on calling for perfume and fire to fumigate it, much to his surprise found some pieces of gold, which a Turk or Arab can scarcely refuse; but in this case he could not think of receiving it, being surrounded by too many witnesses. But he being satisfied that there is no possible risk in lessening our quarantine, and that our intentions were good, has this evening sent his secretary to say that, in consideration of our having passed so much time in the desert and several days in Syria, and out of respect for the firman of the Sultan, with a certain *indispensable backsheesh*, it would be unkind in him to detain us more than another day; we shall therefore be on the move again after to-morrow, and rejoiced to escape from being imprisoned a week or ten days without cause.

# XXXIV.

JERUSALEM, *March 25, 1842.*

Some time since, when I crossed the mountains of Judea, and my eyes beheld the holy city in the distance for the first time, I could not help exclaiming, "Is it possible that at last, after a voyage of six or seven thousand miles from my native land, I am soon to visit the many interesting localities connected with the life and sufferings of our Saviour, from his nativity at Bethlehem to his crucifixion upon Mount Calvary?" most of which is now realized.

My last was from the quarantine at Gaza, after escaping which we entered the city, visited the governor, and in the name of the Sultan demanded an escort, which he readily granted, by sending two mounted gensd'armes who accompanied us to the town of Ramlah, the ancient Arimathea, where resided Joseph who took from the cross the body of our Lord and laid it in his own sepulchre.

There are no antiquities at Gaza, and the traveller looks in vain for the ancient gates connected with the history of Samson. The streets are narrow, and the houses, many of which are situated in gardens, are unglazed, but the location is beautiful, and surrounded with groves of olive and palm trees. Our first day's travel from Gaza, through the land of the Philistines, brought us to a mud village at night, where we proposed striking our tent; but much to our surprise we found the bare-footed sheik and half-clad Arabs of the village would not permit it, asserting that the country was infested with robbers, that the villages were against each other, and that they would not be responsible for our safety. They showed us a mud khan, without any other opening than a sort of door to crawl in, which all Turkish villages furnish the traveller, and some of which are habitable for one night. Being finally obliged to submit and abandon our tent, which was a palace in comparison with this hovel, we struck our lights, and among rats, fleas, and apprehensions of robbers, from either the village or country, we passed a disagreeable night, escaping at break of day scarified with the bites of insects, and looking as if we had the small-pox. The next day we arrived at Ramlah, and were about pitching our tent in an olive grove, when our chevalier, who was mounted on a swift Arab, and who had gone in advance to procure horses to go to Jerusalem, came down upon us, saying there was an American Vice-Consul at that place, who invited us to his house. The invitation was readily accepted, as it commenced raining for the first time since we left Cairo. We were welcomed by this hospitable Greek with a hearty shake of the hand, and soon found ourselves at ease, seated upon a low divan, with the usual cup of coffee and pipe. It was a luxury to be once more under a roof, after sixteen days' hard riding upon the back of a dromedary in crossing the desert.

The day we came to Ramlah, through our anxiety to arrive early, we put our dromedaries on full trot; mine stumbled and came down with me. It was a *long fall*, but I escaped with a slight bruise. Having sent our caravan in advance, we made a few excursions on horseback, and started the following day for Jerusalem. Passing the village of Ludd (Lydda), where the apostle Peter cured Eneas of the palsy, after two hours' ride we commenced the first ascent of the mountains of Judea. The road winds by a rugged ravine, round a detached and barren hill, on the summit of which is the village of Latroun, or Thief's Village, so called from its having been the birthplace of the criminal who repented on the cross, and for whom Jesus Christ performed his last act of mercy.

Soon after leaving this village, we entered the mountains, portions of which were extremely wild and romantic, and abounding with flowers. In some places the road, or path, was almost impassable, and steep with rugged rocks, and we had to lead our horses. This road is not considered dangerous, owing to the great travel from Joppa. We passed several caravans of camels, donkeys, Arabs, and also pilgrims, who presented quite a singular appearance; the men, women, and children in various costumes, and bound for the holy city. After passing the most elevated of the chain of mountains, where vegetation almost ceases, we descended into the Vale of Jeremiah, where we visited the sheik of Abu Gosch, of an ancient Arab family, who formerly demanded tribute of all strangers that passed, and whose tribe occupies the mountains; but his rights having been asserted and maintained against the Sultan, at length his authority was confirmed by his guarantee of the peace of the mountains, and we found several of his guards by the road-side at different points. He showed us his fine Arab steeds, and after partaking of an Arab repast, while seated upon Turkish rugs upon the grass, and an half-hour's conversation through our dragomen, we left, and passed into a deeper valley, called the Valley of Turpentine, near which we came to the brook where the youthful David picked up five stones, with one of which he killed Goliah.

After a few hours' ride over a rough road, where a few olive trees are the only signs of vegetable life, we reached the top of a high hill, when suddenly the anxiously looked for city presented itself to view. We soon found ourselves at the gate, where our bill of health was demanded, and found our caravan had been suspected and put in quarantine; but we were immediately liberated. We made the best of our way to the Convent of St. Salvador, visited the father, and got permission to stop.

The rooms of the convent are small, like prisons, with iron gratings for windows, but are considered comfortable enough for pilgrims, who have fared much worse en voyage. The first morning after my arrival, I attended the Episcopal service, and found a small congregation worshipping in my native tongue; and the words of Scripture which declare that "where two or three are gathered together in my name, there will I be with them," were forcibly impressed on my mind.

I visited bishop Alexander and his family, whose mission was established last winter. The new church is in progress of construction, and bids fair to be a fine edifice.

Having had occasion to visit the palace of the Pacha, which was formerly the location of the house of Pilate, I mounted the flat roof where the panorama of Jerusalem was taken, and saw below me the square of *Harem Scheriff*, a grand and noble retirement for the Turks, which also incloses the mosques of Omar and El Aksar, built on Mount Moriah, where formerly stood the throne of Solomon and the judgment-seat of David; and a certain spot is shown, where the Turks believe Mahomet is to judge the world, assembled in the Valley of Jehoshaphat, below. None but Turks are allowed to visit its sacred precincts. It is prettily arranged with walks, fountains, and a few orange trees. I then strolled along the *Via Dolorosa*, regarding the localities with interest as they were pointed out; the place where Simon assisted to carry the cross; where the crowning of thorns took place; the residence of Simon, the pharisee, &c., until I arrived at St. Stephen's gate, and passed down the ravine near which he was stoned to death. I soon found myself in the garden of Gethsemane, and here the olives have the appearance of great age. Near by was shown the spot where the apostles slept, while Christ went to pray in the grotto near at hand, and where he said, *"Father, if it be Thy will."* The grotto is now fitted up by the Catholics, and lights are continually burning. There is a small chapel near by, fitted up as the tomb of the Virgin Mary. From the valley I ascended the Mount of Olives, which is a round, tabular hill, covered with verdure and a sprinkling of olives. To reach the summit is a long walk, and half way up are the remains of a monastery, built on the spot where *Jesus wept* over Jerusalem, foreseeing how her people should be scattered, and her high places made desolate. On the top of the hill is the ancient church of the Ascension, now a Turkish mosque. Here is an impression made in the rock, to show the last footprint of our Saviour, and many a devout pilgrim concludes it to be as represented.

Here I had the best view of Jerusalem, with its embattled walls fortified with towers, and inclosing the city on all sides, with its seven gates.

The Church of the Holy Sepulchre, the mosques, the Armenian convent, the Tomb of David, the Turkish burial-grounds, the spot where once stood the palace of Herod, &c., all present themselves at one view. The houses of Jerusalem are heavy, square masses, very low, without chimneys or windows, flat terraces or domes on the top, and look like sepulchres or prisons. The streets are unpaved, narrow, and obscure, and said to be generally very dull;

but I was fortunate in arriving here to witness the ceremonies of the Holy Week, the same as I was at Rome, last year. The many pilgrims who come from different parts of Asia, Africa, and Europe, composed of Greeks, Armenians, Copts, Latins, and some Protestants, give the city life as well as variety of character and costume, and create an active demand for the necessaries of life.

My next excursion outside the walls was in passing the gate of the prophet David on the top of Mount Zion, nearly opposite to the tomb of David, and the scene of the Last Supper. Near the gate of Bethlehem we saw some ancient cisterns of Jewish workmanship, which are alluded to in Neh. iii. 16, and Chron. xxxii. 30. Here are also a number of sepulchres cut in the rock and well executed. These tombs are alluded to in Neh. iii. 6. Following the valley of the Gihon outside of the walls, we made a long walk until we came to the cave in which the apostles hid themselves after the crucifixion. Then coming along we passed the Potter's Field, the price of our Saviour's blood. On the opposite bank of the valley of Mount Saba near which flows the brook of Kedron, is the village of Siloam, partly built and excavated out of solid rock; near this is the Pool of Siloam, where we descended by a flight of sixteen steps to the water and found it excellent. A little further on are three ancient tombs, cut in the rock, and called Jehoshaphat, Zachariah, and the Pillar of Absalom—two are nearly square, and adorned with pilasters and columns. In the vicinity is shown the spot where Christ was arrested by the officer of the High Priest, and the *footprint* is cut in the rock to mark the place.

# XXXV.

JAFFA, *April 7, 1842.*

When I wrote you last from Jerusalem, I was about making an excursion to St. John's in the desert; and had also sent a messenger to the sheik of the Bedouins, who was to provide an escort to visit the Dead Sea, the river Jordan, Jericho, &c. Mounted on horses we passed Bab-el-Khalib, or the Gate of the Pilgrims, and soon found ourselves in the environs, passing the cistern where Zadok the priest and Nathan the prophet anointed Solomon king over Israel. It is dug in the rock, the same as the pools of Solomon. We next passed the tombs of the Maccabees, situated on a lofty hill to the right, and in two hours' travel, over rocks and stones, hill and valley, we passed through the village where the convent stands erected on the spot where John the Baptist was born. We proceeded much further, penetrating the desert where he existed in the wilderness forty days upon locusts and wild honey. Some parts of this excursion we found indeed gloomy, without any vegetation, but in others the groves of olives situated upon terraces, with the cultivation of the grape, forming hanging gardens, presented a striking contrast. Near one of these olive groves, from which it is asserted the cross of Christ was taken, a convent has been founded in commemoration. It was dark when we returned; the gates of the city were closed, but having employed the Janizary of the English consul to await our return, we were permitted to enter.

Space did not permit me in my last to speak of that which interests Christians most, viz. the Holy Sepulchre and Mount Calvary. I visited the church the first time alone, preferring to pay my devotions at the shrine of our blessed Redeemer without annoyance. The access is by a narrow avenue, from its being so blocked up with buildings, and there is only one entrance. Over the doorway is sculptured the triumphal entrance of our Saviour into Jerusalem, and to the left is a high tower, the ancient belfry. The first object that I observed on entering was the slab of marble which covers the "stone of unction," upon which the body of Christ was anointed for the tomb, John xix. 39. A little further in I found the nave of a circular form, surrounded by sixteen pillars, supporting galleries, and covered by a dome. In the centre of this area is a small oblong marble building, surmounted by a small cupola standing upon columns. This covers the supposed site of our Lord's tomb.

The Greeks, Armenians, and Catholics occupy the principal part of the church, leaving the Copts but a small part, and the Protestants out of the question. The Catholic service had already commenced, and the display of the robes of the priests embroidered with gold and silver, the goblets and other vessels of gold, silver candlesticks with immense candles burning, the mitres of the priests filled with precious stones, reminded me impressively of the ceremonies of the Holy Week at Rome.

On one side of the Holy Sepulchre upon the pave was seated a group of women and girls, with white veils over their heads and faces partly covered; also others from Bethlehem, with shawls of a yellow color and faces entirely covered. These were surrounded by a guard of Turkish soldiers placed there to preserve order; as, unfortunately, so much jealousy exists among the sects, it becomes necessary; but they look on with indifference and contempt, considering us infidels, and our religion a farce.

The groups of Greeks and Armenians in native costume, the latter with heads shaved and red caps, were scattered around the church, and presented a scene at once novel and impressive. Since the fire of 1808, which burnt down a considerable part of the church, and which was repaired by the Greeks with Russian aid, they have secured the most important part of the church, and it is magnificently fitted up, rich in paintings, images, and gilding. On the north side is the chapel of the Apparition, where our Saviour appeared to Mary Magdalen. There is another altar, in commemoration of the flagellation of our Saviour (John xix. 1). Near the entrance of the church I ascended a flight of steps to the rock of Calvary, where Christ was crucified. Here are two altars, one of them Greek and the other Catholic; both splendidly adorned, the floor of mosaic, the cross with the figure of Christ suspended, and the figures of two women, one on each side. The rear is filled up with pictures, small crucifixes of pearl, and all sorts of devices, lamps continually burning, and suspended ostrich eggs. Between two slabs of marble is a small grating, through which with a candle I could discover the original rock, to all appearance split by the earthquake which followed the crucifixion of Christ. In another part is shown an altar erected on the spot where the soldiers drew lots for the garments of Christ (John xix. 33). Then descending about twenty steps into a rocky court the spot is shown where the Empress Helena discovered the true cross.

These localities have the appearance of truth, and if deception has been practised it was well devised. I attended the various services in the Church of the Holy Sepulchre, but cannot go further into detail, for I must give you some idea of our visit to Jordan. Being informed that the road thither by Jericho was quite unsafe without a strong escort, and being notorious from early antiquity as beset by robbers, evidence of which the poor Levite had when relieved by the good Samaritan, we applied to the sheik of the Bedouins, and myself, my companion and dragoman, started with five Arabs, well armed. Passing the gate of Mount Zion, and crossing the Valley of Jehoshaphat, and part of the Mount of Olives, in half an hour's ride we arrived at Bethany, the village where Jesus raised Lazarus from the dead. The monks here pretend to show the localities of the house of Simon the leper, of Mary and Martha, and the identical fig-tree which the Lord cursed. We proceeded, winding through the mountains and valleys, until towards night we discovered in the distance the long line of black tents, surrounded by herds of goats, sheep, camels, and horses. When we arrived, we found the tent of the sheik ready to receive us, but what a reception in the tent of the Bedouins! Here was man almost in his primitive state. Blankets of camel's hair were spread upon the ground; the tent was inclosed on two sides only. The women and children seemed excited at the appearance of strangers, but soon recovered from their surprise. A small hole was made in the ground in front of the tent, some brush was brought, a few grains of coffee in an iron ladle were roasted over the fire, and at length the indispensable pipe and coffee were passed. The encampment formed a circle of about twenty tents, and while the old men and the most influential of the tribe formed a group in the front of the tent of the sheik, the women and children were employed in driving all the animals within the inclosure for the night. Our evening repast consisted of fresh bread with goat's and sheep's milk, after which we stretched ourselves upon the blankets, surrounded by some fifteen or twenty Bedouins, but not to sleep, as the noise of the animals and the crawling of insects were calculated to give us an early start in the morning. After traversing the mountain where it is said Jesus was tempted by the devil, and over hill and dale, we at last arrived at Jericho, which is entirely destroyed. The only object of interest is the supposed house of Zaccheus. After leaving Jericho we proceeded across the plain for about three hours, until we saw the trees in the distance which denoted the Jordan. We had already discovered a great deal of anxiety on the part of our Arabs in crossing the mountains, on seeing four men on the top of a mountain in the distance, and they remarked that they had lost several camels and sheep, and had had one of their tribe killed, all of which we concluded might be a farce to extort money from strangers; but on approaching the Jordan we discovered a party emerging from a thicket with muskets, and our Arabs were greatly alarmed. We were well armed; a consultation was held; the blessed stream where St. John baptized our Redeemer was in sight; we determined on proceeding at all hazards, and finally had the satisfaction of bathing in the stream and procuring some bottles of the water. The suspected party finally came up, and proved to be friendly Arabs.

The Jordan runs very rapidly; the banks are covered with trees and verdure, and present a very pretty appearance. I was struck with wonder and surprise when I reflected how in ancient times the shores of the Jordan were crowded with multitudes of human beings, while now not a habitation or a civilized being is to be found upon its banks; the only occupants that I saw were wolves and gazelles.

After leaving the Jordan we passed over a sandy plain until we arrived upon the shores of the Dead Sea, which is entitled to its name, it being unruffled, the water very heavy, and consequently very buoyant. I threw in several logs of wood, which floated like corks upon the surface. After washing my hands they were covered with an oily and scaly substance. The flavor of the water is extremely salt and bitter. It is contended by some that fish do not exist in it. I did not discover any shells or anything to indicate their existence. Others contend that fish are found, but of a poisonous quality.

It was not my lot to discover any remains of the lost cities of Sodom and Gomorrah. From the Dead Sea we proceeded across the limestone mountains to Mount Saba, where there is a Greek convent, and arrived just at night at this extraordinary location, which is situated among rocky cliffs and ledges, in the midst of a gloomy mountain occupied only by the Bedouins. On knocking at the gate of this vast monastery, fortified by nature and art, and asking admission as pilgrims and Christians, we were welcomed in; and our dragoman being a Greek, we were received with all hospitality, and enjoyed the repose we so much needed. We here found the monks very polite in showing us all the contents of the convent. They told us that in the middle ages St. Saba, with many followers, occupied the caves and ledges of the rocks which are to be found in the vicinity, and that he had a dream, in which he was directed by an angel to found a convent on this spot, which was finally accomplished. They showed us the ancient chapel in the rock, where were exhibited the skulls of all the monks slain in three attacks by the Turks. One of their number was buried the morning we left, having been there forty years, dying at the age of ninety.

On leaving Mount Saba, we directed our course for Bethlehem, and after a ride of three hours over the mountain, we approached the town by a gradual ascent along the side of a well cultivated hill, walled up amphitheatre-like. On entering the convent erected over the place of nativity of our Saviour, we discovered the remains of a church founded by the empress Helena. Taking lights, we followed one of the priests down a flight of steps, visiting several altars consecrated to St. Gerolomi and others, and finally came to a chamber, in which place it is said Jesus was born. The chamber is from twenty-five to thirty feet long, and about fifteen broad, illuminated by fifty hanging lamps. At the extreme end is shown the ancient fireplace of the house of the Virgin; upon the marble hearth is a plate of gold beset with precious stones. On the other side, in a sort of grotto in the rock, is represented a manger, the place being said to be the identical spot where the babe of Bethlehem was laid. The chamber is adorned with paintings representing the virgin and the infant, and lamps are continually burning.

After quitting this interesting spot, we pursued our course to Jerusalem, where we soon arrived, after an absence of three days; and glad I was to return, having suffered exceedingly with my eyes from the extreme heat and glare of the sun, in crossing the limestone mountains. The weakness of my sight confined me to the house for two days, whereby I was able only to receive the vendors of beads and crucifixes.

On our route from Jerusalem to Jaffa, we took refuge at the house of our vice-consul, at Ramlah, who entertained that evening all the suite of the Pasha of Jerusalem, on their return from Gaza, as also the sheiks of several tribes of Bedouins; and it was an amusing sight to see some twenty persons squatted on the low divan, with their long pipes, all in Turkish costume, with long black beards and turbans, and occasionally a venerable Turk with his beard as white as snow. When dinner was announced, five small tables, about a foot and a half in height, were placed upon the floor, with servers on each; when four persons squatting around each, commenced the repast, eating in silence, without the use of forks, rising when satisfied, and washing their hands, which is done both before and after eating, the master of the house dipping his fingers first in the dish at table, and being the last to leave the table, following the rules of etiquette; all returning upon the divan, and resuming their favorite chibouque and cup of coffee.

We are now stopping in the Saba convent, and waiting an opportunity to go to Alexandria; expecting the arrival of a schooner to-morrow, which is the only communication. This town is the ancient Joppa spoken of in Scripture, 2d Chron. ii. 16; Acts ix. 36 and 42, and is situated upon an eminence overhanging the sea. The houses rise in terraces from the water's edge, and present a singular appearance from the sea. It is like a town of stairs, the streets paved in steps, owing to the inequality of the ground. This port is small, and the rocks dangerous. The view from the roofs of the houses is splendid. The surf comes to an immense height to-day, having had a strong north wind. The environs are beautiful, particularly the orange groves, which abound, extending all over the plains of Sharon, so celebrated in Scripture for their fertility, and the beautiful flowers that grow spontaneously from the soil.

# XXXVI.

VALETTA, ISLAND OF MALTA, *May 14, 1842.*

My only means of passage from Jaffa to Alexandria, where I wished to take the steamer for this island, was on board of a crazy old brig, laden with bones for the manufacture of buttons. The captain and his wife were Greeks, and occupied the cabin, infested with vermin. My companion preferred the deck. I spread my Turkish rug in the yawl-boat, and covered it with the awning of our tent, and resigned myself for a four days' trip. Our servants succeeded in preparing our meals, although surrounded by fifteen or twenty Arabs, Turks, and Armenians, most of them dirty-looking fellows. Some of them were pilgrims from Jerusalem. Entering the harbor of Alexandria an Egyptian officer, who spoke French, approached us in his boat, but without coming in contact. He took our bill of health in a tin box to be fumigated, and then condemned us to a quarantine of ten days. This was annoying and unexpected; but poor Tray was found in bad company, and we marched off to the quarantine prisons, where, separated from others by iron bars and railings, to avoid plague-contagion, we awaited provisions from outside. Our apartments consisted of two rooms, without furniture, and covered with dust. We applied to our consul for supplies and made remonstrances, as the plague did not actually exist where we came from, but persons were dying from the disease in our vicinity, and the guard were obliged to keep our servants from communication with infected subjects, which might jeopardize our lives. Our arms were demanded of us, which we were unwilling to give up. To our great joy, through the united action of the Prussian and American consuls, we were liberated after two days' incarceration in this miserable place. What a relief it was to find a decent hotel, a fair table, a comfortable bed, clean sheets, and tolerably free from fleas and other vermin, after the fatigue and inconvenience of Nile and desert travel, sleeping under tents, in mud huts, and subjected to a thousand annoyances, notwithstanding which my health has improved. But the strong glare of light, and reflection of the sun's rays upon the sand, if it had not produced ophthalmia, had so affected my eyes that I had to abandon reading and writing for some time. Fortunately a pair of green goggles, which I had used among the ice mountains of Switzerland, came apropos. I remained a few days at Alexandria, and embarked for this island in the steamer Great Liverpool, bearing the Oriental mail and passengers. The accommodations are of a superior character. Those who land here must undergo a quarantine of twenty-one days. This being the third annoyance of the kind, I was loth to submit, but comfortable provision being made under British rule, and the desire to visit the island in detail, and then proceed to Spain, made the sacrifice compulsory. This ridiculous farce will in time be modified or abandoned. Our ship came in quarantine harbor without communication with the shore, other than through the fumigating process.

We were taken in a boat, keeping at a respectful distance from the oarsmen, and when at the station the payment of coin was made by throwing it in a bucket of water. Our quarters were comfortable, the servants attentive, the restaurant was well provided. We could receive and pay visits within the ward, but only in the presence of the guards, and without touching each other, being kept at the length of the guardiano's stick. The island of Malta lies sixty miles east of Sicily; it is twenty miles in length, twelve in breadth, and sixty in circumference. The capital, Valetta, was built by the grand master in 1566; it has houses of cut stone, two and three stories high, with balconies; rises to a considerable height like a town of stairs, and is well paved and very clean, under English military rule. The strong glare of light and dust from pulverized stone is bad for the eyes. It has many edifices and public buildings full of interest. The ancient palace of the Knights of St. John, now the residence of the governor, is interesting for its works of art and relics taken in the siege of Rhodes. The Church of St. John, or cathedral, is a gem. Even after one has seen most of the prominent churches of Italy, much of merit will be found in this edifice. The mosaic pave is of precious marble, and the epitaphs of the members of the order are intensely interesting. The city is two and a half miles in circumference. The fortifications are on an enormous scale, and considered impregnable. The harbors are small but safe, containing many frigates and other naval vessels at anchor. The promenade on the bastions gives an extended view.

Although, properly speaking, the island is not much more than a barren rock, it has become, through the industry and perseverance of its occupants exceedingly fertile and well cultivated. The hills and rising grounds are inclosed by walls, to prevent the earth washing away, and form a succession of terraces.

They excavate and export cut stone, for flagging, in large quantities, and with the return vessels bring soil, which, mixed with pulverized stone, is made productive. I have made the tour of the island on horseback, and found the weather hot; in many places they had commenced harvesting.

My servant and a running guide accompanied me to the ancient city of Citta Vecchia. After riding five miles over a dusty but magnificent road, in many places cut through the solid rock, and admiring the small patches of vegetation, we came to the palace and gardens of San Antonio. Here I found a mixture of English and African trees, almonds, roses in profusion, and loquats, a fruit of a golden color, of an acid taste, introduced from China, and very refreshing on a dusty road. We then rode to Citta Vecchia; we were considerably annoyed by beggars. We looked at the old church, containing some beautiful work in bronze and marble, with paintings and frescoes of St. Paul's shipwreck. The relics of stately buildings, rich in architecture, are visible in all directions. Not far distant we were shown a church under which was the cave where St. Paul and St. Luke resided for three months. In the neighborhood are found the catacombs. Descending a staircase we found a gallery, with branches in all directions, forming quite a labyrinth.

The sides contain tombs cut out of the solid rock, without regular order, but with considerable taste. There are several halls, galleries, and places for sacrifices. On the floor was one circular block, about four feet in diameter, flat on the top, with a low edge around it. Above are seen funnels and chimneys leading outside. The ancient Phœnicians burnt offerings to the element of fire on the occasion of every tenant deposited in the tomb. In another direction we visited a village where the poor people voluntarily tax themselves in erecting a commodious church over and around the old one. They have been at work nine years, and require five more to accomplish it.

On Sundays the mechanics and laborers are all sure to turn out and work. When the new edifice is finished, the old one will be torn down and taken out. We passed through several villages containing fine churches, clean and comfortable houses, notwithstanding the poverty of the inhabitants. They are strong Catholics, and speak the Maltese dialect, a mixture of Arabic and Italian. The caleshe, or vehicle of the country, has three windows, one pair of wheels, and the driver runs beside the horse. St. Paul's Bay is quite prominent; the spot where he landed has a chapel dedicated to him.

We passed over some high hills to obtain a view of Mellicha, where the devoted make their pilgrimage.

In the neighborhood are seen caves in the rock, once inhabited. The Grotto of Calypso was pointed out by our guide; we found a man and his wife in it, with a hand-loom, a few cooking utensils, a few old clothes, and a couple of chairs, which was all their stock; a small present made them quite happy. They had, very naturally, never heard of Calypso.

They had a beautiful valley lying below them, with a deep bay and the island of Gozo in the distance. There is much to be said and described in and about the island, but time does not permit, as I embark for Spain.

## SUMMER TRIP, 1842.

The steamer Alecto brought me from Malta to Gibraltar; we coasted along the African shore, sighting Algiers, with its high walls and whitewashed buildings, crowned by its citadel. I was struck with awe and admiration at the sight of the renowned rock of Gibraltar, whose defences entitle it to be called the key of the Mediterranean. I climbed up zigzag roads and stairways, and was shown immense galleries excavated out of the solid rock, which terminate in the battery called "St. George's Hall." Higher up, at the height of thirteen hundred feet, is the rock gun. The number of cannon employed in all the general defences is said to be eight hundred. On the summit, or Telegraph Hill, we partook of refreshments, and looking over a register kept for visitors, I was amused at their comments: "No monkeys visible to-day." "Where are all the monkeys?" "Lots of monkeys to-day." I looked over the parapet wall, and, sure enough, the fine weather had brought out thirty-nine or forty, who were scrambling and chattering among the branches of the scrub trees. It is the only spot in Europe where they are found; heavy penalties prevent killing them, but the dogs sometimes destroy them when they descend to rob the gardens below. St. Michael's Cave is curious for its stalactites, and came in as an additional attraction. The view from the summit over the straits and the African coast, the Spanish town of Algesiras, on the opposite side of the bay, the neutral ground, the walled and fortified city below, was of the most enjoyable character. The alemedas, or promenades, are well laid out, and planted with trees and flowers, which give them a cheerful appearance. The birthday of Queen Victoria was the occasion of grand demonstrations on shore and on shipboard. At mid-day the roar of cannons from the vessels of war, in which our own ship Brandywine took part, and the discharge of thirty-two pounders from the rock galleries, produced such a concussion that my inkstand trembled while I wrote. The night illumination of the eighty-four gun-ship Formidable, and others, was magnificent.

The tents and camp of the General, covered with devices and transparencies, produced a fine effect, and the bursting of rockets lighted up the countenances of the dancing multitude upon the Alemeda.

Eight hours' steaming took me to Malaga, just in time for the festival of Corpus Christi. Our passengers were mostly Moors in Arab dress, Spaniards with steeple-crowned hats and fantastic round jackets, contrabandists in embroidered boots and leggings, provided with goods for their traffic. A grand procession, military and civic, priests, men, and boys with lighted candles, preceded by the crucifix, passed through the narrow streets, and made a long circuit. The balconies covered with flags and drapery of gay colors, and filled with the beautiful senoritas of the true Andalusian type, could not help but add to the attraction. Groups of fascinating creatures with black lace mantillas, fan in hand, giving it that peculiar twirl belonging to the race, were kneeling upon the rugs on the cathedral pave, and casting their captivating glances (perhaps unconsciously) upon the passing strangers. My fellow-traveller, the Spanish Consul from Gibraltar, was *en route* for Grenada; he had opposed the contraband trade, and was afraid of an attack.

Our miserable diligence was drawn by eight mules with rope traces; the driver guides the wheel mules with nose-straps only, without bits, and at times jumps down beside them, whipping up and crying out lustily; so they dash along the rugged roads and on the banks of precipices at the imminent risk of one's life.

The first venta had flat stone floor, a rude table with benches, and a poor breakfast. The chambers were bare walls, no chairs, no bedstead; the people slept upon mats with no notion of comfort. The country has been disturbed by civil wars for the past seven years. Assassinations are frequent, caused by political intrigue, or love affairs. The first night we found ourselves at the town of Loza, situated in a picturesque country, in the midst of luxurious groves and gardens on the south side of a rocky gorge, through which a small river forces its way after passing the rich valley of Grenada. The place is celebrated for two sieges under Ferdinand and Isabella, in 1487, and was taken, it is asserted, through the cowardice of Bobadil. Our accommodations had improved.

We passed the Duke of Wellington's estate, given for services during the Peninsular War; it is a pretty vega, or valley, with a village of cottages. Not far from this place an English party had been robbed. Three horsemen, with long carabines, a brace of pistols, and dirks each, presented themselves and asked them politely to get out and prostrate themselves upon their faces, while one of the number stood guard until the luggage was ransacked. They were then offered some of their own cigars, a drink of aguardiente, and left in the usual gallant manner—"*Vaya con Dios*." Some eight miles from Grenada, we passed the small walled town of Santa Fè, built by Ferdinand during the siege of Grenada.

We had made the seventy-six miles from Malaga, and now saw the magnificent valley for miles in extent, the snow-capped mountains of the Sierra Nevada, with the rivers Dano and Genil forcing their passages out of them. Once Grenada was the pride and glory of the Moors; now it is the admiration of every traveller.

We found a quiet retreat upon the summit of the Alhambra hill, near a lofty tower commanding an extensive view of the city below. The unfinished palace of Charles V., and the palace of the Moorish sovereigns stood hard by. A description of the Alhambra, with its beautiful architecture, the court of the lions, its marble-paved halls, its arabesque walls and ceilings, and the many objects of admiration, I shall not attempt to describe. The cathedral, containing the monuments of Ferdinand and Isabella, the archduke Philip and his wife Joanna, has many attractions. The church of San Juan de Dios is rich in marble. The road to Cordova, a distance of eighty-four miles, we made on mule-back, there being no carriage roads. The first night we slept in a venta, upon a brick floor, among horses, mules, drivers, and others of bandit appearance. We were almost devoured by fleas; there were no beds or other accommodations. I find it worse, if possible, than a Turkish khan. We procured here an escort through the wild heath and across the mountain paths, the roads being infested with robbers. Our guides were old cut-throats, and were considered the safest, as they were to be well paid if they piloted us through in safety; they knew all the haunts of the bandits. At Alcala-el-Real we found a posada well fitted up, and the landlady reminded me of a Dutch housewife for cleanliness, which we were prepared to appreciate.

We made a tarry at Byena, and proceeded then to Cordova, and were rejoiced to arrive, as it is not pleasant to grasp one's pistol in the night at the sound of some slight noise in the bush, not knowing what moment you may be pounced upon.

Passing through some of the small villages, the people looked so wretched one could almost excuse an attack. In other portions of the country the peasants looked well, returning from the fields of ripened grain. We escaped with one arrest, only, from highwaymen. One fine-looking, but swarthy, heavy-whiskered fellow, clad in velvet, with knee-breeches and leather-strapped leggings, pointed hat and feather, long carabine, and pistols in his belt, who carried a whistle to call his comrades, descended slowly from a craggy eminence, greeted our guides, and made his demand, which being extremely moderate we readily granted, and passed on without further molestation.

A part of the journey our guide suggested riding by night, and lying by during the day, thereby escaping the heat, and dodging the highwaymen. We started at six P.M. and halted at seven A.M., partook of a miserable breakfast, stretched our mattresses upon a cement floor, encircled with double streaks of olive oil to keep the fleas from jumping across, closed the shutters to darken the room, and reposed until the hour for dinner, after which mounted our mules again. Cordova is dull and lifeless, a large city in decay; the greatest curiosity is the Moorish mosque of eight hundred and thirty-four columns, now converted into a Catholic church. Approaching the city the country is well cultivated, and the gardens of pomegranates in blossom were quite pretty. How delightful it is for the traveller, while quite alone and exposed to danger, to meet with a familiar face. A singular rencontre took place near Cordova. We had abandoned our mule and taken the diligence, when we were met by a vehicle escorted by gensd'armes, who inquired if we had been interrupted by bandits, when to my surprise out jumped a Frenchman, whom I had last met among the ruins of Thebes and Karnak. "Bonjour, Monsieur. D'où venez-vous? Où allez-vous?" he cried out. I had scarcely time to greet him and reply, when off dashed our animals, and I have seen him perhaps for the last time. From Cordova I came to Seville, rejoiced to find comfortable quarters, get a bath, and put myself in the hands of il barbiero di Sevilla. The services of Figaro were only required in hair-cropping, as the natural Turkish and Arab eight months' growth of beard could be still worn with impunity, but once in England the heavy crop must be harvested, or the little urchins will set up a cry.

While in Egypt an anecdote was related of an old man who had been impressed in the army from his native village. Mehemet Ali had adopted the custom of shaving the soldiery. It was found he had passed the age for service, and was told he might go: "Yes," he replied, "go, where shall I go?" "To your village," was the answer. "The boys and girls of my village will hoot at me," he exclaimed, "give me back my beard or allow me to remain until it grows." Such is the value of a beard in oriental countries. The next acquisition was a valet de place, whose duty is to point out all the remarkable sights of the city, which, when Spain possessed America, was considered the wealthiest of the realm.

The cathedral is one of the finest in Spain, of the Moro-Gothic style; its stained glass historical windows, and its sacristy and other decorations demand attention. The secret councils of the Inquisition were held there. From the summit of la Giralda, the tower built by the Moors, two hundred and fifty years before, and taken by king Ferdinand, at a height of two hundred and sixty-four feet, one has a fine view of the city and suburbs, lying upon the banks of the Guadalquiver. The Alcazar, or Moorish palace, built fifty years before the conquest of Seville, with its arabesque and beautiful colored ceilings, bears resemblance to the Alhambra of Granada. Several days were passed pleasantly and agreeably in the old city. I gazed at its fine Murillo paintings, strolled upon its Alemedas, plucked its delicious oranges in shady gardens, peeped into its theatres, saw its tobacco factory, a monopoly in Spain, where two thousand women and six hundred men are employed making cigars and snuff. I then came down the river to the seaport of Cadiz. The banks of the stream are low; large droves of cattle were seen grazing—and many orange and lemon groves. We passed St. Mary's with Xeres in the background; the latter is celebrated for its sherry wine. Cadiz, while Spain was in possession of her American colonies, ranked next in wealth to Seville, but has declined notwithstanding its free port. The houses are lofty, spacious, well-built; the streets narrow, to protect from the sun's rays; they are well-paved, clean, and pretty. The ramparts are planted with rows of trees overlooking the park. The large squares of San Antonio and Constitucion, in the centre of the city, are where ices, love, and scandal occupy the fair sex until midnight. The steamer Royal Tar brought me to Lisbon, the Portuguese capital. Steaming up the broad river Tagus, the first coup d'œil of the city, with its long quays, public buildings, and handsome streets upon its banks, is prepossessing, but in climbing its precipitous hills, built even to the summit, one finds many narrow and filthy streets and lanes, offensive both to the eye and olfactories.

The sights of the city were done up with usual assiduity. The Royal Palace, yet unfinished, occupied by Don Miguel during his short sway, the prominent churches of the city, remarkable for works of art, the Alemeda, the great opera house, and the gigantic aqueduct of the city, all received their share of attention.

We drove to Cintra, the royal country residence, which was some three or four hours' distance. Our party mounted donkeys, whose heads were dressed with flowers by their drivers, and off we started for the Moorish castle, which is now in course of reparation, situated upon a precipitous height, affording a fine view. The vineyards of Collares were visited, and their products tested. The cork-wood forests where the trees had been stripped of their bark were examined. The waters of the iron spring were not as acceptable as delicious oranges from the hands of a Portuguese beauty, whose charms were not heightened by her white head-handkerchief and capuchin cloak, comparing unfavorably with the black mantilla and beautiful eyes of the Andalusians. We visited the palace, met the king, mounted on a beautiful bay horse, who bowed politely as he galloped over the lawn. The queen was plainly clad, a fleshy lady, riding upon a donkey, her infant in a pannier upon a second, accompanied by a train of liveried servants, altogether a novel cortege.

The excursion was a delightful one. I embarked for England, sighting Oporto, touching at Vigo, and landed at Southampton. I went to London, thence to Liverpool, crossed over to Ireland, visited Dublin, Newry, and Belfast; crossed again from Donaghadee to Portpatrick in Scotland; went along the coast to Ayrshire, upon the banks of the Doon, to the former thatched cottage of the poet Burns, thence up to Greenock, and Glasgow, and across by rail to Edinburgh.

I shall return by another route to Liverpool, and embark for the United States, when I can commune verbally about the magnificent countries passed through.

## EXPLANATORY NOTES.

Finding that this work would be too voluminous for the publication of letters and extracts from journals, from 1842 to 1847, I have concluded to omit almost all correspondence, excepting what relates to European, Asiatic, African, South American, and Pacific coast travel. In the intermediate years of foreign travel, my winters were passed in the South, and the West Indies. Going southerly I varied and changed my routes in every possible manner, in order to pass over almost all the roads and rivers of our country, now touching the capitals of all the western and southern States, and then taking cross roads, through pine forests and everglades, along the banks of low fever rivers with their rice plantations, upon the bayous and streams whose deep alluvial produces the sugar crop, and upon the high and low lands which produce the sea-island and up-land cotton, thereby giving one an opportunity to see the small towns and villages of our country, and to study the characteristics of our people, and the mildness of their peculiar institution, as compared with other countries, and to value the productions of the south. After escaping the rigors of a northern winter in the West Indies, my five upward Mississippi trips from New Orleans, in the month of May or June, would be varied.

After making Natchez and Vicksburg, Mississippi, a visit, I looked into Arkansas—Natchitoches and Alexandria on the Red River, I had already seen. The rising city of Memphis and its producing region demanded attention. St. Louis, from its commanding position and rapid growth, could not be neglected. Louisville and Frankfort, in Kentucky, were not forgotten, and a pilgrimage to Ashland, where the hospitalities of the renowned and beloved Henry Clay can never be forgotten. The populous city of Cincinnati, with its fleet of steamers and its immense commerce, was regarded with pleasure on several occasions. The passes of the Alleghany mountains through Virginia and Maryland gave me a chance to examine the coal mines, to say nothing of the mineral resources of the country. To vary the trips, Pittsburg, the Manchester of America, and Alleghany, its sister city, came in for their share of attention in the visits of their iron works—the smoky atmosphere reminded one of Birmingham, Sheffield, and other manufacturing cities in England.

The mountain rides through Pennsylvania, and the canal trip to Harrisburg, the State capital, were suited to the admirer of nature; a short sojourn among the Germans in the close cultivated regions of Lancaster brought up souvenirs of Hesse Cassel in Germany.

On other northern-bound trips instead of turning east by the Ohio, I would go up the Illinois river to Peru and Peoria, then strike across the prairies to Chicago, or continue up the Mississippi, touching Nauvoo, the former residence of the Mormons, and visiting Iowa, thence up the Fever River to Galena, take a look at the lead mines, cross the prairies in a slow coach, the wild grass and flowers up to the horses' knees, where the cries of the wolf and the scream of wild birds only disturb the monotony of these plains bounded by the horizon. At this early period Chicago and Milwaukie were only in their infancy. I have looked at them again on several occasions since, but more recently what was my astonishment to find them large populous cities, with iron arms extending in all directions, the snort of the iron horse replacing the cries of the wild beasts of the prairies. In due course St. Paul, Minnesota, the Falls of St. Anthony, the head sources of the Father of Waters, Madison, the capital of Wisconsin, with Fond du Lac, Racine and

Sheboygan, had to be seen. The tour of the great lakes, Michigan, Huron, St. Clair, Erie, Ontario, all the cities of Upper and Lower Canada, the running of the rapids of the St. Lawrence, and a return by lake Champlain, formed part of another programme. The interior cities and capitals of Michigan, Illinois, Indiana, and Ohio, were visited partly before any railroad penetrated them, and of course attended with much inconvenience and fatigue. During my stay in the north from time to time the cities of Massachusetts, Maine, New Hampshire, Rhode Island, Connecticut, and Vermont were visited, the cotton and woollen manufactories of Lowell, the whaling mart of New Bedford, and shipbuilding on the Kennebec river, were looked at, as well as almost all the railroad routes with their towns and cities in this and other States.

The inquiry will naturally be, What was the inducement? The answer must be briefly this: I designed going again to Europe, and I wished to familiarize myself with every point in our own country, and to obtain some general knowledge at least of the resources, productions, and characteristics of this vast territory. Emigration had been setting in so rapidly, the interest felt by foreigners was increasing, and the inquiries made by English, French, German, and other races were so frequent that I hoped to be able to answer all general interrogations, if not practically, theoretically. The embarrassment to Americans abroad is frequently great from having too little knowledge of their own country.

An English traveller in Switzerland once asked me why we had such frightful accidents by explosion and otherwise on the Mississippi river, while cases were so rare in England. I replied that high-pressure steamers were employed, and that the navigation was obstructed by snags and sawyers, or trees carried down and fastened in the river-bed. He remarked, that an American had told him our boats were all low-pressure. I replied, that the gentleman was from the north, and had probably never seen a high-pressure steamer.

I trust the reader will accept these explanations as an apology for an itinerant life, and not attribute it all to the passion for travel.

# 1848.
# XXXVIII.

ROME, *May, 1848.*

My voyage across the Atlantic was rather boisterous. We were exposed to the gale the night that the unfortunate ship Stephen Whitney was lost with upwards of one hundred passengers, near Liverpool, while we were approaching the port of Havre. We left Sandy Hook together, and reached the British and French coasts about the same time.

I found Havre much the same as I left it some years since, but instead of coasting along the beautiful banks of the Seine, by steamers, as formerly, to Rouen, and thence by diligence to Paris, I was whirled through in locomotive style in a few hours.

My stay at Paris was only sufficient to make preparations for my southern trip. I took my departure via Orleans, Tours, Bordeaux, Toulouse, Nismes, and Arles; the latter cities, with their vast collection of Roman ruins, are worthy of a visit. At all these places I made a short sojourn, not having touched them in my former travels in France. In my general voyages, I have adopted as a rule varying my route, in order to see the entire country, for which reason instead of going from Marseilles to Genoa by water, as formerly, I took land conveyance to Toulon in order to visit the great French naval station, and the prisons and workshops of the five thousand French culprits.

From Toulon I came to Nice, the city so celebrated for its salubrity of climate, where so many pulmonary patients are sent by their physicians to spend the winter, and where I designed also passing some months. But here I must be allowed to differ in opinion with the faculty, as far as I am at liberty to judge from my own experience. The approach to the city from Toulon, winding along the shore of the Mediterranean with its walled hills, amphitheatre-like, covered with a profusion of olive, lemon, and orange trees, laden with fruit, is truly enchanting. The mild and genial rays of the sun, with the light breeze from the sea, is most grateful, while one beholds in the distance the ranges of mountains covered with snow to their summits. The new part of the city is well built with spacious streets on both sides of the *river* Paglione, or rather mountain torrent, but the old town is quite Italian, with narrow streets, tall buildings, and much filth. The rides and promenades along the coast and over the hills and mountains in the suburbs, can scarcely be surpassed; but the transition from the heat of the day to the cool of night, or from the exposure of the sun's rays to the shade, is too severe for those of a pulmonary habit.

From Nice I took my departure along the coast to Genoa, and over one of the most interesting roads for the sublime and picturesque, I had yet seen. The shore is studded with small cities and fishing towns; elevated at times nearly to the summit of the mountains which project in the sea; the huge and elaborate tunnels are cut through solid rocks which are covered with snow; then a descent upon vineyards and orange groves, with a wide and expanded view upon the bosom of the sea, dotted with fruit and fishing vessels; and around the ever-varying costume of the peasantry and fishermen, the former engaged in gathering the olive and bearing loaded baskets of oranges, and the latter lazily lounging in the sun's rays, or hauling their vessels on the beach, or mending their nets preparatory to a cruise.

From Genoa I embarked for Leghorn and Pisa, where I have passed some time, and where the climate seems more uniform and dry than any other part of Italy, and more desirable as a winter residence for those who have any pulmonary disposition. It is less subject to changes from the contiguity of mountains, as at Genoa and Florence, and is less humid than Naples or Rome. I am quite satisfied, however, that no climate in Italy for the winter residence of an invalid will compare with the West India Islands, or even with the southern part of the United States.

As far as my experience goes the climates of the islands of Sicily and Malta are more desirable than Italy, but Egypt, being dry and warm, is better still; however, I would advise those who are decidedly pulmonary to pass their winters in the West Indies.

The revolutions all about us, and the preparation and marching of troops, both regulars and volunteers, arriving from Naples and Leghorn, and departing from here, have been exciting. The frequent illuminations on the receipt of victorious news from the Italian army, and the tri-colored flags waving from every house in the city, with the roaring of cannon and "le feu de joie" from every window, continued until the authorities found it was best to keep their powder and prevent accidents.

One extreme always follows another; joy is changed into grief; the whole populace in tears at the loss of a battle, the massacre of their brethren—widows, sisters, and mothers are sobbing bitterly; the cathedral is clothed in black, and thronged with thousands, the transparencies in large letters at the ponderous brazen doors breathe vengeance upon the oppressor; the immense catafalque in the centre of the nave is covered with the uniforms, and flags, and all the instruments of war, and shrouded with mourning; the Te Deum is chaunted; the cry is again to arms. The priest in his long robes and girdled waist, and broad brimmed three-cocked hat, heads the movement, the crucifix in hand, for the holy crusade, amid the cries of "Death to Metternich," "VIVA ITALIA, VIVA PIO NONO."

I have spent a month in Rome, and have found no great changes since I was last here, except the political ones. It is pleasant to hear the cry of the newsboy, and see the groups of citizens at the corners of the streets, reading the news of the day; for which they are indebted to the liberal mind of the present Pope, Pius IX. I find fewer strangers at Rome during the services of the Holy Week than formerly, and in consequence of the revolutions about us, the English are afraid to travel, and are deserting the city rapidly, and taking passage by sea for their native isle.

The ceremonies of the church were quite as gorgeous as under Pope Gregory XVI.; the illumination of St. Peter's with its thousands of lamps and torches, was quite as magical, but the Girandola, or fireworks of the castle of St. Angelo, did not take place, to the disappointment of thousands who had not seen it. Report says a conspiracy had been discovered, and several barrels of powder found intended for a general blow-up on the occasion. The Pope, who has a fine-looking person and an amiable face, appeared thoughtful and devout during all the services of Passion Week, pronounced the benediction to the thousands and thousands from the balcony of St. Peter's, preached with dignity at the Feast of the Pilgrims, but I thought washed the feet of the latter with less humility than his predecessor Gregory.

We have been on the eve of civil war, having had a three days' émeute. The Pope, who had headed the reform movement and acquiesced in the arming of thousands of Romans for the crusade against the Austrians, was, in his pious moments, after the Holy Week, prevailed upon by the perfidious counsels of the cardinals to proclaim against the war. As a natural consequence the whole population were interested; mothers, sisters, and lovers, whose friends had gone forth in good faith to fight the battle of national independence, were liable to be taken and shot or hung, without any privileges accorded to an enemy legally enrolled. The National Guard of twelve thousand strong took possession of all the gates of the city, inclosed the cardinals in their palaces to prevent escape from the city, and thus things remained for three days until a reconciliation took place, and a change of ministry.

The carnival season this year was rather dull in comparison with former times; but in addition to the usual parade of masquerades in carriages and on foot, with an ample supply of sugar rouberies which they throw furiously at each other in passing, and the avalanche of bouquets of flowers for the ladies, they have a custom at Pisa of carrying wax torches called Moccolo, which, as nightfall finishes the procession, are lighted, and then the whole line of the river Arno is illuminated with bonfires, which give an enchanting effect. The shout of "Moccolo, Moccolo," from thousands of voices, as they endeavor to tear from each other the wax tapers, amid the shower of sugar-plums and bouquets, was an exciting scene, from which I was glad to make my escape with spotted garments.

# XXXIX.

GENEVA, SWITZERLAND, 1848.

I had taken the precaution at Rome to write to Civita Vecchia to secure a berth by the steamer Capri for Leghorn, but on my arrival I found my chance was only for a mattress on the cabin floor, as some one hundred and fifty passengers had just escaped from the revolution and massacre at Naples, and the steamer was full. We had one of those nights that I had seldom seen on the Mediterranean, stormy and boisterous, with a heavy sea; the horrors of sea-sickness were experienced by all, except some six of us old travellers, who, in place of a four-franc dinner, always paid for in advance, could only get a bowl of soup by bracing oneself in a corner. Chairs were flying about under the table, and one confused, chaotic mass of humanity, men, women, and children, was stretched over the settees and cabin floors, while others kept on deck exposed to a drenching rain.

At the Baths of Lucca I found but few strangers, as they were fearful of an attack from deserted soldiers, and a portion of the Neapolitan army who had been recalled by their despotic king.

At Florence the people caught the general, whose mission had been at Bologna to recall the troops after the revolution of Naples; he succeeded in making his escape, however, but we had a great flare-up in the public place, at midnight, in the burning of his papers and carriage. It was a tumultuous scene; the infatuated mob hissing, groaning, and shouting, and the military with their gleaming bayonets shining, as the flames and cinders rose in the air.

The Grand Duke is much respected by his people, and Tuscany has more liberty than any other part of Italy. I was a witness of the brilliant reception he received by the populace at Leghorn, and heard his address from the balcony of the palace, after which followed an illumination of the city. I have little confidence in the lower classes of Leghorn. They are excitable and tumultuous, and difficult to restrain, and we may soon hear of a general flare-up or civil war. It afforded me pleasure to visit once again our fellow-countrymen, Messrs. Powers and Greenough, whose studios have contributed so much in sculpture to the fame of American artists, and who are so well known in our country. I found several other American artists, both painters and sculptors, at Florence, who promise well for the future. It is one of the most agreeable residences in Italy, but I find fewer strangers here than formerly, as the political disturbances, and the failure of bankers in Paris, have driven them away.

At Genoa all was tranquil, and from thence I took the malle-poste via Alexandria, the great Piedmont fortifications, near which is the battle-ground of Marengo, for Turin. In the absence of the royal family and the bulk of the army it was rather dull. The greatest enthusiasm for the Italian cause pervades all Sardinia, and the Piedmont soldiers, being a brave and hardy race from the mountains, are capable of doing duty; but I fear without support from other sources they will not be able to resist the impetuous and large forces of the Austrians, composed of Croats, Slavonians, and Hungarians.

Turin is a beautiful city, with a population of some two hundred thousand, and is handsomely situated on the river Po. Its boulevards and promenades in the suburbs are strikingly pretty. The palace of Charles Albert is vast and richly ornamented; the collection of ancient armor in the old chateau is more beautiful than any I had seen, except the Green Vaults of Dresden.

The Sardinian Senate was in session, and in company with our Chargé d'Affaires, Mr. Niles, who accompanied me to the Tribune, where was seated the delegation from Milan, praying the union of Lombardy to Sardinia. We heard Count Balbi of Genoa, well known for his liberal views, present a petition for the immediate incorporation of the two countries. It was received with bursts of applause and unanimous acclamations, and rarely have I seen so much enthusiasm in a public body of representatives.

The country from Turin to Ivrea, as the road strikes north to the St. Bernard, is well cultivated, and has an air of comfort; and, in fact, in Piedmont generally is seen much less of that squalid poverty than is met with at the south of Italy.

The valley of Ostia is beautiful in the extreme, for the wild and picturesque, as is also the mountain scenery, and the torrents from the melting of the snows, as they rush by with an impetuosity frightful to behold, and only found in Switzerland in the vicinity of high mountains. To my surprise, at the foot of St. Bernard, in the extreme north of Italy, I found at the entrance of the town of Ostia a Roman arch that in beauty and preservation would surpass the arches of Titus and Constantine in Rome. There is also a colossal Roman bridge in good preservation, although partly covered with the dust of ages, also the remains of an amphitheatre, and other relics.

After a day spent here I proceeded in a one-horse vehicle to a small village at the foot of the mountain, where commences the ascent, and where I passed the night. At the entrance of the inn I started back at the sight of a huge chained dog, with glassy eyes, but soon found it was none other than the stuffed skin of one of those noble fellows who had saved the lives of several snow-benighted travellers.

The keeper of the inn was the guide of the pass. I asked him his terms for his mules and services, and found that he asked double the ordinary prices. Upon expostulating with him he informed me that no traveller had yet passed; that the avalanches were yet unmelted and to be feared. I thought it was all a ruse, but he said he would prefer not to go. I could not retrace my steps; I was well provided with garments, having an Algerine cloak with a hood attached to protect the head, a mantle in addition, with shoes and overshoes. I knew I could not suffer from cold, and I accepted his terms, to leave the following morning with two mules for myself and baggage, and two guides. To my surprise I found all he had said was true. We passed over immense avalanches of snow in the gorges and passages, where it was necessary for the two guides to take one mule at a time, one at the head and the other at the side, to keep me mounted.

We arrived safely at the Convent or Hospice, and I was cordially received by the fraternity and showed the interior of the immense building with over one hundred rooms; its chapel or church is decorated with paintings, marble altars, crucifixes, &c., and would compare with many small churches in Italy. Here is also the monument of Gen. Dessaix, Napoleon's bosom friend, who fell at the battle of Marengo. The Emperor contributed largely to the funds of the establishment. I saw that famous breed of dogs so well known, and also a building where are the bones and dried mummies of those who die in the convent or are found in the snow. The monks are only thirteen in number, and usually change every three years, as the temperature is found too bracing. They informed me that all my guide had said was true; that I was the first traveller of the season; I was quite at home among them, as they had many inquiries to make about Rome and Palestine; and although dinner was served early on my behalf, our sitting was prolonged until I was admonished by my guides it was time to depart in order to arrive at the village at the foot of the mountain before nightfall. There I procured a *char-à-banc* and came to St. Maurice and Martigny, and soon embarked by steamer upon the beautiful Lake of Geneva, passing Vevay, Lausanne, and other towns with all their souvenirs of a former visit during the season of the vintage. The day was warm and beautiful, and the lake placid, and I was quite satisfied having made the pass of the mountains which loomed up in the distance, the peak eternally covered with snow, without having suffered accident or inconvenience.

I find this beautiful town, Geneva, less active than when I last visited it, as the distracted state of affairs on the Continent has operated seriously against the branch of commerce in which it chiefly engaged—the manufacture of jewelry. There are now five thousand workmen without their regular employment, and the authorities, to keep them from open rebellion, are levelling a rampart and filling up the fosses, which gives employ to a vast number at a remuneration of only one and a half francs, or thirty cents per day, barely sufficient to keep body and soul together.

---

# XL.

MUNICH, BAVARIA, 1848.

When I wrote you last I was on the eve of departure for Neufchatel, which is a quiet town, and beautifully situated upon the lake which bears the same name. The rich and varied mountain scenery, the still and placid waters of the lake, the high state of culture of the grape and other products, with the apparent comfort surrounding the Swiss cottages, made it an agreeable trip. Here too they had had their Revolution, and the royalist party, which was under the protection of the King of Prussia, was obliged to give way to the Republican Swiss.

Lucerne offers but few attractions in itself, but an excursion by steamer to the head of the lake, with its ever-varying scenery and localities full of historical reminiscences, gives it additional interest. The chapel erected to the memory of William Tell is seen under the precipice from which he leaped when pursued by his oppressors; also the Grotto of the Swiss conspirators, where they concealed themselves when striving for the redemption of their country. Mount Riga, too, rises in all his majesty in the distance, and is much visited in ordinary seasons by travellers, but in these revolutionary times I find myself quite alone. The landlords complain, and say their callings are gone, for this year at least.

At the beautiful town of Zurich I made an agreeable sojourn, and met with real Swiss hospitality from friends whose acquaintance I had made en voyage. The society is good here, and gave me an opportunity of seeing much of the manners and customs in private life. The hotels are excellent; the excursions upon the lake by steamer, most agreeable. The town is pleasantly situated upon both sides of the stream where the lake discharges itself, and is connected by bridges, and reminds me of Geneva.

From Zurich, I took a northerly direction to Schaffhausen, to see the Cataract of the Rhine, which is well worth a visit; but the fall of a river of only eighty feet, although grand and beautiful, and highly extolled by continental tourists, does not so particularly interest an American who has visited the majestic and indescribable falls of Niagara. This reminds me of an anecdote related of a controversy between an American and an Italian, relative to the beauties and remarkable curiosities of the two countries. The Italian thought he had the advantage, particularly in describing the volcano, and the eruptions of Mount Vesuvius; but the American replied, "Yes, all very true; and we have Niagara, which can drown Vesuvius in less than five minutes."

From Schaffhausen, the steamer takes one along the upper Rhine, which is low and flat in many places, and not remarkable for its beauty. We then entered Lake Constance, which is the largest sheet of water in Switzerland, touching at different points until our arrival at Constance, which has nothing particular to offer for the traveller in the way of sights.

Having made zigzag routes in Switzerland in my former as well as present voyage, and having seen eighteen out of the twenty-two cantons comprising the Confederation, I was quite satisfied to depart for the head of the lake, on my way to Augsburgh and Munich. This latter city, with a population of one hundred thousand, is an interesting place, and contains more to interest a stranger than most of the German cities. It, too, has had a share of revolution; and the late king Louis, who has abdicated in favor of his son, and whose favorite, Lola Montez, created so much noise in the world, has fled to Switzerland. The king had a great passion for the fine arts, both painting and sculpture, and good taste in architecture; and the new part of the city is beautified with piles of immense edifices for the use of the state, and galleries of paintings, statuary, and antique collections. The contrast between the quaint, antique houses, of irregular construction, with high roofs and two tiers of windows in their main fronts, ornamented with scroll-work, and the modern style of buildings, is very great.

The new palace, copied after the Pitti Palace at Florence, is one of the most beautiful in Europe, with floors of various kinds of wood, inlaid in patterns which differ in all the rooms, and produce a sort of mosaic. The cornices, bas-reliefs in marble, fresco paintings, after the fashion of Pompeii and the Vatican at Rome, statuary in marble and bronze gilt, with the damask hangings and tapestry—the magnificence and apparent comfort of these things struck me very forcibly.

For one who has not seen other parts of Europe, some weeks could be employed advantageously in Munich. I have been here several days, and have had constant employment, first in visiting the gallery of sculpture, where I found a vast collection of Egyptian and Etruscan antiquities; those which were broken were well restored by Thorwaldsen. One room is devoted to Egyptian statuary, another to Etruscan, another to Ægina collections, and the decorations of each apartment are adapted to the contents, the floors of marble, and the ceilings in rich fresco and stucco patterns, with gilding. In the room appropriated to Egyptian statuary, I could almost fancy myself back among the ruins of Thebes, and the great temples of Karnak, so natural did everything appear.

The picture gallery is one of the finest buildings for paintings in Europe. The paintings are arranged in the schools of the different masters and countries, filling seven splendid halls, and twenty-three small cabinets. The finest and largest pictures of each school are placed in the centre halls, and the light is thrown down upon them from above; the others are lighted from the sides. The ceilings are in fresco and paintings, all of historical character. There are some one thousand five hundred paintings, selected from seven thousand of the different galleries in Bavaria; and altogether the collection reflects honor upon the late king, who has expended large sums of money from his private purse for the embellishment of his capital, which is now so beautiful, and which a century since was only a small German town. A heavy debt, however, has been created for the state, which, as in all other countries, the good people must pay, whether for honorable appropriations, or the follies and caprices of sovereigns.

Among the public monuments, is one now in process of construction, called the Genius of Bavaria; it is of cast bronze and of colossal size. It is the figure of a female with flowing ringlets, about fifty feet in height, mounted on a pedestal, with a crouching lion at her feet, all of solid bronze. The work is still going forward at the foundry in the suburbs of the city, and will require some time yet to finish it. It will surpass altogether the statue of San Carlo Boromeo, of beaten copper, upon Lago Maggiore, in Italy.

The population of Munich are mostly Catholics, and yesterday being Sunday, I visited the churches, which are not as remarkable, with some exceptions, as in Italy. There is one, the Basilica of St. Bonifacius, which is built in Roman style, after the plan of St. Paul's, about three miles from Rome. It is of red brick, but the interior is beautifully decorated, and supported by sixty-four columns of marble in four rows; it is divided in four arches, with a nave seventy feet high, and fifty feet wide. The pave is of marble with painted ceiling of blue, and beams carved and gilded with a variety of frescoes.

My valet took me in the suburbs in the afternoon, and, as in all Catholic countries, the Sunday afternoon and evening are devoted to recreation, so here also. The gardens were full to overflowing, the tables were crowded with drinkers and smokers, and a full proportion of the fair sex with their peculiar costume, and head-dress called *Riegel Haube*, which is a small bag of gold or silver tissue, with two points like a swallow's tail, and is worn on the back of the head to inclose the hair. It costs twelve or fifteen dollars, and it is the height of ambition of the peasant girl to indulge in it. Music was heard in all directions, and waltzes and dances kept up much later than I had a disposition to stay and gratify curiosity.

What a striking contrast between this and our own quiet Sabbaths at home! But such is the result of early education, and we must learn to exercise charity towards those who differ from us from the fact that they have been taught differently. Ever since the reformation of Luther, such is the strong tenacity of the people to Sunday recreations, that, in many parts of Germany, the dance and promenade in the evening succeed the morning services of the Protestant church.

I was at Augsburgh at the anniversary of the birthday of the Bishop, and was much amused at the immense collection of peasants who thronged the streets in costume, and filled the cathedral and vicinity; many of the women wore head-dresses not unlike those of Munich, but the greatest singularity about their dress was the peculiar mutton-legged sleeve, specimens of which may sometimes be seen on the arrival of emigrants in New York.

The town of Augsburg is old; it has a population of thirty thousand, and is quite a manufacturing place. Some fine bronze antique fountains, the Rathhaus, or town hall, the cannon foundry, and a fine collection of richly ornamented brass pieces, are the principal objects to be seen. The old hotel, which is well kept, dates under the sign of the Three Moors for five hundred years. The landlord brags of his old wines, and takes pleasure in showing his cellars. The old register book is a curiosity, with the names of Napoleon, Wellington, Sir Walter Scott, and a host of others, both kings and princes. In one of the rooms Napoleon received the Augsburg magistrates, and told them with sang-froid, that their city was free no longer, and that the king of Bavaria was now their sovereign. There are other incidents related of the house, and valued by the master. This reminds me of the Hotel Fedder where I stopped in Genoa, where they now show the gilded rooms of what was once a palace, where Daniel O'Connell died. Those who wish to make the pilgrimage will find good quarters, but must not be surprised if a small tribute is added to the bill.

# XLI.

FRANKFORT, GERMANY, 1848.

From Munich I proceeded to Ulm, the frontier town of Würtemberg, on the opposite bank of the Danube from Bavaria. The Gothic cathedral there is the most curious object for a stranger, and is now a Protestant church. The body of this church is the largest in Germany, and is a second St. Peter's in size, being four hundred and sixteen feet long, one hundred and sixty-six feet wide, and one hundred and forty-four feet high, with five aisles; the terrace is unfinished, and is three hundred and thirty-seven feet high. There are some fine old stained glass windows, and some remarkable carved work in the building.

I had once tasted of snail soup in Naples, which, during the season of Lent, is considered a great delicacy, but I did not know, until I came to Ulm, that there was a snail market. They say they export millions of them yearly into Austria, and other parts of the country. They are produced in the vicinity, and put up in casks for exportation.

From Ulm I went to Stuttgart, by diligence. It is the royal residence of the king of Würtemberg, who is so celebrated for his love of horses. I saw him driving a fine pair, of the Hungarian Esterhazy breed, through the park, with apparent satisfaction. The manager of the stables of the Prince is an Englishman. The prince married a Russian princess, the daughter of the Emperor Nicholas, and had some Russian carriages and droskys with a Russian driver in costume—the first I had seen.

This Englishman accompanied me through the Crown Prince and King's stables, and showed the horses belonging to government for the improvement of stock. I counted in all two hundred and ten belonging to the king and his son, and one hundred and eighty for the account of the crown. Arabian, Russian, Hungarian, English, and Persian horses are to be found here. The stables, the harness rooms, and carriage repositories were on a grand scale; but the sovereign people will say when the time comes, "The expenses are too great; we cannot submit any longer to these extravagances."

Stuttgart is a well-built and interesting city, surrounded by hills covered with the grape, with fine palace-gardens and a park, traversed by carriage roads and promenades for some miles.

I went to Kannstadt, some four or five miles from the city, to the mineral springs, which are much frequented by the inhabitants. The railroad passes through the place, and there are agreeable walks to return, for pedestrians, along the valley of the river Neckar, and through the palace park to the city.

From Stuttgart I made my way by diligence to Carlsruhe, and here struck the railroad for Baden Baden. Carlsruhe has not much of interest for the traveller. It is the capital of the Grand Duchy of Baden, is dull, with sandy soil, but being a royal residence, has a very fine park. It is curiously built, and is described by a writer as being in the form of a fan, or rather a wheel—the main streets, like the spokes, all radiate from the Palace, which terminates the vista in every street, so that the citizens who wish to know which way the wind blows need only look to the palace weather-cock.

Everybody has heard of Baden Baden, so famous as a fashionable watering-place, and all who have visited it can speak of the beauty of its locality, surrounded by hills and mountains, and its narrow valley with its delightful shady walks; but this year they are quite deserted. The princes have enough to do to take care of their subjects; citizens remain at home to look after their interests; the blacklegs find their avocation almost gone. There is not one-third the usual number of arrivals, consequently the balls, concerts, and gaming tables are less frequented.

Baden Baden is certainly a lovely spot for the invalid, or the man of pleasure; combining the advantages of public life, or solitude in the dark woods, which can be reached in a few minutes. As I before observed, all have heard of Baden Baden, so all have heard of the Castle of Heidelberg, which is a magnificent ruin, and formerly the palace and fortress of the Elector Palatine. It is situated upon a high hill, and approached by a winding footpath on the side of the city. It was one of the strongholds of the middle ages, and is of different styles of architecture by different founders, and has been burnt at different times and rebuilt. It was last burnt by lightning, and remains a ruin, although parts are quite perfect.

One guide takes you through all the castle, and shows the relics and implements of war yet preserved, mounts the bastions and towers, from which the view is unsurpassed; another conducts you into the cellar of the castle, to see the famous Wine Tun, which is the largest in the world, and contained eight hundred hogsheads, or nearly three hundred thousand bottles, and, it is said, in former times, when filled with the fruit of the vintage, they danced on the platform. This tun will not compare with a vat I once saw in the immense brewing establishment of Barclay, Perkins & Co., of London, which contained four thousand hogsheads of porter.

Mannheim is only a short distance from Heidelberg, and is a city of some twenty thousand inhabitants, but possesses nothing of sufficient interest to the traveller to detain him long. The gardens behind the palaces, and terraces along the banks of the Rhine, are quite pretty. It was once a walled city, but was besieged by the French and reduced to ashes, and now has no protection, which, as experience has proved, saves a city from the horrors of a siege.

The city next on my route to Frankfort was Darmstadt, the capital of the Grand Duke. The gardens of the palace are beautifully laid out, and all through this section of country vegetation is very luxuriant. The rides through the country with the villages and towns prettily located at the foot of the mountains, overhung with clusters of grapes, and surrounded with orchards, make it very interesting for the traveller.

This free city of Frankfort, which I visited some years ago, has more the air of life and bustle, I find, than many other German cities, which may in part be attributed to the fact that there are now many strangers from all parts of Germany, as members of the Confederation, and for the reception of the new Vicar General of the German Union, the Archduke John, of Austria, who has just been received with great honors by the military, succeeded by an illumination of the whole city—a very splendid affair. The immense circular church—now converted into an Assembly for the representatives of the whole German Empire, comprising six hundred, and which with the galleries extending all around, will hold perhaps more persons than the Tabernacle in New York—was filled to overflowing on the presentation of the Prince to the Assembly. I could with difficulty procure a seat by going early, and immense numbers were obliged to withdraw for want of room. Numerous addresses were delivered, to which the Archduke responded. He was dressed in uniform, and accompanied by the whole force of the National Guard to the National Assembly. He looked calm and dignified, with a good expression of face, and is sixty-six years old. His task will be arduous, as well as that of the assembly, to amalgamate the different races and sects of the German and Austrian Empire, and will not be accomplished until more blood flows.

I assure you I was greatly rejoiced to arrive at Frankfort, which is an interesting city, and has many sights to interest a stranger. I was pleased to arrive in a city where I could so agreeably repose myself. The gardens and pleasure grounds which encircle Frankfort, occupy the place of former fortifications, and make a delightful retreat for the inhabitants during the warm weather. The principal garden among the number was beautifully illuminated the night following the reception of Prince John, and as the German bands always afford good music, all the élite were found sipping coffee and partaking of ices, and other refreshments.

This is the residence of many bankers, and here the Rothschilds were born, in the Judenstrasse or Jews' street, and when I was last here I went to see the house where the mother still resided, and refused to give up the old confined quarters for the palace of her son. The condition of the Jews has been much ameliorated here as well as in all parts of Europe.

When I first saw the Jews' quarters in Rome, under Pope Gregory XVI., they were confined within small limits, in narrow, dark, dirty lanes and streets, where the sun's rays scarcely reached them; a population of about six thousand huddled together in filth, by daylight, when the gates were open, carrying on their trade in old clothes, second-hand articles of all kinds, readymade clothing, &c. But thanks to the liberal mind of Pope Pius IX., the gates have been beaten down and the Jews may now be seen locating themselves in other parts of the city, although the mass prefer to keep together.

My health not being yet established, I have consulted a celebrated physician, of the race I have just spoken of, who advises me to drink the waters of Ems, recommended highly for all pulmonary and bronchial diseases, and I shall go via Wiesbaden and Schwalbach to the above-named place, and make trial of them.

# XLII.

### Bath of Ems, Duché de Nassau, 1848.

After leaving Frankfort I came to Wiesbaden via Mayence, by railroad, which is rapidly accomplished, but being familiar with those places my stay was short, and I took the diligence to the Baths of Schwalbach, and from thence to this place, where I bought a Bohemian stained glass goblet, an indispensable article to every water drinker, and took up my position at the fountain in the line of invalids.

Ems has been entirely quiet and tranquil, and seems to stand aloof from the Revolutions all around us. Almost every house is a lodging-house or hotel, and the people and peasantry have an interest in keeping quiet.

About one thousand strangers are here at present, the larger portion in pursuit of health, and society is more select and less gay than at the other watering places. The balls, concerts, and gaming tables are less frequented than in Baden Baden and Wiesbaden. The musical band commences at seven in the morning in the promenade, and continues playing until eight, during which time the drinkers swallow their three or four glasses at intervals of fifteen minutes, while the physicians are mingling with their patients to inquire after their health, and give counsel, if needed. One o'clock is the table d'hôte, in all the hotels, when everybody dines; after which the company adjourn and take coffee in the walks in the garden, listening to the music; or go in parties of pleasure along the banks of the beautiful river Lahn, or cross over the bridge of boats to the opposite side and branch off among the hills and cliffs, by the footwalks which extend in every direction. Droves of donkeys with their drivers are always at hand, and are all numbered, which is a good idea, as they are not all sure-footed, and when one is proved can always be engaged in advance, which is important for the ladies, as large numbers scale the hills and vine-clad heights in this manner.

From six to eight in the afternoon, when the heat is less intense, Ems is seen to best advantage. Then all the visitors appear upon the public walks, and the ladies, of whom there is a large proportion, as it is considered essentially a ladies' watering-place, are promenading in the garden, en grande toilette, or seated under the shady trees listening to the music from the band.

Almost every house has its name, and where I am living, upon the banks of the river Lahn, it is called Lust Garten, or in English, the Pleasure Garden. The high walls with a sort of terrace separate us from the river, with a beautiful garden adorned with plants and flowers, which gives the house its name; in the rear of the garden rise the cliffs to a great elevation, which are walled, and covered with the clustering grape. The town is so shut in by hills that sometimes the heat is oppressive, but in a few minutes one may escape into the woods and winding paths on the opposite side.

Notwithstanding among so many persons there are numbers in good health who accompany their friends thither, and who can enjoy life, and many whose ailings are trivial, and who need not deprive themselves of luxuries, still there are many, very many, real sufferers, who naturally put the best foot foremost, and keep up appearances; but the hollow cough and the hectic flush tell too truly of the ravages of that disease which is so flattering.

One of the vices of these watering-places is that of gambling. The new Kursaal built by the Grand Duke, has a handsome Café, gambling rooms, with hazard tables, and is open from eleven to one o'clock and from three to ten in the afternoon. A large ball-room is attached, with marble columns, sofas, and rich furniture. Although there is less gambling here than at other places, still there is too much, and it is curious that some ladies have also a great propensity for gaming. At a public festival the other evening, on the occasion of the birthday of the Grand Duke (in the Kursaal), I was in company with several ladies, and the husband of one of the number, whom I considered a decided invalid and a man of fortune, was at the gaming table. He had previously won, but fortune had turned against him; he continued to lose; his friends begged him to desist; his wife watched him with tearful interest; I saw the hectic flush upon his cheek, and the perspiration starting from his forehead; he staked the last piece of gold in his purse; suffice it to say he lost, and in an agitated state we induced him to leave the room. A few days later he left for Switzerland.

With the exception of a Russian family whom I met in Nice and Genoa, I have not found any of the Italian travellers of last winter; but one is not at a loss for acquaintances, for here are French, Germans, Russians, Hollanders, English, and a few Italians, and as I have been a sufferer myself, and was in possession of some medical works and treatises for the diseases of the chest and bronchial tubes, which were new, my physician adopted them for his patients, which brought me in contact with them.

We have excursions up along the river to Nassau, about six miles, which can be made by carriage or donkey. Among these, are rides to Kenmau, back of Ems, which can be accomplished after dinner, and where one has a very expanded view from the top of the mountain of the whole country lying below. One goes to Coblentz in about two hours by omnibus, where passengers arrive coming up the Rhine to visit Ems. This, the great bulwark of Germany, and the castle of Ehrenbreitstein, the Gibraltar of the Rhine, standing on the summit of a rock nearly eight hundred feet above the level of the river, opposite Coblentz, together with the defences on both banks of the Rhine, and the Moselle, which there falls into the former, are capable of containing a force which might resist any attack, and are considered impregnable. The road hence to Coblentz is very pretty, and the residents at the Baths frequently go down to do their shopping. In passing the turnpike gate I was amused at the manner of receiving the tolls. The turnpike keeper, instead of coming out and taking the fee, sits smoking his hanging meerschaum pipe, and with a slow movement rises with his pipe in his mouth, and in his hand a long stick with a box on the end, which he shoves forward and receives the coin, he then draws in his prize and closes the window.

The Germans are a quiet, patient, forbearing, good-natured people, but the revolution in France awoke them to a sense of their rights, and the despotism of kings and petty princes, which they are trying to shake off. At Ehrenbreitstein castle I saw them making preparations for the Schleswig Holstein war with the Danes, having just received orders from the Prussian king to send on a body of troops.

These waters are of great service in most pulmonary cases, but I find the free use of them and strict regimen in eating is calculated to weaken the stomach and appetite, and the associating with invalids and hearing their repeated complaints and sufferings, is anything but agreeable, and calculated to operate upon the spirits, as mind has a great effect over matter.

# XLIII.

Copenhagen, Denmark, 1848.

I floated down the Rhine from Coblentz to Cologne, reviewing my recollections of the localities of that beautiful river, rendered doubly interesting from its historical associations and old legends, with all its varieties of wild and picturesque scenery; towns and villages and fertile plains upon its banks; thick forests and vine-clad hills, and old chateaus, and rivers in the distance.

I remained but a single day in Cologne. The great Cathedral, which was begun in 1248, and which would have been, if completed, one of the finest Gothic monuments in Europe, with towers five hundred feet high, has been left in an unfinished state for centuries, but of late years the king of Prussia has made large appropriations towards its repairs and gradual completion. I find the work has progressed moderately, and the king of Bavaria has made a splendid present of stained glass windows, which will be exhibited publicly in a few days, when the centennial anniversary of the Cathedral takes place, and there will be a great re-union of kings, princes, and plebeians. A few years since when I was in Prussia, and travelled by private post, or the conveyances of the country, it occupied much more time in making distance, but one saw the country to better advantage; now the railroads are constructed in many parts, and the traveller is transported from one city to another with locomotive speed.

I came from Cologne to Hanover and Brunswick, and then retraced my steps in order to visit Bremen, and from thence returned, via Hanover, to take my departure for Hamburg, accomplishing the entire distance by railway with less fatigue and in less time than if I had crossed the country, which is a much shorter way; but one is exposed to night travel and the want of pure air, as the Germans have a horror of an open window, and are constantly enveloped in a cloud of smoke. On some of the German railways they have third and fourth class cars. In France and Belgium, and in fact all over Europe, the genteel traveller takes the first class car; not so in Germany, for there the second class is almost as well mounted as the first, and is part of the same car with partitions; the third class receives those who like more air, free smoking, economy, and hard seats. The Germans say that none but princes and fools take first class cars; but if one must pass a part of the night on the railroad, and wishes to be quiet with a car to himself, without society, then they are preferable. On some of the German roads no luggage is carried free; on others from thirty to fifty pounds are allowed the passenger; in some instances for five pounds overweight of the scale, which varies on the different roads, I have paid as much as an American dollar—a caution to those who make long voyages with much luggage.

Hanover, the residence of the old king Ernest, is on the river Leine, with a population of some thirty thousand inhabitants. It is a curious old town, with peculiar Gothic houses, and is remarkable for a superfluity of windows, which, if they were subject to the light tax of England, would soon ruin their owners. The Esplanade, in which stands the Waterloo Monument, a column one hundred and fifty-six feet high, with a statue of Victory, dedicated to the Hungarians who fell in that conflict, presented a gay scene, on the occasion of a Sunday parade of all the troops, prior to the reception of the king of Prussia, who was expected to halt there while on his way to the Cologne celebration.

I had a view from the top of the column of a rich, fertile, and beautiful country lying in the distance, with the turn-out of the citizens and peasantry in holiday attire, after the church service of the morning, and the evolutions of the horse, artillery, and infantry, near the base of the column, and an imposing sight it was. I had seen most of the monarchs of Europe in my journeyings, except King William, who was absent when I was at Potsdam, his residence; but here I had the opportunity of seeing his reception and all his courtiers, with all that famous troop of cream-colored and black horses, of the English breed, from the royal stables.

Brunswick, the capital of another of these German princes, who have so long tried to outvie each other in the splendor of their palaces, parks, &c., to the detriment of their subjects, is a very old city of thirty-five thousand inhabitants. The palace is a tasteful and splendid building. It is said that the old one was burnt by some of the citizens, who were obliged to replace it by a much more costly and beautiful edifice, and the Duke is now sumptuously quartered. The antiquity of the city strikes the eye of a stranger, particularly the gable-ends of the houses to the streets, steep roofs with rows of windows in them, and the immense number of windows in the fronts. The famous corps of Black Brunswickers was parading in the palace grounds—the first of this uniform I had ever seen—and looked frightful. They wore black cloth uniform, slightly relieved, and black horsehair plumes with death's-head and cross-bones; they are said to be valorous, and particularly attached to the Duke.

The railroad depot at Brunswick is very splendid; in fact, in several parts of Germany the depots are furnished in the most sumptuous style, the buildings in some places being like palaces of Gothic architecture, some with towers, and the waiting saloons of the first and second class passengers furnished with sofas and divans, covered with rich stuffs; in short, they have spent too much money for the interest of the shareholders.

On visiting Bremen, I was struck with that air of cleanliness and comfort which one finds in Holland. It is one of the free cities of Germany, lying on the river Weser, and one with which we have a growing trade. I expected to find the steamer Washington there, as her commander, Captain Johnson, came from our section of country; but she lay down the river, at Bremerhaven, and was just about departing. The city has a population of some forty-five thousand, and has fine new white houses upon the streets, which front the walks, and boulevards which extend around the city.

The quantity of tobacco imported from America is immense; it is manufactured here and sent through all Germany, and one sees the names of all our states and towns noted for "the weed" figuring in the shop windows.

The old town is quite like the other German towns, and has some curiosities. The old cathedral has a vault which contains some bodies which have been preserved from decomposition for centuries. But an exhibition of this kind at Bordeaux is most curious; for there are the remains of some twenty persons, whose history is known from the tombstones; when disinterred they were found, from the peculiarity of the soil, with the flesh only wasted. The mummies were placed around the low vault, lighted by torches; and among the number was a colossal man who killed himself by a trial of strength; another, a girl buried in a trance, and now exhibiting all the horrible forms and agonies of starvation and despair, with a portion of her own body devoured.

On my arrival at Hamburg, I found the river Elbe, upon which it stands, blockaded by the Danes, and the merchants complaining bitterly. This city is eighty miles from the mouth of the river, and is divided in many places by canals and crossed by bridges; and in the old town, the houses, bridges, and quays reminded me of Amsterdam. The city has a population of some one hundred and forty thousand, and possesses an immense amount of commerce. The great fire a few years ago has been the means of beautifying that portion of the city which was destroyed, for now the burnt district is rebuilt, and will compare for splendor with any of the continental cities. The old fortifications and ramparts around the city are now, as in many other capitals, thrown down, and covered with trees, plants, and flowers, which afford a breathing-place for the inhabitants, and a delightful promenade.

There are no remarkable collections of art, or curiosities for a stranger, in Hamburg. The promenades in the gardens, the cafés crowded with both sexes, the sight of the water parties, in their gaily painted boats, a stroll through the gardens in the evening, listening to the music, and viewing the dances and waltzes of all classes, is quite sufficient to occupy the time of a traveller. I met here, at the same hotel, an old travelling acquaintance, who left me in the West Indies some three years ago, and who had since made the campaign of Mexico. I allude to Mr. Kendall, of the *New Orleans Picayune*, who is now writing a history of the war. In walking out together, said he, "*Do you see that coffin? There goes another coffin!*" And in fact so it appeared to be. The servant girls and cooks rarely go out without being gaily dressed; at all events, a splendid shawl is arranged under the arm so as to cover a basket in the exact form of a child's coffin; and it matters not whether it is fish, butter, cheese, or dirty clothes for the wash, it must always be covered with a shawl.

Altona, a populous town and a part of the Duchy of Holstein, belongs to Denmark, and is now in dispute; it is in the immediate vicinity of Hamburg, so that the two cities have almost grown together. I there found troops collecting together from the different German states, to go forward to Schleswig and Holstein.

The distance from Hamburg to Lubeck, where I took the steamer for Copenhagen, is about forty-five miles, and is made by diligence. We were three in the coupé, or front apartment of the vehicle; and to my surprise, for the first time in Germany, my companions did not smoke either pipe or cigar.

The free town of Lubeck is a very antiquated place, with its Gothic churches, and venerable public buildings, and has not changed very much in general appearance since the days of its prosperity. Its population is not one half of what the city is capable of containing; and the lifeless streets, in many parts overgrown with grass, tell the story of deserted commerce. There is sufficient, however, of interest here to keep the traveller a day or two, to look at the old paintings and other works of art in the churches, some of which are very superior. One of the paintings upon wood, of the style of the fifteenth century, would compare with those at Florence. It was a representation of the events of the Passion of our Saviour, from the agony in the garden to the resurrection, depicted in twenty-three distinct groups introduced in the landscape, in the background of which appears Jerusalem. Another very curious painting, occupying three sides of one room, was The Dance of Death, with the Pope, the bishop, the king, the merchant, the banker, and others, all in appropriate dress, with dialogues inscribed above them; but the skeleton Death always had the advantage. It has been preserved since the fourteenth century, and is only valuable for the design, which is curious.

The passage from Lubeck, by steamer, to Copenhagen, was made in less than twenty-four hours. This residence and capital of the King of Denmark is a large commercial city, with a population of some two hundred thousand inhabitants. The Danes, being surrounded by water, have naturally become good sailors, and their greatest strength in carrying on the war consists in their fleet, with which they have captured and now have one hundred and ten German vessels in port. It is quite amusing in going from one country to another to look at the caricatures in the shop windows; in Germany, the Danes are escaping from the battle-grounds in awful plight, but here the tables are turned and the Dutchmen have got the worst of it.

The palaces and parks are not very remarkable, but there are some fine gardens and places of resort for the multitude, one of which, the Tivoli, is fitted up with much taste. Those who want amusements, in the way of theatres, jugglers, singing, miniature railroads, or a look at the zoological collections, can have their choice here. The grounds of the cemetery are very extensive and beautifully laid out, as is the case in most parts of Germany, and I have in very many cases visited them. The greatest respect is paid by friends to the ashes of the dead; it is gratifying to see mothers and sisters quietly employed in plucking the weeds from among the blooming flowers, and watering the plants growing over the graves of those they loved. They have a custom here of embanking the borders of the grave with white sand, while on the top are presented beautiful little flower gardens under the shade of the weeping willow and other trees.

This was the birthplace of the celebrated sculptor Thorwaldsen, whose studio I visited in Rome some years ago, and who has since died, leaving the bulk of his property to found a Museum for his vast collection of art. In one of the churches is seen his colossal figure of Christ, elevated on a pedestal behind the altar, with the twelve apostles ranged on both sides of the body of the church, and in an apartment of this same building rest the mortal remains of this great artist, until the museum is complete, when they will be transported thither, and rest with the wonderful works produced by the skill of his hands. It is a large building, centrally situated, with spacious halls and apartments filled with the originals in marble and plaster, or copies in marble of the great works of this man which are found in Italy and all parts of Europe, and it appears only surprising that even in living to an advanced age he could have executed so much in one lifetime.

# XLIV.

CHRISTIANIA, NORWAY, 1848.

From Copenhagen to Gottenburg, in Sweden, is about one hundred and twenty-five miles. The steamer strikes up and through the Straits of Cattegat, touching at Elsinore, the stronghold of the Danes, where there is a beautiful citadel. Helsingburg, on the opposite shore, is visible to the naked eye. The Danes yet adhere to an old custom, and demand tribute of all vessels navigating the North Sea and the Baltic, traversing the Straits, but without a shadow of justice.

Gottenburg is considerable of a commercial city, with a population of forty thousand, and carries on a large trade with England and other countries in lumber from the interior of Sweden, via the canals and lakes. They have here some large cotton mills, sugar refineries, and the largest porter brewery, for the supply of all Sweden, that I have seen on the continent, except in London, and which strangers are directed to as a curiosity. I saw here a full cargo of cotton just arrived from New Orleans, and also one hundred bales of American hops. Our treaty with Sweden is a bad one. They have all the advantages of the carrying trade, and in return they tax our products at a high rate. We are taking large quantities of iron annually from that country, and some attention should be given to our trade with Sweden by those whose business it is to attend to such matters.

The Danes and Norwegians speak one language, but the latter give more force to the words, and are not so effeminate as the former. The Swedish is another language, but it bears resemblance to that, similar to the affinity between the Spanish, Italian, and Portuguese tongues. I have met with many persons who spoke English, as might have been expected, there is so much trade with that country.

From Gottenburg, by steamer along the coast of Sweden, one enters the Gulf of Christiania, with its innumerable islands; touching at the little towns which are engaged chiefly in the lumber and fishing trade, and finally at the head of the gulf is seen the town from which I write, with a population of some thirty thousand, carrying on an extensive trade in lumber, fish, iron, &c. This whole northern country, in the interior, from which I have just returned, having made an excursion to the iron works, reminds one in many respects of the state of Maine. The ship building, pine forests, and salmon fishery, bear analogy to our northern latitude.

They have a great abundance of lobsters of the best quality. Very little fruit is found here, except green apples, and the August cherry, which is yet scarcely ripe; there are fewer flowers than in Italy in the month of May. Such is the difference of duration of heat between the climate of the sunny south, and the more rigid regions of the north. They have yet no fear of the cholera, which is still remote; but at Gottenburg we were kept in suspense for half an hour by the quarantine officers, who suspected the disease had appeared in Copenhagen, although we had a clean bill of health. The potato disease has reached this country, and I see its ravages in many places.

The light summer nights—the day scarcely obscured—the Aurora Borealis, or northern lights—the wild and romantic country of the north—these things strike an inhabitant of the south of Europe who visits this country for the first time.

The Norwegians are a fine race of men, of light, ruddy complexion, and are capable of hard service. They are much attached to their country and pine groves, yet the charm of freedom has drawn away many to our own land. This is the only part of the world that I have yet visited, where there are no Jews. Such is the horror of the race, that ancient laws, interdicting their settlement here, have not been repealed, although repeated efforts have been made. A Jew can only remain twenty-four hours in the country.

There are no curious sights here, as in other old countries; things are more premature, but there are some fine points of view, and nature puts on her gayest attire. I was gratified, however, in visiting an immense new prison in process of erection, for solitary confinement, to find a faithful copy of one in Pennsylvania. A new palace for king Oscar, who is obliged to pass a certain portion of the year here, is now completing. It is a large structure, and for Norway, does very well. The two governments of Norway and Sweden are subject to the one king, but the former has many privileges secured to her.

One peculiarity I noticed along the Norwegian roads. Every owner of land is obliged to keep his part in repair, and the line is marked by stakes with a flat board, on which the name is painted; so that if the road is impassable, the traveller knows of whom to make complaint.

The currency is all silver, with the exception of bank notes to the value of about one dollar, and the expenses of life are nearly double those of Denmark, as all the luxuries of life come from abroad. The currency of Sweden, on the contrary, is almost all government paper, and the rag currency reminds me of our shin-plaster days. A paper rix-dollar is about twenty-five cents, and they have notes as low in value as eight cents of our money; the consequence is, that in getting a piece of coin changed of the value of an American dollar, you have a pocketful of rags in exchange.

The steamers employed on these routes this season are more indifferent than usual, as there are few passengers, and the best class of boats have been hauled off for the use of the government. King Oscar is now at Malmö, on the coast, within five hours of Copenhagen by sea, and has his army all prepared for a move in case the Germans enter Denmark. For the affair of Schleswig Holstein, which is debatable ground as to the rights of the two countries, he will not interfere; but if the Germans move an inch further into Denmark, then Norway and Sweden consider the cause their own.

# XLV.

STOCKHOLM, SWEDEN, 1848.

Since I wrote you from Norway, I have, by means of private post, and public vehicles on the land route, and steamboats upon the lakes and canals, travelled entirely through Sweden; a country of which so little is known, and which is so beautiful and picturesque that I could not help being delighted. This country has been much favored by nature in the development of its internal resources, for its lakes, by the construction of immense canals and locks, which will compare for solidity and beauty with any in the world, have been connected with rivers in such a manner, that vessels of good size with their cargoes, as well as small steamboats, can traverse the entire width of the country, from Gottenberg on the west to Stockholm on the north-east coast. It is less tedious and more interesting for the traveller to vary the means of conveyance.

A few hours' ride from Wenersborg, a small town situated upon a large lake which bears its name, and where it falls into the river Gotha, are the cataracts of Trolhatta, celebrated in all the north as the Niagara of Sweden. There are several falls which are separated by islands, and the scenery is wild and savage, and reminded me of the Niagara, although it is less majestic; I think it preferable to any of the cascades of Europe.

There is a sail by steamer of fifteen hours upon lake Wener, almost the entire length, to Holt, where stages take passengers to Örebro, a fine town, which has the peculiarity of most of the country towns in Sweden, the houses being built of wood and painted red, as well as the outbuildings and fences. There one takes the steamer and passes through a chain of small lakes and canals, amid numerous and picturesque islands, varying in form, with wild and enchanting scenery, bearing some resemblance to the groups of islands in the St. Lawrence.

The approach to Stockholm through the beautiful lake Mälar, with its banks richly cultivated and covered with villas, and occasionally a village, old chateau, or palace, is certainly very beautiful; and the city itself, situated upon seven islands, is only surpassed as a commercial port by Constantinople and Naples, and I consider the locality, in point of natural beauty, the third in Europe.

I have visited the objects most worthy of notice in the city, viz. the palace of the late king Bernadotte, containing all the relics and souvenirs of that monarch, who was a French General, and governed the Swedes for many years without acquiring any knowledge of their language, and as a natural consequence the French became the court language, which accounts for many persons being found here who speak it. His son, the present king Oscar, is educated with the language of the country. One of the churches is a perfect museum, containing a vast quantity of trophies, from Turkey and other parts of Europe, made in the conquests of Charles XII., together with all the relics identified with that warrior prince—the pride of Sweden; his chapeau, with the bullet-hole therein from which he received his death, as also his uniform, is preserved in a glass case. In the vaults lie the remains of all the Swedish kings, in gold gilded sarcophagi, ending with the last, Bernadotte. There are also a dozen stuffed horses ranged on each side of the building, clad in full coat of mail, with riders covered with armor and shields most elaborately wrought; altogether it is a handsome collection, and would bear comparison with the Turin or Dresden exhibitions. The water excursions to the gardens, and villas, and beautiful points of view, interest the stranger; for my knowledge of them I am indebted to the politeness of our minister, Col. Ellsworth. A steamboat excursion of one day to the Drollingholm Palace and grounds, the favorite residence of some of the former Swedish kings, is very interesting. An excursion by water to Upsala, famous for its university and cathedral, and thence by land to the immense and wonderful Dannemora Iron Mines, returning thence via the palace and grounds of Skokloster, which occupies about three days, is not only an interesting but an instructive one, and should not be omitted by any traveller visiting Sweden.

It would be useless to attempt a description of the contents or beauties of the palaces; suffice it to say then, that I was agreeably surprised to find such collections here in the north of Europe; though when I reflected that they were filled with the fruits of the conquests and robberies of General Bragh, from different parts of Germany, it was easily accounted for.

I chartered a carriage at Upsala and posted thence to the mines of Dannemora. I found the roads good, and horses small but fast. The unusual number of gates appeared singular; each farm or plantation has its own, and I suppose one hundred would not exceed the number passed in this voyage. Either my valet or the driver was continually getting down to open gates, where children were not found running to do so, to earn a small copper coin, which I was glad to throw to them to avoid delay.

Sweden is famous for the quality of its iron, particularly for making steel, large quantities of which go to England as well as America. These immense works, with five hundred men employed in the mines, are eight hundred feet deep; the opening would cover acres, and it is frightful to look into the deep chasm. There are millions of tons upon the grounds in the vicinity ready for smelting, which are transported to the different furnaces through the country. The houses and grounds of the village belong to the company, as also the tracts of land for cultivation, and the workmen live on the spot, having their house rent free, and the privilege of purchasing grain at a low rate; they earn *fifteen cents* per day. The only wonder is how families can subsist on such pittances as the poor laborers obtain in many parts of Europe; and the question naturally arises, how can we develope the resources of our country, and pay remunerating prices for labor, in competition with the serfs of Europe, unless by a protective duty, which necessity will oblige us yet to adopt? How many millions of poor starving wretches there are in Europe who would rejoice to have their stomachs filled with the corn bread and bacon of the negroes of the south!

All the necessaries of life are abundant and cheap in Sweden, more so than in most other countries, but the cuisine is horrible. There are no table d'hôtes in the public-houses, and one is obliged to go to restaurants, which are very indifferent. One custom prevails throughout all Sweden, in restaurants, country-houses, and private houses; that is to offer the guest on a side table, what they call schnaps—a species of white brandy, with small particles of smoked salmon or ham, to prepare the appetite. The interior of a Swedish log cabin, in its rustic style, is a curiosity. From the ceiling, by means of network or wood frames, are suspended monthly supplies of black flat rye bread or cakes, with a hole in the centre; the whole battery of kitchen utensils is hung up on one side of a huge fireplace, and as the country abounds in timber the inhabitants need not freeze; the beds are a sort of boxes, hardly wide enough to turn round in, and the pillow is a sort of wedge, in the form of a letter V; in place of coverlids they give you a light feather bed, or one of eider down, which almost suffocates you; yet you dare not throw it off for fear of taking cold.

In the vicinity of the old and ruined town of Upsala, are seen some high mounds, which tradition says were the tombs of the heathen kings of Sweden. They are lofty and curious, and bear resemblance to some I have seen in the western part of our country, so I was induced to visit them. The present king, Oscar, ordered an excavation through the centre of the largest, and walled and piled up the passage as the work progressed, and sure enough, about the centre was found a deposit of human bones, which are preserved and seen through a grate, after passing the line of the passage by torchlight.

The communication by steamer to St. Petersburg is broken up by the cholera, and the want of passengers, as imperial orders by the Emperor to all Russian ministers forbid a passport to other than Russian subjects. If I get into the Czar's dominions it will be with courier passport, as bearer of despatches, and by a circuitous route, via Finland.

Northern Russia with Poland inclusive, being the only parts of Europe I have not visited, and being now in the extreme north, I should much regret not being able to visit those countries, which occupy so deeply the minds of all philanthropists, and which exercise such a powerful influence over the politics of Europe.

I am prepared to make some sacrifices and incur some risks, in order to finish entirely the continental tour, and if I succeed will write you from St. Petersburg.

# XLVI.

ST. PETERSBURG, RUSSIA, 1848.

I wrote you last from the beautiful city of Stockholm, and stated that I intended visiting Russia if a passport could be procured; as in consequence of the revolutions in Europe, the Czar had given peremptory orders to all the Russian ministers not to grant a visé to any but Russian subjects. From this cause, and the prevalence of the cholera, and strict quarantine, no steamers were plying between the two countries.

The only means of entering Russia, therefore, was by taking a small steamer for Finland, then posting one hundred and fifty miles to Helsingfors, where a steamer would be found for Revel, in Livonia, and thence to Cronstadt and St. Petersburg. Through the politeness of our minister at Stockholm, Col. H. W. Elsworth, I was made bearer of despatches to St. Petersburg, but without charge to Uncle Sam, and took my departure on board of a small steamer, with four Finland passengers, who were Russian subjects, in a small cabin with two berths, and two settees. It reminded me in some respects of my expedition up the Nile, from the fact that we were obliged to lay in a stock of provisions ourselves, there being no restaurant on board. My friends dissuaded me from going, and I anticipated but little pleasure; but fortunately the weather was beautiful, and with a little German, mixed with Swedish, and one of our number who spoke French, we understood each other perfectly. In less than two days we had descended the river, traversed the straits, and coasted along through the thousand picturesque islands of Finland to Abo, a pleasant seaport of fifteen to twenty thousand inhabitants. I then took private conveyance and post horses, which went like the wind, on full gallop to Helsingfors, a considerable seaport, celebrated for its sea-baths, and much resorted to by the Russians. I found here a steamer for Livonia, and thence to this city.

This was an agreeable trip through Finland. The rude and primitive habits of the people; the wild, half-cultivated country; the common country inns, with the floors sprinkled with small branches and leaves of the pine tree, which imparted an odor throughout the house; the spittoons, instead of sand, filled with wild flowers—how novel everything was! In the month of June, the traveller can write up his journal at night without candles, as the sun sets at eleven P.M. and rises at two A.M. This is the bright side of the picture; but in the winter, when imbedded in snow and ice, you can judge for yourselves of the amount of pleasure. When spring once breaks, vegetation comes forth rapidly, and from sixty to ninety days the crops are ready for the sickle.

St. Petersburg is considered the most brilliant capital in Europe, although it is situated upon the banks of the Neva, in a low and unhealthy location, and almost on a level with the river; the vast resources of Russia, however, have contributed to fill the marshes and build up the imperial city in all its grandeur, through the genius of the best artists from all countries, and here may be found a little of all which is produced in other parts of Europe. In approaching the city one is struck with the grandeur of the domes and spires of the churches, glittering with gold in the distance, and after entering it, with the magnificence of its monuments and public edifices. There is a good deal of style in the equipages, and the Russian horses are superior. It is less gay now than usual, in consequence of the cholera having made such ravages. The city is intersected by several large canals, in which the water is nearly stagnant, and emits in hot weather unhealthy effluvia. The people often drink the foul water of the canals in preference to incurring the expense of getting it from the river.

In the month of June, the people have a religious fast of three weeks' duration, when they subsist on vegetables and fruits, abstaining from flesh and other nourishing food; which, with an unusual season for changes from heat to cold, augmented the cholera, which reached one thousand cases per day, five hundred of which were deaths. It has almost entirely subsided, or at least is not alarming; and out of the fifty thousand who fled the city at its approach, great numbers are returning from the interior.

We have just returned from a visit to the imperial summer residence at Peterhoff, on the banks of the Neva, between this city and Cronstadt. It is called the Versailles of Russia, and is truly magnificent for its gardens, fountains, statuary, grottoes, and palaces; but will not bear comparison with the beauties of the much renowned Versailles, in France.

When in Pisa, last winter, I made the acquaintance of a Russian family, who invited me strongly to visit them; and on my arrival I found they had preceded me only a few days, and received me with the greatest kindness. The gentleman being the colonel of the empress's body-guard, and the annual fête of the regiment about taking place, I had an opportunity of assisting at the review of the regiment, which was one thousand strong, and one of the best dressed and best disciplined in the world; the platoons are of uniform height, and move as one man, and in line appear like living statues. The ceremonies of high mass were performed in the open air in front of one of the summer palaces, a few miles from the city, with all the pomp and form of the rites of the Greek church; the immense Asiatic gilded silk tent spread to protect from the sun's rays of a beautiful day; the gorgeous services and robes of the priests, with long floating beards, and hair covering the shoulders; the burning of immense wax candles, and the fumes of incense; the whole imperial family en grande toilette; the review of the regiment, after mass, by the Emperor Nicholas and his sons, the grand dukes, on horseback—altogether it was one of the most imposing sights you could behold. After the review by the emperor, the empress and the beautiful new bride of the Grand Duke Constantine reviewed the troops from their magnificent carriage, drawn by four horses, with outriders in jockey style, passing over the beautiful lawn amid the spontaneous "vivas" of the whole regiment, who adore the empress, and are under her particular patronage. The officers of the regiment dined with the royal family in the palace, after which the soldiers partook of a sumptuous dinner, under a long line of tents near the barracks, which were visited by the empress and the new bride, who were saluted by a thousand voices.

The colonel of the regiment and his son conducted me through the tents of the soldiers, and when the word for action was given, it was amusing to see the dismemberment of the carcasses of entire roasted sheep, with gilded horns, whose heads were severed with as much facility as a Cossack would have shown in taking off the head of an enemy. By this same military influence I have had access to the winter palace and private apartments of the empress, which are rich beyond description, and the treasures of the palace in sceptres, crowns, imperial robes, with the decorations in diamonds, emeralds, rubies, pearls, &c., to the value of many millions, all of which was at this time inaccessible to a stranger. I have seen almost all the monarchs of Europe, and I must say that the Emperor Nicholas is the finest looking personage among them all.

Being about six feet in height, with fine complexion and more of the German than Russian caste, well proportioned, with a commanding yet dignified and graceful air, when he appears in full uniform on horseback, one says directly, "There goes the Emperor." He is represented as being one of the most bold and daring of men, with the most indefatigable perseverance and zeal, and his works prove it. With his arbitrary rule of sixty millions of subjects, the largest portion of them uneducated, his task is a difficult one, and extorts praises from his friends, and curses from his enemies.

In matters of politics my lips are sealed, as spies are found in every direction, even among the domestics in hotels and private houses. The passing of the custom-house is most difficult; officers often engage you in conversation hoping to draw out your political views, but I must say that travelling in an official capacity, entitled to courtesy in all countries, my passport excluded me from visitation of luggage, and gave despatch, and the officers were exceedingly polite.

Within a fortress on the left bank of the Neva is a cathedral, rich in relics, which contains the tombs of all the emperors since Peter the Great; and in a cabinet in the Museum may be found all the relics which belonged to that great genius of the age in which he lived. In the suburbs of the city is a small wooden or log house where he resided, and which is now inclosed within another building to protect it from the ravage of time; there is also a boat there, made by his own hands. These to me were pleasing reminiscences.

Russia is extremely rich in mines of gold, copper, and precious stones. Her annual resources from Siberia, where the convicts are sent, are enormous, enough so to support her immense army, which is estimated at over one million men. In the galleries and vaults of the miners' corps, is the finest collection of minerals, metals, precious stones, and marbles, I have yet seen in Europe. Here are found also all the models of industry, from the most simple machine to the entire apparatus for the working of the Siberian mines. The vaults under the building, which are most ingeniously constructed, and into which one descends by torches, are a fac simile of the arches and avenues in the gold, silver, and copper mines of Siberia, with the walls stained in different colors, and particles of ore representing all the different strata, so naturally indeed that one cannot but believe that he is really traversing the mines.

The Arsenal for the manufacture of cannon, and the immense collection of arms and trophies from the early ages, are well worth a visit, though they did not strike me as being remarkable.

St. Petersburg being a European city, one gets but an imperfect idea of the character of Russia, without going into the interior. Moscow is represented as being one of the most attractive cities of Europe, and of quite another style, being oriental in its character.

I shall visit that renowned city, and from thence cross the interior of Russia into Poland, striking the river Vistula at Warsaw. Through the influence of friends I have succeeded in getting a Russian and German passport from Count Nesselrode, purporting to be bearer of despatches, which gives me command of horses at all the stations in preference to others. Agreeably to an imperial order the peasants are obliged to have at all times a certain number of horses reserved for couriers or bearers of despatches. You will hear from me again at Moscow.

# XLVII.

MOSCOW, RUSSIA, 1848.

I came to this city by extra post from St. Petersburg over the imperial macadamised road, which terminates here, a distance of about four hundred and sixty American miles, in forty-eight hours, including stoppages. Our change of horses ordinarily required only three minutes, and in consequence of some little delay on the road, the last ten miles to the gate of the city were made in forty minutes by three horses abreast, the lead with postillion on, coachman and conductor in front, and four inside passengers, the horses on the full gallop. I have never travelled faster in any country, by mail coach, than in Russia.

I wrote you from St. Petersburg, with some details of that brilliant capital, which is, however, modern and European; but whoever has visited it and not gone into the interior, has seen but little of Russia. There are several important towns and cities on the route between Petersburg and this city, Novogorod being one of the principal. The villages of the peasants, which are composed of log cabins mostly, and which, with the immense estates, belong to the nobles, are frequently seen. The serfs, usually clad in a long frock or surtout, made from sheepskin with the woolly side reversed, rough coarse boots or sandals, made from the bark of trees, an old small-brimmed conical hat, with long beard and mustache, and an ugly strap or girdle around the waist, present a rather uncouth appearance. They are conveyed with the land, yet sometimes separately, and are worth about three hundred silver rubles, or two hundred dollars each. The females are much less valuable, and can be bought for one quarter the sum. The usual custom is for them to employ one half their labor for the master, who must be noble, and the balance on their own account. The emperor is disposed to ameliorate their condition, and in time will effect it, but the power and influence of the nobles are so great he cannot directly. There are nobles in St. Petersburg and Moscow, who possess immense landed estates, with from eighty to one hundred and fifty thousand male peasants, and females in proportion, and you can well imagine the princely edifices and equipages these persons can maintain.

I was enchanted with the entrance to this magnificent city at mid-day. The plain where once encamped the defeated Army of Napoleon, in consequence of the Russians burning their own homes and palaces, was in part occupied by a grand review of a portion of the Russian army, the most powerful as a concentrated force, and the best disciplined troops in the world. In the distance, as far as the eye can reach, from some points, can be seen hundreds of temples, churches, towers, of all kinds of architecture, with domes and minarets gilded with gold, the buildings generally painted white or cream color, and the roofs of plated iron, painted green or brown, and presenting a remarkable appearance. I have never yet seen any city in Europe which bears any general resemblance to it, except Constantinople, which for its locality upon the Bosphorus and its general objects, presents itself more beautifully than any other port perhaps in the world.

In this ancient city of the Czars I find reminiscences of the African cities of Grand Cairo and Alexandria. It would be idle to attempt a description of the renowned Kremlin, which incloses within its walls a town of itself, comprising the palace of the Czars, the palace of the Patriarchs, the Senate, the Arsenal, the new palace of the emperor (not yet occupied), the Tower of John the Great, which incloses thirty bells of large and small sizes, from sixty tons weight down, and from which you have a magnificent view; the Cathedrals of the Assumption and the Archangel, which are extremely rich, and dazzle the eyes with gold and silver plating and ornaments. The Czars are crowned here, and here rest the ashes of the emperors prior to Peter the Great, since which time they are interred within the church of the Fortress, at St. Petersburg.

In one of the palaces are five immense saloons, which are entirely occupied for the treasures of the country, and contain riches beyond description. Here are seen the crowns of all the kingdoms that have become subservient to Russia, as well as all the sceptres, crowns, and regalia of the emperors, not including that of Nicholas, which is in the winter palace at St. Petersburg. To give a faint idea of the value of this collection of gold and silver, ornaments, horse armor, &c., I will mention one object which struck my attention particularly for its beauty—a saddle, presented by the Sultan to the Empress Catharine; the pommel is of gold and set with diamonds, rubies, pearls and emeralds, the bridle and straps are dazzling with brilliants; it is said to have cost two hundred thousand rubles or one hundred and fifty thousand dollars. The crown of Peter the Great is said to contain eight hundred and forty-seven diamonds. This collection struck me as being richer than any I had seen, richer even than that of the Sultan or of the crown jewels of England.

The great bell of Moscow, of which so much has been said, and which after its fall remained buried in the earth, is placed upon a circular wall, corresponding to its size, near the tower. Its weight is said to be two hundred tons, and in its composition is a large proportion of gold and silver, contributed by the inhabitants. It is twenty feet high, and twenty-two feet in diameter. A piece of about six feet was broken from it by its fall.

Yesterday I went to Sparrow Hill, some five miles from the Kremlin, to see the convicts examined by the physician before their departure for Siberia. After being presented to the General of Police, the Royal Counsellor, and other officers present, Doctor Haas, who is very kind to the prisoners, and quite unwilling they should leave on a pilgrimage of four thousand and five hundred miles without being in health, or supplied with all that the government furnishes, drew them up in line to the number of about one hundred, men, women, and some children, and asked three questions, to which they answered in Russian. Are you in good health? Are you in want of anything? Are you satisfied to depart? To all of which they gave satisfactory answers, with few exceptions, which were inquired into. The largest proportion were going to the colonies for life; the worst subjects were branded on the forehead and both cheeks, and condemned to the Siberian mines. To-day I saw them take their departure on the Siberian road; prior to which they were conducted by the soldiery to the suburbs of the city, where, in a building adapted for the purpose of confinement, they received from their friends and the charitable of both sexes, supplies of food, clothing, and considerable sums of money. Those who can read are supplied with books by benevolent societies. They were drawn up in line, having a light leather strap from the shoulders to support the chains on their ankles, and received the gifts of the benevolent as they passed them for the last time. I could not help but feel for the poor wretches, guilty as they may be, and followed in the train giving each a small piece of money; they perceived I was a stranger, and some of them, learning from my valet that I was an American, gave a hearty shout.

The weather is still mild and agreeable, much more so than at St. Petersburg, lying several degrees further south and east. It is now the 17th of September by Russian time, but with us the 29th, there being twelve days difference in style. Here the macadamised roads terminate, and those who wish to travel south and east must in most cases have private conveyances and post horses, which are to be found everywhere, but the living is horrible. In the country inns, which are detestable, scarcely anything eatable is to be found; white bread is a luxury. The peasants subsist mostly on black rye-bread and water. The article of tea, which is a favorite beverage of the Russians, may almost always be found, and of the best quality of Caravan, which comes across the country. It is amusing to go into the new park, a favorite drive and promenade in the suburbs of the city, and see a hundred tables belonging to as many girls or women, who furnish the boiling water from as many kettles, to those who come provided with the aromatic plant.

The cholera, which has been frightful the past summer, is now almost entirely subdued, and is wending its way westward. Notwithstanding that the streets are broad, and an infinity of gardens and promenades is scattered and extended on both sides of the Moscow river, with a circumference of twenty-five American miles, still the disease has been awful. With a population of three hundred and fifty thousand, there have been as many as twelve or fifteen hundred cases, and six hundred interments per day. On visiting the city hospital, a fine large structure, admirably adapted to ventilation and comfort, and well deserving a visit from a stranger, I saw only a few cases of the disease remaining.

The great Railroad in process of construction, has met with unforeseen difficulties in the grading, and as the contractors, in order to make the most of it, will procrastinate the work, it will not be completed in all probability short of five years. Our enterprising countrymen, Messrs. Eastwick and Harrison, whose establishment I visited, about six miles from St. Petersburg, and who have employed sixteen hundred men in their foundries and wood-work shops belonging to the government, had a contract for one hundred and sixty-two locomotives, and twenty-five hundred passenger and freight cars, and the emperor gave them four years for their completion. At the expiration of the second year the work was completed and the emperor was informed of the fact, which he could not credit; the answer was, "Will your majesty please visit the establishment?" which he did, and expressed himself in warm terms of satisfaction. Those gentlemen are now engaged in throwing an Iron Bridge across the Neva.

The Russian religion is Greek. It does not acknowledge the supremacy of the Pope, the emperor being at the head of the Church. There is more form visible than among the Latins, and more repetitions of the sign of the cross, and they prostrate themselves in the churches frequently. This is the birthday of one of the Russian saints, consequently one of their festivals, of which they have a great number in the course of the year. Last evening I attended the imposing service of the nuns in the dazzling chapel of the convent of Strachnoy, preceding the anniversary of the patron saint of to-day. The bleeding form of Christ, suspended on the cross, surrounded by burning lights, the reflection of a thousand candles on the gilded images, and the burning of incense, carried my mind back to the ceremonies of the Greek church at Jerusalem, during the Holy Week.

Leaving the interior of the Kremlin by the Gate of our Saviour, where all who pass, by an ancient custom, uncover the head, one passes on the opposite side of the square into the bazaars, which are worth a visit, and where, it is said, there are ten thousand shops, of every branch of industry.

I found here a well-ordered hotel, kept by an Englishman, where I am quite at home, although the only traveller in the house. The landlady tells me I am the only American who has visited them this year, in consequence of the cholera and the revolutions in Europe, with the difficulty of procuring passports.

In Russia, all strangers are obliged to publish for ten days in the public journals, their intention to leave the country; which publication, with the permission of sojourn, is quite a tax. I have, however, escaped all that, and shall depart soon for Warsaw.

# XLVIII.

Cracow, Poland, 1848.

Since I last wrote you at Moscow, I have travelled over one thousand miles in Russia and Poland, by mail coach, private post, and lastly by railroad from Warsaw to this place, having had but one upset, without injury, and the breaking of an axle on another occasion, which obliged me to take the common wagon of the country. These wagons are made almost entirely of wood, with little iron, on low wheels, and very light. There not being any seats, the only resource was to fill the wagon with hay, to avoid the jolting. With a pair of good horses, and sometimes four, on the full jump, and a rough peasant driver, one gets over the road rapidly.

I have passed over large tracts of country entirely level, there being no great elevations in central or western Russia—a vast deal of uncultivated and thin soil—long distances made without signs of habitation or life, and presenting a desert appearance—most parts of the country thinly wooded; and it was gladdening to the eye to strike a town or village, to obtain supplies, but particularly gratifying to arrive in Poland, an old and better cultivated country, with more evidence of civilization, and means to support life. The weather has favored me much, being mild and dry, and the roads in good order.

On my arrival at Warsaw, on the banks of the Vistula, a city with a population of one hundred and fifty thousand, I was struck with its dull and sombre appearance, under the iron hand of despotic rule—liberty of thought and speech being suppressed. Here I found the Russian troops were marching out of the city, to take up winter quarters, after a general review. They were composed of thirty-one battalions of infantry, forty-six squadrons and eight divisions of cavalry, twenty batteries of artillery—in all thirty-four thousand men, ten thousand horses, and two hundred and twelve pieces of cannon. It was a brilliant sight to see them on the move. The Russian government is exceedingly jealous of its rights, and determined to maintain its authority. There are three hundred thousand soldiers ready to march to the frontier at a moment's warning.

A signal telegraph is established from Warsaw to St. Petersburg, but the people here know nothing of the events in Europe. A Warsaw newspaper is a curiosity; it is about six inches square—a double sheet.

On passing the frontier, and coming to Cracow, I was questioned particularly why I was going out of my route on my way to Berlin, as my courier pass expressed; to which I replied I was ahead of time, and wished to see Cracow in passing. The conversation of the officer was of a nature to draw out my views, but I was on my guard. After which, as I was obliged to pass the night there, he was extremely polite, and told me the difficulty he had to obey orders in the visitation of luggage and examination of papers; he was even obliged to take off newspapers as envelopes from packages, to prevent the introduction of news from the adjacent countries.

Europe is in a dreadful state, and as yet there are little signs of conciliation or harmony. Germany with all its great and small kingdoms, with over thirty princes, with its different races, religions, and languages, is as difficult to amalgamate as vinegar, oil, and water, and no man can predict the result.

The horrible massacre at Vienna, the revolution in Hungary, the hanging of ministers, &c., have reached us, and you will see the accounts in the papers. I have been, since February last, either among revolutions, ahead of them, or after them, and have seen the effects produced, so that I have become accustomed to them; but I hope soon to be out of the way of European commotions, and as I have seen all the sights of the Continent with very few exceptions, I shall take my departure for one of the Ocean Isles where may be found some tranquillity, and a better climate for the ensuing winter.

In approaching Cracow, which was formerly a free state or republic, enjoying commercial trade, with a population of forty thousand, it presents a beautiful view with its churches and spires, but on entering it is found lifeless, with but little trade, and a miserable population. It was usurped by Austria in the spring of 1846, after the horrible massacre of the nobles by their own peasants, in Gallicia, through Austrian intrigue, of which you are undoubtedly familiar. The city is antique, and is remarkable for being the former residence of the Polish kings, whose tombs are found in the old cathedral, which was built in the fifteenth century, and which is adjoining the palace, and situated upon a commanding eminence. The cathedral is perhaps richer in treasures and costly gifts, dedicated by nobles, kings, and other devotees, than any north of Italy. In the crypt under the pave of the cathedral into which one descends by torches, are found the massive copper coffins, gilded with gold, of all the Polish kings. Here is also the sarcophagus of the great general, John Sobiesky, with his crown, sceptre, and sword; the remains of Joseph Poniatowski, who fell at Leipsig, and I well recollect the spot where he was lost, and where a monument is erected; likewise the remains of Kosciusko, who is so well known in our own country. They were brought here in 1817. About three miles from the city I ascended a mound of earth one hundred and fifty feet in height, which was raised to his memory by all classes of Poles, who wrought four years in completing it, and even brought portions of earth from the different battle-fields in which he was engaged.

Here is found an immense number of Jews who fled from Spanish persecution in the middle ages, and were granted an asylum by Casimir the

Great. They have a fine opportunity here to traffic in exchanges, as all the coins of Russia, Austria, Prussia, and Poland are known, and here the traveller must make his exchanges. Men and women with bags in their hands present themselves on the arrival of a stranger, and it was my luck to fall into their hands, having Russian funds to exchange, and it required some skill to accomplish it without being fleeced, as I was surrounded by about twenty of them, and they hung together like a chain.

I was interested in passing through a portion of Gallicia to the great Salt mines of Cracow. The country about here is beautiful and picturesque. The town of Wieliczka contains a population of five thousand, and is mostly undermined by the salt works. I met with an exiled Pole in Cracow, who had recently returned from Paris, whom I invited to join me, as he had never seen the mines, and who acted as interpreter in the Polish language. We put on white frocks over our clothes, and hired a number of boys to carry lamps and a supply of torches to illuminate the subterranean vaults. We placed ourselves with the guides in a sort of swing attached by cords to the main rope, and descended to the first stage about two hundred feet. There are four stories to the depth of about thirteen hundred feet. We then by the aid of our lamps walked through the wide and airy galleries into several halls and chambers, then crossed over bridges spanning salt lakes and dived deeper down from one story to another by staircases. It is the most extraordinary work in the world. Here are found one thousand hands constantly employed by the Austrian Government. The mines have been worked since the ninth century; and although one walks for miles through these caverns, which undermine a whole city, passing through galleries one thousand feet in length, and saloons one hundred feet in height, still the supply is inexhaustible. There are immense saloons with candelabra in glittering crystal salt; there is a Gothic church ornamented with the full length figure of Christ upon the cross. Also the statues of saints as large as life; and once a year in the presence of all the miners mass is performed. One of the saloons was in the form of a theatre, and was fitted up for the emperor of Russia when he visited the mines and held a ball there. The illumination of these vast subterraneous caves with torches, throwing the lights upon obelisks and columns, with inscriptions dedicated to distinguished persons, produced an effect indescribable. The rock is hard, and is cut and chiselled, and even powder is employed in blasting it. It comes up in blocks of an oval form, about two and a half feet in length, by immense windlasses, driven by horse power, and is laden on wagons for the different markets to be broken up when received. It is computed that four millions of tons are taken out annually for the supply of the different governments bordering on Austria.

# 1849.
# XLIX.

ISLAND OF ST. THOMAS, WEST INDIES, 1849.

It was my intention on leaving Southampton, to spend a month at Madeira, and proceed to the West Indies by the next monthly steamer, but circumstances prevented it. We had a rough and boisterous passage through the Bay of Biscay, and only reached Madeira, a distance of one thousand two hundred and eighty miles, in ten days. We had about one hundred and twenty passengers, a fair proportion of whom had paid full tribute to Neptune, and for the first eight days there was little contention for seats at table; but after getting in the trade-winds and balmy air from the African coast, the summer dresses began to appear, the awning was struck, and we found ourselves uncomfortably elbowed at our meals.

We had about twenty passengers to land on the island, but to our surprise, on entering the harbor, we found the Portuguese authorities had got frightened by the cholera reports from England, and put all passengers in the Lazaretto for ten days. Having had considerable experience in quarantines in the east, and learning there were only accommodations for one half the number of passengers to be landed, and that one of our number was dying with the consumption, and believing that in the event of his sudden decease these stupid people would consider it a cholera case, and I might be imprisoned for a month, I promptly concluded to continue by the steamer to Barbadoes, the first windward West India Island. We remained in the harbor of Madeira twenty-four hours, exercising the greatest precaution on the part of the officers in the boats to prevent contact in putting supplies on board, and some most amusing scenes took place among the boatmen, who looked upon us all as infected with the disease. One poor fellow had brought out some canary birds in cages for sale, which were handed carefully to a sailor on the foot-ladder, and the purchaser threw the sum demanded in the boat. With the rolling of his boat the sailor caught his hand to frighten him, the passengers gave a shout, and the poor fellow dropped as if seized by an apoplectic fit; his face was of a ghastly hue, and it was some moments before he regained his self-possession. He had exposed himself to a quarantine of ten days.

The town of Funchal had a novel appearance, with its white houses and flat roofs, its steeples, and turrets, and the mountains rising in the distance. The climate was beautiful. We had thrown aside our cloaks and overcoats, and were enjoying the genial breeze, and requiring protection from the sun's rays. Ripe figs, oranges, and other fruits were brought off to us in baskets.

From Madeira to Barbadoes is about two thousand five hundred miles, which we made in thirteen days. It is the most easterly of the Caribbee Islands, and lies in twelve degrees north latitude. Notwithstanding the trade-winds blowing constantly in our favor, the heat and confinement on board of a crowded steamer, under the tropics, were quite sufficient to cause all to rejoice in making this low island, which is seen about thirty miles off, and is about the size of the Isle of Wight; say twenty-five miles in length, and fifteen in breadth. It is richly cultivated, and one of the most populous islands for its size. There are some high lands called Scotland, resorted to by invalids, and from its being the first island that has the trade-winds, it is considered the coolest. We landed at Bridgetown, the capital, upon Carlisle Bay; it is a considerable town, stretched along the shore for two miles, with some twenty thousand inhabitants.

The yellow fever was committing great ravages among the British troops and residents. I stopped but a short time and then took the steamer, to make the tour of the other islands landing and receiving passengers and mails at the English islands of St. Lucia, St. Kitts, Montserrat, Dominica, Tortuga, Antigua, as also the French islands of Martinique and Guadaloupe, affording an opportunity of sailing along all those beautiful and picturesque shores on board of a large and commodious steamer, with but few passengers and mostly islanders, who could point out all the striking peculiarities of each island, town, mountain, and volcano, as they presented themselves. At one glance in passing near the shore, with the aid of a glass, you have in a beautiful slope or valley, the house of the sugar planter nearly lost in the foliage of gardens of bananas and cane fields, with the slender stems of thousands of cocoa-nut trees forming a green fence upon the sea-shore. Then again you have immense rocks or mountains which rise up from the sea, covered with evergreen foliage, their summits hung with white clouds; standing as pillars at the entrance of some deep bay or circuitous cave, formerly the secure abode of pirates. At Martinique they told us that they had had several slight shocks of earthquakes, and when one considers the sufferings from them as well as hurricanes, it is not surprising the people should be excited. The country around St. Pierre is quite pretty, with its cane fields and palm trees, intersected with winding roads and dotted with white houses. The town is regular and cleanly, and looks more European than most of the English islands.

At St. Kitts we landed two fellow passengers from Europe, residents of the island. The town is called Basseterre, and as a writer remarks, the valley looking from the sea, in softness, richness, and perfection of cultivation, surpassed anything he had ever seen in his life. Green velvet is an inadequate image of the verdancy of the cane fields which lie along this lovely valley, and cover the smooth acclivities of Monkey Hill. This hill is the termination of a range of great mountains which thicken in enormous masses in the centre of the island. The apex of this rude pyramid is the awful crag of Mount Misery, which shoots forward over the volcanic chasm. The height is three thousand seven hundred feet, and it is bare and black at the summit. Monkeys still exist in large numbers on this island.

I arrived at St. Thomas at last, alone, having lost all my fellow passengers from England, who were scattered to the four winds; some had preceded me by steamers direct, en route for South America, or to the Leeward Islands, others had left us from time to time in the Windward Islands. I took up my quarters at the hotel, which is one of the best in the West Indies, allow me to say for the information of those who may come this way.

This small island, belonging to the Danes, has a free port, and with its excellent and commodious harbor for shipping, has become the great depot for goods and merchandise for the supply in part of some of the other islands, and the coast of Venezuela. The population is some ten thousand, and is composed of native Creoles, French and Danes, and many German, French, and English merchants, consequently all languages are spoken. The town is prettily built on three hills, rising from the Bay, and surmounted by picturesque conical mountains. The horseback rides are very good, and in four hours one can make the tour of the island.

In consequence of the emancipation of the blacks in Santa Croix, another Danish island, after the insurrection and destruction of property in June last, the Governor gave the negroes here their liberty. The planters complain of the low price of sugar and the difficulty of getting the blacks to work, they being such an indolent race, and it requiring so little to support life in these warm latitudes. The merchants of St. Thomas have suffered much, and cannot either realize for goods sold, or extend sales, and business is paralysed in the West Indies, with all their resources and beautiful climate. The English planters complain of injustice on the part of the mother country, but if they are not satisfied with part payment for their slaves, what will the holders say in the Danish islands who have received no compensation, the mother country being too poor to pay them?

In the French islands they complain of injustice from the new Republic, which proclaimed not only the abolition of all slavery, but universal suffrage, which sent their enemies to the National Assembly at Paris, as members, to vote against their interests. The French Republic will yet do justice to her colonies, I think, but in the interim labor is considerably suspended, and the crops will be much neglected.

The island of St. Croix lies forty miles south of St. Thomas, and schooners run over frequently in six hours. Having some travelling companions who are planters on this beautiful island, I sailed for West End, a small town, and of much less importance than East End at the other extremity of the island. The rides on the island are beautiful and picturesque; the roads are excellent, being mostly level, and bordered with cocoa, palm, lime, and other tropical trees, affording much shade and delight to the eye. The immense cane fields were promising a rich reward to the planter, as the season has been favorable; but the sugar works and houses of the planters, which were formerly annually brushed up and kept in good repair, are much neglected this year, since the burning and destruction of property by the blacks in the insurrection. Some of the planters are complaining for want of help, but others say they get on tolerably, and I thought the gangs under the new system worked very well. It is the intention of the new governor to compel able-bodied persons to work, or be arrested. I had an opportunity of conversing not only with the planters themselves, but with the negroes in their cabins, and found them generally satisfied; and in reply to my questions as to the difference between slavery and freedom, some who had had good masters found themselves worse off than before, as they had medical attendance when sick; others said they preferred to be free and work when they liked.

The season of Christmas at St. Thomas was less noisy than usual, as the Governor issued orders to prevent the usual parade through the streets with masks and music. The life of the judge had been threatened by those who were aggrieved, but the citizen police were out parading the streets, and all passed off quietly.

I found some old acquaintances resident here, at whose hands I received many courtesies rendering my stay agreeable. I am now awaiting the departure of the English mail schooner to visit that part of South America of which the Republic of Venezuela forms a portion.

# L.

Caracas, Republic of Venezuela, South America,

*January 15, 1849.*

The English steamer not arriving at St. Thomas before the time appointed for the mail schooner, I found myself, as the only passenger, entire possessor of the ladies' cabin, excepting an abundant supply of cockroaches and ants, which infest vessels long navigating these seas; but one gets accustomed to these annoyances, however frightful they may appear at first. Our schooner of ninety tons, London built, had the length of hold fitted up in a ladies' and gentlemen's cabin and dining saloon. She carried four nine-pounders, with first, second, and third officers, who mount the naval cap with gold band, and altogether was a miniature ship of war.

We had a strong trade-wind with a heavy rolling sea at times, which, with the unusual pitching of such a small vessel, produced upon me more effect than crossing the Atlantic. The second officer and carpenter were quite sea-sick. We made the distance, however, of four hundred and eighty miles in the short space of sixty-two hours, and I was landed on the beach of La Guayra at eight P.M. with a heavy surf rolling in, the sailors rowing with all their strength, and it really looked frightful, as the harbor of La Guayra is an open roadstead, and much exposed.

"The chain of mountains," says Humboldt, "that separates the port from the high valley of Caracas descends almost directly into the sea, and the houses of the town are backed by a wall of steep rocks, with but a few hundred yards between the wall and the ocean." There are two principal streets which run parallel along between the wall and the sea. The population is about eight thousand. It was destroyed by an earthquake in 1819, and the ruins are still existing in many parts of the town, inclosed by front walls where lots are not occupied. There is no vegetation in the town, and with the exception of Cape Blanco and the cocoa-nut trees of Marqueta in the distance, no view meets the eye except the sea, the horizon, and the heavens. It is one of the hottest places on the globe, the air being stifling during the day, and frequently at night, as the sea breeze is less felt. Along a deep ravine or mountain torrent outside of the town, the change of air is delightful, and here may be seen groups of females and children in the morning, bathing in the cool and invigorating waters which descend from the mountains.

This curious old city of Caracas, lying on ground sloping to the valley, surrounded on all sides by a bold and lofty mountain, with its valleys abounding in sugar and coffee plantations, was partially destroyed by the great earthquake of 1819, of which many temples and buildings in ruins still tell the sad story. It is three thousand four hundred feet above the level of the sea. There are two roads, the old and new; the first is only for mules and donkeys, and is much shorter than the other, say twelve miles in length; the new road is twenty-one miles, and is winding and circuitous. At present there are no carriages running, and the only way of getting here is on horse or mule-back.

In order to reach the place you ascend about six thousand feet, and then descend to the city. I procured a mule at the hotel at La Guayra, having sent my luggage by a mule-team in the morning, and at three P.M., to avoid the excessive heat of mid-day, I started all alone, being disappointed in a companion. My ride was lonely, but the sights were majestic, the road winding zigzag, the bold and lofty mountains towering above with the most gorgeous and luxuriant growth of tropical trees, with immense fields of cactus interspersed, thirty feet in height; the precipice below, with a depth of from five hundred to one thousand feet, was awfully grand.

Towards sunset I found that my mule was unable to carry me, and I concluded I could not get to the city that evening. I stopped at a rude cabin built of cane and mud, and inquiring for a Posada, or tavern, ascertained that there was one a league further, at which I arrived with the intention of resting until morning. I found I could get no bed, but could get a horse; I was told the road was safe, yet I felt that I was incurring risk in the distracted state of the country, and, as I had heard of the robbery of a Frenchman by three negroes, I felt uneasy; I pushed on, however, and arrived in the city at about nine o'clock at night.

This city has a population of some forty thousand, composed of the native population, with full one-half or two-thirds of the half-breeds, Indian, and black. The houses are of stone, one and two stories high, covered with tile, with grated windows and no glass, as in most Spanish countries in warm climates. There are no remarkable public monuments; in the cathedral, in one of the side altars, are the mortal remains of General Simeon Bolivar, the liberator of his country. The state house and reception rooms of the president are not unworthy of this young republic; the senate chamber and house of representatives is one of the confiscated Spanish convents, where the unfortunate massacre of several members took place last year by the military, in consequence of the threat of impeachment of the existing president, Monagas. The ex-president, General Paez, had a strong party, with means to oppose the measures of the new executive, which led to the armament of vessels of war and troops on both sides, as you have seen by the public journals, and consequently exhausted the treasury, distracted commerce, and almost ruined the country.

In a recent contest, several vessels of the Paez party have been seized; and the American steamer Scourge, brought out for them, has been taken, and will be condemned. The city has been thrown into great rejoicing on the part of the existing government, to the discomfiture of the friends of the opposite side, by news from Maracaibo that the castle has been evacuated by the insurgents, who abandoned some of their vessels and fled to New Granada. Flags were flying, drums beating, the church bells ringing, and thousands of blacks were in the streets at nine o'clock at night, crying "Viva la Republica," "Viva la Libertad," "Viva la Constitution," with maddening and deafening shouts. I joined the throng at the house of the president, and found upon the Plaza about one thousand men, of mixed colors, with the black sentinels at the door, in round white cotton jackets and pantaloons, a sort of red pointed fatigue cap, and bare-footed. I entered and found the president, who is a fine military looking man, with black moustache, surrounded by his friends, who greeted him on the suspension of hostilities. I could not help thinking how little these people, without the means of education, know of real liberty, and the value of a constitution, and the respect due to a majority of voices in the popular suffrage. The present government, which is popular with the blacks and lower orders, has been obliged to make great concessions and promises, which would bring anarchy, were they not a mild and easily governed race.

The people are naturally indolent, not having the same stimulant to activity as in the cold regions of the north. Riding in the country as I do daily, on the coffee and sugar plantations, one can see how the lower classes subsist; the wild cane which grows in abundance is used with mud and straw for the sides of a cabin, the roof covered with the leaves of the palm tree, or other material; a shirt, with a pair of drawers, is their only covering; their furniture consists of an iron pot, and a jar, to contain water. Two or three bananas a day are sufficient to support life. Children up to the age of seven cost nothing for clothing. A lovely and equitable climate the year round, with a soil which, with proper cultivation, would produce anything.

The consumption of beef is greater than in any country I have yet seen; and in all parts of the suburbs are seen slaughtering-places for the cattle from the great plains, and a curious and startling sight presents itself of fences made of bullocks' horns. Cattle in large numbers have been sold by those who feared that the government would take them for the army, or for the want of money, at two dollars per head, and delivered in the city at from three dollars to five dollars. The hides are exported, and the flesh is consumed in large quantities by all classes, particularly the lower orders; the price is as low as ten cents per six pounds. I have seen so much of it, that I have almost abandoned eating meat. There are in the country, holders of from two to three hundred thousand head of cattle on the vast plains.

I have just seen an advertisement of an exhibition at the theatre for Sunday night, called the Gran Nacimiento, or Birth of Christ, which usually takes place at this season of the year; and as curiosity led me to see the exhibition, I must describe it to you, to show the peculiar tastes of these people. There were some one thousand five hundred persons present, of all classes and colors; and among them were seen the scuttle-formed hats of the priests, and their black robes, and the white and black mantillas of the dark-eyed damsels of Caracas. The roof of the theatre over the parquette was the vault of heaven, with the mild full moon's rays, and the twinkling of the stars, almost extinguished the light of the lamps in the carved balconies and boxes, which formed the inclosure, and extended to the roofed building in the rear, for the stage and actors. The first act represented eight children dressed as angels, after which appears Mary, and three other angels descend upon a white cloud and announce the conception; the coronation then takes place by the group of angels, with solos and duets, accompanied by the orchestra; after which appears Joseph, in oriental costume, and accompanies his spouse on a pilgrimage. King Herod and others are introduced in the performance, as well as Lucifer, from the burning pit, and his contest with the archangel Michael, who destroys him; finally comes the birth of the infant at Bethlehem, the dances of the shepherds, and the adoration of the three kings. The performers were all mulattoes and blacks.

There is a club-house and reading-room here, kept by an American, which is frequented by the foreign residents as well as the natives.

Our Minister, Mr. Shields, from Alabama, is a gentleman of talent, and a worthy representative of his nation. He occupies the house and grounds of the former president, Gen. Paez, which has protected this property from spoliation. In dining with him I made the acquaintance of two of the members of the late Congress who narrowly escaped when the attack was made upon them, and were much indebted to Mr. Shields, who secreted them in his house for some weeks until the excitement had subsided.

This is an equable and delightful climate, and more agreeable to the senses than either the extremes of heat or cold; the night and morning air is to be avoided by invalids in consequence of the vapors or clouds which sometimes descend, but during the day rise by the attraction of the sun's rays.

## L.*

Danish Brig of War, Ornen,
Island of Beatti, St. Domingo, *January 25, 1849.*

I took the old mountain road from Caracas on mule back to La Guayra to await the Venezuelan mail schooner, bound to Puerto Cabello. I never passed over a more rugged road or one where it was more difficult for a mule to keep on his legs, for rain the day before had rendered the tortuous and winding way very slippery. I left before sunrise, and found the city enveloped in a white cloud or mist, but on arriving upon the summit of the mountain, where commences the descent to the ocean, the sun had risen in all his majesty, and dispelled the vapors upon the eminences, while Caracas was yet invisible, and appeared like an immense misty sea in the valley below.

The rollers or surf at LaGuayra are perhaps worse than any to be found after a storm, except on the African coast, and the roadstead affording no protection, most of the vessels had put to sea the day after my arrival, and I found myself in company at the hotel with the commander of the Danish brig of war, Ornen, or Eagle, who was separated from his vessel, as his lieutenant was obliged to put to sea to escape a lee shore. Being a particular friend of a Danish commander of my acquaintance, with whom I had travelled, and whose plantation I had visited at St. Croix, he invited me to join him. After the storm had abated, with the aid of surf-boats and men, who stripped and forced the boat forwards, we reached the ship's boat, and gained our brig, bidding adieu to the frightful white-caps which had almost entirely destroyed the breakwater of the port, and produced such a deafening noise that I could scarcely sleep at night at the hotel which was near the shore.

One day's sail brought us to Puerto Cabello, a beautiful and safe harbor, which is resorted to for repairing vessels, and for purposes of commerce, as well as safety. It is a plain Spanish town, on level ground, and has nothing remarkable to offer the traveller, except its beautiful rides in ascending the Cordillera of Mountains that runs parallel with the coast, and then winds along the banks of a beautiful small stream to the village of St. Stephen, the resort of the foreign residents in summer. Our brig had formerly visited this port when the foreigners had fears of an attack from the blacks of the country, and as the report of sixteen thirty-two-pounders, and an equipage of one hundred and two men and officers presents a formidable appearance, all passed off quietly. We were received with great hospitality on the part of the German merchants, and the commander and myself had always horses at our disposal.

I had never yet seen in any country such a luxurious growth of vegetation as presented itself along the streams in the valley of the interior. This country produces an abundance of coffee, and cacao, from which chocolate is made, and my eyes had never beheld such a variety of tropical fruits and in such profusion, as in winding along the banks of this little stream on horseback. The coffee plant; the cacao, which produces a sort of seed resembling a large bean; orange and lime trees filled with fruit; cocoa-nut trees loaded with fruit, falling in many instances without being gathered; bananas, which produce the staff of life in the absence of bread, and which, after yielding fruit, are cut down to spring up anew without culture; the beautiful and tall, broad-leafed bread-fruit trees; with the graceful palm, and an immense variety of wild trees and flowers full of beauty. It seems as if nature had been too lavish and wished to outdo herself, and that, too, to an ungrateful people who would not gather through indolence that which was forced upon them.

The new steamer Venezuela, built at Pittsburg by a New York company, for the navigation of the Oronoko river, was at LaGuayra a few days since. At Puerto Cabello I found the officers of the steamer Scourge, which was captured, and lies in the harbor. I think she was unlawfully seized under American colors, although brought out for the revolutionary party.

We sailed from Puerto Cabello to Curacoa in company with the French brig of war, Le Cygne, and arrived a little before her, taking the first and only pilot to enter that pretty harbor, with its narrow and difficult passage, which resembles somewhat, in its fortifications on each side, the entrance of Havana. We had given our salute and been responded to by sixteen guns from the fort, when our rival entered. We were soon visited by the aide-de-camp of the governor, and the officers of the Dutch transport ship and brig of war on the station, from whom we received much civility. Through the politeness of Mr. Slaugard, the governor's aide, horses were procured for the French and Danish commanders and myself to visit the curious caves of Hatto, on the north side of the island, which to me were not very interesting, as I had seen others of like formation on a more extensive scale in other countries; but what appeared to me curious was the continual dripping and formation of stalactites from this volcanic and coral rock, considerably elevated above the level of the sea, and in a country where it seldom rains.

The island is generally arid, and has a barren appearance; an insect has destroyed within a few years almost all the cocoa-nut trees. The trees generally are of a stunted growth, and where they are exposed to the trade-winds they lean or shoot their branches in an opposite direction. The guinea corn is adapted to the soil, and is produced in large quantities. Within a few years the government has introduced the growth of the cochineal, and with success; and Mr. Slaugard accompanied us to the plantations, where we had an opportunity of seeing the production of the cochineal bug upon the cactus plant. The aloes and the tamarind fruit also produce well.

The population of the island is about twenty thousand; the town itself is situated upon both sides of the harbor, which extends back and opens into a large bay for miles in depth, and in both boroughs contains some six or eight thousand inhabitants. The houses are well built, after the Dutch style, and have the external air of freshness of color, comfort, and cleanliness; but the present race sadly represents its ancestors. Nature has withheld her bountiful hand, and I could readily contrast the difference between the people here, and those I had just left. Stern necessity obliges them to be industrious, and in all parts women, men, and children are employed in making a sort of straw or cane, into hats, cigar cases, baskets, &c. The climate is delightful, perhaps the best in the West Indies or the Spanish Main for invalids. The expenses of life are very moderate, but the hotels are miserable, with no reading-rooms or sources of amusement or instruction for a permanent residence.

The language of the common people is the Curacoa, so called, and is a composition or patois of African, Dutch, and Spanish. In families of the best class, and among the officers of government, the language of the mother country is spoken; many speak English and French. At a soirée given to the officers of the ships of war in harbor by the governor, who is a finished gentleman, and much respected, I found several young ladies quite at home in the English and French languages, and also quite proficient in music, though they had never left the island.

One of the sources of revenue of Curacoa, is its salt pans, which we took occasion to visit, upon the borders of the sea. The water from the ocean is let in in sufficient quantities; the sluices are then closed, when the process of evaporation commences, and with the strong rays of the sun produces an abundant yield.

In company with Mr. Ellis, formerly minister at Caracas, who brought out the steamer Scourge for the Paez party, I went to visit the old general, who had chosen Curacoa for a residence, that being the nearest point to the Spanish Main. He was alone and somewhat disconsolate, having heard of the capture of two of his sons, who had been sent to Caracas as prisoners of war; his fleet had been mostly taken and destroyed, and the day before we had seen a portion of the Venezuelan fleet beating to windward in passing Curacoa. He is a man of middle stature, of dark complexion, not remarkable in his appearance or manner, though he has at times when animated a fiery expression of the eye, and is said to have been the best lancer of his country; he speaks only Spanish, and has never had the advantages of much education, but is a self-made man. His son, who came in during the interview, and who generally accompanies his father, speaks English and French fluently.

The slave population is small in the island of Curacoa, but the negroes seem to be well treated and contented. The commerce of the town is chiefly in the hands of the Jews; a fair proportion of the small currency is in Spanish dollars, cut in four parts, to prevent its going abroad; while the piece of five francs passes currently there and in Venezuela for a dollar, and is the basis of circulation.

I could find no vessel for Hayti from Curacoa, and Captain Irminger persuaded me to continue with him to St. Thomas, where I could get the English steamer; and finding myself comfortable on board with my every want gratified, I concluded to do so, as I had abundance of time with an ordinary passage, for the arrival of the steamer. But in this I was disappointed, as we had to contend with a violent north-easter for several days, which prevented our making an easterly course, and finding the current strong to the west, and having reached the south side of St. Domingo, we took shelter in a bay near the False Cape, and despatched a boat's crew ashore in search of wood, who reported that it could be obtained, as also fresh fish from some negro fishermen on the coast. We then ordered the gig of the brig, and with the captain and several of the officers went ashore, where we found two sail-boats and four naked Haytians, who were in want of tobacco and biscuit in exchange for fish. The idea had occurred to me that if I could get to Jacmel by private conveyance, I could cross the island to Port au Prince on horseback, and save much time in beating up against the wind and current to St. Thomas; but I had my misgivings in trusting my life in the hands of these fellows for eighty or a hundred miles along an uninhabited coast; I found also, as far as I could understand the Creole French, that they would not attempt it. We made sail yesterday, but the sea is too strong, and we have taken refuge under the lea of this Beattie Island. The ship would run back to Jacmel and land me, but positive instructions to be in Denmark without delay prevent.

We have just had some fishermen alongside, two of whom appear honest and decently clad, and quite intelligent. For a handsome reward on my safe arrival, they will convey me to Jacmel, so shall leave to-morrow as soon as the weather permits. You will hear from me, if I arrive safe at my destination.

# LI.

JACMEL, REPUBLIC OF HAYTI, *Feb. 5, 1849.*

My last communication was from on shipboard, at anchor under the lee of Beattie Island, where I had every facility for corresponding, as the generous and gentlemanly commander had given me entire possession of the cabin and library on the main deck, from which I had at will a full view of the tactics and manœuvres of a man-of-war vessel, under the most rigid discipline, and manned by the most hardy and fine looking Danish crew I had ever seen; whose health and conduct were the care and pride of the officers, who were intelligent from necessity, as the naval school of Copenhagen obliges its inmates to acquire the English, German, and French languages, in addition to a general education, so that when they are sent abroad as officers they are at home among the great powers.

According to promise the Haytian fisherman came alongside with his boat. The steward had provided my outfit for a three days' passage, and after exchanging gifts, as souvenirs, with my worthy friend Capt. Irminger, whose kindness I shall not forget, I embarked in the frail vessel, half loaded with dried fish, to make a coasting voyage of upwards of one hundred miles to this place.

Although an old traveller, I had been extremely undecided how to act; if I continued with the brig I could not arrive at St. Thomas in time for the steamer, and would lose a month's time, and my letters had preceded me. The coast of Domingo and Hayti was quite uninhabited, except by half-civilized negroes, and the exposure was considerable in making the point of False Cape with a rolling sea. I had however decided, and thought my confidence was not misplaced in my boatman. The weather was very warm, with a full moon, and ordinarily a breeze in our favor; so trusting in that Providence which has protected me through so many wanderings, I waved my hat in response to the salutations from shipboard and shot away before the breeze in order to double the cape before nightfall, in which we succeeded, not however without drenching my cloak with the spray. I never saw a boat more skilfully managed than by these fellows, who hold their lives in their hands in passing that point, where it looked as if we should be engulphed every moment. In twenty-four hours we arrived at the residence of my men, a village called Saltrou, of four hundred inhabitants, living in cane and mud houses, with thatched roofs; and I found to my surprise that we had unintentionally created a great excitement. One of the fishermen whom we had first met at False Cape had reported that he had seen a man-of war vessel, and a white man on board who wanted to be conveyed to Jacmel. I was met at the beach by some negro officers in rusty uniform, and barefooted, who escorted me before the colonel and other officers of this military despotism, whose cognomen of republic is a farce. I was then questioned from whence I came, and the object of my visit. I had my passports en regle, and had taken the precaution to have the visé of the captain of the brig, showing my intentions. The colonel, who could not read, and spoke but little French, began to abuse the boatman in the Creole tongue, for bringing a man from the direction of the Dominicans, with whom they were at war; but his secretary, an intelligent black, and one out of six who could read and write in the village, gave him to understand who I was, and I had taken an independent course in manner and expression, although the only white man or stranger in the place. He was informed, aside, as I learned subsequently, that I might have the village razed to the ground by this vessel of war, if I was ill treated. I then received from the villagers great attention, and the mother of the fisherman, who happened to be one of the élite of the town, provided the best she was capable of. I was detained one day and night, until the formalities of Haytian law were fulfilled in sending information and an escort with me to Jacmel to the authorities of the place.

As good fortune would have it, my boatmen were good and honest fellows, and became much attached to me from my conduct towards them. The colonel wished to separate me from my men, and send me by a barge coming to this place, in company with a group of all sorts of people, to which I demurred strongly, and he finally consented that my boat should convey me, but in company with the other; so I took my departure, and arrived the following day. On my arrival, I was presented to the Commandant du Port, and other authorities, who were in full uniform, and who appeared well, and showed more intelligence than I had yet found. The highest official with whom I conferred relative to crossing the island to visit the capital, Port au Prince, said that he was obliged to send a special messenger to the President, announcing my arrival on the coast from a war vessel, and that he would probably leave about the same time that I did.

The following morning I departed with my guide, on horseback, and at midday was overtaken by a black officer in full costume and well armed, who came up at a full gallop, and inquired if I was the individual he was directed to join. I concluded I was to be ordered back, but such was not the case. He had almost ruined his horse in overtaking me.

The distance across from Jacmel to Port au Prince is sixty-six miles, along deep valleys watered by ever-living streams, and only traversed by horses, mules, and donkeys, there being from eighty to ninety fording-places, produced by the windings of the little rivers. The valleys are rich and fertile in the extreme. The mountains to be crossed are very lofty, and covered with a profusion of verdure and forestry; they present one of the grandest scenes in all the West India Islands, and prove the assertion that the blacks have the jewel-island of all the Antilles; but how mortifying the reflection should be to them, that what was once such a source of riches to France, and to the islands, and what with industry might be made a paradise, is now so woefully neglected, and falling back into barbarism.

Agriculture is very much neglected from the want of a disposition to labor, as the blacks will not work for themselves or others, and their wants are trifling and readily supplied. The government is a military despotism, and exhausts the country by its levies of troops, and taxation. It has a standing force of some twenty thousand men, and is now at war with the Dominicans at the east end of the island.

Port au Prince has a population of about twenty thousand, composed of all colors, with perhaps one hundred whites. It has a fine harbor, and is a place of considerable trade, being situated in an agricultural and cultivated country.

The city is mostly composed of frame buildings, although there are many of other materials, covered with slate and shingles, but it has a dull and dusky air for the want of paint. The Government-House, which is occupied by Soulouque, with the grounds inclosed, is quite extensive, and the array of infantry, cavalry, and artillery within the grounds, looks formidable; but instead of the simplicity of a republican government, it has the appearance of the residence of a tyrant.

I arrived quite à-propos on Saturday morning—the market-day—when the inhabitants of the country come in with their products without a permit. They are permitted to do so from Friday night to Monday morning; on the other days of the week a passport must be obtained, which is quite a tax to them; and although it is arbitrary, and helps the government, it may have a good effect in keeping them from idling their time in the city, instead of being at work at home. Sunday was the gala-day, and the great review of the troops by the President, whom I saw in full uniform, attended by a numerous staff, and some of the companies, who were well dressed, and appeared quite militaire. Several of them looked well in the distance, but their rusty uniforms would not bear inspection. The blacks are fond of military display. Chapeaux, feathers, and gold lace give them great importance, and one sees generals and colonels sufficient for a British army.

I passed a day with the Consul General of France, and the English Vice-Consul, at their villas, a few miles from town. I had met the former in my travels, and now obtained much information relative to the massacre of the colored people by the blacks, last April. He had taken a noble stand in their favor, and had protected large numbers under his flag, in his own house; and having a vessel of war in the harbor, he effected, under cover of night, the embarkment of many of the most distinguished and intelligent mulattoes.

The ignorant blacks, jealous of the mixed castes, whose intelligence and wealth were far superior to their own, had resolved on a general extermination and pillage. Since then, however, a French war ship is constantly in port, and there is now a better understanding between the races. The President, who is a black, had lent himself to his own color, but soon saw the error. Monsieur Rebaud, the consul, has just returned from St. Domingo, and effected the release of one hundred and sixty Haytian prisoners, who had been incarcerated three years. This act, with the fearless exposure of his own life in April last, among the mob, for the preservation of families from massacre, and threatening the President to fire upon the town if more blood was shed, has endeared him much to the colored people of the island.

It has been said that confidence in the common people of the country is rarely misplaced, and that strangers heretofore could travel over the country by day or night without being robbed or molested; and I must add, that in most cases I have been treated with great civility.

In the mountains, at night, we met with the sable troops bivouacked around their camp fires, en route for the war declared against the Dominicans. Very little clothing is required in this climate, and scores of women and girls may be seen washing clothes by the side of the streams, with no other covering than a handkerchief; while the little naked urchins are basking like black snakes on the rocks, in the sun's rays.

I have just returned from the north side of this little continent, whose circumference, by an even line, is about one thousand miles, and am now waiting the arrival of the steamer to proceed to Jamaica. At present, the drought is excessive on the plains, and the heat of the sun almost overpowering; and I can scarcely realize that while I am writing, dressed in light summer clothing, with my unglazed shutters wide open, and the birds singing merrily in the cocoa-nut trees of the garden, that in this month (February) you, at home, are muffled in furs, and have another music in the chinkling sleigh bells. This town, Jacmel, with a population of some eight thousand, stands at the head of a fine bay (the lower town is the commercial portion), and is built along the shore, near which lies the shipping, that takes the products of the country, principally coffee and logwood. The upper town is built on the hill, and in entering the port, presents a pretty appearance; but the effect is soon lost with bad paved streets and indifferent houses. I was pleased to find a number of schools in the towns and cities.

I am gratified in having had an opportunity of seeing a South American Republic, and a Black Republic, both of which are failures, as they have resolved themselves into military despotisms, without the great fundamental principles of religion and education, which I trust we shall always preserve in the United States.

# LII.

HAVANA, *March 22, 1849.*

I started for Jamaica in the English steamer, which proved to be our old New York favorite, the Great Western. After landing at Kingston she proceeded to San Jago de Cuba, giving me nearly a week's sojourn on the island, prior to embarking for the island of Cuba.

Kingston, although quite a large town, was exceedingly dull. The colonists complain bitterly of the mother country; an immense number of estates have been thrown up, the price of labor demanded by the manumitted blacks exceeding the ability of the planter to grow sugar in competition with the slave-holding colonies. Various expedients have been tried by the English to introduce laborers from the East Indies, and have proved a failure. One large planter informed me that the apprentice system was now found to be the best. All captured slaves are apprenticed for a number of years, and not understanding the language of the country, they apply themselves readily to labor, and become attached to the estate on which they are placed, and with good treatment show no disposition to leave. Although Kingston is a quiet and uninteresting town, lying on a slope with wide and unpaved streets, and sandy soil, still many of the houses, constructed of wood or stone, two stories high, setting a little back from the street, with verandas above and below, have an air of convenience for a warm climate. I found a very good and retired hotel, full of English comforts, and kept by an English lady. The hotels generally are only tolerable.

I enjoyed a rest after my fatigues in Hayti, and then made some excursions in the interior. The capital of the island, Spanish Town, offers nothing of interest aside from the public buildings, the House of Assembly, the residence of the governor, and the military barracks for the black troops. The white regiment of English soldiers is stationed at New Castle, an elevated point in the mountains, some fifteen miles from Kingston, where they enjoy better health than they would at the latter place, and can be called upon when needed.

The House of Assembly was in session. It is composed of forty-seven members, a respectable-looking body, the largest proportion of whom are white, though there are some mulattoes and one black among them. The debate was rather interesting, as tending to reduce the burdens of the island, the taxes being enormous for their present reduced resources; but the governor, bishop, and other officials, appointed by the crown, with fat offices, being members of the Council or Upper House of twelve, bolted, I understood, and I suppose had their own way. The Court of Assize was holding its term while I was in the capital. On entering the court-room I found a crowd of blacks and mulattoes, drawn thither by the trial of a negro, who occupied the prisoner's box, for the murder of one of his race in a night fracas. I made my way through to get a view, and hear the evidence, and could not without difficulty command my gravity. The judges and lawyers were in black robes, agreeably to the English forms; the jury were half white, the balance being negroes and mulattoes. The evidence, on the part of the blacks who were present at the fight, was in such broken language, and so contradictory, that the counsel and judges were at times obliged to give vent to a suppressed laugh, and in which I heartily joined, but was soon stopped by the cry of "silence," coming loudly from the mulatto criers in regimentals.

Jamaica is a fine island, and has been one of the most productive of the group. The views in the interior are varied, and the mountain ranges present a great variety of magnificent scenery, and a great diversity of climate; but the island in general has sadly fallen off from its ancient prosperity. The distance from Kingston to Havana, seven hundred and forty miles, was made under favorable circumstances, the ship and passengers behaving well. The portion of the latter who had never seen Havana were struck with the cheerful and picturesque views in the distance, as we approached the harbor, on the left of the narrow channel or entrance of which stands the old Moro Castle, with its bastions well fortified, and on the opposite side the Punta, another strong fort, and the immense Tacon prison, with its imposing exterior.

Being already familiar with the island, nothing struck me as new except such innovations as had been made upon old Spanish customs, since my last visit; but I well recollect the impressions made upon me when I first landed upon its shores and could enjoy the surprise of some of my fellow passengers when they beheld the peculiar construction of the buildings, the narrow streets, and the volante, or carriage of the country. I repeat, a stranger is surprised and amused at seeing such things for the first time, and as these vehicles dash along the Paseo or public promenade, in long files with fleet horses, filled with ladies in full dress, with mantillas instead of bonnets, enjoying the balmy air before the setting sun, they cannot but prove attractive to him.

So much has been said and written about Havana that I shall not attempt a description. Suffice it to say, I found that the same causes which extend the suburbs of our cities have here had their effects, for since a line of omnibuses was established, the environs of Cero have been beautified for about three miles out, and there are now many delightful residences there. When passing the country-house where Santa Anna formerly resided, and where I saw him engaged in his favorite sport of cock-fighting three years ago, a crowd of thoughts came in my mind, of the immense conflicts and conquests growing out of his return to Mexico; and now I find him banished again, and living in retirement in the suburbs of Kingston, Jamaica.

The city, in fact the island in general, is enjoying its usual prosperity under the existing institution of slavery, but in a more grateful aspect than formerly, by reason of the suppression of the slave trade to a great extent. In consequence of the drought the sugar crop will be much less in quantity, but the large prices obtained for it will make good the deficiency.

The Habaneros are fond of music, and have been in raptures with the Opera Company who have now left. They have the Tacon Theatre, an immense structure, the interior of which is chastely ornamented, with boxes separated by slight railings, and open gilded trellised work in front; when filled with ladies in full dress it produces a beautiful spectacle. The Ravels are now doing all the business. The steamer for Charleston has taken the family of children called "The Viennese Dancers," who have done better at Matanzas than here.

The carnival season had ended when I arrived, but having already passed several carnivals here and in different parts of Italy, it was no great loss. The Grand Catalan Benevolent Society Masquerade Ball did not come off as usual in the theatre this year, but was held in three distinct places, on a Sunday evening, according to custom. When held at the Tacon, where I saw it once, with six thousand persons attending it attired in all possible variety of costumes and dances, while outside, the Paseo or public promenade contained many thousands more, under the mild rays of a full moon, dancing to the sounds of banjos, and other discordant music; it was really a novelty, and like all new visitors I enjoyed it, but now I gaze upon it with indifference.

A few days since I met with a travelling acquaintance who had accompanied me, when I was last on the island, to its south side, where we visited the sugar estates, and made ourselves familiar with the whole operation of grinding the cane, and boiling and granulating the extract into sugar. Afterwards we stopped at a small Spanish town at the termination of the railroad, which was exceedingly dull, except on festivals, or to those who take an interest in cock-fighting, for which the Spaniards have a great passion, congregating here in goodly numbers, from town and country, in the arena of a small theatre, twice a week, to exercise this cruel practice, in which one of the combatants must be killed to decide their heavy bets.

On Sunday morning we attended the parish church, where a large number of ladies had assembled, with their flowing white and black lace mantillas, gracefully thrown over the back of the head and shoulders, kneeling and sitting in groups upon their rugs on the stone floor of the church, apparently devout, and watching the changes of the service, while their negro servants in livery were placed beside them. A detachment of cavalry was also upon their knees, and two of the privates in the same position, with drawn swords, were placed beside the priest at the altar. During the several changes of the service the trumpeter of the troops would sound his shrill bugle, and the old walls seemed to shake. Service being done many of the ladies crossed over to the fancy shops, which were all open, to make their purchases. Soon after the country people begin to arrive on horseback, with their game chickens under their arms, and in this way, or in some other diversion, they pass the Sabbath, which to them is considered a festival or holiday.

The steamer Isabel, of the Charleston line, has just left. The evening before her departure her owner, who is from Charleston, gave an entertainment on board which passed off well. The family of the Captain General of the island, and several of the Spanish nobility, with a number of the consuls, and many English, German, and American ladies and gentlemen, to the number of a hundred, after a dance on deck to the music of the band, sat down to a magnificent supper. The steamer lay off in the harbor, and we were taken on board by a steam ferry-boat. The deck of the steamer, which was well lighted up, and a stream of rockets flying in the air, produced a fine effect from the shore.

The season of Lent will soon be over, when the functions of the Holy Week will take place; but having described to you the ceremonies at Jerusalem, and the great and gorgeous display at Rome under Pius IX., I fear I shall have but little to communicate on this occasion. I could have hardly thought while in Rome, one year since, hearing the enthusiastic multitudes singing VIVAS to PIO NONO, that he would so soon be banished from his temporal and spiritual seat.

# LIII.

HAVANA, *April 10, 1849.*

This is the last of the five holidays, during which the custom-house is closed, and commerce suspended. The Passion Week ends to-day, and I have concluded to give you some of the details, without comment, from which you can draw your own conclusions. I find that there is a great difference of opinion among the Spaniards themselves as to the utility of keeping up, in this enlightened day, the observance of customs which were practised in barbarous ages, and are divested in most cases of the imposing and magnificent ceremonies at Rome, during the Holy Week.

Commercial men dislike the prostration and interruption of trade, which continues nearly a week, and which produces great hurry and bustle in loading and discharging vessels, prior to the closing of the custom-house; but on the part of the negro population the festivals are much enjoyed. Dressed in all the finery possible, the sable damsels may be seen with white and black mantillas, and fans in their hands, forming a portion of the church attendants, sitting or kneeling upon the marble pavement, side by side with the wealthy classes, kneeling and reposing upon rugs brought by liveried servants. In the house of worship no distinction is made between bond or free, black or white; all enjoy the same religious privileges.

On Jueves Santo, or Holy Thursday, after ten o'clock in the morning, Havana, the noisy, bustling, active city, is in deep repose, and for forty-eight hours all is silent; not a vehicle is allowed to pass; the bells are muffled; the sentries and military guards have their arms reversed; the flags of all the vessels are half-mast; the altars of the churches and convents are decorated with the figures of angels and cherubim, in gold and silver tinsel robes, bearing in their hands the instruments of torture, symbolical of the crucifixion of Christ. In the Santa Catalina, which, as well as some eight or ten other churches, was illuminated with hundreds of wax candles, and visited by thousands, is the figure of Christ bearing his cross, and borne down by its crushing weight nearly to the marble pave; a little further on are two other figures, representing the flagellated and the mutilated body; the third Christ being in a sitting posture, bound and bleeding from his wound.

The hosts of ladies who scarcely ever appear in the streets unless in volantes, are obliged to make use of their tiny feet, and from the churches wend their way to the Plaza d'Armas, a beautiful promenade in front of the governor's house, where by the light of the moon they can exchange glances and salutations with friends, and listen to fine music from the military band.

On Viernes Santo, or Good Friday, an immense procession, composed of the clergy and assistants in full dress, with torches, assisted by the military with arms reversed, proceeds from the church of San Juan de Dios to the cathedral, where the dead body of Christ is deposited in a sepulchre, in which it remains until the morning of the third day, when, after the performance of mass to the multitude at ten o'clock, silence is once more broken by the pealing of the bells, the roar of cannon from the forts, and the discharges of the infantry who occupy the Plaza or square, in front of the cathedral, all of which announces the resurrection. The negro drivers, who have bedecked their mules with ribbons, drive wildly through the streets; the military shoulder arms, and the flags of the vessels are again hoisted to the tops of the masts.

The following morning the ceremony of Christ going forth to meet the Virgin took place. The almost naked figure of our Saviour, as large as life, upon a platform supported by twelve men, almost concealed from view by curtains suspended to the ground, sallies forth from the cathedral followed by the priests in robes, bearing the host under a canopy with burning incense, while the military and populace are prostrated upon their knees; after having made the tour of the Plaza, amid the showers of bouquets from the ladies in the balconies, the procession marches in the direction of one of the churches, which contains full-sized figures of the Virgin Mary and Mary Magdalene, in rich robes of gold and silver tinsel, who are brought out on platforms upon which they are attached, and supported upon the shoulders of four men each; the latter, espying Christ coming in the distance from an opposite direction, run hurriedly towards him, turn as suddenly and go in pursuit of his mother to communicate the glad tidings, while she in turn rushes rapidly forward to embrace him, when, after a salutation, they proceed together, and are placed within the altar, and mass is said, and the scene is finished.

I observed but a small attendance of whites of the upper classes, at this last described ceremony, but hosts of negroes whose curiosity it gratifies. The sensible part of the community wish it dispensed with, as, instead of being imposing and solemn, portions of it excite the laughter of the crowd.

A grand masquerade ball is announced for Sunday night, at the theatre, which will be attended by probably five or six thousand persons; this will close the ceremonies and performances of the Holy Week in Havana.

The cathedral is an antique, and plain, but noble building, with some good monuments. The most interesting, historically, is that which covers the remains of Christopher Columbus, whose ashes were transported from the cathedral of San Domingo by the Spaniards, when that island was ceded to the French in 1795. The reception of the body at Havana is said to have been august and stately. After it was landed with the greatest pomp, it was conveyed to the cathedral, when, after mass and solemn ceremonies, the mortal remains of the great navigator were placed in the wall behind a bust, in basso relievo, in marble, with the following inscription:

"O, remains and image of the great Columbus,

For a thousand ages continue preserved in this urn,

And in the remembrance of the nation."

# 1850.
## LIV.
### TRIP TO CALIFORNIA, DEC. 20, 1850.

I left New York by mail train for Philadelphia, spent a day there, and then went on to Baltimore and Washington; Congress in session; called upon some of the members: took the train for Aquia Creek, thence by rail to Fredericksburg and Richmond; visited a few friends, and started for Wilmington, North Carolina, all by rail, without any of the inconveniences of corduroy roads as in former days. The steamer took us to Charleston; rough night; second cabin filled with negroes going south, fresh from Virginia plantations; they experienced the horrors of sea-sickness. Left Charleston the first of January, by steamer Jasper, outside passage for Savannah, and Georgia Central Railroad to Macon; passed Sunday, attended divine service there, and continued by rail to Montgomery, in comfortable cars, where more than once before I had made the same journey in open wagons, drawn through the mire by six horses; where the stage could not stand erect; broke the pole at midnight; up to knees in mud, carrying rails on the shoulder to pry out the wheels, and borrowing planters' wagons; carrying lighted pine knots in hand, in the obscurity of the night; lying before a camp fire, upon a buffalo skin; and riding upon an iron-bound trunk, over the hind axle, for one hundred miles. Such, in winter, were Georgia pine-woods roads for travelling, before the railway was completed. Took steamer Daniel Pratt at Montgomery, capital of Alabama, for Mobile, receiving cotton at all the landings. Weather foggy and rainy—made it slippery work. An animated sight in a dark night (the steamer tied up to some tall tree on the river bank) is the sliding down of cotton bales from a high bluff, while camp fires are lighted on the banks, and the five or six furnace doors on the main deck are thrown open, and the red glare of light throws its lurid beams upon the gangs of negroes, singing sailor songs.

An amusing incident once occurred, coming down the river. The excessive rains had made the roads almost impassable. The boats were anxious to fill up with cotton freight, until the guards were under water, and the bales were piled half the height of the smoke stack; and wherever the eye rested, it was on cotton. This valuable freight could not be resisted; but the bales lay some distance up a little bayou. So all hands and a number of passengers started for the point. Each man mounted a bale and came floating down. I selected a large square one, and with two poles came paddling along safely; while some of my neighbors made poor selections, and round went the bales, and they got a good ducking, to the amusement of the bystanders.

Sunday, attended church in Mobile, and left with steamer J. L. Day for New Orleans. Among our passengers were Madame Le Vert, of Mobile, and Miss

Fredrika Bremer, the Swedish authoress, who, like myself, were bound for Cuba. We were laden with cotton, mules, and other freight for New Orleans. Our steamer grounded at midnight on Cat Island, and was so belated we could not arrive in time for the departure for Havana, the next day. I took the ladies under my charge, and escorted them to the St. Charles hotel, where my friends Mr. Brown (late Consul General of Turkey) and his wife, whom I had known in Constantinople, were stopping, with the Turkish Envoy, Amin Bey and suite. Our hotel took fire on Saturday morning, the 18th, and was consumed in two hours. I had just breakfasted with the party, stepped out a half hour, when it was announced that the hotel was on fire. I rushed to the scene, and ascertained that our friends' luggage was saved, made an effort to secure my own, and succeeded in saving the greatest proportion of it. The conflagration extended to the neighboring church and other buildings, and was terrific. Madame Le Vert requested me to telegraph to her husband, and take her to the railway, and she would return home. Miss Bremer, who fortunately was visiting friends, lost nothing, and went over to Havana in company with us. Here we found Jenny Lind, to whom Miss Bremer presented me. She had not seen her since a child, in Sweden. I had attended her concerts in New York. The steamer Ohio, Captain Porter, was present, bound for Chagres, and I embarked in her. The first day, at dinner at the captain's table, a lady seated at my right heard my name, and asked if I was the friend of a cousin of hers, who had stated I was on my way south. I replied that I was, and was pleased to meet with her, and should be happy if I could be of service. What was my surprise, when, on going in the ladies' saloon, I found her with her nurse and four children, the youngest sixteen months old, on her way to California; she had missed her friends, a gentleman and lady, whose boat was detained by ice in the Mississippi, and could not connect at Havana. She had paid a through passage to San Francisco, and was in great distress whether to return or proceed. I was not well myself. I had heard much of the horrors of the Isthmus; my sympathies were with the party, my reputation as an American was at stake, for courtesy towards ladies; the regard I entertained for her friend, induced me to say, "You shall proceed, and I will assume the responsibility." With travelling experience, and a knowledge of Spanish, and such assistance as gentleman passengers could render throughout, there would be no difficulty. On our arrival in the roadstead of the dirty, filthy place, with low huts on both sides of the Chagres river, the sea was rolling in heavily, and we landed with difficulty. The children were lowered in crockery crates, and, the infant in my arms, I was suspended in a chair. I procured supplies from the steamer and purchased some ashore. We were the last to leave the ship. I chartered a dugout, or canoe covered with palm-leaf top and tarpaulin; made my contract in Spanish with some Maracaibo natives to pole us up the stream as far as Gorgona, the price sixty dollars, half down, and half on arrival. I would not suffer them to stop at Gatoon, where the boatmen have their fandangos, but, as we were the last to leave, I insisted on beating the party and arriving ahead. We kept straight on and reached los dos Hermanos, and arrived that night at eleven P.M.; I went ashore and purchased sugar, and strolled through the small street of the village where they were slung up in hammocks, half naked. We waited at San Pablo until early break of day; I kept watch in a sitting posture in the stern of the boat, as I did not like the looks of the natives. We started in advance of the others; a beautiful morning after a rainy night in this hot climate; the scenery lovely; tropical vegetation, foliage of the trees, beautiful flowers, parrots and other birds of plumage of charming character. Difficult poling up the rapids; our men were liberally supplied and stimulated to action, and I was determined to beat the party, in consequence of their want of politeness in not assisting an unprotected family. I arrived at Gorgona in advance, made arrangements for four mules at fourteen dollars each, and three children to be carried on the shoulders of natives to Panama at ten dollars each; the luggage at nine cents per pound. We were all mounted and in the act of departure when the other boats came in sight, and up went the price of mules to sixteen dollars.

The paths were of the worst possible description—deep ravines worn down by the tread of animals, and at certain seasons impassable. The mule of the lady fell, and as I sprang to assist her the branch of a tree caught me by the neck and made an abrasion; while in the act of getting her up down came the Irish nurse spraining her wrist; she was unwilling to re-mount, and declared she was kilt intirely; by great persuasion I got her on again. Then the children separated in the woods from the mother, upon the backs of these half-naked dark-skins, and sadly distressed her. Passing over rugged roads, crossing ravines, deep gorges, the remains of dead animals and bones of mules lying by the way, we came to the tents or shanties of supplies; the occupants looked sepulchral from fever. Piles of empty bottles, were round, and disappointed Californians were returning. The natives did not want to go on, but I pushed them up to the work, anxious for my charge, and a little after sunset entered the gates of the old, desolate-looking city of Panama, and stopped at a filthy hotel. I was never more rejoiced; I had left the last from Chagres, and arrived the first at Panama with all the incumbrance, and the gentlemen voted me a leather medal. The ship Columbus, Capt. McGowan, was in port. I put the family under his protection, feeling satisfied then I had done my duty. The town was infested with gamblers who quarrelled. I heard pistol shots in the room adjoining mine at four A.M. and presently a negro policeman in pursuit of some one, pistol in hand, marched through my room, from a balcony and down the stairs.

The transit of passengers to and from California had already changed the appearance of the decayed city. The American signs were a distinguishable feature, and the movements of animals with freight and passengers, on the arrival of steamers, gave some tokens of life. I waited for the steamer Panama, Capt. Watkins, which was to stop at many points on the coast, en route for San Francisco, coasting along Costa Rica, San Salvador, and Nicaragua, thereby breaking the monotony of the voyage. We had a passage of seven days to Acapulco, where we obtained coals, fruits, and such supplies as were necessary. The heat in the Isthmus was oppressive. Fever cases not numerous, though we had several on board. It was a relief to get ashore for a day at this Mexican town, and ramble over the hills looking down upon its beautiful bowl-formed harbor, surrounded by high volcanic country; I strolled through the poor bazaars, and under the big tree where the natives were selling their fruits and wares; it looked neat, clean, and refreshing in comparison with Panama. A short walk here in an orange grove, with the sight of a few cocoa-nut trees, is a happy change from a crowded ship.

The next point was San Blas en route to Tepic; much annoyed with sand-flies. Stopped next at Mazatlan, a rather pleasant town, pretty well built; called upon some Spanish Senoritas, who occupied a pretty house and garden, and regaled us with fruits, accompanied with good music upon the piano. Dined tolerably well at a French restaurant, at California prices. Our next landing-place was San Diego. After passing Cape St. Lucas and the Gulf of California, the Pacific Ocean is no more entitled to its name. Cold winds and heavy sea, and we suffered from the effects; all the way up to Mazatlan you could see the upper deck covered with hammocks and mattresses; I counted fifty persons stretched upon deck, but afterwards went below; there was scarcely room for the three hundred and fifty passengers. The Panama fever disappeared. We were getting short of coals on the passage, and took in thirty tons at the price of fifty dollars per ton, fifteen hundred dollars. Were obliged to pay three hundred dollars for three thousand pounds of potatoes, at ten cents per pound. I strolled up the mountain which separates the bay from the ocean, and procured wild flowers for the ladies on shipboard. The hills, covered with low undergrowths of bushes, reminded me of the heather of Scotland, with an abundance of quail. The mountain torrents have produced extraordinary formations. We next entered the harbor of Monterey, California, as the sun rose, and for the first time descried the mountains of the Sierra Nevada covered with snow. The contrast between the deep blue water, and the green woodlands, and verdant lawns in the distance, struck us with delight in the first rays of morning sun. We reached the harbor of San Francisco in twenty days from Panama. I was struck with the forest of masts, which exceeded my expectation. Went ashore in small boats; all life, bustle, and activity; city growing rapidly beyond all estimate; stopped at the Union Hotel, a large brick substantial building, the best hotel in the city. Charges, boat ashore, each two dollars; baggage porter, two dollars; hotel bill, board, daily seven dollars; wine, five dollars per bottle; blacking boots, twenty-five cents; refreshments, fifty cents per glass; cigars, twenty-five cents; washing, five dollars per dozen. You will perceive they are gold-dust prices.

At the first breakfast a lady passenger sat beside me whose husband was unwell. I saw a gentleman eating eggs, and ordered a couple; the lady concluded she would try them also. Presently the servant came with a card, saying that eggs were extra; of course politeness induced me to write for four; on inquiring afterwards I was told the price was fifty cents each; the landlord paid six dollars per dozen to accommodate travellers, and if any of the eggs were bad it was a dead-loss. A soirée was given by the boarders, and well attended by gentlemen; the few ladies in the city were present; a band of music was engaged; a magnificent supper provided, with fruits, ices, and champagne in profusion. While the party was engaged in the waltzes I stepped aside for reflection, and asked myself, "Is it actual or magical, when I am told where this house now stands two years since were only seen tents; and that now a large city is rising up where recently were fisher-huts, and all through the magical power of gold!"

It now appears that my suspicions of the natives on the Chagres river are verified, for I have learned that a boat's company of six men, two women, and two children, who were on their way up with us, and whom we passed in the night, were murdered while asleep, and their bodies secreted in the bushes.

## LV.
### TRIPS TO BENECIA, SACRAMENTO, STOCKTON, CALEVARAS DIGGINGS, &c.

I took the steamer Wilson G. Hunt for two days and went up to Benecia, the pacific mail station, where I met my old friend Catherwood, and talked of Palestine matters. Rode out to Vallejo, the newly designed capital of California. The officers of the U.S. Barracks politely offered horses for the excursion; vast quantities of game, and immense number of cattle grazing in the neighborhood, but not a house yet erected, and doubtful if there will be. Crossed over to Martinez, and was amused at the horsemanship of the native Californian or Mexican race, who run their horses at full speed and bring them down suddenly on their haunches. Continued with next steamer to Sacramento up the river; streets muddy, from excessive rain; could not get in the country. The gambling-houses with bands of music in full blast; the miners crowding around with bags of gold, staking their all; the city building up rapidly; every variety of character to be found in this new country, good, bad, and indifferent. So much has been said by others it would be useless to enlarge. Expenses enormous; everybody employed at something. One young gentleman of New York was driving team at ten dollars per day; another, turned carpenter, was shingling a roof at the same wages; never drove a nail in his life until he came here, but necessity knows no law. A single crab costs fifty cents, equal to the price of an egg. With the tide of emigration these things will regulate themselves, and with more resources California will become one of the most productive States in the Union. Returned to San Francisco; took the steamer up San Pablo Bay, and the cut-off to Stockton, in company with a friend, the proprietor of a quartz-mine, in order to visit the gold district. Having procured a strong wagon and a pair of horses, india-rubber covers and blankets, a supply of barley for feed, off we started. The rain came down in torrents; stopped at a ranche and dried ourselves, drove to another, and passed the night in a double bed and mattress on the floor; sack wet through, clothing out to dry by a fire. Price, for horses and wagon twenty dollars per day; feed, each time twelve pounds of barley at two shillings, three dollars; meals a dollar and a half each. Next day rode to Cherokee Ranche; met a party of Americans, with arms in hand, in pursuit of Mexicans, near the Hawk's Eye Ranche, and dared not stop, as they threatened the extermination of the Greasers, as they called the Mexicans. Passed a disagreeable night in a log-cabin. A vagabond of a fellow has just killed a Mexican in the woods near the cabin; the half-drunken scoundrel could not be turned out, and sat before a huge fire; the chimney of logs was carried up outside the rude hut. We lay in bunks upon our blankets and straw. I slept with one eye open, and my six-shooter in hand; finally at a late hour, in came a German in a red shirt and slouched hat, whom I soon recognised as being from Puerto Cabello. He told me, that in the war between Gen. Paez and Monagas he was obliged to fly. He was well connected, I had known his family, and it was a relief to meet him. Next day arrived at Carson's Creek, having passed Calaveras Creek diggings, Angel's Creek, and looked at the rocking-cradles and long toms of the miners, and passed through the villages of tents of the Mexicans who had deserted; met them on the road flying with their women, children, and donkeys.

The lassoing of a bull attracted my attention; the position of the horse, the shot, and falling of the animal, reminded me of the bull fights in Havana and Spain.

We finally arrived upon the summit of a high hill in a mountainous country; the valley filled with tents, and the earth thrown up by the diggers as by an earthquake. We lodged in an open cabin, built of staves rived out of the tree, without floor; a rude pine table; fried beef and potatoes, with coffee, and hot, hard, wheaten cakes was our food. The quartz rock produced abundantly. The opening, ten feet by seven, and ten feet in depth, had already produced the value of fifty thousand dollars. There were three casks in the cabin, headed up, full of quartz strongly charged with gold, besides sacks and bags. This important discovery was not yet known, otherwise it would have been dangerous; we were six persons sleeping upon straw, with a blazing fire, which gave light sufficient for an enemy to point through the opening anywhere, and kill the party. I felt anxious, and was glad to get away within three days. The operation of breaking the quartz was performed with rollers of stone drawn by mules; the more valuable pieces were broken with a pestle; some lumps weighed eight pounds. There were seven partners in this valuable claim. We came down with a quantity of the specimens, accompanied by Jack Hayes, the famous Texian ranger, who exhibited his skill with pistols in shooting the gopher, a little animal not unlike a ground mole. Ground squirrels abound in California, and are destructive to the crops. The scenery was at times magnificent; the thick heather, or undergrowth of the grizzly bear, in some parts is prominent. At one ranche the owner showed us some young cubs. There was some beautiful prairie country, capable of fine cultivation, and excellent grazing, which produces fine horses and horned cattle.

The wood-pecker provides for himself singularly in this country. I was struck with the mosaic appearance of some trees, and on examination found that this bird had bored holes in the thick bark, and set in the acorns for his winter's supply. At one ranche the hogs, sheep, and cattle looked remarkably well. At another stopping point, the owner has a pet ram, who knew a Mexican at sight, and bucked him with his head; he had a perverted taste for an animal, and was very fond of tobacco. His owner had an inveterate hate for an Indian, who had killed a brother of his. The Indians are fast disappearing. I was glad to get back to San Francisco, to prepare for my Oregon trip.

## 1851.
## LVI.

OREGON TERRITORY, *May 5, 1851.*

By the powerful agency of ocean and river steamers, without disparagement to horse and mule force, I find myself transported from the southern mines of California, a distance of some nine hundred miles, and can scarcely realize that I am now writing in a log cabin of the Upper Willamette Valley, in which the first legislative committee of nine persons were sworn in office by the missionary (Rev. Jason Lee) after their election by a mass meeting of the early emigrants, in 1846, to decide if laws should be enacted for the territory. The interpreter, Dr. Newell, who is present, drove the first pair of oxen across the plains, and now occupies his claim of a mile square, or six hundred and forty acres.

After returning from the mines via Stockton, to San Francisco, I embarked with the ocean steamer Columbia for Astoria, and had the pleasure of meeting with an old friend, in the person of the Hon. Thomas Nelson, from Peekskill, recently appointed Chief Justice of Oregon, in company with the Surveyor General, J.B. Preston, and several ladies; among the number were five who came out from the States as school teachers, under the auspices of the Hon. Mr. Thurston, Delegate to Congress, who died at Acapulco, after having crossed the isthmus, and whose death creates a great sensation in the territory. He was a candidate for Member of Congress for the next term, against Gen. Lane, who now meets no opposition. We had an agreeable passage to the mouth of the Columbia, whose far-famed breakers troubled us but little, the weather being favorable. Cape Disappointment at the north, and Point Adams at the south, with its eight-mile entrance, scarcely showed us where lie hidden the frightful sand banks which have so long been the terror of the mariner.

Another hour brought us to Astoria, which lies under the mountain range with a dense forest in the rear, and is a miserable town, without comfort or convenience, just the reverse in short of what you would expect from the name of its founder, and the writings of Washington Irving. We found here a steamer which carried us to Vancouver, a distance of one hundred and ten miles up the Columbia, the river narrowing from Astoria, as you proceed up stream, down to a mile in width, and sometimes less. The shores are mostly high lands, and are covered with impenetrable forests of firs of the most gigantic growth. Vancouver is the military post, and we found here the Mounted Rifle Regiment; it is in a most desirable position, situated upon a beautiful rising plain in an old settled part of the country, the establishments of the Hudson Bay Company being located here, and well worth visiting. They are in an immense inclosure, picketed with piles thirty feet in height, and containing several acres, with block-houses and towers fortified, and inside are immense store-houses for goods, and the dwellings of the governor and employees. Six miles below this point is the mouth of the Willamette, which river we ascended twelve miles to Portland, nearly the head of navigation for three-masted vessels, where we take whale boats or bateaux to proceed to Oregon City, which lies below the falls.

We chartered a boat with six Indian oarsmen, and, as it had a windlass in the bow, and an immense coil of rope to fasten to the trees for hauling up the rapids, we proceeded well until night overtook us within two miles of the town, where the rush of water was too much for us. After making ineffectual efforts until nine o'clock, we abandoned all hope until morning unless we should find shelter in a log-cabin, there being one, we were told, on that side of the Clackamas river. We divided our party of gentlemen, leaving enough for the protection of eight ladies, and commenced pioneering through the dense forest, without the aid of a lantern, until we discovered the timber burning in clearing up the land, and found the log cabin, but our only success was the borrowing of a dug-out to cross the Clackamas and to try to get to town to procure whale boats. Judge Nelson, our guide, and myself squatted in the bottom of this egg-shell canoe, and were paddled across this turbulent stream. We got to town about midnight, worn down with fatigue, our boots and clothes torn from contact with fallen logs, and from crossing ravines; but we were too late to obtain assistance until morning, so the party were obliged to camp in the open boat. Having been recommended to Gen. Gaines, a noble-hearted Kentuckian, who has seen service in Mexico, now Governor of the Territory, I was invited to join him and meet the commissioners now in treaty with the Indians. Our route of twenty-five miles through dense forests, ravines, and cane-brakes, and over prairies and streams, was intensely exciting, and to one who had not had some experience in California and Texas, it would have been startling. I found here three tribes of Indians encamped upon the plain, and was not a little amused by their ball plays, their war and other dances around the camp fires in the evening, and their gambling games which are sometimes kept up noisily all night.

The Yam Hill and Lukamuke bands of the Callapooya tribes are rapidly diminishing in numbers by disease. The Molalla tribe are mostly horsemen and warriors, and are a fine-looking race. The commissioners have just succeeded in effecting treaties with two of the bands, which I was called upon to witness; and it was an interesting sight to see Governor Gaines, Judge Spencer, and Colonel Allen, opposite the three Indian chiefs belonging to each tribe, with the interpreter and secretary, in grave council, while in the interior of the log cabin and around the door were collected many of the tribe, anxiously zealous of their rights, and suspicious lest any one band should get more than the other. The commissary distributes daily the flesh of a bullock, with rations of potatoes, flour, and salt, and the camp fires are constantly smoking. Their horses are hobbled and grazing on the prairie and in the woods; occasionally they mount them, and dash over the plain with the speed of the wind. The distribution of blankets, calicoes, and various articles, will take place when they leave. By the treaties for sale of lands and removals, they are provided with agricultural implements, supplies of provisions and clothing, horses, and in some cases, log houses instead of tents which they now occupy. This is to continue for twenty years, which is liberal on the part of the government.

The French prairies, a few miles from here, are mostly settled by French Canadians, who were the early settlers, having been engaged in trapping. I found one who was with the first expedition of Astor, some forty years since, and who has now his family of half-breeds, and his mile square of land.

From this point we have travelled in the country on the opposite side of the river, and from the summits of the highest hills had some magnificent views of the mountains of St Helena, Hood, and Rainer, eternally covered with snow, and of the immense forest of firs and pines, intervening with prairie land, the whole forming a panorama of surpassing wildness and beauty.

# LVII.

SAN FRANCISCO, *May 20, 1851.*

On my return to this city from Oregon, a scene of desolation presented itself. The boatman who brought me and an elderly gentleman ashore, who had lost property largely, as also friends who had perished in the flames, was ordered to land us on the beach near a hotel which had escaped, as I knew not whether the house where I left my effects was saved; but fortune had favored me once again, for the second time in this voyage—the first being in the destruction of the St. Charles hotel, in New Orleans. As we guided our boat between the blackened piles and charred dock timbers, with scarcely a landmark for a circuit of acres, which had so recently been covered with stores filled with merchandise, the heart sickened at the sight, and the old man, with his grey locks, sobbed aloud and wept, and leaned upon me for support. I took my way up the street, and discovered with satisfaction that I had a home, although thousands were scattered, many without a shelter or a change of clothing. I found the outbuildings and fences burned off the lot, but a change of wind and great efforts had saved our house. You have before this had full particulars of the destruction of property in this, the greatest conflagration that the city has ever experienced, and one which will cause distress and immense loss to many in the Atlantic States. I have never yet found a people who meet disaster with so much fortitude, and who possess the same recuperative faculties.

While the ruins are still smoking, some of the most business streets are being rebuilt, and the rapidity with which the work progresses is magical. The buildings now constructing being of wood and of frail material, are soon erected; and many house-frames were in the market, the remains of former speculations, which enables the builders to advance rapidly. The activity of the workman is exhausting; and as the rainy season has passed, many places are occupied with goods while the roofs are not fully covered, and fortunately the store ships in harbor contained abundant supplies to recommence business.

The temporary buildings must give way in time to fire-proof structures, otherwise another conflagration must be the result, as the winds are high from the north-west during the summer, and calculated to sweep the flames towards the business streets, wharves, and shipping. It was a singular fact that the fire should have occurred on the anniversary of the disaster of last year, and many persons fear the torch of the incendiary on the 14th of next month, that being the date of the second misfortune the last summer. The citizens are now enrolling themselves as a special night patrol.

From early morn until night is now heard the constant serenade of the saw and hammer of the carpenter, and the trowel of the mason. Many who have lost their all, retire in disgust; others start for the mines; others, even after the third or fourth visitation, if they have anything left, try it again, believing that the same elements of prosperity still exist in the country. It is a harvest for laborers and mechanics, and attracts many from other points about the country. The former obtain six dollars per day, while carpenters and painters have ten dollars per day.

I attended yesterday the funeral of a worthy young man who lost his life from over-exertion at the fire, and to-day looked at the ruins of an iron building, with the only survivor out of six who were within during the fire, and who made his escape by the scuttle and passed over the burning roofs of the adjoining buildings, while his brother and the remainder of the party were roasted alive. The streets, being planked, added fuel to the flames, and made it difficult for persons to escape. We have had a shock of an earthquake as a closing scene; it was felt so sensibly as to rattle the crockery of the ladies in the houses, but more positively down the coast, sufficiently there to remind one in a slight degree of Naples and Messina.

The smoke rising from the charred timbers, with the dust and ashes carried by the high cool winds which prevail every evening, makes the climate at present very disagreeable, particularly to those affected with any bronchial difficulty. I shall avail myself of the advantage of a trip down the valley of San Josè, called the Garden of California, where I will have an opportunity of visiting another great source of wealth to the country, the Quicksilver Mines.

# LVIII.

Lahaina, Sandwich Islands, *June 23, 1851.*

In my last communication from California, I think I intimated, at least I meant to intimate, my departure for China, via the Hawaiian group of islands. I have never known the same difficulties experienced by shipmasters in procuring crews; we were considerably delayed, waiting for the sailors, notwithstanding the enormous wages of one hundred dollars per month, which are paid, and which is not in their estimation equal to the allurements of the mines, until they find themselves without means, and obliged to take to their ordinary avocation.

Our list being finally filled by the rapacious landlords, who devour the substance of the poor Jacks, and force them on board after getting them well in debt, we proceeded to sea with a mutinous crew, and nothing but the rigid deportment and treatment of the officers brought them to their duties.

We were becalmed the first four days, which monotony was partially relieved by shooting at a species of Albatross, a large aquatic bird, and by fishing for sharks, of which we had large numbers, and sending an occasional rifle-ball into the backs of the large whales which were playing and spouting about us, producing a sound not unlike the escape-pipe of a Mississippi high-pressure steamer. At length our captain grew weary of the continued calm so near the coast, and charging my only fellow cabin-passenger with being a Jonah, he would now feed him on sea-fowls' eggs, of which we had a supply from the small islands, and shark-stew and steak, which was the last recourse to raise a breeze. As Prince Murat, who died in Florida, said he found all animals eatable except the turkey buzzard, we concluded to take the dishes dressed from a young shark which seemed to be enjoyed by the crew, and, if prejudice had not interposed, the repast would not have been unsavory. Fortune favored us and filled our sails, and in a few days we found ourselves in a latitude of the trade-winds, which blew steadily with agreeable weather until we made the island of Hawaii, with its volcanic fires illuminating the heavens at night; and moderate breezes prevailing under the lee of the island of Moui, commonly known as Mowee, gave us an opportunity of coasting, and examining the peculiar formation of the frightful rocks and chasms of extinct craters, as well as the verdant valleys produced from the decomposed lava. We finally made the harbor of Lahaina, most resorted to by whalers, to obtain fresh supplies of meats, fruits, and vegetables, of which there is an abundance, and here nature presented herself in her most luxuriant garb of tropical vegetation, with cocoa-nut trees filled with fruit, bananas, figs, grapes, melons, &c., reminding us much of the West India Islands, but with an entirely different population. One would suppose from the number of

Kanakas of both sexes, and of all ages, that the inhabitants were amphibious, as they were rolling and dashing in the surf among the breakers.

Some of the most extraordinary anecdotes are related of them. They have been known to swim thirty miles when wrecked midway between the islands, and often stories of credible parties give greater distances. The missionaries wrought great changes; a fair proportion now read and write, and have a capacity for arithmetic; many are members of the church, and their condition is so unlike their barbarous cannibal existence when they were visited by Capt. Cook, who was murdered on Hawaii island, known as Owyhee, that one cannot but thank the cause of the missions. Mr. Balding, one of the pioneers of the work, with whom I dined, and who had resided for twenty-one years among those then barbarians, gave me much valuable information. The native population suffer much from measles and other diseases, contracted in their intercourse with foreigners; and their numbers, not unlike the Indians of Oregon, seem to diminish gradually as the whites supplant them. Their taro is the chief article of food, being a root easily cultivated, and when pounded and baked, or boiled, is called Poi, and it is amusing to see groups squatted around the large gourd shells containing it, while each member puts his finger in and twists it round until well loaded, which he conveys to his mouth. Its consistency is denominated single, double, or three-fingered Poi.

They still have their propensity for raw fish with a sauce of salt water and pepper, which they relish with great gusto. Instead of going in a state of nudity as formerly, the largest proportion now wear clothing, and those who have the means, in the towns, wear the most gay-colored dresses of light materials.

Passages are not unfrequently made in about nineteen days from San Francisco, a distance of two thousand two hundred miles, with the stormy north-west winds, to the tropics, where begin the trades, which will enable those from California who desire a warmer climate to escape a more rigorous latitude. Our passage was only an average one of eighteen days, but looking forward to my embarcation for Hong Kong from Honolulu, eighty miles further on the island of Oahu, I could wish the aid of steam for traversing the ocean waste of five thousand miles, and also to escape with certainty the frightful typhoons of the China sea, in August and September. But I expect at the latter place, the arrival of a clipper ship, which was to succeed us at San Francisco, and will give me an opportunity of seeing King Kamehameha's dominions, of which Honolulu is the great port of entry of the Pacific Islands for the whalers, and also the residence of his majesty. Such information as I think may interest you I will communicate from there.

# LIX.

HONOLULU, *June 27, 1851.*

From Lahaina I came to this place, the capital of the Sandwich group, upon the Island of Oahu, and I find to my satisfaction the arrival of the clipper ship Samuel Appleton, of eight hundred tons burden, by which I shall embark for China. I must say I am agreeably disappointed in the aspect of things here, and the advancement through the instrumentality of the Missions and American residents. During the season for the return of the whalers from their fishing grounds, large numbers of vessels are seen in port, and the conveniences now offered far surpass those of any of the other small islands. It is the residence of King Kamehameha, and all the principal functionaries of government. The town is regularly laid out upon the margin of a deep bay, with an extended valley in the rear, and an undulating country between the high mountain, volcanic ridges extending towards the north part of the island, through which draw refreshing winds, without which the heat would be insupportable.

The houses of the natives are formed of bamboo cane frames, and thatched with wild grass; the sides are covered with like material, which resists the action of the sun and rain. The houses of foreigners are constructed mostly of wood, with verandas, and are well adapted to the climate. Some of the public buildings are of stone.

I found a comfortable hotel, delivered my letters and papers, and passed the first evening very agreeably at a social tea party, where was present the daughter of one of the chiefs, who had been educated, and spoke English well. While sitting in the veranda we heard the most strange, discordant cries, and wailing sounds, proceeding from one of the palaces, and were told there was a new arrival of relatives from some one of the islands to attend the funeral of the princess Kepanonohe, grand-daughter of Kamehameha I., which will take place in a few days, and for which extraordinary preparations are making.

She was an elderly woman, and is now deceased three weeks, and lying in state. I proceeded to the house and found some fifteen persons, old and young, sitting and prostrating themselves on the floor, and uttering deep tones of distress that were pitiable to hear, and calculated to excite one's sympathy, supposing them to be sincere.

I have heard the lamentations of the Jews under the walls of the ancient Temple at Jerusalem, and the hired mourners of Egypt, whose doleful cries rend the air, and who, from long practice, seem to experience all the anguish of the afflicted relative, and I was at a loss to subscribe to the divine command, "Weep with those who weep." These wailings were continued until eleven o'clock, and were the last sounds I heard as I returned to my hotel, half a mile distant. Mr. Wylie, Minister of Foreign Affairs, gave us a letter to one of the chiefs called Paaki, who has the title of Chamberlain to the king; you will perceive there is no want of high-sounding names. We found that he occupied a fine house, which was built by an architect named Charles Nelson, from our town, whom I knew when a boy, and who has resided here for many years. The chief received us kindly, bade us enter, and showed us his establishment. He is a man of muscular frame, over six feet in height, well proportioned, and weighs three hundred pounds; he was dressed in modern style, with white duck suit, and Panama hat, a noble-appearing person, who looked the chief.

He spoke but little English. It is said he prefers his mat upon the floor of one of his cabins, and his dish of Poi, to the refined modes of life. He accompanied us to the palace of the king, which is a fine wooden mansion, recently constructed, and situated in the centre of a square inclosure surrounded by trees, and got up with considerable taste for this country. Some native troops at the lodge presented arms as we passed, to sustain the dignity of the place. The throne room contains the portraits of the royal family, some respectable furniture, and the portraits of Louis Philippe, Frederick, King of Prussia, and some views; which were more than I expected to find in a country so recently reclaimed from barbarism.

The same afternoon we procured horses, of which many are to be found, as the Kanakas are very fond of the quadruped, and proceeded to the north side of the island, through the valley, whose cultivation is mostly of taro, the island-bread. Some three miles from town we left the main road to visit the cascade, a small mountain torrent rushing down the rocks, which is a favorite place for sham battles and diving; and there we found several of the amphibious beings contending for the small pieces of coin which were thrown them in the water. Mounting our horses, we pursued our way through the valley, passing the low mud and bamboo huts, and dense thickets of small trees and bushes, with jagged and crooked branches, almost impenetrable outside of this narrow defile, through which the wind rushed strongly, while the dense clouds were lowering upon the summits of the volcanic ridges above, threatening to drench us, though we escaped dry. We met with considerable numbers of cattle, horses, sheep, and goats, which shows the advancement of the island.

Some seven miles towards the north the ascent is gradual, and brought us to the Pali, a precipice which certainly presents one of the most beautiful views the eye can behold, of the plain below, with its tropical trees and forests, with the ocean in the distance.

The descent is by an excavated road running round the peak, whose height is immense; it reminded me, in some particulars, of the excavation in the mountains of Caracas, under the government of Paez. Tradition says that the opposite and most lengthy peak, which appears to be only a foothold for a man, was occupied by one of the former chiefs, or kings, when pursued by his enemies, whom he hurled headlong as they approached. The following day I paid a visit to one of the young princes, who had been in the States, as also in Europe, the past year, in company with Dr. Judd, and found him in a bamboo, grass-covered house, within the inclosure of the palace grounds, seated upon a sofa; the ground floor was covered with matting, upon which squatted the lightly clad Kanaka women of the household. He conversed well in English, and expressed himself pleased with his voyages. The women are expert riders, and on Saturday of each week the whole town, male and female, who can procure horses, make it a gala-day. The former, who bestride the saddle, wear a bright yellow scarf, extending from the skirt of the dress behind to cover the stirrups in front, and round straw hats with wreaths of flowers, presenting, as they dash furiously along, a picturesque appearance.

I congratulate myself in having again escaped the loss of my luggage, as my fellow passenger from San Francisco has lost a part of his effects, while the remainder was wet through in coming ashore. The reef extends out about half a mile, and the heavy breakers capsized the boat's crew, who narrowly escaped a worse fate. I was fortunately ashore with the captain.

## LX.

HONOLULU, *June 26, 1851.*

The Yankee character for enterprise is admitted to be a peculiar one, whether productive of good or evil. On board of our vessel from Lahaina we received two Americans who had established a circus company in this place with great success, and had gone to the neighboring island to try their fortunes, but were not permitted to play. They had come here to present their petitions, and had numerous advocates, although it was contended by their opponents that the Kanakas were so fond of this amusement that they would exhaust their resources to gratify it. It is contended by some that the laws and regulations enforced by the missionary influence are too rigid, and that while the latter are actuated by good motives, their remedies have proved worse than the disease; that while the most stringent laws have been enacted against immoralities, they are entirely ineffective of good, as it is asserted that the most unblushing looseness of manners prevails in the islands. Another charge is against the teaching in the language of the country, and discouraging the use of other languages; and that civilization cannot advance when hampered by a tongue which, in the words of Onmittee Wyldie, abounds in names for every vice, but is without a name for any virtue, and which is too loose and ambiguous for official correspondence, permanent records, or civil contracts. They say that the discouragement of manly exercises among the natives, such as throwing the spear, and wrestling, in which they were so expert, has gained them nothing but increase of idleness, inactivity, and diminished cheerfulness, which are incentives to criminality. The missionaries, on the other hand, refute the charges alleged against them, saying, that they are not answerable for the acts of the Hawaiian government; that church and state have never been united in the islands; that the penalties imposed upon the people for their abuses in manners exert a powerful restraint; and that the natives are the only true judges, as they understand fully the nature, objects, and operation of the laws. They state that they have taught English as far as possible, but cannot teach an entire people a new language; that they had other work to do, leaving the translation of the Bible until such times as the people could understand it. They have been without doubt instrumental of vast good, having civilized and partly christianized these barbarians. They have had many difficulties to contend with, and those who are now enjoying the benefits of the present state of society, are the first to oppose them. They have without doubt committed some errors in judgment, which is usually the case with reformers who wish to make all classes conform to their standard of right and wrong; but I have generally found them useful, and obliging to the traveller and stranger, and desirous of imparting information; standing as pioneers at the outposts of civilization, and as useful in extending the area of knowledge and Christianity, as the hardy squatter of the frontier, in his advancing the agricultural pursuits of our western wilds.

When we reflect that in the year 1820 the first mission was established among a nation of low and brutal savages, who have been reclaimed from barbarism and instructed in Christianity, it must be admitted that much has been done, although it is contended by many that the population has been vastly reduced by contamination with the whites, and rendered less happy.

The churches, of which there are several, are attended by natives to hear the word in the native tongue, and large numbers are communicants, and follow up the externals, and many are strictly pious, but very many have to be dealt with, not being able to forget their former practices, which causes much labor for their teachers. They have here a House of Nobles, so called, whose acts are published with as much consequence as if they proceeded from the Parliament of England. I have been much amused in the island of Hayti with the supreme authority and dignity of the black emperor, Soulouque; and cannot help but look at some things here as a farce, but the advantages are that there is American talent here to dictate and pull the wires. I have had the opportunity of visiting and coasting through six of the eight inhabited islands of the Sandwich group, which extends between 18° 50′ and 22° 20′ N. Lat., and 154° 53′ and 160° 15′ West Long., and which composes eight thousand square miles with a native population of some eighty thousand—supposed. I am thus particular in describing their locality, as I had previously known so little of these remote specks on the vast Pacific, which were so far removed from us by reference to the chart, that I had never intended to visit them. As you may be interested in the language, I give you the following notice with the translation; it may be of service to those who wish to commence the rudiments at home.

*Fonu—(See Selom.)*

OLELO HOOLAHA.—Ina. e. loaa ana kekahi. kanaka, mahope o ka hooaba ana o keia palapala, e lawe ana, i ka PAAKIA.

*Olelo Hoolaha.*—Ina e loaa ana kekahi Kanaka, mahope o ka hooaha ana i ka Paakai o Puuloa, a me ka ja, paha o na loko, a me ka ja o ku Pa Kuli, a o na Kanaka e loaa ana e laroe ana i ka Paakia i huna ia ma Puuloa, ua kuai ia ku paha a kehahi Kanaka malaili me ka lohe, ole a me ka ae ole o ka mea nono ka inoa malole, e hopo ia no lakou a hoopii ia lakou, a e hookokole ia lakou ma ka ano aihu.

Honolulu.

C. W. V.

## TRANSLATION.

*Notice.*—All persons, after this notice, found taking salt from Puloa, or fish from the pond Paa Kuli, or others, or any person found receiving salt made at Puloa from anyone, except with the permission of the undersigned, will be arrested, and an action of law brought against them for stealing.

Honolulu, June 6, 1850.

C. W. V.

# LXI.

LADRONE ISLANDS, *July 21, 1851.*

The cry of "Land Ho" to the traveller on a sea voyage is always refreshing, but particularly so after having been some weeks out of sight of terra firma. Our ship is deserving of the name of clipper when she has good breezes, and when full rigged is perfectly white with canvass, carrying from thirty-five to forty sails.

We have been running with the trades almost in a direct route from the Sandwich Islands, some three thousand five hundred miles, and have never furled a sail since our departure until yesterday, when appearances indicated one of the much dreaded typhoons, which are so much feared at this season, and which appear in the region of the islands, and extend through the China Sea. The strongest and swiftest ships are unable to resist them; they have their spars carried away, and even their masts taken out, and are not unfrequently lost, as was the case with the clipper-ship Rainbow. The heavens at mid-day were only comparable to the blackness of night, and the whole horizon seemed to be circumscribed; it appeared as if our bowsprit would soon enter into the tar-colored circle ahead of us. The orders of officers were given and responded to by an active crew of sixteen sailors. The orders, "Brail the spanker," "Haul up the mainsail," "Reef the foresail," and so on, were rapidly given until she could be got in safe trim. It proved to be more a deluge of rain than a gale of wind, with terrific peals of thunder, as if all the artillery of heaven was in commotion; the lightning played beautifully and awfully about us.

It was one of those magnificent sights which must be witnessed to be appreciated. If we had not shortened sail we should have run out of it, but prudence dictated the greatest caution, particularly in this latitude. The sailors, as the rain abated, amused themselves like a parcel of ducks, playing and bathing in the water upon deck, before the scuppers could carry off the copious supply.

Our ship is spacious, with fine promenade, quarter and main decks unencumbered. Our cabin is large and handsomely finished, and furnished with accommodations for thirty-two passengers, but there being only two of us we are not elbowed, and find our supplies bountiful.

My companion from San Francisco, is bound to Canton only. I had once made a passage with him from Charleston to New York, and we subsequently met in Havana, and now chance throws us again together under pleasant circumstances. We occupy our time like most others on shipboard, to relieve monotony, by the usual labor of eating, drinking, and considerable sleeping;

of course, also in writing and reading, the latter being the great resource, and my neighbor, being fond of music, whiles away many a weary hour upon his guitar and accordeon.

Our Anniversary of the glorious Fourth, we ushered in by discharging our six-shooters, and ringing the steward's bell, and afterwards firing at a mark, to commemorate the day. Dined patriotically, with sentiments to friends and home, heard an occasional salute from Jack, of the forecastle, carrying the mind back to the scenes of former days. Thus passed the day, and at ten at night, while pacing the quarter-deck by moonlight, under a press of canvas, with a nine-knot breeze, the trade-wind dead aft and sailing on even keel, the ocean calm, and now entitled to its Pacific name, I could not help reflecting upon the events of home, and found, at that moment, judging from our position of latitude and longitude, you were then returning from a Church Oration, or listening to the mid-day salute. Sunday the 6th, was observed as the Sabbath on shipboard, but had been lost in the calculation of nautical time, as we had passed the one hundred and eightieth degree of west longitude, or the world's centre, being the antipodes of Greenwich. We then counted it as ship's time, Monday 7th, and commenced in east longitude. On the ninth day out from Honolulu, we lost sight of the bark Isabella Hine, with which vessel I went to the islands from St. Francisco; we left in company, and kept in view during all this time, which was a little remarkable, showing the equality of sailing of these two clippers—the average runs being from one hundred and sixty to two hundred miles per day, with moderate breezes. The weather has been very hot during the entire passage, the thermometer now standing eighty-six degrees, with an occasional refreshing shower, favorable for fresh supplies, as the old stock of water is repugnant to smell.

As we have had no weather to admit of fishing, such calms not being desirable, our curiosity has not been excited with the sights of whales, sharks, sea lions, or porpoises, of which we had an abundance while going down to the islands; we conclude therefore that we have got away from their cruising grounds. There is nothing to call one's attention, except the water-spouts, which we are disposed to give a wide berth. The moonlight nights are delightful, and the most pleasant part of the twenty-four hours; they incline one to pace the deck, and give him plenty of time to reflect upon the many changes and scenes in life.

Having no opportunity to forward this letter, I shall not close it till our arrival at Hong Kong or Macao.

MACAO, *Aug. 4, 1851.*

Having an opportunity of sending the annexed letter immediately on entering port, I can now announce our arrival, although in the latter part of our voyage we were becalmed and had to contend with the head-winds, after the regular trades had left us, on passing the Bashee Islands in the China sea, where we had reason to expect the south-west trades, or monsoons, but on the contrary had to contend with heavy tide ripples or counter currents, running at the rate of two and a half miles per hour. I assure you it was disheartening to make only twenty miles per day, within three hundred miles of our haven, while liable to meet a stray pirate, or a frightful typhoon, not to mention the sun's rays, which were overpowering; but our for fortunes changed after a few days' reverse, a strong south-wester having brought us in sight of the Celestials with their long tails, who are surrounding us in their sharp, lightly constructed boats, with sails of matting, and are proffering their services for pilotage, supplies of fish, fruits, &c. I have not time to add further, but shall write you from Canton, seventy-five miles up the river.

# LXII.

CANTON, CHINA, *Aug. 20, 1851.*

We arrived at Whampoa, where the foreign shipping lies, some fourteen miles below this city, and where we cast anchor. We were immediately surrounded by a multitude of boatmen, and amongst the rest a host of washerwomen, neatly dressed, with flowing pantaloons and a loose vest which falls over the hips, and is made of blue or black cotton or silk. They crowd around with commendations in their hands, and solicit the preference at the extremely low rate of one dollar and a half per hundred. You can judge of my surprise, who had paid five dollars for the single dozen in California, which of itself was the strongest evidence of the great disparity of population. The hair of the married women is put up in an artistic manner, and the young girls wear the long queue braided, but their heads are not shaved like those of the men. The following day I came up to this city through a perfect fleet of junks, and other boats, with their teeming population, the study of whose habits and modes of life would occupy much time. It is computed that there are eighty thousand boats, with a floating population of four hundred thousand souls, upon the waters of the Canton River.

I was particularly struck with the appearance of the large junks with their painted eyes at the bow, as the Chinese say, *"Suppose no have eyes, no can see."* The Mandarin War Boats carry fifty oarsmen, and their broad-brimmed conical bamboo hats answer as a shield from the sun and spears. The peculiar open stern which incloses the rudder and place for ingress and egress, and the sudden manner in which they turn the boats, surprised me; the neatness displayed on board the small ferry and passenger boats, where families are born, live, and die upon their native element, is without example. They are covered by permanent and also sliding roofs of bamboo matting, and propelled mostly by women with a scull-oar on a pivot at the stern. Some are nicely fitted up and gilded, for parties of pleasure, and are really fine.

The foreign population of Canton is made up of about fifty persons of different nations, mostly occupying a fine range of buildings, called Factories, fronting a beautiful garden of about two acres square, with high walls at the ends, and extending to the river; it is filled with every variety of tropical trees, plants, and flowers, and affords a delightful lounge upon Chinese settees, or a fine promenade upon its cemented walks. In the centre is a neat Episcopal Chapel, and the flags of three nations, ours being one of the number, are flying from elevated flag-staffs. Adjoining the grounds is an extended boat-house which contains the finest collection of race-boats of the most delicate construction in the world, for the regattas of the English and American residents, and for daily exercise, as it is not safe to penetrate into the country;

there are no drives, and in fact horses are rarely seen or used, the dense population and low price of labor with the use of the buffalo, supplying their places. The latter animal is nearly amphibious, and gets a portion of his supplies in low grounds unfit for cultivation; in fact the Chinese, being the most laborious, economical, and indefatigable people perhaps in the world, cultivate every inch of ground, as far as I can perceive in my excursions up and down the river, and along the paddy or rice fields. I arrived opportunely for the Festival of the Dead, but it reminded me more of the Fourth of July at home, from the constant discharge of crackers and fireworks. The flower boats, which are eighty to one hundred feet in length, with cabins beautifully decorated, and literally overhung and festooned with large, beautiful, vari-colored lanterns at night in long processions, with the beating of gongs, and the playing of instruments, in sound not unlike the Scotch bagpipe, produced a most singular effect. The offerings, which are made to the deceased friends and burned in the streets, are made to represent clothes, money, and other articles; and the consumption of prepared folded paper of different colors, some of gold and silver gilt, which are placed together by the masses and then fired, is not a slight tax upon the people. An exhibition of this kind took place at the angle of our house, and our coolies and servants were among the group, after which copper coins, called cash, one thousand two hundred to the dollar, were thrown out to the beggars who were scrambling among the embers. I am indebted to the hospitalities of Wm. Buckler, Esq., to whom I had letters, there being no hotel deserving of the name, and have received many invitations and civilities at the hands of other parties. The servants here are excellent, and anticipate your every want.

I must describe mine to you. His face, as also the skin around his eyes and ears, and his head to the crown, is well shaved; his long, black hair falls plaited nearly to his ankles; his white frock or long vest with sleeves, flows over his flowing pants of white grass linen; he has white leggings attached to his turned up and embroidered shoes, and tied at the knee, and they are perfect patterns of cleanliness, although droll-looking objects.

The usual hour for tiffin, or lunch, is three in the afternoon, and dinner is at seven in the evening. In accepting invitations out, custom demands and admits in this hot climate, a full dress of white, the round jacket included, and your servant to accompany you.

Canton contains probably a million of inhabitants. Ingress cannot be obtained within the walls. I effected an entrance for a short distance, but was soon expelled. The town outside is probably more interesting than within, as the streets run parallel with the walls, and the houses are built close up against them. They are ordinarily one or two stories high, the latter class forming a hollow square inside, with galleries surrounded by merchandise, and arranged for the display of goods. The signboards run up and down, are gaudily painted in various colors in Chinese characters, with tasteful lanterns at the entrance, and in the narrow streets have a gay appearance.

The merchants, mechanics, and artisans, in their many occupations, can hardly be described on paper. The latter are well clad in the costume of the country, and mostly in black, and carry fans or umbrellas. The laborers at this season have the upper part of the body exposed; they carry their burdens suspended from the extreme end of a pliable round shoulderpole, and cry out for space as they thread the dense throng in the narrow passages. At certain hours at night, the gates of the different quarters are closed, and the district is liable for any robbery committed within it. If the culprit is found, his head is taken off at the execution ground, in the open space within the heart of the town outside the walls. Their punishments are most severe, some victims being chopped in pieces, and some flayed alive. The ground was red with gore as I passed through that quarter, from the recent execution of fifteen men for treason; a revolt has lately taken place in one of the provinces, and the rebels succeeded in destroying five hundred of the celestial troops, with the exception of ten who escaped the ambuscade.

The object is to change the present dynasty. Since the late opium war and treaty with the English, with the privileges of trading, many advantages have been gained, and gradually the country will be penetrated, and we shall know more of this peculiar and interesting people, who boast of the highest civilization, and consider all outsiders as barbarians. The maxims of Confucius, who is held in great veneration, teach affection, and obedience towards parents, respect for elder brothers, and esteem on their part for younger brothers. The people are Boodhists in religion, and the doors and entrances of all the shops have figures and offerings suspended, and incense tapers burning night and morning, to keep off the evil spirits.

Temples and Joss Houses, where are placed the figures of their gods, are seen frequently along the river bank, and the great Temple of Honan on the opposite side of the river is extensive and very curious. On entering the gate from the river side you pass under a line of shade trees, and enter three temples in succession, with colossal figures of Joss, seven in number, of giant form, in sitting postures, and in size reminding me of the figures Gog and Magog, in London. The architecture of the buildings is strikingly Chinese, with figures of lions and dragons at the angles. The priests have their heads clean shaved, and the beating of the kettle-drums of huge size, and the sound of their instruments at hours of worship, are almost deafening. The contents of some of the temples remind one of a museum, from the great variety of armor and figures. The grounds attached to the temple of Honan contain a pond for the cultivation of the sacred lotus, or water lily, and granite monuments wherein repose the ashes of the priests, who are buried in a small stone structure, which is inclosed on three sides, within shady bamboo trees;

the blackened and smoky chimney betokened recent use. Eight noble fat hogs are within the inclosure of the temple, and are represented to the faithful as immortal; in the event of accident, however, others are in reserve.

Opium is freely used by the people, and the trade in it has increased to a frightful extent, although contraband, the officials being engaged in the traffic, so that the consumption has increased to twenty-five millions of dollars per annum. This, in a population of three hundred millions, is considered not to be a great excess, but it tells a sad story on the constitution of an habitual smoker. The use of tea is of course general, and spirit is distilled from rice. The Houqua gardens belonging to the great merchant deceased, some few miles above the city, are in good taste, with fish-ponds, artificial cascades and grottoes, and a vast number of fruit trees, plants, and flowers, peculiar to the climate.

# LXIII.

HONG KONG, CHINA, *Aug. 20, 1851.*

This island, the name of which translated is Fragrant Springs (it is certainly supplied with running water, though barren and hilly), is twenty-one miles in circumference, and is situated on the north side of the bay which communicates with the Canton river, to which it is the key. It was ceded in treaty to the English, and is a great acquisition, but has cost them five or six millions in erecting buildings for troops, fortifications, and general improvements, in addition to the large expenditures of English capitalists. It is decidedly an English town, although their numbers are not great therein, though it contains a regiment of one thousand troops. Its being a free port facilitates contraband trade; it has a large Chinese population, and in all contains probably twenty thousand inhabitants. Macao, on the opposite side of the bay, about thirty miles distant, occupied for centuries by the Portuguese, is an agreeable place of residence, but it has, through bad management, lost its trade, and its harbor is quite deserted. It is now used as a place of summer resort, but rents have declined, and the people are poor. The heat of Hong Kong and Canton is very oppressive at this season of the year; we had the thermometer in the latter city from ninety-eight to one hundred for several days in succession, with but little difference in the night. Humboldt says that La Guayra, in South America, is the hottest place in the world, but I suffered more from the heat in Canton than there.

Before leaving Hong Kong, I made an excursion to the Whampoa Pagoda, which is nine stories high, of an octagonal form, and has in the distance a most imposing effect. The duck boats by the river bank attracted my attention; the ducks are driven ashore in large numbers to feed, and at the sound of a bell they rush back to their quarters, from the circumstance that the last one who enters gets whipped for being dilatory. The Chinese have a temple here, also, well fitted up; and last evening it was magnificently lighted by their fanciful lanterns, and a festival called Sing Song came off, with the beating of gongs, kettle drums, and other instruments, and a supply of confectionery and other eatables, inside and outside the building, upon stands, for sale.

There were immense figures of men and animals, made of painted pasteboard strengthened by wires, which were taken out and burned as offerings to their gods. We could expose ourselves with perfect safety among the people, and examine minutely the idols of the altars, feeling a sense of security on British soil which I could not feel in and about Canton, under like circumstances.

I was quartered in Canton in the most desirable part for sights, and some of a most amusing character were constantly seen. One day I counted from my window eighteen stout barbers, who carried on their backs a three-legged stool with straps attached, and in the bottom a chest of lances; they were engaged on, or waiting for, customers in the open court. The operation of dressing the long tail and scraping the pate, in addition to the practice of cleaning the eye and ear, occupies some time, for all of which they get about six cash, or half a cent each. Mandarins occasionally passed in sedan chairs, with suites of attendants, and the hurry of the crowd was observed to allow their mandarinships a free passage. A large wedding procession attracted my attention from the great quantity of presents therein. I counted fifty coolies with loaded hand-barrows, filled with fruit, flowers, confectioneries, cakes, nuts, robes, &c., in rich profusion, preceding the bride, who was conducted to the house of the groom veiled, in a sedan chair, as the tiny feet of the ladies are seldom seen in the streets. They are affianced early by their parents without ever having seen their lovers; and when their intended husbands gaze upon them, if acceptable, they are supported by women across a pan of coals into the house.

They are sometimes rejected, but damages are expected. This leads to unhappy marriages and polygamy, which is recognised by the law, the children having legitimate rights. The river-women all go bare-footed in warm weather, and their feet are of natural size.

The upper classes still continue the bandaging of the feet as a mark of rank, which is eulogized in Chinese poetry. This barbarous practice consists in turning under the small toes of the infant and bandaging them, leaving only the great toe exposed, which system in course of time raises the instep and throws the heel backwards, giving them more equilibrium; the iron shoe is not used, but the wrappers are changed daily. Among the poorest classes, female children are much neglected, and frequent instances of infanticide occur, woman being considered born to drudgery, and not meriting an education.

I came down by steamer, the only passenger, and in the evening found fire-arms brought up and laid on the companion-way; I naturally asked the cause, and was informed there was nearly a million of bullion on board for shipment, and that an attempt had recently been made by a Chinese crew who had concerted a plan with some fifteen forward deck passengers, by previous understanding, for the taking of the shipment of specie, and to cut off the officers while at table, and run the boat outside of Boca Tigris. The plot, however, was discovered in time to prevent it.

Not unfrequently the piratical Chinese attack the junks, notwithstanding all their crews go armed with spears and lances. Now they employ all

Englishmen on board of the river boats which contain treasure. We have had news of the loss of the steamer Pasha, which was run down by the steamer Erie, in the Straits of Malacca, with the loss of several lives, and a large quantity of opium. It was from carelessness, as the steamers had exchanged signals about midnight, but notwithstanding, the Erie at full speed struck the Pasha with her port bow, a little slanting, a few feet abaft the mainmast, and she sank in five minutes, without having time to lower her boats.

This has produced great excitement here, both steamers belonging to the Peninsular and Oriental Steam Co. I think now I can embark with safety tomorrow on board the steamer Malta for Singapore, as more care is always exercised after an accident.

# LXIV.

SINGAPORE, *Sept. 1, 1851.*

Having arrived at Singapore, I will resume my narrative. We had rather a rough passage down, in the face of a south-west monsoon in the China Sea, for a distance of about one thousand four hundred miles. The Malta is an iron steamer of thirteen hundred tons burden, well disciplined and manned by Lascars, or Indians, from Bombay, Chinese as deck hands, and Seedes, or blacks from the African coast as stokers, or firemen, the heat being too great for Europeans.

It was curious to see the variety of costume of the deck hands as they left port; it was Sunday at the time, and they did not doff the costume of the holiday until we left the harbor. I noticed more particularly the gay-colored turbans, white frocks and fancy belts of the Lascars, and the long tails of the Chinese, while many of their female friends were in boats around the ship, keeping up a constant discharge from bunches of firecrackers. We were only seven passengers, English gentlemen and officers of the army, myself the only American. The system adopted throughout by the steam navigation company is to charge enormous prices, more than double the rates of fare of our Atlantic steamers; for instance, from Hong Kong to this place, the passage, including exchange, costs one hundred and seventy dollars, the passage to Calcutta being upwards of four hundred dollars. They furnish a profusion of everything available in the way of supplies, rendering the consumption of liquors, wines, and soda, greater than in the West India line, where each individual signs a card for the steward as he gives his order, and settles weekly, or at the expiration of the voyage.

The English officers and gentlemen are particular in dressing for dinner; considerable etiquette is observed, and they generally occupy much time at table. I am frequently called upon to combat error and prejudice against my country in a variety of ways. The minds of some have been poisoned by such works as those of Mrs. Trollope, and others.

I was told that I was the first overland California traveller. I could answer the interrogations about lynch law, rapid eating or bolting of food at hotels and on board of steamers; and in the latter charges, I could only admit, American-like, that we were a young but fast people, and that we could not enjoy the luxurious ease of old countries, as time did not permit; that pioneer life on the borders cautioned the sovereign people where laws did not exist, to rid themselves of robbers and assassins.

Throughout the East the Punkah is made use of while the guests are at meals; it is a long frame from three and a half to four feet in depth, covered with white cloth, with a fringe running the whole length of the table, and suspended on hinges from the ceiling, to which is attached a cord passing over a pulley, and put in motion by an invisible hand behind a screen, or passing through the wall into the adjoining room. We have three Lascar boys in costume, who are seated on the opposite side of the dining saloon, keeping up a constant circulation of air during meals.

I have been under the surgeon's hands since I embarked, with a slight attack of Hong Kong fever; consequently I could not enjoy my passage, and was disgusted with the sight of eatables and drinkables. I am now quite recovered, and a drive about the environs of this city in a palanquin has had a good effect. These palanquins are small carriages with forward and back seats, adapted for two persons, and on low wheels, drawn by small Sumatra ponies full of spirit. The drivers, or rather runners, are Malabars from Madras, of a dark ebony color. The costume of my man is a white scarf bound round the head, loose white pants coming to his knees, and a red sash about his loins, so that his limbs are perfectly free, and he runs beside the horse at the top of his speed, holding one rein and the trace at the same time for safety and support. These men will run to the end of the island, sixteen miles, if occasion requires. You not unfrequently see persons galloping on horseback, and the man running along to take the reins when the rider dismounts.

Singapore, near the Straits of Malacca, is a small city on a small island, well built by the English. It is a free port, and large numbers of vessels from all parts visit it for purposes of traffic.

Great numbers of Chinese, say as many as thirty thousand, have migrated to this point, and can be seen in every kind of pursuit; they monopolize almost every species of labor, and being more vigorous than the others, can work cheaper at the various mechanical branches. The greatest variety of costume and language is found here, congregating from all the East and all the islands, Singapore being in the high-road from east to west.

I shall proceed to Penang upon Prince of Wales Island, by steamer, and thence to the island of Ceylon, on the other side of the bay of Bengal, where I shall wait for the steamer from Suez, on her way up to Calcutta, and as Ceylon is represented as being a beautiful island, and I shall be there some two weeks, you may expect to hear from me.

# LXV.

Kandy, Island of Ceylon, *Sept. 16, 1851.*

I find myself now one hundred and forty-four miles from Point de Galle, the place where I left the steamer on my route from Penang to Singapore. Galle is a small fortified town which was first occupied by the Portuguese, taken afterwards by the Dutch, and finally acquired by the English, who are now in full and complete possession of this large island, extending from 6° to 10° N. Lat., from the Tropic of Cancer, at the west entrance of the Bay of Bengal opposite the Coromandel coast. It is about two-thirds the size of Ireland, and once contained a large population, but at present only one and a half million. From Point de Galle I proceeded to Colombo, the chief commercial mart, distant by land seventy-two miles, winding along through almost uninterrupted cocoa-nut groves, for some sixty miles, with long lines of thatched cabins, villages at intervals, and the most peculiar and primitive population in many respects I have ever met with. The natives along the coast are copper-colored, with fine features and slender forms; they wear long hair, falling half down their backs when loose and male and female wear two shell combs, one over the crown, and the other of great height to make the coiffure behind; it is difficult at first to distinguish the sexes among the young. The cocoa-nut tree is the chief support; they pay some attention to fishing, however, in the oddest vessels that ever floated, consisting in many instances of simple "dug-outs," with an outrigger of bent boughs, which are lashed to the side of the vessel, and to the end is attached a pointed log, floating on the surface, and if the canvas is carrying the bark over, they balance it by sitting on the outrigger, sailing with great rapidity.

The harvest of the cocoa is now at hand. The milk is refreshing, and quenches thirst; the fruit is not only eaten, but large quantities of oil are made from it for use and exportation. The bark is rotted in pits of water, and bruised, then the fibres are pulled and made into cordage and rope of different kinds. The trees stand from six to fifteen feet apart, and are from fifty to eighty feet in height; large use is made of the liquid that exudes from the off-shoots near the top of the tree, which is distilled into arrack, and the natives may be seen like ourang-outangs, moving from the tops of the trees on the cordage made from the fibre to aid in climbing, while lower down are the earthen vessels in which the juice is collected. After passing through the cocoa-nut forests the cinnamon plantations present themselves, within a range of eight to ten miles of Colombo, and are mostly owned by foreigners.

One of the vices to which the natives are mostly addicted is the excessive use of the betel, which is a composition of the betel-leaf, the areka-nut, and chanam or luire, made from the muscle-shell, to which is sometimes added tobacco; it not only has a stimulating effect, but causes the lips, teeth, and inside of the mouth to appear blood-red, and tends in time to blacken the teeth, which is considered by some a mark of beauty. The stranger, when he first finds himself among a group of dark, ebony Kandians, and copper-colored Cingalese, with a sprinkling of Malabars in the primitive state, and in the costume of our first parents, with their mouths full of betel, imagines he has fallen among demons; at least I did, though I soon became accustomed to the sight.

The old kingdom of Kandy successfully resisted the Dutch and Portuguese, and for a long time the English, as from their fastnesses in the mountains, without roads to facilitate the enemy, the natives were long enabled to keep possession of the interior, after their sea-ports were occupied, and until they finally succumbed to the English. It lies seventy-two miles from Colombo, and fourteen hundred and sixty-seven feet above the level of the sea, and is characterized by the grandeur of the mountain scenery, and its wooded hills and luxuriant vegetation. The climate is very pleasant, its average temperature being 74°. The approach to this place is full of interest and novelty.

You find the paddy or rice fields in the valleys cultivated by the natives, who subsist mostly upon rice, made into curry, adding a sauce composed of cocoa, pepper, ginger, and coriander seed. Most of them are Boodhists, and touch no animal food, it being contrary to their religion to take life. They are often seen with almost naked skins, and hatless heads, their hair tied up in a bunch behind or falling over their shoulders, following black, uncouth, and sluggish buffaloes, which drag a rude wooden plough through the muddy field, inundated from the mountain streams.

Since the English have occupied the country, the colonial government has opened good roads, and much attention has been given to the planting of coffee, which is the chief source of profit, and enables it to place its troops in different parts of the island. An attempt at rebellion in this the most warlike province, two years since, after a considerable massacre, was soon suppressed. The road to Colombo is now much travelled by two-wheeled carts with high covered tops of cocoa-nut plaited branches, drawn by diminutive black cattle, about three or four feet high, with short horns, looking not unlike large calves, but tough and strong. Travelling Bandys are frequently seen; they are about the size of a good dog cart, with a small bullock in the shafts, and a cord running through his nose and over his head, to the sides of which a pair of lines are attached; two or three persons sit inside with their knees drawn up to the chin. The cabins by the road-side are in low and sheltered positions; they are furnished with two or three stools, a few plaited mats, earthen water-jars, a rice mortar, and some few culinary articles. Such of the women as are not engaged in weeding and reaping in the fields busy themselves in preparing betel, cooking curry, or in attending to their children. In approaching Colombo, as also this place, appearances change, the difference of caste, of which they were very particular under the old regime, being still seen.

The Kandians, despising the effeminate combs of the low-country people, wear a gay-colored handkerchief tied around the head, leaving the top exposed; they wear a white or fancy colored cloth of double breadth wrapped around the loins, while Mormons or Mussulmans with turbans, and Hindoos with painted faces, and also Malabars and other races, make up the picturesque masquerade. The Rhodias, or outcasts, a sort of Gipsies, are not permitted to wear any garment other than a sense of propriety suggests. The better caste of women appear here with heads uncovered, a long cloth of single breadth wrapped around the loins and falling to the ankles, and a portion thrown over the left shoulder. They wear silver, crystal, and brass bangles or bracelets, and flat ear-rings about the size of a quarter dollar, and the thickness of a child's tin whistle; the holes of the ears are cut and distended by weights while young, to receive their flat rings; they also wear gold clasps in the top of the ear, which gives them a strange appearance, particularly with the addition of rings in the nose and on the toes. Umbrellas and dried branches of the tallipot tree are much in use to prevent the action of the sun's rays. This is the residence of Governor Anderson, whose houses and grounds are quite pretty. There are some fifty foreigners, inclusive of ladies, as civilians, in addition to a regiment of troops, partly Europeans and partly Malays.

From Singapore we passed up the Straits of Malacca to Penang, on Prince of Wales Island, where we coaled and remained one day, which gave an opportunity for a ride to see the town, and then proceeded to Ceylon, making the distance of some fourteen hundred miles within eight days to Point de Galle, where I left the steamer on my way north to Calcutta, while she proceeded to Suez.

# LXVI.

KANDY, ISLAND OF CEYLON, *Sept. 20, 1851.*

I am surprised to find such remains of civilization among a people who once had a dense population, and were somewhat advanced in the arts, as their relics testify, but who had fallen to the darkest period of the middle ages. The palace of the king, the hall of audience, with its elaborately-carved wooden columns, the hexagonal tower two stories high, and the chief Boodhist temple of the island, formerly under royal patronage, present a front of some six hundred feet of ground, with a wall and moat with drawbridge, supplied with water from a beautiful artificial lake, with a long line of parapet with triangular centres whereon to place lamps during the illuminations, and when the king addressed the people from the balcony overhanging the canal, and witnessed the religious processions with elephants which are annually continued.

These buildings are now all occupied for government purposes, except the temple of Boodh. On its archways and walls are sculptured hideous figures of dragons, and images of gods and devils; the paintings are rude, and bear a mixed resemblance to those of China and Egypt. The present powder-house is in a small building in the centre of the lake, which was a great resort for the king, while the harem-building on its banks is the hospital for sick soldiers.

We have just had a festival day, and I have occupied some time among the Boodhists. Their daily hours of worship are from six to eight in the morning, and the same time in the evening, and on this occasion the noise of the silver tom-toms, or kettle-drums, and the harsh sound of as many instruments resembling the Scotch bagpipe, with their discordant sounds, were almost deafening. One of the sanctums of the temple, which is ascended by a small flight of steps, has two immense pairs of elephant tusks, also the carved and painted figures of devils, to guard the entrance, and the room is about twelve feet square, hung with gold brocade, somewhat rusty. Upon a raised platform, inclosed by railings, and hourly unlocked, is seen a figure not unlike a huge bell, thirty-four and a half feet high, and nine and a half feet in circumference. It is in three pieces, which are joined, and which contain within each other seven smaller caskets; the smallest is supposed by the people to contain the tooth of their god Boodh.

The outer casket, or figure, is ornamented with rich gold chains and gems; the most remarkable is the figure of a gold bird, suspended by massive chains, beset with diamonds, rubies, sapphires, and emeralds. This is considered by the natives the most valuable acquisition in the world. Another of the sanctums contains the figures of gods, of gold and silver gilt, and of colossal size; the entrance is guarded by lions, the altars are covered by sweet smelling sacred flowers, which the devotees of all classes and sexes make as offerings before prostrating themselves and retiring in succession, and which the priests, with shaved heads, in yellow robes, receive. The people came loaded from the country with supplies suspended at the two ends of poles, borne upon the naked shoulder—the usual manner of carrying burdens; and at twelve (noon), the priests partook of a repast. It reminded me of a vegetable and fruit market, with heaps of rice, cocoas, pineapples, and prepared betel, to the use of which the priests are addicted, besides a variety of presents. As I stood alone among these half-clad heathen, who stared at me with surprise, I accosted a boy whose dress indicated Christian discipline, and who, speaking English, was able to give me much information, having been educated by a Protestant missionary.

I saw one marriage party in the country, a few days since; they marry young, and ordinarily in the presence of a witness, and according to caste; where they are of any rank, the parents arrange the matter. The girl in this instance carried presents to the house of the groom, when both parties sat around a pail of paddy and ate with their hands, exchanging balls of rice and cocoa-nut milk, with presents of clothes and jewels. The order of things is reversed here, for it is quite common for women to have two husbands, who seem to live happily together; they think it polite to do so, besides being less expensive; while in the event of the death of either husband, the family is provided for. Boodh came from the east, consequently in life they lie in that direction, but in death they turn the body; the higher castes here burn the corpse, the lower bury it in shallow graves. The funeral pile of the former is a layer of cocoa-nut shells, a layer of husks of the same, then a layer of wood; the nearest relative fires the heap in presence of a priest, and then returns home. Strips of young cocoa-nut stalks split are put up to mark the locality, which is visited after seven days; stones are erected to mark the spot, and a devil called "Sohou-Yaka" is appointed to the care of the burial grounds; at night, the natives will not approach these places, fearing malignant influences. The Boodhists have a great variety of devils, and have the greatest fear of evil spirits, some of which preside over the cocoa-nut, toddy and other trees. The favorite devil of the Kandians is called Gaveleyaka. He takes care of the children, cattle, and grounds, and the people feed him well with rice and curry, to keep him in good temper, otherwise he gets vexed, and they are attacked by the misfortunes against which they strive to propitiate him.

The other morning, at an early hour, in the country, I heard music, and saw lights beaming in the wood. It was, I found, a devil-dance. Some one having fallen sick, it was attributed to witchcraft, and a devil-priest was called to cure him. They had made a house of bushes and put the sick man in it, and had commenced dancing at eight o'clock at night, and the priest was just concluding, and performing a charm of some sort. Taking the leaves of a certain tree, they make up several dishes, and put rice on top with a lighted match, that the surrounding devils may inhale the odor; the priest then says another charm, and commands all other devils to "vamose." He then says they have "put out," and they throw everything in the bushes and leave them there, and he gets well paid for his trouble.

This is a remarkable country for elephants; the government employs them for heavy work on the roads; the immense carts and wagons are drawn by them, and the rollers for flattening the earth are made in proportion to their strength. I visited the stables and saw them on the road, but none have crossed my track, though they are still very numerous in the jungle, and sometimes very destructive to the plantations. I was informed that eleven were taken from this region and shipped to New York not long since, and presuming that you are familiar with the manner in which they were caught, I will not attempt a description. We are subject here to a land leech, which during wet weather is very troublesome, and makes leggings necessary for protection in the grass and woods. A gentleman travelling in our company found the blood flowing freely, not having provided himself with leggings; the natives have remedies against the bite. Ceylon is famous for the variety of rare and precious stones found in Galle and Colombo, which are a source of considerable traffic with vendors. The pearl fishery of the coast was formerly very productive, but of late years it is of little value; the cause is supposed to be over-fishing the original stock of oysters when nearly exhausted.

# LXVII.

CALCUTTA, INDIA, *Oct. 8, 1851.*

I left Ceylon by the steamer Hindostan, on her way from Suez, with the overland mail, having about forty passengers, mostly from England. I now find myself in the so-styled city of palaces, upon the banks of the Hoogley, one of the many branches of the Ganges, and about one hundred and forty miles from the Sand Heads of hazardous navigation, while the jungle, on its lower banks, is haunted with the famous Bengal tiger, a terror to the shipwrecked mariner. Strong indications of a heavier storm than we had already encountered, two days below the entrance, induced our captain to turn back and run south, which was most unusual and unwarrantable, with a well-found steamer of fourteen hundred tons burden, and caused a delay of thirty-six hours, proving an error of judgment.

This city, the capital of the Bengal Presidency, is said to contain from five to six hundred thousand inhabitants, the foreign population not exceeding one thousand, besides the troops. The public buildings of the East India Company, inclusive of the Governor's palace, and private residences of the employees of government, are well constructed, and discover a good deal of taste in their erection and site. The course or esplanade, and general drives along the river banks to Garden Reach (the out of town residences), are extensive and beautiful, and display more luxurious vehicles, and finer horses with outriders, and bearers in costume, than can be found for the same population anywhere in the world. The evening six o'clock drive before dinner being the greatest means of enjoyment in this hot climate, every sacrifice is made on the part of all classes to sport their equipages. I arrived here just after the commencement of the annual Hindoo festival called the *Doorgah Poojah*, during which all business is suspended. The heat is most oppressive, and no white man of any means is seen walking in the streets during the day, but palanquins are in general use. They are not unlike small houses with sliding doors on each side; they contain a mattress to lie upon, covered with matting, and sofa pillows of light material upon which to recline the head, and are supported on the shoulders of four Hindoo bearers, whose black shining skins, reeking with perspiration, denote the fatigue they endure. It is astonishing how fast they get over the surface; they are to be found in all public places and anxious for employment. It is a luxurious mode of travel, and long journeys are performed by Dawk, so called, with relays of men, but to me it is a painful mode of conveyance, and scarcely fast enough for an American. The Punkah here is indispensable; in the large hotel where I am staying, and which equals in size some of our large New York hotels, all the rooms are furnished with them, suspended from the ceiling, and necessity obliges each occupant to employ a punkah driver, who by means of his cord and pulley in the passage, keeps up a constant circulation of air. The great diversity of caste among the Hindoos, makes it necessary that housekeepers should employ a multitude of servants. The punkah driver being inferior, cannot be employed as bearer or body-servant, and he in turn will not wait at table. They must be employed as grooms, coachmen, footmen, cooks, water-carriers, washerwomen, and an infinite number of occupations. In dining with an official in the East India Company's service, of large appointment, who had been a fellow passenger, and who had a large retinue of servants, he informed me that he required fifty for his establishment. Their wages are low and they furnish their own supplies, which are mostly rice and curry, as they disdain the food of the Christians. The Mussulmans, of which I have one, are not so tenacious, and turn their attention to different kinds of work. The expenses of life here are enormous, exceeding those of all other oriental cities. They grow out of the luxurious extravagance of the East India Company's servants, through its extensive patronage, and the officers of the Queen's troops, who not only exhaust their liberal salaries but are heavily in debt.

The native portion of the city, which extends for miles, exhibits a striking contrast to the palaces of the European quarter. The bazaars are worthy of being seen, but having visited those of Constantinople and Grand Cairo, they were no novelty to me. The other evening I attended the "nautches," a species of ball or entertainment given by the native princes some three miles distant from the hotel; driving my buggy through immense masses of the populace, with the continual cries of my servant and footman to clear the track, I made my way slowly, coming in contact with a variety of vehicles in the darkness and confusion. At last I emerged from this chaos of equipages, and managed to get up to the extreme end of the lane to the Sohha Bazaar, where my vision was dazzled with the immense number of torches. The illuminations of the princes were intended to out-rival each other, and were got up with a good deal of fanciful display in oriental style. On pressing among the crowd through the spacious arena of the building amid the display of tinsel and torchlight, I found a large assembly of mixed nations and great variety of costume. The interior was covered with matting and chairs, with divans around the wall for the multitude. The Rajah was very polite, offering his divan with refreshments, and ordered the "nautch" or dancing girls before us to perform their different evolutions, which delight the natives, but to a European are anything but chaste or graceful. They were loaded with ornaments in their ears and noses, and on their necks, arms, wrists, and ankles; their voices were put upon a nasal half key, which enabled them to keep it up much longer.

The Hindoos burn their dead, but the funeral pile is not desecrated as formerly with widows of deceased husbands. In the upper part of the city is found a hollow square on the river bank, enclosed by three high walls, the water-side being open; a large gateway receives the remains of all Hindoos whose friends can afford to furnish the wood for burning. I saw them congregated thither and throwing, according to custom, small broken sticks upon the burning bodies. It was a revolting and disgusting sight to witness the burning bodies, particularly when fuel enough is not provided for their destruction, in which cases they are devoured by hundreds of carrion birds, like the adjutant and vulture. Very many are thrown into the river, and not unfrequently you meet them in passing up and down, though that method of disposing of them is contrary to law. We have just had the great annual Tumasha, and the worship paid to the goddess Kallee, by immersion. I suppose there must have been one hundred shrines mounted on platforms and supported on men's shoulders, representing the goddess in tinsel of gold and silver, surrounded by artificial flowers, with her six arms, and a variety of other figures upon the pedestal. The procession of votaries to consign this inanimate but adored goddess to the holy waters of the Ganges, consisted of thousands of men, women, and children, with bands of music; the tops of houses, terraces, and balconies were filled with human beings. The different priests of the goddess came from different parts of the city, and congregated at the strand, where this rash tide of humanity despatched their deity on her cloudy voyage in the muddy waters of the sacred stream.

The drive up the river to Barrackpore, some fourteen miles, over a perfectly level road, with rows of trees almost the entire length, is beautiful, and a great relief from a heated city. It is a military station, and the country residence of the governor, besides being the finest park in India; there is also found there a large collection of wild animals, among which the giraffe, the tiger, and ostrich are seen in perfection. Ten miles higher up, the French have a small possession called Chandernagore, which they have retained during all the conquests and battles of Europe. It is antiquated, but prettily situated, a small town without back country; their whole force consists of twenty Sepoy soldiers, but the tricolor is floating from the government house. It is a favorite asylum for unfortunate debtors and persons of small means, and is a nuisance in the eyes of the English, but the rights of France and treaties must be respected. The Danes had a settlement near by, which the English bought, but "*la grande nation*" declined selling.

The Hindoos have a great fancy for painting their faces, with a streak down the nose and across the forehead, as well as lines on the cheeks, and bars of a yellow color made from powdered sandal-wood, which looks like gold upon a black ground. The eyes and nails of many are dyed with henna; a part of the foot is also dyed red. A great variety of character is to be found in the bazaars, not forgetting the beggars with daubed faces, and hair filled with ashes; they are not in such favor as the fat Brahmin bulls of the priests, which walk along and eat where they please, until the poor benighted Hindoo raises his hands together to his head, and cries, "Now, good bull, pray go eat at some other shop." The Chinese population are at full liberty to enjoy their opium, to which they are so much addicted, and it is curious to see the effect produced upon them by the use of the drug. You will find some fifteen at a time lying upon couches, inhaling the fumes, which seem to put them in a happy state, after which they gradually recover. The opium leaves its bad effects in prostration of the system, and the habitual smoker may readily be known from the expression of the face and eyes. The manufacture and sale of the article, which is a monopoly of the East India Company, is its greatest source of revenue.

# LXVIII.

Steamer Pekin, for Bombay, *Oct. 20, 1851.*

From Calcutta I came down to Madras, the capital of the Presidency of the same name, by the steamer Haddington, on her way to Suez. It lies some six hundred miles south of Calcutta, and is a city of considerable trade, notwithstanding its bad roadstead, where the surf is most formidable. We landed in a masoolah boat, of great depth of hold, entirely open, built of elastic wood, the joints stuffed with oakum and sewed together, without a nail in the construction, which enables them to spring and give when they strike bottom. These boats are worked by twelve boatmen, who keep up a singular chant or howl as they pass through the almost irresistible surf.

I found here a means of floating, which surpasses the Ceylon or Sandwich Island boats, being more primitive; they are called catamarans, and the natives manage them in the most skilful manner. Imagine to yourself a small raft eight feet in length, of three logs tied together and pointed at one end, which they go out upon, and which, when they return, is untied, and dried upon the shore. One or two men are seen upon these slight supports in the heaviest surfs, like black imps sitting crouched upon their heels and making good use of their paddles. Sometimes they are thrown off and hidden in the waves, but like magic they catch on again. One of the great objects of attraction for strangers is the civil and military service club, about three miles from town, and prettily situated with all the comforts and luxuries of the east. The hotels of the city are miserable.

There is but little to interest the traveller at Madras, which is on a flat sandy plain, with reddish-colored soil. Black Town, the native part, is poorly built, and the people are a cringing, menial, lazy set, kept under great subjugation and treated as brutes by the existing powers. The climate is better than that of Calcutta, on account of the sea breeze, and the drives along the sea beach, which in the suburbs make the place supportable. The jugglers and mountebanks of this country are celebrated, and perform some remarkable feats. We were infested with them in the street in front of our hotel, performing somersets, springing through hoops, and passing over swords, &c., without the aid of spring boards upon the solid earth. Next come the snake charmers, who bring their snakes in baskets, which are placed upon the ground; they then play a sort of bagpipe, after which they blow at the snakes and play again, when they open the basket and a large cobra-de-capello rises up with a peculiar hood spread back of the head, his long neck arched like a horse's; he attempts to strike, but the charmers know their distance. We had half a dozen snakes dancing at the same time, around their masters, while another group was waiting to swallow swords and stones. In landing or going out, self-defence compels one to jump into a buggy or palanquin, as these poor people are very persevering, being better paid by Griffins, or foreigners, than by residents.

The Sepoys, or native troops, appear well on parade early in the morning; they are completely dressed in white drill, and the officers in red coats and white pantaloons. The Madras Presidency has some forty-two thousand Sepoys and eight thousand European troops, which serves to keep all the population quiet between the Bengal and Bombay Presidencies.

Our steamer is slow, making only eight knots an hour at the top of her speed. She has just been caught by a typhoon in the China sea, which has swept away decks, yards, and spars, with a loss of five out of her six boats, and will have to go into dock at Bombay. Since leaving the bay of Bengal, and the last of the south-west monsoons, we have had quiet and beautiful weather, running up the Malabar coast of the Arabian sea. I will finish this letter in Bombay.

# LXIX.

BOMBAY, *Nov. 7, 1851.*

It was my good fortune to arrive here the first evening of the new year, and the commencement of the Hindu festival Tumashee, in which the Parsees unite in a general illumination of the bazaars and private residences, with shade lamps of variegated glasses, and a large display of Chinese and other paintings, the shops being open and occupied by the people of all races, Mahrattas, Parsees, and Hindoos of every caste, but no Moormans, or Mussulmans, the latter having had a religious contest with the Parsees, in which several houses were destroyed and pillaged. The Mussulmans being followers of Mahomet, have a strong aversion to the Parsees, or fire worshippers, as well as the Hindoos, or worshippers of idols. About five thousand of the former had collected at the mosques, and threatened to exterminate the Parsees, causing great anxiety. The Governor ordered out a large special constabulary police, and the troops were in readiness at given signals; the corners of streets and public places were placarded with orders in different languages to close all spirit and opium shops, and restrictions against carrying or selling arms. The great variety of picturesque costumes during this festival exceeded those of any city I had yet found. The display of bandys, drawn by oxen with ribbons of silver and gold-gilt, and filled with women and children, literally loaded with bracelets, nose and ear-rings, amulets, &c., in which the wealth of many consists, surpassed what I had seen at Calcutta. Among my introductory letters I had one to a Parsee house, from which I received much civility, and which gave me an opportunity of informing myself about this peculiar people, who are called fire-worshippers, and of whom so little is known. It is a small sect in comparison with others, and its members are a commercial and trading people; many live in good style, and drive fine equipages, and one of their number was knighted by the Queen for his many noble acts. The bequests of Sir Jamtsejee Jejeebhoy to many charitable institutions rank him as one of the most benevolent individuals of the age. The Parsees are the followers of Zoroaster, who lived about 389 B.C., and who was their lawgiver; his doctrine teaches them to believe in one God. They worship no other Being or symbol like him, and believe in a future state of existence.

They say they take the sun, moon, and fire as emblems of purity, and as the most powerful and obvious evidence of the supreme government, and in performing their five prayers daily they face any of these mighty elements. They are the descendants of the ancient rulers of Persia, from which country they were driven away in the seventh century, being unwilling to embrace Islamism, when eleven thousand were compelled to become Mahometans within twenty-four hours, under the penalty of death. The refugees were received by a lenient Hindoo prince, who gave them shelter and protection provided they would agree to certain stipulations. First, To throw away firearms. Second, To lay aside the original costume and adopt the peculiar one which they now wear. Third, not to kill or eat a cow, that animal being one of the favorite idols of the Hindoos. Pressed by necessity, they adopted these and other restrictions, and offered a solemn pledge, to which they still adhere. They wear a white garment and girdle around the waist, composed of seventy threads, about as large as a lady's stay-lace. These are worn as insignia of religion. Children after seven years old wear it, and parents are morally responsible for them till they are ten years of age. If they die before ten, they are considered innocent, and are supposed to go to heaven. They feed and clothe their poor in a liberal manner. They drink wine and eat animal food, with the exception of beef, veal, and pork; have one wife, and are betrothed in infancy; the males marry at fourteen, and the females at twelve, and the marriage festival and procession costs some thousands where it can be afforded.

My Parsee friend will marry his son of fifteen to his bride of twelve in a few months. They cannot eat with us or drink out of the same vessel that we do. I accept civilities among the Parsees, but we eat at separate tables, and I have noticed among the most devoted a prayer murmured over me, and a glance of kindness. The Hindoos cannot assign any reason why the body should be burned, the Mahometan why it should be interred, nor the Parsee why it should be placed in a circular, high-walled, amphitheatrical cemetery, where the bodies of men, women, and children are placed in separate exposures for decay, and destruction by birds of prey; and they deny the assertion made by their enemies that the condition of future existence is denoted by the part of the body first attacked by the birds. I saw one public and one private cemetery of the kind on high hills; no one was permitted to enter. The position of Bombay, in Lat. 18° north, at nearly the head of the Indian Ocean, with a good harbor and sea-breezes, with its suburbs and fine dwellings, and forests of cocoa and date trees along good drives, makes it more agreeable and less hot than Calcutta. Within the inclosure of the old fortified town stands the arsenal, mint, cathedral, and other public edifices. I attended the cathedral last Sunday, but found few worshippers, although every appliance for comfort and ease. I counted fourteen long punkahs suspended from the ceiling, and as many men employed outside pulling the cords. Open rail pews, bamboo seats with arms, marble pavement, and a free circulation of air, but poor preaching and bad delivery, had driven the congregation away. The dock-yard here is the finest in the East, and is resorted to by all vessels for repairs; I noticed in it a frigate of the Imaum of Muscat, built of teak thirty years old. The mint for coining—the chief coins are rupees, nearly the size of half-dollars—is admirably well arranged, and would do credit to any country. They had nine presses at work, and were turning off one hundred and fifty thousand daily, out of the sycee silver, which comes from China, in payment for opium.

Having visited the hospital and benevolent institutions, to see what was doing for humanity in this part of the world, I was induced to visit the most extraordinary institution I had ever heard of: a hospital for diseased animals, established by the Parsees. I found there not only hundreds of horses, oxen, buffaloes, goats, and other cattle, but dogs and cats, which are never killed, but are allowed to enter the hospital gratis, and are kept until they recover or die. The great curiosity is the caves of elephants, on an island opposite Bombay. Taking supplies, we started early, in a covered boat; the tide being down, we were carried a long distance on men's shoulders, to the shore, and around the mountain side through the trees to the bungalow of the Sepoy guard, and then entered the cave to see the Hindoo idols. The entrance is fifty-three feet wide, the height of the ceiling eighteen feet, and the depth one hundred and forty-three feet; it is nearly as wide as deep, and is supported by massive pillars, carved out of solid dark trap rock.

In the recess in the rear is seen a gigantic tri-formed god. Brahma is in the middle as creator, with placid face and jewelled cap. Vishnu, the presiding deity, is represented with a beautiful face, and with the sacred lotus flower in his hand. Siva, who fills up the other side of the tri-formed gods, holds a cobra serpent; he frowns, being the destroyer. From the chin to the crown of the head is six feet, the caps are three feet more. There are steps behind the bust where a Brahmin might have hidden for priestly imposition. The courts of death are at the right and left, as are also pilasters and figures fourteen feet high. There are various chambers and large colossal figures of divinities within the cave, which to me were interesting, being of a different style of sculpture from either the Egyptian or Chinese idols, and were once very beautiful, though they have been much defaced by the Portuguese in the early possession of the country. A few miles from town, on Malabar Point, is the place of pilgrimage for the Hindoos. It is a village with a community of some five hundred persons or more, subsisting upon charity. It is situated upon the side hill, inclosed by walls, and descending towards the ocean, with a water-tank, or large reservoir, some hundred feet long and square, and about twenty ghauts or stone platforms, to descend, and is surrounded with houses and temples. The front verandas are filled with bells of all sizes, and the idols of various deities. The half-naked priests, with painted faces and long hair and beards, were sitting in groups, quarrelling for the division of the spoils.

I had a good opportunity of seeing the mode of worship here, notwithstanding that the jealousy of the people allowed me to go no further than the threshold. One family came covered with jewelry, and had their own priest. Vessels filled with water were suspended over the stone of fertility, which constantly drips upon the flowers placed upon it; and the devotees touched each other's hands, and went through various acts of devotion before the idols of the five different gods, while offerings were made.

# LXX.

ALEXANDRIA, EGYPT, *Nov. 24, 1851.*

I have felt more like writing you since I left Bombay, where I confidently expected advices from friends, which I have been deprived of for some months; and having heard indirectly, without particulars, of the death of a beloved sister, I was anxious to arrive at this place, where I am put in possession of that which is so highly valued by the traveller—letters from home. From Bombay I embarked with the Achilles down the Indian Ocean to Aden, some one thousand six hundred and forty miles, situated near the entrance of the Straits of Babelmandel, and recognised in her an old acquaintance, having made a passage by her from Glasgow to Liverpool, some years since.

Aden is the coal depot of the Peninsular and Oriental Company's line of steamers, and here we were obliged to wait during three days for the arrival of the steamer Erin, which replaced the Precursor, that had been caught in a violent hurricane and disabled, at the mouth of the river, below Calcutta. The Erin is the steamer that sunk the Pasha, by collision off the coast of Malabar, some time ago. I feel thankful in having escaped typhoons, hurricanes, and accidents, of which many have occurred while I have been in the East, and hope to be favored for the future in my peregrinations, until I once more return to my friends and native land. Aden is a strongly fortified place, called the "Gibraltar of the East." It was constructed by the East India Company, in order to resist the encroachments of the Arabs, and is situated in a desert country, without a sign of vegetation, a portion of it being in an extinct volcano. It is one of the most disagreeable spots in the world for a long sojourn, with no attractions aside from the camp, and all necessaries come from abroad when the Arabs do not choose to supply them. The heat at times has been almost insupportable; the Red Sea is considered the Tophet of the East by travellers. Not unfrequently in summer, passengers become perfectly exhausted, and some sudden deaths occur. The shores in general are barren and arid, with high volcanic mountains at intervals, with exceptions, of course, as we sighted Mocha, which is forty miles above the entrance of the Straits, and is celebrated for its choice coffee. We passed the usual landing-place for Mahometans proceeding to Mecca. We had about forty passengers from Bombay, and northern India, mostly officers on leave, or retired pensioners; among the number were several ladies, and twelve children, going home to be educated, so we were not at a loss for juvenile music. We made the passage up the Red Sea in five days and a half, and found, as we advanced towards Suez, that the weather became cooler.

Mount Sinai and the localities designated as the spots where Moses and the Israelitish army crossed, were pointed out and commented upon. As we approached Suez the sea narrows, and a place some thirty miles below, where the water is thirty fathoms, or one hundred and eighty feet in depth, is said by the Arabs to be that where Moses crossed. It is twenty miles wide, and the rise and fall of tide is very small; so that the most sceptical must allow the crossing to be quite as miraculous as the sustaining of vast bodies of people in these arid plains and mountains for a long sojourn. The arrangements are now very perfect in crossing the isthmus, and it scarcely merits the name of desert in comparison with the fifteen days' journey across the Arabian sands to Palestine, during my former travels in the East.

The Pasha deserves great credit for his transit accommodations. At Suez, a dirty village upon a sandy plain, is a large stone hotel, and in approaching the town a small steamer meets and conducts you to the wharf, where camels in large numbers are ready to convey luggage and cargo across to Cairo, a distance of eighty-five miles. They are started off, and passing us, we are sent in vans with two high wheels, and a double shaft for two horses or mules, with a pair of leaders. These vans contain six persons and their luggages, and are changed every five miles. There are four places for supplies on the desert, where most articles can be obtained desirable for comfort, including couches to repose upon during the halt. I found them so much improved since I was last in Egypt, that I was agreeably disappointed. The road is beaten by constant travel, except that there is heavy sand in some places. The greatest objections are the rays of the sun, and the fiery sand, which affect the eyes; but it is of short continuance, as we cross in sixteen hours. The supply of water, and, indeed, every trifling article, must be carried on the backs of camels. The transit across the isthmus and down the Nile from Grand Cairo to the canal at Atfeh to Alexandria, is in the Pasha's name; and arrangements are being made for the construction of a railway between the first and last named cities.

At Grand Cairo I found that great changes had taken place since I last visited it, not only in the hotels, but in the general appearance of the city. The most beautiful edifice, or monument, is the new alabaster mosque, with its nobly gilded domes and interior decorations, its lofty minaret towering above the citadel, and inclosing a catafalque in one corner, with the remains of Mehemet Ali, who had massacred the Mamelukes at a spot hard by, one only escaping by a fearful leap, killing his horse under him. I once described to you my visit to, and reception by, this extraordinary man, whose remains I am now gazing upon, while a thousand reflections cross my mind. Turning my eyes from the spot, there stood in the distance the almost imperishable pyramids, and the Nile, flowing without change, bathing the land of Goshen as in days gone by. The bazaars were filled as usual with an immense multitude of men, veiled women, and children, and donkeys, and camels. The streets being very narrow, our carriage was preceded by a runner, cracking his heavy whip to clear the passages. I find small, but not uncomfortable steamers now coming from Cairo to Atfeh, the termination of the Mahmoud canal, making with the current some twelve miles per hour; also barges for passengers, towed by small steamers on the canal, with very fair living accommodations. Alexandria has become more like a European city; the suburbs near the banks of the canal are occupied with the residences of foreigners, and the vicinity of the Obelisk, or Cleopatra's needle, and Pompey's pillar, looks less deserted than formerly.

# LXXI.

STEAMER SEVERN, ISLAND OF TENERIFFE, *Dec. 22, 1851.*

From Alexandria, Egypt, I embarked on board of the steamer for Malta, with the privilege of continuing to Gibraltar or Lisbon, to await the arrival of the steamer from England, on her way to South America. The weather was heavy and boisterous for the first two days, which caused some delay, and required four and a half days to make the passage of eight hundred miles to Malta.

Our leisure time was passed in rowing about the harbor, viewing the English fleet; and I amused myself in the Lazaretto in visiting my old quarters where I was confined in quarantine twenty-one days, coming from Egypt during the prevalence of the plague. The fortifications are very strong, and the island is an agreeable place for sojourn in the winter; the rides to the bay where St. Paul was shipwrecked and landed, and where a chapel is erected on the spot; the so called Grotto of Calypso; the Church of the Knights of St. John; the ancient catacombs; and the general drives and views, make it well worth tarrying at; but having been all over the ground, there was no incentive to remain, so we proceeded to Gibraltar, one thousand miles further, with beautifully fine weather, coasting along the bay of Tunis, with Sicily and Algiers in view, and then branched off to the opposite coast of Spain, passing close to the bay of Malaga, with white-capped mountains in the distance, and the famous quicksilver mines of Adva at their base, until we approached the frowning rock of Gibraltar.

Those of our passengers who had never passed along the Mediterranean, enjoyed all the sights and various changing views; I, however, could not feel the same interest, except in the way of reminiscences of past scenes. Gibraltar, as you are aware, is considered invulnerable; its strength surpasses any fortification in the world, and as long as Great Britain retains her present ascendency, it would be useless to attempt its capture, as starvation of the garrison would be the only successful artifice. We were informed here that the French had just bombarded Tangier, on the opposite coast of Morocco, and knocked down the town about the ears of the Moors. On the opposite side of the straits is Ceuta, a strongly garrisoned fortress belonging to the Spaniards; the straits here are seventy-two miles wide. The current was setting into them at the rate of two miles per hour, and always running in the same direction. The nearest point to the African coast is St. Cruzes, towards Tarifa Light, on the European side; it is seven miles wide.

Gibraltar is considerably improved, many new buildings having been erected, but its contraband trade with the south of Spain is now much reduced, and the people complain of hard times. Trafalgar Bay, famous for the victory and death of Lord Nelson, lies only a short distance north. I don't recollect, while travelling in the beautiful country of Malaga, Grenada, Seville, and Cadiz, to have said anything of Portugal, to which my travels were also extended, at that time, but at the risk of repetition I must remark that Lisbon is prettily situated on the Douro, about twelve miles from its mouth, and were it not for the dark aspect of the city, the effect of climate upon the sandstone, it would show to great advantage, situated as it is upon an undulating surface, with portions of its pinnacles looking like a tower of stairs. It is much cleaner than formerly, filthy streets then being its chief characteristic. The trade of Portugal has declined, and the government and people have become more and more impoverished. They have had no rain since last May, and the country is suffering. Processions were being held from the churches to invoke the Virgin for refreshing and copious supplies of the vivifying element. One of the most extraordinary mosaic pictures of large size is the Annunciation of the angel to the Virgin Mary; it is here in one of the churches, and is said to have cost a million of dollars. The stone aqueduct which rests upon several ties of arches, and supplies the city with water, is considered a stupendous work; it is much shattered by a former earthquake. The promenades and gardens are tolerable, as are also the quays and public squares, but the port seems deserted by merchant vessels. A part of the English fleet lay in the river, and among the number was one which, although small in comparison with the other craft, had given evidence of her sailing qualities to the world, and all eyes were directed to her. It was the little, low, raking-masted yacht, America.

I found myself once again on board the ship Severn, having made a passage with her in the West Indies, under the same commander, three years since. We had a mixed company of passengers, consisting of duchesses, countesses, not forgetting Lady Wortley, who visited the United States some time since, military and civil officers, South American Spaniards, Portuguese Brazilians, Frenchmen, Germans, and English, some twenty of whom we left at Madeira for the benefit of their health; the rest will continue to Teneriffe, Cape de Verde, Pernambuco, Bahia, Rio Janeiro, &c., where we land and take supplies of coal. The rigid formality of strict English society is confounded with the life and liberty of the different races thrown together, and five languages are continually heard at table.

Madeira is a pretty and picturesque island. Its vineyards, which are its only resource, have acquired for it a lasting name; its climate is renowned, and is much resorted to, particularly by English invalids, the number of whom amounts ordinarily to about three hundred, who are a source of great profit to the poor people, subjected to Portuguese rule. The harbor of Funchal is an open roadstead, and as there was a heavy rolling sea the night before our arrival, the landing was bad, especially for ladies, but once ashore, horses and palanquins were at command. The latter are so unlike the conveyances that bear the same name in the East Indies, that I must describe them. They are in the form of colossal shoes with the front part cut or pared down one-half, the heel being a support for the back, as you sit upon cushions with head erect; they are supported by rods attached to the pole, each end of which rests on the shoulders of a man, and in that way you are carried up and down hill, having a sort of top to protect you from the sun's rays.

Madeira lies two days south from Lisbon, and Teneriffe one day and a half from Madeira. There are nine islands in the group; the people are generally poor. The chief town is Santa Cruz; it is pretty well built, and streets are clean; wine is its chief means of support. There are some fine views all through the islands; the peak of Teneriffe is the most remarkable, towering some twelve thousand feet high, and covered with snow.

# 1852.
# LXXII.

BAHIA, BRAZIL, *Jan. 2, 1852.*

From the island of Teneriffe, on the opposite side of the Atlantic, we proceeded south to the Cape Verde islands, and stopped one day to receive coal at St. Vincent, but had difficulty in getting a supply, as fever and starvation had destroyed one hundred and fifty out of the small population of six hundred, and laborers were procured from the island of St. Antonio, and fed and kept by the English consul, who is the agent of the Cape of Good Hope Steam Company. Several coal-vessels were waiting impatiently to be discharged. A small American whaler had lost her mate, and five of her crew, and the captain was not expected to survive. We were besieged for medicines, which we gave as liberally as we could, and also landed the contributions of flour, corn, &c., from Madeira. Our passengers were much alarmed, particularly the Brazilians, who imagined that they inhaled the pestilence with every breath, and brought forth large supplies of cologne and volatile salts. The purser, doctor, and myself were the only persons who landed, and we found the people dying from sheer exhaustion; many would not take the medicines which we offered them. Such squalid wretchedness I hope never to witness again. We had constant trade-winds from the N.E. for some days, with warm, delightful weather, and when we crossed the line, the sailors, not having forgotten the former visits of Neptune, amused themselves and the passengers, by dressing in couples, one on all fours under a sack, imitating a donkey, with long ears and false tail, mounted by a third, and beaten with sticks by the whole cavalcade.

The following day these jolly fellows listened with attention to the prayers and services of the Church of England, which were read by the officers. The first land we sighted towards the American coast, was the island of Fernando Norona, some three degrees south of the mouth of the river Amazon; we ran close under the rocky shore. It is used by the Brazilians for transportation of prisoners, and rarely visited. Whaling vessels sometimes touch, and for supplies of cattle and vegetables. The scenery of the island appeared enchanting. We arrived at Pernambuco, Lat. 8° south, sixteen hundred miles from Cape Verde, in advance of the usual time, which gave us a good opportunity of seeing the city, and riding several miles in the country. The view from the steamer, the natural reef of coral rocks, fifteen miles in length, forming the harbor; the town of Olinda on the hill to the north, with its white houses amid groves of green cocoa-nut trees, strike the beholder as exceedingly beautiful, and I found the town more cleanly than I expected, as the Brazilians, like their predecessors, the Portuguese, are renowned for filth. The city is prettily situated on three islands connected by bridges; it has some nine thousand population, one-third whites and two-thirds slaves; the buildings are high and well-constructed, but the interiors are poorly furnished; the narrow streets are offensive, but those of tolerable width are in better order. We found immense numbers of mules and horses, which come long distances from the interior, laden with cotton and sugar. The foreign population is small, some five hundred in all, French, English, and Germans; the latter predominate in the Brazils, as several colonies of them have been formed under the auspices of government. Of Americans there are only eight or ten; their numbers are usually small, but they are to be found at all commercial points of importance, and to them we are indebted for the great luxury of ice, which the people here had been deprived of for a long time; we could also obtain supplies of fruit.

We have some disaffection on board among passengers of different races and tastes, as to the supplies, and a committee was formed to wait upon the commander, who is a worthy and excellent person. But the system of the West India and South American Steam Co. which allows the captain equal to one dollar and eighty-seven and a half cents per day per head, wines, sodas, and other refreshments being ticketed, and settled for weekly, is found obnoxious by many passengers, who pay monopoly fares, and is entirely different from the liberality displayed by the Peninsula and Oriental Company, who, notwithstanding the mail contract and monopoly systems, are much more liberal in their provisions and accommodations. But with the increase of American steamers, their influence will be felt, not only in this respect, but more particularly in point of speed. The English mail contract throughout the East exacts only eight knots running time, and the West India and South America nine knots per hour, which is slow work for one accustomed to American steamers. Necessity is driving the English to a higher rate of speed, and the company is now constructing new and faster boats to run to Chagres, in order to prevent the tide of travel from setting to New York. We found two American whalers in quarantine at Pernambuco, which had touched at St. Vincent, and had some fever on board; we had obtained a clean bill of health, and having no sickness, we were permitted to pass. It was a great relief to get a drive of six miles, in the country where nature appears so beautiful even during the heat of this, their summer, with the thermometer at eighty-five, passing through groves of cocoas, palms, breadfruits, tamarinds, oranges, and other tropical trees, with melons and other fruits to satisfy thirst. We first learned here that war had been actually declared between Brazil and Buenos Ayres, and that the government had granted a loan and part of the fleet to blockade the port of the latter, while the Banda Oriental attack with the land forces. The son of Gen. Manzilla, and nephew of Rosas, the Dictator of the Argentine republic, is a fellow passenger; he promised to accompany me in the interior of Buenos Ayres, but the shock is rather astounding, and we can only learn the facts at Rio Janeiro.

The entrance to Bahia, or Bay of All Saints, is really beautiful; it lies four hundred miles south of Pernambuco, and the entrance is seven miles broad; its fine harbor is protected from all winds, and the rich country about it receives the waters of several small rivers. Americus Vespucius discovered it in 1503, under the patronage of the King of Portugal, and his carrying home a species of dye-wood, which, when cut, resembled coals of fire, gave Brazil its name, from Brazas, or coals. Bahia owes its foundation to the fact of the captain of a shipwrecked vessel in 1510 having his life spared by the Indians, after most of the crew were killed. The town is divided into two parts, the Praya, or Citada Baxa, under the hill, and Citada Alta, above, which appears quite antique. The descent is difficult, but by well paved roads and cadeiras or ornamented chairs supported by two negroes, which are in general use, it is quite practicable. The streets are clean, as Yellow Jack has improved the habits of the filthy Portuguese. New Year's day is kept here as holiday, and our passengers enjoyed themselves in visiting the public gardens and riding about the suburbs, while a party of sixteen dined together at the hotel on the summit of the hill, with a fine view of this magnificent bay, which in some respects recalls the harbor and site of Naples in miniature. The hedges are of lime trees; grapes are in season, bananas and melons abound; the seedless orange here is superior to that of any other part of the world. The public garden is situated on the boldest and most commanding height of the old town, one side looking upon the ocean, and the other upon the bay, with iron railings to prevent falling down the precipice.

The large Jaca tree which furnishes fruit larger than the cocoa, and affords fine shade, is found here. Formerly the privilege of the whale fishery was sold for a considerable sum, but at present it is reduced. The island of Itaporica, in the bay, has some oil establishments, and whales are occasionally killed; the flesh is much admired by the negroes, and is found in the market for sale. There are extensive plantations in the country, with two or three hundred slaves, and large quantities of sugar, cotton, and tobacco are produced. It is the Havana of Brazil for the manufacture of cigars. Large quantities of American flour are imported, but the food of the common people is farina made from the root of the mandioca. There is a fine race of negroes here, and they appear better dressed than I had expected to find them; but from what I can learn, their condition will not compare favorably with the negroes of our Southern States, whose enhanced value in the absence of the slave-trade induces kind treatment aside from motives of humanity.

# LXXIII.

Rio Janeiro, Brazil, *Jan. 13, 1852.*

From Bahia, I came down by steamer, a distance of seven hundred and twenty miles, under the most favorable circumstances, in three days, making the moderate average of ten miles per hour. The entrance or mouth of the harbor lies between two small islands, and is one mile wide and skirted on each side by immense masses of solid rock, six hundred feet high, if not higher; the hills are steep and fortified. The view of this splendid harbor is majestically grand, increasing in size to eight or ten miles, and in this gulf are many small islands distributed about and occupied by small villages: the sheet of water is fringed with green verdure, bright villas, and immense high craggy peaks of mountains, forming one of the most beautiful pictures. The city lies low in a valley, and appears from an elevated spot of a semicircular form; the streets run at right angles, with public squares without trees, but as the Brazilians and Portuguese idolize filth, don't expect much in the way of cleanliness. The hotels are vile for a city of three hundred thousand people, even if one-half are negroes; in this warm climate, with the thermometer in the month of January at 92°, you can well imagine the annoyance from vermin in badly conducted dens. I was obliged to fight a bloody battle the first night with the bugs, who disputed possession, and the following morning I abandoned my quarters for better ones. There is a considerable French population here, and one street is supplied with every variety of Parisian fancy goods, so much so that one for the moment would almost imagine himself in Paris; but he would soon be undeceived on demanding prices, and finding them double or treble what they are in France, the Brazilian duties being from eighty to one hundred per cent. on many articles, which offers a premium for smuggling. It is said the customs are here ten million dollars, but the Emperor receives four hundred thousand per annum, and has now a war on hand with Buenos Ayres, and a force of from thirty to forty thousand men to be kept up. As some one must pay for this, it falls upon the consumers, and for the benefit of those who expect to reside here, I will state that the expenses and luxuries of life, inclusive of carriage hire, exceed those of Calcutta or London. The country is rich and fertile; sugar, coffee, and hides enter largely in the exports. Our people know how to appreciate Rio coffee, particularly along the valley of the Mississippi, and we have become for our population the largest consumers of coffee in the world.

I have escaped the odoriferous smells of the narrow streets and the heat of the city for a few days, in visiting the new city and private summer residence of the Emperor Pedro II. called after him, Pedropolis, where he has founded a colony of Germans, in the valley of the mountains, two thousand four hundred feet above the level of the sea and about twenty-seven miles from

Rio, and where the temperature of the air is from 68° to 70° Fahrenheit, while in the city the thermometer ranges from 85° to 92°. We proceeded by a small steamer across the bay, winding among many little islands in a second bay, and thence up a small meandering river to the landing-place, where we took land-carriage to the base of the mountains, where our vehicle containing four persons was drawn by four mules, over a zigzag, well constructed road, with parapet walls and stone arches for the mountain torrents, built by government at heavy cost; the entire distance was accomplished in seven hours. The panorama of the bay and city in the distance from the crowning point is superb. There were some fourteen hundred families of Germans composing this colony, and they have employment upon the roads, in the erection of houses, and improvement of the town, which is well laid out, with streams of pure water passing through it. Many fine mansions have been erected by city gentlemen; the Emperor is building a palace of solid construction, which has already occupied four years, and cost two hundred thousand dollars, and will require two years more to complete it, as the work progresses slowly, and is a fat job for the builders. Many of the Germans have sold out their grants of town lots, and bought lands in the neighborhood, which they are cultivating, and I could almost imagine myself in parts of Switzerland, for the style of the dwellings, and the costume and figure of the German peasants carried me back to Faderland. As long as the Emperor spends money freely, all will work well, but if his patronage is withdrawn the place will decline, it being too expensive for the masses and too difficult of access.

I saw here a group of German girls in Bloomer costume, with a part of the palace band, who were playing from house to house. I met with an American on his way to the diamond mines, some five hundred miles in the interior—a persevering pioneer from old Kentucky, who had not been home in twenty-four years. He had married a Portuguese who had died, and he had his family with him, who had been educated in England, his second wife being an English lady. He had some two hundred hands engaged in his business—a profitable one, as Brazil exports some four million dollars' worth of diamonds annually. Droves of mules were constantly passing to the different mines of gold, diamonds, and other precious stones in the interior. I was shown some handsome specimens said to be worth two thousand dollars per ounce in the rough. The Emperor and Empress are seen almost daily in their promenades about the suburbs or through the town, with a small escort, and sometimes quite alone; the people speak well of their kindness and liberality. The Emperor is only twenty-four years of age, and his consort, the sister of the King of Naples, is his senior by three years, and not at all remarkable for beauty. I saw them at the opera last evening, in full costume; they appeared to advantage, it being the close of a gala day, the Emperor having received at his palace all military officers of distinction. He was clad in full military dress;

he is of good stature, with a well developed figure, a face of the Austrian or Russian type.

The frigate Congress is now in port, proceeding to Monte Video, and our Minister, Mr. Schenck, whose health is somewhat feeble, accompanies her. If the city of Rio Janeiro is remarkable for its filth, and the depravity and immorality of its inhabitants, it can boast of the beauty of its suburbs, which extend for many miles. La Gloria and Botafogo, and other villages situated upon the little indentations and bays, are very pretty, and nature is very prolific in her supply of fruits and flowers. One of the most beautiful drives is to the botanical garden, some six miles from town, the road winding along the beautiful bays, the shores lined with the villas of foreigners and wealthy residents, and the gardens filled with a great variety of fruit trees and flowers peculiar to the climate. I found in the botanical garden avenues of stately palms, not unlike the cafetals in the island of Cuba; a bamboo labyrinth, and an acre or more of the tea plant, as a reminiscence of China; a grove of cinnamon trees of large size, equal to those of the island of Ceylon; and in fact, all the productions of the tropics except the cocoa-nut, which I have lost sight of since leaving Bahia. The city is supplied with water from the mountains by aqueduct, and some three hundred tanks have lately been placed at the corners of the streets; but I drink river water of an underground culvert in the city. The offal is carried in vessels upon the heads of the negroes at night, and thrown upon the beach and in the harbor.

It is only surprising that the yellow fever does not always exist here; it is a blessing instead of a curse, if it only improves the cleanliness of the people. The currency of the country is government paper, from one milreis upwards. Of gold there is considerable, of the value of twelve dollars each piece; there is no small silver, but the quantity of copper in circulation is enormous. It is not as bad as in China, where twelve hundred small coins go to the dollar; but here, if a milreis, valued at sixty cents, is exchanged, you obtain a thousand reis; the smallest coin is valued at ten reis, making it necessary to ballast equally well your pockets; but fortunately, however, ferry boat and omnibus tickets go well, and remind one of our own shin-plaster days.

# LXXIV.

Monte Video, *Jan. 20, 1852.*

The continuation of the South American line of steamers is maintained by the Prince, of only four hundred tons burden, which takes the mails and passengers from Rio Janeiro to this place and Buenos Ayres, one hundred and twenty miles further up the river. It is always agreeable to meet with old acquaintances, and in this instance I was surprised to find that our captain had formerly been in command of a mail packet from St. Thomas to La Guayra, which had carried me down to Venezuela. Our passage, of something more than one thousand miles, was made in a little over four days.

Monte Video lies at the north of the Rio de la Plata, one of the largest rivers in South America after the Amazon; it was discovered in 1515 by Juan Diaz de Soles, who proceeded as far as 34° 23´ south latitude, but was killed, as were also his crew of four men. A few years later Sebastian Cabot, who went to discover the Straits of Magellan, and penetrated as high as the conflux of the Parana and Paraguay, some two hundred leagues, had a fight with the Indians, and succeeded in taking their treasures of silver from Peru; and supposing the supply inexhaustible gave the stream the name which it now bears, Silver River. It is over a hundred and fifty miles wide at the mouth, but at Buenos Ayres it is reduced to forty. The influence of this formidable river is seen by the water being colored more than four hundred miles at sea. The position of this port is desirable on account of its ready access and geographical position; it has a temperate climate, and moderately dry winds from the land to counteract the humidity of the sea air. It once had a population of seventy thousand, which has been reduced to twenty-five thousand by a nine years' siege, which was successfully resisted with the aid of the French, who have paid for some years annually forty thousand dollars per month to sustain the place against the besieging army of Oribe, at the head of the Buenos Ayrean forces of the Dictator Rosas. I found that the town had suffered severely, particularly in the deserted houses and crumbling walls; the pavements of the streets are badly broken up, and everything had the appearance of desolation; but the siege being raised last October, much life and activity have since been displayed in repairs, and the blockade has been removed from vessels proceeding to Buenos Ayres.

Oribe, the tool of Rosas, has now retired to his quinta, or farm-house, and is said to be poor. His army was headed by General Urquizas, in connexion with the allied forces of Brazil, and those of the provinces of Entre Rios and Uruguay, and they are now proceeding to "beard the lion in his den," having crossed the river Parana, on their way to Buenos Ayres by land, while the Brazilian fleet are occupying the river. The French have eleven vessels of war now in port, and in the town are quartered fifteen hundred troops, reminding one of a garrisoned town in France. Brazil has now taken upon herself the charges of the war, and relieved the French; she has a large number of German troops employed, and the Monte Videans feel sanguine that with an army of thirty thousand men on a good war footing, they will be able to overcome any force that the tyrant Rosas can produce, although his infantry and cavalry are estimated at from twenty-five to forty thousand, by far the greatest force ever brought together in South America.

The houses here have mostly azoteas, or flat roofs, which afford a fine promenade for the ladies, who have the advantage of seeing all that passes over the parapet. Notwithstanding they have suffered so severely, and have made such sacrifices, many families having been beggared, they support an opera which is well attended, and the fair sex looks as graceful and charming as in most Spanish towns.

I am now proceeding to Buenos Ayres, where I will finish this epistle.

# LXXV

BUENOS AYRES, *Feb. 1, 1852.*

My first impressions on approaching this city were highly favorable, the line of shore appearing fresh and verdant in comparison with Monte Video after its long and devastating siege. The city, built upon the banks of the river, some thirty feet high, with its forts, and public and private buildings and temples, as seen in approaching from the outer roadstead, looked quite imposing. The outer anchorage is five or six miles from the shore, and only vessels of a light draught of water can get to the inner anchorage, half a mile from town, where small boats carry you towards the shore, and you take large carts, drawn by a pair of mules, nearly up to their backs in water, from the many obstructions in the river. At the landing the son of General Mansilla and myself were met by the captain of the post and several other officers, dressed in the Rosas, or sanguinary costume, which every native is obliged to wear, viz. a red vest, a ribbon of the same color around the hat, and one at the button-hole, with the inscription, "*Viva la Confederacion! Mueren los salvages unitarios!*" (Long life to the Confederacion! Death to the savage Unitarians.) The offices of the Government, I noticed, were painted red, and everything indicated that I was in the country of a despot. The misnamed republic of Buenos Ayres extends along the Atlantic from the Rio Negro south to the Rio de la Plata, along the shores of its estuary to the southern bank of Parana, near to Santa Fè. Its soil is fertile, and affords the finest of pasturage for cattle. Millions of horned cattle and horses run upon the pampas, or plains, and its exports in hides, horns, jerked beef, and tallow, are immense. Its climate is most agreeable; we are now in midsummer, and the thermometer seldom goes higher than 85°; every variety of fruit found in warmer latitudes may be produced here; but the energies of the people are blunted from the excessive abuses of the tyrant Rosas, who has been for twenty years the governor, so styled, but really the modern Nero of the world. I had heard of his many acts of atrocity while at Montevideo and Rio, but was unprepared to believe the thousand charges alleged against him, until I learned from those who had passed through the reign of terror, and who are protected by their consuls, whereby they can express their minds, although not loudly, that half the wholesale butcheries which have occurred here for opinion's sake, cannot be portrayed. I came here with the intention of crossing over the pampas and the Cordillera mountains to the west coast at Valparaiso, which is about twenty days' travel on horseback; but I find that I cannot proceed ten leagues from the city without the strongest probability of being assassinated by stragglers or deserters from both camps; so I shall have to abandon my intention, and proceed to Rio Janeiro, retracing my steps twelve hundred miles in order to procure passage by a British steamer going through the Straits of Magellan to take her position on the west coast line from Chili to Panama. The most intense excitement prevails in the city. Levies are made of all the native forces, from boys of ten years of age up to old men of eighty, who are called out daily at three p.m. by bands of music for the purpose of drilling until sunset; all places of business are closed, and the poor people, who have no means of support, must work at night to keep from starving. Husbands and brothers are dragged off to the army, often leaving their families entirely destitute.

The residence of the dictator, called Palermos, a beautiful drive about three miles from town, where millions of dollars have been spent in reclaiming a marshy country near the river bank, is intersected by canals and lined with avenues of willows which grow in great profusion and afford a fine shade, as do also oranges and other fruit trees. The drives through the country are beautiful, and the whole arrangement is of a princely character. The review of the troops, whose barracks are within the inclosures, was an interesting spectacle; they were dressed in red cloth-caps, with coats of the same color; gaucho pantaloons of white, with heavy fringe at bottom, and as a finale the whole regiment, say three thousand strong, responded to the cry of "Viva la confederacion!" "Death to the fool and traitor Urquizas!" "Death to the savage Unitarians!" All of which I listened to with horror and disgust, and thought, "It will not be long before your tunes are changed," and I have just had the satisfaction of seeing them flying to the city for safety, as an engagement has taken place several leagues from the city, in which two thousand of Urquizas' cavalry put to flight some thousands of their opponents, who made good their escape as fast as their horses would carry them, throwing away all their accoutrements of war, even to their blankets.

It is an exciting time, and the issue will soon be known. Rosas is leaving the country. To prevent the approach of the enemy, all the supplies of hay and provender are embargoed for the use of the troops, and prices have been advanced from two to three hundred per cent. The currency of the country is all paper, and the dictator has supreme control of the bank of issue. Ounces of gold command three hundred and five dollars of paper. He has gone to the camp, as he must make a stand at the head of his army to encourage his people, who secretly wish his reign of tyranny over; his daughter, Manuelita, whose political character is quite established, has left Palermos. It is surprising that the combined nations of the earth should have so long sustained such an infamous government, but the facts are that the world has not been enlightened on the subject; foreigners have been protected by the policy of this chief, and the wily arts of the second in command, his talented daughter, who has many good traits of character, have inveigled Chargés and Consuls, who have received such high favor at court, that they have been infatuated and blinded to the monstrosities of the father, while the governments that they have represented have remained in ignorance of the true state of things. Our former Minister, Mr. H——, on his departure, wrote one of the most fulsome and disgusting of letters, very flattering to the vanity of these persons; but our present Minister conducts himself as an American should, with proper sentiments for suffering humanity. The government is seizing private horses for the use of the army; the crisis is approaching, and in a few days we shall know the result.

# LXXVI.

Steamer Prince, off Montevideo, *Feb. 5, 1852.*

My last was written the day before the final blow was struck by Gen. Urquizas, at the head of his forces, upon the camp at Santos Lugares. The battle commenced at six in the morning and terminated at ten; the first shock was received by the cavalry of Rosas, who were put to flight and completely routed. At twelve o'clock the lancers had fled around in the city, announcing that all the cavalry had been destroyed, and it is supposed that four thousand infantry and horsemen have been slain or wounded. The ministers and consuls of the different nations, as well as the commodores and captains of the vessels of war, English, Spanish, Swedish, Sardinian, and American, conferred together and resolved to bring their marines ashore to protect the lives and property of their countrymen, and applied to Gen. Mansilla, he being in command of the city, who replied that at six P.M. he would give an answer, but within half-an-hour he sent word by an officer that they could land and take such measures as they wished, at the same time requesting the assistance of a deputation of ministers to carry a flag of truce, and sue for terms, and cessation of hostilities. The city was filled with troops, and the greatest possible excitement and confusion reigned; but the policy of Urquizas is pacific, and we may now hope that all will be harmonious soon.

The steamer Locust has just come down and informs us that Rosas and his daughter escaped under cover of night in a small row-boat disguised as sailors, and bare-footed, their shoes having been drawn off by the mud. They were passed by the Locust on board the British steamer Certain, and it is supposed that he will go to England, where it is said he has large investments in the funds. This news of the downfall of the tyrant is received with great demonstrations of joy in Montevideo, and succeeded by the merry peals of all the church bells, and an illumination. Mr. Schenck, our minister from Rio, is with us on his return, having gone down with the frigate Congress, Commodore McKeever, whom we left at Buenos Ayres.

I could have wished to have remained a few days longer to know the final result of the affair, but as there is only a monthly steamer of the mail line, I must avail myself of this occasion, to be able to meet an anticipated opportunity by steamer to Valparaiso. While at Buenos Ayres I visited the Salideros, which is one of the most remarkable sights. It is well known that the slaughter of cattle is unprecedented here, and the execution is remarkable; some of these establishments dispose of from five hundred to eight hundred per day. They are driven in from the estancias in herds, in inclosures made of sharpened stakes placed upright, and sufficiently high to prevent escape; this inclosure is gradually contracted and separated by means of hoisting gates, until the animals are closed compactly near the slaughtering sheds, where they are lashed by the horns and drawn to a ring in a cross piece of timber, over a truck cart upon a railway, where they are quickly despatched by a single blow of the knife in the neck, back of the horns; they are drawn up by horse power acting over pulleys; fifteen in eleven minutes were disposed of in my presence. The hides are removed, and dried or salted for exportation; the meat is jerked or cut in slices for drying, and sent to the West Indies; the horn is peeled, and the pithy particles within are used for making fences or bridging places or roads; the offal is put in immense reservoirs, containing two hundred barrels each, of which I counted ten in the establishment. Large pipes from an immense boiler convey the steam into these repositories, and the tallow runs out of tubes at the bottom like molten lead, and is put up in tierces while in a liquid state for shipping. The refuse of the vats is used for making steam, and in fact every particle of the animal is consumed, except the blood; the ashes from the bones answer the purpose of guano, and are contracted for in quantities. In consequence of the war and the uncertain tenure of this kind of property, which is liable to be taken by the army, cattle have been sold at two dollars each, our currency. It is a horrible and disgusting sight, but it forms the chief branch of commerce of this country. We will now carry the war news to Rio, which will be gratifying and relieve the treasury.

# LXXVII.

Steamship Winfield Scott, Pacific Coast, *March 17, 1852.*

When I last wrote you I think I was returning from Monte Video to Rio Janeiro, to obtain a passage in a new steamer which was expected out from England, designing to continue my voyage through the Straits of Magellan, and up to Chili, but I found myself disappointed. Soon after this, the arrival of the noble ship from which I now write gave me an excellent opportunity to do so, being well commanded, and having accommodations for six hundred California passengers, while we are but two in number. The detention at Rio, on my second visit, gave me the advantages, or rather the annoyances, of the Carnival season, as it is there conducted. For three days from twelve at noon until night, it was unsafe to appear in the streets, where you ran the risk of being drenched with water, the contents of colored wax balls of the appearance of lemons, thrown by ladies, gentlemen, and children; in fact, all classes entered into the sport, from the doors and balconies across the streets. The Carnival commenced on Sunday, Washington's birthday, and for three days business was mostly suspended. I had taken a social and quiet dinner in the suburbs with our minister, under the protection of a large and magnificent star-spangled banner, recently received, and floating in remembrance of the Father of his Country, to whom we are so much indebted for gifts possessed by no other people. In returning my vehicle had to run the gauntlet amid the showers of lemon balls. Theatres were crowded with masquerades, which I did not attend; having looked in upon them, however, the evening previous, which was the commencement, I found thousands of spectators occupying the boxes, and a multitude dancing with a violence that I had scarcely ever seen in cold latitudes. Prior to the Carnival they had an annual ball for charitable purposes, to which I was invited. It was given in an immense building in the centre of a long inclosure called the Garden of Paradise, but it appeared to me more like a Purgatory. Several thousand persons were present, to whom every variety of iced refreshments were offered; the extreme heat of the saloon, which was nearly one hundred degrees, and the ridiculous costume of the gentlemen (black coats and pants) oppressed me so much that I was induced to leave at an early hour. The ladies wore more dresses of rose and pink than of white, which appeared to add to the heat, and were sparkling with diamonds more attractive than their persons, but less diversified in complexion, the Portuguese race not being remarkable for beauty, while the color here is much mixed.

Our ship, which is about twelve hundred tons burden, took in eight hundred tons of coal and put to sea, and at the expiration of four days and a half we found ourselves at the mouth of the Rio de la Plata, with muddy water and no soundings, two hundred miles from shore, which shows the force of this river. We saw nothing of interest along the coast, except immense flocks of aquatic birds, opposite the Guano Islands. At the termination of nine days and a half we were in Lat. 52° south, at the entrance of the Straits, Cape Virgin at the north, and forty miles wide. The cold having increased gradually, we had made accession of clothing, and put up a stove two days before. Our steamer hove to off the cape, and we entered by daylight, with a cold, strong head-wind; the banks were from one hundred and sixty to two hundred and fifty feet in height; large numbers of walruses or sea-cows basked in the sun, and many birds of large size flew foolishly in and through the rigging. Guanacoes and ostriches are seen on the Patagonia shores, and the country appears dreary and barren.

I became interested as the scenery improved in grandeur and majesty, and occupied a place in the pilot-house, being well muffled up in overcoat and cloak; still it was cold and cheerless, and I could not avoid reflecting upon the inconveniences of a shipwreck. The first narrows dividing the Patagonian coast from Terra del Fuego are about nine miles long, and one mile and a half wide, with strong tide ripples, and we can see distinctly the two shores; the water is of a greenish river color, but quite salt. The Indians, of whom some few are seen, trade for beads, petty trinkets, liquor, ammunition and lead, of which they make balls, and with which, attached to the ends of cords, they entangle the legs of the ostriches. In the afternoon of the day we entered we had passed the second narrows, with Elizabeth Island in view, in an open bay, when we espied the first small sail, and supposed it to be some man of war's boat, cruizing with the French flag, bearing down for us. We were heading off and should have passed her, had we not accidentally observed the tri-colored flag half-mast, when we altered our course and came up. We discovered a French lieutenant clapping his hands with joy, and crying out in his native tongue, "We are shipwrecked!" When shall I forget the scene of excitement and ecstasy manifested by himself and his six men composing the crew, as well as ourselves, on learning their condition, and being the means of saving them? His launch was twenty-one feet in length, and six feet wide, with mainsail and jib; it contained his supplies of red wine, salt-beef, and biscuit, but was leaky, and kept two men bailing; they could not have lived twenty-four hours longer. The facts are these: The French brig of war, Entreprenant, coming from the Pacific on her way to the Falkland islands, had entered a false bay, of which there are many, and the constant westerly winds resisted every effort of her crew of one hundred and thirty-five men to get her out; they were surrounded by mountains of snow and ice, without any chance of escape. At the expiration of eleven days, the launch started in pursuit of relief to Port Famine, a penal settlement, and the only habitable neighborhood along the straits. On arriving there they found that the convicts had risen and massacred the governor and other officers, and escaped, after hanging and burning the captain and owner of an English brig and an American three-masted schooner, taking possession of the vessels and all the treasure obtainable. The only recourse for the launch was to continue with the wind towards the Atlantic, when fortunately we met and saved them from a frightful death. The lieutenant explained to me the position of his ship, which I interpreted to our commander, who readily consented to go in pursuit of her. The next day we discovered a sail, and heard the discharge of guns, and found it to be the brig of war, which had just emerged from the bay, after an imprisonment of eighteen days. A perfect calm had enabled them, a desperate effort of their oarsmen, to tow her eight miles out into the strait, when the commander, Count Pouget, espied us, and expressed his obligations, sending a letter to the French Commodore at Valparaiso, requesting me to call upon him personally with the Captain, and to receive his thanks. The two ships parted amid the general rejoicing of all parties.

We had a cold but beautiful sail through scenery of the most majestic and romantic character, mountains rising from two thousand five hundred to three thousand feet in height, with jagged forms and snow-clad, with the gilding of the sun's rays upon them.

There are various kinds of scenery as you pass west. Sometimes the peaks resemble those about Rio, high and conical; I almost imagined myself among the ice-mountains of Switzerland, and then again, in the scanty undergrowth of some localities, in Norway. With the strong westerly winds in some parts, the stunted trees rise from the sheltered side of rocks to a level with the summit, and seem as if cut and trimmed off at the top, and all the branches extend towards the east. The mountains rise in succession, retreating as you approach the ocean, the influence of the salt-air melting the snow and bringing down avalanches, while those in the rear are constantly white, and those on the margin are of grey granite in layers. On the shores of South Desolation we descried the smoke and fire of the Fuegean Indians, who came off in bark canoes, making signals with seal skins; the men, women, and children, notwithstanding the severe atmosphere about us, were nearly in a state of nature. The distance through the straits from Cape Virgin to Cape Pillar is two hundred and seventy miles, the most southern point being Cape Froward, in Latitude fifty-four south; our distance from Rio Janeiro to Valparaiso will be three thousand and six hundred miles, and the views through the passage are certainly among the most rough, wild, desolate, and exciting in the world. When the California trade first opened, many small vessels passed through, but now the clippers have replaced them, and a sail is rarely seen.

We had fine weather until we approached the Pacific entrance at Cape Pillar, which is a singular rock or column, five hundred feet high, when a heavy gale of wind, with a strong current from the west, set in, bringing in tremendous seas, which nothing but the immense power of steam could resist; the smallest accident in the machinery must have dashed the vessel on the rocks. The qualities of the ship have now been fully tried, and nobly has she conducted herself for three boisterous days, with but slight damage to the wood-work about the guards. She rode the billows handsomely, through a perfect white sea of foam, and rarely have I seen or enjoyed more grand and majestic waves. During the squalls we had some magnificent rainbows, which appeared to approach the ship in circular form, like colossal wheels, until almost within grasp. We also saw large numbers of albatross, with wings measuring from eight to ten feet from tip to tip, and with two joints, which gives them the most graceful motion as they skim over the waves.

My travelling companion from the Bay State is making his first voyage, and has suffered intense agony of mind for fear we should be lost. He says he has already seen the tusks of the "elephant" off Cape Pillar, and for two nights he did not close his eyes in sleep, as he thought every moment we should be capsized by the heavy roll of the waves; I, however, had full confidence in the ship and officers. My friend says he must try to get home by land, as the value of the ship and cargo would be no inducement to him to pass through the same scenes again. The weather is now clear, the winds are hushed, the sea is smooth, the nights are brilliant, with the white Magellan cloud in the heavens, as an index for the mariner, and the weather is becoming warm and pleasant. We have passed Ascension, and are now approaching Valparaiso, where I shall leave the steamer and proceed after a few days to Santiago, the capital of Chili, ninety miles in the interior.

# LXXVIII.

SANTIAGO, CAPITAL OF CHILI, *March 24, 1852.*

On entering the harbor of Valparaiso, I was struck with the number of vessels anchored in its deep bay, sheltered from all but the northers, which are at times most destructive to shipping. It has great depth of water, say from sixty to eighty fathoms, near the shore; from the broken and peculiar formation of the many clay-covered hills in the background, with deep ravines, and huts, and frame dwellings clustered on the side, above the narrow city below, it appears not unlike a town of stairs, the dry and parched appearance of the summits affording no vegetation, there having been no rain for many months. Much movement and commercial life are there; the shattered buildings of last year's earthquake are mostly repaired; the hotels are very fair; the number of foreigners large, and the population upwards of fifty thousand. The civil war of last autumn having ceased, the newly elected president has been received by all classes on his arrival from the capital, and remains the guest of the city. He is a lawyer, and occupies a high judicial position; he is the first civil governor Chili has ever had; his opponent, General Cruz, who attempted to nullify his election, was defeated with the loss of four thousand men in one battle.

I had brought letters from Rio Janeiro for the officers of the flag ship Raritan and St. Lawrence, and had gone on board the former to pay the commodore a visit, when the latter entered the harbor, having left Rio two weeks before us, going round the Horn; but our ship had made the quickest passage on record—fifteen days and twenty-two hours, moving time, via the Straits. A salute of thirteen guns was received, and nine returned, agreeable to rank. The Portsmouth has also just arrived from Rio. Mr. Peyton, our Ambassador here, tells me that he has just received advices from Ecuador, that General Flores has been fitting out an expedition from Callao to Guayaquil, and the presence of this ship will be required there. These South American Republics, which do not merit the name, are almost always in confusion, you perceive. We found that the American vessel which had been seized by convicts at Port Famine, had arrived in the harbor of Valparaiso, having been rescued from the pirates by an English steamer; the ringleaders will soon be executed. I regretted to learn that the owner, who was barbarously hung, and whose body was burned, was an acquaintance, he having on one occasion conveyed me from New Orleans to Havana; I saw him last at San Francisco. The Captain is now here, accompanied by Mr. Duer, our consul at Valparaiso, prosecuting claims against the Chilian government; but I fear it will be very slow work. The usual mode of travel from Valparaiso, a distance of ninety miles, is in biloches, a sort of heavy gig with two and three horses, each mounted by postillions, the outside ones attached at will by heavy straps at each side of the shafts, and fastened with hooks to a heavy saddle; the riders attach or detach themselves at full speed, going with the greatest velocity up and down mountains and over a desert country, where nothing is seen but bushes and scraggy shrubs in a sandy soil. A few places are seen on the road where peach and pear trees, as well as grapes, are found, but the country is destitute of water most of the distance. The horses are driven ahead in a drove, and changed as required.

The Bilocheros have the habit of racing; a certain rivalry exists between them, and where opportunity offers they go at full speed up and down the hills, and over the plains, regardless of horse-flesh, which is only nominal in price. We made the distance in twenty-four hours, passing part of the night at a small village, where the fleas disputed possession stoutly, and we were glad to make a start at three in the morning to escape them. We had clouds of dust from the large numbers of laden mules and ox-carts. The entire elevation is some two thousand five hundred feet to the base of the Andes, a chain of Cordilleras, which show their snow-clad summits beautifully as you approach the delightful and extended valleys of Santiago, and it is gratifying to discern the well watered plain, with its long lines of poplars and willows in the distance. Bridges are thrown across the river, or mountain torrent, which is not unlike the Po at Nice, and the rides along the banks of the stream in this genial climate, with its vineyards and fruit trees, amply compensate for the trouble of getting here. The rides up the mountains give you a fair view of the city, which is extensive, and has a population of some ninety thousand. It is the residence of all the foreign ministers, and the seat of government; it derives its revenues from silver mines, and its agricultural products; it has a good supply of red porphyry for sidewalks; its streets are wide and long, and paved with small pebbles; its houses are mostly built of adobe, or unburnt brick, which resist the shocks of earthquakes. The cathedral is rather dangerous, being somewhat shattered. There is a corps of United States astronomical engineers here, whose observatory is placed on the summit of the little hill of Santa Lucia. I find an acquaintance here, in the person of the French minister, whose family came out with us in 1849. One of the church festivals has just taken place by torchlight, in the Alameda, the pride of the city, a promenade of a mile in length, with six rows of tall Florentine poplars, and pure streams of running water the entire distance.

Large numbers of ladies are seen in church-dresses, with black mantas covering the head; the people are not of the pure Castilian type as in the south of Spain, many showing signs of descent from the Indian race. The countrymen all wear the ponchos, of various colors; the poncho is a blanket with a hole in the centre, through which the head is passed, and falls over the shoulders. The women of that class wear men's panama-hats, with long hair plaited, and falling in two parts over the back. It is curious to notice the primitive manner in which some things are done here. The watering of the streets is done by a muleteer on the back of his animal, which carries two small twenty gallon kegs, one lashed on each side; these are filled at the top from the fountain. When he arrives at the dusty spot he pulls the cork from the bottom and starts his mule on a trot until the contents are scattered, and then returns for fresh supplies. One of the curiosities shown here is the first house built by Valdivia in 1560. It is a one-story adobe dwelling, with gratings above near the roof, in order to give ventilation and light, and to prevent attacks of Indians by openings below; it has had additions since. The wheat crops are excellent, and the exportation of flour and beans from Chili to California is very heavy. We visited the chacras or farms in the valleys, where thousands of bushels of grain were exposed in heaps in the open air, without fear of rain, having been trodden out by cattle, and numbers of men, employed at fifteen cents per day, and found, were throwing up the wheat to the breeze, which carries off the chaff and winnows it perfectly. Labor is improving, however, and in the cities fifty cents per day, and one dollar twenty-five cents for mechanics, are paid, in consequence of the great emigration to California. Two vessels lately sailed thither with two hundred emigrants each, and from personal experience I know that very many Chilians are found in that country. Vast sums have been realized here from Eldorado for products, and large mills are now being erected in the south for the supplies of that market, though too late, I think, as Oregon can produce immense quantities when once the population becomes more dense. The transportation of products from this capital to Valparaiso is performed by heavy ox-carts, many with covers resembling small round-top houses with windows; these covers are a protection during the winter months, which commence in June, also against the sun's rays in summer, which has already passed; they travel now mostly by night, with a brilliant sky, and you see families of women and children occupying their tenement by the desert roadside, or cooking the supplies brought with them. They train their oxen not only to pull, but to hold back the load by the horns; they have four yoke for the immense zigzag cuttings, a mile and a half in the ascent; they then reverse the order of things, and the poor beasts are seen behind, with heads bowed to the ground, holding back, and almost tripped off their legs, and not unfrequently off go the whole troop down the precipice and are dashed in pieces.

A nephew of the president joined me in coming up from Valparaiso, his family having left earlier, and we overtook them and dined on the road. They were going to his chacra, in another direction. At the little village where we stopped at night, he introduced me to the Catholic curate of this poor place, who regaled us with cakes and matte from Paraguay; matte is the leaf of a tree much in use as a substitute for tea and coffee, and sucked through a tube; we passed the evening in conversation and smoking cigarettes, until the time came to be devoured by fleas in bed.

The English steamers touch at half-a-dozen towns on the way up to Peru, giving an opportunity of passing a day at each. I shall embark from Valparaiso in a few days for Callao and Lima.

# LXXIX.

Lima, *April, 1852.*

My last was from Santiago, the capital of Chili. I now address you from the renowned city of Lima, the seat of government of Peru, having in the interim touched at many of the small ports along the coast from Valparaiso to Callao, spending part of a day at each. Our first landing-place was Coquimbo, where are some important copper mines and smelting furnaces. The town, which was the seat of the insurgents in the last civil war, is about two leagues from the little port. Our steamer was the Santiago, recently from England, and she proved rather a failure, making only one hundred and ninety miles in thirty hours. Her machinery became heated, the wheels dipped too much; they attempted to account for it, however, by the bad quality of the coals. We arrived the following day at Oasco, which is surrounded by a small valley, very grateful to the eye, in comparison with the volcanic and iron-bound coast. The next point was Caldeva, the port of Copiapo, fifty-two miles distant, where the first South American railway was during the past year put in operation by American mechanics. We landed there one hundred and forty passengers of mixed classes, bound for the mines. They were a noisy set, grasping at table, and continually dancing their Samba Queca on deck; there were also some amusing groups of half-Indian and Spanish races, in costume of the country.

We received there considerable quantities of silver in bars, destined for England. It was a great relief to find our passengers reduced down to twenty-five, as the living had been poor, and a change was much needed. No good excuse could be offered for neglect, as the price of passage was enormous; but nothing to warrant American competition, as the line is now firmly established, with large capital, and determined to drive off all opponents. Our next point of debarkation was Coliza, the only port of Bolivia, a miserable town of huts, with only three wells of water, which is divided out among the inhabitants in proportion, from small kegs on the backs of donkeys. The mountains about it are barren, and not the slightest sign of vegetation is seen. Silver and copper induce people to live there. We visited the guano deposits, where about one hundred state prisoners were at work putting it up in sacks for exportation. The following day we arrived at Iquique, where one of our fellow passengers is established, though he is now from Valparaiso on his way to England. He was evidently the Alcalde of his miserable town, which relies mostly upon saltpetre for its support; not a blade of grass or drop of water is to be seen, reminding one of the shores of the Red Sea; still about one thousand persons exist there. A small mill grinds the wheat brought from Chili; seventeen Chinese were employed on it. Many are brought over to the coast and sold for a limited period for their passage money. The escape steam from the machine distils the salt water, which is sold at six reals, or seventy-five cents per keg of eighteen gallons. Fruit and vegetables are brought from Arica, eighty miles further down the coast. The village looks like an Egyptian one, being composed of mud huts thatched with leaves. The mules and donkeys are the most miserable specimens, dying with thirst, and wading in the salt water, laving their mouths and picking up sea-weed. These animals come down laden with saltpetre, one day's journey, and the mules return immediately; the donkeys generally rest a day or two, but frequently their drivers are unwilling to pay a real, or twelve and a half cents, for a bucket of water, so the poor brutes are compelled to return without a drink. Our friend's house and stores were large frame buildings near the beach, two stories high, with balconies, and comfortably furnished and supplied.

I was particularly struck with his despidida, or farewell departure, after a residence of nineteen years. A handsome collation of fruits and wine of various kinds was served to his friends, and among the number appeared a lady of the country with her child. She was dressed in velvet, with a rich China shawl, diamond necklace and ear-rings, and fingers loaded with precious stones. While the champagne corks were flying I had a glance from the balcony over the desert with its heavy sands and rocky mountains in the distance, and could scarcely realize my position; but the figure of Commerce presented herself among the shipping and explained the circumstance. The town of Arica appeared like an oasis in the desert, the streets being paved and well laid out; the houses were built with flat roofs, and there were two churches, badly shaken by earthquakes. Our Consul had very comfortable quarters, with a fine garden of fruit and flowers. The country in the interior in many places is productive, but the chief fertility consists of silver mines. Islay, the next town, is difficult to access, being high and rocky; it has some decent houses, and is the port of Arequipa. Water is brought in by aqueducts, and it was a refreshing sight to see the donkeys drinking at will. I called with a friend upon an old Spaniard, whose two daughters gratified us with music upon the piano, even in this almost uninhabited country, and seemed contented with their home and climate. The following day we found ourselves at Pisco, celebrated for its wine and liquors. We mounted horses and rode in the country, visited some of the vineyards, and returned to town about two miles from the beach; it happened to be Palm Sunday, and we visited the cathedral built by the old Spaniards, saw the procession and entrance into Jerusalem, by knocking at the side-door, and heard some extraordinary music. Palm branches were distributed, and the motley group of half-castes, Indians, Negroes, and Spaniards dispersed. We had the day previous picked up a launch with six men, who had been out twenty-three days from Valparaiso, and without water and provisions for two days. We supplied them with biscuit, beans, candles, wood, and water; not forgetting cigars, which were among the first articles which they demanded.

Our final landing-place was the Chinchas Guano Islands, the present great source of wealth of the Peruvian government; a supply still exists for perhaps a century, sufficient to pay the interest on the national debt of some twenty millions of dollars, the bonds of which, from being almost valueless, have advanced to par in England. I was surprised to find ten ships and brigs waiting for loads. One can scarcely realize that the immense deposits or hills have been produced by birds, but the flocks which are seen, and which are prohibited from being destroyed, and the known voracity of the species, reconcile one's doubts, particularly in a climate where it never rains.

The use of the guano has long been known in the interior of the country; it is transported on the backs of animals to the valleys, irrigated by the waters from the melting snows of the Andes. The people, I learn, are substituting negroes for the Chinese, as the latter, being disappointed in this kind of servitude, have frequently destroyed themselves by hanging, many in groups, joining hands and leaping over the precipice, in the belief of restoration to their happy homes. I arrived here at the commencement of the Passion Week, and found that all Lima had had the peste, or plague, a species of yellow fever; it had nearly exhausted itself for want of victims, but strangers of course were expected to take it. The Italian opera company, of seventeen persons, just arrived from the north, were all taken, save three, and out of our number of twenty-five at the hotel at table only five were left. I have been exposed, with my fellow-passengers, but in consequence of having had the original Yellow Jack, have thus far escaped. The churches of Peru are the finest in South America; there are about fifty-two in the city, with a population of ninety thousand persons. They date their riches and luxury in the time of the Spaniards. Some of the temples were decorated with a great variety of flowers, in vases furnished for the occasion, by private families, forming avenues of tropical vegetation through these deep edifices, while the light of a thousand candles illuminated the high altar, and disclosed the faces of hundreds of the beautiful Limanians of the Andalusian race, who were kneeling in their rays, in black shawls or mantillas; after a short prayer they rose and visited other churches. I visited twelve of the most important in the evening, and found, as in Havana, that at these festivals, some new attractions are held out for visitors, who continue the rounds until overcome with fatigue. In one church the last supper was represented by Christ and his twelve apostles, sitting at a well-covered table of fruits, flowers, and wine, the approach to which was difficult, on account of the rush of negroes and half-castes. In another church the figures of the soldiery and the crowning with thorns were represented; a grotesque zapatero, or shoemaker, in a crouching position, looking up with a huge pair of spectacles, seemed to excite the mirth of the common people. The balcony of my apartment faces the Plaza, or Cathedral Square; at the right is pointed out the spot where Pizarro lost his life, fighting nobly; in the crypt of the cathedral is shown what are called his remains.

On Noche Buena, the night after the Passion Week, the whole square was roasting and stewing. Negroes were there in great numbers, with fire and cooking utensils; hot fritters boiled in oil, sausages, garlic salads, and *aguardiente*; and there were booths, or stands, on three sides, with every variety of trinkets for sale, and an immense concert of Indians, negroes, and other races; while in front, respectable ice-cream and confectionery stands accommodated the gentlemen and ladies with seats, and cooling drinks, made from fruits and ice, brought from the mountains, seven leagues distant, on the backs of mules. The river Rimac flows through the city, and running water passes through many of the streets. The mountains around are arid and forbidding, without the least verdure; but by irrigation the gardens of the valleys are made productive. At a charge of four reals, or fifty cents, the railway, eight miles in length, brings passengers from the port of Callao. It is a new construction, and has an elevation of five hundred feet. The chief place of resort for the Limanians, are the ocean baths of Churillas, whither I propose going.

# LXXX.

Steamer Quito, *April 29, 1852.*

The old Spanish custom of bull fights is still kept up with all its vigor in Lima, and the long looked-for combat came off after the church ceremonies of Passion Week had ended. Having, as a traveller, witnessed this barbarous sport in Spain, where it is countenanced by the nobility and the dignitaries of the government, I was induced to attend it here chiefly to observe the ladies in their saya mantas—a garment which entirely prevents recognition, as it leaves one eye only exposed. The sayas are falling into disuse, and not seen so often as formerly in the public streets, except on festive occasions. Any lady may be addressed, but under no circumstances can the veil be removed by force, without calling down the vengeance of bystanders. An immense building of circular form stands near the Alameda; it is a public promenade, with palcos or boxes for parties and families, and seats in the form of an amphitheatre, capable of containing some seven thousand persons. The authorities of the city occupy a prominent place, as well as the military officers and judges. A programme is sold, containing the names of the twelve bulls to be killed, and describing the characteristics of the prominent matadores, two of whom, father and son, have recently arrived from Spain.

The trumpet sounds; mounted horsemen come forth and clear the ring; others appear with lances in hand; and then appear six flag-men with red and yellow scarfs, round jackets, and short clothes of silk and velvet, embroidered with gold and silver lace, shining knee-buckles, and silk stockings. The sliding gate is opened, and in rushes the tortured bull, with his eyes glaring, and makes for the horse, but is diverted by the blazing colors of the scarfs. Sometimes a mantle is thrown over the shoulders; the animal pursues it, when the wearer dashes it aside and dodges the infuriated beast, escaping behind a side partition fence, while he takes after another, and barbed arrows with feather or paper plumes are planted in his neck, causing him to roar and paw the dust, and make another attempt at his adversary, in which he sometimes upsets horse and rider, goring the former, to the delight of the multitude, whose cries and waving handkerchiefs attest their pleasure. After the ineffectual efforts and hair-breadth escapes of the actors, the matador, while attracting the bull with his red flag, with one thrust of his long sword gives him a mortal stab, which passes through the neck and heart, and appears between the fore-legs. The enthusiasm is then at its height. The trumpet sounds, the gates are thrown open, two pairs of heavy mules appear, bedecked with feathers, and mounted by two riders. The head of the defunct is raised upon a pair of small wheels, and attached by the horns to the traces; the band strikes up, the dead carcase is removed under the full gallop; the gates are closed, and a new victim soon appears. I felt it a relief to escape and stroll along the beautiful Alameda, upon the river bank. The ride to the baths of Churilla, a few leagues from Lima, is over a heavy, sandy road, dusty, dreary, and of no interest.

The Indian village situated on the bay is much resorted to during the summer months. The bath-houses are of cane or reed, and form a sort of labyrinth, with a few flat stones in each for seats; they are occupied by both sexes, but are rather exposed. Gambling seems to be the order of the day, or rather night, as all classes, male and female, enter into the sport, it being the ruling passion of the Peruvians as well as the Chilians. Among the passengers in the diligence or public conveyance was a grey-headed, thin-visaged, lank old man, whose whole dress, including his poncho, would not have sold for *twenty dollars*; yet this confirmed old gambler had amassed two hundred thousand dollars in play, and notwithstanding that he was lame with one foot in the grave, his passion, which was the object of his visit, must still be gratified. Many persons have private residences for the enjoyment of the sea breeze and bathing, but they are of a primitive character. Ludicrous dances in grotesque costumes are performed by the negroes, which help to pass their evenings.

Lima is considered the gayest city on the South Pacific coast, and enjoys a mild, equal climate, being uninfluenced by the near approach of the mountains, and of a much more agreeable temperature than the same latitude on the opposite side in Brazil. The houses, which are two stories, have balconies of latticed work, which gives the ladies an opportunity of seeing all passers in the streets. The ladies are less celebrated for constancy than for sprightliness, grace, and beauty, and are a far superior race to the men, who are much inferior to the Chilians. The use, or rather abuse of the saya manta was formerly a means of intrigue even in the presence of husbands and brothers, as exchanges of robes were easily effected. The adoption of European costume is fast reducing the use of this garment.

To a stranger the alarm created by a shock of an earthquake upon the natives appear ridiculous, as they rush out of their houses into the open square, and if the shock is in the night, of course in undress; all who experience these shocks, however, are soon overcome by the same kind of terror. The earthquake of the last century swept Callao and its entire population into the sea. We had a considerable shock a few days since, while I was in a heavy stone and brick building, used in part for a museum, and where some interesting specimens of antiquity of the times of the Incas are found, as also mummies from the Indian mounds, and the portraits of the former viceroys of Peru. I was examining these objects attentively, when I found myself suddenly alone, with the balance of the party making for the inner court or square, crying out "*un temblor!*" The dust was flying about me, and I followed hurriedly; I observed that the sky was remarkably bright, that there was a perfect stillness of the elements, and that the air was filled with birds in confusion; however, it soon passed, and without damage.

The steamer from which I write is new; she is just out from England, this being her first trip. We are fortunate in having fresh supplies and attentive servants, with few passengers, and every comfort. We have just met the Santiago, and exchanged civilities, and received English papers from Panama. I learn from her captain, who has just recovered from the pest, that all my fellow passengers from Valparaiso, who touched at Callao and Lima, with one exception, were attacked, and among the number a family of seven persons. I find I have great reason to be thankful in having escaped.

We shall make the distance of eighteen hundred miles in seven and a half days, passing nearly one day at Paita, which has a fine harbor, and was formerly resorted to by whalers for supplies; they now go to Tumbes, seven leagues above, where water is to be had, with which water Paita is supplied, not a blade of grass or a drop of the liquid element being produced at the latter place, the few plants there in boxes being looked upon with much pleasure. It is far superior to many other small towns along the coast. There are some comfortable houses built of cane, and covered with flags, which earthquakes cannot shake down easily, and several long and narrow streets which afford shade. An extraordinary event had just occurred, it having rained for a part of a day, for the first time in seven years. The natives are mostly Indians; a quiet, docile, and well-looking people. The residents seem satisfied with their position and climate; they say that they are deprived of vegetation and water, but that they can get supplies from along the coast; that they are not infested with venomous reptiles and noxious fleas, the accompaniment of rank verdure, and that the people die of old age, citing instances of ninety and one hundred years longevity. I had made a passage with the son of the English Consul, whose father had been there for nineteen years, and enjoys the climate. I breakfasted and lunched with him, with some other guests from the ship, and certainly there was no want of the good things of life, even in such a desert place. The reputed wife of General Bolivar resides here; she was with him in many of his campaigns, while Liberator of South America. A friend took me to her house, and I found a stout, fat, but well featured elderly lady, in her hammock, which I learn she rarely leaves, unless for her bed. She had her two poodle dogs nestling beside her; she received us kindly, and conversed intelligently and in a diplomatic manner upon matters of politics. She is a great friend of General Flores, whose expedition is now approaching Guayaquil with fourteen hundred men, and with the prospect of overthrowing President Urbini, of Ecuador, who, she says, was educated by General Flores while former President, to whom he proved an ungrateful wretch. I found there the daughter of Flores with her husband and aide de-camp, awaiting news from the seat of war. This lady, who once lived in Lima in almost regal style, now subsists upon the charities of her numerous friends. As I had once visited the tomb of Bolivar in Caraccas, and received the hospitalities of a cousin bearing his name, in his rancho, near Porto Cabello, the old lady seemed interested in me, and insisted on my joining her in smoking a choice Havana, an occupation which she appeared to enjoy.

To-morrow we shall arrive at Panama, which place I had not expected or hoped to see again, and I can scarcely realize the fact that since my last visit I have made the circuit of the globe, and since my departure from home have passed almost the entire length of North and South America on both sides. After fourteen winters' travel in southern latitudes, and several years' absence at intervals from home, I find that my table of distances amounts to six hundred thousand miles, from the snowy regions of Canada, Norway, and Finland in the north, to the barren shores of Patagonia in the south—having traversed by sea and land, at different periods, almost all the practicable portions of the earth, in making the circuit of the world. Although what has passed appears not unlike a dream, my ambition for the present is satisfied, and I have reason to thank a kind Providence, whose protecting hand has carried me through almost all the perils of life, and has been the means of preserving a constitution endangered by the severity of northern winter-climates. I shall proceed via the isthmus to Havana, and thence to New Orleans, on my way home, where I hope to arrive in the early part of June.

# 1853.
# LXXXI.

PARIS, *Jan. 31, 1853.*

Since I left the Pacific coasts of Chili and Peru last spring, I have hesitated about afflicting you with correspondence, and thinking and hoping that my voyages around the world were complete. Time and circumstances, however, have since carried me to Cuba (by the way, it is my eighth visit), and I have traversed the waters of the Gulf of Mexico to the city of New Orleans; steamed up the mighty Mississippi and Ohio rivers for the sixth time; besides visiting Canada and Niagara. Notwithstanding the thousand incidents constantly occurring, I held my peace. Having left my native village in the latter part of November, in pursuit of a more genial climate, I find myself once again on European soil, and in the capital of the French empire. So many important events have transpired since I left home that you will pardon me for once more taking up my pen, and breaking silence. Our steamer took the southern passage in crossing the Atlantic; the early part of our voyage upon the edge of the gulf-stream was delightful, until at length a famous combat arose among the great opposing elements. For five successive days we had a continuation of the most violent gales, more properly speaking hurricanes, such as our officers had never experienced, and it was with difficulty that I could recall reminiscences of equally grand and awful scenes. The good ship Hermann, although obliged to manœuvre, or lie to, as the sailors term it, for thirty-six hours, at last got the mastery over Neptune: and when we arrived in England, we found that the steamer Washington had been disabled, and obliged to return. The same gales had carried destruction along the entire coast. The then approaching holiday season of Christmas was anxiously looked for, in England, particularly by the poor, for charities are more freely exercised at that time, and the English markets and butchers' stalls are beautiful to gaze upon. But instances are rarely if ever known, as in our favored land, of the working classes trudging home under the weight of turkeys, geese, or chickens for a Sunday or Christmas dinner. How little do we know of the miseries of the laboring population abroad, and how slightly do we appreciate, as a people, the eminent advantages which we enjoy in our own favored land!

The universal practice of giving *étrennes*, or presents, on New Year's day, among the Parisians, has led to the granting of privileges to *boutiques*, or temporary wooden shops, along both sidewalks of the Boulevards, for one week before, and one week after the first of January; they form a continuous bazaar for more than a mile, composed of all the indescribable knick-knacks and fancy articles that the ingenious brain of a Frenchman can contrive to gratify youthful taste or fancy, dolls and cheap jewelry figuring largely. This exhibition, with the flood of humanity to the extent of some hundreds of thousands, military, foreign, and domestic, in every variety of costume of holiday attire, added to the gay equipages and liveried servants, struck me as one of the great sights of the capital.

The season thus far has been remarkably mild; we have had much rain, but no winter, and fears are entertained for the future crops should the mild weather continue. In the *Jardin des Plantes*, some trees indicate the putting forth of new leaves.

This being the gay season, and Paris full of strangers from all parts, opportunity is not wanting for the gratification of the most fastidious. One would judge, from the announcement of balls, concerts, and theatres (of which latter I think there are thirty-two, of all sizes), that they could not be sustained; but on the contrary they are fully attended. The work of Madame Beecher Stowe has caused a perfect furore in Paris. Authors and editors run a steeple-chase in their hasty translations, which pour from the press with exaggerated engravings to gratify the tastes of the eager purchasers. Two large rival theatres, the *Ambigu Comique* and the *Theatre de la Gaité*, conceived at the same moment the idea of dramatizing Uncle Tom. The *Ambigu* won the race by a few days with immense success, but the *Gaité* followed close after; and now may be seen the *affiches* everywhere, and large transparencies in front of the theatres, emblazoned in great letters, "*La Case de l'Oncle Tom.*" My curiosity as an American, besides my familiarity with the institution of slavery as it exists at the south, induced me to visit the *Ambigu*, where I found the piece well mounted, with superb decorations, but full of exaggeration. The cries of the blood-hounds in pursuit of fugitive slaves; the brutal conduct of the masters; the tender scenes of separation; the discharge of fire-arms; the sale of negroes in New Orleans, all helped to bring the ladies' handkerchiefs into frequent use; their tears, however, were readily dispersed by some ludicrous scene not in the novel. At the *Gaité* the scenes are entirely changed, the state of Kentucky being the theatre of action. The sale of Uncle Tom, the flight of George and his wife, Eliza with her infant child, the crossing of the Ohio upon the ice, the arrival in Canada, the land of promise, amidst the most beautiful tropical vegetation, were greatly exaggerated; but worse than all, and shocking to the moral sense, Uncle Tom, who was a perfect black, was represented as the father of Eliza, a beautiful quadroon. One of the Parisian editors lately remarked that he was not at a loss to decide which condition was the most deplorable, that of the well-fed and well-clad negro in bondage, free from care, or that of the thousands of poor creatures in Paris, who shiver in the garret of a six-story tenement, after a hard day's service for one franc, or twenty cents, to sustain their starving families.

The Parisians are emphatically a theatre-going people, and they have juvenile theatres expressly for nurses and parents with their children; of course the latter imbibe the passion early, and Sunday being their gala day, all places of amusement are naturally crowded. It would appear that all Paris is dancing at present; the imperial court dances, the ministers of war and of state dance, and the senate is preparing to dance, all of which is gratifying to the fancy dealers of the capital. The great event of the season took place yesterday, Sunday. It was the marriage of the Emperor at the cathedral of Notre Dame. The civil marriage was performed at the Palace of the Tuileries, the evening previous, by the minister of state, in presence of the family of Napoleon. After the ceremony was concluded the Countess Montijo was reconducted to her private residence in the Champs Elysées. Yesterday presented one of the most gorgeous pageants that Paris has ever witnessed. It would occupy too much time and space to attempt a description, and it would be useless to repeat what may be found in the public journals. The distance passed by the cortège from the Tuileries to Notre Dame, more than a mile, gave the Emperor, as he proclaimed in his speech to the Senate, an opportunity of presenting as he desired, to the army, and the French people, the bride of his choice, and if one could judge from the vast multitude which thronged the streets, the quays and bridges of the Seine, the windows, balconies, and every point which could be occupied, not only Paris, but the whole country was represented. The brilliant cortège left the palace at twelve M., preceded by detachments of mounted lancers, cuirassiers, guards, and divers others, followed by the imperial family and ladies of honor, in glittering state carriages with liveried coachmen and footmen, drawn by four and six horses with beautiful caparisoned harness, and a long train of foreign ambassadors, representatives and members of the Senate; then appeared the magnificent equipage of the Emperor, surmounted by an imperial crown, with sides of plate glass, drawn by eight white steeds, with plumes and gold-gilt trappings, containing himself and beautiful bride, responding gracefully to the salutations of the multitude. The same carriage was used but once before, at the nuptial ceremonies of Napoleon I. with the Empress Josephine, so much beloved by the French people. A double hedge of bayonets on each side of the line of march, composed of the regular troops of the national guard of Paris, prevented encroachment. The interior of Notre Dame was festooned with great taste and much splendor, while the exterior was enveloped in floating banners. The archbishop having performed the imposing marriage ceremonies, the cortège returned by another route, giving the masses the opportunity of seeing their imperial majesties.

The vast interior of the *Place du Carrousel* was one living mass of humanity, awaiting the return and appearance of the happy pair upon the balcony of the Tuileries; at length they appeared and bowed to the multitude to close the scene. While men and boys were crying the sale of effigies and medals of the Emperor and Empress, amid the anxiety and excitement of a French population, I could not forget witnessing a review of the troops by Louis

Philippe, on the same ground, and his then enthusiastic reception. Time makes great changes, and what may be the fate of those in power to-day! The French are fond of pageants, and always ready for a change. As long as commerce flourishes, and the condition of the laboring classes is tolerable, things go on smoothly; but amongst the thinking and reading portions of the community, who are deprived of the liberty of speech, and the press, there must be a deep hatred of the present dynasty.

Louis Napoleon has certainly had an eventful career. An exile, a prisoner at Ham, he returned to France after the fall of Louis Philippe, under the provisional government, and was a member of the National Assembly when I visited that noisy assemblage in the autumn of 1848. On my departure for Italy in 1847, all was quiet under the royal rule of Louis Philippe; on my return, the trees of liberty were planted throughout Paris, the public buildings proclaimed in large capitals, "*Liberté, Egalité, Fraternité*"; the press was free and untrammelled, also liberty of thought and speech, as was seen placarded upon the bulletins. Things have changed. Liberty is crushed; her name, with those of her sisters, is scrupulously effaced from the public monuments. The constitution was declared, and there was an extensive display of two hundred thousand troops, and gorgeous decorations and fireworks upon the *Place de la Concorde*. I hoped that the government would become consolidated in a true republic, but I had my misgivings. The next news brought the election of Napoleon as President for four years; afterwards his power was extended for ten years; next came his famous *coup d'état*; then followed the proclamation of the Empire, and yesterday his marriage. The telegraph has proclaimed the joyous event to all France, and now all that is required is the confirmation by the Pope, which may probably take place next spring.

Within a week the Carnival commences. I am preparing to leave for the south of France, and Spain.

# LXXXII.

BARCELONA, SPAIN, *Feb. 28, 1853.*

After the marriage of the French Emperor in Paris, whence I wrote you last month, we had nothing remarkable until the Carnival, and nothing notable then except the *fête du bœuf gras*, or the Sunday promenade of the fat ox. This novel ceremony seems to be a vestige of remote antiquity, and has been preserved up to the present time, as it gives the multitude an opportunity of diverting themselves. It appears that the poor fishermen of *Lutèce* formerly adored the zodiacal bull, and as late as 1711, in constructing a sepulchre under the choir of the church of *Notre Dame*, several *bas-reliefs* were found, one of which represented a bull clothed in sacred orders. It is the remains of the equinoctial spring ceremonies, when the sun entered into the zodiacal sign called Taurus, and the people of the agricultural provinces conducted the bull in great pomp with the sound of various musical instruments. This being altogether novel, I must describe it to you. The procession was got up by the butchers of Paris, who formed a cavalcade of one hundred and fifty persons on horseback, provided with various costumes, from the time of the crusades down to the court robes of Louis XIV., and guards of the Emperor Napoleon. This procession, with bands of music, was followed by an immense fat ox called Père Tom, or Uncle Tom, raised in Normandy, decorated with bouquets of flowers, ribbons, and laurels, followed by an immense gilded car drawn by six white horses, with the figures of several heathen deities, Venus being surrounded by a bevy of young girls, dressed in white with garlands of flowers. The day was occupied in their visits throughout Paris, to the imperial palace, the various ministers of the empire and foreign embassies, the police departments; and finally the poor beast, having slowly dragged his heavy carcass of two thousand three hundred pounds about town for the amusement of the populace, brought up at the *abattoir*, or general slaughtering establishment of the city.

Indications of approaching cold weather after the extremely mild season, induced me turn my face towards Spain. The railroad from Paris soon conducted me to *Chalons*, upon the *Saône*, whence I took steamer the next day for Lyons, the great silk-manufacturing city of France. Small steamers are employed upon these rivers; they are constructed of iron, very long, but exceedingly narrow, not much wider than an ordinary Erie Canal boat, but with the strong current they dash along at a frightful rate when the rivers are full. They are provided with jointed smoke pipes, to pass the numerous bridges.

On one occasion descending the Rhine we were obliged to lie-to, not being able to pass under the crossings from the heavy inundations, but in this instance the want of water prevented our continuing further than Valence; I took the diligence some sixty miles to Avignon, where the railroad conducts us to Marseilles. The sail upon the Saône and Rhône, with their numerous manufactories, agricultural towns, and villages, and wine districts, is quite entertaining to the traveller. A large population is engaged in the culture of the grape, but I have seen only two drunken men since I have been in France, and those seemed to be the amusement of groups of boys and men who surrounded them. We were caught by the first snow-storm of the season, and the mistral blew with its full force. The almond trees in blossom felt its effects; it will probably shorten the crop.

This being my third visit to Marseilles, I have nothing to write about it, except its progressive condition in commercial importance. The new port, in course of construction, an extraordinary enterprise, is progressing rapidly. The old port, which was small and crowded to excess, rendering vessels liable to entire destruction in case of fire, and the difficulty of egress, induced the creating of an artificial port of solid masonry. Two days' delay gave me an opportunity of embarking for this city, where I find a temperate climate, being sheltered from the northern blasts by the high mountains of the Pyrénées.

Barcelona, for size, is the second city in Spain, and the first in importance for manufactures. It is a walled town with ramparts as promenades around it, closely built, narrow, and rather intricate streets, and tall houses, mostly of stone. The Muralla or sea wall affords a good promenade, and a fine view of a harbor rather indifferent for vessels of heavy tonnage, with a commanding fortification called Mont Juich on the summit of a high hill overlooking the sea and the city; the latter is cleanly kept, and in good order, and well worth a visit. The suburbs of the city for some miles are occupied in part by manufacturing villages, and among the number is a large town called Gracia, resorted to by summer residents to escape the heat of the city; it is a pleasant retreat. The population of the city and suburbs is two hundred thousand. The province of Catalonia is perhaps the most industrious and enterprising portion of Spain. The Catalonians, whose language is a *patois*, pride themselves in being more advanced than the Castilians. In 1835 the first steam-engine was introduced in manufacturing, and from the unfounded prejudice of the working classes the establishment was destroyed by the populace. But at present steam is freely used, the supply of coal being brought from England; the mountains of Spain abound with the article, but the want of communication precludes a supply from this source. Railroads are being introduced moderately; the only one yet constructed in this department is from Barcelona to Mataro, a town along the coast. It runs along the sea-shore some seven leagues, passing through fishing villages.

The Spaniards are famous for their public promenades or *almedas*, and the *Rambla* is the chief attraction. It presents a gay, picturesque sight on Sunday, when thronged with all classes in the holiday attire of the country. The two principal theatres are situated upon this promenade, as well as the great hotels, which gives one an opportunity of seeing the sights from the balconies. The Barcelonians boast of the largest theatre and the most luxurious *cafés* in the world. Certainly the Eliseo is nearly or quite as large as La Scala in Milan. The club room, called the *circulo*, and the *casino*, adjoining the opera and theatre, are fitted up with great taste, containing libraries, and many periodicals of the day from France and England. There is a numerous French population here, and the character of the people is not so decidedly Spanish as further south. In times of reaction or opposition to the government, this place is generally at the head of the movement. This is perhaps attributable to the superior intelligence of the people, and to its proximity to France. The direct commerce is trifling with the United States in American bottoms, but the exportation of wine, oil, soap, brandy, and dried fruits, is very large; these articles are sent to Havana in Spanish vessels, which in return bring cargoes of cotton and sugar from the Southern States and Cuba.

The American corvette Levant is now here, having been detained some time with small-pox on board; her destination is our naval station at Spezzia. The health of the crew is now good, and the ship is looking finely. I was kindly received by the officers; and the Levant being the only American ship in port, and myself the only American traveller here at present, it was gratifying to be once again under the protection of the stars and stripes. The climate is mild, but the mornings and nights are cool. One would suppose, from the manner in which the Catalonians are enveloped in their large Spanish cloaks, which cover their noses, that the thermometer was below zero, while the same atmosphere in New York, in the month of April, would be considered delightful. Strange as it may appear, in our hotel, with seventy rooms, there is not a chimney; and when fire is absolutely required, we make use of *braseros*, a flat brass vessel with raised edges, which contains live coals, and ashes from well burned wood, in place of charcoal, to avoid suffocation from the gases.

The chief amusements are the promenades, *cafés*, opera, theatres, and bull fights, at all of which the fair senoritas assist. The bull fights I described fully last year from Peru. They are not so famous here either for their bulls or swordsmen as in Seville or Madrid; neither will the ladies compare for beauty with the graceful Andalusians. In all public places you are enveloped in cigar smoke; the lobbies of the opera during the scenes are filled with devotees of the weed, whose smoke penetrates throughout the house, and by common consent is tolerated in all public and private houses and conveyances.

The lower orders are poor; they fare meagrely, and are poorly rewarded for their labor. The city is not remarkable for its public monuments. The cathedral is a noble Gothic structure, and possesses some works of art, but it would be idle to compare it or the other churches with those of Italy.

# LXXXIII.

PALMA, ISLAND OF MAJORCA, *March 10, 1853.*

My last letter was from Barcelona. I was then preparing to visit this island, and notwithstanding its proximity (it is only one hundred and fifty miles distant) and its belonging to Spain, one has to go through all the silly formalities of procuring a Spanish passport, with the *visé* of the American Consul, and a certificate of health from the *Casa de Sanidad*, which latter is a sure and easy mode of robbing the traveller. I embarked on board of a small weekly steamer for Palma, the capital city, on the south side of the island, situated upon a deep bay, and having a good and secure harbor for large vessels, and a fair trade with Havana. I was agreeably surprised in finding a city of forty thousand persons, occupying a healthy and eligible position, with many fine public buildings, some of which are very antique, denoting its great commercial importance when it enjoyed the trade of the Levant.

By reference to my books I find that the Romans granted it the privilege of a colony; it was afterwards conquered by the Arabs, who made it the residence of their kings, and it continued such after the conquest of Don Jayme the First, of Aragon, in the year 1229, and its most extraordinary monument of that period, commenced during his reign, is the citadel, upon the summit of a high hill, about one mile from the city, commanding a most extensive view of the town and sea. In the centre of it, passing over a deep and wide moat, by a drawbridge, one enters a tower of Cyclopean construction, of great height, and by easy circular stairs of heavy stone arrives at the summit, from which the eye beholds one of the most magnificent prospects of the entire valley and the suburbs of the city, dotted with cottages, and olive and almond trees in blossom. From the prisons within there was no escape, particularly from the lower one, where the culprit passes a final trap, never to be withdrawn.

Some comfortable quarters are fitted up for the use of the governor during the heat of summer. The polite and civil colonel of the governor's staff conducted me in his cabriolet with the aid of an extra mule, nearly to the summit. I have received, by the by, many marks of courtesy from the commandant of the marine as well as other Spanish officers in Barcelona, to whom I was recommended, notwithstanding that our national character has suffered through the acts of the filibusters in the island of Cuba. The houses and the streets of the city are clean, and the population industrious; the hotels are poor. The chief branches of industry are those of the *zapateros*, or shoemakers, whose work is exported to Havana, and the abundant supply of olive oil for the manufactories in the suburbs, of the famous castile soap. The exportation of wine, dried fruit, and almonds, is also very considerable. The language of the country is the Mallorquin, a *patois* of the Arab, Spanish, and French languages; the common people do not speak the Castilian. One of the finest estates is that of the Conde de Monte Negro, about three hours' drive from town. The Cardinal Monte Negro, now deceased, while at Rome made a famous collection of antique statues, and founded a museum on his estate, which is surrounded by valleys of orange, almond, and olive trees, with vineyards upon amphitheatred walled patches of earth extending up the mountain side, and affording the most changeable and picturesque views imaginable.

The little town of Soler, some five leagues distant, on the north side of the island, with a population of eight thousand, is almost entirely dependent upon the culture of the orange. The high mountain over which one crosses is unproductive, but the valleys are extremely fertile, and the scenery is varied. The roads are indifferent; their zigzag windings and tropical views bring to mind the mountains of Caraccas, and the heights of Brazil, and although I rode behind a mule, in a rude sort of gig without springs, with low cover to protect me from the sun's rays, not sufficiently elevated to wear a hat, my driver perched upon a rude box at the tail of the mule, with a cudgel in hand, now yelling hideously expecting to increase his speed, then jumping down in disgust at the obstinacy of the animal, and trudging along on foot, I felt fully compensated by the magnificent prospect in the distance, and a growing appetite for even a Spanish dinner, tinctured with oil and garlic. My driver attempted to describe the objects about us in Spanish, but finding himself embarrassed, he branched off in his own jargon, presuming that I understood him perfectly.

I had ridden through orange groves on horseback in the West Indies, plucking the fruit in passing, but I was not prepared for a league square of orange trees loaded with their golden crop, the branches extending over the walls, uniting and forming an arcade across the narrow streets on entering the town. Soler is situated about two miles from the port, along the banks of a mountain torrent, the sides of which are strewed with fallen oranges.

This is the fruit season, and many small vessels are employed in carrying cargoes to Marseilles, and other ports in France and Spain. Those that are picked by hand and delivered on board, are worth two rials vellon, say ten cents per hundred; such as fall from the trees, detached by the wind, are worth the same price for *five hundred*. I was struck with the fine faces of the children, and the Arabic type and complexion of the women. The people are poor but industrious, and their wants are few. They have bread, some meats, *garabanzas*, a species of pea much in use, with oil and wine; the latter, of the choicest quality, is called *malvoisia*, or *alba flor*, and enjoys a high reputation in Barcelona. The little port is round as a bowl, and placid as a lake, entirely protected, and landlocked with high projecting cliffs above its narrow and bold entrance, and bears resemblance in miniature to Acapulco, on the Pacific coast. A few fishermen only reside there, and a few small orange vessels are seen.

The peasants of the country are very primitive in their costume, wearing broad-brimmed conical hats, and long pantaloons, girded about the loins, with goat skins which cover their shoulders; holes are cut in the side of the undressed hide to pass their arms through, and the entire form of the reddish-brown skin, with the tail in some instances, is suspended down the back, presenting a grotesque appearance. The women wear men's straw hats, with handkerchiefs round the head and under the chin, and round, white, expanding collars, falling a foot in length, with a priestly look, and the groups of both sexes on foot, and mounted upon donkeys, carrying panniers loaded with charcoal, wood, and products of the soil, form a droll caravan. Their copper coins are about the size of small dress-coat button, and nine of them are given for a rial vellon, valued at five cents; and singular as it may appear, the people refuse the copper coin of the main land, while the circulation of five franc pieces is current here, as also in Spain. The old-fashioned pistareen, or peseta, is in general use. In most things they are full a century behind the age, but the light of civilization is beginning to extend here as on the main land. The climate is delightful, nature prolific, and the people in general honest, civil, and polite. I could prolong my stay with pleasure, visiting other portions of the island, but I must not, as I proceed to Valencia, which lies one hundred and fifty miles opposite, on the Spanish coast.

# LXXXIV.

VALENCIA, SPAIN, *March 22, 1858.*

I am in the ancient city of Valencia, surrounded by many antique buildings and relics of Moorish architecture peculiar to the south of Spain. The city contains a population of sixty thousand, and has a fine old cathedral, from the tower of which is seen to advantage the verdure of the valley in the extreme distance, irrigated by water drawn from a mountain torrent which passes near the city, and which at this season presents little but a gravelly bed. The mulberry is cultivated largely, and the production of silk and velvet is the most important branch of industry. There are many churches adorned with fine old paintings by the Spanish masters. The ceilings of two large saloons in the *Casa de la Ciudad*, or City Hall, are of heavy timbers, about a foot apart, and ornamented with an infinity of carved allegorical figures of most exquisite workmanship, in a high state of preservation; they belong to the thirteenth century, and differ from anything I have ever seen before. Notwithstanding the foreign and civil wars, the code of laws of that period, written on parchment and illuminated with the most precious designs and colors, is almost as perfect as when written. The city library, of four thousand volumes, has also some of these gems of antiquity, the labor of a lifetime, executed in the calm and quiet cloister of the monk, free from the cares and anxieties of the world. Aside from museums, churches, paintings, statues, and Moorish architecture, my time has been employed in visiting the public institutions of the city, and the manufacturing establishments peculiar to the country.

The Presidio, or state prison, which has two thousand convicts, each of whom has his occupation in the different departments, reminded me of Sing Sing, with this exception: that here almost all branches of industry are prosecuted, and often to the detriment of the poor free mechanic, which is not the case with us. The most interesting portion of their employments is the weaving of velvets of rich colors. The manufacture of our staple cotton enters largely into the production of common cloth; basket-work, shoemaking, blacksmithing, and the making of chairs and furniture are important branches, also. The kitchen department, and the extreme cleanliness of the whole institution, refute the charge of filthiness, so frequently alleged against the Spanish race. Not a soldier is employed; the prisoners stand sentinel over each other. No cells are used; the mattresses are rolled up and suspended according to number, to be spread in large airy halls. The obstreperous and unruly wear chains; they seem to be easily governed, although many hard subjects are found among them. The hospital is an immense establishment, covering a large extent of surface; it comprises three departments, for the infirm, the reception of new-born infants, and the lunatic asylum, and contains in all some six hundred persons of both sexes. The sick are in charge of sisters of charity, whose devotion is well known. I can scarcely say what is most painful in this establishment—the groans of the sick and suffering, the pitiful cries of the new-born and abandoned infants, or the wild ravings of the maniacs. Certainly sympathy is excited, and our moral nature is exercised, but we experience a sensible relief in escaping the inclosure of so much concentrated misery. The same system is practised here as was until recently in Paris; the poor or culpable mother puts her charge upon the revolving wheel, which places it in the hands of the nurses, for whom there is one large apartment; there are forty of these nurses, each one in charge of three suspended cradles rocking upon a pivot from the walls. The arrangements are perfect, but the pitiful cries of one hundred and twenty infants of tender ages induced me to pass hastily to the apartment of the larger children; I saw groups of them at table, of the ages of two years and upwards; they appeared happy and joyous.

The insane were classed according to their malady, in different departments; there were some fifty at dinner when we entered, who behaved well. In the next apartment, containing about twenty, we were addressed by one who had in hand a bowl of pottage, and who, in the most eloquent and appealing language, complained loudly of barbarous and despotic treatment, and want of nourishment; the keeper replied in reproachful terms, when a combat commenced between them which threatened to compromise our safety, as the maniac got the advantage of our guide, who escaped with the blood trickling down his scratched figure. We pacified the surrounding group with presents of cigars, which they sought for eagerly; in the next department they were the most violent, and were placed in chains, with their arms strapped and rendered powerless; they begged lamentably to be released from captivity. Iron cages still exist in the prison, but the use of them is now abandoned; not so in Egypt, where I saw the poor maniacs in cells like wild beasts, in a state of nudity, with collars about their necks, attached by a chain, and climbing the iron bars.

The article of tobacco in Spain is a government monopoly, and various manufacturers of cigars and snuff are found in the principal cities; the *estancos*, or shops for their sale, are appointed throughout the kingdom, producing a net revenue, under the best administration of affairs, of nine millions of dollars per annum. The establishment here is an immense solid stone structure, resembling a palace, three stories high, and employing three thousand eight hundred female operatives in making cigars, and two hundred men in cutting smoking tobacco. The director informed me that they had orders ahead to the value of sixty thousand dollars, and had not hands sufficient to supply them. Every department of the upper stories is occupied with females, there being from six to eight at each table; these tables are placed in double rows on each side of halls some three hundred feet in length, of a quadrangular form; the centre of the edifice is an open court. They commence at seven A.M., and leave at six P.M., bringing their simple repast with them in the morning. The basement is occupied as store rooms, in which are found all the different qualities of Havana and Philippine tobacco, not forgetting eleven mammoth hogsheads of one thousand pounds each, which I recognised readily as the staple of Kentucky and Virginia. I once visited the factory at Seville, where eighteen hundred females are employed, and thought it an extraordinary sight; but I was astonished to see such masses of the tender sex as were here, and the amount of work they performed.

The entire process of the silk manufacture, from the opening of the cocoon to the making of stuffs for ladies' robes, is an interesting study. One large and well regulated factory that I visited employs from two hundred and fifty to three hundred females. In the upper story of this building are seen one hundred and twenty girls, placed in rooms sixty feet long, with a permanently set kettle in brick-work, and pipes of hot and cold water supplied by the engine pumps. The cocoons are put into the warm water and circulated with small brush brooms; the silk attaches itself to the fibres, and by motive power is drawn off on reeling machines. The worm is dislodged from the cocoon, and the silk completely drawn off; it then passes into the hands of the spinners, and thence to the weavers, and finally appears as the choice fabric of Valencia.

The manufacture of porcelain of various designs and colors, is curious for one not familiar with the method. The preparation is made from ground clay, moulded as in our brick and pottery works, then kiln-dried for fifteen hours, then passed through a composition of liquids, which is immediately absorbed, and which whitens it; it then goes into the hands of the artist, who designs with a brush the different figures and colors; it is then dried in kilns with faggots, for sixty hours. The principal trade is in squares for floors and staircases. Tiles for the domes of churches are also made of different colors. Valencia has a miserable harbor, which is now undergoing reconstruction; the roadstead is bad and dangerous, and it is at times impossible to land or embark, on account of the breakers. On landing from the steamer, which came from Barcelona, and which lay a mile distant from the shore, escaping from the surf on one side, we were beset by a clamorous horde of tartana drivers, each determined to have his portion of the spoils. The luggage has to be carried and examined at the custom-house, and thence transported from the village of Groan to Valencia, a distance of three miles.

The tartana is an odd-looking and hard riding vehicle; it is the carriage of the country for all classes. I can only compare it to a butcher's cart without springs; it has a baggage-wagon top, seats suspended lengthwise, slightly raised from the axle, with heavy netting for the bottom, and steps in the rear;

the driver has his seat on the shafts. The wealthy manage to fit them up with springs, and have them cushioned inside, with glass windows fore and aft, and tastefully painted; they are large enough for a family, and the captivating glances from the flashing eyes of the dark-browed senoritas, peeping from the openings, compensated in some degree for the ill-looking conveyance.

# LXXXV.

MURCIA, SPAIN, *March 29, 1853.*

Leaving Valencia, by steamer, we arrived at Alicant the morning of Palm Sunday. The city contains some twenty-five or thirty thousand inhabitants; has a small artificial harbor, a tolerable roadstead, and is the seat of considerable commerce. It is well protected by a fort on the summit of a volcanic rock, of a dull grey color. The houses are clean and well built; but they suffer here from drought, having had but little rain for several years, and large numbers of the peasantry have emigrated to Algiers. The cathedral was crowded with groups of men, women, and children, bearing palm-branches, artificially braided, and fancifully ornamented with ribbons and sugar-plums, with which they paraded in the procession to the sounds of violins and bugles. The priests, in full church-robes, followed by the multitude bearing torches, passed out of the church, making a circuit, and returning knocked for admittance at the closed doors, which were finally opened to the triumphant group, a symbol of the entrance of Christ into Jerusalem. The huertas, or valleys, in the distance, irrigated by artificial means, are rich and fertile, and produce olives, grapes, and a succession of crops. The palmtree flourishes in certain localities, and the fresh dates are not to be despised. From Alicant I proceeded to Carthagena by steamer, some hundred miles. Carthagena is in a decayed state, for the want of commerce; still it is the best port of Spain on the Mediterranean. King Charles III. made it a naval establishment; the fortifications, bulwarks, hospitals, arsenals, and ropewalks, are upon a magnificent scale, and well worth a visit; but it has a dull, inanimate appearance, only a few naval vessels being there; the trade is mostly with English craft, bringing coal for the foundries in the neighborhood, and taking cargoes of lead in return. The mining of lead and copper is a very important branch in this portion of Spain. I visited some works which are extensively carried on by English capitalists, but I thought the lead ore which I once saw in Galena, Illinois, was superior in quality. There is a Presidio, or government prison, at Carthagena, which contained one thousand two hundred persons, employed like those described in Valencia. Large numbers were engaged in braiding Esparto, a species of mountain grass, which is made use of for sacking, carpeting, and various purposes. Not a little amusing was it to see groups of male convicts engaged in the unmanly employment of knitting fancy stockings for ladies.

From Carthagena I came to the capital of the old kingdom of Murcia by diligence, a distance of about thirty miles, and arrived in time to witness the principal ceremony of the Holy Week. The road passed through a dull and uninteresting country, traversing a grey volcanic region for a considerable distance across the mountain, without vegetation, when the fruitful valley of

Murcia appeared of a sudden, not unlike an oasis in the desert. The irrigated valley is prolific in orange, lemon, mulberry, and other trees. The city contains forty thousand inhabitants; it is very quiet, being the residence of many aristocratic families, as may be seen from the armorial bearings on the fronts of the houses. The streets are narrow, and the buildings fancifully painted. There is an air of ease and comfort about the male peasantry, with their gay striped mantles, and the fancy embroidered drapery of the women, in groups on festival occasions, fills up the picture. The public walks, here, are very agreeable. The view of the Vega, or valley, from the Cathedral dome, and the circular city, with its blue flat roofs and cane pigeon-houses, is charming, as also the prospect of the country in the distance, with its drooping palm trees and flowery fields and gardens. The cathedral rises in divisions not unlike a spyglass drawn out, and surmounted by a dome.

The Holy Week has just drawn to a close. Having passed several of these festivals in Jerusalem, Rome, Havana, and Lima, I was anxious to witness the religious ceremonies, here, and compare them with those of the countries I have named. I find they outstrip the latter in the detail, but are less grand and impressive. The people pride themselves on the rich wood carvings of one Francisco Larcillo, who lived in the last century, and whose work is found in the churches, also in the figures which form part of the procession, and which are admirably executed. It was curious to watch the country people, of both sexes, in their gay Spanish costumes, crowding the streets to see the figures personifying the acts and sufferings of Christ; the Saviour being represented to the life, supporting the weight of a heavy cross, the woodwork of which was covered with tortoise-shell, and tipped with gold, his hair streaming at full length, and the blood trickling from the wounds of the golden crown of thorns. The platform rested upon the shoulders of twelve men, who were provided with crutches with which to rest themselves at the stations. The figures of Mary, the mother of Jesus, Mary Magdalen, and St. Peter, with the keys, were upon similar platforms, covered with silks and satins, tinsel and gold, with a profusion of artificial and natural flowers. Among the number is Christ and the Twelve Apostles surrounding the table of the last supper, which is abundantly supplied with meats, fruits, and confectionery, very tastefully arranged. The almost naked and bleeding form of Christ submitting to the flagellation, is represented by the hideous figure of a monster who has fallen from exhaustion, while others are drawn to take the cords that bind him to the stake. The immense procession is headed by bands of music, the priesthood in full regalia, the military and civil officers, followed by a company of Nazarenes in armor, with lances, who go through a sham fight, the whole succeeded by the military, and as many as five hundred persons, bare-footed, of all ages and sizes, dressed in white cotton cloth hoods and skirts, their loins girded with cords. The hoods or masks contain two holes for sight. The persons who wear these masks support a black crucifix of some weight upon their shoulders. The streets are crowded to excess, and the balconies are filled with sparkling-eyed senoritas and groups of friends. The anxiety of the crowd to get a peep at the procession, with the confusion, made it more a festival or jubilee than a religious ceremony. The night procession with torches, after the crucifixion, with the lifeless and mutilated body of Christ, surrounded by his weeping mother and the attending groups, was more quiet, and more solemn and imposing. High mass was numerously attended in the Cathedral on the morning of the Resurrection, when at ten o'clock the bells of the city churches thundered forth the glad tidings that the Saviour had risen, and induced many to huzza it. I had to take refuge in a shop for a half hour from the merciless peltings of those on the house-tops and in the balconies, who threw ashes, sand, and earthen missiles, not unlike the Brazilian wax-balls of lemon size, filled with water, only more difficult to dispose of. It was a temporary diversion, and was taken in good part: but some funny scenes and dirty faces were the consequence.

Having visited on a former occasion all the southern cities of Spain, and having now completed the eastern coast on the Mediterranean, I must turn my face towards Madrid, and have a fatiguing ride for upwards of two hundred miles, in heavy lumbering diligences, over rough roads, with miserable Posadas, or inns. The roads are now considered tolerably safe, being protected by civil guards, who have arrested and shot many of the highwaymen.

I shall take Aranjuez, the Versailles of the Spanish court, en route to Madrid.

# LXXXVI.

MADRID, *April 15, 1853.*

Ensconced in the bedina, or front compartment of a huge lumbering diligence, at two o'clock in the morning, I left Murcia, behind eight mules, a postillion, and two drivers, with the prospect of a hard ride, over a very uninteresting country, of sixty Spanish leagues—which are unlike any other for length—the "Camino Real," or royal road, being neglected, and in consequence of the winter rains, in horrible order. The wheel mules are attached to the pole, and guided without bits; the others draw by long straggling ropes; the coachman sits in the box with his long whip, and his assistant, who jumps down from time to time and pelts the animals with sticks, stones, and mud. The postillion rides a horse beside the first led mule; he is required where the roads are the worst, and he keeps the track. The mules all have their titles, and seem to understand the incessant cries, from the India-rubber lungs of the driver, of Carpintero, Zapetero, Carbonero, and the whole catalogue of names. The long ears of the animal named, are pricked up, and his best efforts are made under the cut of the lash, or the whizzing of a stone past his head.

We pushed through a dreary and uninteresting country some twenty leagues, with occasional fertile valleys and indifferent villages, to the Sheffield of Spain, the town of Albacete, where we passed the night. It is noted in Spain for the manufacture of arms. Population ten thousand. We were soon surrounded by venders of poniards, stilettos, and small punalicos, or knives, which the women are said to conceal in their garters. The Spaniard is very expert in the use of the knife, and with it concealed under his capa, or cloak, is a dangerous enemy. The inns are generally great, barn-like stone buildings, with open patios, or courts, for the entrance of animals and vehicles. The rooms are generally dirty, with no furniture except cot-beds; and after an oily garlicky supper, the fleas, and kicking and thrashing of the mules all night, one is prepared for a comfortable nap in the diligence over a rough road. The bread is generally excellent throughout Spain, and chocolate can always be procured.

We made long, tiresome distances, over barren treeless plains, with no water for irrigation, and no signs of birds or animal life, when we would suddenly strike a fertile valley, tolerably cultivated by the scratching process of rude ploughs, but without hedges or landmarks, to denote proprietorship.

At break of day, and late sunset, the peasants may be seen mounted on donkeys, or carrying their implements of husbandry, after the hard toils of the day, returning to their mud or stone hovels, comfortless and cheerless, not unlike the country people in the interior of Sicily, who congregate in villages in like manner, and for a motive similar to the one which actuates them here—safety from the hordes of bandits which the wars of the Peninsula have produced. The guardias civiles, whom we met from time to time, have made sad havoc with the Ladrons, shooting several, and taking many prisoners, so we came through in safety.

Some of the villages of La Mancha through which we passed, were very poor, with many beggars; others appeared comfortable, and the people gay and cheerful, notwithstanding the heavy exactions and badly administered government. The country, however, was full of historical interest, as at the left, not far distant, lay Argamasilla del Alba, in the prison of which Cervantes wrote Don Quixote. Near the villages many flat, square, open threshing floors, were found, for bruising the grain with the feet of mules and oxen, after the custom of oriental countries. I was forcibly reminded of the exploits of Don Quixote as we approached the village El Toboso, the reputed residence of the crack-brained knight of the windmills; for here the mills were numerous, and used for grinding the grain of the country. They look not unlike giants in the distance, and hence it was perhaps that the Don assured Sancho that they might get elbow-deep in adventures. It was a festival day with the peasants, and the dulcineas, with their half Swiss, half German appearance, in blue and green petticoats, with handkerchiefs tied under their chins during the Cachucha, the national dance, and castanets in their hands, and their Cabeleros, in low crowned, high rimmed, velvet-bound hats, with fancy colored, round clothes, jackets and leggings, had a happy effect.

On the morning of the third day we breakfasted at Ocana, memorable for a battle in 1808, in which Marshal Soult, with twenty-five thousand men, put to flight sixty thousand Spaniards, through good generalship; the French killed five thousand and took twenty-six thousand prisoners, with the loss of only one thousand six hundred men, a stroke of luck reminding one of the famous Texian fight at San Jacinto. The town was pillaged and almost destroyed—the people left poor and miserable. The diligences and other vehicles concentrate here from the south and east, and give it some importance.

From Ocana we passed through a hilly, dreary, and treeless country, until suddenly, as if by enchantment, burst upon the view the fertile valley and banks of the Tayos, upon which is situated Aranjuez, the early summer residence of the royal family, the spires and cupolas of the palace and outbuildings, looming up like signals for the benighted traveller in the desert waste. Here is found the only railroad, which enters the capital, a distance of nine leagues. As I design visiting the palaces and the gardens when the trees are in full bloom, I shall defer my remarks until that time.

Upon a small eminence, approaching Madrid, is seen a monument denoting its geographical position, in the centre of Spain. Madrid is, comparatively speaking, a modern city; for Spain having risen under Charles V., who, gouty and phlegmatic, found the cool bracing air from the mountains adapted to his complaint, he deserted the ancient capitals of Valladolid, Sevilla, Granada, and Toledo, and fixed his residence upon several hills upon the banks of a small river, almost dry in summer, at an elevation of two thousand four hundred feet above the level of the sea. It was declared the capital by Philip II., in 1560. The country about is flat, and without trees; it produces but little, the climate being changeable; but being the residence of the royal family, and seat of the government, with its three hundred thousand population, from all parts of the empire, as well as strangers, it became the grand focus of attraction and extravagance, exhausting the revenue and the resources of Spain, both foreign and provincial. Every article of use is brought from abroad, or from the provinces, over the caminos reales, or royal roads, which branch off, but meet north and south. Notwithstanding the aridity of the soil, the lavish expenditures of former governments have, by means of irrigation, produced magnificent shaded drives and promenades in the suburbs; among the number figures the Prado, the resort of all fashionable Madrid in the evening. It is ten thousand feet in length, and two hundred feet wide, with fountains and statuary. The salon, or part most frequented, is about one thousand five hundred feet long, and is occupied by promenaders of both sexes, in full dress, while thousands of ladies in mantillas, seated in chairs, are being passed in review by Cabeleros smoking their cigaritos. The side carriage road is occupied by a long procession of brilliant equipages and liveried attendants. It is necessary to sprinkle the grounds, as the fine grey dust is prejudicial to dress, and destructive to the eyes and lungs.

The Spaniards think there is only one Corte, one Madrid in the world, and it is not surprising, for the resources of the country concentrate here. The palace is beautifully situated, and one of the finest in Europe. The Royal Museum contains the famous national paintings of Murillo and Velasquez, as well as some of the best gems of Raphael, Titian, and Michael Angelo; and the immense galleries of all the different schools of European art, demand several days' close examination. The chief public amusements are the theatres and bull-fights; in the former, you see the national dances in all their perfection; in the latter, which are attended by all classes, to the extent of some thirty thousand persons, eight or ten bulls, and seven or ten horses pay the forfeit of their lives. One of their famous matadors, or swordsmen, died recently, and was interred with great pomp and ceremony, his coffin being exposed, covered with a black pall, for twenty-four hours before the high altar, surrounded by tall burning wax candles. The stately, silver-mounted hearse, with waving black plumes, was drawn by four horses, in black drapery, followed by a large number of bearers with torches, and one hundred and ten vehicles, several of which were of the nobility; then followed a multitude of the middling classes, while the balconies were filled with ladies.

Near the Palace, on the opposite side of a beautiful circular promenade, surrounded by trees and the statues of the former kings of Spain, is situated the opera-house, a fine edifice, erected by Ferdinand VII. for his convenience. The night piece to the close for the season is Fra Diavolo. We had a full house, the queen, as well as the ex-queen Christina and daughters, being present.

Things are in a bad state in Spain; the treasury is bankrupt; the abuses of the general government are great; constitutional privileges are only in name; the taxes and imposts upon the farmers are heavy; the people in the interior are poor; the liberty of the press is abridged; and all this in a country possessing every variety of soil and climate, and rich in its productions, both agricultural and metallic.

The all but universal want of honor and good faith of the royal family and upper classes of society is notorious. The queen mother, one of the wealthiest capitalists of Europe, is grasping and avaricious; undertaking enterprises with great benefit to herself, but disastrous to the tax-payer. The people detest her, but are currying and subdued when she presents herself.

I was in the Cortes when Bravo Murillo was defending himself from the charges alleged against him for his acts in granting railway privileges while minister. The House of Deputies is magnificently fitted up; but the members, in handsome attire, with white kid and colored gloves, and gold-headed canes, differ from our working members, surrounded with their budgets and documents, and up to their eyes in paper, ink, and public journals. The opposition were exposing the acts of the government in influencing the public elections, thereby securing their own instruments of power. This could not be endured, and a royal order closed the Cortes. The excitement soon passed over; for what can the reformer do when the whole force of the army is ready to put down any attempt, and when that arm of strength is the only official department sure of pay, even when other branches of the public service are neglected? My opinion is that the day is not far distant when a change must take place in the affairs of this ill-governed country.

# LXXXVII.

The Escorial, *May 1, 1853.*

On this busy, bustling day at home, I find myself wandering quietly and solitary through the untenanted gorgeous palace of the Escorial, with its minute combinations of convent, royal cemetery, and residence of the former kings of Spain. My guide is nearly seventy years of age, and has been blind for the last fifty-six years; yet he is active, mounts the cupola through the numerous passages, and describes the particular localities and points of view. This immense edifice measures seven hundred and forty-four feet by five hundred and eighty feet, and the entire square covers more than three thousand feet. In the centre is the chapel, surmounted by a dome. There are, so says the guide, sixty-three fountains, twelve cloisters, eighty staircases, sixteen court yards, and three thousand feet of fresco work, commenced in 1553, and finished in 1584.

The chapel has three naves three hundred and twenty feet long, two hundred and thirty feet wide, and three hundred and twenty feet to the top of the cupola. It is built of granite, in fine proportion, and superb for its simplicity, with richly decorated altars of jasper, and various marble and bronze gilt statues of great size. The painting, statuary, frescoes, and other ornaments are in proportion, to give you a faint idea of this immense work. Philip II., half monk, half king, died here in 1598, boasting that from the foot of a mountain he governed half the world with a scrap of paper. The lavish expenditure of millions upon millions could only have been supplied from newly discovered America.

From Madrid the distance is eight leagues by diligence, most of the way over a barren, desert country, where the immense glowing piles are discovered, at the base of the mountain, with its small village which is resorted to in summer by the citizens of Madrid, to escape the heat, glare, and dust of the city. The royal family never visit here, as it is the resting-place of their deceased relatives. The lawns, gardens, and promenades are pretty, as is also a miniature country house, ornamented with marble arabesques, rich paintings, and all the paraphernalia of a palace. Philip II. accumulated some seven thousand relics, which are preserved in five hundred and fifteen shrines. The French carried off much of the bullion of gold, but the exhibition is still sufficient to satisfy the most fastidious. The Pantheon, or burial-place, is a vaulted chamber under the high altar, approached by green and yellow colored jasper staircases, by torchlight; it is an octagon-formed chamber, thirty-six feet wide, and equally high, where in niches repose the kings and mothers of kings, the sexes being on opposite sides. The hosts of monks who were formerly here under the patronage of the king, no longer exist; and the services to the departed dead, and the few living who repair here, are performed by a limited number of priests.

Since I last wrote you from Madrid, I have visited the antiquated city of Toledo, and the summer residence of the royalty at Aranjuez. From Madrid to Toledo is twelve leagues, over a dull, dusty road, with straggling villages; among the number Illescas, which merits its reputation of having served up a stewed cat to Gil Blas, instead of a hare; but on approaching the venerable and imposing old city, the country improves, and is tolerably cultivated. It is built upon an almost impregnable rock of seven hills, and is two thousand four hundred feet above the level of the sea; the river Tayos rolls through the gorge which separates it from the opposite eminence; it has only one approach by the land side, which is protected by mammoth towers and castellated walls. The diligence enters on the outside road, which is of modern construction, and can only pass through the old gates and the narrow and circuitous lanes by means of cutting places for the form of the hubs to pass. It was a relief to escape from the heat, and glare, and dust of Madrid, and find oneself in the elevated, fresh, and invigorating atmosphere of this old city, with its shaded terraces and huts, protected from the sun's rays by tall, substantial, Moorish-like houses, with clean courts, not unlike those of Seville; and although it was gloomy and tomb-like, its dilapidated population having dwindled down from two hundred thousand to fifteen thousand, it was an agreeable change from the noisy, bustling capital. My eyes having suffered from the dust, which in Madrid, at this season of the year, amounts to an epidemic, I wore blue goggles. I went quite opportunely, however, to see the town in convention, as the following day the ex-queen Christina and daughters came to see the Cardinal, her confessor. It being her first visit to this old city, it was quite a festival day; the priests were in full regalia, and the troops under arms; high mass was performed in the old cathedral; this, and the firing of cannon from the towering platform of the Alcazar, the banners, curtains, and counterpanes suspended from the balconies of the curious antique Plaza, gave the old city an animated appearance. Christina, in her gracious, smiling, and captivating manner, responded to the salutations of the people, who at heart despise her for her intriguing and audacious disposition. She was remarkably well, and appears nearly as young as when I saw her in Rome during her exile.

In the heart of the city towers one of the finest cathedrals in Spain; it is two hundred and four feet wide, and its central nave is one hundred and sixty feet high. It is a perfect museum of art, architecture, sculpture, and painting, which cannot well be described on paper. The illuminated stained glass windows, when seen at sunset, resembled rubies and emeralds. The view from the tower is very extensive. The chiming of the many ponderous bells, coming upon you while in the tower, is deafening. There are various churches and galleries, of antique and Moorish architecture, which occupy one's time to advantage. Toledo, famous for its arms, has still its government manufactory, which employs about two hundred men; it is situated about one and a half miles from the city, on the banks of the river, and is well worth a visit. Although the machinery is dull and heavy, the work turned out is very superior. The finest armory I have seen was in Madrid, which has a vast collection, and contains a variety of ancient as well as modern blades. The collection of horse and warrior armor is of the choicest and most exquisite composition. The blades are of fine temper and polish, and so elastic that they can be coiled like the mainspring of a watch, and packed up. The collection of new arms in the form of all the antiques, Arab and Turkish, in use, is very interesting. The introduction of fire-arms was destructive to the interests of Toledo.

From Toledo I proceeded along the river bank six leagues to Aranjuez, through a rich agricultural and beautiful country, the property of the queen; it was sparsely populated, and little productive, from its unnatural tenure. The shady avenues for nearly a league approaching the royal abode are agreeable. The court resides here until the middle of June, when fevers sometimes prevail from the miasma of the river, then the town is quite deserted, and royalty departs to La Granza for the summer and autumn, until it returns to Madrid. Nature was in her prettiest attire, the vast and extensive gardens were filled with shade-trees of all countries. In the long walks, studded with thickly covered foliage, among the flowering fruit-trees, the fountains abundantly supplied with water, the statues and groups of Neptunes, Tritons, Dolphins, and hosts of allegorical figures, among the singing of birds, and the murmuring of the cataracts of water, one is transported as if by enchantment into a fairy land. The workmen were all busy in getting the grounds in order for the arrival of the queen.

I returned to the capital. The usual display of military took place at the departure of the queen, whose absence gave me an opportunity of seeing the royal stables, carriage houses, and harness rooms, which are among the richest in Europe for equipage. Some of the antique carriages were superbly decorated with gold and silver. The stable contained two hundred horses, one hundred and fifty mules, and one hundred and fifty equipages, which can be turned out on state occasions with appropriate harness and trappings. The employees in and about the palace are about eight hundred in number, so a very good idea may be formed of the expenses of a monarchical government, and an easy solution of the enormous imposts and taxation. Spain, with a population reduced from twenty-four millions to thirteen millions, pays the queen two and a half million of dollars per annum, while the glorious Republic of double the population, considers twenty-five thousand pretty good pay for a President. How often, while standing at the gates of the walled cities, noticing the wrangling between the officials and the hardy peasantry of the country, who are obliged to submit to the impost upon every article of production, have I reflected upon our free and untrammelled farmers at home, enjoying liberty of action, opinion, and religion, and free from passports and spies. How much we have to be thankful for, and how much we undervalue the privileges we possess.

I shall proceed across the mountain to La Granja, the last royal seat I have to visit, and shall continue to the ancient cities of Leyena and Valladolid.

# LXXXVIII.

VALLADOLID, SPAIN, *May 9, 1853.*

Leaving the Escorial I proceeded on horseback, with my guide, across the Guadarama chain of mountains, which divides old and new Castile, a distance of some nine leagues to San Ildefonso, the residence of the Court in the months of July, August, and September, about eighteen leagues from Madrid. We had had rain at the Escorial, which proved to be snow on the mountains. The road was constructed in 1749, by Ferdinand; at its extreme height is a marble lion, five thousand feet above the level of the sea. The view from the summit, with the valleys and villages spread out like a map, was very beautiful, while the tall forest pines with their white mantles among the jagged rocks, and the cascades from the melting snow, were truly Alpine, and reminded me of the Simplon. Here, also, Napoleon crossed on Christmaseve, in 1808, with great loss from the extreme cold, leading his army in person, and in his impatience leaping from his horse, and walking on the snow, encouraging his troops. During the winter the road is frequently impassable; but notwithstanding that my horse was plunging through snow banks in the narrow passes up to his middle, I felt little inconvenience from the cold under the rays of the mid-day sun, and the highest pinnacles once past, descending rapidly into the valley, a two hours' ride carried me to the village of La Granja.

In 1722, Philip V., while hunting, discovered this Granja, or farm house, of the Segovian monks, and being of a retiring disposition, bought the site, and commenced building a palace, and laying out the grounds, levelling rocks, forming lakes and fountains, which surpass many in Europe, for there is no want of water here. The gardens are planted in avenues and adorned with marble statues. There are twenty-six great fountains; among the number are the baths of Diana, with twenty female figures. The fountain of Fame throws water one hundred and twenty feet high. The mountain rises abruptly here eight thousand feet high; the snow on the craggy, rocky sides and forests, the fresh vegetation of spring in the valley, and the mountain cataracts, produced one of those magnificent sights which are so difficult to describe, and so hard to forget. The season was still backward, as the fruits of spring ripen in autumn: everything was artificial; rocks were levelled and hollowed to admit pipes and roots of trees, and earth brought from the plains. The expenses were so enormous, that this infatuated king died owing forty-five millions of reals. The palace is pleasantly situated, and looks over the royal grounds; the royal apartments are light, airy, and well finished, but not strikingly magnificent. The saloons have some fine paintings and statuary, but many of these works of art have been removed to Madrid. Here, in January, 1724, Philip V., who was a bigot and hypochondriac, abdicated his crown and resumed it the same year, after the death of his son, being urged to become a king again by his wife, who was tired of private life.

Here, Ferdinand VII., in 1832, revoked the decree by which he had abolished the Salic law, and declared his daughter, the present Queen Isabel, heiress to the crown, which act brought upon Spain her civil wars, and the imputed succession of "Don Carlos," for here were carried on the court intrigues by Christina, who induced her royal husband to sign the document while on a sick bed. Ferdinand died in 1833, and then commenced the civil wars, which distracted the kingdom. In the same palace, in 1835, this same Ex-Queen Christina, in turn, was deprived of her royal privileges, and forced by the soldiery to proclaim the democratical constitution of 1812, after which she was exiled until the present restoration of things took place. A few leagues further on is the old Castillian city of Segovia, with its giant houses and balconies; it resembles Toledo somewhat; the population is reduced from thirty thousand to nine thousand. Its position is cold and bleak, three thousand three hundred feet above the level of the sea, surrounded by picturesque old walls and towers. Here is the most remarkable Roman Aqueduct I have yet seen. The steep banked rivers of the Erisina and Clamores which girdle the city, were difficult of access, and induced the ancients to bring the pure stream of the Rio Trio several leagues by this aqueduct. It has several angles from two hundred to nine hundred feet, to break the force of the water; the arches rise in proportion as the ground deepens, until they become double; the upper tiers are uniform; the three central ones, which are the most stupendous, being one hundred and two feet in height. This mammoth work is of solid granite blocks, without cement or mortar, of similar form to those in the Campagna of Rome. This immense structure was probably erected by Trajan, but nothing is known of its history. According to some antiquarians, it was built by one Lucinus, but the common people call it the Puente del Diablo, or devil's bridge, because his Satanic majesty was in love with a fair Segovian, and offered his services for her affections, which she promised him provided he would build an aqueduct in one night, which he did. One stone, however, being found deficient, the church decided the contract void, and Satan was foiled. The lower classes believe the story, and give no credit to other accounts. The aqueduct was respected by the Goths, but broken in part by the Moors of Toledo, in 1071, who destroyed thirty-five arches, which remained in ruin until 1483, when Isabella, Queen of Spain, repaired them. One of the finest old Gothic Cathedrals of Spain is Segina. From its square tower, covered with a cupola three hundred and six feet high, is a beautiful panoramic view of the city with its gardens, convents, aqueduct, and La Granza, lying at the base of the towering mountains.

Valladolid, the city from which I write, has no diligence communication with Segovia. I was therefore, obliged to make a circuit of ninety miles to reach this point, spending a part of a day at San Raphael, the angle of two roads in a miserable Venta, a halting-place for muleteers; it was an open, barn-like barrack, with a stone floor; a huge kitchen, black as night from the smoke of the past twenty years; the ceiling hung with sausages, garlic, bacon, and dried calf skin, while the sides were covered with the whole battery of the cuisine, not forgetting a strolling tinker at work repairing the copper vessels. The huge fireplace in the centre, was some ten feet square, rising conically through the roof, not unlike the smoke-stack of a furnace. The grape-vine fire burned brightly, surrounded by dark-visaged and bearded muleteers in their bandit-appearing costume, singing and cracking their jokes, awaiting the contents of the various copper pots distributed upon the embers and suspended over the flames. In manner I was awaiting my puchero, one of the best Spanish dishes, divested of oil and garlic, and composed of beef and vegetables boiled. My appetite was arrested, however, by the bleating cries of a poor calf three weeks old, which was being massacred by the fire-side. It had no effect upon a poor famished soldier, who had entered and ordered a bowl of broth and a morsel of bread, which seemed to restore him until he disclosed his poverty and inability to pay. In vain he solicited relief from those present; the cook took his handkerchief in payment, and drove him away. I interceded and relieved the poor man, to the satisfaction of the guests, but the cook looked daggers, for he had lost his prize. Travelling in the interior of uncivilized Spain is doing penance, but one is amply compensated for it in the enjoyments of the large cities, and in the examination of the monuments and works of art.

Valladolid was, in the sixteenth century, the seat of royalty, and as such was adorned with splendid edifices, under Charles V.; but its beautiful river and fertile country were abandoned for upstart Madrid, situated in a desert plain, to gratify the caprice of a monarch. Its population dwindled from fifty thousand to half the number. Buonaparte made sad work with the convents in 1809, as the relics of art now collected in the museum testify. Some of the finest specimens of woodcarving by Juan de Juani are found here, while exquisite and elaborate façades of convents in marble still exist in perfection. All the public archives of Spain are preserved at Simancas, a town and castle about two leagues from here. The strong castle, surrounded by a moat, was a well selected site when the capital was here; but it is now too far removed from Madrid. There are some thirty rooms filled with state papers, the correspondence of foreign governments and the provinces. The papers of the Inquisition are very numerous; also war orders and original dispatches of the Grand Captain, letters of the different monarchs, the correspondence of Christopher Columbus, the Inventory of Isabella's jewelry, and her last will and testament besides the title deeds to the Duke of Wellington's estate.

Napoleon ordered the most curious documents to Paris, as he had already plundered Vienna and Rome. Some eight thousand packages and bundles were sent to Paris, but after the battle of Waterloo most of them were restored. The French soldiers destroyed large numbers, as the strings were useful, and the papers served to make beds, and to light camp fires.

Documents bearing date in the 13th and 14th century are dry and perfectly preserved, as are those of the present day.

There is sufficient of interest to occupy one pleasantly a few days, but having diverged considerably from the main route, I shall proceed to Burgos, celebrated for its Gothic Cathedral, and from thence branch off to the left and visit the Basque provinces of the north. Having strong recommendations here to the husband of the Infanta, or king's sister, who occupies the palace of Philip III., I was hospitably entertained. It was in this palace that Buonaparte was lodged, and he looked out of the window upon two of the noblest specimens of religious Gothic art in the world; the interior is destined to destruction, but the exterior sculptures of these convents still remain in their purity. Invited to dine *en famille*, I found myself with a little circle of five persons, the seat of honor being reserved for me beside the Infanta. A sumptuous repast and choice old wines were served by three full-liveried servants, after which the conversation turned upon our beloved country, who found a defender present, and one disposed to portray her beauties and capacities as far as was consistent with his position. The evening closed agreeably at the opera. You will probably hear from me again from Santander or Bilboa, in the north.

# LXXXIX.

SAN SEBASTIAN, SPAIN, *May 23, 1853.*

From Valladolid to Burgos, some seventy miles by diligence, the road was dry and dusty, and the country uninteresting; the villages were poor, and the soil badly cultivated. The land tax, and the conscription for the army, are discouraging to the cultivator of the soil; the youth are liable to be taken and forced to quit their native country, and sent to the Island of Cuba, or the Philippine Islands, as was the case recently while I was in Santander. Some two hundred were sent off in a crowded vessel at this unpropitious season, to arrive in the yellow fever months at Havana.

The city of Burgos was sacked and burnt by the French army in 1808, and its population of fifty thousand dwindled down to twelve thousand; but it is mostly rebuilt, and presents a tolerable appearance. The great attraction for strangers is its Gothic Cathedral, one of the finest in Spain, and of great antiquity, having been commenced in the year 1221. It was respected by the French during the war. This immense edifice has two towers with spires of open stonework, which in the distance appear as light as lace-work, and one wonders how it can endure this blustering climate. The chapels are as large as some churches, and filled with tombs of sculptured marble and stained glass. The white stone of some of the interior walls and buttresses inclosing the choir represents in sculpture the life of Christ, his agony, the supporting of the cross, the crucifixion and ascension; the building, like other edifices of the kind in Spain, is a perfect museum of art, pictures, statuary, and carved wood. The ceremonies of the Ascension were consummated while I was there, in the presence of a vast assemblage from town and country, giving one a good opportunity to observe the variety of character and costume.

From Burgos to Santander, the northern Atlantic shore of Spain, is ninety miles; the first portion is dreary and badly cultivated, and the hills are high and arid; but suddenly some of the most charming valleys appear, and the face of nature as well as the condition of men changes, as we approach a commercial port. Santander is an important trading town of sixteen thousand souls; it has fine stone quarries, and the air of activity of trade. There are large quantities of flour exported to the island of Cuba, which is protected by a heavy duty against our American productions, and should Spain lose this jewel of the crown the blow would fall heavily upon the grain-producing countries of the north. Another eighteen hours' ride, after leaving Santander, brought me to Bilboa, the capital of Viscaya, situated upon the little river Nervion, which divides the old and new town, and is navigable from its entrance at Portugaleta, a small town, to the city. Bilboa lies in a gorge of hills, and has a damp climate; the vegetation is luxuriant, the country is most romantic and picturesque, and the town has a population of some fourteen thousand. Although still in Spain, appearances have changed, as the Basque provinces of the north, comprising Alava, Viscaya, and Guipuzcoa, forming the mountainous angle of the N. W. of the Spanish Peninsula, are the home of the aboriginal inhabitants who were never subdued or expelled, but were the first to sally forth from the mountains and beat back the invading Moors, a feat from which they derived their nobility, which afterwards extended throughout Spain; they consequently enjoy certain privileges not granted to any other portions of the country. They are free from conscription, or, as the Spaniards say, blood-tax, and are exempt from land-tax, stamps, and a variety of imposts, to which other parts of the empire are subjected. They regulate their church matters, and construct their own roads; hence the great and striking difference discernible in the manners, agriculture, manufacture, and general well-being of the people.

Tobacco is the great government monopoly in Spain, but here it is free, cheaper, and of better quality than elsewhere, which affords a great opportunity for the contraband trade. It is a great annoyance in Spain to have your luggage searched in every town you arrive at; mine has already been examined some fifteen times, without leaving the territory, or having any Spanish property in addition to my own. The Basques are a strong, hardy, and athletic race; they were invaded by sea in the year 879 by the Norwegians, and partly overcome, which accounts for their light complexion and form. The women perform the work of men. Arriving at the diligence office and giving the name of my hotel, as an American I felt mortified on seeing my trunk moved off on the head of a woman; but I soon discovered it was customary, and submitted.

Their holidays are celebrated with song and dance and ball playing. On Sunday the public promenade near the Cathedral was filled with children of all ages, with their nurses, enjoying the dance, while on the opposite banks of the river, within fifty yards of the Basilica, were assembled some one thousand grown persons, male and female, of the middle and lower classes, forming various groups and circles, in their curious costumes, dancing to the sound of tambourines and fifes, until fatigued, taking refreshments, or returning to the church, which, during the month of Maria or May, is a perfect flower garden. Banners were suspended from cords extending from the church to the refreshment hall.

From Bilboa to San Sebastian, is another eighteen hours' ride, through a most luxuriant, charming and picturesque country. The farms are small, some only five or six acres—just enough for man, wife and family to work with spade or prong fork, which turns up the mould a great depth. The valleys and hill sides are covered with trellised grape vines, and reminded me much of Switzerland; indeed the people resemble the Swiss from their hardy habits and attachment to their country.

A fair was held at Bregada, a town at which I halted; it was a festival day in the villages. It rained, but not sufficient to stop the dance of the peasants, who stood in brogues made of skins, tied with strings, and were cutting it down in the mud, the water oozing out from the openings. The women, with hair in long plaited tresses and heads tied round with handkerchiefs, seemed to enjoy it hugely. The language no one but those bred in the country pretends to understand. Authors differ as to its history. One asserts that Adam spoke Basque, and that it was the language of the angels, and was brought pure into Spain before the confusion of tongues at Babel; another says, that angelic or not, it is so difficult that the devil, who is no fool, studied seven years in the Bilboas, and learned only three words. The use of various tongues in the same empire is a source of great evil, and causes distrust and jealousy, giving despots great advantage. The Basques proper are not understood out of their jurisdiction; the Catalonians are not understood by their neighbors, the Valencians; the Majorcans have a jargon of their own; the Gallicians are in like manner mixed up with the Portuguese. The Andalusians do not speak the true Castillian, consequently it is only in Castile and a part of Aragon that the language is spoken in its purity; quite unlike the enlightened republic of our country, where free education and the liberty of the press, and constant unrestrained communication absorb all other tongues, and make the English language general and intelligible through the land. This is the last important town in Spain before crossing the frontier of France; the distance now to Bayonne is only eleven leagues. San Sebastian is built on an isthmus under a conical hill which rises some four hundred feet above the sea, and is crowned by a castle. The approach is made easy by walks planted with trees, and here are found the graves of many English officers, to whom monuments have been erected, with the inscriptions in their own language. It was the theatre of several sieges between the French, English, and Spaniards, and the town was sacked and destroyed. The new town which is of rectangular form, with its plazas, shops, arcades and tall houses with balconies of uniform appearance and color, looks quite un-Spanish. It has a handsome beach, and is much resorted to in summer for sea-bathing. The greatest difference is observable between these Basque towns and those in the south, for the attractions here are those of Nature and not of Art. The fruits of the north are found here. Fruit is abundant in the mountains, and many valleys and points of view on the road carried me back to the magnificent scenery of the valley of the Schuylkill and Delaware. I find myself far removed from the orange groves, but apples are here in profusion, and the tables are served by the light Chacoli wine and cider of the country. The solid balconied stone manor houses of the wealthy appeared like fortresses, bearing their armorial shields sculptured over the portals, for the Basques pride themselves on being the original nobility of Spain. The law of primogeniture still exists as in England, but with the modification that the inheritor may dispose of one half of the inheritance; and as they are a money-getting and commercial people, the purse is getting the ascendency over title. Having formerly seen the south and west of Spain, and in this journey the east, centre and north, I have had a fine opportunity of judging of this peculiar country, closely bound together under one form of government, but composed of as different materials, in point of language, manners and costume, as of soils and climates, full of provincial prejudices, but loyal to the crown, unanimous in religion, and opposed to foreign innovations. In private life civil and polite to the stranger; warm friends, but implacable enemies. I shall now proceed to Bayonne; thence to Pau, and the famous baths of the Pyrenees, in the south of France; thence I shall return, via Bordeaux, Rochefort, La Rochelle, and Nantes, on my way to Paris.

## XC.

PARIS, *June 20, 1853.*

From San Sebastian to Irun, the first frontier town on the high road to Madrid, we rode along the coast through a wild, scraggy, shrubby country. At that place I was relieved of my Spanish passport, and *visé* for France with an additional charge of two francs. We soon crossed a small stream which separates the two countries; the little bridge was guarded on each side by sentinels, one of whom examined the passport to see if it was properly *visé* to leave Spain, the other if it was *en règle* to enter France. We were accompanied as far as the frontier by two distinguished refugees from France, who had received a visit from their families at the first town, but dared not cross the line under pain of transportation to Cayenne.

I had previously met with several in different parts of Spain, who had narrowly escaped by crossing the Pyrenees, exposed to hunger, cold, and exhaustion. Over this bridge had passed half a million of French troops during the invasion of Spain under Buonaparte, half of whom never returned alive. The luggage once examined at the frontier custom-house, a few hours carried us to Bayonne, through a rich and cultivated soil, with fine houses dotting the country, so unlike the uncultivated wastes in the interior of Spain. Bayonne is an old, walled, seaport town, of considerable commerce, situated upon both banks of the Duoro, with shady ramparts and pleasant wooded environs. Its citadel was the key of Marshal Soult's position in 1814, and was the scene of one of the most bloody conflicts between the English and French, which cost the lives of two thousand men. Here the Bayonnais used their knives in the muzzles of their muskets, which gave them the name of bayonets, and introduced that weapon in modern warfare. A few miles from Bayonne is Biaritz, much resorted to for sea-bathing; the shore is high, rocky, and iron-bound, but the bays are sandy, and the village, with its snug cottages and tenements, has somewhat the air of our own Cape May.

From Bayonne I diverged to the east to Oleron, along the base of the Pyrenees, in order to visit Pau, a place much frequented by foreigners for the mildness of its climate, and to make excursions to the celebrated watering-places. Pau is a lovely and attractive spot; its natural scenery is the admiration of all visitors; the beautiful chateau of Henry IV. is in the centre, upon a very commanding position. It is now undergoing repairs, and preparing for the reception of the French emperor in July.

Les Eaux Bonnes, the favored resort of the Countess Montejo, the present empress, and Les Eaux Chaudes, or hot springs, are situated in the mountain gorges of the towering Pyrenees, where we found excellent hotels, and all the recreations and diversions, and agreeable winding walks which nature and art can contrive, and which induce thousands of fashionables and invalids to resort thither during the hot months of summer.

The bathing establishments are on a stupendous scale. The valleys are teeming with a numerous and industrious population in their simple garb, and we see women and children with their simple utensils of husbandry in hand; the little patches are worked by hand, as the land is divided in small parcels, and frequently women are seen holding the scratching sort of plough, while the husband takes the place of the horse, or vice versa, when the representative of the animal is fatigued. These simple peasantry, who are buried in snow six months of the year, now employ every moment of their time to provide their winter supplies. They look forward with great pleasure to the arrival of the empress in July.

From Pau, in another direction, a distance of forty miles, lies Tarbe, a considerable town in a beautiful valley. I stopped there to visit the Hara, a government establishment which contains one hundred and twenty of the finest horses in France, imported from Europe, Asia, and Africa, for the improvement of the race. Thence I proceeded to the baths of Bagniere de Bigore, a pleasant town, famous for its hot ferruginous baths, and greatly resorted to. The largest marble manufacturing establishment I had ever visited, I found here, employing some one hundred and fifty hands. The great variety of marble found in the Pyrenees enables the stone-cutters to work to great advantage; the execution is on a larger scale than in the mines of Carrara, in Italy, where a large population is employed, but upon smaller work. Here the huge blocks are sawed by water power, and the work, from heavy altar pieces down to ladies' ornaments, is skilfully and delicately wrought.

Not unlike our Kentucky farmers, who produce large droves of mules for the Southern States, the mountaineers here derive a handsome profit from the raising of these animals for the Spanish markets. In France horses are almost universally in use, while in Spain the hardy mule endures better the coarse fare of the road. In making my excursions I found myself reduced from a Spanish diligence with eight or ten mules, to a pair of horses and caleche, as the summer lines were not yet established. Another twenty hours' ride from Pau, brought me to Bordeaux, upon the banks of the Garonne—the city most renowned in France for its wines, and having an extended commerce to all parts of the world. Bordeaux will soon be in direct connexion with Paris, by means of railroad, a distance of some three hundred and fifty miles, in ten to twelve hours. I found that the city had improved extensively since I visited it in 1847. It was then a fatiguing ride by diligence, but it will soon be a pleasant trip from Paris. Instead of returning by the same route, I descended the river by steamer to Blaze, and thence passed through the beautiful grape districts en route to Rochefort, famous for its arsenal;

there, as well as at Toulon, the French marine is seen in its perfection. The town is regularly planned, with wide streets, well-paved sidewalks, and large gardens laid out in miniature, in the form of the Tuileries of Paris. The walls or ramparts are planted with shade trees, which have attained an immense size, and form beautiful promenades.

The head-gear of the peasant women is the most peculiar in France. They wear plain white or embroidered caps upon a form suited to the head, rising eighteen inches in height, the top extended like a fan; the elderly women are more moderate in their patterns, but the young girls seem to rival each other in the quantity and quality of the floating material. The next town en route is La Rochelle, in striking contrast to Rochefort for cleanliness and beauty. Its commerce consists chiefly in the exportation of brandies, as the region of country about Cogniac is almost exclusively devoted to and dependent upon the spirit trade.

From La Rochelle I proceeded to Nantes, one of the principal cities of France, situated upon the Loire. I arrived on a Sunday morning, and large preparations had been made for a church festival and procession from the cathedral. Nantes, like all other towns in France, as well as Spain, has its octroi duties, and every article of consumption pays its tribute at the gates, for the municipal support of the city. The conductor of the mail coach had carefully concealed a leg of mutton and a basket of peas for his festival dinner. His negative reply to the general question, if he had anything to declare, did not satisfy the officer, who, after a diligent search amongst the luggage, brought out the unfortunate treasure, which was put upon the scales, weighed, and taxed, much to the annoyance of its owner, as well as the detention of the passengers and mail. The houses and balconies of several streets were hung with tapestry, and adorned with garlands of natural and artificial flowers, immense altars with gold and silver tinsel ornaments occupying the angles and squares through which the procession passed, with long lines of musicians, the military, the church, and civil officers, followed by a thousand girls in white robes and veils—all got up with French delicacy and taste; it had a happy effect. At Nantes I first availed myself of the railroad, as I had made a long detour along the coast in order to visit the places named, avoiding other cities on the main route which I had formerly visited. It was with no small satisfaction that I took the express train, at the rate of forty miles per hour, for Angers, an antiquated city within, surrounded by a boulevard of noble trees upon the former rampart. It has a famous castle of immense size, built by the Roi d'Augon; it covers a large surface, and has seventeen towers. A fair was held there at the time, which attracted a large concourse of people. My next stopping point was at Amboise, where I visited the chateau which was the property of the Orleans family; it is eligibly and magnificently situated upon the banks of the Loire, and is a perfect fortress in itself. Here was shown the apartments where Abd-el Kader and his suite were confined nearly six years, as his captivity in the chateau of Henry IV., at Pau, was of short duration. The gardens and grounds, upon an elevation more than one hundred feet, are very picturesque, and here he delighted to pass most of his time. In one corner of the grounds which he occupied are seen the mounds of twenty-six out of ninety Arabs who died during their confinement. The country through which I passed was the garden of France. It was a continuous village; the cultivation was close, and the small farms abounded in products of every variety; vineyards and fruit were in profusion: cottages and farm-houses were almost within gun-shot of each other. From Amboise I continued by railroad to Tours, which contains one of the finest cathedrals in France. The fast line soon carried me to Blois, to visit its famous chateau, partly restored under the administration of Louis Philippe; the interior wood-work, painting, and gilding, are of the most choice execution. From Blois to the modern and unfinished chateau de Chambord, belonging to Henry V., the present legitimate incumbent to the French throne, is five leagues distant from the main route. I was well repaid for my ride. The structure is gigantic, the style of architecture is of varied character, and is a souvenir of monuments of different European ages, as well as Oriental styles. The buildings were never finished, but appropriations have been made by government to continue the work. The grounds inclosed occupy about eight miles square, with several villages of tenantry. Orleans, the next large city en route, has one of those mammoth Gothic cathedrals so much bepraised; but I have spoken so frequently of the works of art, that the subject must have become tiresome to you. The city was full to overflowing, and with much difficulty I procured quarters; the agricultural and horticultural fair and cattle-show produced such multitudes as we see in our own State. Finally, I was not a little rejoiced to return to Paris, after the fatigue of a somewhat protracted voyage. I might have gone into detailed accounts and filled several sheets since I last wrote you, but I desisted, as my eyes have not recovered their full force since I left the glare and dust of Madrid. I expect to leave Paris the early part of July, on my way home.

# 1854.
# XCI.

MARSEILLES, *February 27, 1854.*

My apology for not writing since my departure for Europe, in November last, is of the most plausible nature. I have been under the care of two of the most scientific oculists of Paris for the past six weeks, for the relief of a species of ophthalmy, produced by the excessive glare of light, and fine dust during my journeyings in Spain last year. Finding myself partially relieved, and once again on my winding way, I will briefly state that less than a month had elapsed from the time I stepped on board the fleet and gorgeous steamer Arctic, for Liverpool, before I found myself in the great Babylon of modern times, London.

After a hasty visit to the manufacturing establishments of Manchester and Bradford, looking in upon the famous steelworks of Sanderson & Son, and the cutlery shops and depots of Joseph Rodgers & Son (both of Sheffield), spending a Sabbath in the old city of York, and enjoying the chanting of melodious voices, from a numerous choir in its much renowned Cathedral, I made an excursion to a cheese fair, where I found John Bull up to his shoulders in tons of choice Cheshire and Stilton.

The powerful agency of steam, and the perfection of the railway system, soon transported me across England to the eastern counties, the land of my ancestors, famed for its agriculture and game; thence to Yarmouth, the old town celebrated for its fisheries and sea-bathing, with its labyrinths of lanes, numbering from one to a hundred, through its very centre; only accessible for donkeys and foot passengers, impenetrable to foes without, and impracticable to home police in case of revolt. The herring fisheries were prodigious, and I recognised the cut of the Hollanders, who were attracted thither with their vessels. Providence in his wisdom had caused the ocean to yield a substitute for that which the soil this year refused, and in return for ingratitude the surplus was thrown upon the land.

Several excursions were made from the city of Norfolk to the farms of some of the branches bearing our family name, over well macadamized roads, and through highly cultivated grounds, surrounded with hawthorn hedges, inclosing herds of Devonshire, Hereford, and other famous breeds of cattle, not forgetting the flocks of Southdown and Leicester sheep, feeding from hurdles, upon the large Ruta Baga turnip; the scenery is interspersed with game forests belonging to the lords and nobility; they were delightful to the eye. But it was necessary to look further, and inquire into the working of the system. The products of the country bring high prices, but tithes and taxes reduce them. Labor is ill rewarded, and the distinction between the rich and the respectable poor is too strongly marked. The cry is for reform, and the British Parliament will be obliged to listen to it. One of the parties whom I visited pays eighty pounds, or four hundred dollars, church-tithes annually, in lieu of one-tenth part of the crop, and without the enjoyment of any of the advantages, for he is of the reformed religion, and has a small church upon his grounds.

The season was cold and wet, unfavorable for a long sojourn in England. I remained some ten days in London, revisiting some of the public monuments and works of art, which I had formerly described to you; also, the famous brewery establishments of Barclay, Perkins & Co., and Henry Meux & Co., which are among the great sights of the metropolis; the former, particularly, has been visited by thousands of strangers since the expulsion of Gen. Haynau, the Austrian butcher, by Barclay & Perkins's draymen.

These works are gigantic, covering several acres of ground, and employing millions of capital. The quantity of ale manufactured on the average is equal to a thousand barrels (of thirty-six gallons) each per day; the gross quantity is four hundred thousand barrels each per annum, which enters into ordinary consumption, as ale and porter are the general beverage of the nation, and its first source of revenue under the excise is the malt and hop-tax. It is curious to look over the stables of one hundred and fifty of their mammoth dray-horses; the name of each is lettered over the stall. A small engine is used for cutting hay and straw, and cracking the grain, for feeding.

I attended the Smithfield Cattle Show, which gave me an opportunity of seeing the finest specimens of English and Scotch fat cattle, of the choicest breeds I had ever seen, the famous heifer of Wm. H. Worrall, of Dutchess county, being the only exception for her age. Prince Albert took the first prize for the finest exhibit of pigs.

Having attended the State Fair at Saratoga last autumn, I was better enabled to judge of our Poultry Show, which certainly compared favorably with the exhibition which took place while I was in Norfolk. The drove of Kentucky cattle, after a long drive to Saratoga, will be admitted by those who saw them to have been a beautiful sight, and gratifying to American pride.

Having made a sort of pilgrimage through one branch of my ancestry, I was anxious to visit in detail the work of another branch, the Guy Hospital in London, founded by Thomas Guy, whose honored name I bear. This noble Institution, one of the most celebrated in the world for its usefulness, was founded in 1722, upon a gigantic scale, in the Borough, across London Bridge. The founder, a bachelor, who had amassed a large fortune in trade and in the South Sea Expedition, conceived the laudable project of establishing an institution for all time, for the relief of suffering humanity. The buildings are airy and spacious, the residences of the governors exceedingly comfortable. He lived to complete the work, and enjoy the pleasure of its fruits for some twenty years, leaving an endowment of two hundred thousand pounds. The grounds have been enlarged, and new structures have been added with all the recent improvements for heat as well as ventilation, and it is now capable of containing from three hundred to four hundred patients, with a degree of comfort and cleanliness almost equal to a well regulated hotel. A small lunatic asylum, separate and distinct, is within the grounds, inclosed. The museum is a collection of wax figures, for the use of medical students, portraying almost all the diseases to which the human family is liable; it is a separate building, and is equal in merit to the famed exhibitions which I had visited in Montpelier in France, and Florence and Bologna in Italy. The institution is in the most flourishing condition, thanks to the legacy of the generous Mr. Brooks, who left it his entire fortune, upwards of a million of dollars. Medicines are distributed to all who apply, which privilege is abused, as I noticed in attendance, in airy, comfortable halls, in one wing of the buildings, seated upon benches, scores of men, women, and children, many even handsomely dressed, who, through avarice, avail themselves of this charity; but the will of the testator must be observed.

Notwithstanding the agitation of the Oriental Question, and the high price of provisions, I found Paris in the midst of its holiday festivities. The government understands so well the wants and desires of the small dealers in fancy articles, that all sorts of amusements are encouraged, whereby money is put in circulation. Several magnificent balls have been given by the Emperor at the Tuileries. The Municipality of Paris has also given grand balls at the Hotel de Ville. Masquerade balls take place weekly at the Grand Opera. The condition of my eyes prevented my joining in many of the gaieties of Paris. The evening of my presentation, however, to the Emperor and Empress, I assisted at the Court Dress Ball at the Tuileries, where were present some three thousand persons, and it was certainly the most brilliant affair I had ever seen in Europe before. We were some twenty-five persons in the saloon adjoining the imperial apartments, awaiting a special presentation; after which, following in the train of the ladies of honor to the grand saloon of the Marshals, the dense multitude opening in line, we formed ourselves in front of a sort of throne, with an orchestra for the music alone. Their Imperial Majesties being seated, were surrounded by the ex-king Jerome Bonaparte, the Grand Duchess of Baden, and other distinguished members of royalty. The Emperor opened the ball with the wife of the Ambassador of Belgium, the Empress dancing with the Minister of Austria; the quadrille was made up by the Minister of Finance, Mr. Fould, and Marshal Magnan, and their partners. The dance then became general in the vast saloons adjoining, and the music of an additional fanciful kind. Waltzing was followed by beautiful young ladies and their cavaliers, who aspired to the privilege of displaying themselves in the presence of the Imperial group. The vast gilded saloons of this immense palace were brilliantly illuminated from suspended candelabra; the great variety of uniforms, Military, Naval, Diplomatique and Civil, Turkish, Greek, and Hungarian, and others, with the rich costly robes of the ladies, certainly presented one of the most magnificent spectacles the eye could behold; diamonds, emeralds, rubies, and other precious gems, were dazzling to one's eyes.

Mr. Mason, our Minister, appeared in court dress, notwithstanding the request of Secretary Marcy to all diplomatic functionaries to appear only in plain garb, which instruction should have been made positive, if made at all, and it would not have led to the unpleasant incidents already experienced by our representatives.

As simple citizens of the Republic, we must subscribe to the rules of foreign courts, or exclude ourselves from such festivities; consequently necessity obliged me to take my rank as aide-de-camp, with a sword and chapeau. One of the most "observed of all observers," was a German Prince, the Duke of Brunswick, who was a burlesque on royalty. He wore a peruque with curls, thick rouge on his face, a court dress emblazoned with gold and precious stones; white doe-skins, with diamond knee-buckles; silk stockings, and pumps with diamond shoe-buckles; his epaulettes were of topaz and diamonds, the scabbard and hilt of his sword were of gold, beset with emeralds, rubies, and brilliants; his breast was covered with orders and massive gold chains, encircled with gems; even his chapeau was decorated in like manner. In a word, he was an eccentric, and in my eyes a vain and conceited personage.

The early refreshment saloons, and the two o'clock supper halls at the two extreme ends of the banquet rooms, were visited by the imperial party, after which they retired.

The entertainment was sumptuous, and what might be expected from imperial munificence, with the art and taste of the French *cuisine*.

From Paris to Chalons, by railway, eleven hours' ride, a night's repose, and eight hours' descent of the Saone by steamer, through what would be a picturesque country at a more favorable feature of the year, and one finds himself at the great silk manufacturing city of Lyons.

The navigation of the Rhone was interrupted by low water. Last year I made half the distance to Avignon by steamer at the same season; now I had no recourse except a twenty-four hours' ride in the diligence; two hours' additional by railroad brought me to this commercial city of Marseilles for the fourth time. Of course I have nothing new to offer you.

I propose visiting two islands of the Mediterranean, which I have not seen, and of which little is known by travellers. The first, Corsica, which gave birth to Napoleon, is improving; but the other island, Sardinia, remains in a primitive state, so I shall probably meet with something that will interest you.

# XCII.

AJACCIO, ISLAND OF CORSICA, *March 12, 1854.*

I wrote you from Marseilles, the great southern commercial port of France, where much activity prevailed at this season among the vessels, in consequence of the excessive imports of grain, through the failure of the French harvest. I responded to the civilities of our Consul, in dining with our Chargé d'Affaires from Naples, and embarked the following day for Porto Torres, a small seaport upon the island of Sardinia, a distance of some two hundred and fifty miles, by steamer, touching at Corsica. A heavy sea and head wind delayed us; the journey occupied some thirty hours. Thence I proceeded to the principal city, which is called Sassari, and contains a population of some twenty thousand persons.

I found the people more benighted than in any of the other islands of the Mediterranean I had yet seen.

The population of the entire island is estimated at three hundred and fifty thousand; its length is one hundred and fifty miles, and it is from sixty to eighty miles in width. It belongs to the kingdom of Sardinia. The peasantry live in villages, and, not unlike those of the interior of the island of Sicily, go long distances to cultivate the soil, and may be seen at early morn in their coarse black cloaks, with hoods as substitutes for hats, and dark leggings below white cotton pants extending to the knees, trudging out with their donkeys, which bear their implements of husbandry.

The women and children, while watching their flocks of sheep and goats, have a sort of distaff in their hands, and spin with their fingers the coarse wool which serves for their rude covering.

In the mountains large numbers are found who have no habitations, and live in a state of barbarism, covering themselves with skins, bruising grain between two flat stones, and making a sort of paste which is cooked upon the ground, after the fashion of the Arabs on the desert sands.

The country is infested with bandits. Game is abundant, and fire-arms are kept by all who can afford them. Life is unsafe, and comforts are scarcely known in the cities; certainly not outside of them.

The roads are somewhat protected by gens d'armes, who are useful in pursuing the banditti. We picked up eighteen gens d'armes on the road; they say that the bandits fly at their approach, but if cornered, fight desperately.

My casual travelling companion was going to see a person under sentence of death for the murder of his brother; the culprit was in his employ and confidence, but he basely shot him in the back while they were riding their horses quietly along the road. My companion's object was to ascertain what induced the commission of the crime. The custom is to execute the criminal, if possible, upon the spot where the assassination was committed.

The soil is fertile, but poorly cultivated, and thinly inhabited. The island has but little commerce. The olive groves look well, and furnish oil in abundance. Cork forests abound.

The town of Sassari is encircled with walls and gates; the streets are narrow, and badly paved; the houses are of stone, lofty, but filthy; the inhabitants are dirty. A very small portion of the people seem in easy circumstances. They have a theatre, which is not indifferent, as all the Italian races must have an opera. The cathedral, built in the thirteenth century, is the only respectable monument of antiquity which I found.

The clergy swarm, the profession being resorted to as a military exemption, and more profitable than that, without regard to fitness or qualification; consequently they have a bad reputation.

I could not have believed that I should have found, in such proximity to the continent, a people so behind the age, and so far below the standard even of the Corsicans under French rule.

I was not sorry to escape and get to this place, some seventy miles by water, where one finds the journals from the continent, and a much higher state of civilization, and where fire-arms are prohibited, which is producing great changes in the habits of the people.

Ajaccio is situated upon a gulf of some ten miles in depth; it has about fifteen thousand inhabitants, and contains some fine public buildings; unfortunately, however, it has but little commerce. It is the birthplace of Napoleon, who is the pride of the Corsicans. The house where the hero was born still stands in an obscure part of the old town, upon a little square called Piazza Letizia. It was in those days considered a fine edifice. The identical spot is shown, and the circumstances related of his birth, on the return of his mother from the solemnities of the mass on Assumption Day, 15th August, 1769. The property has been purchased by the present Emperor of France, who has appointed a person to guard it, and preparations are now being made for its restoration.

The family of Bonaparte was of the ancient nobility, and originated in Florence, Italy. Charles Bonaparte, the father, was appointed Deputy of the nobles of Corsica, in 1779, and died in Montpelier, France, in 1785, being only 38 years of age. His wife, Letitia Burnolino, born in 1750, gave birth to thirteen children, all born here; five died young, and the remaining eight comprised one emperor, three kings, one prince, one queen, and two princesses.

A monument has been erected in the public square, to Napoleon, by his nephew, Napoleon III., since his elevation in France.

The Hotel de Ville contains the portraits of the family, and a good life-like statue in marble, of Jerome, while king of Westphalia.

In the Grotto Napoleon, about a mile from the town, after winding through olive-groves, the ambitious boy delighted to pursue his youthful studies.

The public promenades, adorned with orange trees and almonds in bloom, the gardens filled with olives and a profusion of tropical fruits, afford a grateful sight, after escaping from the chilling winds of the continent.

All through the south of France I had noticed great activity in the movement of troops for embarkation for the East. In descending the Saone, our steamer's deck was occupied by the conscripts, mostly young men, who were leaving home and quiet occupations for the first time perhaps, for the uncertain chances of war. They are distributed to points where actual duty is not required, replacing well-formed troops who are sent to the seat of war. Some thousands who had been held in reserve until needed are now sent from Corsica for the marine and land service.

Under the French system, every able-bodied male is liable to army duty, at twenty-one years of age. On a certain day, which is publicly proclaimed, the parties draw for their chances. In the absence of the young man, his mother or some other authorized person draws for him. He is then liable, and when the call is made he must either supply his place or serve; even after an absence of years, on his return, he is seized for the service. Eighty thousand men are thus drawn annually; the term of duty is seven years. The necessities of the nation have not required the number drawn; but now the balance or reserve of four or five years past is called upon here, more particularly to fortify the marine. The Corsicans from the mountains make good soldiers, and distinguish themselves as officers, and are a brave and warlike people. The sea-coast furnishes good sailors.

It is curious to observe the difference in the habits, customs, and governments of two islands which at their extreme points nearly touch each other, at least by a chain of small islands. In Sardinia the language is a patois, and changes in character from one point to another, partaking strongly of the Italian on one side; partially of the Arabic in the south; and in the west slightly of the Spanish; while here the French is commonly understood, though the Italian patois is the language of the people. But what can be expected where every restriction is placed upon communication?

I had my passport examined and *visé* five times in Sardinia, at considerable expense, notwithstanding it bore the Ambassador's visé of the kingdom of Sardinia at Paris, for which he had exacted his fee. All these checks upon intercourse, and these annoyances, only tend to put a little pocket-money into the hands of officials.

In Sardinia, tobacco is cultivated, but the Government seizes the product, and pays its price. The sale of cigars is a monopoly, consequently the quality is very bad, and the prices are double those of this place, where the people are exempt from the tax which exists on the article there, and also in France.

I was strongly reminded of the Basque provinces in the north of Spain, at Bilboa and St. Sebastian, where the people enjoy a similar privilege in the free sale and manufacture of the weed. There, as here, the poor employ themselves in making cigars, which are superior to those for which you pay double at the government shops on the peninsula. The consequence is that everybody smokes by common consent.

One of the most remarkable features in the Corsican race is the spirit of vengeance, which for centuries has existed among them, and which is most difficult to eradicate. Thanks to the government of the emperor, the carrying of arms is strictly prohibited here, and eight thousand gens d'armes are scattered over an island three hundred and sixty miles in circumference.

A most salutary, but arbitrary law, applicable to the case, arrests and imprisons the parents, family, and friends of an outlaw or bandit who has fled to the mountains, or is concealed. In this way his maintenance is cut off; and a reward is offered for his head. Frequent instances have been known where persons have harbored bandits through fear, and have performed the execution of the law, and divided the reward with the gend'armerie.

Instances were not rare, before such rigorous measures were adopted, of sending anonymous letters demanding sums of money, or submission to the consequences. Families exterminated each other. The mother guarded sacredly the linen of a murdered husband, until her son was capable of resenting the act, when his vengeance was excited by the blood-stained garment of the father. A gentleman acquaintance informed me, that when he came on the island, some years since, he gave a little soirée, to which were invited the *élite* of the little town where he resided. His daughter had misplaced her handkerchief; observing another upon a hat, she took it up and discovered pistols, and could not conceive the object. When the party retired, the report of fire-arms was heard in all directions. The friends and servants of the parties opposed had chosen the opportunity for revenge.

This characteristic is said to have existed since the wars with the Genoese, and the feuds that grew out of those contests.

The people are hospitable and civil, and a stranger can now travel over the island in perfect safety, if he comports himself properly, and avoids exciting their prejudices.

Steam communication with the continent, and the light of civilization, are producing considerable changes in the condition of this people.

# XCIII.

BASTIA, ISLAND OF CORSICA, *March 24, 1854.*

Having secured my place in the coupé, or front seat, of a small and rather rickety diligence, I started for Corte, a military station and town of some five thousand inhabitants, about the centre of the island, passing through a picturesque and mountainous country, some three thousand to four thousand feet above the level of the sea; the road was in good condition, but at times, in winter, it is impassable for the snow.

The mountain tops and tall pine forests, still covered with their white mantles, in striking contrast with the bloom and verdure of the valleys below, spread out like a map, presenting new beauties at each turn of the vehicle in ascending the zigzag route, upon the amphitheatred walled roads.

The Corsicans, under their great leader Paolo, defended themselves nobly in these mountain passes against their invaders, the Genoese; the loss of the French troops, before they were conquered, was estimated at twelve thousand men.

Aside from the temperature, I was forcibly reminded of the kingdom of Kandy in the island of Ceylon, which is about an equal distance from the coast, in the mountains, and which could not be conquered by the English until roads were constructed for the transportation of their troops.

The hardy Corsican mountaineers subsist upon the chestnuts which abound here; a species of cake, or bread, made from the flour, is their only aliment, aside from the milk of their sheep or goats. The skins and wool supply their covering; the cheese and surplus chestnuts are bartered in the towns for wine, and what they consider the luxuries of life. The varied temperature enables them to produce wine of good quality, olive oil, figs, oranges, raisins, lemons, apples, pears, and nectarines; but, in general, the Corsicans are not ambitious in culture, contenting themselves with small tracts of land; the necessaries of life are few indeed.

They are great aspirants for position in military pursuits, persevering and indomitable, and frequently rise to rank in the French army. Most of the villages can boast of one or more of their members who have distinguished themselves.

Notwithstanding all the efforts of government, assassinations are still committed, and the old family spirit of vengeance cannot be fully appeased; some important cases among the upper classes are now pending.

At a village in the mountains, where we halted, a case had recently occurred. A party of eight or ten were at play, of which they are fond, when an altercation took place; two of the number left, the landlord discharging a double-barrelled gun as they left the house; he deliberately reloaded, in the presence of the others, and, accusing a third of taking part in the affray, shot him dead; he then loaded again, embraced his family, and escaped in the mountains. The magistrate of the district, questioning those present, and calling them cowards, asked them why they did not prevent the crime; they replied that the persons assaulted were not friends or relatives of theirs.

In the vicinity of Corte there are some valuable quarries of blue marble. The Palais de Justice, now being erected here, has large and massive columns of that material transported thence.

From Corte, the road passes to the north-western part of the island, and to this place.

Bastia, a small and indifferent port, now in process of improvement, is a city possessing a population of some twenty-five thousand, heterogeneous races; it is the chief commercial point of the island, and the seat of government.

The old town, with its lofty stone buildings, narrow tortuous streets, built upon the hill-side, and rising from the water's edge, is really curious; it reminded me of the Grecian island of Scios, and Joppa in Palestine, resembling at certain points a town of stairs.

The new part of the town struck me with astonishment; it had broad streets, with mammoth stone structures, five stories high, cream yellow, and white, with modern green sashes; a new public square, and a handsome Italian marble statue of Napoleon; good hotels, cafés, and baths; markets, finely supplied with fish, game, and fruits; besides a delightful climate, protected by the mountains from the northern blasts. It struck me as a sort of paradise, after what I had seen in the interior.

The secret of its prosperity is its trade with Leghorn and Marseilles, and it being the residence of a race possessing considerable enterprise. Many persons from Cape Corte, just above, and here also, have made fortunes in the West Indies.

The views from the heights, upon the Mediterranean, with the islands of Cabraya, Elba, and Monte Cristo, are very pretty, and a drive along the coast, bordered by amphitheatred walls for the culture of the grape and olive, is not without interest.

A few leagues from town, upon the mountain side, somewhat elevated, is a curious cave, much resorted to, and particularly worthy of a visit, since it is one of the most unique of its kind that I have ever seen. I taxed my memory to find something to compare with it; it is not the cave of Matanzas in extent, neither is it that of the island of Curaçoa, nor the Catacombs of Egypt, nor the Salt Mines of Cracow, which two latter are works of art; but it is a perfect gem of a grotto. At this season of the year it is very dry. It is private property, belonging to a government officer, who has erected near by a stone cottage with stalactite chimney-pieces of beautiful proportions, and miniature flower gardens among the rocks, and an observatory with a delightful prospect upon the sea and fishing villages; it is a rustic retreat for parties of pleasure in summer from Bastia. The grotto at its entrance is walled, and the door is bolted. Its guardian, for an established fee, will light it up with forty lamps; its depth is about one hundred and fifty feet. Stalactites form there in summer from the dripping of the water. The great variety of forms presented is really enchanting. One imagines himself for the moment in the illuminated chapel of a Gothic cathedral, with pillars supporting the roof, the half-formed pointed column rising gradually by crystallization, resembling with its lamp a huge church candlestick; the flowing white drapery falls upon the tomb of the departed, and the weeping willow is seen with its drooping branches. Forms the most grotesque are presented to the imagination. The stalactites are as white as alabaster; one could visit the cave without soiling his white kid gloves.

In going to the grotto, we leave the carriage road, which is only partially completed, and take the mule path for nearly a league, passing through the fishing village of Brando, where stands a small church dedicated to their saint, Our Lady of the Vasina, to whom annual pilgrimages are made on the 7th of September. The sailors of the island, in cases of peril or extreme danger, make certain vows; and it is curious to see the results and read the names and circumstances as related by each. The walls are curiously carved with figures and scenes. Here may be found an exploded gun, with a description of the miraculous escape of the holder by the intervention of the patron saint; white robes, and satin shoes, wreaths of flowers, and other insignia of the funeral rites displayed by females saved from the tomb at the last moment; representations of narrow escapes from shipwreck, the angry waves lashing the frail bark, the lightning falling upon the masts, and the Virgin appearing and conducting the vessel in safety; one person is falling from a citadel; others are escaping from the monsters of the deep.

They have a curious custom here, which would not answer in our country of progress. Their houses are of stone, and lofty, from four to five stories high, and arched throughout, little timber being used other than for flooring. Consequently fires are unknown. The contractor puts up his building, and sells the different stories, whereby there are as many owners as stories; the stairing is in common, consequently neglected and filthy. The gaping, dark entrances, without doors, in the night, seem to invite the perpetration of crime.

The modern buildings have doors, which are closed at night, as in Ajaccio, where assassinations drove the mayor to the issue of a general order for front doors, without exception.

I was strolling quietly last Saturday, which was Beggars' Day, the only time in the week the police allow that class to ask alms publicly, amusing myself in distributing among a group of urchins a quantity of chestnut-flour cakes, which they were looking wistfully upon, when I found myself surrounded by a crowd of beggars, old, infirm, and lame, in tattered and torn rags, or garments of many colors. Distributing my coppers among them, I was glad to escape, and soon found myself near the entrance gate of the city.

Upon looking up, I saw the Republican motto, effaced under the Empire, but still peeping through—"Liberté, Egalité, Fraternité."


Conviction, the most positive, strikes the mind, of the entire incapacity of such masses of ignorance, superstition, and poverty to appreciate the blessings of pure republicanism, as it is enjoyed in our favored land.

Their republicanism means license and anarchy. The moral and social condition of the people must first be improved, and the blessings of general education diffused; their early prejudices for monarchy must first be eradicated. In a word, to be a good republican, one must be educated, or driven by the tyranny of rulers to adopt a home in a country where the rights of all classes are respected.

The surplus agricultural population of the Italian states of Parma, Modena, and Lucca, migrate after the harvest to this island, where there is a demand for manual labor. They are now returning in swarms with their hard-earned savings out of thirty sous per day. It is computed that some twenty thousand visit the island annually; and being exceedingly frugal, they take considerable sums away with them, which helps to impoverish the people here.

Having seen the birthplace of Napoleon, as described in my last letter, from Ajaccio, and being familiar with most of the localities of his exploits, I cannot resist visiting his place of imprisonment upon the island of Elba. There are also extensive iron mines, which are represented as very remarkable.

# XCIV.

SIENNA, ITALY, *April 7, 1854.*

I reached Leghorn just in time to catch the little steamer Gilio, of one hundred and fifty tons burden, which composes the entire Tuscan government marine, with the exception of a few small feluccas. She makes regular trips to the island of Elba, for the conveyance of troops and their supplies. After passing the usual strict examination at the Custom House for the contraband articles of cigars and fire-arms, as Leghorn is a free port, and going through the farce of signing passports, I embarked for Porto Ferrayo. This strongly fortified place bears some resemblance to Malta, and appears almost impregnable; the streets are well paved with flat stones; the houses rise upon the side hill, and are approached by flights of stairs and passages; the crown of the lofty, craggy cliffs is surmounted by immense fortifications, well mounted and manned. The town has a population of five thousand, and about one thousand troops. By means of a fosse, the tide-water is permitted to surround the city. From an angle of the wall on the summit of the citadel is a small observatory, erected by Napoleon, which gave him views from all points of the compass. The house where he lived, a few miles from the city, still stands, and is now the property of Prince Demidoff, who is erecting a palace which will contain all the relics which have been preserved of the Emperor. The island of Elba is only about sixty miles in circumference, and about fourteen hundred troops are kept there by the Tuscan government. The bays and shores are picturesque, and the valleys are fertile. There is great suffering this year in consequence of the failure of the grape, wine being their principal resource. I procured a conveyance to Longone, a free port on the south side of the island, now a fishing town. The immense citadel commanding the height was built by the Spaniards while in possession. It is now dismantled, and unoccupied, except as barracks for the land guard, and is fast going to decay, looking mournful and desolate. Trees are growing where once was heard the busy tread of the military, and goats are feeding and cabbages growing where once was piled the shot for the enemy. From Longone to Rio there is no carriage road, so I mounted a pony, with a guide to run beside him, and passed over a path through a hilly country, to the great iron mines. I had heard of the richness and abundance of the ore; I had seen the extensive mines of Dannemora, also mines in England and America, where the work is mostly subterranean; but was not prepared to find an inexhaustible mountain of iron, where three hundred men were employed in cutting down and blasting out the ore, which ranges in richness from forty-five to eighty per cent.; four hundred donkeys were wending their way by zigzag paths, laden with this valuable product.

The village has an active appearance, but is of a dirty red color; there were vast inclosures for the ore, like huge coalyards, where it was piled preparatory to loading for different ports for smelting. The brick-dust colored earth, which remains after the excavation, has a shining and dazzling appearance, from the particles of minerals in it. The gardens of the valleys on the margin of a small rivulet, with their orange and lemon trees, form a striking contrast in the view. The Grand Duke farms out the privilege to a company for twelve millions of livres, about one million eight hundred thousand dollars. From Elba I returned to Leghorn, which city has been materially improved and enlarged since my last visit; but being still in a state of siege, and protected by Austrian troops, the same civil liberties are not enjoyed there as formerly. The little island of Monte Cristo, lying sixty miles north of Elba, is thirteen miles in circumference. It has been purchased by a wealthy Englishman, who has retired thither with his family, and is now erecting his buildings upon it, employing many Italians from the mainland in carrying out his improvements. He is building a yacht at Leghorn, after the model of the America, and putting in an engine, which will be a pretty affair. From Leghorn by railway a half hour's ride brings us to the old city of Pisa, with its memorable Leaning Tower, Duomo or Cathedral, Baptistry, and Campo Santo; the latter is considered sacred from its containing a portion of the earth brought from Jerusalem, in which repose the dead. It was agreeable to me to visit the spots I had frequently trod during a long sojourn in this old city, and to find numbers of those I had formerly known, still pursuing quietly the same course without change. A branch railroad took me to Lucca, to call upon some old acquaintances, and, on my return, I proceeded to Florence, the capital, and residence of the Grand Duke, and the seat of the arts of Tuscany. However captivated, and even infatuated, one may be upon a first visit to the solid, massive, and majestic palaces, with their beautiful frescoes, their well-filled galleries of sculpture and paintings, the colossal bronze statues of the public fountains, the decorations of the churches, the chaste and delicate mosaic work of the altars, it is not to be expected that I should now go into raptures upon a third visit to Italy.... The eye tires in gazing upon vast collections of works of art, and finds relief in escaping to the beautiful and extensive ducal gardens of the palace, where one may enjoy the works of nature amid long avenues of shady trees, listening to the sound of bubbling fountains, with groups of nymphs, heroes, gods and goddesses, in marble, as mute, silent auditors. Returning from a ramble, I took my favorite seat in the café Doney, much resorted to by strangers, and reflected upon the events which occurred during the revolution of 1848—the granting of constitutional privileges, the liberty of the press, the marching of troops against the enemy, the illuminations of victory at night, the songs of patriotism, the wailing and lamentation at the defeat of the Italian troops in

Lombardy, the funeral mausoleums, and the lighted candles over the uniforms and arms of the victims in the churches, the transparencies and anathemas of the clergy, the mournful procession of the masses by torchlight with the crucifix at the head. All had passed away, liberty was crushed; the Austrian troops now occupy the ground and keep down revolution; the police are active and vigilant. One cannot drive to the Casino, a favorite forest ride, without showing his passport at the gate. Within three days from one's arrival, a protectional passport must be procured, at an expense of twelve pauls, or a dollar and twenty-five cents. In my reflective mood, up tripped a flower-girl, in her picturesque Florentine costume, with flowing Leghorn hat and red ribbon, basket in hand, and presented a bouquet, with the salutation "Come sta signore, Come sta su Amico?" It was pleasant to be recognised and awakened from my reverie; but the excellent person of whom she inquired, and who had occupied so frequently the same seat beside me at table, had finished his mortal career.

The ancient city, Sienna, from which I write, is situated upon an elevation of some thirteen hundred feet, rising from the borders of a dry and dreary tract of country. Many of the streets are narrow, and impassable for carriages. This is one of the few points in Italy I had not seen, and I make the visit on my way to Rome, for the Holy Week. Its lofty antique palaces are the monuments of its former grandeur, while a Republic and rival of France. It possessed then two hundred thousand inhabitants; the number is now reduced to twenty-five thousand. The Cathedral is a fine old structure of the 13th century, and contains many beautiful works of art. The mosaic-work of the choir is covered with planks, to shield it from the tread of visitors, but a fee to the custode enables one to see the flight of the Israelites from Egypt. The wood carving of the stalls of the choir of the 13th and 14th centuries is exquisite, but not superior to work of the same style found in the old churches of Valladolid. Some of the frescoes of Raphael, representing different events in the life of Pius II., are remarkable for their color and preservation. The choir books, of large size, on parchment, are beautifully illuminated, and resemble a collection at the Escorial. In the chapel of one of the churches, begun in 1220 and finished in 1465, is a large, beautiful, and celebrated picture of the Madonna, by Guido; the Siennese claim the honor of being the earliest in the art of painting. I was struck with the preference of the pretty women for this chapel, and was led to inquire its history. In fact, the ladies here are celebrated for their beauty. The public palace, with its lofty tower in the form of an escalop shell, and its circuit of one thousand feet, sloping down like an ancient theatre, and filled with the peasants of the country on a market-day, is a gay and novel sight.

The people of this district speak Italian with greater purity than the inhabitants of any other part of Italy—they are the reverse of the Milanese, Genoese, and Neapolitans, who have a distinct patois of their own, which tends to prevent that unanimity and nationality so much required for the future welfare of Italy.

# XCV.

ROME, ITALY, *April 20, 1854.*

Once again in this old city, the mistress of the arts, and at the close of Passion Week with its gorgeous functions and church ceremonies renowned throughout the world. On two former visits, one under Pope Gregory XVI., the other under the present Pope Pius IX., I attempted to describe the magnificence and splendor exhibited on these annual festivals. It would require volumes to speak of modern, aside from ancient Rome, with its one hundred and fifty thousand population, now largely augmented by foreigners from every clime; its three hundred churches, rich in sculpture, paintings, and frescoes; its three hundred and thirty-five palaces, and thirty villas; its five hundred streets and two hundred and seventy-three lanes; its one hundred and forty-eight public piazzas or squares; its aqueducts, bridges, and twelve Egyptian obelisks, aside from its fifty public fountains, more bountifully supplied with water than perhaps any city in the world.

As to antiquities—they abound on all sides, an evidence of what Rome was in her glory, an inheritance of which she cannot be deprived, and in which now consists her chief resource. Being destitute of commerce, without the annual concourse of strangers to the seat of the Catholic church, the modern city would dwindle down to a village. I find since my last visit that the hotels have increased in number and size, and that the shops for the manufacture and sale of mosaics, cameos, and other objects of art, have been enlarged and beautified. Gas has been recently introduced to a limited extent, and telegraph communication extended to Florence north, and Naples south; but here public or government enterprise ceases. The railroad system was vetoed, the Pope's advisers deciding against it. Beggars are as abundant as ever, and in the country pauperism is fearful. The short crops of the past year, and the over taxation of the badly administered Italian governments, drive many to mendicity from necessity. One requires leather pockets to carry copper coin in to supply the tribe, for no sooner is one hungry swarm satisfied than another as hungry arrives. This is the most disagreeable feature of Italian travel.

I came down from Sienna by post, a distance of some one hundred and twenty miles. And here, to draw a comparison in favor of our own happy country, abounding with plenty for which we cannot be sufficiently thankful, I must cite the fact that in some of the mountain villages the number of beggars was so great that the conducteur, to my horror, provided himself with a dog-whip to resist their importunities. The paper currency of the country is at a discount of seven per cent. Since the Republic an issue of a million of dollars has been made in copper coin, like large medals, of five Baiocchi, equivalent to five cents each, which in the scarcity of gold and silver enters into general circulation. We required a large sack to pay postillions. Everything is quiet here under the protection of some seven thousand troops, who may be seen daily on parade, and standing guard throughout the city; they are very civil and under good discipline. The weather has been delightful during Holy Week; the city thronged with strangers, every means of conveyance in requisition, the almost daily visits to St. Peter's and the Vatican, with the other sights of the city, gave much animation. The heavy carriages of the cardinals, with wheels and bodies of gold and silver gilt, the famous black horses with massive gold plated harness, with two coachmen and three footmen in richly embroidered livery, added greatly to the scene. On Palm Sunday took place the presentation to the Pope of the cardinals in full regalia, bishops, priests, the noble guard, princes and foreign ministers in full costume, and the kissing of his Holiness's slipper; then came the blessing singly of palm leaves tastefully wreathed and braided, of which some three hundred were provided for the officers and soldiers of the army who had made special application for them. The rush of thousands to witness the ceremonies of washing the feet of twelve pilgrims by the Pope in person, in St. Peter's; their banqueting at a well furnished table in commemoration of the Last Supper; the services in the Sistine Chapel, the beautiful music of the Miserere, and the Lamentations of Jeremiah; the exhibition of the Holy Relics; the nails which it is said fastened our Saviour to the cross, some of the wood of which is shown; the handkerchief, inclosed in crystal, with which Santa Veronica wiped the face of Christ; the baptism with oil and water of a converted Jew and a negro girl at the Baptistry of Constantine, and the ceremonies of confirmation at the Basilica of San Giovanni de Laterano; all were calculated to keep up the excitement of strangers, and employ them fully during the Holy Week.

Having witnessed these ceremonies for the third time here, as also on a similar occasion at Jerusalem, with all the rites of the Greek and Latin Catholics, Armenians, and Copts, not omitting the extravagant exercises of Spain, Peru, and the island of Cuba, the scenes have become so familiar that I cannot describe to you the gorgeous display under the same impressions as formerly. Still it must be admitted that high mass on Sunday, at the close of the week, the Pope officiating in person in the vast edifice of St. Peter's, in full pontifical robes and jewelled mitre, surrounded by thirty or forty cardinals, with a host of bishops and other members of the clergy, in their rich attire; the temporary loges festooned with red damask drapery fringed with gold, and occupied by the Princes of Prussia, Saxony, and France, in uniform; the Swiss Guards, with helmets and coats of mail; hundreds of the fair sex in black church dresses; hundreds of soldiers with fixed bayonets, and again other thousands of the masculine race in dress coats and white kid gloves—the whole together presents perhaps the most dazzling group of court, religious, and the military display in the world. At the close of high mass the Pope, in his pontifical chair, supported upon the shoulders of twelve bearers in red silk costume, with a brilliant cortege, is carried to the balcony of St. Peter's in the presence of the expectant multitude of some fifty thousand persons, composed in part of cavalry and infantry. The vast square as I saw it from the top of the colonnade was one dense mass of humanity; heads were uncovered during the brief service, then the whole multitude at a given signal fell upon their knees, and the benediction was pronounced. The bells of all Rome send forth their merry peals, the thundering cannon of St. Angelo roar along the Tiber, and the crowd disperse. The evening illumination of the cathedral St. Peter's with its immense façade of colonnades, and three domes brilliantly lighted as if by magic, with eight thousand lamps, closed the ceremonies and sights of the week. The exhibition of fireworks took place the next evening, with fine effect, at the Porto del Popolo, one of the gates of the city. The former Girandolo from the Castle of San Angelo, representing the eruption of Mount Vesuvius, when the waters of the Tiber seemed in flames, was a magnificent spectacle.

I have never seen so many strangers in Rome as during the past Holy Week. My last visit was during the European revolution of 1848, which prevented general travel; we have visitors now, however, from all countries, though fewer Russians than usual. The Coliseum has become a great resort by moonlight; groups of ladies and gentlemen may be seen climbing its old and antiquated walls, or wending their way through its melancholy corridors by torchlight, which has a happy effect, bringing out their beauties more boldly, and hiding the deformities and decay visible by daylight. While standing upon the heights of this vast ruin, whose broken walls have contributed to the erection of many of the palaces of Rome, and reflecting that sufficient material remains for the construction of a small town, one cannot but be struck with the grandeur and power of the former in comparison with the present fallen race. While figuring to myself the grand and imposing spectacle of the mammoth amphitheatre, under the patronage of the Roman emperors, filled with the élite of the city, during the gladiatorial contests, and the combats of the wild beasts, rushing out from their dens in the vast arena, I could find no better comparison in miniature for the enthusiasm of the multitude in the well filled galleries, than that which is shown at the barbarous bull fights of Spain and Peru; the ancients, however, carried off the palm for brutality by throwing the innocent Christians among the wild beasts. The stranger in Rome, however fastidious, may have his taste gratified, and his time constantly occupied here, after repeated visits; his labors for the first trip may be pleasant to the mind and refreshing to the eye, but they are arduous.

The long picture galleries and avenues of statuary of the palaces, the suburban drives to the various villas, as well as the villages Frascati, Albano, and the falls of Tivoli, with the picturesque costume of the peasants, all afford variety.

The antiquarian strolls among the triumphal arches of the Roman emperors, the broken columns of the Forum, or wanders among the ruins of the palaces of Nero and Cæsar, and the baths of Caracalla. When the eye tires with the sight of marbles, bronzes, or the interior decorations of churches, which are perfect museums of fine arts, by the old masters, one can mount the dome of Peter's, or the Campidolio tower, and grasp the seven hills of ancient and modern Rome, with all their beauties and all their deformities, not forgetting one pretty spot which it is profitable to visit, and where, under the shady willows and rosebuds of the Strangers' Cemetery, he can read the epitaphs of his friends or countrymen whose career is ended.

# XCVI.

NAPLES, ITALY, *May 12, 1854.*

I came to this city over a route which I once had occasion to describe to you, passing through Albano, the pleasant summer resort of the Romans, and crossing the once much dreaded pestilential Pontine marshes which have been improved by drainage. I spent a night at Terracina, the frontier coast town of the Pope's dominions, passed Gaeta the following day, where his Holiness was exiled under the protection of the King of Naples, during his political troubles, and found myself here within forty-eight hours, from Rome, after three searchings of my luggage and five examinations of my passports.

You will naturally ask, "How have you passed your time on a third visit to Naples?" The question is easily answered. The half a million of population of this city and its suburbs is a study in itself. The race of lazzaroni deserve special attention; the beautiful garden, Villa Reale, with its fountains and statuary, on the borders of the bay, now abounding in foliage and flowers, is an agreeable retreat for those who occupy the large and commodious hotels which overlook these grounds. Or there is a ride along the coast to the ruins of Baiæ, the Grotto Pozzoli, or a quiet stroll through the grounds of Prince Roca Romano, an old gentleman of much taste who devotes his entire time to the embellishment of his villa, and is very civil to strangers. Aside from its beautiful position on the bay, its arbors, flowers, and tropical fruits, it has a collection of rare birds and animals, also a miniature museum, where I found preserved the Eyeless Fish from the Mammoth Cave of Kentucky, the gift of an American. The grottoes excavated on the margin of the sea are adorned with statuary and lighted on festival occasions; they contain a goodly number of flying fish of a bluish color, which are regularly fed, and of larger size than those found for sale in the markets of Curaçoa. A steamboat excursion to the island of Capri, to visit the Blue Grotto, occupies a day. The steamer lies off and on the rock; the passengers in small boats enter through the narrow opening at a favorable state of the tide. Sitting in the boat the hat touches the rock, so small is the entrance. One is struck with the beautiful mercurial-like color of the vaulted natural roof, and the great depth of the azure and limpid water. The boatmen for a fee throw themselves in, and to all appearance come out dripping with shining quicksilver.

Mount Vesuvius is now quiet. Having on a former visit ascended the summit and descended one thousand feet to the verge of the boiling crater, and with difficulty (from a change of wind) regained the point of descent, suffering from the inhalation of the sulphurous vapor, with boots burnt off, I had no desire to renew my acquaintance with it. I joined a party of ladies to visit the

Hermitage about midway to the top of the volcanic mountain, where an excellent view of Naples and the valley is obtained, and a good idea is formed of the rolling action of the lava in its destructive descent upon the plain, and also of the fertility of the gardens which are formed from decomposed lava and cinders, and which produce the Lacrima Christi wine, which here enters in as part of a cold collation. A melancholy accident has just occurred. A young German gentleman, who breakfasted at our hotel in full health the morning of his ascent to Vesuvius, was brought down a corpse. While on the summit a small portion of the earth gave way and he was precipitated down the chasm; his cries were heard by his companions for an hour, but before cords could be obtained from below he had ceased to breathe. A few days may be spent profitably and delightfully in visiting the ancient cities of Pæstum and Salerno, and the villages of Amalfi, Minori, and Majori, all lying on the sea-coast. Things have changed since I first trod the silent streets of Pompeii; then it really appeared like the city of the dead. Many excavations have since been made, the results of which are mostly to be found in the Great Museum of Naples; now the railroad passes by, and the station of Pompeii is an important one. If those who still sleep under the cinders and lava of these entombed cities could awake to the shrill whistle and hoarse cough of the locomotive, they would be as much startled by them as they were by the fiery flames and ashes of Vesuvius. Invalided sentinels are quartered to protect the relics of antiquity from the ruthless hand of travellers. Many gates are to be opened, and of course the purse strings must be frequently unloosened. The ride along the railway to Castelmare passes through a number of sailing ports. The rock excavation gives a good idea of the quality and variety of lava as it rolls down to the bay.

The drive from Castelmare to Sorrento is most picturesque. The views of the Bay of Naples, and the islands of Capri, Ischia, and Procida, from bold rocky cliffs surrounded by orange groves, which abound here, have been much extolled, and I was almost inclined to become as enthusiastic as others, as I listened to the harp players, and watched the graceful forms of the peasants in the national tarantula dance.

The anniversary or festival of the patron saint of Massa, a small village across the mountain, took place while I was here, so, mounting a donkey, I found myself, preceded by about a dozen priests in black robes and three-cornered hats, mounted like myself, with boys beating the sides of the stupid animals. Our train was considerably augmented by peasant boys and girls in holiday costume trudging along, and we finally found ourselves in the square of the parochial church, which presented the appearance of a fair.

The temporary booths were supplied with all the eatables and drinkables requisite. The countrymen occupied their time in the examination of goats, sheep, and pigs, and in making sundry purchases, while the villagers and country lasses, with tidy white veils, were listening to a full military band playing church music during high mass. The priests of the surrounding villages were in full regalia, and the interior of the building was hung in red drapery fringed with gold leaf borders. Small cannon were mounted for a grand volley, which was given, after which these simple people returned home as much enchanted as if they had witnessed the pompous ceremonies of Rome, and heard the thundering cannon of San Angelo. My boy had loaded the donkey's head with rosaries of stringed filberts and chestnuts, which fruit were much sought after by those who had not attended the festival.

The royal residence of the king at Caserta is well worth a visit, and easily reached by railroad. It is fourteen miles from Naples; the king spends most of his time here. The palace is one of the most extensive in Europe; the interior, aside from a few of the saloons and the staircase, is not remarkable. The grounds, gardens, and parks are eleven miles in circumference; they are well supplied with water, which is brought twenty-seven miles by aqueduct, forming some beautiful cascades. The soil is rich and fertile, and the Botanical and Horticultural Gardens very fine. In many respects I was strongly reminded of the royal grounds of the Court of Spain at La Granja, but the fountains here, and statues in marble and bronze, will not compare with similar works there.

The military force of the kingdom of Naples is one hundred thousand men. There are three regiments of cavalry and infantry stationed at Caserta, and soldiery and sentinels may be found at all points where one goes. The police are very rigid. For instance I retired to bed early the night of my arrival; at eleven P.M. I was roused by a rap at the door; I asked what was wanted; a peremptory order was given to open; I struck a light, and in marched two officers in uniform, who inquired if I had a passport. I replied in the negative, my passport being in the hands of the authorities at Naples. "Have you a *Carta di Segiorno?*" or permit; fortunately I had provided myself with one, or I should have been marched off to the Carcel. I was then questioned as to the object of my visit, and how long I intended to stay, all of which was exceedingly vexatious.

The flower and fruit season is fairly opened, and the sun begins to make one look for a shady spot. The glare of light is fatiguing to the eyes, and as I am a sufferer I shall make my way north to Genoa and Turin.

I shall take the steamer, notwithstanding the recent frightful accident and loss of the Ercolano from this place, caused by collision with the Siciliano, whereby forty-nine passengers and crew, in a few minutes, at midnight, were sent into eternity. It is attributed to gross carelessness, for it was proved that not an officer was on the deck of the Siciliano when she struck the unfortunate steamer. The culprits are in prison awaiting their trial. Many persons are now going north by land, but without doubt the caution now exercised will for some time at least make steam travel safer.

# XCVII.

Turin, Kingdom of Sardinia, *June 5, 1854.*

Our steamer was a French one, and the commander having reputation for skill and caution, the little boat of two hundred and twenty horse power was inundated with passengers from Civita and Leghorn.

It was ridiculous but amusing to notice the rigor of the Neapolitan police. At the quay, before embarking, one has to have his baggage examined, or to slyly slip a piece of coin into the hands of the sentinel; then he passes to the office and gets a permit to embark, notwithstanding that his passport has already been *visé* by his own minister, the Neapolitan Minister of Foreign Affairs, the Inspector of the Marine, and a permit de sejour has been granted previously—all of which costs several dollars, for the benefit of the Neapolitan officials.

Once on board, you suppose yourself clear of the annoyance; but it is not so. Another scene of counting heads and calling names, to be sure that none are on board without being regularly labelled.

Our boat had arrived from Sicily, and what with Sicilian and Neapolitan passengers, every berth was occupied.

After leaving the bay of Naples, the sea was sufficient to quiet many passengers, and to give a seat at table, which by right could be retained. The following day, at Civita Vecchia, there came a rush of passengers from Rome, on their way to Leghorn and Florence. Fortunately the weather was fine, with a quiet sea; had it been otherwise, with hatches down, those below would have suffocated. Tents were pitched for the ladies on deck, and mattresses scattered about for the gentlemen. Such a democratic party of one hundred and thirty-seven passengers I had not met lately. It comprised a French consul and his family, and Greek servants, from Turkey, Italian counts and countesses, marquises, Spanish generals, English nobility, North and South Americans, German and other travellers, with all the dialects and tongues of Babel.

In such cases most parties are willing to conform to circumstances, although those who embarked first with us had great reason to complain of the abuse of the directors. The first breakfast was at nine, and dinner at four, and those who had to wait for the second and third tables were to be pitied.

At Leghorn we remained ten hours, and received as many passengers as we had landed; so our condition was not much improved.

My trip was just the opposite of one which I made last winter from France to the island of Sardinia, on board of a steamer of great size, when I occupied the entire cabin, the commander being my only table companion.

I rejoiced to get ashore, in the thriving city of Genoa, with civil custom-house officers and few police nuisances, breathing the air of constitutional liberty, and lodging in one of the former palaces, now the Hotel Feder—the inconveniences of the passage made me appreciate good quarters. I found myself casually occupying the apartment where the great Irish agitator, O'Connell, breathed his last.

Notwithstanding several visits to the City of Palaces, I spent a few days profitably. I shall not again describe the contents of the churches, the style of architecture, the marble and gilded decorations of the costly edifices, of the famed republic, but simply state that the intricate streets and numerous lanes, with their tall houses, not unlike those of Venice, have charms after leaving the broad and quadrangular streets of many of the cities of Southern Italy. Horse power is in requisition only in the broad streets and thoroughfares; but it is curious to watch the multitude threading their way through the winding passages, with little shops on each side—the women particularly, with white veils suspended from their heads, and falling over their shoulders.

The cafés and refreshment rooms are, as in all parts of Italy, supplied with the melody of harpists and violin-players of both sexes, who make the circuit, and pick up the crumbs from a musical people.

The gardens and promenades of the Aqua Sole, on the height commanding the harbor and valley, are frequented by all the beauty and wealth of the city on Sunday and other festival days.

On my last visit here Charles Albert, the liberal king, had undertaken the Italian cause against Austria, but had lost his throne, and died in exile.

Then the journey from Genoa to Turin was a fatiguing one of twenty-four hours; now the great railroad is open, and the trip is made in five hours. The distance is one hundred and ten miles; the work was done by the government at an immense expense. The tunnels (one of which, three miles in length, is a stupendous work) are all of arched masonry. Too much money was expended in the construction of this road to permit any interest to be paid: it cost over two hundred thousand dollars per mile.

Turin of late years has made greater advances in improvements than any of the cities of Italy; it may be attributed to its liberal government and the concentration in it of many thousand exiles, including many wealthy families from Lombardy. The full liberty of the press is enjoyed here, and quite as much liberty of speech as is consistent with constitutional government.

The great difficulty in harmonizing or bringing about a union of the Italian states, will be the different dialects. Here the Piedmontese patois is spoken. The journals are in Italian, also the shop signs, and the theatrical performances; but strange to say, the conversation of almost all classes is in the patois, and it is only the shopkeepers and the educated classes who speak Italian or French to strangers. In Genoa, another dialect prevails. In Milan, Venice, and Naples, they have their patois, and cannot understand each other. All this contributes to jealousy instead of unanimity, and enables designing rulers to keep the people in ignorance. The general introduction of railways and common schools would bring about a change.

The Constitutional Anniversary has just passed off with great satisfaction. The son and successor of Charles Albert, king Emanuel, is popular with the masses. He assisted in person, a few days since, at the opening of the new railroad to Suza, at the foot of the Alps.

A famous Amazon race came off on a recent festival day. The parade ground was about three-quarters of a mile in circumference; circles and stands were erected, similar to those in a race-course, to accommodate twenty thousand persons, the centre being occupied by the ladies of the royal household. Thirty thousand persons were spectators. The ladies rode well in the steeple-chase, their horses clearing the bars and mounds with frightful leaps; but they clung to their steeds beautifully.

Just before sunset there was a circus performance on a grand scale. Among the riders was a Hercules in the shape of a mulatto, who galloped two horses, standing erect, one foot on the back of each, and supporting one of the Amazons on his shoulders. The deer hunt was a failure. The deer was but little alarmed, and took it very kindly: the dogs sympathized with the deer, and some of them took to their heels in another direction, much to the amusement of the crowd and the annoyance of the manager, who made an explanation and gave an entertainment for the benefit of the poor.

Turin is, I believe, the only city of Italy where clubs are tolerated. The principal one is composed of the most respectable persons of the city, and occupies a commodious palace, with all the advantages of a library, reading-room, rational amusements, and an excellent table. Through the politeness of Marquis Palavecini, who, with his bride, was with us in southern Italy, I found myself registered upon the privileged list for a fortnight. Upon the tablet of sixteen invited guests, composed of counts, marquises, and barons, two of the number had no title; one of whom, however, was of the sovereign people from America; he dined at the round table d'hôte of eight with the diplomatic circle of Spain, Prussia, Belgium, and Naples. The liveried servants, and the presence of distinguished personages, did not seem in the least to suspend his appetite or prevent his enjoyment of a good dinner.

Turin, with its population of nearly two hundred thousand, its broad and well-paved streets, its long line of porticoes surrounding the public square and extending along the principal thoroughfare, protecting from sun and rain, has its attractions. Its position upon the banks of the Po, with long avenues of shade trees throughout the suburbs, affords fine views. The collection of antique horse armor and coats of mail in the palace, is the finest in Europe after the collection of Madrid.

The scarcity of grain this year diminishes the size of the bakers' loaves, and the outcry of high prices is general, particularly among the poor, whose principal sustenance is bread and wine, both of which are deficient.

Turin is celebrated for its pipestem bread, a peculiarity of the city.

It is laughable, at the table d'hôte, to see each person take a handful of sticks nearly a yard long, and amuse himself in cracking this crisping and delicious article.

The coming crop promises to be abundant. The wheat appears of a strong and hard growth. The heads of rye begin to turn already a golden color; and the hay harvest has commenced. The strawberry and cherry season is passing, as I noticed apricots are already in market.

# XCVIII.

PARIS, *June 30, 1854.*

I find myself once again in the bustle and activity of this great city, after my return from Italy and Switzerland. My last communication was from Turin. The railroad to Suza, recently opened, brought me to the foot of the Alps, where the diligence, with its ten mules, was in readiness to ascend Mount Cenis, whose lofty crest was buried in snow. The rich and luxuriant growth of the valley is gradually lost as the dwarfish and stunted trees appear; the cold winds from the frozen surface and the absence of vegetation prove that the summit is nearly reached, and the traveller rejoices in the descent to the verdant and smiling valleys of Savoy. The macadamized, winding, and zigzag roads upon the borders of frightful precipices are, however, well provided with parapet walls, and tall poles or landmarks indicate the route when it is blocked with snow. The Government has also constructed, at intervals, one-story cottages, with roofs and bare walls, as a temporary refuge for benighted travellers. The passage at this season of the year is comparatively easy, and unlike what I had to contend with in crossing the St. Bernard, some years since, during the same month, upon mule-back, wading through snowbanks in the mountain gorges twenty feet in depth. The scenery is less grand and majestic than that of the Simplon, or great road of Napoleon, which I once passed in the month of October, upon jumpers made of hoop poles, and drawn by a single horse, for one person alone, under constant dread of avalanches and mountain torrents.

A seventy-four hours' ride brought me to Chamberry, and thence three leagues further to Aix, celebrated for its baths from the time of the Romans, some of whose monuments are still found. It is situated in a beautiful valley, between a double chain of mountains, with most picturesque eminences, bordered by the Lake Bourget, some twelve miles in length. This pleasant little town, with a Savoyard population of three thousand, derives its principal support from the influx of strangers during the bathing season. Almost all its inhabitants—loungers, doctors, &c.—draw a portion of their revenue from the rent of their dwellings.

From its position between France, Italy, and Switzerland, it is a convenient and agreeable place for invalids. The waters are of iron and sulphur, and the supply is more abundant than any I had ever seen, and of a high temperature. The quantity discharged from the rock into the Royal Bathing Establishment, which is situated against the sidehill, is sufficient to turn an ordinary mill-wheel. The building, a handsome structure, is composed of four divisions, comprising thirty-six pieces. Here are found swimming and simple, as also vapor baths; shower, vertical, and oblique douches; with the volume and force of the shock required, or all the shades and varieties possible. There are also two dark underground rooms, whose high temperature of sulphur has given them the name of Division d'Enfer, or Hell Division; there is one for females as well as males. Two streams of hot sulphur water break upon the place, while clouds of steam make the atmosphere suffocating. While the invalid is in this he receives the shower-bath, which must produce an active effect. All the employees of the establishment are in uniform, and, when there are many visitors, they have full employment. The alum-water is most used for drinking, it being less heavy for the stomach than the sulphur-water, and its odor less disagreeable.

The Douchers employed in the baths are said to be very clever in their mode of friction, rubbing the limbs, and cracking the joints of rheumatic patients. I had no occasion for them, however. I have not yet forgotten the shampooing or vapor-bath at Constantinople, where one is almost scalded, and every bone of the body seems to be broken; then you are laid out in a winding sheet to be revived with coffee and sherbet, and finish off with a chibouck, or Turkish pipe. These waters and shady grounds being suggested as a relief for an eye-difficulty, I was induced to make a sojourn of some ten days at this pleasant spot. There are not the same attentions here as at Baden Baden and Wiesbaden. The Casino, however, is a handsome edifice, with spacious grounds and gardens, to which visitors subscribe, and have the privilege of a reading-room, a café, and restaurant; a military band plays morning and evening, and in the dancing and concert halls. The most corrupt places are the public gambling-rooms, where are seen groups of both sexes around the roulette tables, and the bankers with their little rakes in hand drawing in or paying out; the glittering gold dazzles the eye of the novices, and frequently induces them to stake their last Napoleon. The government has farmed out this establishment, with the promise that no officer of the crown, or citizen of the place shall be allowed to gamble—a very excellent provision; but the influx of strangers keeps up the traffic, and affords occupation for those who have a taste for play. I arrived in season for the festival of the baths. The programme was attractive, and calculated to draw a large assemblage from the neighboring villages. The firing of cannon, ringing of bells, and church service, the eating and drinking at the baths, made it a sort of Fourth of July affair; it was succeeded by donkey races, closing with an illumination under the tall elm and sycamore trees, with bands of music, and the national dances of the peasant girls and boys in their gay and picturesque costume. A display of fireworks added to the enjoyment of this simple and happy people, who seemed to disperse with reluctance. Rides upon the mountain, fishing, and excursions upon the lake, make up the pleasurable employments of visitors. A lady and gentleman, who came in company from Turin, joined me in an excursion down the lake, to visit a convent containing the royal tombs of the house of Savoy, which, with the chapel, are exquisitely wrought. The intermittent spring was also visited; at intervals of ten or fifteen minutes a rumbling noise is heard, and the rush of water (the volume being the size of a man's body) soon fills a natural basin, when it gradually ceases, to be renewed after taking breath, as it were, from exhaustion. We had embarked upon this placid lake, when a heavy squall came up; the Lilliputian sea became agitated, and the little sail of the frail bark fluttered in the wind; the lady went into hysterics! The idea of being shipwrecked in that manner was ridiculous to me. We made for the mountain shore, and, ensconced under the rocks, escaped the driving rain, until it beat the little billows into subjection. The fright was sufficient to draw forth a promise from the husband and wife not to go sailing again this summer.

From Savoy I went into Switzerland; it was my third visit. I found at Geneva many changes since I was last there: a portion of the old rampart had been thrown down, and streets opened and built upon. Beautiful as it then was, reposing gently upon the margin of the lake whose name it bears, it is rendered more beautiful by the march of improvement; new hotels are being added to those already existing. The opening of railways in France has brought Geneva within twenty-eight hours of Paris, which time will be shortened when other projects are carried out. In visiting the principal of an institution at Geneva, I found eight American boys from different parts of the Union. The little fellows seemed quite delighted to meet with one who was from their native land, and familiar with most of the localities they came from, and, more than all, acquainted with some of their parents. They seemed happy and contented, and under good discipline.

The country never looked better; the prospects of the farmer are encouraging; the disease of the vine, which has made such havoc and caused such loss in southern Europe with those whose only resource is the production of wine, has not yet appeared, and strong hopes are entertained that the vine will escape it. In sections of country where for scores of miles the cultivation of the grape is as general as Indian corn or wheat in our country, the failure and consequent distress may very well be conceived.

I formerly described the chateau of Voltaire, and the few relics remaining of that philosopher. It is situated at Ferney, a few miles from Geneva, and is frequently visited by strangers. The present proprietor has beautified the grounds and remodelled the edifice. He was my travelling companion by the mail coach to Dijon, and amused and interested me much with many anecdotes of this singular man, as well as the remarks of visitors, strongly prejudiced for or against that peculiar philosopher.

I am not yet decided what course I shall take from Paris, but you will hear from me in due time.

# XCIX.

AIX-LA-CHAPELLE, *July 25, 1854.*

The facilities for travel have so greatly increased since I first visited Europe in 1841, that I can scarcely realize that I am now writing from Aix, in Prussia, and that a portion of my last letter from Paris was descriptive of the baths of Aix en Savoie, in the north of Italy, where I was some six weeks since, thence passing through Switzerland to the French capital, making a considerable sojourn, with excursions to Versailles, Enghien, Fontainebleau, &c.; proceeding to Belgium, visiting Brussels, Liege, and the waters of the Spa. These points were all familiar to me, consequently only agreeable as souvenirs of the past. I found Brussels the same miniature Paris, but augmented in size, and containing some two hundred and forty thousand of population, partaking less of the Flemish character than formerly; the houses, shops, and streets very cleanly, with a great amount of industry. Dogs are there turned to account, and seen drawing carts as in Germany. The window shutters of the first floors of many of the houses are supplied with small projecting mirrors, for the convenience of the ladies, as in Holland, enabling them to see the foot passengers up and down the sidewalks, without showing themselves obtrusively. The Park opposite the royal residence, and near the former palace of the Prince of Orange, is a miniature Tuileries, and affords an agreeable promenade. The manufacturing town of Liege, upon the banks of the Meuse, in a fertile valley with most romantic scenery, is well worth a visit. It is noted for its manufacture of cloth and fire-arms. Owing to a free use of coal, the old city is black and dirty, not unlike the manufacturing districts of England. The most delightful valley is that of Spa, celebrated for its ferruginous waters, which are highly charged with iron. The country is fertile; the roads and public walks are bordered by tall and expansive shade trees. The winding alleys, little pavilions and look-outs from the heights, give great variety, and induce one to sojourn here, as the lodging houses and hotels are good and clean. The cuisine for reading, music, and play are attractive, and encourage many English to visit this picturesque spot, as the route is so practicable by way of sea to Ostend, and a railroad being within six miles, families are enabled to get here with little difficulty. The place is famous for painted fancy articles of every description, which are its only commerce; consequently it is a neat, genteel, and quiet watering place.

I had called upon our Minister at Brussels, and upon the Prussian Ambassador, and found them both absent, but had the pleasure of a rencontre with them at Spa. The only privileged bank or roulette in Belgium, is at the springs; the owners are very liberal, and contribute largely to the entertainment of guests. A handsome ball and illumination was given while I was there.

Aix has forty-eight thousand inhabitants, and numerous hot mineral springs in and about the city. Its name, Aquæ Grani, and its origin and prosperity, date back to the Roman era, when the Proconsul Granis and his legions stopped here in their passage from the Gauls to Germany. Its healing springs decided Charlemagne to make it his favorite sojourn with his numerous court. It was the place for crowning the German emperors, from Louis le Debonnaire, in 873, to Ferdinand I., in 1531. There are eight huge sulphur baths, to which are attached good and commodious quarters, giving invalids the advantage of bathing without exposure. At this season of the year the baths and hotels are full; the arrivals thus far reaching several thousands; the names of strangers arriving from all sources are published daily in a small sheet, with their places of residence. The city lies in a valley, and is defended by the now verdant hills, which protect it from high winds; it may be considered a desirable place for health during the inclement season. The principal places of resort for strangers and citizens, within the city, are the Kurhaus, containing library and reading rooms, the concert halls, and a ball-room with a garden, enlivened with an orchestra in the evening. There may be found here a large re-union of ladies and gentlemen, wherein most of the languages of Europe are heard. The fountain Elise, and the garden adjoining, are most frequented in the morning by those who imbibe; glass in hand you see them strolling under the pavilion, reconciling themselves to a disagreeable draught, with an air from the military band. The municipality has here the benefit derived from the gaming tables, which has enabled them to erect a fine new hospital. It is curious and instructive to notice the passion for play—the anxiety manifested upon the countenances of those not accustomed to this unfortunate vice. It is not confined to the male sex, but numbers of beautiful and fashionably-dressed ladies are seen surrounding the tables, staking or drawing in with tiny rakes the glittering pieces of gold. From a height called Louisberg, is presented a beautiful panorama of the city and suburbs. The avenues for a drive and walks through the woods are really charming; an excellent restaurant, erected by the city authorities, with occasional fêtes and bands of music, are among the attractions. As I was strolling alone through the forest, towards evening, I reached a culminating point on an eminence, where I had one of the most magnificent landscapes lying before me, and my mind was involuntarily carried towards home. I heard the shrill whistle and the tread of the iron horse in the distant valley beyond me. I could almost fancy myself gazing from a certain knoll, upon which I have often stood, a little south of Poughkeepsie, with the distant hum from the railroad trains. Although nature had done much, art had not yet accomplished what was required. I looked in vain, however, for the majestic Hudson, whitened with sails, and the towering summits of the Highlands, and awakening from my reverie, I came to the conclusion that there are but few spots which nature and the work of man, combined, have rendered more attractive and agreeable than the Spring side of our beautiful city.

The remains of Charlemagne, the most powerful of Emperors, lie in the old cathedral founded by him. It has now withstood the ravages of more than a thousand years, having been consecrated by Pope Leo in the year 804. It contains many relics preserved in gold and silver cases set with precious stones. The most valuable of these relics were presented by Queen Isabella of Spain, in the sixteenth century, and are only opened once in seven years, for a fortnight, which occasions the pilgrimage of thousands of believers at that time. They are taken from their envelopes of silk, covered with cloths of gold and silver, and beset with jewels. They consist of a white cotton dress, supposed to have been worn by the mother of our Saviour; the linen with which the infant Jesus was clad; the cloth upon which the head of John the Baptist was placed; and the sack with which Christ girded his loins.

A large portion of the population is employed in the manufacture of cloths, silks, pins, needles, and various branches of trade. The Americans are among the best customers for cloths. We had a small fair here the other day. The country people stared and gazed and made their little purchases; mountebanks, menageries, trained monkeys and dogs, flying horses, and albinoes were plentiful; there were moving wax figures of Christ and his disciples at the table; and a living representation of his condemnation and flagellation, with verbal descriptions in German. Lager beer, cheese, and pipes were in general demand.

It must not be supposed that these people know nothing of California. I saw once a panorama of the trip to the land of gold, via the Isthmus of Panama. My curiosity led me, a few evenings since, to look in upon a much vaunted panorama now exhibiting here, painted by two artists who had crossed the plains. The gold diggings, the view of Sacramento city, the descent of the river to Benicia and San Francisco, were tolerably executed. A frightful shipwreck upon the Mexican coast made the audience shudder; the South American pirates seizing and burning a vessel, made them promise without doubt, to stay quietly at home. The beautiful tropical vegetation of Nicaragua was enchanting, but the serpents were frightful. Finally, after a long voyage, via Havana, we were brought safely to the port of New York. The Battery and Castle Garden, with a multitude of shipping, were before us; the spire of Trinity church soared up high; large and beautiful steamers with upper deck saloons were represented—the Reindeer being just ready for departure. The description given as the canvass rolled by, was interesting, although exaggerated; but when, in conclusion, the above-named steamer exploded, with five hundred passengers on board, I thought it was carrying the joke too far. I told the exhibitor, at the close, that we admitted the explosion and the loss of seven lives, but as the tide of emigration was great from Germany to America, we could not afford such wholesale slaughter.

# C.

BATHS OF EMS, DUCHY OF NASSAU, *Aug. 20, 1854.*

In the little village of Graefrath, a few leagues from Dusseldorf, in the kingdom of Prussia, lives an oculist, who is celebrated throughout Holland and Germany, and whose address was given me at Aix-la-Chapelle. Requiring his services, I went in pursuit of him, and found, to my surprise, from two hundred to two hundred and fifty patients, who make a sort of pilgrimage there from all quarters. His success with royalty has given him several badges of honor, which he wears, and has made the village a place of sojourn for the afflicted, who are its chief resource. The doctor is kind and liberal in his treatment of the poor, and no respecter of persons. Each takes his turn, and I considered myself fortunate on my first interview, in meeting with the rank and file; it gave a fair opportunity of witnessing the sufferings of the partially blind, young and old, in the different conditions of life, and studying the hopes and fears of this pitiful class of invalids, and of thanking Heaven that my difficulties were small in comparison with those of many others present. Obtaining the necessary remedies for treatment, I was advised to proceed to this place, and make use of the waters.

Dusseldorf, which I had just left, is renowned for its school of modern paintings, and has three galleries now open, which contain many gems of art. It is also the residence of some three hundred artists. The gallery in New York, which bears its name, as we all know, contains a good collection of pictures.

I shall say little of the city so famous for its Cologne water, its vast, unfinished cathedral, its church with the bones of the eleven thousand virgins, which I have described on former occasions, but simply say I took there the steamer to ascend the much-vaunted Rhine, so full of interest, with its thickly settled villages, the rich vegetation of its banks, whose amphitheatred walls are covered with the vine which has given such celebrity to the Johannisberger, Rudesheimer, and other choice wines, its old castles upon the verge of the mountain crags, with its many legends, all of which are calculated to call forth the enthusiasm of the tourist. The day was fine; the long but narrow and tolerably fleet iron steamers made rapid exchanges of passengers at the principal villages, adding to the interest of the trip. The awning was spread as a protection from an August sun, and dinner served on deck to a numerous party of different races and tongues, who seemed to enjoy exceedingly not only the charming panorama but the light and delicious beverage produced from such clustering vines as covered the mountain side. This being the fourth time that I had navigated this stream, I could gaze upon its beauties with less emotion than formerly, and, must add, for the grand and majestic, the scenery of the noble Hudson surpasses the Rhine, although the former is deficient in variety of detail. The frowning castle of Ehrenbreitstein (the Gibraltar of the Rhine), and the smiling banks of the Moselle, which here discharges its waters, denote our arrival at Coblentz; and a two hours' ride brings us to the village of Ems, deservedly noted for its picturesque and charming site, lying in the valley, upon the margin of the little river called the Lahn, skirted by mountains on both sides. I find myself somewhat at home here, being lodged in the same quarters in which I spent a month in the summer of 1848.

The discovery of the thermal waters of Ems dates from an early period of antiquity. When the Roman legions, under Augustus and Tiberius, occupied these mountains, they erected baths in honor of the nymphs, protectresses of the mineral waters, whose fountains mysteriously came from the earth. After the decline of the Roman power, they were lost sight of until the twelfth century, when Ems passed under the domination of the Counts of Nassau. It was not until 1803 that the house of Nassau erected the convenient and commodious buildings now forming part of this establishment. Since my last visit the improvements have been considerable to accommodate the great number of invalids who come here in search of health. Ems being a village with no other attractions than its beautiful rides and walks, everything has been done to render it agreeable; large and fine hotels have been erected, where every comfort may be obtained. The band plays morning and evening; the Kursaäl is a fine architectural structure for concerts, plays, and general reunions. The gardens are agreeable. The walks and romantic sites are covered with pavilions, accessible for pedestrians and donkeys—which latter abound, with red side-saddles with cushioned backs for ladies, and it is amusing to see the competition among the drivers: groups of both sexes, young and old, are seen winding up the serpentine ascents, presenting a droll appearance. The waters of Ems are celebrated for the relief of bronchial, pulmonary, and nervous diseases; more than one half of the visitors are ladies. Here one meets princes, dukes, counts, senators, merchants, etc., with their wives, daughters, and friends; Russians, Poles, Germans, Hollanders, Danes, and Frankfort Jews, whose object is certainly the restoration of health. The usual term for employing the waters for bathing and drinking is four weeks, and the hours from six until eight A.M.; you see at the hot sparkling fountains of the Kesselbrunnen and Kruenchin from six hundred to eight hundred persons, with fancy-colored Bohemian glasses in their hands, sipping the not unpleasant bi-carbonate fluid, and after a promenade at intervals of from a quarter to half an hour, returning to the same, the band playing all the while inspiring airs. At one P.M., there is a table d'hôte in all the hotels, and parties who occupy lodgings change, if desirable, from day to day, and are more generally thrown together, and seem to become more acquainted, than at many watering places. At six P.M. all congregate at the springs, and after imbibing and strolling through the grounds, to the sound of a march or waltz, disperse; at eight, all is quiet, and the trees, plants, and flowers are left alone in their glory. Such as choose to sup at the Kursaäl, and repair to the concert and gambling saloons, do so.

The waters of Nassau are renowned, and are a source of wealth to the Duke, who is commander-in-chief of this little province, which contains only three hundred and sixty thousand inhabitants. Large quantities of Seltzer water are exported over Europe.

In the history of this little duchy of Nassau, the discovery of one of its springs, as told by a traveller, is so full of simplicity that I cannot refrain from repeating it. It seems there was once a heifer with which everything in nature seemed to disagree; the more she ate the thinner she grew; the more her mother licked her hide the rougher it became; the flies of the forest would not bite her; she was never known to chew her cud; but, hide-bound and melancholy, her hips nearly protruded through her skin; no one knew what the matter was, and no one could cure her. At last, deserted by her owner, she was abandoned for lost. A few weeks after, she appeared among the herd with ribs covered with flesh, eyes like a deer's, and skin as sleek as a snail's; her breath smelling sweetly with milk; every day seemed to re-establish her health. The incident was so striking that the herdsman was induced to watch her; he perceived that every evening she wended her way to an unknown spring of water, from which she refreshed herself and returned to the valley.

This circumstance was nearly forgotten by the peasant when a young Nassau lady began to show the same symptoms as this heifer. The herdsman heard of her case and advised her to try the waters, which she did, and became one of the plumpest girls in the duchy.

Deaths never occur here, at least they are not known, for the poor patient is quietly disposed of at an hour when none but the undertaker is on duty. The sympathies of the living are not thereby excited, and the bright side of the picture is the only one gazed upon.

This water-drinking, bathing regimen and daily routine becomes monotonous where necessity demands it, and one is rejoiced at the approach of the period when he is exempted by the physicians. The latter are found invariably in the morning promenades, to consult with their clients. But for fear you will be gorged and saturated with mineral waters let us change the subject.

The eyes of all Europe are directed to our country; its gigantic strides, its wonderful progress excite the admiration of those who sympathize with our republican institutions, and the envy of those who detest and fear the march of democracy. The loss of the better classes of German emigrants, who leave the country with means, is a source of anxiety to the crowned heads, and every obstacle is thrown in their way to prevent emigration.

# CI.

Frankfort-on-the-Maine, Germany, *Sept. 20, 1854.*

I have, within the last month, touched and visited so many points that I scarcely know how to go into detail in the short space of one letter.

I went from Coblentz up the Rhine, whose beauties from that point to Mayence I shall not attempt to describe. I embarked at Biebrich, the residence of the Grand Duke of Nassau, whose grounds and parks must not be neglected, and went by vehicle to Wiesbaden, the great thoroughfare, as a watering-place. Its hot chicken broth fountain, with its numerous pipes, supplies scores of hotels and bath houses. Its Kursaäls, with play rooms and dining halls, got up on a grand scale, with the adjoining galleries, filled with fancy shops of infinite variety, attract the stranger. The lovers of secluded and sheltered serpentine walks, bordered with flowers, but deprived of the autumn scenery, may find comfort and delight at Wiesbaden; and children may gambol upon the grass, and feed the ducks in the little artificial lakes, while the lordly white swan sails along and claims his authority. The weather was dry and fine. I had got away from the rainy streak, and all was pleasant; but as I was not a stranger in Wiesbaden I shortened my visit and resumed my march. From thence, by railroad, I came to this free German city. From Frankfort we go to Homburg, within two hours, by railroad and omnibus. Among the thirty odd divisions into which Germany is unfortunately cut up and divided, this small landgrave is perhaps the smallest, and will die out with the death of the present incumbent, who is already old. It will pass into the Duchy of Darmstadt adjoining. The celebrity of the waters of Homburg for dyspepsia, its superior position for high and varied scenery, and the privilege granted by Count Alexander for gambling the entire year, a privilege which exists only here, have made Homburg a flourishing village. The sum paid for the privilege of gambling is thirty thousand dollars annually. The bank is not only able to pay this large sum and give greater favors to players than other banks, but has expended an enormous amount upon the buildings; the saloons are the most gorgeous of the kind in Europe, and play is higher and more general here than at any of the watering-places in Germany. Ladies are among the heaviest players. It is a strange and fascinating passion, and leads to great abuses. I will cite an example: on Saturday evening I noticed a lady risking a large number of sovereigns, with unusual nonchalance. The next morning I saw her at the English Episcopal Church. My curiosity induced me to see, on returning, if the same person would enter the gaming rooms that day. To my surprise I found her at her post, with her pile of gold before her. I had heard that in this district, surrounded by Germans, there existed a colony of French, and I was induced to pay a visit to their village, which interested me much. I found a neat pretty settlement of one thousand souls, the descendants of thirteen Protestant families who escaped from France after the revocation of the edict of Nantes, under Louis XIV., and were protected by Frederick II. They have a church which cost thirty thousand florins (twelve thousand dollars) and two institutions for boys and girls, where children from different parts of Germany are educated in French. They always converse in French among themselves, and have preserved their language remarkably. They are all familiar with German, and talk with outsiders in German, the language of the country. They have several branches of industry in cotton, flax, and wool. It was curious and novel to witness this happy, tidy, industrious little community, surrounded by other villages quite impoverished, and in a little territory about equal to the size of one of our counties, heavily taxed to keep up the dignity of a court with palace and grounds, with its quota of military; but how hard is the fate of a poor man with a family toiling and striving for the pittance of eight groschens, only twenty cents per day, as several have told me when I have stopped and asked the price of labor, and in this almost famine year. When they hear of America they are eager to be off, but the means are not provided.

From Homburg I proceeded to Darmstadt and Manheim, in order to make a detour to Speyer, which is celebrated for its Cathedral. At Manheim the river to Ludwigshafen, on the opposite shore, is crossed by a bridge formed by some thirty iron flat-bottomed boats of canal-boat size, fastened together, upon which the structure is laid, with draws for the passage of steamers, as is the case all along the Rhine. An hour's ride by railroad carries one to the old town of Speyer. It was once populous, but is now reduced to six thousand inhabitants, and contains only one object of interest, a cathedral, which may be considered the pride of Germany, as uniting the work of the best modern artists. This cathedral, which was commenced under the Emperor Conrad II., in the year 1030, has been burnt and rebuilt three several times, and now, under the auspices of the king of Bavaria, in whose dominion it lies, has been renovated in the modern style, with exquisite taste, differing so widely from the antiquity which we so constantly find in these old memorable edifices, that the contrast is the more striking and more gratifying to the eye.

On my return I went to Heidelberg and Baden Baden. I visited all the points I had formerly seen and described to you, but none struck me as new, or worthy of description. Heidelberg is a lovely spot for scenery, and Baden may claim the preference as being the gayest and most charming watering-place in Germany.

In getting out of the cars I was greeted by an old travelling friend in Italy and Germany—our Consul at R———m, formerly a bachelor, but now married and here with his wife. We were soon joined by two former acquaintances, the American Minister from Belgium, with his sisters and cousin. We made a very pleasant excursion party in two carriages, and for three days castles tenanted by grave ancestors, and patriots, situated upon high mountain tops, and in dark-wooded forests, were hunted up and examined. The party was not disposed the less to climb the moss-covered walls of the schloss or chateau to points where the most extended views might be obtained. A trout and game dinner in the country, well served, restored us from the fatigue attending such exercise, and we drove to town in time for the evening band and concert.

I left for Strasburg, in order to descend the Rhine, which I had not seen from that point to Mayence, and also to change the route. A sad sight presented itself at my departure, another evidence of the uncertainty of life. A new car, in three compartments, with extended roof and balcony all round, and doors opening from the sides, was put on, which car I chose to take, notwithstanding the Germans say that none but princes and fools travel in first-class cars; the second-class is good, but the third-class is very rough. I was standing on the balcony when the cars moved off, and saw a well-dressed man, who had escorted three ladies and just taken leave of them, come out. Finding he was late, he attempted foolishly to get off while the train was in rapid motion; he tripped, fell under the wheels, and was cut in two under our eyes; only three of us witnessed the accident. I gave an alarm hastily, and succeeded in stopping the train. My sympathies were strongly excited for the afflicted ladies, and his only daughter, who is now an orphan.

Lightning speed soon carried us to Kehl, on the left bank of the Rhine, and then we took an omnibus across the bridge of boats to the French Alsatian shore, where, after the usual delay of visitation of passports and baggage, we passed a few miles further, to the well-fortified city of Strasburg. It has ninety thousand population, and is noted for its cathedral and tower of a remarkable height (I believe the highest in Europe), also for its extraordinary clock, with machinery denoting the changes of the weather, the action of the hours, &c. At twelve at noon an anxious group assembles in the building to witness the performance of the figures upon the frontispiece of the mammoth clock. When the grim figure of Death, hammer in hand, strikes the hour of twelve, the figures of the twelve Apostles revolve in succession, and make reverential bows before Christ, who in return pronounces the benediction. A huge cock, perched above, flaps his gilded wings strongly, and crows three times with a voice sufficiently strong to make a tame chanticleer take to his heels. The original clock, which I was shown years since, has been removed, but is still on exhibition. Its inventor, who was suspected of the design of building a second for another city of France, had his eyes put out; he then revenged himself by breaking certain springs which baffled the ingenuity of others to replace.

During high mass I noticed a group of emigrants paying their last addresses to the Virgin before embarkation. I had seen the healthy, robust men and women on the road with their heavy chattels marked for America. They told me they were going to Wisconsin, and had friends there.

Embarking upon a small steamer, a few miles of canal navigation bring us to the Rhine, and down its circuitous current we go at a rapid rate, mostly through a flat country, without much of interest except the towns of Worms and Speyer, which I had already visited by railway. I debarked at Mayence, and returned again to this busy, active city, with its sixty-thousand population, noted for its money operations, fairs, seat of the German diet; its numerous picture galleries, public buildings, and its beautiful suburbs, are attractive to the tourist.

# CII.

Hanover, Germany, *Oct. 20, 1854.*

Since I wrote you from Frankfort, I have visited Hesse Cassel.

The chateau of Wilhelmshohe, the summer residence, about three miles from town, with its hydraulics, and the effect produced by the cascades and jets d'eau, are superb. The great cascade is nine hundred and fifty feet long, and forty feet wide, interrupted by basins from one hundred to one hundred and fifty feet apart, as the water descends from a high hill, the summit of which is covered by an octagon tower, surmounted by a colossal Hercules of bronze, club in hand, thirteen feet high. Walking through the grounds alone, I could scarcely realize the fact that twelve years had elapsed since I climbed up the height and peeped out of a little opening within the huge club which the gigantic figure holds in his hand; that I had wandered, since, nearly twice around the globe; had been exposed to all the accidents and casualties of life, in every variety of climate; and that I found myself, through a protecting Providence, on the same spot again. I should not have made these remarks but from hearing of the frightful loss of life by the steamer Arctic, in which I came last to Europe, and have reason to believe that four of my fellow-travellers, who were in Rome during the Holy Week, and who accompanied me in excursions from Naples, have perished. I was waiting the departure of a steamer from that city to Leghorn, when we heard of the frightful catastrophe, and sinking of the Ercolano by the steamer Siciliano, an affair similar to the one just mentioned. This deterred these persons, among others, from taking the sea route, and they left by land. My logic has been, usually, after an accident, to take the same means of conveyance, as more care is then exercised.

From Cassel, I went by post to Gottingen, famed for its University, with some six hundred pupils, and its extensive library.

The contrast between the railroad travel of the present day, with its rapid transition from one city to another, and the slow mail coach of the past, was striking; and I was reminded fully of my first journey through Austria, Hungary, Prussia, and Saxony, by all sorts of fast and slow conveyances, when all the countries named had not two hundred miles of railway. It was certainly tedious, and occupied much time; but the country was seen to better advantage, and the halts at small towns and villages were entertaining and instructive, and gave a better idea of the people and their customs than the present lightning line of communication.

Although great improvements have been made, the people seem to toil as formerly for the necessaries of life, and the weaker sex is made to bear largely its share of the burden.

Not only are fine-looking, healthy girls seen constantly in the fields, performing men's labor, but in the cities they perform the most menial service of wood-sawing, sweeping streets, and loading carts with offal. How often I think of our blessed country, the paradise of women, and the thousand advantages they enjoy there, in comparison with their sisters in continental Europe. Not only is the sex compelled to perform a full quota of the service, but the brute creation must also perform its part. I have often thought how odd it would appear with us, to see the butchers' and bakers' carts, and milk wagons, drawn by collared and harnessed dogs, and the novel sight of single cows, or spans of cows, coming to town with loads of grain or vegetables. The truth is, when carpenters and masons obtain but fourteen groschens, or forty-two cents, per day, and laborers from twenty-five to thirty cents, and the necessaries of life are at the present dear rates, every measure is resorted to for earning an honest living.

The lager, or encampment, of fourteen thousand men, is situated in the suburbs of the city. The citizen army is composed of thirty thousand men.

We have just had a sham fight, which was seen to great advantage from a hill in the vicinity of the plain upon which the manœuvre took place, and gave a good idea of the battle-field. The approach of the marching forces, to the sound of drum and fife, and shrill tones of the bugle, and the bayonets glittering in the sun's rays, were exciting. The cavalry was led by the king in person. Then came the conflict, the thundering noise of the cannon; the continued volleys of musketry from the infantry; the reconnoitring movements of the riflemen; the dashing charges of the horsemen, half-buried in smoke; the retreats, the reforming of the ranks; the advantages gained and lost; the leaps of the horsemen over artificial stockades and sloughs of water; the queen and royal family, with liveried outriders, drawn by and mounted upon magnificent steeds, hovered around the borders of the battle-field.

The thousands of citizens on this festival day crowning the heights, and the enthusiasm manifested, gave interest to the scene.

## CIII.

BREMEN, GERMANY, *Nov. 21, 1854.*

My last was from Hanover. I now write from this free port and commercial city, situated upon the banks of the Weser, which river divides the old and new town. Its gardens are laid out in English style, giving the new town a neat appearance, and many improvements have been made since my visit in the summer of 1848.

Small vessels come to the city, but the larger class of steamers and ships remain at Bremen harbor, a few leagues below.

The chief trade is with America. The quantity of cigars manufactured from our tobacco is enormous, employing some thousands of persons, and scattering the manufactured article throughout this land of smokers.

The number of emigrants forwarded to America is scarcely credible.

In most of the German cities, under the "Rathhaus," or town hall, is a wholesale and retail wine cellar, the profits of which accrue to the church, bishopric, or city authorities, according to the circumstances of an early granted privilege. Since the German reformation the right here belongs to the municipality: and the cellars under the town-hall are shown to strangers as among the prominent curiosities of the city. The long succession of basements contains the choice qualities of Rhine wine, in huge oak casks, varying in size, the largest containing thirty-six thousand bottles of "*Rudesheimer*," of the vintage of 1806. The heads of the mammoth casks are well braced by cross pieces, with sculptured allegorical and historical figures in wood, and highly gilded. In one room, the god Bacchus, and his followers, of life size, all gilded and crowned with wreaths of grape vines filled with fruit, are seated upon the centre of one of three large vats, dating back as far as 1624. One of the cellars most renowned for quality is called the Rose, and another the Twelve Apostles, from its containing only twelve casks, whose names are painted upon metal plates, which are attached to the heads. The wine in these casks is the delicious, light *Hockheimer* Rhine wine of 1718. The rivalry lies between Peter, Simon, and Judas. A manager is appointed by the city authorities, subject to the supervision of the director, and monthly reports are made. City funds are appropriated, and the supply is kept up from the last vintages, so that the public may be supplied with a pure article at moderate prices. A large old sign, in the *Rose Keller*, has the following inscription, literally translated from the German: "What to the stomach, to the body, and to the heart, health, vigor and spirit can give, can console the afflicted, can revive half dead persons, yields this Rose wine."

## CIV.

Hanover.

Hanover lies on the small river Liene, and is the royal residence. It contains the city palace, the summer palaces and grounds; among the number is the *Herren Hausen*, with fountains, orange and botanical gardens. In the latter is a palm house, of iron and glass, a crystal palace in miniature—which is unique of its kind. It is kept at an oriental temperature, and almost all the varieties of palm and date trees familiar to me in the East and West Indies, are to be found there. The mausoleum, at the extremity of the ground, is a snug edifice, containing the royal remains of the late king and queen. The beautiful, full length figure of the deceased queen, in white Carrara marble, is a fine specimen of art, and is very like the much-admired reposing statue of the queen of Prussia. The wilds and forests of the king, extending for miles in the suburbs, give the citizens a variety of walks and drives in different directions.

It is evident that the Germans, unlike the English, never paid for light and air in the shape of a window tax. The old part of the city is literally a town of windows; many are beautified with plants and flowers, fancy screens and porcelain views, which give it an enlivening appearance, in contrast with the gable-ended, projecting, overhanging houses.

The *Konigliche Hoftheatre* is a pretty monument to the memory of the late king, Ernest Augustus, standing upon a beautiful site, two hundred and eighty feet front, and one hundred and ninety deep; the front portico is surmounted by life-size statues of twelve celebrated writers and composers, among whom are Goethe, Schiller, Mozart, Beethoven, Shakespeare, Molière, and others. The interior decorations are luxurious for Germany. In the middle of the front range of boxes, is the king's loge, the inside of which is white and gold, covered with the royal arms; outside are velvet curtains.

The theatre is regarded as instructive and moral, and is unlike what it is in many countries. I was accompanied thither by a very worthy minister and his wife, and the daughter of another divine, whom I had travelled with up the Rhine, and who accidentally visited the city.

The officers of the army, nearly a hundred in number, are obliged to subscribe monthly; their uniform gives the theatre a stiff, military air, unlike that of the Thalia Club, which has fifteen hundred members, or annual subscribers, with reading rooms, billiard rooms, refreshment saloons, and a theatre four times per week, which is fully attended by the respectable middle classes of ladies and gentlemen, and looks quite democratic.

The Museum Club, of which I am a member, is composed of three hundred, a large proportion of whom are active or retired civil and military officers.

Here all is marked out by rule. So many branches of trade of each description are allowed by royal authority. Application must be made for permission to engage in an occupation; if it is considered that there are already sufficient of that branch, the applicant is refused.

Such is the fondness for title or rank, which pervades most classes, that the smith, shoemaker, tinman, or tailor, is delighted when he attains the privilege of putting up the royal arms on his sign, to signify that he is employed by his Majesty.

We have had a German Fair, which brought together a multitude from the surrounding country and cities. Aside from the cattle show, I was struck with the varieties of manufactured articles, the exhibition of toys, curious costumes of the peasant girls, the playing of mountebanks, and the general consumption of honey cakes.

## CV.

BRAUNSCHWEIG, GERMANY, *Dec. 26, 1854.*

My last was from Hanover. Braunschweig, the capital city of the duchy, notwithstanding its princely residence and forty thousand inhabitants, has not the life and activity generally observed in Hanover. The palace and grounds of the Herzog, or Duke Wilhelm, merit attention. Having no wife, or family, his court is not brilliant in proportion to the royal family of Hanover, although his own private revenue and ducal appointments are equal to two hundred thousand dollars of our currency; a very respectable sum for a population of two hundred and fifty thousand. The former Duke, who had his palace burned over his head, and was chased from his country for malconduct, I had occasion to speak of last winter, at a court ball given at the Tuileries. The present duke is the last of his family, and, being without issue, the reversion goes to the Prussian crown.

Christmas is an important festival in Germany; the city presented a gay appearance in consequence of the many preparations for this event. The market places were covered with Tannen Baumer, or fir trees, with booths and tents filled with every variety of fancy articles, for presents, not forgetting a profusion of honey cakes in every form, for which the town has a celebrity. All classes must have large or small fir trees standing upon platforms, some of which are decorated with inclosed garden houses in miniature, and other designs.

Returning here in time for the Christmas-eve ceremonies, which I had a good opportunity of seeing at a friend's house, you will pardon my describing, at this holiday season, what may interest the young. In the centre of the saloon stood a small tree, nearly the height of the ceiling, its branches hung with variegated colored glass balls, round cakes, nuts in gold-and silver-leaf foil, confectionery of various kinds, the infant Jesus in a lying position suspended from the branches, the whole interspersed with wax tapers. The tables were spread with a variety of clothing, and other useful and ornamental articles for the children of from eight to fourteen years of age, who were anxiously waiting outside the closed folding doors until the illumination took place; then, each one rushed to his or her table, expressing childish astonishment and delight. Once recovered from their emotions, the parents were surprised in turn by the children, who had prepared a miniature tree and many little articles of embroidery, wrought at intervals unknown to the elders. The expressions of wonder and joy are general. Grandmothers, aunts, and nieces, had been industriously employed for the past three weeks in preparing gifts. The servants next received their presents. The evening closed with refreshments.

Speaking of Christmas Eve, I am reminded of Polterabend, or Nuptial Eve: some evenings since, I was startled by extraordinary sounds upon the sidewalk, opposite my house, and on inquiring, found that it was caused by the throwing of glass bottles and a perfect shower of old crockery plates, which singular custom was the greeting of the friends of a young lady who was to be married on the following day; and, at the appointed time, the carriages arrived to take the lady-bride to the church over which the minister-groom presided. I have passed houses, where the front entrances appeared as if a family quarrel had made a perfect wreck of the porcelain.

The people in Hanover are dazzled with palaces, horses, carriages, and liveried court-dresses, and servants. Ladies look with admiration upon the queen, and her richly-clad maids of honor; children exclaim, "There goes the pretty little crown-prince and the princesses!" And how often have I observed in theatres and concerts the patient people waiting a half hour or more the arrival of the royal suite before the exercises commenced, when the impatient Americans, in similar circumstances, would have brought down the house over the ears of the manager. Then the cringing manner of the employees and military officers, keeping an eye on the king: when he applauds, the applause becomes universal, while, if he is silent, a meritorious artist receives, perhaps, not the slightest compliment.

One great source of annoyance in Germany, is the great variety of coin and weights in use among the thirty and more different empires, kingdoms, duchies, and landgraves, whereby we must always lose in exchange in going from one point to another. An effort has been made in the Bund, or confederacy, at Frankfort, to bring about more uniformity, but the great quantity of base metal, of little value, in use in some districts, causes the measure to be opposed.

## 1855.
## CVI.

BERLIN, PRUSSIA, *Feb. 27, 1855.*

When I last wrote you from Braunschweig I was on the eve of departure for Berlin and Vienna, and thought it not improbable that I might go again to Italy; but the severe winter weather coming suddenly on induced me to quiet myself in comfortable quarters in this city, where from the conveniences for heating with the use of wood, the cold is less felt than in some parts of Italy. Hamburg, Magdeburg, and Potsdam, *en route* to Berlin, I had once visited in summer, under more favorable circumstances, consequently my stay in them was short.

I was reminded in Magdeburg that Martin Luther, one of the great men whom Germany has given to the world, and to whose former abode in Wittenburg, where the Reformation commenced, I had wended my steps, was a poor student there, and often sang in the streets to assist in supporting himself, as many others are doing daily. Potsdam is to Berlin what Versailles is to Paris. Frederic the Great made it a lovely retreat for the court. Here are seen the apartments of the great warrior nearly as he left them, remarkable for simplicity; the truck-bed upon which he slept, his writing-table blotted with ink, silken covered chairs partly torn by his dogs, and the plates upon which they were fed.

The windmill stands behind the palace of Sans Souci, an emblem of justice in Prussia. Though the story is well known I cannot forbear repeating it. The great Frederic, wanting to buy the mill with the grounds, to augment his gardens, was resisted by the miller, who gained the lawsuit. The king erected the present large mill for him. Since then the descendants of the miller, being in embarrassed circumstances, offered to sell it to the late king, who would not accept the offer, but settled a sum sufficient to enable the family to retain possession, saying the mill belonged to history, and was one of the monuments of the country.

It is now some years since I strolled over the grounds of the Kremlin in Moscow, and it was a reminiscence to find here a little chapel belonging to the Russian colony, surmounted by three domes, of miniature Kremlin form, and beautifully fitted up by the royal munificence for the Greek service.

While in this capital on two former occasions in summer, it struck me as being lifeless. We have cold weather, with ice and snow; the splendid sleighs and horses, adorned with variegated colored feathers, present a lively appearance. The city appears full of life and gaiety; the opera and theatres seem well attended, dancing and music being striking traits in the German character; balls adapted to all classes are continually taking place. The Kroll establishment of the Brandenburg Thor which corresponds to Niblo's in New York, but is on a more stupendous scale, and compares favorably with anything in Paris for its elegance, among other entertainments, has lately given masquerade balls. Curiosity induced me to attend one, in order to compare it with those of other countries, and found, as I expected, that the people are not adapted to this species of amusement, as in Spain, and in the colonies, where, during the carnival, all classes unite in these diversions in every variety of costume, assuming particular parts, and sustaining them admirably. I had passed a far more agreeable and rational evening, under the folds of the stars and stripes, at the house of Gov. Vroom, of New Jersey, our present worthy representative at the court of Berlin, on the anniversary of the birthday of Washington. There were some twenty-five in number present, representing different States of the Union, who responded to the calls, sentiments, and toasts naturally called forth by the handsome entertainment. The night was cold, cheerful American grate-fires were blazing, and the party conversed together upon home topics. My mind wandered as I saw the beautiful silk banner hanging against the wall, to the last occasion I had had of commemorating this festival. It was at our minister's house in Brazil, three years since, we mustered a small party of half-a-dozen; the flag was flying from the balcony overlooking the beautiful bay of Rio Janeiro, and the doors and windows were thrown wide open to get a breath of air, the perspiration starting from every pore, and this in the height of a South American summer on the 22d of February.

Most of the Americans here are students who have the advantage of lectures in the University on law, medicine, botany, Egyptian antiquities, and other subjects.

The royal library contains five hundred thousand volumes, and has a public reading-room for students and strangers, who, when recommended, can obtain books the day after their application, to take to their homes. German is badly spoken by the common people of Berlin; the educated classes in society speak the language purely.

You are aware that for many years I have not passed a winter in a northern latitude, and notwithstanding that the present is considered a rigorous one, it is not so cold as we have it at home; still I have felt it sensibly, and suffered while exposed out of doors. Having procured good quarters in a central position, in the vicinity of churches, universities, the museum, opera-house, reading-rooms, with a southern exposure, I should not say that Berlin life is disagreeable, notwithstanding my occasional longing for the balmy temperature and ripe fruits of a West Indian climate. The heating apparatus is called "Ofen;" I have two of them in my apartments. They stand like monuments of white porcelain in the corner of the room, eight feet in height, four feet wide, and two feet deep; they are useful and ornamental; are heated morning and evening, and throw out an agreeable and uniform heat, without any of the noxious vapors of coal. The windows are double sashed, as in Russia, and plants, of which the German people are fond, are flourishing in my parlor.

# CVII.

PRAGUE, BOHEMIA, *April 5, 1855.*

Since my last from Berlin, I have revisited Dresden, the capital of the kingdom of Saxony, and am now again in the old city of Prague, the former residence of the Bohemian kings.

While in Berlin, our minister addressed a note to Baron Humboldt, the world-renowned traveller, desiring an appointment, at his convenience, to present an American of some experience, which note was promptly responded to. We were cordially received, and passed an hour very delightfully in the society of this venerable old gentleman, now eighty-five years of age, surrounded by books, charts, and a little museum of his own collection.

The noble old man is still active, and fully retains his memory; he speaks fluently the English, French, and Spanish languages. He inquired ardently about countries it had fallen to my lot to visit, which he had not seen, and expressed regret at my early departure, which prevented further civilities on his part.

He is a great favorite with the king, and is of course a royalist; but he has much sympathy for our country, and regrets the late filibustering movements for the unlawful seizure of our neighbor's possessions.

Dresden is noted for having the finest collection of paintings north of the Alps, the work of three hundred and thirty-four masters; the masterpiece is Raphael's Madonna. A number of years had elapsed since I had strolled through these galleries, containing upwards of two thousand pictures, and I saw them with renewed pleasure.

Dresden is also noted in Germany for its musical associations. Madame Goldschmidt, formerly Jenny Lind, has made it her residence. As I had made her acquaintance through her countrywoman, Miss Fredrika Bremer, in the Havana, politeness induced me to pay my respects; she was absent on a tour to Holland.

From Dresden to Bodenback, the Austrian frontier, is two hours' ride by railway, with a delay of an hour when the passports are demanded, certificates given, examined, and then exchanged, and the luggage changed.

The railways in north Germany belong in part to the different governments, and in part to incorporated companies. Here the cars are differently constructed, being larger and capable of containing more persons, resembling somewhat the American; while in most parts of Europe they are like the English ones, with separate apartments, of coach-form, for eight passengers.

The Austrian custom-houses and police are extremely rigid, and they keep, I am informed, a sharp eye upon Americans since the affair of Kosta. Perhaps the warm reception of Kossuth in our country, and the late European Congress of American Ministers, has had its influence.

In order to show you the smallness of the custom-house here, I will state that I was detained a full half hour in the payment of duty upon twenty-one cigars, which, with the official stamp, were taxed at thirty kreutzers, of which the officers retain one-third. I told them the document was worth the money, as an evidence of pitiful meanness, which I had found in no other part of Europe. On a former occasion, in entering Vienna, my travelling companion had two sealed and fifteen open letters of recommendation seized, which were addressed to different parts of Europe. The next day he was cited to the custom-house, and found two sheets of foolscap paper written over, and a fine of twenty florins imposed, which he resisted, as he spoke German, and threatened to apply to our Minister, when he escaped with the charge of five florins upon the sealed letters.

On entering my room here, I was immediately furnished with a printed sheet, to fill up for the police, with my name, birthplace, occupation, married or single, age, where now from, time of stay, religion, &c.

The language of the Bohemians is unintelligible to the Germans; and I am assured that there are native born persons here, among the lower classes, who cannot make the slightest communication in the German tongue. The names of the streets, and signs, are in both languages.

The strength of Austria, which contains a population of seven millions of Germans against twenty-nine millions of the different races, consists in the variety of languages and religions, as is the case with the British East India Company, through the jealousy and religious feuds of Hindoo, Buddhist, Parsee, and other castes.

I am told that throughout the Austrian domain as many as eighteen languages and dialects are spoken.

The Jewish population is some twelve thousand; it occupies a certain portion of the city, formerly inclosed and locked at night, though now all the barriers are removed. Their old synagogue and churchyard are curious; the former is the most antique in Europe, being considered one thousand years old. Its walls are dark and dusky as those of a prison, and for centuries have remained unrenovated. Here is suspended a banner, presented by royalty, some five hundred years since. The laws of Moses, written upon rolls of parchment, in the Hebrew tongue, and many other curious relics, are exhibited.

The new edifice is a pretty building, and when illuminated at night, in its peculiar style, has a handsome effect.

As I am just departing for Vienna, I shall be there in time for the prominent ceremonies in the Cathedral of St. Stephen.

# CVIII.

Vienna, Austria, *April 26, 1855.*

A ride of eighteen hours by rail from Prague, the Bohemian capital, brought me to Vienna, the imperial city of Austria, passing through Brunn, a town of some importance, leaving Austerlitz and its battle ground on the left. A former visit to the places named, taking Iglau and Czaslau en route to Prague, over much tedious and uninteresting country, occupied five days; but by the aid of the iron horse the journey is now accomplished in the time mentioned. I find the old city quite unchanged; so unlike many of our American cities, where, on a return visit, after a few years' absence, one can scarcely recognise the localities formerly familiar to the eye.

I arrived here in time for the festivals, at the close of the Holy Week, and found the old Cathedral of St. Stephen's filled with the multitude as I had last seen it on the occasion of the annual departure of the devotees or pilgrims to the mountain chapel of Maria Zell. It seemed that only a brief interval had elapsed; but hundreds of those whom I then saw have probably made the pilgrimage from which there is no return, while I have been permitted, during the lapse of fourteen years, to pass three similar annual festivals under Popes Gregory and Pius, in Rome; another at the tomb of our Saviour, in Jerusalem; one in Murcia, in Catholic Spain, and two in Havana. The altars here, bedecked with natural plants and flowers, reminded me of a much greater horticultural display on a similar occasion in Lima.

The new chapel has been erected in commemoration of the preservation of the young Emperor from the hands of an assassin; and, on the anniversary of his marriage, about a year since, a brilliant mass was performed in presence of the imperial family. Notwithstanding the attempt upon his life, he seems to have full confidence in the loyalty of his people. I met him recently with an aide-de-camp only, walking in the vicinity of the palace, and we saluted each other politely. I met the mother of the emperor in the palace garden, in like manner, with a lady of the court and a servant, and she also responded politely to my civilities.

The empress, who is of the House of Bavaria, appears youthful, and rather pretty. She is not yet nineteen years of age, and is much esteemed by the public for her simplicity of manner.

On the occasion of the recent birth of a princess an amnesty was granted to many prisoners.

The Prater, with its dense forestry, is the grand lounge, where thousands may be seen on a fine day, and occasionally the cortege of the Imperial family.

The trees are now in bloom, and the country wears a pretty appearance.

The police are very rigid; I found myself closely catechised at the bureau, when I presented myself for an Aufenthalt's Karte, or permit to remain longer than six days.

The language of the people is corrupt German, but the educated classes speak the language in its purity. The many tongues here spoken make it a sort of Babel.

The Slavonians, who number sixteen millions, extending throughout Bohemia, Illyria, and Dalmatia, and whose language is difficult, seem to have the faculty of acquiring other languages; they are of the Czeck race, one of the three families Mech, Lech, and Czeck, who occupy Poland and Russia; and, although they are remote from the others, they understand much that is said in conversation. The Hungarian or Magyar language has not the slightest resemblance to the Slavonic or German, being an eastern or Asiatic language, the Magyars having migrated from Asia to Hungary about nine hundred years ago.

There is a vast deal to be seen in the capital of Austria. Its amusements are abundant. The Strauss Band, so justly celebrated, gives Sunday and holiday concerts in the Volks or People's Garden.

Schönbrunn, the Imperial summer palace and grounds, is within a few miles of the city.

The pretty neighboring village of Heitzing is overrun in summer by denizens of the city.

The immense summer palace has one thousand and three hundred rooms. I passed through fifty-two of the principal apartments, many newly furnished with elegance and taste, and rich in historical and family paintings, reminiscences of the legions of Napoleon, and of his son, the young Duke of Reichstadt.

The park contains the largest menagerie or collection of wild animals, and the best exhibition of rare birds I have seen in Europe, the present emperor having a fondness for natural history. The vast inclosures, of some acres, are of a circular form, radiating from the centre, with walls, and barriers, and outbuildings for the winter, heated to an African temperature, for the giraffes and other animals that require it.

The glass summer-houses, resembling military barracks in size, contain all the varieties of tropical vegetation.

Upon the summit of the hill, in the rear of the Park, stands the Gloriette, a massive stone structure, three hundred feet long, and sixty feet high, with columns; it is an Observatory, whence one gets a good view of Vienna and the Danubian banks.

A favorite excursion is by rail to Laxenburg, the favorite summer residence of the young Empress; she manifests, I think, good taste in her selection, nature is so beautiful here; and shade and retirement must be a great relief after the blaze and excitement of court life, particularly for one who is remarkable for her quiet primitive manner, and her fondness for fishing, so my guide informed me; her liege lord's passion is for the chase, which brings him out of his bed at four o'clock in the morning.

The art of man has produced upon the level surface of the Park, elevated mounds and islands, from the earth thrown out to form ponds for fishing and sailing, in which ponds scores of neatly painted boats are seen; grottoes are formed from heavy blocks of stone brought from the mountain quarries. Upon a small island, called Franzenburg, the miniature Ritterburg Castle is a perfect gem, with its castellated walls and towers; it has several rooms adorned with horse and war armor, and all the antique weapons of war artistically arranged; coats of mail, and lances used in tournaments, etc.; the sculptured oak-ceilings, three hundred or four hundred years old, the paintings, furniture, decorations, marble statues and portraits of the Hapsburg family, illuminated glass windows, cabinets of vases, relics of gold, silver and precious stones, form quite a museum, and give a correct idea of the grandeur and magnificence of the original.

The Viennese have their Baden, a place of summer resort for invalids, and noted for its beautiful mountain scenery, and its valley, called Helenenthal; but it cannot be compared favorably with the celebrated Baden-Baden in any particular, aside from its sulphur waters, which resemble those of Wiesbaden in smell and flavor. It lies twenty miles from Vienna by rail, and is well worth a visit.

The great gala-day of the year is the 1st of May, when nobility and plebeians, great and small, resort to the Prater, and is looked forward to as the chief event of the season.

A sojourn of nearly a month will give me an opportunity of revisiting much that I had seen formerly, and acquiring a better idea of the peculiarities of the different races of mankind.

# CIX.

PESTH, HUNGARY, *May 9, 1855.*

In my last, from Vienna, I remarked that I should remain over the 1st of May jubilee, when all classes feel it incumbent on them to hail the return of springtime and flowers—and to sip their coffee, drink their beer, and enjoy themselves according to their means.

The long shady avenues of the Prater are crowded with observers, regarding the double procession, up and down, of closely hemmed carriages, with liveried footmen, filled with the beauty and wealth of the capital, following in the wake of the many gilded and brilliant court equipages containing the imperial family and ladies of honor, foreign ambassadors, &c. Within neat inclosures, in summer houses, are seen the nobility, dining sumptuously, as Royalty also dines here, on the occasion. But what is more novel, is the Wurstel Prater, on another avenue, and its novel surroundings. Here are found Punch and Judy, or Marionettes, flying horses, miniature railroads, with weighing machines, theatres, boat and revolving swings, panoramas, bands of music, and scores of recreations for the masses, mostly permanent establishments for the summer, coffee-houses, with thousands of tables under the trees; and bread and cheese, sausages, coffee, and light beer, disappear in marvellous quantities, at short notice, and, strange to say, in that vast multitude, I only saw one partially drunken man, a soldier. No fighting, no quarrelling, all harmony, all were in pursuit of rational amusement, rich and poor, men, women, and children.

The Imperial Steamship Company employ their steamers upon the Danube, the Save, the Drave, and Theiss, and terminate their line at Galatz, where the Lloyd line for Constantinople connects. The steamers are small, but much improved since I was last in this country, being constructed after American designs.

From Vienna to Presburg, the banks of the river are low, with nothing of interest, except the battle-ground of Wagram. Presburg is prettily situated, with delightful environs. A bridge of boats crosses the river here; I counted twenty-nine boats in passing over to the forest promenade, which is much resorted to, and contains a summer theatre and refreshment houses. The town has forty-two thousand inhabitants. The Cathedral, built in the year 1090, was the crowning place of the Hungarian kings; it has some remarkable statuary in metal. The festival of the recently declared dogma, by the Pope, of the immaculate conception of the Virgin, took place while I was there—which brought out the ladies in large numbers, and Hungary may boast of the beauty of her daughters. Upon the summit of the hill overlooking the town, still stand the royal castle walls, burnt in 1812, and from which a magnificent view of the city and Danube is obtained.

Descending from Presburg, the river becomes wider; at this place is the celebrated chain bridge, finished in 1849, and one of the wonders of the age; it is fifteen hundred feet across.

Komorn, *en route* between the two cities named, has seventeen thousand inhabitants, and possesses one of the strongest fortifications in Europe. In the revolution of 1849, the Hungarians held out for a long time, and finally gave it up voluntarily.

Gran, lying below, has an equal population, and is the residence of the Primate of Hungary, Cardinal Rudnay, who has erected a cathedral, which is not yet finished. From this place the steamer runs between porphyry rocky shores, whose scenery resembles that of Saxon Switzerland. One of the striking features of the river scenery is the thousands of water mills built in boat-form, and occupied, after the ice disappears, for the grinding of the products of the country. Hungary is rich in wine, wheat, horses, horned cattle, and sheep. The quantity of wool produced is enormous—Prince Esterhazy's estates counting their thousands of shepherds.

When I travelled through this country before a railroad was suggested, it was by "Bauer" or Farmer's Post, in a rude wagon, upon hay seats, with four raw-boned nags upon the full gallop. I had an opportunity then of judging of the dependent condition of the serfs. Since that time they have been made free by the Ex-Emperor, their freedom growing out of the revolution.

I counted yesterday a procession of three hundred and thirty-five men and women coming over the bridge, with banners flying, and crucifixes in the hands of the priests, after a four days' pilgrimage to Mount Calvary, which I had seen from the steamer; the chapel is on the summit of a hill, with different stations in ascending. They came in singing, and looked pretty well jaded out. The populace stood along the sidewalk, in masses, to witness the return; they were mostly of the lower classes, and poorly clad.

Offen, opposite this place, has a population of thirty-two thousand. It was in possession of the Turks for one hundred and fifty years, at different times, and in 1684 taken from them; but the traces of its possession by the Musselmans are still left, particularly in its baths, which remind one of old Stamboul, from the heavy massive work, columns and domes; among the number the poor people's bath costs a kreutzer (three-quarters of a cent). My guide led me through the dense vapor produced by the copious supply of flowing water of a high temperature, and I could scarcely discern an object; but presently figures appear to the eye, as one passes through the mist: there sits a woman washing her clothes; another washes her children; then come men and boys, old and young, diseased and sound, promiscuously thrown together. There were twenty-nine in all, but the bath is capable of containing one hundred and fifty.

The idea is certainly repugnant, and discovers a low state of morals—the blending of the sexes together in a state of nature. With the perspiration rolling out of every pore, I was glad to make my escape.

An excursion to the Kaiser Bad (Emperor's Bath), a few miles by steamer, gives an opportunity of seeing fashionable invalids, bathing in, and drinking the waters.

The fortification which commands the summit at Offen, and from which Pesth was bombarded during the Kossuth war, and which contains the palaces of the Palatine and castle gardens, is now occupied by the Erzherzog Albrecht, and is a town in itself; and, from its commanding position, one has a fine view of the country villages and retreats in the rear, as also of Pesth and the whole surrounding country. Here stands a new monument, erected to the memory of General Heutzi and Oberst Alnoch, and four hundred and eighteen other Austrian officers and soldiers, who lost their lives in defending the place against the Hungarians, who occupied the heights in the neighborhood. Many buildings on both sides of the river still retain the marks of the cannon and musket balls, and many are entirely destroyed, giving an idea of the destruction caused by the revolution, and of the ravages of war.

In Presburg, the Hungarian's nationality seems to be, in a measure, absorbed by the German's. Here, he stands out more in his native form. The shop signs are chiefly Hungarian, and unintelligible to most foreigners. The journals are in both languages, German and Magyar. The officers and troops are from other parts of the Austrian provinces, while the Hungarian soldiery are sent to Vienna, Lombardy, and other points. The language is unlike all the other living languages of Europe, being of Oriental origin, and difficult to acquire.

## CX.

Saltzburg, Austria, *May 25, 1855.*

From Pesth I returned to Vienna, and made my way up the Danube to Linz, a sail of twenty-four hours, which would be lessened did they not lie by at night for the Strudel, where the river, breaking through its rocky barriers, divides into three parts. The most navigable portion is through the whirlpool, on approaching which a cannon is fired, as only one vessel at a time can pass this narrow point, which is from thirty to forty feet, where the fall is three feet in the distance of five hundred feet. Up to the last century, vessels and crews were frequently lost, but by the blasting of rocks, it is no longer hazardous, and bears no comparison to the running of the rapids of the St. Lawrence.

From Nussdorf, the starting-point on the main branch of the Danube, one hour's ride from Vienna, as the steamer advances, leaving the already beautiful environs for which the latter city is noted, the scenery becomes bolder, the stream is divided by islands, and, as the Germans estimate, one quarter of an hour across. As we proceed, an old fort presents itself, with its associations in the thirty years' war; the hill sides are covered with green leaves of the grape vines. Then we land at Tulm, one of the oldest cities on the Danube. Here Rudolph of Hapsburg figured in 1278; and the plain in the environs contained the sixty thousand men, in 1683, who rescued Vienna from the Turks. Further on at Gottweih, is a Benedictine Convent, founded in 1072, standing seven hundred feet high. Still advancing, new objects of interest are coming forward, comparing favorably with the Rhine travel. We landed the prelate of the Benedictine Abbey at Melk, a market town at the foot of the mountain. This immense edifice, looking more like a huge palace than a cloister, built between 1702 and 1736, stands one hundred and eighty feet high, on a precipice hanging upon the river bank. It has been frequently besieged, but is defended with bastions and arms which Napoleon, after the battle of Asperne, established in it from its important position, lying on the highway of the army to Vienna. He levied heavy contributions upon the monks' wine cellars for the use of the troops.

As we mount the stream, we see scores of boats, containing from fifty to eighty persons, with flags flying, and singing lustily, on their pilgrimage tour to Maria Tafel, which upwards of one hundred thousand visit annually.

At one of those small villages we landed a certain Baron B. and his family. He is a Minister in Vienna for one of the German States, and was taking his family for the summer to his chateau, with parks and grounds of four thousand acres attached.

His family consisted of the lady, two daughters, and three sons, with a French governess and male preceptor, and an equal number of servants. I had made their acquaintance through a friend, and found them an excellent specimen of the nobility of the land. The young ladies were nearly as familiar with the French and English languages as with their mother tongue. As we were detained for coaling the steamer, I was invited to visit the chateau, on shore. Cannons were fired at their arrival, and the peasantry flocked down to salute the return of the party. It was annoying and mortifying, as the weak-sighted old women and children kissed my hands, mistaking a simple American for an Austrian Baron, as I escorted the ladies to the house.

The general tourist, of course, comes in contact with all classes of society, and necessarily has an opportunity of studying character. It was my fate this trip to fall in mostly with the upper classes. No sooner had we left the party named, than a quiet young gentleman, a Russian, approached me, and made some inquiries about my route, and I found he was disposed to join me in my excursions. When cards were exchanged, the following day, at Linz, I found that another Baron was announced, which did not prevent the Republican and the Autocrat going along harmoniously together, particularly as the former had circulated more generally than the latter. He is still with me, and disposed to continue to Munich.

Linz is the last town of importance on the Danube belonging to Austria. It was there that I abandoned the river in order to make the most interesting tour through this portion of the Empire. Linz has thirty thousand inhabitants; the suburbs are very pretty; the laying over of passengers, and exchange of steamers, with its internal trade, give it some advantages. A festival day was occupied here in surveying the town and its environs, and in looking at the interesting groups of peasantry, in peculiar costume, in and about the churches.

The second Eisenbahn on the continent, with a flat rail, is here; it was moved by horse power, until this spring. A small locomotive was put on and run from Gmunden Lake, via Wells and Lambach, where a tiny little steamer makes the trip in an hour, through most romantic and enchanting scenery.

It was a reminiscence of the early days of railway travel; the venerable coach cars with small, low wheels; the narrow bed and strap rails; the snail pace movement, avoiding the danger of what we formerly called snake heads, from the breaking of the thin rail, and its flying through the body of the carriage.

Omnibuses run from the head of the Lake to Ischel, a celebrated Austrian watering-place of two thousand inhabitants, the bathing resort of the Emperor, who is now erecting a new summer residence.

The valley and mountain scenery of the Salz-Kammergut, and the position of this place, thirteen thousand five hundred feet above the level of the sea, can scarcely be described for their beauty. The Government Salt Works here are on a stupendous scale, and are a source of great revenue.

The governments derive large sums from the sale of wood, which is seen piled by thousands of cords upon the banks of the Traum and Ischel streams, and the quantities dashing down the mountain torrents from the melting of the snows, afford a curious spectacle. All possible contrivances, through barriers, to unite the floating masses and aqueducts to bring the required quantities together, for piling and drying, before they are sent to navigable water for sale, or for the boiling of the salt flowing through pipes from the bowels of the mountains, are seen.

The town from which I write has a population of less than twenty thousand; it is in a most romantic position, and is full of interest. The birthplace of Mozart, with a monument to his memory, an immense cathedral of freestone and marble, and the fortification upon the summit of Monchsberg, make a lovely picture in the distance. The rock was tunnelled between 1763 and '67 by Archbishop Sigismund III., four hundred and fifty feet through, twenty-two feet high, and twenty-two feet wide; it forms one of the entrances to the city, and resembles somewhat the grotto of Posilippo, near Naples.

An excursion for a day to Konigsee, an inclosed lake, with its occasional precipitate rocky walls, and water six hundred feet deep, with its echoes and the rumbling sound of the avalanches from the towering snowy mountains, from seven to eight thousand feet high, rowed in flat bottomed skiffs by two lusty women with men's black hats, is something novel, to say the least. The Hunting Chateau, the Ice Chapel, and the Cataract, come in for a part of the interest, and one is rejoiced to get back to the little hotel of embarkation with an appetite for Lachsforellen, or salmon trout, and the wild game of the country.

We returned by Bechtesgaden, a small town, occupying a high picturesque position, and celebrated for wood, horn, and ivory cut work, similar to the Swiss ware. The population are in part employed in this business; their manufactures find a market abroad, and were it not for the continual annoyance of custom-houses and travel, one would be tempted to fill his trunk and carpet-bag with their pretty trifles.

The Salt Works at Hallein, about seven miles from here, which I have just visited, are of an entirely different character from those of Cracow. Instead of the rock salt being excavated from the bowels of the earth, the mountains are filled with the saline material, which is extracted by means of fresh water introduced into the pits, and then conveyed through wooden logs to the two salt establishments in the valley below.

The ascent to the summit of the Durenburg, from the town, is about two and a half miles; it is rather tiresome to climb, but the constant changing views relieve one from the fatigue. When we arrived at the house where the descent begins, we rested ourselves, before entering, in a cooler atmosphere; and giving our hats and superfluous garments to our valet, with orders to meet us at the place of egress half way down the mountain side, we put ourselves in miner's costume, with a cap and heavy buck-skin gloves, to relieve the friction of the cables or ropes, in sliding down the rollers.

Preceded by our Steiger, my Russian companion and myself, flambeaux in hand, entered the gallery of Obersteinberg, and passed two thousand two hundred and twenty-eight feet to the first Rollen, or inclined plane of forty degrees. The gallery road bed is of plank, with wood rails on each side for the truck carts to remove the sand, after the salt is extracted, and for the bringing in of materials to support the sides and roofs of these narrow passages. Branch avenues, right and left, extend in different directions in the mountain. The Rollen leads from story to story, as we descend (there are five stories in all), until we find ourselves one thousand five hundred feet below. They are formed of two parallel ranges of round slippery beams, joined at the end, and connecting from top to bottom. One places himself behind the miner-guide, who carries the torch, sitting astride with one thigh resting on a cable rope, grasping the same with the right hand, which serves to moderate the speed, and to establish his position, and then with locomotive motion finds himself two hundred and forty feet below in short notice. As we pass through the different passages, a fairy scene suddenly presented itself: a hundred lights are reflected in the splendid sheet of water, three hundred feet long, and one hundred and eighty feet wide, and our ferry boat, by means of a rope and pulley, is drawn down to the opposite side, when we continue our march.

This is one of twenty-two similar lakes, where fresh water is introduced, and the saline properties for a month absorbed, when it runs to the salt houses for the process of boiling and crystallizing. The mines date from the fifteenth century. The quantity annually extracted is four hundred thousand centners, of one hundred pounds each; it may be increased if needed. In 1761 the mines fell in, and fossil salt was discovered. A museum, or collection of specimens, with monuments to the memories of the founders and Emperors, are within these deep recesses.

The egress from the mine below is through a narrow, calcareous stone arch, two and a half feet wide, six feet high, and six thousand feet long, commenced in 1541, and finished in forty-two years. One comes out seated astride a car running upon a slanting rail bed, drawn by one boy, and pushed by a second, at full trot. When the distance is half accomplished, the light through the opening looks like a brilliant star in the distance, and one hails with pleasure the cheering blaze of day.

# CX.*

RATISBON, BAVARIA, *June 8, 1855.*

From Saltzburg, near the Austrian frontier, I proceeded by mail coach eighty-five miles, through an interesting country, to Munich, formerly described, the Bavarian Capital, deservedly renowned among the lovers of the fine arts, as the modern Athens of Europe, and celebrated throughout the Fatherland for its Bayerisch beer, being to Germany what London is to England, for its extensive manufacture of that beverage.

The museum and studio of Schwanthaler, the celebrated German sculptor, is a source of great interest, and reminded me of Thorwaldsen's collection at Copenhagen.

Munich is celebrated for its *Erzgiesserei*, or Bronze Foundry, and for its glass paintings; the latter work is finely executed, and the new church windows which display it are strikingly beautiful. The colossal bronze statue of Bavaria, a female figure of victory, with a huge lion reposing by its side, was not complete when I saw it in 1848, but is now upon an eminence commanding the Theresien Meadows, standing upon a pedestal of thirty feet, which gives it a height of eighty-four feet. It weighs one hundred and fifteen tons. A staircase of sixty-six stone and sixty-five iron steps leads one into the head, where two benches of cast metal accommodate twelve persons; it is a rather warm berth at this season of the year. I found the great equestrian statue of Washington, for the capitol at Richmond, Virginia, in process of construction at the foundry; it will probably require considerable time for its execution.

A few miles from the city one relieves the eyes, and escapes picture galleries, in the shady avenues of the royal summer residence at Nymphenburg, with its fountains ninety feet in height, and its beautiful sheets of water, winding through this vast inclosure, which occupies two hours' walk in the circuit. The Botanical gardens are not devoid of interest. The supply of water is more copious than in any royal site I recollect having seen in Europe, except the Neapolitan Caserta, and La Granja, in Spain. The deer park, in the vicinity, is also a pleasant drive for the ladies and children, who occupy themselves in embroidery, drinking their beer, and feeding the young animals out of their hands.

In less than two hours, one rides from Munich to Augsburg, by railroad.

The old town has considerable of interest in its churches, architecture, monuments, &c. It being my second visit, one day at Augsburg sufficed, as I was *en route* to Ratisbon, and had to make the circuit by railroad to Donauworth, in order to descend the Danube. A little iron steamer, eighty feet in length, and narrow in proportion, with a tiny cabin, came to the place named as the head of steam navigation, with a small party of first-class passengers. We darted down the rapid stream at a lively rate, at times walled in by precipitous limestone rocks; the scenery was highly romantic and picturesque, with much to interest, but compared unfavorably with the views described in my last, from Vienna to Linz. We landed passengers at Menburg and Ingoldstadt, important towns, and in eight hours' sail found ourselves at this place.

As I have formerly remarked, most of the German governments have different weights, coin, measure, and regulations. One day one has fifty pounds luggage free, and paper money in use; cross the boundary, as is the case here, no baggage is allowed; it must be paid, for even moderate distances, at one cent per pound. If you happen not to have changed your money, you submit to a heavy discount. My Russian friend had a large sum of Austrian paper florins over, and lost forty guldens or sixteen dollars, by not exchanging as I advised him, and was consoled by the money changer, saying: *Mann muss lehr geld zahlen.* One must pay for experience.

Regensburg, or Ratisbon, whence I write, is beautifully situated upon the south bank of the Danube. It was formerly the seat of the Imperial Diet; it has a population of only twenty-four thousand, but is an interesting old city, with enchanting shady walks surrounding the city, giving the occupants breathing room. Sunday being *Frohnleichnamstag*, or Corpus Christi, the service in the old cathedral was fully attended. This vast Gothic edifice, built in the year 1400, was crammed with furniture, offerings, pictures, and relics, which destroyed its beautiful proportions, until King Ludwig, with the eye of an artist, in 1838, saw its deformity, and ordered a general sweeping out, and renovated its magnificent illuminated glass windows, representing the life of Christ and historical Bible scenes.

Strolling from one church to another, I found the current setting across the river to the *Dreifaltigheitsberge*, upon the summit of which is a pilgrimage church with fourteen stations and monuments on the ascent indicating the bearing of the Cross, and sufferings of Christ, up to the Crucifixion. So I fell in with the train, and passed over the old stone bridge, one thousand and ninety-one feet long and twenty-three feet wide, placed upon thirty arches of thirty feet in width, and well worth remarking, for the early period of 1140. Once on the top, I found the ground occupied mostly by Bauern, in their novel costume. The girls in short frocks of fancy colors, with balloon sleeves, and silver chain across the corsage; the men in red vests and short-waisted coats, with two dozen silver and gilt buttons thereon, about the size of a half dollar.

Tents and booths contained the eatables and drinkables. Service was going on, and the temple jammed full. A thunderstorm came up, and I took refuge in the house of the church guardian, in a small room ten feet square, with a bed in one corner, thirty small prints of saints hanging around the walls, a table covered with mugs, ham, and sausages, eight persons, and cigar smoke in clouds.

The weather soon cleared up, and after dinner I found the town deserted. Protestants and Catholics escape the city, and the society gardens, as well as the public grounds, are crowded. The musicians are playing, and the adjacent environs are planted with trees, among which stand large buildings, over deep cold beer cellars, for summer use.

The former Abbey of St. Emmeran, now the residence of the Prince von Taxis, one of the wealthiest nobles of the country, is one of the lions to be seen. His picture gallery is not large but select; his stable of sixty horses is a choice pattern of neatness and convenience; his riding house is adorned with many equestrian groups of ancient combatants by Schwanthaler, and is a gem in its way. The family chapel and vault will compare favorably with those of the kings of Prussia and Hanover; add to which, he has a large brewery in connexion, in active operation, which was erected and worked by this order of monks. Under the roof of the same previous ecclesiastical establishment, are the refreshment rooms for the sale of the article manufactured. What strikes the stranger here is the universal use without the abuse, and it redounds to the honor of the German character, for the rarest spectacle is an inebriated person. In the deep and dark recesses of the Rath House here are seen the whole apparatus of the inquisition; parts of it I had seen in Italy and Spain, but here it is completed. I saw the latticed screen of the judge, with his desk, and the bored holes for candles; the penitential benches for culprits, while listening to the groans of comrades inducing confession; the chair of pointed spikes, resembling a flax hetchel, upon which the victim sat, with the stone weights suspended from his ankles; the platform upon which the naked body lay during the scraping of the skin from the back from head to foot; bolts in the floor to fasten the feet, and heavy fifty pound weights, attached to the arms, while the shoulders were strained by the windlass; with a variety of other tortures too horrible to describe. The seat of the doctor is also shown, whose business was to decide how much the sufferers could endure, without expiring under the treatment. Also cells with small openings through which the prisoners received their food; they were chained in such a manner that they were obliged to sleep with the blood flowing towards the head and heart, inducing, as was believed, contrition; there were dungeons, too, in which they were let down, with no opening except from above, cutting off all hope of escape. In witnessing such an exhibition it is consoling to reflect that civilization has made much progress since the last century, when these hellish instruments were in use.

# CXI.

WIESBADEN, DUCHY OF NASSAU, *June 20, 1855.*

From Ratisbon, I went to the famous Walhalla Temple, occupying the summit of a rocky cliff upon the banks of the Danube, about two hours' ride from that city, composed entirely of marble, stone, and metal, and of which I must attempt a feeble description.

It seems that the artist ex-king, Ludwig, as early as 1807, when crown-prince, and while Germany was bowed down under French despotism, conceived the design of erecting a monument to the memory of the meritorious sons of the Fatherland. As early as 1821, German sculptors had already prepared a portion of the busts, when the preparatory ground-work was commenced, and on the anniversary-day of the battle of Leipsic, 18th of October, 1830, Ludwig, then king, laid the foundation-stone, and which he opened complete in 1842; the cost of which is reported, but probably incorrect, as I notice an article in a public journal, saying that during his reign forty millions of guilders, say seventeen millions of dollars, were expended in the fine arts, and constructing and beautifying churches, palaces, and temples. A considerable portion is represented as out of his private purse.

The majestic Walhalla stands three hundred feet above the water level, and the ascent is effected by double flights of broad marble steps, three hundred and fifty in number, uniting upon wide platforms, and then recommencing in like manner until the height is reached, giving a magnificent view of the river and surrounding country, as also a front view of the edifice. The terrace wall is built of many-cornered cyclopean blocks of stone, and from the second division corresponds with the underground foundation of the building, nearly one hundred feet in depth. The length of the wall from this platform, from north to south, is four hundred and eighty-three feet, and width two hundred and eighty-eight feet. The temple, bearing some resemblance to the ancient Parthenon at Athens, is two hundred and thirty feet in length, one hundred and eighteen feet in width, and sixty-four feet in height. It has seventeen marble columns on each side, and eight each, front and rear, thirty-one feet high, and six feet in diameter.

The gable pediments contain the splendid marble sculpture work of Schwanthaler, each group comprising fifteen figures. The one at the north occupied that artist eight years. The colossal form of the national hero, Herman, ten feet high, forms the centre of the group in the final struggle with the Romans, whose leader has struck his sword in his own breast to avoid the sight of the overthrow of his legions. From the time of Roman and Greek antiquity, perhaps, so large a gable-group has not been seen, being seventy-two feet in length. The inside is one hundred and sixty-eight feet by forty-eight, and fifty-three feet to the roof, and may be considered a rare gem. The floor is of polished white, yellow, and black marble mosaic; one draws on felt overshoes to slip and slide over the surface. The roof is of gilded bronze plates, with three plate-glass windows to admit the light, the crossbeams of sky blue, and stars of gold, with full-sized figures of gods and heroes. The various polished marble sides contain tablets and busts of one hundred and sixty of the most renowned and distinguished Germans. The different divisions are protected by six figures of Victory, in white Carrara marble; these female forms, with extended wings, are the work of the celebrated Rauch, at Berlin. The bas-reliefs, executed in Rome, of the same material, extend entirely around the hall, two hundred and ninety-two feet in length, in eight divisions, and mark the history of the German race, settlement of the country, conquests, arts, religion, knowledge, &c.

From Ratisbon, twelve hours by mail coach brings one to the old city of Nuremburg, the most antique in Germany. Its former population, ninety thousand, now counts fifty-two thousand; it is surrounded by a wall forty feet high, upon which are seventy-two towers and bastions; the four towers of the principal gates are built in the form of cannons. Its cathedral and churches are remarkable for their old illuminated glass windows, woodcarving of the altars, and life of Christ, by the renowned artists Veit, Stoss, and Adam Kraft; also paintings from the original school of Albert Durer and his master, as early as 1485. A remarkable old cemetery contains the tombs of the artists named. The venerable château, erected in the tenth century, recently fitted up for the royal family, who are soon expected, is worth a visit, not only for the view, but its contents. In the courtyard is a large linden tree, seven hundred years old. The city hall, built in the sixteenth century, is a fine structure, and contains remarkable stucco-work of that period, and paintings of Albert Durer, particularly the triumphal procession of the Emperor Maximilian I. The bridges over the stream which runs through the city, the fountains, monuments, and style of architecture of the old town, generally interest travellers. Nine hours by rail transports one, via Bamburg and Würzburg, through an interesting and varied country, to the free city of Frankfort-upon-the-Main. Being on my way to this favorite resort for a rest, and the use of the waters, I tarried but little on the Rhine, and as these points are as familiar as old acquaintances, nothing strikes one as new. Wiesbaden I find on each repeated visit much improved; the usual concourse of guests is from fifteen thousand to twenty thousand annually; its position on the slope of the Taunus hills, gives it the beautiful valleys that surround it, and the advantage of healthful and recreating excursions to the mountains.

I shall remain here a few days longer, then make my way to Paris, for the Exhibition, after which I may conclude to take steamer to my own Vaterland.

# 1856.
# CXII.

PARIS, FRANCE, *Jan. 28, 1856.*

You have been kept advised from time to time for so many years past of my whereabouts, that I fancy you inquiring, "Where are you? What are you doing? What kind of passage had you out?" and the like. The heading of this epistle will show you that I am once again, and for the tenth time, in the great metropolis of the continent, which is a sort of culminating point for European travellers going and returning. The first day of January, for the first time in some ten years, I was permitted to remain late enough in the north to unite with the denizens of our great Empire City in keeping up the good old Knickerbocker custom of wishing a "happy new year;" on the fifth I stepped on board the good steamship Pacific bound for Liverpool.

We stood shivering upon the upper deck, gazing after those left behind us, until reminded of the comfort of a cabin.

We soon found ourselves at Sandy Hook, in the commencement of a northeast snow storm, and with much difficulty disposed of our pilot. One of the roughest and most boisterous nights followed. Those of our passengers who were at sea for the first time, suffered all the horrors of sea-sickness. Our gallant ship combatted nobly the mountain waves, the decks were swept from time to time, and one life-boat was carried away; so passed the first twenty-four hours. Sunday morning, the sixth, I found three passengers out of fifty-eight at breakfast, and our dinner was not served as usual, "*à la carte,*" as the cook's galley had been flooded and things temporarily deranged.

We had a succession of head winds and snow flurries for several days, with seldom a nautical observation. The first day we only made sixty-five knots, as we could not see to run, but our noble ship did her duty, and made up for lost time, doing the passage in twelve days. I had just taken up the papers from New York, and noticed that the snow storm ashore was one of the worst ever experienced by that venerable gentleman, the oldest inhabitant.

Passengers at sea are disposed to accommodate themselves to circumstances, and being more dependent upon each other for the means of passing the time than ashore, generally make themselves as amiable as possible. Our commander I had formerly known; our steward had catered to my wants from Panama to San Francisco; we had several gentlemen and ladies—old acquaintances—and passed our time as pleasantly as our rolling and pitching would permit. We had a great variety of character for so limited a number of passengers—American, English, French, German, Italian, and Spanish, who finding your humble servant was familiar with their several countries, rather taxed his vocal organs in the exercises of their different languages.

Once landed at Liverpool, the great commercial mart of England, our party were soon scattered to the four winds. I started for Chester, one of the oldest and most curious towns in England, with its porticoes and colonnades which enable the pedestrian to walk long distances without exposure to sun or rain, and remind one of Bologna.

The Marquis of Westminster, one of the wealthiest noblemen of the kingdom, has a princely palace and parks in the neighborhood well worth a visit.

From Chester I proceeded to the great manufacturing city of Birmingham, and on to Bristol, in the west of England, a large seaport upon the Severn, with its suburban places of resort, Clifton and Hotwells, much frequented by families and invalids during the winter, on account of the mildness of the climate, and the picturesque and romantic scenery. The first steamships, the Sirius and Great Western, were sent to New York by a Bristol Company. It is a curious old city, but contains nothing very striking for the traveller.

Bath, renowned by the bards and poets, lies upon the Avon, and has some forty thousand inhabitants; it is prettily situated and well built; is celebrated for its hot springs, and is quite full at this season of the year with invalids. The weather was mild for the winter; the fields were still quite green, and vegetables were exposed in the gardens. The Great Western Railway passes through Bath. The living is good, after the English style, roast beef, mutton chops, plum-pudding, Cheshire and Stilton cheese, ale, porter, and old port wine, being the chief articles of consumption; there is no *table d'hôte* at the public houses; parties dine separately at hotels in a very unsocial manner.

The approach to Birmingham via Wolverhampton, for twenty miles along the railway line, early in the evening, presented a curious spectacle, and reminded me of a close proximity to the infernal regions; the hundreds of furnaces for the manufacture of coke, iron, and steel, throwing out their lurid glare of light and smoke, whose fires rarely die out, surpassed those of any part of England I had seen, and filled me with awe and admiration of this immense branch of industry.

Coming over the Great Western Railroad to London, there is much to admire, and many places worth a detour or a visit; among these are the Universities at Oxford, and the residence of the Queen at Windsor Castle, all of which I had formerly seen.

At Sydenham, twenty miles from London, now stands the Crystal Palace. Its lofty towers, two hundred and forty feet in height, are not yet complete; its elevated position commands the whole country; the parks are being beautifully ornamented. It so far excels what it was when I saw it in Hyde Park, at the time of the Exhibition, that I shall not attempt to describe it. Suffice it to say, the Egyptian, East Indian, Moorish, and Italian departments, representing so faithfully the architecture, painting, statuary, and inscriptions of those countries were to me an invaluable souvenir. The Oriental department, kept up to tropical heat in midwinter, with fragrant plants and flowers, fish swimming in the fountains, birds chirping and singing in the presence of huge Indian deities upon the façades of temples, almost transports one to the banks of the Ganges.

A return to the city, with its teeming population of two and a half millions, crowded thoroughfares, bustle and confusion, soon dispels the illusion. The winter is no time for sight-seeing in London, as the smoke or fog oftentimes prevent your seeing more than a few steps before you; indeed at eleven A.M. the gas lights are sometimes still burning. All navigation upon the Thames is suspended; horses and vehicles and foot passengers grope their way in the dense obscurity.

The communication from London to Paris, via Dover and Calais, or Folkstone and Boulogne, is made in twelve or fourteen hours, at an expense of three pounds five shillings, say fifteen dollars. The English railway fares are more than double those of the United States. The same remark will apply to the general expenses of life.

The Parisians are preparing for the Carnival, when masked balls will be all the rage, and the *"Bœuf Gras"* or fat ox, will be paraded through the streets on *"Mardi Gras"*.

# CXIII.

FLORENCE, ITALY, *May 2, 1856.*

Yesterday, the 1st of May, a gala-day in many countries, happening to be the anniversary of the Ascension, it united the church festival and the annual rejoicings of citizens and peasants; all business being suspended, and the entire populace at liberty, there was an unusual movement of the masses, and from early dawn until night might be seen the working-classes with their baskets of provisions, and flasks of wine, making their way to the shady groves of the Cascina, or royal farm. The wealthy denizens, in carriages, reserved their drive until towards evening, to enjoy the music of the band, which had already assisted at the church exercises and processions of the morning.

Having left the gay throng, I wandered along through the forest upon the banks of the Arno, listening to the changing notes of the nightingale, until I came to the junction of another stream, which arrested my progress. I was startled by the tread of the iron-horse in the distance, on his way to Leghorn. My thoughts, with more than locomotive speed, carried me back to the advantages enjoyed through steam power. One year before I was strolling upon the shores of the Danube, through the shady woods of the Prater, watching the movements of the people, and the gay cortege of the Imperial family of Austria, on a like occasion. The same power had since conveyed me twice across the Atlantic, through our Western States, and to the head waters of the Mississippi, and how much reason I had to be thankful for my almost miraculous preservation from the perils attending that power which I had so recently praised, in the superior qualities of the steamer Pacific, in my last passage to Europe. If she be now unfortunately added to the list of lost, it makes the sixth of the first-class steamers gone to the bottom, from which I have escaped within the past few years.

My reverie was broken by the appearance of a group of ruddy-faced peasant-girls, some with broad-brimmed straw-hats and long ribbons floating in the breeze, and some with pearl necklaces and crossed ear-rings. It was a bridal party. Some of the girls were remarkable for their beauty and freshness of complexion, notwithstanding their exposure to hard labor in the vineyards. The bridal portion of the peasant girl consists in the dress and valuable ornaments presented to her by the groom a few days before the marriage.

As I returned through the broad and solitary avenues, I met at intervals the forest guards, of which there were ten in number, in picturesque hunting dresses, with rifles in their hands, and plumes in their hats. Then I came to the joyful and giddy throng—music, dancing, eating, and drinking.

Winter is past, spring time has come once again, and all strive to be happy. Little country urchins are offering children miniature corn-stalk cages containing crickets, whose singing qualities they proclaim to inquiring nurses.

The annual races were held recently for three days in the same vicinity, which attracted large numbers of the upper classes of the community. The concourse of beauty and fashion in carriages was quite different from what it is with us, and gave strangers, of whom large numbers are now here on their return from Rome and Naples, a fine opportunity of seeing the aristocracy, and witnessing the sports of the turf. Curiosity led me to be present on one occasion, and I found things went off better than I had expected. Considerable interest was manifested by many for the success of a horse mounted by a negro jockey, rather a rare personage in this country, but poor Cuffy was almost distanced. It seemed to me, however, the fellow was not disheartened, for I saw him in the evening sipping his ice with a well-dressed white woman in a respectable café. I cite this as one of many examples seen in England and on the continent, however shocking it may be to the American mind to witness, of the practical amalgamation of the races carried out among the sympathizers of poor Uncle Tom.

Inasmuch as all Europe have had their demonstrations of joy upon the return of peace, so also has this government manifested its satisfaction in a jubilee. I suppose even the Duchy of Parma has done the same, although recently put in a state of siege, growing out of the frequent attempts at assassination of government officers. All fire-arms must be given up, and strangers are closely watched.

The people are looking anxiously for the publication of the articles of peace, hoping that Italy may also have real cause for rejoicing.

Although the carriage horses here are of large size and well-proportioned, there is quite a passion manifested for small ponies of the Shetland stock, for little tiny wagons, well adapted to run over the hills, and glide in and around the city, over the well-paved streets.

My ears have been bored several days past with the continual chiselling of the *Scarpellini*, or stone-cutters, who are repaving the street under my windows, and the solid arched stone bridge over the river. From seven in the morning until seven in the evening, with an hour's intermission for a frugal meal, they are measuring, picking, and cutting huge granite blocks into suitable forms, close jointed; the street has no sidewalk, the descent being gradual from the houses, and the water carried off by culverts from the centre. It is a pleasure to look upon such beautiful work; a carriage rolls without impediment, and where there is an ascent it can be nitched or chiselled, as may be needed, for the foothold of horses. These poor mechanics earn from thirty to forty cents per day, our currency, and consider themselves well paid, notwithstanding the increased price of provisions, while large numbers in other pursuits have only the miserable pittance of from one to one and a half pauls per day, say from twelve to eighteen cents.

Begging in the capital is prohibited by law, but tolerated in consequence of the distress of the poor. Public beggars are frequently unworthy of charity, but a Howard would have a fine field here for the exercise of benevolence. The other day, emerging from the Palazzo Pitti, or royal residence, wearied in gazing through long galleries at the pictures of Raphael, Rubens, Titian, Salvator Rosa, Murillo, Carlo Dolci, and a host of other celebrated painters; at the statuary of renowned artists, the allegorical frescoed ceilings, and seeking relief in the shady walks of the Boboli, or palace garden, my attention was arrested by the Ducal family riding out with a splendid equipage. Happy children of wealthy families fed the gold fish in the basins surrounding the fountains, decorated with the colossal figure of Neptune, with the waters of the Ganges, Nile, and Euphrates gushing forth, while nurses and liveried servants were in attendance.

Continuing my walk quite into the suburbs, and reflecting upon the concentration of so much treasure in the hands of the nobility, and the inequality of society in monarchical countries, I accidentally met a little boy quite alone, poorly clad, with dejected air, trying to gather a few sticks. On inquiry I found he had eaten nothing for twenty-four hours, and had left his poor mother and four children in a suffering state. His hunger was soon appeased at the first baker's shop, and it was pleasant to see the little fellow going to the relief of the others with something more substantial than his errand called for.

After repeated visits to the same city, one becomes so accustomed to the remarkable sights which first attract the stranger, that if he attempts to describe them he scarcely knows where to begin.

We pass and repass the Palazzo Vecchio, an old palace of Grecian and Etruscan architecture, with its lofty tower of the thirteenth century, and its gigantic figures, at the entrance, of David slaying Goliah, and Hercules slaying Cacus, with but slight notice, casting a glance at the open gallery opposite, with its pretty front of columns and arches, containing the beautiful bronze figure of Perseus and Medusa, with the bleeding head of the latter severed from the body, the marble group of a young Roman warrior carrying off a Sabine female, whose father is prostrate at his feet, the statues of priestesses, figures of huge lions, &c.

One strolls along through the city, on some church festival, to the Duomo, or cathedral of the thirteenth century, the walls of which are of black and white polished marble, four hundred feet in length. The front never was finished, but a project is now on foot for its completion. The square tower, or Campanilla, of Arabic and Greek architecture, of white, black, and red marble, stands beside it, and rises two hundred and eighty feet in height. The baptistery, of octagon form, somewhat resembling the Parthenon at Rome, stands opposite and completes the trio.

The bronze doors are exceedingly beautiful, with festoons and foliage prettily wrought. The marble columns, the altars, the twelve statues representing the Apostles and the written laws, the trophies of victory, won by the Republic against the Pisans—these, with other adornments here, become so familiar to the eye, that when one drops in on some festival occasion, or christening, his attention is more directed to the personages and ceremonies than the contents of the edifice.

Instead of wearying you with descriptions of works of art, I would rather revert to the beauties of nature, at this season of the year, in the neighborhood of Florence. The rides, walks, and views from the surrounding hills, are now most agreeable and rarely excelled.

# CXIV.

BOLOGNA, *June 3, 1856.*

Before leaving Tuscany, I passed a couple of days in revisiting Siena, from which place I wrote two years since on my way to Rome. It is accessible by railroad from Florence. Although dull it possesses much of interest, and its airy mountain location induces many to spend a part of the summer in it. Its delicious water, from a fountain constructed in the year 1193, and famous for its quantity and quality, is spoken of by Dante, in his Inferno. The people, however, do not consider it the best substitute for their favorite wines, which they have been in some measure deprived of by the partial failure of the grape crop of late years; they look forward, however, to a good return season.

The cathedral, the position of which was once occupied by a temple dedicated to Minerva, is a masterpiece of Tuscan Gothic architecture, incrusted without and within with black and white marble, of the fifteenth century. Notwithstanding the eye may tire of gazing at churches and their contents, still this old edifice, constructed by the celebrated sculptors of Siena, will well bear re-examination, and the mosaic pavement, among the most celebrated in Italy, is a study in itself, consisting of sculptured history, the story of Moses, also that of Joshua, and the emblems of cities once in alliance with Siena; the elephant of Rome, with a castle on his back; the lions of Florence and Massa; the dragon of Pistoia; the hare of Pisa; the unicorn of Viterbo; the horse of Avezzo; the she-wolf of Siena, in memory of Romulus and Remus; and many other animals and armorial representations of the different cities and republics. Abraham's intended sacrifice of his son is most esteemed. The art of description in mosaic as early as the fourteenth century, strikes many persons with surprise; but it appears from the pavement which I saw in one of the disinterred houses among the ruins of Pompeii, and which represented the battle of Darius with the Persians, that the art was known before Christ, Pompeii being buried by the irruption of Mount Vesuvius in the year 72. The painted glass of the year 1549, with the busts of all popes down to Alexander III., and some original frescoes of Raphael, are all well worth attention.

Some years since, coming to this city, I employed the Vetturino mode of conveyance, taking the mountain route, with the privilege of stopping when and where I pleased, with an agreeable party. For the first trip it was decidedly pleasant; we had a fine view from the summit of the Apennines, of the Adriatic and Mediterranean; now halting for a rest, or gratifying our curiosity; again strolling off to visit some remnant of antiquity, and passing the night in some solitary inn or obscure village; then came a scramble to the top of a hill called Monte di Fo. High up over the rocks there was a small volcano, some fifteen feet in circumference, disgorging its bright flames much to the satisfaction of some of our party, who had not yet climbed Vesuvius or Ætna, or seen Stromboli in a state of eruption. As we are apt to judge by comparison, I naturally looked at it as a small specimen of a volcano. Having since seen the burning mountains and craters of the Sandwich Islands, I was not ambitious to retrace my old route, so I took the railroad to the old city of Pistoia, with its wide, straight, and well-paved streets. It contains some objects worthy of notice, but appears dull for want of population; it was famous among the ancients for the defeat of Catiline, and in more modern times for the factions of the Guelphs and Ghibelines.

The country around is rich and fertile in the extreme, being amongst the best cultivated in Tuscany. At this season of flowers and early fruits, the hedges and climbing vines in festoons upon the trees, forming continuous arbors, present a gay and cheerful appearance.

From Pistoia, taking the coupé or front compartment of a diligence, in company with a French baron and his lady, and nine passengers inside and on top, besides a heavy load of baggage, with from four to seven horses, and a pair of oxen for the steepest ascent of the Apennines, we accomplished the distance of fifty-four miles in thirteen hours, along a most picturesque and romantic route, winding around the brink of precipices and upon the margin of mountain torrents, with their deafening roar, not apprehensive of avalanches of snow which I have sometimes dreaded in Switzerland; they have an occasional land slide here. We passed one spot, in particular, where twenty-four persons lost their lives.

Crossing the frontier into the Papal States, we had, at the first custom-house, the usual scenes, such as I described to you two years since, in going south; also swarms of beggars, blind, halt, and lame, affording an opportunity of disposing of small coin, no longer of use in the adjoining territory.

Descending the mountain, following the course of the river Reno through a beautiful valley, the road lined with the tall poplars of Lombardy, we arrive at Bologna, the second city in size, and first in commercial importance, of the sovereign Pontiff Pius IX.; it is pleasantly situated upon the river just named, and famous for other things besides its sausages. History reports its existence, under the name of Felsina, as an Etruscan town, previous to its capture by the Boii, who changed its name to Boina, and in time converted to Bologna. 653 B.C. it received a Roman colony, but suffered by civil war; it was restored by Augustus after the battle of Actium, and afterwards became one of the most powerful cities of Italy.

It is now commercial, with a population of seventy thousand. It is the most remarkable city for porticoes I have ever seen. It is rainy to-day, but you may walk for miles without an umbrella. About three miles from the city, on the summit of a hill, is the church of the Madonna, the ascent to which is fatiguing; it has a continuous arcade, containing six hundred and forty columns, constructed at the expense of different ecclesiastical establishments, and the bequests of the rich. We went up the carriage road in our vehicle, putting in advance of the horses a pair of oxen. From the summit is a vast and extensive view of the neighboring mountains, the extended valley, and the city, almost at our feet.

A curious old tower stands nearly in the centre of the city, called Asinelli, erected in 1109; it is said to be three hundred and twenty-seven feet high, and inclines four feet. Another, near by, built about the same time, is one hundred and forty feet in height, and inclines eight feet from the perpendicular. They are constructed of brick, and have been restored at different periods. A slight shock of an earthquake would tell a sad tale for the neighbors. A canal, or race, runs through the city with an abundance of water, supplying the mills. The Piazza del Duomo, or principal public square, upon which stands the venerable cathedral, the Government House, and other public buildings, has a noble but antique appearance. Here is a colossal statue of Neptune, in bronze, by the celebrated Giovanni of Bologna. This gigantic figure holds a trident, one foot rests upon a dolphin, and at the base of the four angles of the pedestal are seated four female figures, with their hands across their breasts, from which issue jets of water; their nether limbs, terminating in the form of fish, are seated upon huge dolphins, whose nostrils spout the liquid stream in the basin beneath. The Campo Santo, or burial ground, ordered by Napoleon in 1801, is interesting to visit.

Bologna boasts of giving birth to Guido, Domenichino, Annibale Caracci, and of course has a good gallery of paintings. Its anatomical collections, with the one in Florence, are the most curious and extensive in the world. Its university is supposed to have been founded by the Emperor Theodosius, in the year 425 of the Christian era; others say by the Countess Matilda, much later. It is said to have contained six thousand students once, and professors in proportion; its celebrity is not now so great. Some of the palaces are well worth seeing, for those who have not seen Italy generally.

Strangers, I notice, make but a short tarry here generally, but push on south for Florence and Rome, or further north to Milan and Venice. I design to reach the latter place in a few days, after visiting Modena and Mantua.

# CXV.

VENICE, ITALY, *July 1, 1856.*

The Duchies of Modena and Parma (the latter is in a state of siege since the assassination of the Duke), were among the few points in all Italy I had never visited; so I was induced to diverge from my route to this city to look in upon these little courts, whose fortified capitals contain some forty to fifty thousand inhabitants each, and whose territories might bear some resemblance in size to the little states of Rhode Island and Delaware, surrounded by their more opulent neighbors; but the usual forms of visitation of baggage, examination of passport, and other annoyances of the police, must be submitted to.

The strict censorship, and tax upon the home press, and the suppression of liberal foreign journals—even those of patriotic Sardinia, across the frontier, are forbidden—and keep the people in ignorance. The country is rich and fertile, closely cultivated from necessity by a redundant population. The palace of the Duchess Regent of Parma is strongly guarded by Austrian soldiery, which is also the case in many parts of the Pope's dominions.

Strangers are looked upon with suspicion by the authorities, as they well know the masses are much dissatisfied with the result of the Peace Congress at Paris, having hoped for reform in Italy; they fear, therefore, an outbreak of popular resentment. The parade and pomp observed by the small potentates of Italy and Germany, aping their superiors in all the forms and etiquette of court life, to the exhaustion of their subjects, often brings to my mind the burlesque on royalty of the black emperor Soulouque, before whose palace entrance I noticed more ebony soldiers than I had ever seen Cossacks before the winter palace of the late Czar Nicholas.

From Parma I proceeded north-east some forty miles, passing over a perfectly level agricultural country, with waving fields of wheat, rye, hemp, hedges of trees, and festoons of climbing grape vines. The peasantry were picking the leaves of the mulberry for the silkworms, which are here a great source of revenue.

We crossed the rivers Po and Olio in scow boats, and came to Mantua, renowned for its gallant defence during several sieges. This Lombardian city and fortress, which contain some thirty-five thousand inhabitants, have been much strengthened under Austrian possession, and look impregnable. There are some objects of interest, but not sufficient to detain the tourist long.

Crossing a famous stone bridge over a river, seven hundred and eighty yards in length, at a distance of three miles, one is rejoiced again to strike a railroad, which conducts to this extraordinary city. Had it not been for several days' indisposition, I really think I should have enjoyed this my third visit to this unique city as much as the first. After having escaped the noise, bustle, and dust of continental cities, it is a great relief to get where you are surrounded with comparative quiet and solitude, away from the rattling of carriages and tread of horses, with free circulation of salt air from the lagoons of the Adriatic, and particularly during this season of salt bathing. I am located on the Grand Canal near the Piazza San Marco, and am annoyed with the continual chattering of the Gondoliers, whose songs are inspiriting, but whose noisy disputes are disturbing to the temporary invalid.

You are aware that Venice is built upon many small islands, mounted upon piles, and connected by means of bridges and canals in the lagoons, thus separated from the sea. I will not undertake to describe this wonder of the world, the seat of the Doges; the vast commerce of its two hundred thousand inhabitants in the fifteenth century, now reduced to one hundred and twenty-five thousand; its gorgeous palaces, its magnificent churches, its narrow streets, its theatres, its valuable collections of art by the old masters, and its four hundred and fifty bridges, connecting one hundred and thirty-six islands with its water communication by one hundred and fifty-four canals. The natural bubbling of a fountain is unknown, and horses are objects of curiosity; thousands of gondolas and other craft supply the places of carriages, both private and public; you step out of your palace or hotel door into your vehicle to be transported for pleasure or business, as in a cab. The Grand Canal winds in the form of an S through the city, and is divided into two parts.

A gay scene presents itself these bright moonlight nights, with the hundreds of boats, containing families, beautifully dressed ladies, and a fair share of strangers, floating gracefully along, while the balconies of the antique marble palaces of Gothic, Byzantine, and other styles of architecture are filled with their residents. The grateful and refreshing breeze disperses the smoke of the lovers of good cigars, and new objects of attraction are continually presented to the eye.

We will here step out for the present and wind our way through the narrow streets lined with tiny stores and shops filled with all that art and taste can conceive of, following the multitude like a swarm of bees through the intricate lanes and alleys from four to twelve feet in width, in order not to lose our way; we will suppose it is eight or nine o'clock in the evening, and they are proceeding to the public square San Marco, which has been lighted with gas since my last visit here. Venice has some four hundred cafés, and here under the porticos of the palaces forming the large piazza, or square, are twenty-five of them, with thousands of chairs and benches for the accommodation of the immense throng, where fashion and beauty partake of ices, and other refreshments, listening to the music of the Austrian band, the interim being filled with the songs and recitations of strolling minstrels. Baskets of confectionery are moving about in the crowd, and groups of promenaders saunter along the well-paved and commodious piazza, which has scarcely a particle of dust to soil their beautiful dresses. There in front stands the Cathedral San Marco, now nearly eight hundred years old, with its symmetrical cupolas and façade of porphyry and other antique marbles, its scriptural figures in golden mosaic, and its four bronze horses brought from Corinth, taken to Paris by Napoleon, but afterwards restored.

There stands the Campanilla, three hundred and thirty-four feet in height, from which a fair view may be obtained by daylight, and near by is the Doge's Palace, in all its grandeur, communicating by the Bridge of Sighs with the prisons. The columns of the Lion of San Marco and Saint Theodore stand towering in bold relief as you approach the water's edge, where hundreds of gondolas are waiting to receive their precious freight.

This is the bright side of the picture. My letter is now too extended to give in detail the private communications of those who suffer in spirit and in purse from the arbitrary exactions of the power which now gores them.

# CXVI.

Como, Lake of Como, *July 29, 1856.*

Recovering from temporary indisposition at Venice, I made up for lost time in revisiting several cities already seen, such as Padua, Verona, Milan, Bergamo, Vicenza, and made several detours to visit points that I was not familiar with, such as the Lago di Garda, whose beautiful waters will compare favorably with Lago Maggiore and Lago Como.

The whole distance from the fortification of Peschiera to Riva, at the head of the Lake, is made by a small Austrian steamer in six hours, touching at the different villages upon its well cultivated banks, abounding with millions of orange and lemon trees—a source of a great profit for exportation. This region is protected by mountains, some as high as six thousand feet, with deep blue waters, romantic waterfalls, amphitheatred walls, olive groves and climbing vineyards all around. Although in the north of Italy, approaching Switzerland, the climate in winter is mild, and fogs are quite unknown; the Lake never freezes.

Proceeding to Milan, the Lombardian capital, by rail and land conveyance, I was induced to strike off south-east to visit Pavia, noted for its University containing nine hundred students, and its collection of anatomy and natural history. Twenty miles distant is Lodi, rendered memorable by Napoleon in the famous battle crossing the bridge over the rapid river Adda. I found great preparations making for the festival of the patron saint of the city, whose remains, dating from the fourth century, were being transmitted from the old vault in the basement or crypt of the cathedral to a new sculptured marble tomb. The sarcophagus was of solid silver, with double crystal plates inserted in the sides and cover, exposing to view the skeleton; the bones were joined together with silver wire, and reposed upon a couch of silk and velvet. The rush of the multitude was so great, I could scarcely gain access to the altar; men and women were there with rosaries and handkerchiefs in their hands; and a priest in attendance was busily engaged in passing these articles over the relics of the consecrated saint; after which, when communicated to an afflicted part, they were thought to give relief.

The beautiful plains through which I passed are irrigated at will with abundance of water; the aqueducts were lined with willows, and other trees, affording shade the entire length of the road between the two cities. The rice plantations are beautiful indeed, surpassing in verdure anything I have seen of the kind in the Carolinas or East Indies; but the miasma is productive of fevers, and the peasantry live in villages remote from the inundated fields.

Each city has its objects of interest. Padua boasts of the villa of Petrarch in the vicinity; its stupendous church of the patron saint Antonio; its University with fifteen hundred students, bearing upon its walls the antique armorial insignia of the many noble youths educated there; its library, its anatomical collection, and fifty-five thousand inhabitants.

Verona, rather more populous, has its attractions; its old amphitheatre, in the same style as the Coliseum at Rome, one thousand four hundred and seventy feet in circumference, with forty-five rows of seats, and with places for twenty-five thousand persons, is in remarkable preservation; in the arena is now erected a *Teatro Diurno*. These day-theatres are without roofs; the performance commences at six P.M., and is generally frequented. The tomb of Juliet, in an old convent, is only of interest for the romantic story of herself and of her lover Romeo. The house of the Capulets also exists. The position of Verona, divided by the river Etsch, with its high hills strongly fortified by the Austrians, is almost impregnable withal, and picturesque; it has become, with its garrison, a second Mantua.

Vicenza, a smaller city of thirty-five thousand population, has its antique public square, government house, palace of justice, with arcades worth looking in upon, and a fine view from the summit of a hill in the suburbs. A covered gallery some two thousand feet in length leads the pilgrim to the convent of the Madonna of the Mountain. An antique Olympic theatre in the city attracts strangers. From the benches of the amphitheatre I was struck with a singular perspective receding from the stage of a miniature city of Greekish architecture, representing streets, houses, and professions. While examining the old structure of wood, decorated with ornamental figures, I made some comparisons which were responded to by my conductress, a beautiful girl of light complexion and golden locks. Upon questioning the girl, I found that she spoke English, although of Italian birth; every city and province has its peculiar tongue, and only the educated speak Italian. It is in Tuscany alone where the language is spoken in its purity. I have been in dining rooms where there were several groups at the tables speaking Neapolitan, Genoese, Milanese, and other dialects, without understanding each other, yet all were Italians. One can well conceive the difficulty of regenerating a people where such objections to unity are met with, and where local prejudices are so strong. One fine morning in Milan, twenty-one guns announced to us the telegraphic news from Vienna of the birth of a princess to the House of Austria. Notwithstanding the disappointment (a prince had been hoped for), great preparations having been made at the Duomo for the celebration, it came off in this world-wide renowned edifice with the usual pomp and ceremony of church, civil, and military parade.

The Corso Francesco in Milan has many elegant cafés, which were quite desolate for two or three days, in consequence of the seizure of foreign journals giving the debates in England upon Italian affairs. The old papers were read and re-read, and almost worn through; the evident disgust and under-toned denunciation of the powers that be could not pass unobserved.

# CXVII.

ZURICH, *Aug. 16, 1856.*

Leaving the beautiful lake of Como, with its lovely villas, cultivated gardens, vineyards, and picturesque views, I started for Switzerland, via the lake of Lugano.

The Austrian frontier of Lombardy is soon reached, and one finds himself in the Canton of Ticino. Upon crossing the bridge of Chiaso into Swiss territory, one soon discovers the effect of free government and liberal principles in the public schoolhouses, in the culture and manufacture of tobacco, in the relief from annoyances of passports and examination of luggage. A quarter of a mile from there, tobacco is a monopoly, and its growth is prohibited; here it is produced in considerable quantities, and manufactured for exportation.

The town of Lugano, prettily situated upon the borders of the lake, surrounded by romantic scenery, is considerably frequented, and foreign journals may be read there without the intermeddling of the censor-police.

On the opposite side of the lake is the village of Castigleone, in Austrian territory, at the foot of a steep mountain; it is accessible only by land, over the Swiss high-road. Here the people enjoy comparative freedom, and are exempt from military proscription; but in these mountainous regions of Switzerland many women are afflicted with huge swellings of the neck, which are frightful to behold, and are attributed to the water of the country.

Among the twenty-two Cantons of Switzerland, there were four which I had never seen; neither had I yet passed the Splugen and St. Bernardino, which are of great interest; so I was induced to finish the work. The St. Bernardino must not be confounded with the great St. Bernard, which I passed some years since on mule-back, with my guide, in the early part of the month of June, among the avalanches and snow banks twenty feet deep, and was happy to find refuge among the monks of the convent, who greeted me as the first traveller of the season, and were longing for the news of Rome during the Holy Week. The Simplon I had formerly crossed in the month of October, upon a sled for one person, made of hoop-poles, with my trunk lashed thereto. Mount Cenis I passed two years since, on my way from Turin to Chamberry, under favorable circumstances, without exposure or fatigue, and now with the lateness of the season I had nothing but beautiful scenery to expect, four months of the year being considered free from danger.

From Lugano I proceeded to Bellinzona, in an open carriage, having a fine view of the valleys and lakes in the distance below; it was a five hours ride. We departed at midnight. With the early dawn we found ourselves climbing up the zigzag mountain sides, among its scattered villages, and houses of rude stone construction, whose slate-roofs were secured from the high winds by huge stones; the shepherds were in simple costume, tending their herds of goats and sheep; the limited culture of grain was still green, while in the valleys it was already harvested. We breakfasted at a village of five or six houses, mostly inns, near the summit of the mountain, covered with snow, where the stunted pines show that vegetation nearly ceases. This place, called Bernardino, had some one hundred and fifty visitors making use of the waters, which are strongly charged with iron; this and bracing mountain air and climbing walks are particularly strengthening for some constitutions. The mountain once passed, the gorges and ravines of the Splugen and Via Mala are singularly grand and beautiful, with every variety of romantic and picturesque scenery. At one moment I could imagine myself, on some accounts, upon the mountains of Chili, from the winding and circuitous road; then again the descent into one valley for some miles, brought to mind our own Alleghanies from Frostburgh to Cumberland. But the Via Mala caps the climax for its excavations, bridges, stone-covered arches and tunnels, deep ravines and precipices, where the head-waters of the river Rhine, gushing and foaming between high ledges of rocks, may almost be leaped. The warm rays of the sun, the cheerful villages, the grape fields, the farmers gathering their grain, the disappearance of the chestnut-trees, upon the fruit of which the mountain peasantry subsist, the throwing off of overcoats, the Italian tongue replaced by the German and Swiss, all show conclusively that we are in the valley, and across the Alps.

The Rhine receives another branch at Reichenau, and requires another bridge to cross it; this bridge is directly in front of the chateau where Louis Philippe served two years as a schoolmaster.

We are in the Canton Grison, the largest of Switzerland, and at five P.M. we find ourselves at Chur, a post town of five thousand inhabitants, in a lovely country. After eighteen hours ride from Bellinzona we were disposed to rest, and take a few baths at Pfaffers, some miles beyond.

The place just named has become somewhat celebrated of late years among the Germans, and is much resorted to for its healing waters, and its elevated position in the mountain gorges. There were some two hundred and fifty visitors. The Duchess of Orleans, with her family, passed the summer at Ragatz, and now Count Nesselrode is expected.

From the last point named, in the Canton San Gall, I proceeded across the country to the Wallenstadt Lake, upon which steamers are employed, and by diligence to the head of Lake Zurich. Lake Zurich, with its well-cultivated borders, numerous villages, and many steamers, I have seen before; still the whole trip was full of interest. Our boat was crowded with tourists of all races. One heard all the different languages, a perfect Babel, or confusion of tongues, which is not to be wondered at, as the present railroad and steamer facilities bring at this season of the year multitudes from all sources over the beaten tracks and most accessible parts of the Swiss territory. Among our passengers was a party of young men from one of the Swiss Cantons, with their arms, flags, and distinguishing badges, going to the Turn-Verein yearly festival, at Winterthur, a two hours ride by rail from this city. I was curious to witness this celebration, represented by delegations or companies from the twenty-two Cantons of Switzerland. A large building was put at the disposition of the Union, with an inclosure in the rear, and stages were erected for ladies and gentlemen who desired to see the gymnastic exercises, leaping, jumping, climbing, etc. A tower was constructed, covered by the colors of all the Cantons. The prizes, many wrought by the ladies, were suspended within; judges were appointed to decide upon the merits of the performers; and it must be admitted that among the number, which was upwards of five hundred, some extraordinary feats of agility were performed. The free use of arms and target firing, which I have noticed, and in which they are expert, and which would not be allowed in despotic countries, reminds one of home, and the freedom of the people there.

Switzerland has also its Baden, which may be reached by rail in one hour from this city. It is a charming place of resort for those who cannot go to the banks of the Rhine. The German watering places have more attractions, and the waters are more salutary.

I am desirous of seeing the upper portion of the Cantons St. Gall and Appenzell, after which I purpose taking the Lake of Constance via Schaffhausen into Germany, where I hope to use the waters of Wiesbaden, which were of service to me the early part of last summer.

# CXVIII.

WIESBADEN, GERMANY, *Sept. 15, 1856.*

Zurich is not only justly celebrated for its lovely position and beautiful lake, and its good hotels, but for its increasing silk trade, which rivals to some extent that of Lyons in France. It now has connexion by railway with the industrious canton of St. Gall and the Lake of Constance.

I was struck with the marked progress the Swiss have made in the manufacture of cotton, and noticed in several places many large factories, four and five stories high, comparing favorably with the mills in the villages of New England. The raw material used in the eastern counties is mostly Egyptian; transportation is long and tedious, via Trieste or Venice over the railway and mountain routes.

St. Gall is appreciated by the ladies. Its ten thousand population live and thrive, and its merchants grow rich, out of its fancy embroidery trade, now greatly extended in our country.

The inhabitants of the Canton of Appenzell, situated from one thousand to fifteen hundred feet above the level of Lake Constance, are mostly engaged in this kind of labor. The Canton is nearly equally divided between Protestants and Catholics, who live separately, scarcely ever intermarrying, and pursuing different styles of work. The country is a grazing one; the people subsist mostly upon cheese and milk. The supply of wheat and rye comes from Bavaria, Wirtemburg, and Austrian Tyrol, and from Roorschach, upon the Lake.

It is curious to see the occupants of all the houses in the villages and in the country, boys and girls, men and women, when not engaged at other work, busy with their forms and patterns before them, plying the needle. In the villages the children commence at eight years old, but in the country they put them at it at the age of six. As persons advance in years, and their sight becomes weak, they perform coarse work. The houses are all constructed with a line of front windows, close together, for the admission of light. The gain derived from this kind of labor is about ten cents per day, upon the average. The Catholic portion of the Canton still adhere to all descriptions of light work; the others turn their attention more to Vorhang Stuckerei, or curtain embroidery, dresses, and under-garments, and succeed better. One of the worst features in this early application is the entire deprivation of education, and the consequent ignorance of the masses.

Weisbad is an agreeable, quiet resort in that mountainous country, with good hotels, shady walks, pleasant company, but with little virtue in its waters. A number of the party who had not climbed mountains, and seen the sun rise, started off at three A.M. for a peak some thousands of feet high. My souvenirs of Norwegian, Chilian, Teneriffe, Spanish, and Sicilian sunrises and sunsets were still vivid, and I declined the invitation.

A very excellent view is had from a mountain called Peter and Paul, a few miles from St. Galls; this view extends over the Lake of Constance, Bregenz in Tyrol, Lindau in Bavaria, Friedrichshafen in Würtemberg, and Rorschach, which is a part of St. Gall, six miles distant. At Bregenz, the St. Gebhardsberg, or mountain, a place of pilgrimage, is the most frequented. The great festival is on the birthday of St. Gebhard (August 27), who, in the 12th century, was Bishop of Constance, and whose history is rather interesting. The church, built upon the site of the old family castle, was commenced by a hermit in the year 1670. The ascent is rather fatiguing for three-quarters of an hour, but one is well repaid for the labor. A magnificent view is obtained from its summit over the lake and surrounding country. Here the Rhine flows into the lake.

At Lindau, where I once had debarked *en route* for Augsburg and Munich, a tedious mail-coach ride, I now found the railroad complete, and at Friedrichshafen another to conduct one to Ulm and Stuttgart, over a road which I had travelled formerly at snail's pace. When I was first in Europe, in 1840–42, and travelled pretty generally over the continent, I found only six pieces of railway, and now we have a perfect network in all directions; except in Spain, Southern Italy, Greece, Turkey, and the extreme northern regions, facilities are constantly multiplying. The transport from one point to another is without loss of time, as formerly; consequently, the tourist has more opportunities to see the cities.

The length of the lake from Bregenz to Constanz is about thirty-eight miles; then, by steamer, you take the meandering Rhine, as it flows out through the valleys, with its hills, chateaux, and vineyards, to the town of Schaffhausen, near the falls. Coming down the lake, before landing at Friedrichshafen, we met the Queen of Würtemberg and suite, on a pleasure excursion. The steamer was decorated with flags, and salutes of cannons were exchanged. The presence of the royal family in the palace and pretty grounds forbids the entrance of strangers, but the gate-keeper, in the absence of his royal mistress, could not resist the silver-key, and conducted me throughout. Here royalty is inclosed in high stone walls, with an ample park, trees, shrubbery, and flowers, bubbling fountains, and elevated shady look-outs upon the margin of the beautiful sheet of water; surrounded with luxuries and liveried servants, it is unconscious probably of the want and privation of many within a stone's throw. But if Germany is satisfied to support thirty-two princes and potentates in pomp and extravagance, we have no right to complain.

The city of Constanz has nothing of great interest, aside from its antique cathedral, built in 1052, and now in process of restoration, and the old building and saloon of the famous Council of 1414–1418, with their contents.

We left there at twelve A.M. and arrived at Schaffhausen at five P.M. Passengers dine on deck *à la carte*, and enjoy the varied views in passing.

I found great changes since my last visit to the falls of the Rhine. The huge rock upon which stands the castle, containing picture galleries, sale rooms and Camera Obscura, has been tunnelled, and the stone arches for the railroad bridge are being constructed across the river. We visited all the attractive points of view, and shortly after ferrying across with our light skiff, in the misty clouds of spray and the deafening roar, and getting in the large Hotel Webber, on the summit of the hill directly in front of the waterfall, there came up a severe thunderstorm, and in the dulness of the night, the repeated flashes of lightning lent additional interest to the scene. The weather cleared up, however, and the full moon's rays gave us all the advantages of a night view. An hour's ride brings one by diligence to the frontier of the Duchy of Baden, and seven hours more, to Freiburg, which is one of the cleanest towns I have met with. Streams of water course through all the streets. The Cathedral, built by the celebrated Erwin von Steinbach, the architect of the Strasburg edifice, with a tower almost as high as that of the Cathedral; the illuminated glass windows; things there attract even when one is fatigued with works of art.

Here we strike a lightning line, or "*Schnell Zug*," which carries one to Baden-Baden.

This being my third visit, I was not induced to make a long *séjour*, but came by rail to Frankfort on the Main. I spent a day or two at Homburg, in the vicinity. My object was to get to this place to avail myself of the benefit of these waters for bathing and drinking; and here I am, up at six in the morning, and at the hot, boiling spring, guzzling my three or four glasses, at intervals of a short walk, with no lack of company. Then comes a bath, repose for a while, warmly covered, and afterwards a light breakfast. There are two *table d'hôtes*, at one and four P.M., and music in the morning at the Healing Fountain, and in the afternoon at the Kursaal, with its beautiful shady walks through the extended grounds.

# CXIX.

HANOVER, *Nov. 15, 1856.*

I came down the Rhine to Cologne and Dusseldorf, and took the road to Elberfeld, a large German manufacturing place, worth looking at. Its trade in woollen, cotton, and silk goods amounts annually to some twelve millions of our currency, and is well known to our importers.

The cross road took me to Dortmund, another manufacturing town, on the main road leading to this capital. Stopping at Ham, a branch road to the north conducted me to the old catholic city of Munster, which I had never seen, and gave me an opportunity of visiting some acquaintances with whom I had crossed the Atlantic. The gothic antiquated town hall of Munster, with its saloon, memorable for the Westphalian treaty in 1648, is of unusual interest, as well as its cathedral, three hundred and sixty feet long, and one hundred and twenty-five feet wide, with two towers. Upon the tower of the St. Lamberti church, two hundred feet high, were placed in three cages the corpses of the leaders of the rebellious Anabaptists. The arches and colonnades of the houses of the principal street are not unlike those of Bologna; they afford protection from sun and rain, and give the city a peculiar aspect. Munster has a population of twenty-five thousand. Many public and private literary and charitable institutions, and agreeable suburban walks, make it a pleasant residence.

A few hours ride brought me to the royal Prussian Salt Baths of Rehme, whose Director and wife I had promised on an ocean passage to call upon, should I ever find myself again in this part of Germany. The grounds are well laid out, and large improvements are in progress. The mineral salt works in the neighborhood are supplied with water from a depth of two thousand two hundred and fifty feet, sufficiently warm for the supply of the Baths. The season was about over, and most of the guests had departed.

An excursion to Minden, upon the river Weser, five hours from Bremen, with a population of twelve thousand; charming walks and drives in the vicinity, with old friends, with reminiscences of mutual dangers escaped at sea, and the occurrences and events of the interim; so a couple of days slipped by agreeably, and I found myself again on the road for this city, the residence of the King of Hanover, where I made a halt some two years since, of which I gave you some details at the time.

The deceased King Ernest, who had a great passion for horses, had one of the finest stables in Europe. The present king is blind, but he rides a horse handsomely. In company with one of his councillors, I met him a few days since in a deep wood, his steed on a gallop, and his adjutant beside him. The adjutant held a check-rein attached, and gave the signal for a salute, when the king made a graceful bow; his infirmity would scarcely be noticed by a stranger.

When last in Austria I noticed the use of horse flesh as food, and now I find its introduction here also. I have before me a newspaper advertisement, with the figure of a capering horse, and three hands, with index fingers pointing to a plate of prepared food, with the announcement that at the slaughter-house stall may be had daily tender horse-flesh, liver, and stewed meats, with warm strengthening sauces, at all hours. Of course the poor avail themselves of this supply at low prices.

## 1857.
## CXX.

BERLIN, PRUSSIA, *Jan. 7, 1857.*

After an absence of nearly two years I find myself once again in the Prussian capital, and when I recognise my former friends and acquaintances who have remained stationary, and answer their interrogatories, I can scarcely believe that most parts of Europe have been revisited by me within this short period; the Atlantic crossed and re-crossed; the head waters of our great Mississippi gazed upon; and I return here without finding any noticeable changes. I tell them from my own experience, that in 1844 the prairies were crossed from the head of Illinois river navigation to Chicago, and from Galena to Milwaukee, in ordinary coaches, with indifferent accommodations for man and beast; that wild waving grass and flowers bounded the horizon, and scarcely a sound was heard except the cries of the wolf and prairie hen, when the places named were villages. Then I tell them what great cities, with teeming population, I found in their stead during the past year, with lines of railway, expanding like arteries from the human heart, spreading life and activity in all directions. If they are inclined to doubt statements which appear fabulous, the fortunate presence of a famous bill of fare, of the Chicago Hotel, gives demonstrative evidence of the progress of civilization.

The Americans are becoming notorious on the continent as extensive travellers, which is not surprising, as our country is so extended, and the opportunities for locomotion are so great. During my first visit to Egypt it was rare to meet one of my countrymen; but five years since I was informed at Grand Cairo that more of them, than of English, had gone up the Nile that winter.

Our political system is to Europeans an enigma. A well-dressed person, at a public table, asked me how large a court Buchanan would have, and the emolument he would receive; and seemed greatly surprised that we had no court, and that the salary of twenty-five thousand dollars per annum would not equal the livery expenses of some crowned heads; and that the emoluments of four years would not equal the christening expenses of the imperial infant of France; that we travel without passports; that the press is as free as the air we breathe; and that our national army is scarcely seen or known.

Christmas-day I found myself the only stranger at the table, in a family gathering of twenty-five persons. The Germans dine much earlier than the French. At half past two P.M., an abundant repast, with various kinds of Rhine wine, was served, enlivened with the usual touching of glasses, and toasts. At the close of the dinner, the host struck up a hochlied, or hymn, accompanied by one of the ladies on the piano, which hymn was followed by shaking of hands and congratulations. The gentlemen retired to smoke, and the ladies amused themselves with dancing and waltzing. An hour later, we were seated again at the table, with coffee, conversation, and recitations from the younger members of the family. There was a constant change of diversions: juvenile violin players, exquisite performers upon the piano, vocal music, dancing, tableaux vivants, &c., kept the company incessantly occupied until about half-past ten, when *abendbrod* was announced. This meal (literally evening bread) consisted of a copious hot supper, not unlike the dinner, and required a stronger stomach than mine to digest, at that late hour. At midnight, with cordial salutations, after having enjoyed every moment of time, the company separated.

When the bulletins announced that the *Eisbahn* was in condition, hundreds of persons of both sexes might be seen upon the ice of the *Thiergarten*, or Royal Park. A small fee admits you on the ice, where seats are prepared, and gardrobe for clothing; supplies of skates are on hire, with servants to strap them; there are chair-sleds for those who do not skate, or for lady invalids, drawn by gentlemen skaters; and hosts of fashionable and beautiful city ladies, gracefully waltzing and performing various evolutions, or gliding rapidly in groups over the frozen surface; it is a pretty and characteristic scene of winter life in this region.

With the present railroad and steam advantages, travellers are brought together singularly. At the hotel, a heavy-whiskered gentleman at my right opened a conversation in German—the language spoken at the table—which was for a time continued, when it struck me suddenly who he was, and I asked if he recognised me? I received a negative reply. I asked if he had travelled in Egypt? He answered, "Yes, but many years since." "True," I responded; "you called upon me in Jaffa, in the Holy Land. You made the passage to Alexandria with us; you are an American," and I called him by name. We were both mutually surprised and delighted.

I notice across the street, outside of the double window sashes, heavy coarse curtains drawn up, which are lowered at night to protect from cold and storms. What are the white and colored objects hanging against the glass, and what do the flower-vases contain? They are a counterpart of the porcelain variegated transparencies suspended from mine, with similar tulips; but it strikes me that my two India rubber trees, with their long green leaves, are more attractive. The people are very fond of these window decorations.

The droschki drivers, thickly clad, are dozing upon their seats. Here comes a customer. The driver gives him a ticket, as he enters, with the number of his vehicle, in case of reclamation, in default of which he is amenable to the police. He receives so many checks from his employer daily, and is responsible for them.

Our American ladies are shocked at seeing women sawing wood, carrying coal, making mortar, working upon the land, and performing all sorts of manual labor. A pair of harnessed cows before a wagon containing five or six ruddy-faced, thick-waisted, bare-headed, or cap-covered, country costumed *bauerinnen*, or peasant women, is quite a ludicrous sight.

This last sentence, I notice, partakes a little of the German form of writing. It must be atmospheric. In the works of some German writers, one sometimes reads a third of a page before finding the meaning of the sentence, the construction of the language having the advantage of keeping up and increasing attention to the end. The word which least defines the subject is placed at the beginning of the sentence. Then come those words which define it in a higher degree, so that the word which most determines the meaning of the phrase, is at the end. It is one of the richest and most beautiful of living languages for its literature, but exceedingly difficult to acquire, and few Germans speak their language grammatically. Dialects are found all over Europe; and in many parts, the distance of a few miles changes the *patois*. In no single country, for its extent, is a language (notwithstanding the slang, or provincialisms) so generally well spoken, as in the United States. With a knowledge of English, the traveller may visit all parts of our country, with slight exceptions, and hold intercourse with all classes, which cannot be done even in some parts of Great Britain.

Unconsciously this letter has been drawn out to an unusual length, and I fancy I hear you cry out, "Halten sie an!"

# CXXI.

Breslau, Silesia, *Feb. 10, 1857.*

On my way south to the Austrian capital, instead of taking my former route, via Dresden and Prague, from which cities you heard from me two years since, I have made the detour to this place ostensibly to visit a travelling acquaintance, who had passed several months with me in Turkey, Greece, Egypt, and the Holy Land.

Breslau, with its suburbs, has a population of one hundred and twenty-five thousand, and has its attractions for the students, nine hundred of whom attend the University, which has a public library of three hundred thousand volumes. There is an interesting Zoological Museum, some antique churches, and other objects worth seeing. The public walks upon the former bastions, now planted with trees, with views upon the river Oder, whose branches traverse the city, are quite pretty, but fevers are the natural result there in summer. It is a bustling, active, trading city. The carnival season is now at hand. At a citizens' masked and unmasked ball, given at the theatre, I noticed more variety of costume, more characters assumed and carried out with more life and animation than is generally manifested in Germany on similar occasions. I was struck with the contrast, having in Berlin recently attended the first of a series of three balls, given at the grand opera-house, and attended by the king and royal family. The attendance consisted only of those whose names guaranteed the privilege of a ticket, and ladies could not appear without the expenditure of large sums in dress; foreign ministers, civil and military officers, were covered with orders. The galleries, passages, and stairs, as well as the rear of the stage and parterre, which were planked over, were converted into a tropical garden of plants, flowers, and festoons of laurel. There was an excellent orchestra, and the supper halls were well garnished with dainties and substantials. The quantities of diamonds, emeralds, and rubies, with the scores of gas-lights, dazzled the eyes; the value of these baubles, properly applied, would prevent any further increase of taxation, a subject which is now agitating the country. The ball was numerously attended by the leading nobility and the whole retinue of the court; beauty and ugliness were there in the richest and most extravagant apparel. The variety of characters and uniforms in the waltz and dance, was undoubtedly calculated to strike one at first glance with wonder and admiration, but with a certain amount of restraint; the guests did not seem to enjoy themselves very much.

I adverted in my last, or meant to if I did not, to the practice of duelling still kept up by the German students, and winked at by the authorities, and even the professors themselves, who not unfrequently wear the marks of old duels upon their faces. Many clubs exist among these youths, whose different colored caps denote their members. They have their different places of rendezvous for pastime, drinking, and smoking.

An opportunity presented itself recently at Berlin to witness this foolish and shameful spectacle, which some consider a source of amusement. They fight for fifteen minutes, unless one or the other cries enough. The weapon is a straight sword, somewhat over three feet long, with a sharp blade; the end is about three fourths of an inch wide. The duellists are clad in a leather suit, the whole body protected except the head; the neck is bound with a scarf, and the right arm heavily bandaged with cloths; it is supported by a second during a halt, while a third stands with a sword to parry side-blows. Judges give the word of command, keep the time, and decide the contest. The students of both corps sit and stand around, smoking their pipes, without manifesting any particular concern, further than regards the manner in which the work is executed. It is incumbent upon each member to pass the ordeal, and the others have no hesitation in taking a hand for amusement. A cut upon the face or head, sometimes the loss of an eye, or a broken nose, is not unfrequently the result of this barbarous relic of the days of chivalry. I am happy to say that our Americans, with two exceptions, avoid this foolish exposure; one of whom has a mark upon his face, which he will always carry. Disgusted with the whole system, I was glad to escape.

The German railroad companies are yet far behind in the comfort of their cars. In France, the coaches are heated with vessels of hot water under the carpet; going last winter from Paris to Marseilles, I found it as comfortable as in a parlor. From Berlin to this place I noticed that only the ladies' carriages were warmed with bags of hot sand; fortunately, I obtained a seat in one of them. I learn that from hence to Cracow, and also to Vienna, in Austrian territory, they are not warmed, and shall make my arrangements accordingly. The people in these latitudes in winter accustom themselves so much to the use of furs that they don't seem to require this precaution.

The houses, cafés, and places of amusement, are well warmed, and one suffers less from cold than in northern Italy.

Since the release of the royalists from the Swiss prisons at Neufchatel, and the anticipated call of the Prussian Landwehr to the battle-field, the war excitement has cooled off, and the community have been excited with the judgment and execution of Verger, for the murder of the Archbishop of Paris.

# CXXII.

VIENNA, *March 15, 1857.*

The movements and doings of this gay and mixed population during the Fasching, or Carnival season, may be of interest to you. I notice in the papers that in the city proper and suburban cities, there have been given in all over one thousand public and private balls during the festival season. The corners of many of the streets were provided with transparent lights, announcing the different balls, from the Citizens', Jurists', Lawyers', Professors' and Students', to the Cab Drivers' and Servant-girls'. It seemed as if the chief occupation was dancing, and all were disposed to employ the time until the beginning of Lent, when the famous musical Strauss and Sperl Bands could lay down their instruments, and a tired population repose their wearied limbs. It is computed that an inveterate dancer here, in the waltz gallop and dance, will travel over several English miles of surface in the course of the night. The Burger Ball, given in the Palace, was a brilliant affair; some two thousand five hundred persons present. In the absence of the Emperor in Italy, his father, the Archduke Charles, represented him. Fanny Ellsler, the danseuse of so much notoriety, who is now a resident of this city, was among the number of guests. She was bedecked with diamonds, and was in conversation with the Archduke. Prince Metternich, the renowned Austrian statesman, even at his advanced age, was present. Vienna is noted for its beautiful ladies; they belong to a variety of races, the city being a concentrating point, during the gay season, for the fair daughters of Hungary, and of the Bohemian, Polish, and Italian provinces.

The education of young ladies is more superficial here than with us. Music, dancing, and the languages, seem to be the most important branches of an education; not that all other acquirements are neglected, but that the practical is not considered so essential as in our institutions at home.

The Emperor, Empress, and suite arrived day before yesterday from Italy, and were received at the railroad depot by a large body of Italian residents, who addressed thanks for the Emperor's acts of clemency in Lombardy. He was received by the citizens in large numbers, who formed a line of protection for the imperial cortege to the gates of the city, where the Burgermeister and authorities of the metropolis attended him.

The Italians have gained through his visit a Viceroy, in the person of his brother, who is to reside at Milan and Venice alternately, dispensing with the military government of Radetzky. Political refugees have been pardoned, and granted the privilege of returning. Confiscated property has been restored; the revolutionary events of 1848 buried in oblivion; the prisons for felons have been in many cases opened, and a sort of jubilee produced among all, except those whose national prejudices cannot submit to Austrian rule. Culprits and cut-throats in despotic and monarchical countries never divest themselves of the sheet anchor Hope, for the marriage of a Prince, the birth of a Princess, or an accession to the throne, bring amnesties frequently. These are paraded and published as acts of magnanimity; and with their consummation, not unfrequently come many breakers of the peace and pests upon society.

On Washington's birthday, the Secretary of our Legation and his Austrian wife, our Consul and family, and some eight or ten American students and travellers, accepted a sumptuous dinner at the house of our patriotic Minister, Judge Jackson of Georgia. The stars and stripes of our beloved country were attached to the wall, encircling the portrait of the illustrious father of his country, whose memory we are proud to honor.

A twelve hours ride by rail brought me from Silesia to Vienna. At the Austrian frontiers our luggage was visited as usual, and our passports examined. I designed revisiting Polish Cracow, by taking a branch line to the left, but as the cars were not heated, declined doing so. I made some remarks relative to the discomfort and slowness of the train, which were responded to by one of the officers of the company, who was passing over the road in consequence of a collision which had occurred the day before, attended with loss of life and property. We Americans are so frequently called upon to reply to the gross calumnies upon our steamboat and railroad disasters, that I was curious to see if an account of this accident would appear in print, but I never saw it. The officer remarked that it was very important to keep it secret, as the apprehension of the travelling public would affect the interests of the road. The press being under censorship, and the government being a party in the construction of the road, we can understand the silence.

# CXXIII.

TRIESTE, *April 15, 1857.*

The distance from Vienna to this free Austrian port is about three hundred and fifty miles, which, upon the completion of the railway, in the month of August, will probably be accomplished in eighteen or twenty hours; I was once four days in accomplishing the same route.

The Semering Pass is about fifty miles this side of Vienna. It is a gigantic work, and excites the admiration and wonder of all travellers. The immense arches of the granite aqueducts spanning the mountain torrents, and the road winding in a serpentine manner, with extraordinary curves, through the valleys, penetrating the huge long tunnels in and out, afford a fine rear view. The iron horse climbs continually up the ascent, to a height of two thousand seven hundred and ninety feet; then a tunnel four thousand feet long is passed, and the rail continues to Murzuschlag, in connexion with the southern or Trieste road, to Gratz, in Steyermark, or Styria, a city with a population of some sixty thousand inhabitants, the residence of the Archduke John, uncle to the Emperor, whom I saw at the German Congress of nine hundred, in Frankfort, in 1848, when the city was illuminated, and he was proposed for the Emperor of United Germany. I saw him here under other circumstances, sitting quietly in a provincial theatre. The town is beautifully situated in a healthy position, and in it are some objects of interest.

March is a bad month in Vienna for coughs and colds, and suffering from the same, I made my escape to Gratz, where I spent several days to recruit, and then took the railway to Laibach, distant some one hundred and twenty-five miles, noted for the Congress of sovereigns in 1820.

At Marburg, some fifty miles south, the German language, badly spoken as it is in Styria, begins to be lost; and at Cilley, in Carinthia, a language, entirely unintelligible to the Germans, is found. It is the Sclavisch tongue, which is used by many millions of Austrian subjects.

At that period I was travelling by post, which prevented a visit to the great quicksilver works of Idria, which demanded a ride of twenty-five miles over a bad road, some one thousand five hundred feet high, over the mountains. I had always regretted having lost the opportunity of seeing those immense government mines, and I now resolved to make up for it, notwithstanding that the season was early for the trip. Having in the interval of time visited the Almedan quicksilver works, in the Valley of San Jose, California, the silver mines of Peru, the lead mines of Galena, the iron mines of Sweden and of the Island of Elba, my curiosity was the more quickened to inspect this mountain of quicksilver ore, particularly as I had recently heard a series of lectures on these subjects, at the University in Vienna. Procuring a close carriage and a pair of strong horses with a driver, for a three days' excursion, I was enabled to accomplish this tour, and also to visit the renowned Grotto of Adelsberg, on my way to Trieste.

The village of Idria, of four thousand population, lies in a valley of a round bowl form, with an abundance of water power. The ascent of the mountain is by zigzag roads, with at intervals a peasant's cottage, bleak and dreary; the summit once reached, we can scarcely realize that a smiling village, with gardens and fruit trees, exists in the low grounds. There are seven hundred men employed in these works. A ticket of admission is granted, a miner's suit is provided, and a guide, with lights, procured, all to be paid for in turn. The descent commences through narrow arches and long galleries, of a man's height, of stone work; then by flights of steps cut in the rock, from seventy to one hundred and forty in number, leading from one gallery to another. They are more fatiguing than the salt mines at Hallein. Some two thousand steps are here made to the fourth gallery, whose perpendicular depth is seven hundred and fifty feet. At a depth of three hundred feet I noticed that the timbers employed in the passages were charred, and learned that only a few years since fire had occurred by accident, which cost the lives of many miners, whose bodies were drawn out after suffocation. A portion of the pits have also been flooded with water; the steam and water pumps were exhausting it. The heat at this great depth is apparent, and the miners who are on duty with picks and axes, and blasting the rocks, have a warm berth of it. The poor fellows, in shirt and trowsers, with the dull light of the lamps in the close murky atmosphere, sweating at their toil, look certainly haggard, and excite one's sympathy when he learns that the recompense is only sixteen kreuzers (or fourteen cents) per day. The government furnishes flour and fuel at fixed rates, which are less than current prices. The ore in some cases will average sixty parts, and the liquid quicksilver is seen in the pores of the stone formation. They turn out annually from two and a half to three million centners, of one hundred pounds each. The price is now low, being about fifty cents per pound.

The ascent is by steam or water power. From the bottom, seven hundred and fifty feet, a perpendicular square shaft communicates with all the galleries, for hoisting the ore. One puts himself in a square box, of solid wood construction, with a board seat, supported by four chains from the corners, attached to a rope cable, and trusts to its strength and the movement of the water wheel to see daylight once again. The reflection is anything but agreeable; for should an accident occur, not a vestige of frail humanity would remain. The ascent on foot is too fatiguing, although many persons prefer it.

The smelting furnaces here are on a large scale, as also the manufacture of red vermilion from quicksilver and sulphur combined, under the action of great heat. It is a singular fact that those employed in these works not only lose their teeth early in life, through the salivation of the mercury, but the atmosphere being impregnated, young people of twenty-five years of age show the same signs of decay. They had recently four shocks of earthquakes, and a house near the pits was considerably cracked, but the miners said the vibrations were only slightly felt below.

A singular idea prevails, not only in this country, but in other parts of Europe, among certain classes, which reminds me of the days of Miller. It is the prophecy of the destruction of the world on the thirteenth of June, by a comet. I have seen several newspaper articles confirming the probability. I tell the people they must emigrate to America, where the vicinity of icebergs will keep them thawed out.

A seven hours' ride brought me to the cave of Adelsberg, recently visited by the Emperor, Empress, and suite, on their return from Italy. Some three hundred laborers were employed for several months, carrying in sand for the purpose of making dry walks, repairing the bridge over the rushing waterfall, which loses itself here and appears again some miles distant, and in the preparation of the twenty thousand lights, along all the passages, and the grand illumination of the Dome of Neptune chapel, whose death-bell music is produced by beating sticks upon the suspended stalactites, and the riding school, organ, altars, and the ascent to Mount Calvary, with its twelve stations. The roof from the base of this enormous cave at this point is scarcely visible, but from the summit of Calvary, it is strikingly grand. The immense dancing hall is used once a year, for the people's festivals. The distance walked over is probably four miles. I cannot describe the beauties of this nature's wonder. Thousands of columns are formed and are forming, from the dripping, and one can see the most exquisite imitation of curtains, and drapery like lace of various colors, and the imagination conjures up a thousand forms of animals, antiquities, Hindoo and Egyptian deities. The amount expended for the Imperial reception was twenty thousand guldens, or ten thousand dollars. I happened along at a favorable time, as the decorations and evergreens were not removed, and the cave was perfectly dry; and I fortunately found two Austrian officers who were willing to join in employing twelve guides and torch-bearers, for lighting up, with one hundred and forty wax candles, in order to examine the old, as well as the newly discovered grotto, and see all to advantage.

Another six hours by mail coach, and we were on the summit of the mountain, descending to Trieste, with the beautiful placid waters of the Adriatic before us, the blue sky and an Italian sunset above us, the almond trees in bloom, and the city lying at our feet, with its hundred thousand inhabitants, and the flags from the ships, of all nations, waving in the mild and gentle breeze. The sight of the sea is refreshing after so long an absence, and on this occasion the elements conspired to make it particularly striking. The growth of the city has been rapid, and great changes have been made since I was last here; the new part is most substantially built; the streets are wide, and paved with flat slabs. The costumes are various, from all parts of the Levant and Archipelago. It is a perfect Babel for languages.

# CXXIV.

VENICE, ITALY, *May 15, 1857.*

A seven hours' passage by steamer brings me across the head-waters of the Adriatic from Trieste to this city. The contrast between the rumbling noises of rolling wagons and carriages over the broad, well-paved streets of the trading city, in addition to the heat and oppression from clouds of dust from the calcareous mountain roads, to the clean, quiet quays and landing-place of the steamer at Venice, strikes the stranger upon his first visit, away from noise and dust, and breathing a pure salt atmosphere. We left Trieste with the beginning of a howling *Bora*, or north wind, which, being after us, had no other effect than to quiet most of our passengers, giving them a taste of the horrors of sea-sickness. Both cities are free ports, and notwithstanding they are under Austrian rule, the dissimilarity is very remarkable in every particular. The dialect is different; the currency is metallic, the Lombardian states never having accepted the paper medium of the Empire, being the only exception in all the Austrian provinces; their weights and measures are not the same; the habits and customs of the people are quite unlike. In Trieste commerce predominates, and early hours are observed; here it is the reverse, the habits of the people are late, the dining hour being five P.M.; the theatres commence at nine and are out at twelve or half-past twelve; many places of refreshment are open at midnight, and others never close; during the heat of summer, the bright moonlight nights are almost wholly passed in the open air, or in excursions in gondolas, and the quietude and tranquillity of the city induces repose by daylight.

It is now nearly a year since I wrote you from Venice, and this being my fourth visit, I will not reiterate the remarkable sights of this remarkable city. Sunday evening I was standing upon the Rialto Bridge, which crosses the grand canal, admiring by moonlight the marble palaces with their quaint architecture of Byzantine, Gothic, and other styles, when I noticed the steeple of St. Apostoli, illuminated in the distance; and on inquiry, I learned that it was a festival in honor of the admission of a priest to full privileges. How many lanes or passages, called *calle*, from four to twelve feet in width, in this labyrinth of a city, I travelled, I know not; but prosecuting my tortuous way through the multitude, I came at last to the Campiello, or little square of the church, whose neighboring houses were gleaming with lighted torches. Bengal lights and rockets were exploding in the air; the cafés were filled; the masses, mostly the working classes, were out, the brunettes without bonnets; the booths of the Fritolero, with their bright copper kettles of boiling oil, preparing pastry, were quite surrounded; dark-eyed damsels were overhanging the balconies, listening to the sound of a guitar, or the merry song of a gondolier, whose tiny bark lay in the canal underneath. I had so often witnessed similar spectacles, that I should have been almost unconscious of the novelty, but for the presence of an American friend on his first visit, whom I was desirous of gratifying; his expressions of surprise awoke me to a sense of the peculiarities of the scene. As gondolas are used by strangers generally, who are unacquainted with the intricate passages which require long experience, much of interest is lost. One steps in his bark from the hotel door, and is rowed from church to church, from palace to palace, as well as to the theatre, by means of these intersecting canals, without the necessity of dodging in and out, and around corners, and over bridges; when time and experience permit, however, the land-route is of great interest, for one learns thereby the characteristics of the people; one may walk for miles, and find always something new and interesting.

Isolated as is Venice, every comfort and luxury can be procured here, and one naturally seeks out the sources of supply. The flower girls trip along in the morning under the porticos of San Marco, presenting strangers with early-plucked roses. Fresh butter and milk are found at the cafés. The water carriers, mostly country village girls, in funny costume, wearing boys' fur hats of peculiar form, with feathers, are trotting bare-footed along with a pair of small copper kettles suspended from flat elastic rods over their shoulders; the markets are well supplied with shell and other fish; the landing-place for vegetables is filled with boats delivering their cargoes; the water barges are moving up the lateral canals; the wood market furnishes its quota; foreign vessels contribute the colonial supplies; oranges, cherries, strawberries, green peas, asparagus, are seen in all parts exposed for sale, and the stranger looks in vain for any signs of vegetation, or the bubbling of a fountain. The *gardino publico*, the work of Napoleon, at the extreme end of the city, where, within a given circuit, horse exercise may be taken, is resorted to more by foreigners than by natives. Eight of these strange quadrupeds are kept in hire for the purpose. They are now regarded less as a curiosity than formerly.

Italy is the school for music, and the nursery of the arts; but dramatic artists must not expect to acquire fortunes in it. The operas and theatres are frequented for the purposes of coquetry, and the exchange of salutations replaces visiting to a certain extent. Shakspeare's Othello, or the Moor of Venice, translated in Italian, has had several repetitions lately here; it loses in the translation, but the scene being laid here, the costume of the Doges, the canals and bridges in the decorations, give it additional attractions. It is curious to see the cushioned and richly furnished gondolas by the light of a full moon, driving up like cabs to the front door steps of the theatre, taking in the well-clad aristocracy, or such as live remote, and do not wish to thread the narrow streets on their way home.

# CXXV.

LUZERNE, SWITZERLAND, *June 12, 1857.*

In order to vary my plan in proceeding north into Switzerland, I was obliged to again take Verona, Vicenza, Brescia, and Milan, en route. It is not a year since I described to you my visit to these cities, and my excursions upon the Lago di Como, Guarda, and Lugano. I now wished to accomplish the last of the five great passes of the Alps, the St. Gothard, and include Lago Maggiore once again in the circuit, having last year crossed the Splugen, and on former occasions Mount Cenis, the Simplon, and the great St. Bernard.

From Milan, I took the poste to Sesto Calende, on the Lake Maggiore, where our passports were visé, as we were leaving Austrian territory. The next landing place on the opposite side, in Sardinia, is Arona, near which stands the bronze monument of San Carlo Boromeo, sixty-six feet high, upon a pedestal forty-four feet in height, to the head of which I had once ascended by an inner staircase. The remains of the saint are in a crystal and gold coffin, in the crypt of the Domo of Milan. We soon reached the islands called Isola Madre, Isola Bella, Isola Pescatore, belonging to the same family, and noted for their beauty. The two first are perfect gems. Isola Bella, with its palace, picture galleries, terraced gardens, fountains, tropical vegetation, gold fish, guinea fowls, &c., gives it the air of a little paradise. The length of the lake may be made in five hours, to Mogidorro, where an omnibus conveys you to Bellinzona, from which point the road strikes off over the Splugen Pass to the right, which I took last year from Como. I now passed in to the left, by diligence at the foot of the mountain, to Airolo, where I passed the night. Leaving in the morning, our horses climbed steadily up the zigzag walled roads, until at mid-day we reached the Hospice, a height of six thousand eight hundred and sixty-eight feet above the level of the sea, where we partook of refreshments, and commenced the descent. The height is, you will perceive, seven hundred and sixty-two feet less than that of the location of the convent on the great St. Bernard, the highest habitable point in Europe, once described to you, and which is one thousand feet above the growth of timber. The mountains were snow-capped, the weather was fine, and we suffered but little from cold. The snow banks did not affect the passage. During eight months in the year sleighs are used. Some of the passes, which are subject to avalanches, are protected by long galleries, over which the huge masses slide into the gorges and ravines below. One of these galleries is one hundred and eighty feet long, and twelve feet wide. The melting snow produced beautiful cataracts, and the foaming and rumbling of the waters were at times deafening, particularly near the Teufel's Brücke, or Devil's Bridge, over the torrent Reuss, ninety-five feet in height, about four thousand feet above the level of the sea. The dangerous passes, on the verge of precipices hundreds of feet perpendicular, are protected by parapet walls. In two instances, from the encroachment of the snow upon the border of the deep chasms, our wheels were blocked with loaded wagons going in contrary directions, which obliged us to dismount, and caused some delay. The scattered stone houses of the peasantry in the valley, from the lofty eminences, looked like birdcages, and the cultivated patches in the green fields I could only compare to brown rugs which had been washed and were lying out to bleach upon the grass. The descent in the valley, the wild, romantic scenery of the mountains, the deep greens foliage of the pines and cedars, the neat and airy Swiss villages, the herdsmen, with flocks of goats, the peculiar costumes of the peasants, the roaring of the torrents, and the splashing of cascades, were well calculated to keep up a lively interest, even in one who had traversed most of the mountains of Europe. The village where William Tell was born, and the spot where he is represented as having shot the apple from his son's head, lent an historical interest to the route.

At Fuelen, the head of the lake, a small steamer was in readiness to conduct us, in two hours and a half, to Luzerne, one of the prettiest positions for a town in Switzerland. I had made the tour of the lake some years since, and was then, as now, struck with its majestic and magnificent scenery. The hotels here are excellent.

At the period alluded to, my health did not permit the ascent of Mount Riga; I have now accomplished it. An hour's sail, by steamer, takes one to Waggis, where horses and guides are procured, and where the ascent to Riga begins. The mountain lies free on all sides, and stands on one of the most interesting points, in reference to its beautiful views, also its near approach to the great chain of the Alps, and the neighborhood of so many lakes and valleys; I counted eleven of the former. Its height is five thousand five hundred feet. Its extensive view, not only over north, east, and west Switzerland, but also over a part of Germany, well repays the tourist, if he be fortunate enough to have clear weather, in which one is often disappointed. The road or path is good, but it is laborious on foot, and places for rest and refreshment are found. The better way is, for ladies and gentlemen not accustomed to climbing, to take horses; in three hours the ascent is made. A cold water cure establishment is found half way up. The Stafelwirthshaus is about a mile from the summit, and on the extreme top is the hotel called Riga Kulm, where we passed the night. We were favored with a fine sunset, after which the horn sounded for dinner, which our party enjoyed under the bracing atmosphere. The sky was serene, and the moon in the full. We retired early, and the echo of the morning horn saluted us a half hour before the sun rose on this grand and imposing spectacle, whose beauties cannot be described with the pen.

Cloaks and overcoats were in requisition, a warm breakfast enjoyable, and we descended by another route to the village of Kussnacht, where a vehicle was chartered to convey us to Luzerne. My next may be from north Switzerland, or from the banks of the Rhine.

# CXXVI.

BATHS OF EMS, DUCHY OF NASSAU, *July 14, 1857.*

About the time I left Luzerne, in Switzerland, the sympathies and anxieties of the public were highly excited by the report of fire and explosion in the railroad tunnel, which is to intersect that city with Basle. Twelve persons, who had volunteered in the rescue of upwards of forty workmen who were thus suddenly cut off, had perished in the attempt. When our passengers took the diligence to cross the mountain, in the depths of which the accident occurred, three of our number took a short cut across, hoping to obtain some information of the sufferers. It was melancholy to reflect that so many human beings were probably suffering the agonies of death under our very feet, without our being able to relieve them. I learned subsequently that thirty-three corpses had been taken out and interred. A horse was found slaughtered, but not eaten.

The Swiss cars are constructed after our American model; passengers see the scenery of the country better from them than from the coach cars generally in use in Europe.

A railway ride of three and a half hours, by express train from Basle, brings one to Baden-Baden, upon the west slope of the Black Forest, in one of the most beautiful valleys of Germany.

A few days' sojourn, and I proceeded to Homburg, which is much frequented; but neither that place nor Baden-Baden was as full as I found them last year.

At Wiesbaden, however, I found larger multitudes than I had ever met there on my former visits. This I attribute in part to the facilities for play, newly granted by the Bank.

Having detailed to you, on former occasions, the baths, qualities and uses of the waters, amusements and excursions, it will be needless to go into repetition.

In addition to the plebeian movement, it would seem that royalty has turned out in every direction. The King of Bavaria and ex-Empress of Russia were at Baden-Baden; the Emperor and Empress of Russia are at Kissengen; the Grand Duchess Constantine and her suite live opposite to me, occupying the entire building called the Panorama, belonging to the Ducal Kurhaus, where I am lodging. Having seen all these imperial and royal personages in their own territories, my curiosity is not excited; but it is a curious spectacle for an American to witness the sycophancy and idolatry of the masses for crowned heads; and one naturally asks himself, "Are such people capable of enjoying any other institutions than those they have been educated to adore?"

Those who remain at Ems, do so ostensibly for health; and no waters in Europe are so valuable for bronchial diseases, incipient pulmonary disease, nervous complaints, and many other difficulties; the fair sex predominate.

The Russians have the privilege of travelling since the treaty of peace; the presence of the wife of the Grand Admiral Constantine has brought large numbers here. The other evening, on the occasion of her birthday, the Duke of Nassau gave a grand celebration. In the middle of the little river Lahn, which flows through the valley, opposite the quarters of the Grand Duchess of Constantine was an illuminated barge, with thirty musicians. The Swiss Cottage Restaurant, upon the hill-side, was brilliantly lighted; and on the opposite mountain-ridge was a display of Bengal lights, and other fireworks, which produced a pretty effect, much to the edification of visitors and the peasantry, who seemed to enjoy it highly. Last night a ball was given by this lady in the honor of the Russians.

One is elbowed on all sides by Dukes, Duchesses, Counts, Countesses, Barons, and Baronesses, and the whole aristocratic race.

The German aristocracy are easy and approachable. You find that you have made the acquaintance of your neighbor; cards are exchanged; you see, perhaps, the arms and title of a Count, Baron, or some high functionary or dignitary, in return for which you give him a plain American address, without a handle to the name.

The demoralizing and destructive practice of open gambling is only tolerated in the German duchies, and is a source of great revenue to their rulers. In France it is prohibited: Prussia has withheld the grant at her watering places: in Belgium it only exists at Spa: Sardinia has stopped it at Aix les Bains. But all the efforts of the great princes have not yet succeeded in destroying the system established at Baden-Baden, Homburg, Wiesbaden, and Ems.

Next month I go to Paris, and expect to be in the United States in September.

# 1858.
# CXXVII.

MARSEILLES, FRANCE, *Jan. 15, 1858.*

I must apologize to many of my friends and acquaintances whom I could not have the pleasure of seeing during my last short sojourn at home, and also for my sudden departure, which was the result of cold and indisposition.

From the time I left New York, on the 25th of last month, I experienced no cold weather until recently in Paris, where the prevalence of the *grippe*, or influenza, induced me to take flight for a more congenial climate. Our passage by the steamer Fulton was one of the shortest and most comfortable winter passages I ever made. Christmas and New Year's festivals were passed in Paris. The great city, as usual at this joyous season, was extremely gay.

The Boulevards, from the Madeleine to the Bastille, a distance of three miles, were lined on both sides with booths, offering every variety of fancy and useful articles for presents and use, as at this period all classes expect gifts and souvenirs, which tax the ingenuity in the selection, and the purse in the acquisition. In this manner several millions of francs change hands. The number of Americans is much less than usual this season, but at a ball given by our Consul in Paris, I should judge that three hundred of both sexes were present.

The crisis is less visible in France than in most of the countries of Europe. One would scarcely infer from the manner in which the theatres, operas and masked balls are frequented at the opening of the carnival season, that a money panic existed in the capital of France; in fact very little publicity was given through the press, as the Emperor had declared the thing a humbug, and not intended for his Empire. At the grand Hotel du Louvre, near the Tuileries, where I lived, I noticed that the number of arrivals kept up pretty well for the season. It is the St. Nicholas of Paris, and a stupendous structure, far exceeding anything of the kind in Europe as a hotel, for its style of architecture, decoration, magnificent marble staircases, luxuriant dining and reading rooms; the former has splendid crystal candelabra and six hundred gas lights at the six o'clock table d'hôte. It is better adapted for travellers who have been accustomed to warmer heated apartments in winter than most French hotels, as the halls and passages are heated by registers throughout. Russians, Americans, English and Hollanders are the best paying guests. The French, with more strict notions of economy, are unwilling to pay for the extravagant outlay and parade. The transition from the recent cold in Paris to the mild temperature of this region, which one reaches in the short space of twenty hours by rail, a distance of five hundred miles, is most striking. Here the almond trees are in blossom, and the silvery leaf of the olive has a more cheerful aspect. The contrast is more marked now than before the construction of the railroad; I once experienced a similar change, but after a tedious journey of four days and nights; the lightning line now accomplishes it in less than one day.

The community is now excited, as well as all France, at the recent attempt on the life of the Emperor, which, had it been successful, would have put all Europe in a blaze of revolution. Marseilles is particularly interested as a commercial port in the preservation of the existing dynasty, since its growing commerce with Algeria, as well as its other interests, would suffer by a change of government.

It has been suggested that the Emperor designed visiting Africa, and the project of railroads has been proposed. The Kabyle districts and warrior tribes having been subdued by the French troops, a good opportunity is offered of visiting the northern part of Africa; and, as I wish to escape the cold changes which occur even in Italy in winter, I have decided to embark for Algiers, where I shall find a race of Moors and Arabs differing perhaps from the Bedouins of Syria and Egypt, and find many monuments of Moorish architecture more antique than those of the Alhambra of Granada, and the Alcazar and Giralda of Seville, continued after the Arab conquest of Spain, I shall be able to judge of the effects and progress of French civilization over barbarism, and shall in addition have something to communicate.

I notice many changes and improvements, each time I return to this point of departure for Italy, Spain, Egypt, and other lands on the Mediterranean.

# CXXVIII.

ALGIERS, AFRICA, *Feb. 1, 1858.*

Notwithstanding we had some boisterous weather in the Gulf of Lyons, our voyage across the Mediterranean brought us in less than forty-eight hours in sight of the African coast. The city seen from the sea with its triangular form upon a steep slope, appears like a white mass of chalk surrounded with verdure. The Arabs compare it poetically to a diamond set in emerald and sapphire. Its primitive appearance, as occupied by the Dey before the conquest by the French, in 1830, is greatly changed by the opening of wide streets near the base, and the erection of buildings of modern style, and public squares and gardens. The new port and quays give portions of the city an European air.

The blending of Moorish and French architecture, and the great variety of costume worn by Arabs, Moors, Jews, Spaniards, and government troops and officials, strike the stranger with astonishment; and had I not been familiar with Egyptian, Turkish, Greek, and Continental races, I should have been as much astonished as some of our fellow passengers seemed to be.

The day of our arrival was fine, and the sun's rays warm, as the thermometer in winter always keeps considerably above the freezing point, although the Atlas Mountains in the distance are at times tipped with snow. The venders of fresh dates, oranges, bananas, and other fruits, advised us of a much warmer climate than we had left.

The summit of the triangle is crowned with the chateau La Casbah. A half league to the left of this ancient fortress, the last residence of the Dey, stands the famous Fort of the Emperor, the explosion of which, by the French, in 1830, decided the fate of this well-fortified city.

Algiers was founded by the Berbers Mosgan tribe of the BeniMezarhama, and the companions of Hercules the Lybian, who left the army of the hero and fixed themselves here. It then became part of the Mauritanic Cæsariene.

On the fall of the Roman empire, it became the prey of the chief of the Vandals, and was destroyed. It was reconquered by the Arabs, who armed piratical vessels, which became so formidable that the Spanish king, Ferdinand, fitted out an expedition, and occupied a small island in front of the city, where the lighthouse now stands. The Algerines called to their aid the celebrated pirate, Barbarossa, who was checked by the Spaniards. Furious with his defeat, he seized and killed the sovereign, and took possession of the city.

All the efforts of the Spaniards were defeated, and the fleet destroyed by tempests or otherwise.

The brother of Barbarossa, Kair-ed-din, with the aid of thirty-six thousand Christian slaves, for three years united the island with the main land, and formed a port for his vessels. After his death it became the property of the Turks.

The city suffered various changes of masters, and was desolated by plagues and earthquakes, and other scourges, too numerous to mention, until the French Consul-General was insulted in 1827, which led to a strict blockade, maintained in 1829, and finished with thirty-five thousand troops in 1830, by blowing up the fort mentioned, which commands the city; the Dey was shortly after transported to Italy.

I notice the results of the earthquake of last year in many of the mosques, as well as private buildings. The government botanical gardens, on the seashore, beyond the pretty residences of the Europeans, in the village of Mustapha, are worth visiting.

Here are found date trees filled with fruit, sugar-canes, bananas, oranges, lemons, indeed all sorts of tropical fruits and productions, calculated to encourage the Arab races in agriculture; and as the caravans of mules, donkeys, and camels, pass along loaded with articles for market, their owners and drivers can see what the labor of man is capable of producing. The principal agricultural colonists are Spaniards and Maltese. The French, it would seem, are unwilling to leave La Belle France, excepting those engaged in commerce and mechanical operations; their ideas are still confounded with apprehensions of fever, the attacks of Arabs, the ravages of lions, jackals, hyenas, and other beasts of prey, the legitimate result of the thousand and one narratives of returned soldiers. The government makes every effort to induce colonists to accept concessions of land, but the work moves tardily, and they learn with surprise that thousands and hundreds of thousands of Germans and other Europeans emigrate to America, while Algeria affords a home for all who choose to accept it. The truth is, these people are tired of monarchy and military rule, and breathe freer in the United States, with a brighter prospect for the future.

The theatre is a structure of some pretensions; a ball was recently given there, under the patronage of Madame Randon, the wife of the Governor-General of Algeria, for the benefit of the poor, and was well attended by the élite of the city. The balcony of the first tier was occupied by about fifty Jewesses, in full Algeria costume, and produced a pretty effect. They wear vests or bodices of colored silks, embroidered with gold; sashes and flowing robes of rich stuffs; head-dresses of silks, or conical caps made of gold coins; headbands of diamonds, as well as necklaces of emeralds, pearls, and rubies; armlets of gold, with jewels piled on in profusion, producing a blaze of light eclipsing the gas of the establishment. The second tier was occupied with quiet, grave Musselmans, with the red fez, and white turbans. These two classes, of course, do not dance, but watch intently the fashionable crinoline-dressed European ladies, joining in the giddy waltz or polka upon the stage or platform below. The foyer, or saloon, was fitted up for refreshments and gaming, and I noticed that both Jews and Musselmans of the wealthy class like the excitement of play.

The whole of Kabyle is subject to French rule, since the conquest of last autumn, and all is tranquil in that direction. Having lost all hope of recovering his liberty, the Arab, formerly accustomed to a wandering life in the interior, must now see the necessity of fixing himself on the soil in the neighborhood of towns and villages, and supplying the markets with his productions. Their habits of economy and frugality enable them to accumulate and hoard money; their consumption of French articles is small, however; consequently, the money concealed or kept out of circulation is a loss to the empire. The possession of this large territory by France, say two hundred and fifty leagues of coast from east to west, and fifty leagues from north to south, may prove in time a source of revenue, but at present it is attended with great expense. The outlay is some twelve millions of dollars, the receipts about two millions. It is a fine military school for the fifty thousand troops employed in keeping possession. If once properly colonized, it would give France a full supply of grain. As to the product of cotton, I doubt if it can ever be cultivated here in competition with our Southern States, notwithstanding the proposition of introducing the apprentice system for negroes from Soudan. The African wheat and barley are of excellent quality; corn is tolerable; tobacco can be raised in great quantities, but the quality does not compare with ours. At the Museum or Exposition of Industry, I have examined all the products of the provinces. In the event of a general war in Europe, and a rising of the Arabs, France might be obliged to abandon the interior and occupy the sea-ports only.

We have had some rain, and the roads are bad. As soon as they improve I shall go in the interior, and reconnoitre the ground, visit the towns and villages, and attend the fairs of cattle, sheep and horses.

# CXXIX.

Medeah, Province of Algiers, Africa, *Feb. 15, 1858.*

Medeah is built in amphitheatre form, upon an inclined plane beyond the first chain of the Atlas Mountains, some twenty-three leagues south of Algiers; it is some three thousand six hundred feet above the level of the sea, and is rather difficult of ascent. It is the site of the ancient kingdom of Tittery.

Medeah has been occupied four times by the French troops, since 1830, and indefinitely in 1840. The hostilities of 1830 demonstrated that so long as the Arabs were free to organize forces in the mountains and make sudden attacks, there was no safety. The occupation of this point with troops makes it perfectly tranquil. Abd-el Kader, whose prison I visited at Amboise in France a few years since, and whose exploits are often brought up in this country, gave the French much trouble.

One of the greatest achievements was in the zigzag road constructed by the French army through the gorges of the river Chiffa, some four leagues in length, which enabled them to conquer the country of the warrior Arabs of the mountains. The points of view through these rocky passes, with their precipices, towering masses of rock above, and deep chasms below, in many places without parapets, look frightful in making the ascent. I was reminded by it of a road constructed by the English in the Island of Ceylon, which I once described to you, and which was the only means of conquering the mountain King of Kandy. In one of these mountains there are large numbers of monkeys, which may be seen clambering up the rocks and branches of trees, and basking in the sun's rays. Gibraltar is the only point in Europe where they exist, and they are supposed to have been introduced there from Africa. One passes through several large towns on his way to this place. Douera, which was a camp in 1830, is now quite a town, with a wall around it, and gates for protection, and the imposition of octroi duties. The country produces cotton, tobacco, cereal grains, and pasturage for animals. When water is not abundant, as they are subject to drought on the plains, wells are dug for irrigation.

Boufereck was the first post established on the plain of Misidza, in 1830, when the army advanced to Blidah for the first time. It was then humid, surrounded with marshes and bad exhalations. It was known for a long time as the cemetery for soldiers and colonists; but it is now quite healthy. The weekly market of the Arabs, bringing in all the tribes from the surrounding country, with horses, cattle, goats, &c., is a striking feature in that settlement. The inclosure of the grounds is ample, with a mosque adjacent for the Mussulman to say his prayers in. One often sees them by the road-side prostrating themselves towards Mecca in the east. Often in towns and cities you pass from the bazaars and densely-crowded streets directly into the mosques, with fountains of water in the court, as in Constantinople, where they wash their feet and trip in upon the matting and carpet rugs to pay their devotion, while you hear the cry of the muezzin from the lofty minaret adjoining, calling the faithful to prayers. The mosques are generally plain, with whitewashed walls, and lamps suspended, as well as ostrich eggs strung upon cords. Some, however, are of beautiful Moorish architecture, with an infinity of columns, and a great variety of arabesque work. The mausoleum or tomb of the Marabout is much venerated, being a sort of pilgrimage for the devout believer.

An anecdote was related to me in visiting the edifice erected to the memory of the Marabout; it is upon a hill, a beautiful position, outside the walls of Algiers.

The Koran forbids the use of wine and all alcoholic drinks, still the holy man indulged freely, being supplied by the persecuted Jews, who took this way to obtain the favor of the chief of the sect. There being a sort of veneration for idiots, this besotted individual was once aroused by the cries of the people, that the enemy's vessels were off the port and approaching the city. With difficulty awakened from his stupor he cried out, "Where are the infidel dogs? Give me a whip and I will lash them off the surface of the great deep." Reeling on the seaside he slashed away upon the calm surface of the water, venting his anathemas and imprecations. As fortune willed it, one of those sudden tempests arose, not unfrequent in this latitude, and the vessels were driven off or dashed to pieces. He was shrewd enough when he witnessed this singular phenomenon to take advantage of it, and exhorted the people to exhibit greater faith for the future. A temple was erected over his tomb, and his memory perpetuated to posterity.

I passed a couple of days at Blidah, some twelve leagues from Algiers. It is the chief place of the first military division, at the foot of the Little Atlas mountain. It has a population of fifteen thousand Arabs and foreigners; it is surrounded with a belt of foliage, forests of orange, lemon, fig, olive, and palm trees, which give it the air of a delicious garden. The Arabs call it The Voluptuous. In 1825 it was visited by an earthquake, which entirely destroyed it, with one half of its eighteen thousand inhabitants. On the 23d of July, 1830, after the occupation of Algiers by the French, the General advanced to this place, and was well received, but in returning was attacked by the Kabyles.

The European part of the town is well built, with regular streets, public squares, cafés, and a theatre; the Arab part has narrow streets, low, one-story, whitewashed houses, with a single door or hole in the wall for entrance, and little portholes or latticed windows for the women to peep out. The women are rarely seen in the streets, and never in the mosques; when they come out they are closely veiled in white shawls, which show the eyes only.

The Arab market at Blidah exhibited horses, cattle, grain, dried fruits, hog skins, or rather wild boar skins, filled with olive oil, wool, charcoal, &c.; the Arabs buy iron, hardware, coffee, sugar, thread, and such things as are actually necessary.

I visited the haras, or government stables of the Arabian, Persian, and Syrian stallions, some eighty in number, one of which, El Haz, presented by the emperor, cost forty-four hundred dollars.

The environs of Blidah are enchanting; the supply of water for irrigation, from the mountains, is abundant, and the climate lovely even at this season of the year. The Arab poet, Hamed Youssef, said, "They call thee a little city, I call thee a charming little rose." I was reminded of a lovely little spot, called Soler, in the island of Majorca, where one rides for miles through orange groves, which, like those of Blidah, are exported to France. I noticed, in passing through the village of Ben Mered, an obelisk erected to the memory of twenty-two soldiers who were attacked by three hundred horsemen of Ben Salem, in the year 1842, and all killed after the most heroic resistance. Only one, a sergeant, who was wounded and left for dead, could give the details. The young sergeant, in the midst of the conflict, fell, mortally wounded, with the words upon his lips, "Friends, remember that the French never surrender, but defend themselves to the death."

The Arabs in this part of the country are now turning their attention to agriculture; the plough merely scratches the surface, and without doubt, is the same used in the primitive days of Abraham. Herds of sheep and goats are seen in the mountains with Arab boys and dogs.

# CXXX.

Constantine, Africa, *Feb. 27, 1858.*

Returning from Medeah to Algiers, I embarked on board of a French government steamer for Stora. We landed troops at Delys, Bougie, and Dzidzelle, and after a two days' run, arrived at Stora, and proceeded to Philippeville to procure a conveyance for this city, which is situated some seventy miles in the interior.

Constantine is the Cirta of the ancients, the Cossentina of the Arabs. It is situated upon the river Rhumel, at the point where the torrent crosses the elevated mountains to penetrate the upper basin of the plains of Milah. The ancient capital of Jugurtha is now the chief city of the eastern province of Algeria. It lies some eighteen hundred feet above the level of the Mediterranean, upon a triangular plateau. This plateau is surrounded by the two branches of the river, and crowned by the heights of Mausourah and of Sidi-Merid, from which it is separated by deep chasms and precipices, at the bottom of which courses the Rhumel, with its wild and magnificent cataracts. It has the aspect of a lofty island, with its high rocks, almost perpendicular, rendering the city almost, or quite, invulnerable, with its strong gates and fortifications. Constantine has been the scene of great events in the grand history of Africa. The founder of the city was said to have been a Greek adventurer, 250 years B.C. Marva reigned over the Mumides. It was in turn occupied by Masinissa and his sons. Juba sided with Pompey, and was chased by Bogad, king of Sittius, who founded a Roman colony.

Cæsar undertook great works, and one finds many of the old walls, ramparts, and inscriptions remaining. The ancient aqueducts, the ruins of which still stand, some forty feet high, about a mile from the city, are said to be the work of the emperor Justinian. The invasion of the Arabs destroyed the opulent city, and it passed from one to another among all the African conquerors; it was in the hands of the Turks in the sixteenth century, and afterwards in the hands of the Deys of Algiers, many of whom were assassinated.

The last, Hadz-Ahmed Dey, kept it the longest, but it was by oppressing his subjects. From 1826 to 1830 he cut off the heads of some three thousand of his people, and committed the most revolting deeds. At that time the French government denounced his acts, and named the brother of the Bey of Tunis his successor; but he managed to keep possession until 1836, when Marshal Clausel attacked them, at the head of an insufficient army, but was driven back from this stronghold, and obliged to retreat.

The next year, however, a body of ten thousand men, with the second son of Louis Philippe in the avant garde, took the city by assault, General Damremont losing his life in the attack. I find his monument in an inclosure of the ancient casbah or fort, near the caserne and hospital grounds, which are now crowned by large structures. I have just visited them in company with my present travelling companion, a captain in the Russian army, sent out for general observation. The French officers have shown us much civility and attention, making our stay here agreeable.

The reservoirs constructed by the Romans upon the summit are repaired thoroughly, and contain a full supply of water for a long siege. The view from these points is of the boldest character. The city is now divided in two quarters, Arab and French, and offers the most striking contrast.

The Arabs said that Constantine was a rock in the middle of a river, and that it would require as many French to take it as ants to take an egg from the bottom of a pot of milk; but in this they found their error, and concluded it was the will of the Prophet. The trade of the city with Biskarah is large in dried dates, and with Setif and other ports in wool; ostrich feathers, elephants' tusks, and gold dust are seen in small quantities. At Philippeville, on the coast, I found some English officers who came out to join the famous Jules Gerard, the lion slayer. They were going to form a camp in the neighborhood of Bona, further up the coast. I shall probably meet them again when I get up there, and learn what success they meet with. The conductor of our stage has assured us that at one point near El Cantour, a dreary mountainous country, lions are known to follow the vehicle when driven to extremity for want of food. Not a very pleasant prospect for a traveller. I saw the skin of a famous fellow, some sixteen feet in length, recently killed. The jackals, hyenas, and wild boars are abundant; the latter may be seen in quantities in the market places, filled with olive oil, which is brought on the backs of camels. We passed through sections of the country entirely uninhabited, where the wild olive and cork wood grow in abundance. In the settlements they engraft the domestic olive, which does well.

The Arab cultivation here is meagre and primitive; the plough is drawn by a camel and donkey yoked together—rather a ludicrous sight. If the Arab has a surplus of grain, or the price does not suit him, having no barns, he buries it in pits prepared for the purpose. His tent can be transported easily with his small household effects, consisting of a few earthen or copper cooking utensils, or he can throw up a mud hovel and thatch it with the leaves of the date or other trees.

He mounts his horses or camels, with his wives and children upon their backs, and emigrates to another place where the land suits him better. The women, whose faces we occasionally get a peep at, wear a profusion of bracelets, anklets, and huge rings from the top and bottom of the ears. One would suppose them too weighty for this tender part to sustain. In the city the wives of the wealthy Moors are beautifully clad with ornaments; they are fond of monotonous music and the lascivious dancing of the professed dancing girls, not unlike that of the dancing girls of Egypt. The fair daughters of Judea, whose faces are always uncovered, have preserved their type of beauty here. I have seen the howling and whirling Dervishes of Constantinople, the adoration of brazen bulls in India, the prostration of the Chinese before their heathen gods, the Parsee worship of the rising sun, the dancing of Shakers, as well as most varieties of worship, but I have never yet witnessed such a horrible exhibition of fanaticism as in a little temple here. The building was a plain one, not unlike a whitewashed Mohammedan mosque, with arches and columns, ostrich eggs strung upon cords, and suspended lamps. Upon the matting and rugs squatted a centre group, of musicians, with tambourines and tamtams, a sort of kettle-drum. Around the walls were seated rows of men and boys. My companion and myself crossed our legs, tailor-like, in line with the devotees, and awaited the working of the spirit.

Then commenced monotonous, plaintive singing, accompanied by the musicians moving their heads backwards and forwards until the sounds became wild and discordant, when a huge, dark, Bedouin-faced figure unrolled his turban, threw down his red fez, while a heavy tuft of long hair floated over his shoulders like the mane of a lion, then his eyes rolling furiously, and his head swaying as if it was on a pivot, he threw himself among the crowd, raving and snarling like a dog, and attempting to bite all who came in his way. At length he was appeased, with horse nails, scorpions, &c.; he licked red hot iron, much to the enjoyment of the audience, who indulged in the wildest strains of music and songs of delight. After which performance, dancing, the most extravagant and arduous, was continued until several fell frothing at the mouth, and were carried out of the circle. This curious spectacle continued about two hours on the Musselman sabbath, which is Friday. It was curious to see the boys imitate the shaking of the head and body of the leaders of the sect. The turmoil ceases at intervals, prayers are muttered, incense burned, and the parties take breath only to renew the frenzy and excitement. On the public square you see snake charmers and jugglers, who rival those of Madras.

# CXXXI.

TUNIS, AFRICA, *March 13, 1858.*

From Constantine, the capital of the eastern province of Algeria, seventy miles in the interior, I proceeded to the sea-coast at Philippeville and Stora, to embark for Bona and Tunis.

Philippeville is a modern French town on the site of the ancient Russicada, with an open roadstead; Stora, a league distant, serves as a seaport, and is protected from almost all the winds. Philippeville has a future, being the commercial and military centre for Constantine and eastern Algeria. The environs are picturesque and productive of tropical fruits. The remains of a Roman amphitheatre are found there, also statues, Corinthian columns, and the cisterns or reservoirs which formerly supplied the ancient city. Nine of them have been repaired, and now furnish the town with water.

From Stora I came by steamer to Bona, the seat of the second military division. This city was constructed in the year 497 by the Arabs with the remains of the ancient and beautiful city of Hippona, about two miles distant. It was founded by the Carthaginians and called Ubbo. It lay at the foot of two hills, with the river Seybouse passing by, and vessels came up at that time to the city. In the year 709 of Rome, Scipio, a fugitive, beaten by the tempest, took refuge here with his little fleet, which was destroyed by Sittius, the lieutenant of Cæsar.

In the year 429 A.D. the Vandals besieged Hippona and destroyed it in part. It was retaken by Belisare, but the Arabs took it again in 697, and transported to Arabia the present French town of Bona. The kings of Tunis built the Casbah or citadel in the year 1304. It has changed hands many times, and has been burnt and destroyed; in 1832 the French took complete possession. Many improvements have taken place; the country is tolerably cultivated in the environs, and some fine works have been established.

We had cleverly got to sea from Bona when a sudden norther came down upon us and obliged our steamer to take refuge under the lee of a fort and projecting cape; after it subsided we pushed on the next day to the Bay of Tunis, and landed at the village and port of Goletta, some twelve miles from the city; it can be reached by land or water, the latter way by a salt lake.

Here, in this city of one hundred thousand inhabitants, the largest proportion of whom are Arabs, one finds himself out of the pale of French civilization. In Algeria life may be considered tolerably safe, but here, such is the fanaticism of the Musselman, and so little the respect paid to Christians, that one is naturally cautious in his movements. The mosques cannot be entered as in Constantinople, Algiers, and other places; the cemeteries cannot be defiled by infidels. The five gates of the city are closed at six in the afternoon. All persons found out by the armed sentinels after seven in the afternoon, without lanterns, are taken to the guard-house and released upon the consul's application in the morning. An instance of intolerance occurred last June, which created a sensation far and wide. I passed the gate recently where the Jew (you will recollect the circumstance), meeting with some obstacle, anathematized Mahomet; he was maltreated, thrown into prison and condemned to be executed, and notwithstanding the protestations of various consuls, was decapitated and literally cut into pieces by the exasperated populace. The French sent down a squadron, and at last obtained redress from the Bey, in promises for the future privileges of Jews and Christians. Here one finds African life in its natural condition, beyond the reach of French officers and soldiery.

The miserable, sallow-looking troops are dressed in round jackets and pantaloons, with the fez, or cap of red cloth, ill adapted to a hot climate. The streets are narrow and wretchedly filthy; all the offal is thrown into them, and where hogs do not exist as scavengers, the dogs, who are always numerous, supply in some measure the defect. When it rains, the black mud is difficult to wade through, as there is no pavement, and pattens are brought in requisition. The stench from filth is abominable.

The bazaars are interesting to visit, on account of their display of rich silks, costumes, smoking pipes with amber mouth-pieces, otto of roses, embroideries of all kinds, and rich trappings for saddles and bridles.

The Arab cafés, with their thirty to forty inmates, sitting cross-legged, sipping coffee in little cups, and listening to guitars and national airs, are curious to look into. The little barber shops are found everywhere, and busy enough are their masters, shaving the skulls of the faithful. A pile of shoes is always at the door, as the Arabs step upon the mats and rugs, and then draw their shoes off, and draw their feet up under them. You are elbowed in the streets by negroes and Arabs of the different races, dark-eyed boys, camels and mules laden with olives, olive oil, fruits, and vegetables, and surrounded by the cries of vendors, and the confusion of tongues. The exterior Moorish architecture of some of the mosques, and the light and airy minarets, are attractive to the eye as you look up and espy the Muezzin crying out the hour of prayer. The supreme power is vested in the Bey, who has several palaces in the city and country. He is now residing some nine miles hence, along the shore, whither I have been to witness an Arab fantasie, or display of horsemanship.

An artillery regiment lay encamped directly opposite the immense palace, with its latticed windows, domes, terraces, and four hundred and fifty inmates, including the harem, eunuchs, servants, officials, and relatives of the Bey's wives. Two huge, uncouth, painted lions were seen over the inner porch; sentinels, stacks of muskets, and officers, civil and military, were in the front of the doors, together with the sons of the sovereign, and when the Bey presented himself at the window, the equestrian exercise commenced. There were forty horsemen, accompanied by two Kadis and three Scheiks of tribes in the interior, who were dressed in the most luxurious costumes of silks and embroidered cloth flowing robes, their arms, saddles, and bridles glittering with gold and silver filigree work. Starting at some distance, they came down singly, and in groups of three or five, upon full gallop, drawing and discharging their carabines as they passed by, and suddenly reining up and whirling their guns in the air—a most exciting and wild scene, beautifully executed. Others were dancing their horses to the sounds of drums and flutes, and making all sorts of evolutions around the sentinels, describing a figure eight, and embracing the sentinels without treading on their toes. The homage paid was recompensed by rich and costly presents sent out to the victors.

While the authorities are revelling in luxuries, the poor suffer the penalty. Three thousand troops have just been sent out, to be absent some months, for the purpose of collecting taxes and imposts, which are enforced by the bayonet.

The country is beautifully fertile and productive. We rode through miles of olive groves. The Bey has a famous oil mill, driven by steam power, under the direction of Europeans. The olives, when fully ripened, are sent in panniers upon camels' backs, and crushed by machinery; the oil is then pressed out. Our Consul and some others made up a party for Gomart, twelve miles distant, where we found some catacombs; but to one who had seen those of Thebes they afforded but little interest.

The friends we visited occupied a palace which had been built by Christian slave labor during the piratical days of this people. The amount of labor performed in the construction, with its fountains, basins, orange, lemon, and date groves, must have exhausted the patience of these poor prisoners.

The ancient city of Carthage lies along the sea shore, some twelve miles from Tunis, and is quite accessible by carriage drive. We visited Mr. Davis, the gentleman employed by the British government in excavating the antiquities, and accompanied him in these explorations. The site of the great temple of Esculapius is plainly visible, and a portion of the foundation walls and staircases. He has forty men employed, and we discovered the basements of several houses where the mosaic floors were quite perfect and very beautiful. Many large boxes have been sent to the British Museum. The ancient port of the city is still distinguishable.

The traces of the aqueducts are well defined, and large masses of stone still stand. The reservoirs for water, seventeen in number, are in the best state of preservation; they are evidently of Roman construction.

The circuit of twenty miles, where stood the great city, is now under cultivation, scarcely leaving any vestige of existence above the surface.

# CXXXII.

Tripoli, Coast of Barbary, Africa, *April 1, 1858.*

The land route from Tunis is attended with so much fatigue and risk, that I took the steamer for Malta, and embarked for this port, where we arrived in the midst of a violent norther, the waves dashing violently among the breakers, and landed, much to the satisfaction of all concerned; particularly, two Turkish Beys, with their harems, from Constantinople, who were my fellow passengers. The women were under lock and key, but notwithstanding the sea-sickness of their liege lords, as well as the eunuchs, I noticed the jealous glances cast outside of their berths from time to time.

There are two small hotels at Tunis, but here, none; and as I had letters for our Consul, Mr. Gaines, I accepted his Virginian hospitality. This territory, which extends to the Egyptian frontier, is under Turkish rule, and the now presiding Pacha is Osmand Bey, a worthy old gentleman, to whom I was presented, and with whom I had a long chat through his interpreter. Coffee, sherbet, and confectionery were served, and long pipes, or chibouks, of jessamine wood, with amber mouth-pieces encircled in diamonds, gave the Latakia tobacco a good relish. As strangers are seldom seen here, the communication being rare, it is rather gratifying to resident consuls and others, to extend facilities. I am the first native American visitor, the consul tells me, since his residence here of nine years. An English government steamer brought down a gentleman whose friends reside here, and who has done service in the Crimea, and is now appointed consul in Russia. His friends, being mine, have given me an opportunity of joining in the festivities and recreations offered to the officers. Horses have been put at our disposition for social and shooting parties in the country. Dinners and evening parties have been constant, and the time passed pleasantly. Consuls here, as well as at Tunis, wear the uniform and cap with gold band, which is much respected by the natives.

As our dragoman goes round the city with his silver-headed massive stick, it is quite amusing to hear the sergeant present arms in Turkish as the sentinels are passed. There are some four thousand Turkish troops here from Constantinople. The population is chiefly Arab, with a sprinkling of Jews and Maltese. The city contains fifteen thousand inhabitants; it is much cleaner than Tunis, and is in a healthier position, and warmer, being further south and nearer the desert. The country between the sea and the sandy waste is very picturesque; it is mostly cultivated by means of irrigation, as the Persian wheels, driven by cattle, are seen in all directions, attached to the wells.

The date groves in all quarters, interspersed with olive, fig, and almond, give it an oriental appearance. The scenery, as well as the costume and habits of the people, is African. Every variety of color may be seen, the ground being contiguous to the races of the Sahara and the starting point for Timbuctoo. The weekly fairs upon the beach are most primitive. Sheep, goats, and camels are driven in and butchered upon the sand. You see the Arabs squatted, barefooted, or in red and yellow sandals, around piles of skins, fruits, vegetables, or grain; tinkers, in little date-leaved tents, repairing copper cooking utensils; itinerant barbers plying their avocations; donkeys loaded with wood and charcoal; squalid figures, black, brown, and yellow, cooking a scanty meal of pumpkin, red pepper, and oil; others indulging in the national and savoury repast of kouskous;—and a thousand other sights and eccentricities that we, as civilized beings, can scarcely dream of.

The previous war steamer that was down here brought the English Vice Consul, and among the guests two English ladies. The Pasha gave a review of the troops and a picnic in the country. He drove one of the ladies in his own carriage, followed by a cavalcade—so unusual a thing for a Musselman, that the Arab women thought he had taken a new wife, and commenced chanting a merry song, much to the lady's annoyance.

A splendid dinner was given to the officers, with abundance of wine, contrary to the usage of Musselmans, but in accordance with the Pasha's notions of propriety; and when the lady left he presented her a beautiful pony. He is more European in his conduct than Turkish, and has set an example for others in having only one wife.

Visiting a country-seat a few days since, I noticed upon an observatory overlooking the seat the wooden figure of a hand nailed up, a custom, I presume, in accordance with that of more civilized countries, where horseshoes are fastened over the doors, to keep off the witches. I asked if it was to keep off the evil eye, and the reply was that the carpenter would not continue his work until it was fastened there. We frequently see the impressions of hands, in red and black marks, upon the buildings; such is the superstition of the natives.

The birthday of Mahomet will soon take place, when it will be unsafe for Jew or Gentile to appear in the streets. For several days before the festival the Marabouts or holy men commence eating Indian hemp seed, which produces delirium; they then rush out, shaking their heads and bodies violently, followed by men and women chanting and shrieking. They then perform miracles by swallowing knives, nails, glass, and putting red hot shovels to their tongues, and sometimes their fanaticism induces them to maltreat or tear to pieces Jews and Gentiles; and the Pacha warns Consuls to keep their protégés or servants at home, as he cannot be responsible for them.

We have had some excellent gun practice from the English gun boat Vigilant, now in port, in honor of the Pacha. The distance fired was nearly half a mile, with two sixty-eight pounders; she carries also two thirty-two pounders. The target was a rock in the roadstead, painted white. Rounds of shot, shell, and grape, were fired with much precision. After the conclusion, and the partaking of a collation, the captain carried us in his gig to examine the effect, and we found chain shot and broken shell.

I am invited by the commander of this beautiful screw steamer, of six hundred and forty tons, to occupy a part of his cabin. Although I had paid my passage on board the steamer which has already departed, my friends induced me to stay a few days longer and accept the invitation. The old Pasha was to have been on board, but a plea of indisposition excused him. Several consuls and vice-consuls were among our number. On another occasion we had a trial of firing at a floating target, which in this case was a barrel sent adrift, with a couple of sixty-eight pound shot suspended to keep it steady, and an old flag staff stuck in the bung. We then described a circle of a half mile, and fired while in motion; the shot told remarkably as line shots, and the surface of the water sometimes looked like the spouting of whales. The English have now one hundred and thirty, large and small, of this class of steamers or gunboats. The Vigilant carries ninety men, and has an engine of two hundred horse power, with a screw twelve feet diameter; the boilers and machinery are below water mark; she draws twelve feet of water, and is admirably calculated for destruction.

Within the harbor of Malta, and encircled by the strong walls of these immense and world-wide renowned fortifications, lay the flag ship and part of the squadron of Admiral Lyons. Having once made a quarantine of twenty-one days there, coming from Egypt, which quarantine is fortunately abandoned now, besides spending ten days in sight seeing, nothing stuck me as new.

# CXXXIII.

GRAND CAIRO, EGYPT, *April 10, 1858.*

I reached Malta on board of an English war steamer, in time to connect with the Peninsular and Oriental Company's packet, with the India overland passengers. An agreeable passage of three and a half days brought us to Alexandria, and instead of taking canal and river boats as in former times, occupying four days, I proceeded by rail to this city in eight hours. The distance is about one hundred and thirty miles, and the road is to continue to Suez, across the little desert, some ninety miles more. There only remain some twenty miles to complete it, when Alexandria and its port will be in communication with the Red Sea. The Pasha has constructed this great work at his own expense, and must ultimately derive a large revenue from it, as the tax upon each passenger crossing is ten pounds or fifty dollars.

This being my third visit to Egypt, I am able to judge of the changes that have taken place, particularly since the introduction of the railway. In 1842, when I first made the ascent of the Nile to Upper Egypt, we met only four passenger boats; the past winter the number has been forty, which is much less than usual, owing to disturbed monetary relations throughout the world. Then, Alexandria was a village, surrounded with the ruins of the former city. Now, it is a place of large commerce, with a population of seventy or eighty thousand, and instead of camels to carry one's luggage, and donkeys to ride up a miserable hotel, one finds carriages and four-horse omnibuses around the railway station. The whistle of the locomotive, and the cry of "clear the track," is calculated to wake up the most lethargic races. When I passed through Egypt in 1855, *en route* from the East Indies, I was struck with the changes. We descended the Nile in a steamer from Cairo, which was a great improvement.

Pompey's Pillar and Cleopatra's Needle still stand, towering high, as solitary spectators of the progress of the age.

I find here some familiar faces; the Dragoman who accompanied me to Upper Egypt and crossed the desert to Palestine, meets me with a smile; Paul, who is spoken of in Stephens's work on Egypt, I find again. I have just visited the Mausoleum of the great man Mohammed Ali, the regenerator of Egypt, with whom I once passed an evening with accompaniment of the chilbouk or pipe, sherbet and coffee, talking over the affairs of this country. He was of humble origin, but through his military prowess and energy of character rose to the throne, conquered the Bedouins of the desert, massacred the Mamelukes, dug canals, regulated the embankments of the Nile for irrigation, forced the natives into the army and into useful employments, introduced the growth of cotton, built a fleet, which was destroyed by the allied forces, erected manufactories and palaces; in a word, he was a tyrant, but a benefactor in advancing civilization.

He succeeded in creating a Dynasty for his family, and his remains now are inclosed within the walls of the new and gigantic alabaster mosque, with its pointed minarets, standing upon the citadel inclosure, within the walls of which the unfortunate Mamelukes were shot, one of whom only escaped by jumping his horse over a steep precipice.

I find here some of my countrymen, and a few English, who are returning from the Nile trip, as the season is about over and the water low. In June the rise commences. Some are making excursions to Heliopolis and to the Pyramids, others visiting the bazaars and Schrubra, the garden of the Pasha, which, with its brooks, fountains, fruit, and flowers, is well worth a visit.

The great vehicle of locomotion for the multitude is the donkey, which threads the crowded and narrow streets at a rapid rate, flogged by the boy running at his heels and keeping up the cry of "right, left, legs, arms," in Arabic words. The veiled women ride crosswise like men. Officers in gay costumes go by on richly caparisoned horses; droves of camels laden with merchandise, and Arabs with hog skins on their backs, filled with water for sprinkling to keep down the dust in this warm climate. The smell of otto of roses and other perfumery keeps under other disagreeable odors as you ride through the bazaars. Then comes the cry of avant couriers, who run before and behind carriages, staff in hand, to make way. The Court passes in European carriages with gilded trappings, and outriders in fancy-colored Oriental costumes, the women of the Harem scrupulously veiled, only their black round the eyes being seen. Then comes a drove of goats for the supply of milk. Altogether it is a mixture, such as cannot be described, of all races, colors, variety of dress, but must be found in this city of three hundred and fifty thousand inhabitants, where, particularly as the kemsing winds have just set in, custom demands that every person should appear and snuff the air. The festival continues three days, and the people are out in their best attire.

Two of our guests have just started for Jerusalem, via the desert. Their caravan consisted of twelve camels, a dragoman and servants, with camel drivers, &c., an English lord and his companion. The Arab Scheik taxed him five pounds or twenty dollars per head for the use of the animals alone. I was thankful I had not the same journey to repeat; for to be perched up sixteen or twenty days upon the back of a dromedary is no small task. Another party have left for Memphis, also to visit the monster Sphinx, the Pyramid of Cheops and others, the establishment for hatching chickens by heat, &c., I enjoy these things as souvenirs, having on a former occasion seen and mounted the great Pyramid at Gizeh, crept into the interior chambers and breathed its dust of ages and its close atmosphere. Its dimensions are seven hundred and thirty-two feet square, and four hundred and sixty feet high, and it covers some twelve acres of ground. There are many smaller ones, which are almost equal in size. Herodotus says that one hundred years were employed in constructing the two largest. Pliny says seventy-eight years, and the number of men three hundred and sixty thousand. The facilities for travel in Upper Egypt are greatly increased since my first visit; then we had to procure a boat and dragoman by the month; every article of supply, with cooking utensils, had to be purchased, and a suitable cook selected. The Reis or captain and his crew of twelve men were paid by the month; every delay was to them a profit. Now a dragoman takes upon himself the entire outfit and supplies, relieving the party from all responsibility for a stipulated sum, averaging from five to eight dollars a day per head, according to the numbers. The charges on the Peninsular and Oriental steamers are about sixteen dollars per day. The passengers are abundantly supplied, as you will see; coffee and tea early in the morning, soda water if wanted, breakfast at nine, lunch at twelve, with ale or porter, dinner at four, with four kinds of wine, tea at seven, grog or hot drinks at nine P.M. The servants form themselves into a band and play from eleven to twelve M., and from eight to nine in the evening, for which passengers contribute. The consumption of provisions on board this line is excessive. The French and Austrian steamers have two substantial meals only, and charge considerably less.

There is a general complaint throughout the East of the increased hotel charges and the expenses of life since the Crimean war. I intend returning to Alexandria, and embark via Jaffa for Beyrout. I shall probably visit Damascus, the Cedars of Lebanon, and the ruins of Balbeck from the latter place. When I was in Palestine before, the Maronites and Druses were at war, which prevented travelling in the mountains. I now hope to avail myself of the present opportunity.

# CXXXIV.

CONSTANTINOPLE, *May 1, 1858.*

I find myself at a remote point from Grand Cairo, having extended my route in order to visit the Crimea and other parts of the Black sea.

On our arrival at Jaffa we found some thousands of pilgrims waiting opportunities to embark for their homes. Immense numbers had been at Jerusalem, but as I had passed the Passion Week once in the Holy City, had climbed the Mount of Olives, wandered through the Valley of Jehoshaphat, bathed my eyes in the Pool of Siloam, refreshed myself at the Brook of Kedron, swum in the Jordan and reposed at Bethlehem, I was unwilling to lose first impressions by a revisit. At that period, after a voyage across the desert of sixteen days upon camelback, the Land of the Philistines and the Gardens of Sharon were quite refreshing, but now steam has revolutionized travel, and distance is quite annihilated. There were several steamers in the dangerous roadstead taking away the pilgrims. One of the number had been wrecked and stranded in a late gale, and twenty-nine of her passengers and crew lost. We took away some three hundred, mostly deck passengers, consisting of Greeks, Copts, Armenians, and Latins, from all the countries of the Levant. Such a beggarly looking party of all races and costumes it would be difficult to scrape together. They were penned up like cattle on the deck, men, women, and even children; and you may imagine what effect a heavy sea produced upon the party.

We coasted along the shore of ancient Tyre and Sidon with Mount Carmel in full view, and debarked at Beyroot, a pretty town with picturesque environs, backed by the mountains of Lebanon, and occupied by the Druses and Maronites.

After a sojourn of a few days I took passage for the island of Cyprus, interesting for its historical reminiscences and famous for its sweet wine; then proceeded to the island of Rhodes. The old city is in a dilapidated condition. Earthquakes have made sad havoc from time to time, one of which is said to have destroyed the great Colossus. The old streets of the Knights of St. John, with their armorial insignia upon the fronts of the houses, are well preserved.

Smyrna I found improved. The rebuilding of good, substantial stone houses upon the sites of the burnt districts, where miserable, rickety wooden buildings stood, has greatly changed the appearance of this large commercial city. The fruit trade brings vessels of all nations into its capacious bay. A view from Mount Pagos, where are the remains of an old Genoese fort, embraces one of the most beautiful of panoramas.

Having had three passages by the Lloyd Austrian steamers, I there took the French Messagerie, imperial packet, via the Dardanelles and Sea of Marmora, touching at Gallipoli and other points, for Constantinople.

My souvenirs of this renowned capital of the Sultan are now revived. The visit to the Seraglio and palaces, the church of St. Sophia, the mosques of Sultan Mahmoud and others, and the tombs of the distinguished monarchs, is made by means of a firman. The visits to the bazaars, excursions on the Bosphorus, and to Scutari on the Asiatic shore, and the sweet waters of Europe and Asia, are delightful beyond description. And as I gazed from my windows from the lofty Frank quarters of Pera down upon the Golden Horn, separating old Stamboul from Galata; the Bosphorus, dividing the two continents; the lofty minarets of the white mosques; the deep evergreen cypress of the cemeteries, in contrast with the blooming trees of the Seraglio Point gardens; the forest of masts of all nations; the numerous war and commercial steamers, I am led to exclaim, "This is certainly the most magnificent view of the kind which the eye can behold."

Rio Janeiro for its majestic scenery can only surpass it. The Bay of Naples has its peculiar beauties. The harbor of New York we all admit is lovely. Stockholm, situated upon its seven islands, is entitled to consideration. San Francisco can boast of a noble sheet of water, as well as many other countries, but the palm must be awarded to the position of the Turk.

The allied armies have fought, bled, and expended great treasure, but one discovers few changes for the better. The improvements are in the European quarter chiefly. The sick man may linger along for an indefinite period, but it is doubtful if he can be resuscitated.

We are in the midst of the Ramadan, or fast of the Mussulmans. The faithful partake of neither meat nor drink from sunrise to sunset, during forty days, and consequently cannot be very good-humored. Joyous voices may be heard at the evening meal if one dares thread the narrow, ill paved streets, lantern in hand, and prepared to resist the multitudes of half starved dogs without masters, who are the public scavengers, and breed, live, and die in the streets.

The minarets are now illuminated, and present a pretty appearance on a dark night. During the war the mosques were easily entered, now greater rigor is exercised, and the devout follower of Mahomet who makes his five ablutions daily, washing his hands, face, and feet, at the fountains in front of the mosques, and fasts from morn till night, cannot look with favor upon the Christians eating and drinking, and treading the sacred precincts of his Holy Temple, and defiling it with their unwashed feet.

They look with surprise and astonishment at the wars of the sects in Jerusalem, at the threshold of the Church of the Holy Sepulchre, and the

Turkish soldiery preserving order at the point of the bayonet. Fortunately for the reputation of Christianity the late ceremonies of the Holy Week passed off without scandal in the sacred city.

The Greeks, notwithstanding the efforts of consuls to suppress rejoicings after Lent is over, have had their fireworks, discharges of cannon, &c., with loss of limbs, much to the annoyance of the Turks. The Latins have their rejoicings, and illuminate as in Rome, and the faithful will have feastings and a jubilee when the season of Ramadan comes around, and the penalties of the Koran are complied with.

We have here three Sabbaths: on Friday the Turkish bazaars are closed; on Saturday the Jews keep their Sabbath; and Sunday all the Christian races keep theirs, at least a part of the day. Those who wish to make purchases should select the early part of the week.

Steam has here made its innovation. We formerly had only the small egg-shell caique for the waters about the metropolis; now steamers for ferries and excursions are employed, and packed full. A bridge of boats connects old Stamboul with Galata, across the Golden Horn. Many more carriages are employed, richly gilded with gold. The ladies of the harem are seen more frequently riding out; and the white gauze veils, disclosing only the eyes and nose, seem to be lighter in texture than formerly, showing more of the beautiful features of the Georgian and Circassian beauties.

The currency of the country is unsettled; little but paper and copper is seen; consequently speculation has increased, and the people complain of increased charges making Constantinople one of the most expensive cities in Europe.

# CXXXV.

SEBASTOPOL, *May 12, 1858.*

The voyage from Constantinople up the Bosphorus and to the head of the Black Sea, was made in forty hours, on board of the new steamer Grand Duke Constantine. This was her first trip, and with fair weather, a comfortable one. The Russian Company, through a guarantee of five per cent. interest for a term of years, from the government, have ordered in all fifty steamers, to compete with the Austrians and French in the navigation of the Mediterranean and Black Seas; and it is thought by the travelling public that competition will reduce the extravagant charges on these lines, which is detrimental to commerce.

The great grain city of Odessa suffered but little during the war from the allies. It lies somewhat elevated from the harbor, with private houses, rather scattered, covering great distances, and large public and private buildings of cut sandstone; its unpaved streets, and the immense number of droskeys, grain carts, and other vehicles, with a light clay soil, make it one of the dustiest cities I ever was in. The birthday of the Empress was celebrated in the cathedral, and as a holiday, and in the evening there was an illumination upon the Boulevard, an elevated drive commanding a fine view of the harbor; and the turn-out of fine horses, and carriages filled with ladies in rich robes, presented a scene seldom equalled.

A Russian passport had to be procured for the Crimea. For the information of all those who design visiting Russia, I would say, bring nothing printed, as all books, maps, &c., are seized at the custom-house and sent to the censor office. On leaving, one must advertise three times in the paper his intention of quitting the empire, in order to show that he has contracted no debts, or committed no offences; then a passport will be granted by the police. When I travelled through Finland and the north of Russia, I was provided with documents as bearer of despatches, thereby avoiding all annoyance of examination of luggage, and met with much civility.

I embarked for Eupatoria at twelve A.M., and was landed the following day; it is the first point of debarkation of the united squadron. The town is partially destroyed, and is a small miserable place. The batteries of the allies are still recognizable near Wind Mill Point; these and the Jewish synagogue, of much beauty for this country, are all of interest to be seen. I posted to Sympheropol, the capital town of the Crimea, a distance of seventy-two wersts, or fifty-four miles, passing salt lakes, which are productive, and worked largely for exportation; a long distance of rolling prairie country, with little timber; occasional small streams, with valleys and shade or fruit trees, thinly settled, bearing some analogy to parts of our western country. The city has fourteen thousand population, and is rather pleasantly situated. The hotels are bad throughout the land, and war prices are still maintained. The Greek churches are the prominent monuments, with a great profusion of ornaments, outstripping the Latin Catholics in decoration. From Sympheropol I took a two horse fourgen, a sort of covered baggage wagon, there being no post route to Bourlouk, or the battle field of Alma, in company with a young Russian officer to whom I was recommended, and who kindly offered to accompany me. He had received two orders for his zeal and bravery in the battles and eleven months' occupation of Sebastopol, during the siege, and was a valuable guide and companion. His sister owned the land and village which stands near the scene of combat. The Russians burnt the huts of the Tartar peasants, the mansion house, and stacks of grain, to prevent their falling into the hands of the enemy. We made the thirty wersts, and arrived at nightfall. After the national dish of the Tabaif, a sort of vermicelli paste, baked, with honey and tea, which can be procured all over Russia, beds were made upon the divan in the new stone cottage, and to my surprise and delight I slept upon the folds of the stars and stripes of an American flag, preserved from the wreck of a vessel on the coast.

In the morning, our accomplished hostess, who spoke French like a native, mounted her horse, and we rode over most parts of her possessions, some seven wersts square, comprising the battle grounds, and the different heights and valleys occupied by the Russian, French, and English troops, crossing the Alma at different points, visiting the cemeteries of thirteen thousand slain of both armies, and reading the epitaphs on such few tombs as had been erected.

The route of the invading forces can yet well be traced, by the quantities of woollen and cotton cloth fragments, leathern straps, cannon balls, and débris of all kinds. It was a melancholy sight, and made my companion sad when he recollected many of his companions who fell upon the field.

The name of Alma is taken from the Tartar for apple, of which large orchards existed in the valley, and along the water course. The country was desolated by the war, and the fruit-trees and crops were destroyed; but the people are now returning and building up their little cabins, and commencing the cultivation of grain and the vine, of which they give one-tenth to the land proprietor. The predominant race are Tartars, and they speak corrupt Turkish; they are Mussulmans, or of the Mohammedan religion, and are an indolent people, and without enterprise.

I here left my companion, and had a lonely ride of some twenty wersts over a high rolling prairie, some mountainous country, and deep valleys, which brought me to Batschi Seray, the former residence of Tartar royalty, and could scarcely help believing I was passing the long streets of a Turkish town; their costumes, habits, bazaars, carts, and market stands, all indicating the same. I visited the old palace, with its inclosures, mosques, minarets, cemetery, and tombs of the Tartar kings, some twenty-four in number, before it fell into the hands of Russia. The style of architecture, the fountains, gardens, and chambers of the harem, are strictly Turkish.

Some four wersts hence, on the top of a mountain, is a most curious old Jewish walled and fortified town, called Tschufout Kale, which formerly contained one thousand or more families, but is now reduced to thirty. It reminds one of Pompeii, or the city of the dead, and is fast tumbling into ruins. They date back their emigration from Jerusalem in the early centuries, and while persecution reigned were in their fortresses, but are now scattered to the four winds. The Rabbi and his companions have still the old synagogue, and are well supported by the absentees. Not far distant is a fraternity of monks, who have the steep mountain side walled amphitheatre-like, and a monastery and chapel built in the grottoes of the rock, with the altars and interior decorated with images in gold and silver. On the outside façade, where the precipice projects, are seen the colossal figures of Christ, the Virgin Mary, and Apostles, in figures of gold, which are visible for a mile, and are attractive as a pilgrimage. The lamps and candles are kept constantly burning, as at Bethlehem.

After making these excursions, I proceeded to Sebastopol. Through unavoidable delay, I arrived at nine P.M. of a dark night, upon the shores of the north bay; there were no accommodations for travellers, an unusual heavy sea was on, and the boatmen were unwilling to cross without extortion; I succeeded, however, in getting across safely with my Tartar guide, and found among the ruins of the town one of the two little inns erected since the destruction of the city. Such a scene of devastation as I found, when awakening next morning, I had not pictured to myself. Out of one hundred thousand inhabitants, comprising soldiers and marines, only eleven thousand remain, and one can only judge by the light of lamps and fires, where they live at night; some in barracks, cellars, and corners of buildings where the walls are standing, rudely covered over. The temporary frail huts thrown up, remind one of Texas in its infancy, or the early frame houses of California and Oregon. The government has erected a Greek Church, buildings for servants of the crown to reside in, and individuals have put up some good stores for places of business; but dwellings are scarce, and rents dear.

It is painful to gaze upon the beautiful but ruined walls of palaces, libraries, club rooms, churches, hotels, and private residences, either destroyed by the shot and bombs of the enemy, or exploded by the Russians. You are so familiar with the localities, as shown by charts during the progress of the war, that I shall not attempt a description, but merely state that my time has been occupied in strolling over the devastated city, visiting the ruined docks, aqueducts, and hospital sites, mounting the famous Malakoff and Redan batteries, riding out to the different camp grounds of the English, French, Sardinian, Russian, and Turkish troops, visiting portions of the cemeteries, of which there are said to be three hundred and fifty in number, and a half million of men mouldering in the dust. Cannon balls, bombs, and bullets are still strewn in all directions. Teamsters are employed in gathering and drawing them to the magazines. Some curious persons have lost their lives by picking up and throwing down infernal projectiles, which exploded.

The camps look like decayed villages of rough stone huts; some of the walls of the English are whitewashed, and the door-ways paved with coarse stone, carrying out ideas of comfort. A little frame building is still standing and preserved in a valley, near a spring of water, on our way to Inkerman, some twelve wersts from town, where we dismounted and refreshed ourselves. It was the pavilion of Lord Raglan. On the summit near at hand is a monument to the united forces engaged in the battle; it was raised by the British army. One of the English burial grounds is well inclosed, and has many tombstones. The descent to the plain, and scene of strife at Inkerman, through which the Russians advanced, is a deep gorge, with high palisades of white sandstone, quarried out of the building material of Sebastopol.

Our countrymen are succeeding well in destroying and fishing up the fragments of the Russian wrecked vessels which obstructed the harbor. I have just had the satisfaction of being on board one of the four flats, or caissons, of twenty-five horse power engine each, and assisting at the first success in raising a twenty gun schooner. There are twenty-four sunk, large and small. It is curious to see the divers go down, with their india-rubber suits and helmets, glass eyes, and a keg of powder under the arm for explosion; also the fishing up of copper, iron bolts, portions of the wreck, &c.

# CXXXVI.

YALTA, *Crimea, May 20, 1858.*

A few miles down the coast from Sebastopol, are to be seen the remains of the ancient city of Chersones, and the little bay and port upon which it was situated. It is most interesting to the Russians, as being the spot where the first Bishop Vladimir was converted to Christianity from Paganism, which was the means of establishing the Greek Church, the prevailing religion in Russia.

A chapel is now found upon the spot, where resides a venerable priest, with his colleagues. A new and large church is to be erected upon the site of the ancient temple. During the war, the French, in cutting entrenchments, made discoveries of some valuable relics of marble and sculpture, which are now visible. Under the Tartar dynasty the old city was deserted, and went to decay.

On my way to Balaklava I made a detour to look at the Kamisch camp grounds, and to visit one of the wildest and most romantically situated monasteries to be found. It is called St. George, and with its church, convent, outbuildings, and hanging fruit gardens, on the south side of the craggy cliffs, is well calculated to attract attention, and was known and respected by the army of invasion.

Balaklava is now a miserable village, but when its little basin was occupied by the English and French vessels it must have produced a lively effect. The streets and roads approaching it are well paved as left by the troops. The track of the railroad is still discernible. The black coal depositories show where the iron horse was stalled. The heaps of broken bottles show the consumption of the troops, and reminded me of the Ranchos on the Isthmus of Panama after the passage of an army of gold diggers. The high rocks at the narrow entrance bear the white letters painted by the English—"Powell Point," "Castle Bay," "Cossack Point," &c.

We have had blustering winds and an unusually boisterous sea, so say the residents, giving an opportunity of judging of the fierce waves of the Black Sea along the iron bound coast, which shipwrecked so many of the vessels of the combined squadron.

I here left my horses and droski, and took the post, the usual mode of quick travel in Russia. I had taken out a Padorozna from the authorities for horses from Balaklava to Alushta and then to this place, in order to take the steamer for Theodosie and Kertch, upon the straits of Azof. In this manner I can visit the whole length of the south coast of the Crimea of any interest. The distance to the place named is one hundred and fifty-two wersts, of three-fourths of a mile each, for which one pays six kopecks per werst; the greasing of the wheels at each post station is twelve kopecks, and a gratuity to the driver in addition. Your vehicle is changed at every station. It is a rude wagon, without springs, built in the form of a scow boat cut off at both ends, and about eight feet long, with low wheels. The seat is a net of ropes from the hind stakes, with quantities of hay or straw. The same for the driver in front. Two bony nags are attached, and you are now at his mercy. The horses are kept on the run, the extreme distances in Russia making it necessary, but woe to the traveller who is not accustomed to it. It is wild and furious travelling.

The post houses are furnished by the crown, and are known by the high, square, box-like posts of white and black colors, with distances marked thereon; for instance, on the main line, to St. Petersburgh two thousand two hundred wersts, and in like manner on the side roads. A sitting room is furnished with a sofa, chair, and table, and in case of bad weather, or no inn, one is under shelter, and sometimes something may be found to eat.

The Russian nobility travel in their own carriages, and carry their tea machines for preparing tea, heavy fur cloaks for sleeping, &c. The best and largest hotel in Odessa, for example, gives you a plainly furnished room, with an ofen for heating purposes, if required, and a bed without linen, for from six to ten francs, say from one dollar and twenty cents to two dollars, per day. Bed covering, towels, and lights are charged extra. You take your meals in your own room, or at the restaurant, for which you pay *à la carte*, at the time, or it is put in your bill. You will thus perceive a wide difference from our American plan.

At my first station from Balaklava, I found the Tartar village of Bidar, quite deserted during the war. The occupants of this beautiful valley, filled with pear, apricot, and other trees, had left for Constantinople, and their return is not permitted. In the hands of an industrious people, it would be very valuable.

My next relay crossed the mountain pass, where the sea, valleys, deep precipices, and vineyards presented themselves instantly on the passage of a tunnel, very like a mountain road from Genoa to Spezzia, celebrated for its beauty.

The zigzag road, with short curves, was driven over more rapidly than within my experience, the horses on full trot, or galloping down the mountain. I could hold my seat with difficulty, but said nothing. I timed my watch at the foot of the mountain, and found we had made fifteen wersts in three-quarters of an hour. The Russian youth turned towards me for a look of approbation, pocketed his Navodki, and was soon off for Alupka, the palace of prince Woranzow, the most magnificent private affair; perhaps, in Europe. The grounds, gardens, and vineyards occupy miles, beautifully situated on the Black Sea, sheltered from the cold by a southern exposure. The palace, or castle, is of Gothic architecture, and was finished in 1852 by an English architect. It has been building many years, and is of Crimean granite. Six noble lions, of Carrara marble, in Canova style, standing, crouching, and sleeping, guard the staircase on the water side. Pavilions, a Greek church, a mosque, flowers, fruit trees, and miles of drives, comprise the beauties. Such an outlay as three millions of roubles in this remote country, can only be expected of a Russian noble with two hundred thousand serfs, or more, besides immense wealth differently invested. He lived to accomplish this work, and died, leaving an only son, who resides in Paris.

My next point was Orianda, the new palace and grounds of the ex-empress of Russia, who has never seen it, but is expected this summer. The palace cost only half a million of roubles, or four hundred thousand dollars. It is neat, substantial, well arranged, and is furnished richly, but in good taste. Several of the rooms and fountains are after the Pompeian style.

This is the resort of Russian nobility for the autumn months, during the grape season. Many have estates and splendid residences, but are seldom here. I have chosen the best season for visiting this region.

The little village from which I write is in the midst of lovely gardens, the trees now in full bloom. The grape vines are putting forth their leaves. The mountain side is dotted with occasional Tartar villages of rude cottages, the peaks in the distance contrasting with the green sea, whose waves are breaking upon the gravelly beach, with no sign of shells. The water is saltish, without smell from sea weed.

The only decent hotel I have yet found in the Crimea, is the little one here upon the seaside, kept by a Frenchman and his English wife, both of whom were servants in a Russian noble family. It is a luxury, indeed, with its neatness and comfort; and meals are served up in one's one room, according to European taste. I am the only guest at present. The lulling sound of the waves induces repose, which I much needed, and I am quite unwilling to leave the spot.

The only person in the town who speaks English, except the landlady, is her little boy, who converses also in French with his father, and Russian besides. I find the German more useful than the French for the traveller in this region who does not know Turkish or Russian, as there are several colonies of Germans.

This country being new and sparsely settled, money has less value, and the luxuries of life are difficult to obtain without great expenditure, which will prevent visitors or permanent residents from coming here.

The valleys abound with pasturage, and cattle may be raised in quantities; but the Tartar race is lethargic, and works only when necessity compels. They tell me fresh butter cannot be had at even a rouble, or eighty cents, per pound. Their wants are few, and the pipe is their only solace.

This being the fast of forty days my Fourgon driver, to whom I offered refreshments, refused, but watched the waning sun, procured a bottle of boza, a sort of acid drink made from flour, and bought a wheaten cake, and the moment the last rays disappeared the poor fellow swallowed his morsel, and drained his draught with a good relish. If the land could be relieved from this race by sending them to Turkey, and their places occupied by German colonists, it might be made a flourishing country.

I attended yesterday a village interment. The corpse of the defunct was in an uncovered coffin, draped with crimson plush, and supported by bearers by means of cords two or three feet from the ground. After the ceremonies in the pretty little Russian chapel on the top of a hill, with its stained glass windows, tiny turrets and spire, surrounded by flowers and plants, the body of the man, preceded by the noble-looking Greek priests in full robes, with long flowing hair and beard, crucifix in hand, chanting a funeral hymn, and friends carrying burning candles, was borne to the neat cemetery, where further ceremonies were performed. When the crimson lid, with the white figures of the cross upon it, was nailed on and lowered in the grave, the despair of the women, as they were called upon to throw stones and earth upon it, was frightful, and brought to mind that command of scripture, "Weep with those that weep." Home, with near, and dear, and departed friends, came suddenly in the memory.

The service over, a large dish of rice, covered with raisins and sugar, is passed to the priest, who applies the spoon, and it then goes the rounds, the boys and idlers coming in for the balance.

# CXXXVII.

### TIFLIS, CAPITAL OF GEORGIA, *June 6, 1858.*

From Yalta, I embarked for Theodosie and Kertch, upon the Straits of Azoff. The former place is designated as the terminus of the railroad from Moscow, as its harbor never freezes.

Kertch was partly burned by the allies during the war. Its population is some fifteen thousand. It has a good harbor for vessels bound either for ports in the Black Sea, or going up the Sea of Azoff for cargoes of grain. There were some fifty sail of all kinds at anchor.

In company with the French and English consuls I rode some fifteen miles to the Sea of Azoff, visiting also some extensive Tumuli, or mounds for cemeteries, in which have been found very interesting relics, supposed to be from the reign of king Mithridates, 132 years before Christ. They are quite similar to those I once found in Upsal, in Sweden. The masonry is in a perfect state of preservation. The prairie country extends for miles about the city, and hares are found in great abundance. Our horses and dogs gave them a fine chase.

I took a steamer at Kertch for the Asiatic side of the Black Sea, passing along the Circassian coast with its towering snow-capped mountains. The small ports or roadsteads are occupied by the Russian military, which cannot get a foothold in the interior.

Heavy weather prevented our arrival at Soukum Kale until the second day. It is a bad roadstead, but beautifully situated amid the greenest and most luxuriant vegetation, reminding me of the West Indies or the coast of Venezuela, by its prolific growth. The little colony being among roses and acacias in full bloom, the air is odoriferous with perfume. The inhabitants are, however, virtually imprisoned, the heights being occupied by barracks, and troops who cannot go beyond a certain limit.

The villages of the Abasiens are seen in the distance, and we would fain have taken horses for a ride thither, but were warned not to walk even, beyond a certain point, under the penalty of a ball from the enemy. Notwithstanding the chief of the tribe is friendly and under pay from the Russian government, and we saw him and his harem on board of a steamer put at his disposal, still his people are not reliable, and the Russians cannot penetrate the country, but are obliged to make a detour by Redout Kale, where we landed the following day.

It is bad, like all the other roadsteads along the coast, and frequently the semi-monthly steamers cannot land, and passengers are obliged to wait a month to embark. The breakers were rolling strongly, but we landed at the mouth of the little river Orion, at the miserable town, among such a rough, bandit-looking race as one seldom sees. The captain of the post was very civil, and invited my companion and myself, to dine and occupy part of his miserable quarters, until we could lay in a stock of provisions and supplies for voyage in the interior.

I had imagined and was prepared for a rough time in visiting these regions, but the reality far exceeded my expectations. A Russian officer, attached to the General's staff of the Circassian army, accompanied me, and was provided with a Poderozna, or authority for horses and escort. He came directly from St. Petersburg, and found himself equally disappointed.

We were provided with saddle horses for ourselves and others for our luggage, and supplied with Cossack guides well armed. We made seventy-two wersts in this manner, passing through a lovely country, among trees of great growth and freshness, and woods in places filled with wild grape-vines. There are no general roads, and we travelled mostly by paths.

Our first night was passed under the roof of an old peasant, with his wife, and a little boy and girl in ragged clothes, as our companions. The one-roomed hut was thatched with straw, and had an opening in the side for the escape of the smoke from a fire built on the earth floor in the centre. A few eggs roasted in the cinders were all that could be procured, with the exception of a small kettle to boil our tea water in, and a few bundles of straw upon which to spread our blankets. We had forgotten candles in our list of supplies, and I was quite amused at the manner in which the deficiency was supplied. The woman had some yellow wax, and tore off a strip of her shawl to make the wick, upon which it was twisted.

When we arrived at the village of Marvan we procured post horses over natural roads, in the rudest vehicle in the world, upon seats made of hay, with ropes stretched across.

The country is diversified, consisting of valleys, prairies, and mountains. The mountain roads have been made by the Russian troops, who are found throughout the country, but are miserably made and dangerous. Many small and rapid streams are crossed. Nature in her primeval state presents many beautiful views. The distant Circassian mountains covered with snow, and the plains, remind me of California and Oregon.

Agriculture is of the most primitive kind. Wooden ploughs drawn by eight yoke of oxen are used. Cattle and horses are seen in abundance, but the people have no idea of comfort or luxury. Their caps are of sheepskin, the curled woolly side out. They carry from twelve to sixteen bone or reed cartouche boxes sewed on, or attached to the breast of the dress, and with their long carabines on the back, and cutlasses at the side, are always prepared for an attack of the enemy. This has from long use become the national costume.

The villages more remote from the coast are almost entirely under ground. The huts have the front part raised to the height of half a story, and the roofs run back to a level with the ground, covered with sod and earth; and there they burrow, surrounded by a beautiful and fertile country, capable of producing everything, but still in a state of semi-barbarism.

We were five days making the distance. The stations where horses are changed are mostly miserable affairs—infinitely worse than in the north of Russia, and exceedingly filthy. There are some exceptions, where supplies can be procured. One who makes this journey is called upon to suffer privations and fatigues of all kinds, and any one but a Russian or an old traveller would be disheartened at the outset. This season of the year is the most favorable, and the voyage to this place is now accomplished.


This city is curious to visit in many particulars. It has a population of sixty thousand, composed of a great variety of races, Armenians, Persians, Georgians, Turks, Jews, Russian military, and some twelve hundred officers, who are not permitted to go out without their swords, as the whole country is in a state of war with the Circassians.

Prince Bariatanski is the Viceroy, and has supreme power. There are some three hundred thousand troops scattered over this whole territory, to defend the mountain passes from the attacks of Schamyl and the Circassians, and to keep open the communication with the North and the Caspian Sea.

The city is upon the banks of a rapid river or torrent, and is surrounded by high hills, which renders it now very hot. There is a strange compound of civilization and barbarism here. There is a handsome theatre, bazaars, the palace and garden of the Viceroy and of the former King, now occupied by his son, a fine botanical garden newly laid out, well built bridges and houses for officials, and a colony of Germans living neatly and comfortably, while beside them are the early inhabitants of the country, whose huts are scarcely above the surface, and who live among fleas and filth.

Droskies and other fine carriages and horses, extravagance in the dress of the females, and beautiful Georgian ladies of the upper classes, with their picturesque head-dresses, abound.

Russian gold and silver flows like water; a hundred millions of rubles are expended yearly to keep up the war, which has lasted now thirty years, and is still without much prospect of a close.

This former capital of the Georgian kings, which is some three hundred and fifty wersts in the interior, was abandoned to the Russians about the beginning of the present century; the people finding themselves no longer able to resist the attacks of the Persians, Turks, and Armenians, who ravaged the country and carried off the women and children as slaves.

The commandant of the city, who speaks Russian, German, and French, has shown me many civilities. The only consuls here are the French and Persian; to the former I am also indebted. The hotels are execrable. The French adventurers have succeeded well in the introduction of Paris fineries, as money has but little value; comparing favorably with California in its infancy.

All advise me to pass up through the Circassian mountains to the north, as the weather is now hot, and there is less danger and delay from avalanches, and the passes are less infested by bandits. I shall probably go in company with a Russian officer, and have an escort when necessary.

---

# CXXXVIII.

Piatigorsk, Circassia, *June 12, 1858.*

I must give you some details of the trip to this place, across the Circassian mountains, and over the fortified road dividing the territory of Schamyl; to the right coming up towards the Caspian Sea and the Circassians, and on the left bordering on the Black Sea.

We left the scorching city at five P.M., and were glad to escape the intense heat. We made two stations, thirty-four wersts, when horses were not forthcoming until early the next morning. The station was one of the most miserable on the route, and between filth and vermin we were glad to leave at four A.M.

My companion, a Georgian captain in the Russian service, and myself occupied a Tarantas, a wagon of the country, with a carriage body mounted on long poles, the servant in front.

At seven o'clock we discovered that the baggage had been cut away from the rear of the vehicle, entailing considerable loss to my companion. My own baggage was fortunately in front. Information was given to the officer in command at the next village to send Cossacks in pursuit of the offenders. The wheels of our vehicle showed signs of weakness, and the smith's services were called to cut and renew the tires, much to his advantage, as those who travel in carriages are expected to pay.

Towards sunset of the second day we commenced the ascent of the mountains over a miserably rocky road, at a snail's pace, with eight yoke of oxen, and arrived at a station where the night was passed. It was a lovely evening, pleasantly cool, and the snow-capped peaks of the mountains of El Brus and Casbeck, from fourteen thousand to sixteen thousand feet high, by the light of a full moon, were magnificent to gaze upon.

An early start, with relays of horses at each station, carried us over the zigzag winding roads, which are without parapet walls. The drivers are exceedingly expert in the management of their three horses abreast, coursing along the margin of yawning precipices, hundreds of feet in depth. The mountain torrents and the remains of avalanches did not retard our progress. The season, however, favored us, as travellers are sometimes detained for weeks.

The wild and savage appearance of the country, the rudely constructed roads, the primitive costume of the people, who are partly dressed in skins, and nearly all armed, the fortified passes, the galleries in the rock, the narrow defiles occupied by the Russian soldiery, to prevent the attacks of the Circassians, and the feeling that you are liable to be arrested and carried into captivity, or shot by them, kept up a different state of feeling than that caused by ordinary travel.

We passed several fortresses well provided with soldiers, arms, and ammunition, to protect the road. The men are employed in constructing or repairing the route, as the Russian soldier performs the most menial service, and is not exempt until after twenty-five years. The term is, however, reduced under the present emperor. His pay and supplies are a mere bagatelle, and he is a machine, obeying the will of his officer.

The road is now considered tolerably safe, with the exception of the stations where a ball may be sent through the unsuspecting traveller.

The Russian troops are gradually hemming in Schamyl on one side, and the Circassians on the other. Both are Mussulman races, but have little intercourse, as Schamyl is the leader of a fanatical people who repose all confidence in their chief. The pasturage and tillage grounds have been taken from them, and they are now more closely lodged in the fastnesses of the mountains, and with less means of life. The Circassians on the Black Sea can obtain contraband supplies from Turkey, via Trebizond, and can dispose of their children to advantage, the girls looking forward with pleasure to the sale and prospect of occupying an important position in the harems.

During the war of the allies, Schamyl made a descent when least expected, and carried off two Georgian princesses and their children. They suffered much from cold in the mountains, although well treated. The ransom demanded by the robber chief was his son, who was taken by the Russians when eight years old, and sent to St. Petersburg for his education, besides eight millions of roubles. They not knowing the value of money, ten ox-carts loaded with small coins were forwarded, with his unwilling son, now grown to manhood in civilized society, and the exchange was made, much to the satisfaction of distressed families and friends.

The Circassians are most dexterous horsemen, and fond of adventure among themselves. A man who has not shown acts of daring is little considered; while if he can bring down the enemy, or take him captive in order to obtain a ransom, he has done acts worthy of the consideration of the people. One year since, in the place from which I write, the little son of a physician was picked up by a mounted Circassian, and carried out of sight before the alarm was fully given. A ransom of a thousand roubles was demanded, but the government is opposed to the payment of tribute, and he is still among them.

We arrived the third night at Vlada Kaukas, prettily situated upon a rapid river, or mountain torrent, a pleasant town of Russian creation, the residence of the officials of the district, civil and military, containing the barracks, hospitals, &c. The houses are built of stone, wood, and unburnt bricks, many covered with iron roofs, painted green, as indeed are almost all the Russian churches, which produces a cheering effect after seeing nothing but straw roofs in the interior.

We could here renew our supplies, as it must be remembered nothing can be obtained to eat or drink on the road in these wild countries. The stations are furnished with a few chairs, or wooden sofas, to pass the night upon, and a Semivar, or tea machine for hot water, with which to prepare your own tea, can always be obtained. All other appliances for sleeping, and to support life, you must carry with you, or starve.

At the place named we were detained one day waiting for horses, as the commanding officer had ordered all the post horses for the use of Cossacks, who were in hot pursuit of the enemy, who had committed some depredations.

We were glad to have passed the seat of difficulty in good time. We were not allowed to travel at night, and the whole line upon the steppes, some two hundred wersts, was occupied, up to our arrival at this place, by Cossack sentinels at intervals of a few wersts, generally three together, mounted upon a platform erected upon four poles adjoining their cabins. Each is furnished with a ladder to ascend by, and a straw cover to protect the men from wind and rain. Mounds of earth are also often thrown up as observatories, and their horses are always saddled and bridled ready to pursue the enemy.

Huge stone crucifixes point out the spots where the unfortunate Cossack peasants, sent down for colonization and cultivation of the soil, have been killed.

Some of the Circassians have submitted to Russian rule, and occupy their villages unmolested. A few reside in the Russian towns, consequently they know all that is occurring, and act as spies when necessary. They are a fine-looking race of people, and their costume is picturesque. I have heard Russian officers who have known them personally say, that if they had their way they would not wage war against them, while others go for extermination.

Circassia is to Russia, what Algeria is to France—a military school, a means of patronage for officials, and a source for decorations and honors, at the expense of the empire in general.

On the main road towards Staverpool, at the little town of Gorgiesk, fairs are held twice a year for general supplies.

A detour of thirty-four wersts brought me to this place. Within a circuit of forty wersts are found hot and cold, sulphur, iron, salt and soda springs. I design visiting all of them, and will speak of their qualities in my next. This place derives its name, Piatigorsk, from five small picturesque mountains within sight. It is romantically situated, and may be made a lovely spot.

There are six sources of hot and cold sulphur water, and the government has expended large sums in erecting baths and laying out the grounds in imitation of the Germans; but the distances are so immense, the bad roads and want of accommodations so great, that the Russians prefer going to Germany, now they can have passports. There are some four hundred here, where two thousand might be accommodated with private lodgings. I am the only foreigner here. The military band plays morning and evening, and the little Russian boys and girls, profit in waltzing and dancing upon the gravelled walks under the shade trees, to the delight of mothers and governesses.

# CXXXIX.

STAVERPOOL, NORTHERN CIRCASSIA, *June 22, 1858.*

In my last from Piatigorsk I stated my intention of visiting the other mineral sources. Of these Gelesnovodski furnishes hot iron water, and is one of the few in the world of the hot ferruginous kind. It is romantically situated some twenty wersts from the place above named. It is a village of Cossack peasants, who were whitewashing and brushing up their rude cabins, built of branches of trees trellised or woven together, with a mud coating on both sides, and a coat of white for appearance. The roofs are entirely of straw, and of the most primitive style. A few decent houses have been erected, and the government has built some ordinary baths, and the woods and grounds have some walks and drives cut through. I went out in company with the Director of the Baths at Piatigorsk, which was fortunate, as the season had fairly commenced and no hotels were open, but being introduced to a certain baroness just established in her own house, we had a very respectable dinner.

Some thirty wersts in another direction is the most remarkable soda fountain I have ever seen in any country, called Kissnovodski. Here the crown has expended considerable sums in the erection of bathing buildings of massive masonry. The promenades through the woods are in good order for visitors. The source is about ten feet in diameter and throws out four hundred gallons per minute, bubbling up like soda water or sparkling champagne, being highly charged with carbonic acid gas. It is slightly charged with iron, and is delicious either with or without wine. It is used at the close of the season for bathing and drinking, giving extraordinary strength to the muscles of the body. Such a spring in a civilized and settled country, where there were facilities to get to it, would be a mine of wealth. Salt springs are also found about midway in going out.

A Tartar village lies to the right on the way to the springs first named, and also a village of German colonists about midway, which I visited a few days since in company with a party of Russian officers and their wives. I learned from an old German that the government gave them the use of lands in common, with certain immunities. I also found here an old Scotchman who had nearly forgotten English, having come out with the first missionaries, of whom none now exist. Both these old people had friends in the United States, and you can well imagine their joy and surprise at seeing an American for the first time.

I have had occasion to pass nights in Cossack houses, when horses were wanting at the stations, or it was unsafe travelling after dark, and when the only room in the post station was occupied, and I found the contrast between the tidy, comfortable cottages of the German settlers, and the filthy dwellings and habits of the Cossacks, Tartars, and Kalmucks, most striking.

Their villages are generally from twenty to twenty-six wersts apart, and are about a mile square, with a mud wall or brush fence and embankment all round, and sentinels at the gates. The houses, barns, and sheds are thatched with straw, and sufficiently remote from each other to guard against fire. The streets or roads are one hundred feet in width, and many are planted with trees.

The plains are used for pasture and tillage, and at nightfall the oxen, sheep, goats, and hogs are driven in by the shepherds, when all the boys and girls of the village turn out to drive their respective animals into the fold. They cultivate the ground, and harvest their crops at great distances from the villages, and always go armed.

They are the pioneers of Russian civilization, accustomed to border warfare like our squatters with the Indians. The government sends down villages of them from the river Don, granting them certain privileges, for which they are obliged to keep the Circassians at bay and furnish certain numbers of guards or sentinels, who change about, and are ever ready to pursue the enemy. As fast as portions of Circassian territory are acquired, fortresses and troops advance, and the Cossacks follow up and settle upon the lands. It is a sort of semi-barbarous civilization.

For a distance of some two hundred wersts we have seen no wood of any consequence, the whole country consisting of immense steppes or plains. The small water courses furnish brush for making wicker fences and frames of houses. Artificial turf is made from the straw, hay, and deposit of the barnyards, dried in the sun, and cut in brick form in summer for winter fuel. The ox-carts and wagons are entirely of wood, not a nail being used in their construction. I have counted from fifty to eighty loaded carts at a time, and not a particle of iron could I discover. The wood must be brought long distances from the mountains. The timber for building at this place is brought some six hundred wersts, or four hundred and fifty miles, by land. This is one of the best countries in the world for railroads, and if occupied by Americans the enemy would be conquered by the locomotive.

I passed a couple of days with a Russian nobleman at his village, making a detour of some thirty wersts, on a side route upon the banks of a little river where was quite a forest. As the question of the emancipation of the serfs in Russia is now the absorbing topic, I availed myself of the invitation. In many particulars it reminded me of the plantations in our southern country. Two years ago the village of cottages was burned down, when the proprietor immediately built brick kilns, having materials and wood on the spot, and reconstructed the houses better than before. He is one of the few Russian nobles who attends personally to his estate, and has much of the American in his composition for contrivance. He has three hundred and eighty-four serfs. They work three days in the week for their lord, and three for themselves. He had erected a flouring mill of very rude construction, with several run of stones. Little iron was made use of, as such supplies come from Moscow, and are very expensive. He also had an undershot wheel in the little creek or river for supplying his large garden and fruit trees with water by irrigation, as the steppes or plains suffer much at times from drought. The little girls of the village were busying themselves with gathering mulberry leaves for feeding silkworms, as he had erected a building for the purpose. The women and men were employed in all kinds of agricultural work. He has his overseers, but is quite practical himself. His family was absent, but his home was comfortable, and I was treated most hospitably.

He was willing to join in the manumission of the serfs, now the commands of the government fall upon him. If the serfs are liberated, he can rent his land to them, also sell or rent horses, oxen, &c., and if he employs them, pay wages. His domain is about ten miles square.

Staverpool is the seat of government for northern Circassia. It is a town of fourteen thousand inhabitants, built upon a pretty site in the midst of a picturesque country, and surrounded by hills, and valleys, and groups of forest trees. It is pretty well built, and contains a cathedral, and churches, with domes, spires, and roofs painted green, as usual, presenting a fine appearance. In all Russian towns the churches are the most striking ornaments.

I was presented to the governor, dined with generals and colonels in the service, and passed an evening at a re-union of the citizens in a beautiful woody grove, with a building for dancing and supper, at which figured the glittering uniforms of officers in all the different branches of government employ, and some pretty ladies, handsomely dressed. Paris modes and fineries find their way to the most remote parts. Two Circassian princes, in full costume, were among the number for their first time in civilized society; but like our Indians, did not express surprise at the giddy waltz, or the music of the military band.

# CXL.

TAGANROG, RUSSIA, *June 28, 1858.*

From Staverpool I had five hundred wersts to travel in order to strike the waters of the river Don, at Rastoff, a town which thrives through the increasing grain trade. From thence I came in a tug steamer to this city, on the head waters of the Sea of Azoff.

The scenery on the route is little varied, consisting of vast steppes, or plains, with seldom any timber to be seen, and Cossack villages every twenty wersts and upwards. Immense droves of cattle, sheep, goats, and horses are frequently observed grazing, and cultivation is somewhat better and more general than in the country I had passed through before.

The natural roads over the prairies are easy for horses and for travellers, but quite monotonous. Posting is less difficult, and less dangerous, from the attacks of freebooters, being out of the district of the Circassians, but it is almost as difficult to obtain supplies on the road.

When horses were obtainable, we kept on until late at night, as my companion assured me there was no danger. He was familiar with the roads, and, notwithstanding others lay by through apprehension, and postmasters would not furnish horses after dark, he said at the point where we were, the Circassians could not seize us, and get across the line of sentinels by daylight; besides which, at this season they had their engagements, and can also be traced through the grass. As I was anxious to get on to catch the weekly steamer, I allowed myself to be convinced, and can now rejoice at being out of the reach of the Abassiens, Mingraliens, Georgians, Circassians, and Cossacks.

A few evenings since, at one of the rude stations where we passed the night, a pleasing rencontre for my friend was the meeting of a general en route for his post on the shores of the Caspian. They had not met since they were cadets together, some fifteen years before. He was provided with some choice sherry and some old Havanas, which gave additional zest to an evening in a barbarous country.

This pretty, well-built town, occupied in part by Greeks, who have made fortunes in the grain trade, was sadly mutilated by the fleets of the allies. Many of the ruined houses and magazines have been restored. I counted thirteen cannon shot in the front of the house of an eccentric individual, who had made his repairs, and stuccoed the balls, mosaic like, in the front. The lower part of the city, under the bluff, was entirely destroyed, and the upper part, on the hill, badly damaged.

There are some two hundred vessels, of different nations, in the roadstead, waiting for cargoes of flint wheat, or the lighters loaded with the ordinary kinds, brought from Rastoff, or higher up in the Don. Large quantities are transported from the river Wolga to the Don, and floated down. The fisheries of the river are also important, and quantities of caviar are made from the eggs of the sturgeon, for exportation. The hide, wool, and tallow traffic is also considerable.

A monument to the Emperor Alexander, who died here after his visit to the Crimea, is erected upon the public square. The so-called palace, a large mansion house, where he died, is visited generally by Russian travellers. The room he died in has an altar in it, and the priest who was with him in his last hours still lives, and presides on festive occasions. I noticed here, also, that a few stray shots of the enemy had done their work.

I found one village near Rastoff almost exclusively occupied by Armenians. Their churches are handsome edifices, and will compare favorably with the Russian churches for beauty of architecture, and the towers and cupolas painted white, with green roofs, have a pretty effect. The interior decorations are not unlike the Russian Greek churches, which, in paintings, images, crucifixes, lamps, and candles, are more overloaded than the Latin Catholics.

The Armenians are generally a money-getting race, and surpass the Jews in financiering.

Among the different races which I have found in this country, the Kalmucks must not be forgotten. They remind me of the Chinese as far as traits of feature are concerned. They are mostly employed as shepherds. Their huts are made of a sort of felt, under which husband, wife, and children are grouped together. They use for covering the skins of sheep, and live upon black bread and loppered milk. They kill no animal for food, it being contrary to religious prejudice; but when one dies, I notice the great iron pot is partly filled with water, and placed over the fire in the middle of the tent. The intestines of the beast are boiled with slices of pressed common tea, which comes overland in the shape of cakes, and a soup is prepared for the whole family.

Russia comprises such an infinity of races, some half-civilized, and some barbarian, that it is not surprising, notwithstanding the upper classes are educated, and have the surface, or gloss, of high civilization, that one often discovers the traces of barbarism when least expected. They are hospitable in general, and I have received many civilities at their hands; but nevertheless the proverb, "Scratch the Russian a little, and under the surface you find the Tartar," in many instances is not incorrect. They are trying to improve their condition, but what can be done by a people who rely upon the will of one man, whose word is law?

The routine of Bureaucracy is fearful. The laws are a mass of ukases issued by the different emperors, and many remain dead letters. For instance the Emperor Nicholas, hearing of a great conflagration from the use of lucifer matches, issued an edict prohibiting their introduction, which does not prevent the general use of them; still the ukase is not countermanded. The abuses of officials are also startling. The government was robbed to a great extent during the war by persons who are now living in splendor. Many were detected who had sent their ill-gotten gains to the bank on interest; these sums were confiscated.

The crown has now reduced the rate of interest from four to three per cent. on bank deposits, hoping to induce the people to invest in railroads, but they say they would rather have three per cent. certain than risk their money in new undertakings. There is no spirit of public enterprise among the people, and if there was, every possible obstacle would be thrown in the way by the officers and employees of the government.

The circulation is mostly the Government Bank paper, which is prohibited from coming in if once taken out, and when one leaves the country, to buy gold and silver he must pay a handsome advance, as both of the precious metals bear a premium, and the bank can only be called upon for small sums. The natural consequence of such a state of things in any country is advanced prices for all articles of consumption.

If the last emperor had employed one half the vast sums expended in keeping up a gigantic military force, in improvements to the roads and rivers, and in railways, he would have been a great benefactor to his people.

Much is hoped and expected from the present emperor, who is willing to be guided and advised, while Nicholas was obstinate, and his will was law. I find more liberty of speech and action among the people now than when I first visited Russia, ten years ago, when every one felt as if his neighbor was a spy.

# CXLI.

ODESSA, *July 6, 1858.*

At this season of the year Odessa is only livable and visible after a rain storm, such as we have just had. It then appears to advantage, as the houses are of stone, well built, with metal roofs painted green. The soil is clayey, and the streets broad and unpaved, so that the hundreds of ox carts loaded with grain and the immense numbers of droskies produce a perfect cloud of dust, exceeding anything of the kind in the world. In winter it is very muddy, but at this period of heat without rain, it is a sort of purgatory. In twenty-four hours it will be dusty again, notwithstanding the heavy fall of rain we have just had, rendering the streets extremely difficult to cross. There are magazines or stores in the city for fifteen million bushels of grain.

A great annoyance to travellers leaving Russia is the procuring of passports. All the necessary measures must be taken at the police in person, and the intention of departure must be advertised three times in the Russian Journal, which appears only every other day, making a delay of a week, if fortunately no holiday or festival intervenes. At every point you are taxed for stamp paper, advertising fees, and other items, to sustain the hordes of officers. Your pass for interior travel is taken from you, and a new one has to be made out. Your original pass must be visé by the minister or consul of the country you design visiting, and another is not forthcoming until the chief of the police certifies there are no civil or criminal charges alleged, and then, perhaps, it is too late for the weekly steamer, thereby detaining the stranger against his will for perhaps a fortnight. I am now only in possession of my books and maps, which were seized by the Censor when I entered Russia. The obstacles thrown in the way of travellers should be noticed by enlightened Governments. Through the assistance of the Governor, to whom I went in person, I shall get through with less difficulty. The last act signed is by the Quarantine Officer, without whose visé one cannot get on board of the steamer. Is it any wonder that the progress of this great nation should be retarded? Where would the United States be if our system was as contracted as the European?

I came from Taganrog to Kertch, stopping at Esck, a new town just growing up, at Mariopol, and at Berdiansk, the latter a little city of commercial importance, but whose trade may now fall off, its privileges having expired.

In order to build up a new city, as is the case with Esck, which reminds me of one of our new towns in the West, the commercial tax upon a merchant is taken off for ten years, if he will erect a store at a certain cost in the new city. Large dealers in Moscow, or other cities, find it to their advantage to make the outlay, without ever seeing the property. The system strikes me as a forced one, and after the term expires the town may decline.

The ex-governor of Kertch and myself were the only persons landed at Esck, and the governor drove us around in his drosky, and to his house for refreshments.

I passed a day at Kertch, where I met the newly appointed consul for Soukum Kale, whose family I knew at Tripoli. We visited the governor actual of the city, and dined with the English consul, where were present Spanish, Neapolitan, Sardinian, French, English, and Tuscan ministers and consuls, and I found myself the only non-official at the table, which, however, did not prevent our great nation from having a representative.

I next embarked for Odessa, touching at Theodosie, Yalta, Sebastopol, and Eupatoria, all of which places I had visited before. A telegraphic dispatch had been received announcing the plague on the Barbary coast, where I was last winter, and to which I gave little credence. The alarm, however, was great, and it looked as if we should have to make a quarantine of fifteen days, as the steamer had come from Trebisond, in Turkey. The whole thing was ridiculous; but the passengers at Theodosie were not allowed to land at first, and the excitement among the ladies was quite intense. Having made two quarantines formerly, after crossing the desert to Jerusalem, and from Egypt to Malta, I was also glad to escape.

At Sebastopol I found our countrymen had recently raised a Turkish steamer taken by the Russians during the war. I examined her hull, and found it sound. The engines and boilers were in good order. The upper wood-work of pine was much eaten by the worms, but the painted work was not touched. They have heretofore had every difficulty to contend with, and have divided the property raised, or exploded and fished up, equally with the government; but the crown is now disposed to be more liberal, and the company are to have all they save, giving half the chains and anchors to the government, and are to raise the frigate Vladimir gratis. The wharves are covered with old copper, iron bolts, fragments of wood, water tanks, &c., &c.; altogether, it is a curious collection. It is to be hoped they will succeed, particularly as the English Times has indulged in a side thrust at both Americans and Russians, by announcing the failure of the Americans, and that the harbor must remain blocked up until the worms destroy the wrecks.

Our anniversary was not forgotten by our consul, Mr. Ralli, a wealthy Greek merchant, who has had the honor and little pay for the last twenty-four years. He drove me to his country-seat, where a sumptuous dinner and fine old wines were provided, and toasts heartily drank to the memory of the father of our great country. As the writer was the only native born present, of course a few words were expected from him.

Whether it was by accident or design I know not, but a later invitation was offered from Mr. Matthew, the late English consul at Philadelphia, now consul general here, to dine the same day, but deferred for a subsequent one.

He protests his innocence in the affair of the recruits, which caused his removal, and looks back with pleasure upon his sojourn in the States, where he left many warm friends.

The terminus of a railway in all countries awakes a spirit of speculation, which I was struck with at Theodosie, the projected terminus of a railroad from Moscow, which may be a long time yet in construction. The people were brushing up and making repairs in the dull-looking town, and property was already out of the reach of buyers.

In the suburbs is a Tartar village of mud huts and thatched roofs. While strolling through the Musselman district with my map in my hand, and tourist glass directed to the chain of hills, with their line of windmills, I was surrounded by men, women, and children, whose curiosity was excited to know, either from motives of interest, or dread of having their houses torn down, where the iron horse was to come in, they having of course an indefinite idea of a railroad.

The Russian steamers on the Azof and Black Seas are of English or French construction, and are now manned by Russian officers. Three of the steamers among the number I have sailed in had none but Russian servants, speaking their language only, which is awkward for such strangers as have no knowledge of the same, particularly as the passage tickets include dinner only, and all other meals and refreshments are extra, so that at the end of the voyage the items for the traveller increase the expense from a third to a half. The English and American system is the best for sea steamers, where all is included and payable in advance. For the information of those who desire, it may be remarked that Russia is one of the most expensive countries in Europe to obtain the comforts and luxuries of life in.

# CXLII.

BADEN, AUSTRIA, *July 28, 1858.*

Our steamer left Odessa at six P. M., and the next morning at sunrise we found ourselves at the entrance of one of the mouths of the Danube, with Sulina, the Turkish port, at our left, a small ill-built wooden town, its position reminding me of the Balize at the mouth of the Mississippi, with low banks and marshy soil, covered with reeds and rank vegetation. Large numbers of vessels lie straggling along the wooden wharves, waiting for a favorable wind, and tug boats to tow them up to their destined ports for cargoes of grain.

We had but few passengers; among the number was a Georgian Princess, the grand-daughter of the last King, whom I had met with her husband, a Russian colonel, in their own country. This lady is the sister of the Princesses taken captive by Schamyl, who were ransomed by the Russian government, as mentioned in a former letter. The meeting was the more agreeable, because quite unexpected. The society of a young and beautiful Georgian woman, with all the simplicity and amiability of the lady, speaking the English and French language fluently, as well as her husband, a man of large experience in Circassia, was calculated to make a long trip less irksome than it would otherwise have been.

At four P. M. we arrived at Galatz, in Moldavia, a city of some forty thousand inhabitants, where we changed steamers, remaining there thirty-six hours, awaiting the arrival of the passengers from Constantinople.

A larger boat was now furnished, constructed after the manner of our American river boats, with a saloon on the main deck, abaft the wheels, an upper promenade deck, and a number of cabins upon the forward deck. Our numbers being considerably augmented, the heat was oppressive, and mosquitoes brought back reminiscences of the Alabama and Apalachicola in the spring time.

We landed at Giurgevo, in Wallachia, a small town, the port of Bucharest. Both Galatz and the place named lie upon the river bank, but the principal parts are upon bluffs above. Galatz has a mixed population of all races. As the Principalities are subject to Turkey, the coin of that country is in use, as well as that of all the neighboring states, and the numbers of money-changers installed at short intervals upon the sidewalks, present a curious spectacle.

The language has much of the old Roman in its composition, and one is struck with the names of streets and persons upon signboards bearing analogy to the Italian. The dresses of the peasants also struck me as resembling those worn in Italy. The original inhabitants were evidently

Romans. Their sympathies are, however, more Russian, as they profess most generally the Greek faith.

The river is quite serpentine in its course, and the scenery as we advanced became more varied, groups of forest trees and better cultivation being seen. Turkish villages lie along the left banks with their mosques and minarets, and Wallachian and Moldavian villages on the right.

We passed Silistria, celebrated for its defence by the Turks and defeat of the Russians with a loss of twelve thousand men; landed and received passengers at Mikopol, and at the strongly fortified town of Widdin, and arrived at the Eisernen Thor, or Iron Gate, where the low stage of water obliged the landing of passengers, and we took wagons for the distance of a few miles and found a small steamer of light draught of water, which conveyed us through the pass between high mountains of the boldest and most romantic scenery, a miniature Switzerland, to the town of Orsova, the frontier line of Hungary. Here all the luggage was discharged and carried to the Austrian Custom House for examination. Tobacco, sealed letters, and playing cards were handled without mercy, and some of the passengers had to pay heavily.

We made a halt at Belgrade, the last point in Turkey, and at Semlen near the mouth of the Save. The Hungarian shores were alive with cattle, horses, and sheep grazing.

At Widdin we took on board its Governor, Ismet Pacha, and suite. I found him an intelligent and liberal-minded man. Our sleeping apartments being contiguous we had frequent interviews, and I found he entertained a high opinion of American character and enterprise. He has occupied many important positions, and tells me he has always protected the Christians.

An unpleasant affair has just occurred at Belgrade in the attack on the English consul by a Turkish soldier; he escaped without serious injury. This, however, with the recent massacre at Jiddah, and the murder of the Greeks and attack of the Christians in Candia, have produced a painful impression throughout Europe.

The voyage up the Danube, although offering much of interest, is rather monotonous, occupying seven days from Odessa to Pesth, in Hungary, where the railroad can be taken for Vienna. The distance probably does not equal that from New Orleans to Louisville, which occupies less time, and our steamers afford better accommodations to passengers at one-third the cost.

The Danube Steamship Company have one hundred and five steamers in all, besides barges for towing. The capital employed is very large. Last year, with the outlays for wharves, new boats, etc., they were deficient over a million of guilders. With the further extension of the railways, and the probable free navigation for all flags, the success formerly obtained is questionable.

I spent a couple of days in the capital city of Hungary, which I formerly described to you. It is a fine, well-built, and well-paved city, offering many objects of attraction. Near Orsova the spot was pointed out to us where the crown of Hungary, secreted as it is said by Kossuth, was discovered. A small chapel is erected on the spot.

From Pesth I took the railroad to this celebrated Austrian watering-place. It is abundantly supplied with hot and cold sulphur baths, and swimming schools for ladies and gentlemen. A most charming, romantic, and picturesque country lies about it. The town has a population of four thousand, and there is about an equal number of guests. It is only an hour's ride by rail from Vienna, and consequently much frequented. The bath houses are well built structures, with comfortable quarters for families or private individuals; the ladies and gentlemen have separate entrances and dressing rooms, but generally bathe together in deep square baths, surrounded by a gallery for the use of friends or spectators. They use bathing dresses, which are numbered. It is rather startling at first when one enters, to find a party of gentlemen and ladies walking about, their heads only above water, and engaged in cheerful conversation. Private baths may be obtained, but the masses prefer passing the hour in society, talking over the affairs of the day and making arrangements for excursions and dinner parties.

# CXLIII.

BATHS OF TÖPLITZ, BOHEMIA, *Aug. 21, 1858.*

From the baths of Baden, in Austria, I came to the old capital, Vienna, which I found dull as usual at this season of the year, as all who can get into the country make their escape. A grand work of improvement is in progress here. The old Bastei, or walls which fortified and surrounded the city, are being torn away and levelled. The concentration of business and residences in the city had increased the average occupancy of houses to seventy persons each, or double the number of any city in Europe, and the want of room for extension had caused the building up of some twenty-five suburbs, towns and villages. The admission of light and air will lessen the mortality, which was in greater proportion to the population than in other well-regulated cities.

We came from Vienna to Prague in one day, by rail. Having visited this city repeatedly, and, I think, described the same, I will not hazard a repetition.

Four hours by rail brought me to this celebrated watering-place, which has been used for the last thousand years. The distance now traversed by the locomotive within a day, cost me more than five days' travel, by the posts of the country, before these conveyances were introduced.

I found Töplitz much changed since my last visit, years ago. The railroad now connects it with Dresden, the Saxon capital, within a few hours. The town has about six thousand inhabitants, and the number of guests throughout the season equals that amount. Besides numerous hotels, almost every private house furnishes lodgings, and has a particular name, which one would suppose would exhaust the whole vocabulary of words. There are some eighty bathing establishments of all kinds, capable of accommodating four thousand four hundred persons daily with warm baths.

The many romantic walks and drives, the park grounds of the chateau of Prince Clary, to whom the buildings, bath, and spacious garden where I have taken up my abode belong, all afford an infinite variety for the stranger. The majority of the visitors, however, being here ostensibly for health, there is less life and animation than at the watering-places on the Rhine. The character of the guests is less varied. Russians, Germans, and Poles predominate. Only a few French, Italians, English, or Americans are here this season. Indeed the baths generally are less frequented since the late crisis, and the complaint is general in cities as well as places of summer resort, of the falling off of travel.

In the Austrian dominions gaming is not allowed, which pays all the expenses of the great bathing establishments in the little German Duchies, and attracts a different class of society. Here a tax is levied upon every visitor, called Kur- und Musik Taxe, which I hold the receipt for in Baden and here, and as I design visiting Karlsbad and Marienbad, I shall not be forgotten by the collector or by the Barmherzige Brüder, who presents himself as soon as one gets comfortably quartered in his hotel, for a subscription for the infirm poor of all nations, who are received and treated gratis.

We rise at six A.M.; drink of the mineral waters agreeably to medical advice; walk until eight; partake of coffee, milk, and plain bread, without the accompaniment of fresh butter; bathe at ten; repose, without sleeping, in warm clothing, and avoid stimulants, fruits, acids, and fat or greasy food, as long as under treatment.

This place is indebted to Frederick William III., king of Prussia, who visited it annually for nearly a quarter of a century, thereby prolonging his life, and expended yearly about the same sum our President receives for his full term. Consequently the citizens, as well they could, have erected a monument upon what is called King's Hill, to the memory of their lamented guest.

There is, as usual, a theatre, concert rooms, a shooting house for target exercise, coffee saloons, and music in the open air, all calculated to sustain the drooping spirits of sufferers. I find more persons in little wagons, and chairs upon wheels, drawn or pushed about by servants, than at other baths. I have met with many paralytic cases, but the waters are used for such a variety of diseases, that it would be difficult to enumerate them. Many finish the cure here, after making use of other springs in the early part of the season. It is interesting to hear the counting up of so many more baths, and so much more water to be drunk, before they can escape the exactions of the physicians, and can set their faces towards home, or upon intended travels.

For now nearly a month the friends of monarchy have been expecting the birth of a prince or princess to the crown of Austria. If the former, one hundred and one guns would announce the happy event; but if the latter, the news will fall upon them like a cold shower bath, as I observed two years since in Milan, where the authorities had the great cathedral decorations prepared for the occasion; when the tidings came of another female heir, twenty-one guns only hailed the news, and the celebration was a failure. Amid the expectations of the interested, I notice in the public journal that the empress's health continues good. I also translate literally an article of court news from the same journal, as follows:

"*The Little Wagon of Princess Gisella.*—In Laxenburg the little Princess rides often in a little wagon, to which is attached a little donkey. The governess rides upon a similar animal by her side. The sight is extremely delightful, and excites the most intense interest among the park visitors." Comment is unnecessary.

The birthday of the emperor has just been celebrated by the firing of cannon, ringing of bells, high mass in the church, and music by the band, all of which it is incumbent upon the officials and employees to perform. In order to be conversant with the affair, I attended the dinner given in commemoration, but it struck me that it went off with little enthusiasm, and without that spontaneous effusion of patriotism so marked on public occasions in our country.

Since my last visit, two years since, I find the currency somewhat better. The shinplasters for ten kreutzers, or eight cents, are supplanted by an alloy, and the national bank, on the 13th of October, will make an effort to resume specie payments. It has three hundred and eighty millions of paper guilders afloat, equal to one hundred and ninety millions of dollars. The government of Austria has a debt of two billions of guilders, or one billion dollars, and it is every year increasing the debt. The interest is equal to fifty millions of dollars yearly. What would we think in our country of such a load upon its shoulders? The resources of the country, it is true, are great; but the whole territory does not equal in superficial area the state of Texas. Every source of income is squeezed and pressed out, while the farm laborer obtains only twenty-four kreutzers, or twenty cents per day, not enough to keep body and soul together.

# CXLIV.

MARIENBAD, BOHEMIA, *August 29, 1858.*

Karlsbad lies thirteen hundred and seventy feet above the level of the sea, in a deep narrow valley between steep projecting granite rocks and hills, upon the margin of a little serpentine stream, and from the many points of lookout reached by circuitous paths, gives enchanting views and panoramas. Upon one of the ragged jutting points stands a bronze deer, indicating the Hirschsprung. As the story goes, the discoverer of the Sprudel, or hot bubbling spring, which throws out forty-five buckets of water per minute, was the Emperor Karl the Fourth, in the year 1379, while in pursuit of a deer, which leaped over the precipice, pursued by the dogs, and when found was in a cooked condition in the boiling element.

The town has about three thousand inhabitants, and the Kurliste calls for about four thousand visitors during the season. What is called the wiese, or meadow, is formed of two long rows of houses built against the rocks fronting on the little stream Tepel, spanned by bridges, promenades bordered with shade trees, a quantity of little shops filled with wares and ornaments of every variety, offering a lounge for the ladies. Both sexes sit in the open air and take coffee and refreshments, and the parties are more thrown together, making it more like a family circle than in many other bathing places.

The different springs are so arranged with galleries as to protect from the sun and rainy weather. The walks and ascents are of the most wild and romantic character. Savage scenery and deep woods of thick forest trees, affording exercise and protecting from heat, abound. Altogether the natural attractions are almost unsurpassed on the continent. Baden-Baden and Karlsbad are two of the watering-places of Europe, where within a few minutes' time one may escape the noise and excitement of the multitude, and find himself solitary and alone, admiring the works of nature.

The heat of the spring is 165° Fahrenheit. Objects encrusted with the deposit of this water are polished and prepared in different forms, the colors resembling the lava of Vesuvius, and are quite an article of commerce. Here is seen the crucifix upon Kreuz Berg. Now one stumbles upon a monument to the memory of a benefactor who has built a new walk, or extended balconies or iron railings; then one imagines, in a narrow defile in the rocks, he is entering a graveyard, with slabs to the memory of the deceased, but on reading the engravings in different languages, he finds they are tributes and songs of praise from invalids to the waters for restored health.

After a halt of a few days at this agreeable place, I proceeded to Marienbad. It is also a lovely spot, with newer arrangements than Karlsbad, better bath houses, and larger and better hotels. It lies one thousand nine hundred and thirty-two feet above the level of the North Sea, and contains only about one hundred and twenty private houses. Nearly six hundred thousand jugs of this water are sent out, and it finds its way to all parts of Europe. The entire spring grounds form an English park, with trout brooks running through, and are particularly adapted for those who wish to escape the bustle of the world to take care of their health while here in this quiet valley surrounded by hills and pleasant walks. Nature and art together offer everything for the recovery of the lost blessing.

The sources here, as well as at Karlsbad, are various, and the springs are built over. The Krews Brunnen has a colonnade of seventy-two Ionic columns, with a long hall connecting for bad weather. Before the same is the promenade, under the shade of lofty trees, with music morning and evening. Every guest has his vari-colored Bohemian glass, and takes his turn at the fountain of health, at intervals of a quarter of an hour, with a walk in the meantime.

A bright Sunday morning at Karlsbad announced the long expected birth of an heir to the Hapsburg dynasty. The bulletins gave the information that it was a crown prince, and accordingly a hundred and one guns were fired, all the church bells were rung, a Te Deum was performed, and the officers military and civil, with their trappings and orders, paraded through the streets much to the edification of the peasants, in their picturesque costumes, who were attracted to the town by the holiday. At night the hills were illuminated with the lights representing the double-headed eagle, with the letters F. J., a twinkling star, and E., signifying Francis Joseph and Elizabeth.

The great achievement of the submarine telegraph strikes all with amazement, and the masses begin to comprehend that America is considerable of a country. The peasants have heard that grain in our country is sowed, harvested, threshed, and cleaned by machines, instead of manual labor, and the inquiry is, how is it possible?

Our failure in commercial affairs, through extended enterprise, improvements, and fast living, made Europe feel our importance, and from which it still suffers. We retrenched, stopped buying goods, and economized in public and private outlays, which cannot be done here with their standing armies and expensive court charges; and now I remark our banks are loaded down with specie, new gold discoveries are added to the stock, and only the movement of commerce is needed to put the wheels again in motion.

What would our farmers say if every head of cattle sold, paid a tax of two dollars for slaughtering privilege, and smaller animals in proportion; and every sale of houses and land from five to ten per cent. to the crown.

Hotelkeepers and owners of private houses, for neglect in announcing to the police the harboring a friend or stranger over night, have to pay from five to ten guilders.

# CXLV.

Copenhagen, Denmark, *Sept 12, 1858.*

I had not the remotest idea of revisiting this northern region when I wrote you last; but such are the extraordinary facilities of locomotion in this age, that one finds himself within a few days transported hundreds and thousands of miles. I was on my way to Swinemunde, on the Baltic, for sea bathing, when I heard that my old friend Captain Irminger, with whom I visited Caraccas, La Guayra, and Porto Cabello in Venezuela, and the Island of Curaçoa, and who landed me on the small island of Beati, south of Hayti, many years since, from the brig-of-war Örnen, was now residing in this city as admiral of the Danish fleet, and I felt that I could not resist the desire of seeing him again.

I can scarcely realize the fact that at this time last year I had just returned home for a visit, and have since passed over so much ground in Europe, Asia, and Africa. It seems but yesterday that I was climbing the mountains of Circassia, or travelling rapidly over the steppes of Southern Russia, or wandering through the ruins of Sebastopol, passing in review within the year Arabs, Egyptians, Turks, Circassians, Georgians, Greeks, Hungarians, Moldavians, and a host of other races; but when I reflect that space is now almost annihilated, I must be reconciled to the fact, and turn my attention to the quiet and peaceful Dane, and mark the changes, if any, since I saw him for the first time.

From Marienbad I came twenty miles to Franzensbad, not remarkable for its position, but somewhat for the healing qualities of its waters, of which about two hundred thousand jugs are sent away, and about two hundred invalids visit it annually.

What struck me as most singular are the Schlambäder, or Turf Baths, charged with alkali, salt, and iron. One large bath house is adapted to this use. A number of men are employed digging and wheeling in turf, which is broken and ground in a mill, not unlike the breaking of clay for brickmaking. A steam engine of sixteen horse power is employed for this use, as also for pumping and for the heating of the water reservoirs. The bath tubs are mounted on wheels, filled with the black mixture, like thick mud, and rolled through the inner courtyard and in the outer door of the bath rooms. The patient takes his bath and then jumps into another of equally hot water, for washing and cleansing himself. The cost of such a bath is only half a dollar. They are said to be extremely strengthening after the use of other baths and water drinking, and particularly useful in rheumatic and paralytic afflictions. A couple of days was quite sufficient to familiarize one's self with the springs, grounds, advantages, and disadvantages of the locality.

A ride of thirty-five miles by post, and one bids adieu to Bohemia, in Austria, and strikes the frontier of Saxony on the railroad to Leipzig, a city celebrated for its fairs. It has seventy thousand inhabitants, and is surrounded with pretty garden suburbs. Among the number is Gerhard's, where is the monument to Prince Poniatowski, who lost his life in jumping his horse across the little stream Elster, which runs through the city. This was at the famous battle of Leipzig, of 1813.

I arrived on a Saturday evening. The next morning service commenced in the Protestant churches at half-past eight, and continued till half-past ten. Numerous congregations attended, and listened to earnest, faithful preaching. During the exercises all places of entertainment are closed, but opened afterwards for necessary purposes.

The beautiful walks of Rosenthal, and oak woods, that extended to the village of Gohlis where Schiller wrote his Don Carlos, were fully occupied with promenaders after dinner, and the many public gardens filled with the multitudes partaking of their coffee and lager beer, the men smoking their pipes and cigars, women embroidering and listening to the bands of music, and children with their nurses amusing themselves upon the grass. All seemed happy and quiet, and as the evening approached some wended their way to the summer theatre, in an open garden, others to their homes. Such are the customs, and such the force of education even in the land of Luther's reformation.

I made a halt of two days at Leipzig by way of reviving my recollections, and spent a day at Halle, on the river Saale, noted for its university—a very old city, of thirty thousand inhabitants, offering nothing of particular interest. The railroad passes through Gotha, Dessau, and Wittenburg, all of which places I had formerly seen in detail before this mode of conveyance existed here. As I partook of some refreshment at Wittenburg, which I once described to you, I inquired if the old town was as much a place of pilgrimage as formerly. The reply was to the contrary, since the railroad passed through the people had no time to stop. It had once cost me a long journey to visit the houses where Luther and Melancthon lived and wrote, and where they lie buried.

I also looked in upon friends at Berlin, whom I had left eighteen months before, a picnic party in the country being the result, and made a visit to the grounds of Baron Humboldt, where the remains of the illustrious traveller's parents are entombed.

Governor Wright drove us to Charlottenburg, the royal residence. At the opera in the evening the young crown prince of Prussia was present with his new bride, young Victoria. A sojourn of three days in a city which I had visited so repeatedly, and in which I had almost gained a residence, was brief, but I was *en route* for the salt breezes of the sea, and two days later found myself walking ashore from the good steamer Geiser in the well known port of Copenhagen.

The admiral accompanied me up the coast by steamer some thirty miles to Helsingsen, and visited the famous old castle of Kronburg and its fortifications, whose thirty-six pounders reach the Swedish coast opposite, but as the Sound dues are now compromised with all foreign powers, the neat and formerly flourishing town looks cheerless. The neighboring bathing place, Marienburg, if once brought into notice, would help to revive it.

Omitting the Dardanelles, few straits are so much used by vessels as this passage. A strong north wind was bringing in many ships, while almost an entire fleet were at anchor waiting to get out.

The settlement of this knotty Sound question is a source of gratification to all ship navigators, and the result, I trust, will be quite as advantageous for Denmark.

A ride of twenty-two miles from the city to the castle of Fredericksborg, with the visit to the beautiful grounds and the interior of the immense edifice, with its richly decorated saloons, halls, church, and picture galleries, and return, occupied a full day, even with fast horses and equipages from the royal stables.

My friend ranks as chamberlain to the king, and presented me to his majesty, whom we found with his master of ceremonies on a fishing excursion. He is passionately fond of angling, and had already caught sufficient for a good dinner, which he had served in a little summer-house, upon a small island in the lake. He received me cordially, and we had a long chat in French together, and he assured me I should always be welcome in Denmark. I enjoyed a lunch in the palace, a stroll in the flower and fruit gardens, and through the extended park, and immense and majestic Black Forest, a glance over the beautiful lakes and picturesque sheets of water, and the return drive to town, and the setting sun found me at a family dinner with one with whom I had passed through many interesting scenes nine years before.

# CXLVI.

SWINEMUNDE, PRUSSIA, *Sept. 20, 1858.*

In my last communication from Denmark, space did not permit a description of many objects of attraction in and about Copenhagen, which might afford pleasure and information to the tourists, most of whom, however, wend their way to the south of Europe.

The celebrated Danish sculptor, Thorwaldsen, left his fortune for the founding of a museum, in the court of which repose his remains, surrounded by the models and many of the originals of all his great works of art. The government collections of antiquity, from the earliest occupation of the country, when hatchets and weapons of stone were only known, marking the various periods of civilization, and improvements from wood and stone to iron and steel, are of great interest.

The visitor can form a pretty accurate idea of Iceland, Lapland, and Greenland life from the many objects of costume, boats, sledges drawn by dogs, &c., in use in those countries. The suburbs of the city abound with beautiful gardens, and places of public resort for concerts, summer theatres, and amusements for the masses, who flock thither on festival occasions. The now gay appearance of the city, and the air of comfort among the people, struck me favorably, having seen them first during the Schleswig-Holstein war, under disadvantageous circumstances.

By steamer I came to this place, from which I write, lying upon the island of Usedom, about fifty miles from Stettin, upon the river Oder. It is a harbor, bath, and garrison city of five thousand inhabitants.

The abolition of the Sound duties has proved of great advantage to Stettin, to this place, and indeed to all the Prussian ports of the Baltic. They should thank our government for the initiative measures in the matter. Denmark felt aggrieved, without doubt, at our obstinacy, but eventually it will probably be for her interest, as the revenue fund, the respective sums contributed by different powers, will perhaps quite equal the former receipts, particularly after passing through the hands of many office-holders.

The communication daily between this place and Stettin, up the river, the departure and arrival of sailing vessels, steamers for Sweden, Denmark, and Russia, gives an additional interest to bath guests, whose numbers amount to perhaps a thousand at some periods of the season. The bath-houses for both sexes lie about a mile from the town, upon a beautiful sandy beach, and are reached by shady walks for those on foot, or by good carriage roads. The excursions are by steamer to the island of Rugen; by carriage to another bath called Herrings Dorf, prettily situated among leafy groves, with a delightful and invigorating salt atmosphere. A village of fishermen is found in the vicinity, who furnish a good supply of the eatables of the briny sea. The weather is still mild, the water sufficiently warm, and the baths are considered serviceable until the first of next month. It being however late, the majority of the guests have departed, leaving the theatre players with a light audience, and the weekly balls thinly attended. The house owners can repose for the winter upon the summer harvest, until spring, when the whitewashing, painting, and little flower gardens must be looked after, and made as attractive as possible, to the eye of the tenant.

The new fortifications here are of remarkable strength and beauty, effectually protecting the narrow entrance to the harbor. The brick lighthouse, two hundred feet in height, ascended by a spiral staircase of three hundred steps, is provided with the French Reflectors, and can be seen for many miles. A view from the top over the sea, the river, and the surrounding country, well repays the climber. Our worthy German vice-consul, Herr Krouse, and his excellent family, have offered civilities tending to make my sojourn very agreeable. The soil is sandy, the streets unpaved, and in some respects I am reminded of Cape May; but an excursion a few miles brings one to dense pine forests, then to fertile pasture fields, where fine crops of hay have been gathered; then come turf meadows, with inexhaustible quantities of fuel, which, strange to say, after being dug over a few years is found to be renewed. These belong to the Crown, that leases them out for a term, for extracting or cutting, and derives a large revenue therefrom. Then we ascend a high hill covered with beech trees, affording an extensive and enchanting view of the neighboring country. At one point some four thousand acres of land are covered with water, or shallow lake, which is in process of being reclaimed, or pumped out, after the system of Holland. Altogether, the country has attractions for one accustomed to sights where nature is more lavish of her gifts; but those from the flat lands of the north of the kingdom, who smell salt water for the first time, are quite in raptures, and chant the praises of the baths of Prussia's most prominent watering-place.

On inquiry I find the laboring classes are better paid here, as is the case in most sea-ports, than they are in the interior. In Denmark the condition of that class seems easier, and there are less dispositions to emigrate. The female portion of some parts of Germany are the most entitled to sympathy. They are made slaves and beasts of burden, and ill paid for their services. Even in hotels where the wirt, or master, taxes in his bill eight silben groschen (or twenty cents per day) for service, not including the *porter* or *boots*, the poor domestics get in many cases only twenty-four thalers (or eighteen dollars) per year, and where the good will of the traveller makes a donation in many cases it is extorted from them under penalty of dismissal. More would emigrate if they had the means to get away, and would be industrious and valuable citizens in any country. The tender feelings of Europe, through incendiary works and pamphlets, have been so excited that, as Americans, we are called upon to rebut the charges of inconsistency of slave-holding under our republican system, as if *we* at the north were responsible for the south, and can only reply that millions on the continent might well envy the well-fed negroes upon southern plantations.

It is to be regretted that our laws are so lax in the punishment of crime, and that so many high-handed examples of public outrage occur, all of which are portrayed in glowing colors in the European journals.

# CXLVII.

FRANKFORT-ON-THE-ODER, PRUSSIA, *Oct. 15, 1858.*

Having formerly seen Austrian and Russian Poland, whose capitals are Cracow and Warsaw, I was induced to make the detour on my route from Dantzic to look in upon Posen, the chief city of Prussian Poland, which by rail was soon accomplished.

Among the forty-five thousand inhabitants ten thousand are Jews. I came in on Saturday, their Sabbath day, and on a festival occasion, and thus had a good opportunity of seeing the multitude, as also the wealthier classes, upon the promenade, and the many pretty faces of the Hebrew women. They have recently erected a splendid synagogue, as is the case in Frankfort-on-the-Maine, Pesth, in Hungary, and other places. The Jews, as a people, are acquiring wealth and importance, and making advances in science. Had they the same privileges enjoyed in our country, the distinction between the races would not be so marked.

Among the twenty-three churches of the city, a number of which I visited on the Sunday, the newly rebuilt Dome of the thirteenth century contains the Golden Chapel, in which are placed the bronze gilt statues of two Polish kings there interred. High mass was being celebrated in the Latin and Polish tongues when I visited it. The original Bauer, or peasant costume of the country was well represented. It is picturesque but somewhat ridiculous, fashion's innovations not having yet reached it.

In the Stanislaus Church, which is of strict Italian architecture, with its marble statues of saints, illuminated glass windows, altars, pulpit decorations and paintings, I could fancy myself in the Pope's dominions.

The Poles are decided Romanists, and cannot be converted readily by the Russians to the Greek faith, or by the Prussians to the Evangelical. The Prussian or German population is about one-third professing the Protestant and reformed religion. The balance are Israelites and Catholic Poles.

The city is fortified in the strongest manner, with walls, batteries, gates, and trenches, throughout the entire circumference, and contains immense barracks for the soldiery, stables and magazines of supplies for quite an army, if required. Several thousand troops are here stationed.

One sees no prospect for the regeneration of Poland. To occupy a position under the government the young must acquire the German language, notwithstanding their prejudice and hate of their subduers. They are divided up between three powers, and get little sympathy from the great nations they looked towards for relief. Little by little their identity will be lost, and they will become part and parcel of the governments which deprived them of their liberties.

When I look upon and examine the bulwarks of defence newly erected, and in progress of erection, at Swinemunde, Stettin, Konigsberg, here, and at Custrin, I am not surprised that from one-third to one-half of the whole revenue of Prussia is employed in the army department. These are besides only a small portion. Look at the immense establishment of Ehrenbreitstein, the Gibraltar of the Rhine; at the fortress of Mayence, and the many others on the frontiers. How thankful should we be as a people that we are not obliged to tax every article of food put into our mouths, every garment we wear, and abridge all pursuits and pleasures to sustain masses of soldiers and hordes of officers for defence against our sister states, thereby employing the youngest and most active of our youth, incapacitating them for other pursuits, and demoralizing the society of wives and daughters.

Dirschau, where the road branches off for Dantzic, has one of the finest Gothic station houses which I have seen in the north of Europe. The line belongs to the government, and the iron bridges over the river Weichsel or Vistula at that place, and over the Nogat at Marienberg, in connexion with the old castle, formerly the seat of the grand masters of the German Order of Knights, altogether attract many visitors. The old town in itself, for its antiquity, is worth a visit, but the castle is of much interest to Germans. It was built in the thirteenth and fourteenth century, during the conquest of the country, and rebuilt by the government from 1819 to 1820. The saloons are beautifully arched, and one of them is sustained by a single column gracefully supporting its burden not unlike the branches of the palm tree. A cannon ball still sticks in the wall, thrown by the besieging Poles, from which the centre pillar barely escaped.

The portraits of the Knights, with their names and coats of arms, were, for me, in some respects souvenirs of the original Knights of St. John, from which the order sprang, and of whose monuments I found so many in the islands of Rhodes and Malta. The antique figures, weapons, and coats of mail are to the people very curious.

Frankfort-on-the-Oder is in steam communication with Stettin. It is a dull city for a population of thirty thousand persons, although active during its four annual fairs, when it overflows with purchasers and sellers from all parts of Germany. Many of its warehouses are afterwards closed until the season returns, which gives it a melancholy appearance. Its suburbs and gardens, however, are pretty, as indeed they generally are in Germany, and the people have great taste for flowers and plants, as is noticed in the windows of the humblest village cottage.

I had passed through here twice before, but now I hold up for a rest, for which this city is well adapted, where nothing remarkable demands attention. It is a mistaken notion that the tourist lives a life of pleasure and indolence; on the contrary, untiring labor, application, and energy are required to enable him to profit by his travels. One is rejoiced at times to get to some quiet spot where no obligation is felt to take advantage of the sojourn, and have time for repose and to review the ground passed over.

The government is building new salt stores here upon the river bank, that article being a monopoly. Strolling along I observed some sixty men employed driving piles for the foundation, with only two drivers. I counted thirty men, each with cord in hand, a wooden handle thereto attached, and all fastened to the main rope. At a given signal up went the hammer, and down it fell upon the head of the pile. I was so astonished at the loss of power I asked the overseer why he did not use a machine, and that with six men I could accomplish more work than with his sixty. He answered they had none. I observed he would save the cost in a few days. Then an officer remarked that machines were a great curse, as they deprived the laborer of employment. The other dissented thereto, and added that they could not get men enough even at ten silben groschen (or twenty-five cents) per day. Think of that, where coffee is from thirty to forty cents per pound, sugar fifteen cents, and meats and rents in proportion, and tell me how the poor man lives!

A few days ago I met at a station an under forester in crown employ, with his wife and four children. He was being transferred from one domain to another. I asked him how much salary he had. He replied, ten thalers per month, or one hundred and twenty per year, equal to ninety dollars of our money. I inquired, "How can you get through the year?" The reply was, "I must; rye bread is now cheaper, and water costs nothing." A young girl was also waiting with a free passage ticket from her brother in America, via Hamburg to New York. Her position was evidently envied.

# CXLVIII.

Hamburg, Germany, *Nov. 5, 1858.*

In the extreme north of Germany lies the grand duchy of Mecklenberg, a country less visited by travellers than most other parts of the Vaterland, whose institutions are peculiar to itself, and which is not included in the Zollverein, or Tariff Union. As it was the last of the German States I had not seen, I was desirous of visiting it. The lines of railroad from Frankfort-on-the-Oder, where I last wrote you, conveyed me to Schwerin, the capital of the Duchy.

It has a population of twenty thousand, and can boast of one of the finest schloss, or palaces in Deutschland. Wonders never cease. I was astonished to find this new Gothic edifice, which stands upon a small island, and upon which some millions have been expended, and could only wonder how in the nineteenth century the potentate of a small territory could gather together and expend such sums in extravagant construction. The saloons, halls, and dining-rooms, as well as bed-chambers, are luxuriously finished and furnished in modern style. A spiral staircase from the first floor to the upper apartments is of black marble, and the railing of bronze gold gilt. The church, or chapel, is richly decorated, and the windows are of stained glass. Several sentinels were under arms; permission was granted, for a fee, to inspect the whole premises, with the hot-houses, and obtain a fine view over the beautiful lake, reminding one of the sheets of water in the western part of our state.

The peasants are still attached to the soil, without the privilege of obtaining title for lands. The landholders own large estates, and are wealthy. The duties upon importations are light. This class of citizens can obtain at small cost all articles they require. The crown is possessed of an immense domain, which brings in large revenues, enabling the grand-ducal family to expend large sums without extorting from the land proprietors; but inquiry may be made, "who pays?" the answer naturally is, "the labor of the peasant." Time will make a change. The downtrod workman, if he can raise the means, will find his way to America, and they will have to introduce hired cultivators from the neighboring countries, or abandon the system.

Rostock and Weimar are their sea-ports on the Baltic; the former has a population of twenty thousand, and is quite noted for its shipbuilding. I found many vessels lying in ordinary for want of employment, growing out of the commercial crisis, and but few on the stocks.

Mecklenberg not being a manufacturing state, and the wealthy land proprietors not being able to loan on home securities, turned their attention to interest in shipbuilding, and are groaning over their losses.

A horticultural, agricultural, and mechanical exhibition was being held, which was of interest. The farm implements were of a heavy character, and capable of much improvement. As in most German towns, the walks and promenades have received much attention. The old fortifications and ramparts have been planted with shade trees and flowers, and afford a delightful stroll for the inhabitants.

The Blucher square, or place, contains the bronze monument erected to the memory of the marshal, celebrated at Waterloo, who was born in Rostock, in 1743. The parks, grounds, and lakes in and about Schwerin are as lovely as could be desired; but the residence city, notwithstanding its arsenal, port, and other public buildings, has the air of a forced growth.

An hour's ride by railroad brought me to this great commercial, free trade city, with its population of one hundred and sixty-five thousand.

The great fire of 1842, which burnt over seventy-one streets and squares, and destroyed nearly two thousand houses, was the cause of making the new city as beautiful as it now is, and one sees no traces of the great conflagration; but, on the contrary magnificent rows of tall, solidly constructed houses, public buildings, churches, exchange, immense hotels, of American internal arrangements, a number of which are situated upon the Alster Basin—a fine sheet of water, with broad avenues and sidewalks surrounding it. The streets of the old city are narrow, and paved with round cobble stones, dirty and dreary, making the contrast more striking. Almost continuous walks upon the site of the old walls surround the city, and are planted with shade trees and shrubbery. The view of the harbor and the Elbe, with its shipping, and the forests of masts, obtained from a height, is truly grand.

Hamburg being strictly a commercial city, and divested of the military parade, titles, orders, and the pomp of a court of monarchical cities, strikes an American coming from other parts of the continent, as being more like a Republican metropolis. The peculiar costume of the women water-carriers would be exceptional. Altona, in Holstein, belonging to Denmark, has almost grown into the city.

The gates are closed at night, and toll must be paid by every person passing, according to the lateness of the hour. The currency of the city is its peculiar kind—*shilling, and mark Banco*; the former worth *two cents, and sixteen for mark*. The traveller in Germany, in passing from one frontier to another, must dispose of the small coin of the country, which may be of no value after a few hours' ride by the railway. A gentleman bound for Russia, whom I lately met in the cars, wished to purchase some fruit for his wife. He was on his way from Paris, did not speak German, and pulled out a handful of coin which he had received in change along the road, none of which would pass. The train was almost moving, and he was giving up in despair, when I came to the rescue. Mecklenberg, Denmark, and even Bremen change, is of little value here, although only separated by the frontier. A story is told of a Frenchman, who, starting on a tour through Germany and Italy, as an experiment put a twenty-franc gold piece in his vest pocket, changing the same into the currency of each country as he passed, and on his return found the entire sum had gone into the hands of the money-changers.

# CXLIX.

HANOVER, GERMANY, *Nov. 29, 1858.*

I thought I had quite finished up my peregrinations in the north of Germany, but I found I had left unvisited parts of Schleswig Holstein, which, since the war of 1848, has occupied so much of the attention of German and Danish diplomats.

This country is populated mostly by Germans, and that language is generally spoken, but it is governed by Danish officers and the military, in as mild a form as possible; the ill-will and hatred of the inhabitants, however, is so great, that little social intercourse is kept up between them. The currency is Danish, but German coin passes for nearly its value, as the trade with Hamburg, and the direct communication by railroad with Kiel and Schleswig, keeps up the German influence, to the detriment of Copenhagen. After long delay, and bitter recriminations and threats, the Danish king has granted many concessions, and a constitution for self-representation. The people hope, and, with Germany, desire its union with the Vaterland; but the balance of power is such a delicate question in Europe, and the jealousy of governments towards each other so great, that the matter may be put off until, perhaps, a revolution brings a change. The quickest and easiest communication with Copenhagen is, via Kiel, by rail, a distance of seventy miles from Hamburg, where steamers are found in readiness for embarkation.

Every stranger that visits Hamburg, if time permits, should make an excursion in Holstein, if only to get a passing view of nature's beauties, of picturesque lakes, meadows, and fields, with their hedges.

Were it not for the three gates, one would scarcely know he had left Hamburg in driving through the city of Altona, in Danish territory, to take the railroad for Kiel, as the two cities are nearly grown together.

Kiel has some fifteen thousand inhabitants. Its environs may be called beautiful. The forests of beech and other trees along the water's edge, with bathing places, and some elevated points of view, make it a desirable summer residence. It evidently has much improved of late. The country mansions and gardens bear testimony of the fact. The fish market is abundantly supplied, and what is better, there is no duty, as is the case the moment the German frontier is crossed in the interior. Among the delicacies, in smoked articles, are the "Schnebel," and large sized eels, which are exported in great quantities to the interior. The oysters used in Germany are mostly from the North Sea. They are much smaller than ours, and have not unfrequently a coppery flavor. Salmon and lobsters come mostly from Norway. Hamburg is celebrated for its basement rooms, or Kellers, where are found all the dainties that land and water furnish.

Kiel has its monuments, public buildings, and attractions, but nothing very striking to the general traveller. Its harbor is fine and deep, and here lay at anchor, near the shore, the entire fleet, at one period during the war with Russia.

The terminus of the railroad which leads to this city is at Harburg, the new rival of Hamburg, upon the Elbe, and only eight miles from the last-named place. When I was last there, in 1855, the inundation of the river had flooded the island of Wilhelmsburg, carrying away houses, cattle, and crops, and destroying millions of property in the lower part of the metropolis. Hundreds of persons were shelterless. We were aroused at midnight in the midst of a terrific rain storm, by the alarm guns warning the occupants of basements and one story dwellings, to save themselves from drowning. When we took the steamer for Harburg, in passing the island we saw only the tops of trees where now I pass in an omnibus, over a well cultivated country, with dusty roads, and the people complaining for want of rain.

A few miles below lies Stade, a small town of six thousand inhabitants, which gives the name to the Stade Zol, or imposition of the River Elbe dues, which our government is trying to induce the Hanoverian authorities to renounce.

Harburg has made much progress, and grown to be quite a city under the protection of the Hanoverian government, and favors in the way of duties and manufactures.

The route to this place is an uninteresting one, tying in part over the Luneburger Haide or Heath, which is without cultivation. I perceive, however, that advances are made in the way of irrigation, and it is pleasant to see entire waste lands, by the use of water, made to produce bountifully. It called to mind an experiment of a rice garden, and olive and almond trees, which Mehemet Ali produced upon the white sand of the Egyptian desert, by the use of the Persian wheel, driven by oxen; and it struck me that the Arabs regarded him little less than Deity.

Having formerly described what was of most interest in this city when I made it a temporary residence, I can only add that the population has increased, the city limits extended, and many new improvements have been made. The large cotton and carpet factories flourish in consequence of the great protection in the tariff. Rents and living expenses, as well as taxation, are increasing, but workmen are better paid than formerly, as the country was chiefly agricultural and there is now more demand for labor, growing out of the manufacturing.

The King, although blind, is building a new palace, and has just called upon the Stande or Chambers, for an appropriation of *six hundred thousand thalers* for the work, as far as completed.

A fair has been recently held here, which for a stranger is well worth seeing. One day only is allowed for the furniture sale, and it is held in a different part of the city. Every variety of household article is exposed for sale, brought in from small neighboring villages, which gives the poor a chance to buy cheap. It is curious to see the stream of wagons and carts, drawn not only by horses, oxen, and donkeys, but single cows and spaniel dogs in harness, the drivers cracking their whips. Now comes a load of countrywomen, in fancy colored short corsets and jupes, then the Bauer, or peasant, with his high-topped boots, long-tailed coat, and big bright buttons. The market-places were filled with booths and venders from other cities, with every variety of articles, attractive and for use; jewelry, wearing apparel, and pumpernickel, or honey cake, in great quantities, an indispensable article for the multitude. The good-natured country people, with their Platt Deutsch, or land dialect, seemed to have a good time of it, and the national dishes of sausage and saur kraut, with light beer and pipes, were in great demand.

Here in Hanover, and also in Celle, a town of ten thousand population, which I lately visited, the language spoken by the upper classes is the most pure in all Germany.

# 1859.
# CL.

*Berlin, February 23, 1859.*

The great event of the season was the birth of a prince to the crown of Prussia, and the first grandchild of Queen Victoria. Demonstrations, congratulations, and addresses have been made to the royal parents by the Lord Mayor, and other dignitaries of London. The street upon which I live, leading to the Palace, was crowded with vehicles, containing the nobility, civil, and military officers in full uniform, advancing to the royal residence to inscribe and present themselves in honor of the happy event. Crowds of persons were standing upon the sidewalks for many days afterwards, gazing up at the windows and walls which inclose this precious jewel of a monarchical people. The students have since had their torchlight celebration for the occasion.

In these reverences and a thousand other ways, through titles and orders given to all persons of any distinction, wealth, or merit, is the aristocratic band so linked together, that the very children imbibe that love and respect and awe for the royal family till it seems engrafted in their very natures.

In political matters you are kept fully advised through the European journals. As I suggested in my last, things look ominous for the future. The money and commercial marts are still agitated, and uncertainty prevails. France continues steadily her military preparations; Sardinia the same. Austria is stubborn, and sends further supplies of troops into Italy. Diplomacy is hard at work to prevent a general European war, and, if the issue must come, to confine it to the Peninsula. A slight outbreak at the present moment would put all Europe in a blaze. The demand for saltpetre in the London markets, even from the smaller powers, and the prohibition of the sale of horses shows that they fear the result, and must be prepared, if not against the enemy, against their own people. Cannon foundries and manufactories of arms are in full blast in different countries.

The horrors of a European war, the destruction of life and property, the anguish of widows and orphans, the demoralization of invading armies, the cost of maintaining the same, and the entailment of debt, are not to be portrayed. Already Austria and Sardinia are in the market for loans, consequently there is a depreciation of the whole outstanding debt in the hands of the public.

Since I visited the Crimea I feel myself better able to judge of consequences. The ruined and battered fortresses and public and private edifices of Sebastopol, Kertch, and other points, the graveyards of the half million of souls of Inkerman, Alma, and the Malakoff, all testify to the melancholy results. However, the question of the whole Italian race, suffering under the bonds and chains of tyrants, cannot be longer delayed, and we shall probably soon know the decision. Either the evacuation by Austria of the Papal States, and the duchies of Modena and Parma, and abandonment of her tutelage, with a system of reform, or war, must be the result.

Some persons contend that war, like cholera, or other epidemics, in over-populated countries, is as necessary as a thunderstorm to clear a sultry and vitiated atmosphere, to sweep off a part of the redundant population, lessen competition, and give the survivors a chance to earn their bread. More humane means can be substituted in the favoring of emigration to the vast regions of unoccupied territory, not only in Europe, but in both Americas.

While all Europe is in uncertainty, America stands without anxiety, as a looker-on. In the event of a European war her breadstuffs would find a ready market. Capitalists, looking at the uncertain tenure of things here, would turn their attention to investments on the other side. Emigrants, to escape army duty and save what little they have from destruction, would take refuge in this land of liberty. Her Mexican and Cuban question could be settled without the interference of foreign powers, who would have occupation at home.

Our Treasury it seems is exhausted, and loans are made in time of peace. We pay our President twenty-five thousand dollars a year. I notice the French Senate have granted Prince Napoleon eight hundred thousand francs, or one hundred and sixty thousand dollars, as expenses for his marriage to the daughter of Sardinia's king, and two million francs, or four hundred thousand dollars yearly. In the event of widowhood she is to have forty thousand dollars, our currency, and a palace to her use. All that for a cousin of the Emperor. What would our honest yeomanry think of such outgoes with us, which are mostly made up by indirect taxation upon each and every article consumed by rich and poor?

Yesterday we celebrated the birthday of Washington at a splendid dinner given by our minister, at which assisted some sixty persons of both sexes— Americans residing in or passing through Berlin, naturalized Germans, Consuls and Senators from Bremen, Stettin, &c. Baron Humboldt sat vis-à-vis with Gov. Wright under the folds of the American flag. Toasts and speeches, as customary on such occasions, were made, and all passed off to the satisfaction of guests. Some fifteen or more of our states were represented, and were called upon for a sentiment or a toast, which, under the exhilarating influence of champagne, was generally well responded to, and brought forth some amusing and historical reminiscences of the American revolution. Portraits of the Father of his country, of Humboldt,

Webster, and others, and the beautiful engraving of Washington crossing the Delaware, were suspended from the wall. An artist gave a toast which was rather a strong one in a monarchical government, and in a less enlightened age perhaps we would not have had the privilege of meeting together to commemorate the birthday of a republican victor; it was to "Humboldt, the King of Science, whose shoes most kings are not worthy to unloose." The venerable old man is now in his ninetieth year; he is fond of ladies' society, who adore him as a traveller and writer. He has remained a bachelor. His memory is fresh and vigorous; I asked him if he recollected my presentation by Gov. Vroome, some four years since, and the conversation about the island of Ceylon. "Yes," replied he briefly, "and Singapore also," and then recounted information derived from other sources since.

# CLI.

Frankfort-on-the-Maine, Germany, *March 22, 1859.*

I left the agreeable city of Berlin with mingled feelings of regret and pleasure. To get rid of an obstinate attack of bronchitis when all other remedies fail, my usual course is change of climate, and I put myself on the road for Dresden, the Saxon capital, as well as the business city of Leipzig, which I next touched. I had visited it before on different occasions and described it to you, and it offered but little new.

I thought I had seen the thirty-two empires, kingdoms, duchies, landgraves, and other imperial, royal, and ducal residences of Germany, but recollected an unexplored tract through the Erzhogthum of Weimar, and of Gotha and Coburg, the latter duchies celebrated as furnishing husbands for most of the Princesses of Europe, Prince Albert of England being one of the number. As I was at a loss to know what route to take for a change in such an emergency the smallest favors are thankfully received.

It is really curious and interesting to look into these little Dutch settlements, and scrutinize the efforts made by these pigmy potentates to imitate the regal residences of great sovereigns, as I once described to you, from Port au Prince, Island of Hayti, that the guards and cannon at the entrance of the Imperial gates of the black despot looked as formidable as those of the Emperor of Russia. But the people have there wrought a change, and Soulouque is a wanderer. In time similar changes will take place in Germany.

The towns of Jena and Nuremburg, and the battle-fields of 1806, with the bivouac of Napoleon upon the height called Landgrafberge, are all of much historical interest. The town of Weimar has thirteen thousand inhabitants, and lies upon the slope of a beautiful valley, through which runs a limpid stream. On the opposite side are elevated commanding grounds, upon which stands a new caserne containing an entire regiment of one thousand men. The town appears neat, is well paved, and has the air of a regal seat, without much trade or commerce, where the residents are in part dependent on the government, or persons whose means allow them to enjoy the advantages of such facilities as cannot be obtained in the small villages or upon the land.

The large and beautiful palace contains rooms with fresco paintings consecrated to the poets Goethe, Schiller, Herder, and Wieland, who were patronized by the then existing duke. The summer cottage of Goethe, *vis-à-vis* to a rustic resort of the duke, in the wood, is still in the possession of the poet's family. At twelve A.M., the band played before the palace. A Greek chapel is found here, as well as in several German courts, in consequence of Russian marriages. The mother of the present duke is sister of the ex-emperor Nicholas. So you perceive how the family alliances are calculated to divide political influences in the Fatherland. The library has one hundred and fifty thousand volumes, also a good collection of medallions and objects of art. A fine large theatre is supported. The park is prettily laid out with rich and rare plants, hot-houses, and a summer palace for the duke. All these and much more might be added from a little domain of three hundred thousand inhabitants, about one-third that of New York and Brooklyn, with a salary of two hundred and eighty thousand thalers, say two hundred and twenty thousand dollars our currency. Horses, carriages, liveried servants must be kept up, three thousand troops entertained, and—who pays? These princes have generally large land incomes in addition to salary, and in this case Russia contributes a portion.

The territory of Gotha and Coburg is smaller. The population of Gotha is one hundred and twenty thousand, Coburg forty thousand, making one hundred and sixty thousand in all. The town of Gotha has fifteen thousand inhabitants, and is beautifully situated upon a side hill, with water running through all the streets. The new part looks well, but the old dull, and not so fine as Weimar. The Schloss or palace stands upon a high hill called Hochberg, and is of quadrangular form, some four hundred feet or more in extent, with a high tower. The grounds are extensive, and the terrace is compared by some to that of Windsor in England. The view is very extensive. The alleys and public walks around the little city are strikingly beautiful. There are several other palaces and summer residences belonging to the Duchy, a library of one hundred and sixty thousand volumes, a collection of coins consisting of some forty thousand pieces, a Chinese cabinet, galleries of pictures, copperplates, etc. One naturally wonders where and how such collections and public buildings have been put together and paid for, and by whom. The theatre is a fine building, and a regular company is kept up.

The Duke receives one hundred and forty thousand thalers from the land yearly, say one hundred and five thousand dollars our currency. He was absent with his wife in Berlin at the christening of the infant Prince of Victoria, whose mother is his niece, the daughter of Prince Albert. He has no family, and at his death Gotha and Coburg fall to Prince Alfred, the second son of England's sovereign, who is now in the navy. The present Duke is a soldier, and lives in a small palace, like a sensible man, and is esteemed by his people. The army contingent is sixteen hundred troops. All these things are very pretty to gaze upon, and quite attractive to travellers who look only upon the surface, but talk with the people a little and get their views.

The manufacturing of lucifer matches has become a heavy business for exportation. You can scarcely believe it that in this unhealthy occupation girls are employed at three and a half silver-groschen, or nine cents, per day, whose food consists of potatoes and rye meal cooked together, who scarcely know what it is to get a piece of meat. In Erfurt, an old city of thirty thousand inhabitants, where nothing of interest offered except the cathedral, dome, and the fortifications, I mounted the steeple for a view and to look at a bell of great weight, here considered a wonder, and called the Maria Gloriosa. I asked the girl who conducted us if she had ever heard of the Moscow bell, which is really of monstrous size. She did not even know the name. I inquired if many visitors came, and what she earned. She replied the sexton paid her twelve thalers the quarter year, or thirty-six dollars our currency, yearly. The gifts of visitors she must hand over, or they would be taken from her. One cannot but pity such objects. I then said I will pay the sexton and what we give is extra for your use. People complain of untrusty servants, of peculations and unjust reckonings in short weights, etc. I tell them it is their own fault; they have driven them to dishonesty by low wages, which makes slavery on the plantation a preferable position.

My next halting-place was Hesse Cassel, from whence the English imported troops to fight against us in the revolution. I saw a review of the Gross Furst, or Elector. He has a passion for military. The country has nine thousand soldiers, but in case of war the number demanded by the German confederation is twelve thousand. The people are not satisfied with their elector. His salary is eight hundred thousand thalers. He has a large family, and his wife was the daughter of a hotel-keeper, consequently his children cannot occupy his place, and it is said instead of spending his money at home for the good of the people, it is sent to England, or used, in the purchase of estates in Bohemia, for the future provision of his heirs.

I have twice before visited Cassel, and described to you its position, its suburbs of Wilhelmshohe, the great artificial cascades and fountains, and other gigantic works executed with English gold received for the sale of Hessian soldiers.

I have said nothing about politics. The excitement in Germany has been great, but no unity of action. The Austrian papers lash Prussia for her neutral policy. The attacked journals reply that they are ready to defend the interests of the Fatherland, but unwilling to assist in the perpetuation of tyranny in Italy, and in the total want of religious toleration in Austria. The *brochures*, or pamphlets, in Paris, advising the conquest of the Rhine provinces, have done more to wake up the German population than anything else.

# CLII.

FRANKFORT-ON-THE-MAINE, GERMANY, *April 22, 1859.*

The free city of Frankfort is historically known since the eighth century. It is the seat of the Deutsche Bund, or German Confederation. In the old Roman Hall in the Rathhouse, or City Hall, where the German emperors and kings were chosen, the full length portraits, in costume, of the entire line are exhibited. In the Dom Kirche, or cathedral, is found the monument to the memory of Kaiser (or Emperor) Gunther, of Schwarzberg, dated in the year 1352; also the tombstone, under date of 1371, of the Ritter, or knight Rudolph, of Sachsenhausen, which little town lies on the opposite side of the river Maine, connected by a stone bridge twelve hundred and sixty feet long and thirty-three feet wide, resting upon fourteen arches.

Strolling through the settlement the other day I found the streets narrow, the town surrounded by a wall, the egress by the same gates through which one goes in, and the language of the people almost unintelligible and quite different from those who come in contact with the world where pure German is spoken.

Last Sunday I found myself in the Protestant, St. Paul's, Church, consecrated in 1833, on the site of the old Roman Barfusse Kirche. It is in an elliptical form, built of square freestone blocks. While listening to the tones of the immense organ, my mind was carried back involuntarily to the events of 1848, when I had seen this edifice used for the General Assembly of nine hundred delegates, presided over by the Grand Duke Johan of Austria, whom it was proposed to elect emperor of all Germany. The torchlight and window illuminations of the city upon his arrival was a striking feature, but it was all a flash in the pan—an entire failure. The revolution was soon over. Austria had gained the battle of Novara over Sardinia, and reinstated her power. France was again quiet. The kings of Europe, who had in the presence of the enraged masses promised constitutions and all else required, soon found the people themselves disunited, and began to contract their strength and forces, and finally refused to perform any of the acts named.

The central position of this city gives it a decided advantage for trade and commerce. The activity of the eighty thousand inhabitants is striking in comparison with the ducal residence of Darmstadt, an hour's ride by railway, with its long broad streets and population of thirty thousand, but looking dull and dreary as a village. The railroad in an hour conveys one to Wiesbaden, in a half hour to Mayence, and in an hour's ride by omnibus and rail one arrives at Homburg.

The baths of the first and last-named places are now open for the season, but it is too early for many guests. On festival days they are full, and the sums of gold lost and won upon roulette and *trente et quarante* are scarcely credible. A Russian nobleman attracted the attention of the numerous bystanders recently, as he used only gold and one thousand franc bank notes, a pile of which he had before him, and won and lost equal to one thousand dollars, our currency, upon the turn of the wheel—now reducing his capital, and then increasing. The bank of Wiesbaden paid its shareholders thirty-one per cent. dividend the last year, after expending fabulous sums in the embellishment of the gardens, fountains, magnificent Kursaal, and reading rooms; and after giving semi-weekly balls, hunting parties at the close of the season, &c., &c., besides paying to the Duke of Nassau a large annual sum for the privilege of fleecing the public. It is an interesting study to see how these things are managed at Homburg and Wiesbaden. In addition to the immense expenses for laying out and beautifying the grounds with trees and flowering plants, the best restaurateur from Paris is employed to furnish a table d'hôte in the superb ornamental gilded and frescoed dining hall at a moderate price, thereby attracting strangers. The omnibus line receives a portion of the fare from the bank, making it easier accessible. The entrance to the reunions is gratis. Musicians, and even the police taxes, and other charges upon passports are paid at the expiration of the season by the company. Many families spend the winter at Homburg, where the bank is kept open the entire year, and they enjoy without charge the use of reading-rooms, with papers and periodicals in all modern languages. The managers, however, calculate adroitly upon the general average. If the father or mother do not play, the son or daughter, or friends perhaps will, and they can extricate so much gain per head on the average. Ladies are not free from the vice, large and small sums being risked by the fair sex. The bank even employs them for that purpose as a decoy. The Landgrave, or petty prince of this piece of land, about the size of one of our small counties, receives a handsome annuity.

The system is immoral and wicked, and ruins many families; but as long as Germany remains disunited, cannot be suppressed. At the close of the last business season at Wiesbaden, there were, I learn, as usual, many who had lost all, and could not get away. The bank in such cases advances the means, takes a note or draft for the same, and if not paid, the party does not return, consequently it is clear of them, and don't incur the odium of suicides through despair.

The old town of Frankfort, with its narrow, tortuous streets, gabled-end projecting houses full of windows, is curious. Outside the walls surrounding the city are magnificent shady walks, highly ornamented with shrubbery and plants. The season is forward, and the trees in full bloom add to the beauty of the promenades. The suburbs are well laid out with broad streets and superb houses, occupied by the wealthy. It has become a favorite residence for strangers, being so central, and in connexion with so many attractive watering-places and cities.

The Jews are here very numerous. Many of them are bankers, at the head of which is the original house of Rothschilds. In the same neighborhood has recently been erected an immense freestone synagogue.

In the Burger Verein, or Citizens' Club, an institution established on an extensive scale, I find among other correspondence some of our New York papers.

Frankfort and Leipzic are celebrated in Europe for their fairs. Two are held here yearly. The Oester Messe, or Easter Fair, now exists, and lasts three weeks. The quay along the River Maine and the public squares are occupied with booths filled with wares from all parts of the country. The concourse of merchants and buyers from neighboring towns gives activity to the place. Of course amusements are provided for guests, and America comes in for a part. There is an immense circus from Berlin, in which Jas. Robinson, the most celebrated bareback rider in the world, is employed, making his summersets over star-spangled flags and ribbons, backwards and forwards, with the agility of a cat. Bands of volunteer musicians from other cities, and Tyrolese minstrels, find themselves here, who make the rounds, and whose notes are heard from morn until late in the night, and who adopt this method of picking up the crumbs. The theatre is crowded; the flying horse machines and puppet shows please the children; gaping crowds are listening to the marvellous tales of outcriers at the entrance of travelling menageries, museums, camera obscuras, and of the fat girl nineteen years old, weighing six hundred pounds; the railroads profit by freight and traffic, and lager beer, sausages, and cheese are in the ascendant.

The political situation of Europe exerts a baneful influence upon all general trade. The complaint on all hands is prostration of business. The game of chess now playing between France and Austria is discouraging to all classes. They would prefer open hostilities to indecision. The belligerent parties have gone so far that we must soon see the bloody sword of war, or the olive branch of peace.

# CLIII.

PARIS, *May 24, 1859.*

I find myself once again in the great European capital. It is now a month since you heard from me last at Frankfort, Germany. I then left for Baden-Baden soon after the opening of the season. I never saw the country look more smiling and lovely. Nature had put on her most beautiful spring attire, and indeed nothing in Europe can surpass the natural scenery of the suburbs of this renowned watering-place.

The little city was brushed up as usual, and every hotel and lodging-house awaiting anxiously the arrival of guests, but in this I fear they will be woefully disappointed this year. The anxieties and financial difficulties growing out of the war, and the bitter feeling manifested by Germany towards the French, will prevent the usual rush of visitors. Few persons were there, and the magnificent gas-lighted saloons, with their bands of music, had few occupants. The employees of the gambling tables looked wistfully at every stranger, hoping their business will soon commence.

The past month has been full of exciting events. Austria has renounced negotiation. The war decree has gone forth. Sardinia has been invaded. The French Emperor with his troops has been called upon for relief. Austria is intriguing and stimulating the German powers to unite with her in fortifying the Rhine. The German press was most violent against the French Emperor, giving him the most opprobrious names and calling it a war of conquest. Austrian securities have fallen from eighty-five to thirty-eight. Frankfort held some fifty million florins of that national paper. The war loan was rejected and Austria made an arrangement with the National Bank, which only last year resumed specie payments, to grant a loan of a hundred millions in small circulating notes, making the same a legal tender. Up went the price of specie. The bankers and commercial classes suffered, and large failures occurred. Commerce and trade were paralysed. I met two Hungarians, who were leaving for the United States, who were fortunate enough to obtain specie at a loss of thirty-five per cent, against paper. This stubborn act of Austria lost her the sympathies of Europe, excepting the small German states, Bavaria, Wirtemburg, Hesse Cassel, Baden &c., some of whom are connected by family ties. Prussia has stood and still stands firm in resisting the warlike disposition of the small states of the confederation, observing an armed neutrality until the real interests of Germany proper are attacked.

The French people who opposed the war are now almost universally in its favor. The triumphal departure of the Emperor, his reception in Piedmont, the subscription to the French loan of more than four times the amount, justifies this belief. The report of a secret alliance between Russia and France, and the advancement of a corps of observation upon the Austrian and Prussian frontier, caused great consternation on the continent. The English funds fell five or six per cent., and many dealers and brokers were ruined by the panic which ensued. The Tory cabinet was denounced by the English. The report proved untrue. Then came the declaration of neutrality by England.

War declared, the French army were transported south by rail, and then crossed the Alps, while other regiments went by steamers on the Mediterranean to Genoa. The departure of the troops, the enthusiasm of the populace, the martial display and equipage of war has kept up a lively interest. The reports of the first battle and victory of Montebello are received, and we are anxiously waiting the news of further engagements. The national guard are the protectors of the city, and few regular troops are seen, which is another evidence of the popularity of the war of Italian independence.

France is engaged in a righteous cause in effecting the liberation of Italy from the yoke of tyranny and bondage of Austria. Having passed so much time in Italy, I may be permitted to judge of the hatred of foreign domination.

Sardinia was worthy of assistance, being the only really liberal and free government in the south of Europe. The Emperor, sagacious as he is, wanted the Italian question settled; and through the proposal of Russia for a congress, in which Austria dared not show her hand, he brought the matter to a focus. The occupation of the army, the glory of France at the head of European civilization, and the confirmation of the dynasty were needed. All these things had their influence. Austria was put in a false position. The result is war, and if confined to Italy good may grow out of it. If Germany attacks France on the Rhine, then the war becomes general; but the French government and press are doing everything possible to suppress such a move. The public journals are now unanimous in favor of Italian liberty, and the war cry is, down with the Austrians, and their expulsion from the shores of the Adriatic.

Last year this time I was riding and walking over the battle-grounds and fields of Alma, Inkerman, Kamiesch, Eupatoria, and Kertsch, where half a million lie buried, and probably some curious tourists among the number.

The death of the king of Naples has delivered that beautiful land of a tyrant. Probably the neutrality of the young king may be accepted. He is a cousin of Victor Emanuel, king of Sardinia, but the queen mother is the second wife of the deceased king, and of the house of Austria. She has been intriguing for the accession to the throne of her eldest son, and troubles are expected.

Strangers are getting away by small steamers in crowds, without comfort or accommodation. The war will make it very inconvenient for travellers. The

Lloyd steamers in the Levant are withdrawn to the neutral harbor of Malta. The French have already blockaded the ports of the Adriatic and taken many Austrian prizes. I am thankful I have nothing undone in that direction, and can remain a neutral spectator.

# 1860.
# CLIV.

Tetuan, Coast of Morocco, Africa, *February 15, 1860.*

After a short sojourn in the French capital, I took the rail for Marseilles. The distance of five hundred miles we made in twenty hours, in comfortable cars, warmed by shallow metallic vessels filled with hot water, and placed under the feet. This was even shorter time than two years since, when I passed over the same road to embark for Algeria.

It is now nearly four months since the declaration of war on the part of the Spaniards, who at vast expense have landed an army of thirty-five thousand men upon the coast of Morocco. Tangiers being well fortified, although blockaded, they could only land at Ceuta, a point occupied by them for convicts. A distance of six leagues then had to be made by land along the coast to the small river Tetuan, where they encamped in presence of the Moors, who occupied the heights and the city of Tetuan, which is upon an eminence six miles from the coast. A great battle was fought, and finally the city was besieged. The Moors in great numbers occupied the heights, and coming down in masses from the mountains headed by the brothers of the emperor of Morocco, harassed and attacked the Spaniards. They were, however, dislodged and cut up by the latter, who report in killed and wounded two thousand of the enemy and two hundred of their own; but verbal reports here say they lost one thousand in killed and wounded. The latter were sent away immediately to the hospitals of Malaga and Cadiz. Finding resistance useless, orders were given to evacuate the city, and the Moors fled in every direction in the mountains, but the Jews, a much oppressed race, remain, as also do the old and disabled Moors.

The city, which contained a population of some thirty thousand, now presents a strange aspect, the narrow streets being filled with soldiery, mules, and donkeys. The Jews have suffered much from pillage at the hands of the Moors and Kabyles of the Riff, who are not unlike their pirate associates, and the doors of a great number of houses are still seen broken open by these marauders, who regarded neither friend nor foe. The Israelites are rejoiced at the result, as such was the intolerance of the Mussulmans that they were obliged to take off their shoes in approaching a mosque.

Subscriptions have been made in different countries for the Jews who are at Gibraltar, who have been obliged to abandon the ports of Morocco. An agent has just arrived here with supplies for the sufferers in Tetuan, who stand much in need.

I scarcely know how to describe the singular scene that presents itself. On entering the roadstead I counted some forty-five steamers of different nations, including several Spanish war vessels, besides a large number of small sailing vessels, also several tugs for the purpose of discharging and towing, while feluccas, scows, and small boats loaded with merchandise and munitions of war were scattered about in the mouth of the river to the landing place near the square tower or citadel. The beach and quays are covered with cannon, bombs, balls, wheels for mounting, scores of pipes of red wine, boxes, bales and packages of all kinds for the supply of the army, and for venders and speculators in and around the different camps.

The first camp presented itself near the shore, quite in repose. Horses, mules, and donkeys were feeding. The soldiers were preparing their dinner over little fires of sticks, and from the little tents of the Spanish venders were heard the cries of oranges, cigars, liquors, and every conceivable article which can be disposed of to the troops. A temporary fort had been thrown up of earthwork and the branches of the cactus, which attains the height of a small tree in this climate, and cannon were planted at the angles and other openings to prevent surprise. Little tents for the soldiery, for six each, were spread upon the ground; those of the officers are of larger dimensions, and more comfortable.

As we proceeded further, martial music was heard in the distance, and an army of horsemen with lances came up followed by infantry and cavalry. Four thousand fresh troops had just arrived, and the road was lined with mules and horses, already jaded out with hard service, carrying provisions to the camps. Here and there was lying a poor animal who had drawn his last breath, while disabled Moorish cannon and balls were scattered about.

To the right and left the encampments were seen, and the music of bands was heard, mingling with the national airs of the Spanish soldiers, who appear happy, notwithstanding the fatigue of the campaign in an enemy's country during a rainy season, with the accompaniment of cholera, which has cost the lives of many thousands. The weather is now, however, dry, and favorable to the health of the troops.

The orange gardens, with the olive and other trees, look fresh in the valleys, which extend for miles around, and the well whitewashed walls of the city glisten in the sun's rays, so that one who was not familiar with Mussulman cities and structures would imagine its contents beautiful. The camp of Gen. O'Donnell is placed upon a plateau near the entrance, and over the fortified archway is already inscribed *"Puerta de la Reyna,"* or Queen's Gate.

As soon as the entrance is effected, one finds the streets narrow and dirty. The houses are one and two stories high, with small courts in the centre and lodging rooms above. Fountains abound, as in all Moorish cities, for the washing of the feet of the faithful before entering the mosques. The principal mosque upon the great square is already occupied by the cross, and the burning wax candles beside the Virgin, in singular contrast with the suspended ostrich eggs usual in Mussulman temples.

Scarcely any accommodations can be found for strangers at any price, and such as can be found at enormous prices, remind me of California in its early days. Fortunately our steamer is supplied with all the comforts and conveniences, and we may go and come when we please.

The presumption is that the Moors will now sue for peace, which Spain will probably be glad to accept, as it will be difficult to penetrate a country where several millions of barbarians are found. If report tells the truth, the resources of the Emperor of Morocco in treasure are enormous, the result of hoarding from his ancestry down, and if the Spaniards can extract a few millions towards the expenses of the war, they will relieve themselves of a heavy burden, and put an amount of gold and silver in circulation now lying idle.

The Spaniards have landed already rails and ties for a short railroad for the transport of heavy war material to the city. They have also commenced a telegraph, probably for communication with Madrid, or to give the Moors an idea of European civilization. It struck me as curious that they should do in Africa what they have been so backward in accomplishing in their own country.

# CLV.

MOGADORE, COAST OF MOROCCO, *February 29, 1860.*

My last from Tetuan, informed you of its occupation by the Spaniards and the flight of the Moors, which has created the greatest burst of enthusiasm and national feeling throughout Spain; and if we can judge from the Spanish journals, which are filled with the events and incidents of the war, the praises of the army are being sung in all parts of Spain.

Gen. O'Donnell has been created Duke of Tetuan. Report says the Emperor of Morocco has sued for peace, and the Queen's counsellors have demanded the permanent possession of Tetuan and twenty millions of dollars in part payment of the expenses of the war. It now remains to be seen if the Emperor will accede to the proposition.

Our steamer received orders to discharge her cargo at Gibraltar, where I took up my quarters at the hotel for a few days. Having visited this strongly fortified key of the straits twice before, and once described it to you, I will only add that no practical changes have taken place. The garrison of six thousand well-equipped and well-disciplined troops is kept up. Only a portion of the English and French fleet, which were sent here when the war broke out, now remain in the bay. The gates of the city, which inclose twenty thousand souls, including troops, are closed at sundown and opened at sunrise. A permit is granted for visitors who are not lodged in the city, which is good till the evening; but a longer sojourn requires application at the police. There the steamers coal which are bound up the Mediterranean, and to England and Portugal. The supplies are drawn from Spain or the coast of Morocco, and vessels from different sources. The natives, by derision, are called Rock Scorpions, and are mostly Jews and Spaniards. The Spanish is commonly spoken, although the schools are in part English. The streets are kept neat and clean. The houses rise one above another, like the sides of an amphitheatre, to a great height, and the ascent requires considerable climbing.

On the summit of the rock, with its frowning batteries and tunnelled galleries, with cannon pointing in all directions, is seen the telegraph; and by it, in the brush and scrubby trees, are monkeys grinning and climbing, the only representatives of the race in Europe, and who would have been extinct long since did not heavy penalties prevent it. On the African side, the mountains are infested with them.

The carnival season was being enjoyed by the masqueraders, but the balls and costumes were rather sorry affairs in comparison with those of Madrid, and other large cities of Spain.

Gibraltar is a free port, and gives employment to merchants and traders, who are celebrated for their sharp and acute transactions. The captains of vessels whom I met, who had put in for repairs or in distress, say they are worse than Key West wreckers. Smuggling and contraband trade with Spain has fallen off, however, with lower duties and the close of civil wars.

The weather was cool for the season. Snow was seen upon the African mountains, and bad reports of cholera came in from Tetuan; large numbers were dying among troops and residents. I had seen sufficient evidence of its existence, and concluded it was safest to be out of the district.

The American gunboat Iroquois came into Gibraltar and took our consul, Mr. Brown, to Tangiers, being the first consular return to Morocco since the war began, when those of all nations, with their families, decamped, and all the subjects of foreign governments who could, did likewise. The only consul in the whole of Morocco who remained, was the English, Mr. Hay, at Tangiers, who received express orders, and was protected by war vessels from Gibraltar, that port being considered blockaded.

Finding our steamer was going all along the Moorish coast, and thence to the Canary Islands, I concluded to embark. Our first stopping place was in thirty-six hours, at Casa Blanca, where we landed the French and Portuguese consuls, who were old residents, but, like all others, had abandoned their posts, fearing the fanaticism of the Moors, and the loss of their heads, as the wild Arabs don't distinguish among Christians as to what race they belong. We remained a day. The Moors had heard of the taking of Tetuan, and were uneasy, and less sanguine. These two gentlemen we left, but the thought was painful, that they were running the risk of losing their lives in their own houses.

We next proceeded to Mazagan, an old fortified city of six thousand inhabitants. It is of square form, with strong walls and ramparts, situated upon an iron-bound coast. It was built some centuries since by the Portuguese, who protected it by cannon on the land side as well as the sea, and occupied it for a long time during the height of the commercial prosperity of Portugal. At length, from the encroachments of the Moors, however, they were obliged to abandon it. Before leaving, they mined it in every direction, and then by stipulation removed their population and supplies. The keys of the city having been given up, the wild Arabs rushed in, and filled up the deserted streets and houses. While looking for booty, a doubloon was discovered, and eagerly seized, which was attached by a thread to a concealed pistol, which exploded the mine, and blew up the greater part of the city, causing great destruction of life, and satisfying the vengeance of the Portuguese.

The old subterranean cisterns, or reservoirs, still exist, and are worthy of their authors, reminding one of the old Roman and Carthaginian masonry. The city is now mostly of one story buildings, with flat roofs, except consular and a few other private houses and magazines. Europeans make themselves as comfortable as possible amidst the filth which prevails ankle-deep in the narrow streets, and smells, badly suited to the olfactories, from dead dogs and cats. The English consul being absent, I noticed a dead donkey lying near his house. Himself and his colleagues had all fled the country, and cleanliness was out of the question.

The Jews from all these points along the coast had been removed, or made their escape as far as possible. Outside the walls of Gibraltar, I saw some five hundred tents, furnished by the English government, where about thirty-five hundred had congregated, and some eighteen hundred still remained. The government had given rations daily, and the French government made liberal allowances for such subjects as were under the protection of its consuls. It was a curious sight, reminding one of the descriptions of the camp of Israel. Men, women, and children, in the African Jewish costume, were performing the culinary operations of the separate households. The canvas streets had their names. The ground floors were whitewashed, or limed against infection. English sentries were on patrol, and all well regulated.

The country about Casa Blanca and Mazagan is fertile, but badly cultivated, and produces wheat and barley of excellent quality. Cattle, sheep, horses, and donkeys are kept, but the camel is the principal beast of burden. The export of horses is prohibited; other animals pay a considerable head tax. Poultry and eggs are abundant and cheap; gum, wool, and grain were the chief articles of export before the war.

We left two European merchants who had their houses there, and proceeded to this place, Mogadore, the farthest point on the Morocco coast, at which a steamer lands, and which is the chief city for the trade of the capital, Morocco, that lies one hundred and ten miles in the interior.

This is, for a Moorish city, strongly built, and is surrounded with walls. The houses are one or two stories high, and well whitewashed. The bastions and fortifications are upon a rocky shore. The small island of Mogadore forms a breakwater against the northerly storms; but like all African harbors, this is only a roadstead. The vicinity consists of desert for some miles, and then agricultural and grazing country. The town is dry and clean, reminding me of Tripoli, on the Barbary coast, for cleanliness, as Mazagan and Casa Blanca compare with Tunis for filth.

The sight of a steamer, being the first for six weeks, brought the whole population out. The walls and battlements were crowded with Arabs from the country, there being twelve hundred who had come in to protect the city from an expected attack of the Spaniards. The long white woollen mantles, or cloaks, and red caps, covering their swarthy bodies, the natural growth of black beard, and the long carabines, presented a strange aspect, as they looked grim and surly upon the Christians, and wondered what business we had there.

The women, with their heads covered with white veils, and feet with yellow boots, looked slyly at us out of one or both eyes, or were peeping through the blinds as the strangers passed.

Here we have a Jewish quarter, also, which is locked at night. The daughters of Israel are very fair, and some of them beautiful; they don't hide their faces like the Moorish women. Some disorders had occurred, and some of their houses been broken open and pillaged, for which they had no redress, as all foreign consuls were absent.

The climate here is delightful, being from seventy to seventy-five degrees Fahrenheit, and never varying more than ten degrees throughout the year.

One of our passengers, an English merchant long in this country, had left his house in possession of a trusty Moor, and found all satisfactory. Indeed, the residents among the Moors have more to apprehend from pillage on the part of the wild hordes of the country, than from those of the city. My friend, at whose house I am, will not remain, although he speaks Arabic, but will go on to the Canary Islands with us, with the intention of returning when the war is over. Another of our passengers, a merchant, who was born in a Mohammedan city, will remain and take his chance.

No sooner had we landed than we were surrounded and followed by groups of friends and listeners, who followed close on our heels to the house, which was closed by main force to prevent intrusion. Soon after, the familiar and monotonous songs of the Arabs, accompanied by primitive violins, reached my ears from the gallery. There sat five musicians, whose music and song was spiced from time to time with a peculiar howl or whistle from two blind women, which I at first took for the escape of steam from the steamer.

To my surprise the health officer, when he came off, spoke English and French. He looks the Moor in costume, with his patriarchal white beard, and is now seventy-six years of age. I have been to his house to-day, and found him squatted, legs crossed, upon a divan, taking his repast of tea, instead of coffee, with oranges, dates, raisins, pomegranates, and a liquor which he offered us, made from figs, from his little table about two feet high. His father was an Englishman and his mother a Spanish woman. He has been forty-six years in Morocco, having come as interpreter to an English gentleman who wanted to travel in the interior, and was there murdered. His speaking Arabic saved him from the same fate. When the war broke out he sent his family to Gibraltar, and is now quite alone.

# CLVI.

BATHURST, RIVER GAMBIA, WEST COAST OF AFRICA, *March 10, 1860.*

From Mogadore we proceeded to the island of Lancerota, one of the group of Canary Islands, landing and spending part of a day at the principal town, Arecife, whence the island of Forteventura is in plain view.

The product of these islands, since the failure of the grape crop, consists mostly of cochineal, as the salubrity and uniformity of the climate are admirably adapted to the raising of the cactus plant upon which the insect feeds. The principal islands, Lancerota, Teneriffe, Gomera, and Palma, contain some one hundred and eighty thousand population.

My immediate destination was Santa Cruz, in Teneriffe, the capital of the Canary Islands, and the seat of the Spanish Governor. The approach to the well whitewashed town, with its large roadstead, backed by high mountains of hard basalt and soft pumice stone, of which it is built, is very picturesque. In the distance looms up the Peak of Teneriffe, said to be fifteen thousand feet high. The atmosphere was clear and soft, and overcoats and cloaks were no longer needed. They have had an unusually wet season, and apprehend a loss from excess of humidity in a climate where it rains usually so little.

Here I found several Germans, who had spent most of the winter in Madeira, four degrees further north, and give the preference to this climate. The accommodations, apartments, and society I have found better there than here.

The town is clean and well paved, with good roads, and a fair hotel. The island is evidently volcanic, as the wild and irregular masses of rock around the town testify.

Camels are here used as beasts of burden, showing conclusively they can be employed over similar roads on the overland routes in the United States, as well as on the sands of the desert.

My intention was, if I arrived in time at Santa Cruz, which I had before visited some years since, to take the West African Coast steamer for the Gambia river, and from thence down to Sierra Leone. In this I was not disappointed; after a few days' delay I embarked. The steamer from Fernando Po, on her return touched at all the ports along the Grain, Ivory, and Gold Coasts of Guinea, and several passengers were landed and lodged at our hotel. They reported the season as being most favorable for a visit; the fevers, which had desolated the settlements, existed no longer: but their yellow and jaundiced appearance was not encouraging for the traveller. Having been so much in tropical climates, and having had much experience in fevers, I hope to pass unscathed.

On board of the good screw steamer Athenian, with favorable breezes and increasing heat, in four days we made Bathurst, near the mouth of the Gambia River, one thousand miles from Teneriffe. The approach to this English colony up the broad serpentine river is directed by a negro pilot.

The public and private buildings are well and substantially built. The beach on one side is sandy, and the tide leaves a road bed for equestrians at the ebb. The date, mango, and other tropical trees give the place a picturesque appearance. The garrison is composed of English officers, and native black soldiery. The epidemic has made sad work among the whites; out of seventy-one, twenty-one died.

The negro population is upwards of five thousand, who live in reed huts, upon streets laid out at right angles, the different tribes in their respective quarters. They present a curious sight for the European, a fair proportion requiring only the garments of our first parents, Adam and Eve. Mothers carry their young, not unlike the squaws of our Indian tribes, upon their backs, but with this difference, that the little black urchin is nestled in the folds of a cotton shawl or girdle around the waist, the child being in the hollow of the back. The little boys and girls instead of clothing are supplied with strings of beads and amulets, as ornaments, and to keep away the evil spirit.

The river is navigable beyond Macarthy island to the cataracts, which are some one hundred and eighty miles from its mouth, and trading stations are found as high up. There are some thirteen tribes under different chiefs, and several different languages and dialects are spoken. The country is unsafe to travel in without a sufficient force for protection. It was here that Mungo Park, the renowned traveller, commenced his explorations, and it is supposed that he was killed on the Niger, after losing his soldiers and marines by fever and exhaustion. One of our fellow passengers, a colonel in the service, owned a farm ten miles from the town; his house was attacked, several killed, and he had a narrow escape.

I find much hospitality on the part of the inhabitants, which is quite natural when they have a steamer from Europe at long intervals. The Governor of Gambia, Col. D'Arcy, and his interesting wife, to whom I was recommended, offered me their house. I dined with them and passed an evening; breakfasted with our consul, a Brazilian by birth; visited several other of the prominent residents; and rode some miles along the coast, passing by the English burying ground, which seemed fast filling up. The government house belongs to the crown. It is a fine mansion, pleasantly situated among tropical trees and flowering plants. Negro soldiers as sentinels at the gate reminded me in this particular of the entrance to Soulouque's palace in the island of Hayti.

A number of French vessels are in port loading with ground nuts for making oil; many dry hides are also shipped. The trade of Senegal, the French colony, lying farther north, is of considerable importance. I find here a small vessel loading with peanuts, or ground nuts, for Boston; she hails from Salem. The down-easters are the most enterprising mariners in the world. They are met with in the most remote quarters of the globe. I have found them where I thought no trade could be furnished—up the Red Sea, the Island of Sumatra, Zanzibar, and other places, picking up coffee, spices, gums, and all sorts of products, in exchange for hard biscuits, coarse cotton cloth, lumber, wooden clocks, and an infinity of Yankee notions. The captain of this small vessel is quite a youth; he had his head cut and his nose broken by a mutinous sailor, but he came off victorious.

While at Teneriffe, the war steamer San Jacinto, belonging to the American squadron, watching the African slave coast, came in port. She was proceeding to Cadiz for repairs, as her machinery was out of order, and the nearest point was Spain. Capt. Armstrong was in command. Several of the officers were from our state. They had been cruising eight months, and, as you can imagine, were pleased to meet with one who could give direct news from Europe and the United States.

# CLVII.

Sierra Leone, West Coast of Africa, *March 14, 1860.*

Two days' steaming brought us from Bathurst, Gambia river, to this, the oldest English settlement on the west coast of Africa. It is situated upon a broad bay at the entrance of the Sierra Leone river, with high hills and peaks in the distance. The soil looks reddish, like that of New Jersey, but is thoroughly charged with iron. The vegetation is decidedly tropical, producing palm oil, ginger, spices, gum, bread-fruit, oranges, bananas, pineapples, etc. The heat is oppressive.

The fever epidemic has destroyed fifty-eight out of ninety-eight white residents within thirty days. The Catholic mission is closed, the bishop and the priests under his charge having died. The other missions also suffered, but not to the same extent. One of the prominent colored missionaries of the English Episcopal church I found to be a native of Charleston, South Carolina. He had lost his white German wife by fever.

I visited the schools for the education of the young males and females, and found them getting on very well in their studies. The sons of negroes who have been slaves in other countries, and who are traders and general dealers, appreciate the importance of education; but those of the villages and in the suburbs live in that listless manner characteristic of the negro. They perform but little labor, sufficient only to procure rum and tobacco as luxuries, for nature furnishes yams and other necessaries of life without much effort, preferring to bask and sleep in the rays of the broiling sun, which are death to the white man.

The French consul, to whom I had a letter and with whom I dined, drove me to his villa on the shore, some miles from town, a beautiful spot, where nature appeared in all her loveliness; but the insidious fever had closed the mission edifice in the neighborhood. We drove through villages at different times and in different directions up and down the coast, among hedges of lime trees twenty feet high, filled with fruit, resembling the wild vegetation of Venezuela. The umbrella-topped palm grows in profusion. The oleander and other hot-house plants with us, standing fifteen feet high, in bloom, as in the West Indies; pine-apple bushes laden with fruit are growing in a wild state; and the wide-spreading branches of the mango offer opportunity for repose, but the threatened fever for the white man breaks the charm.

The African fever this year has carried off thousands of the negroes also. The present population, mostly black, is computed to be forty thousand. The garrison is English, but the officers only are white, the soldiery consisting of natives and captured slaves, who are apprenticed. The vessels in the harbor during the epidemic, a few months since, lost in some cases captains, officers, crews, and even the cats on board, leaving the vessel riding alone at anchor. We don't sleep ashore as yet on any occasion.

The few white residents left are most hospitable, and my letters were such as to furnish all the civilities the settlement can afford. A wealthy German merchant, who has a native wife, as most persons have on the African coast, did all the honors for the Vaterland, a German missionary, whom I knew at Teneriffe, and who had left for his health, having given me letters.

The thermometer stands at from eighty-eight to ninety-seven in the shade, so that a piece of ice from the steamer, sent as a present by the officers of our ship to their friends and acquaintances, is esteemed a great luxury. White umbrellas are in vogue.

The next steamer will bring out the new Governor and English Bishop, his predecessor being dead. The Spanish consul and vice-consul both died, and the acting French consul has just been decorated by the Spanish Queen for services rendered during the crisis.

The English steamer Pluto is in port, having just returned from St. Helena after the capture of the American bark Orion with eight hundred and fifty slaves. These are apprenticed for a number of years, and a bounty of five pounds or twenty-five dollars her head is paid to the officers of the ship by the English government in addition to the thirty-five shillings per ton upon the hull. The vessels are then condemned and sawn in two. Several such half hulks lie on the beach here. I noticed two American schooners in port, fine rakish looking vessels, appearing as if they were for what they call here the "black-bird trade." Our American officers, whom I met in the Canary islands, complain that they cannot get prizes, as the English have spies all along the coast and get information, which they can afford to pay for, as John Bull pays such large prize money, while our people pay only in sympathy.

An amusing incident has just occurred. A negro soldier came on deck and handed me a note. I found he spoke but little English jargon, which the negroes use, and I asked him where he came from. He said he was a captured slave, and now received half-pay for military service. At that moment he recognised a Portuguese passenger as the man who had sold him on the coast. His eye glistened with anger as he spoke to the person, and said, "You sold me." The Portuguese could not recollect him, as he was one out of one hundred and sixty which he admitted he bought, and sold at a profit of twenty-eight dollars per head. On further conversation, the negro admitted that he was now very glad of the change.

The brig Harris, an American, has lately been taken. The English had watched the vessel for a long time as suspicious, and, in fact, knew what it was up to, but it is policy for them to wait until the negroes are on board; thus they get apprentices and the bounty money. In the evening the Englishman visited the ship, the cargo was already on board, the hatches closed, and some negroes lying on deck, who were reported as native sailors of the coast. The crew were pulling the tails of pigs to make them squeal, to prevent the hearing of noise from the hold, where officers stood with revolvers, threatening the negroes if they did not keep quiet. The hatches were down twenty minutes. The commander left, satisfied that the game was not yet bagged, and went away, when an English captain informed him that he had seen the negroes going on board. Had it not been for this information the American would have been off. He was watched, boarded, and commanded to haul down his flag and give up his papers. The American denied the right to board him, according to treaty. Then, said the commander, I will detain you until I find an American cruizer, and you will be delivered up and tried as a pirate. The effect was produced, and a compromise took place. The Englishman turned his back, the flag was hauled down, and the papers were thrown overboard, officers and men permitted to leave with their effects, and the vessel seized as a prize, without nationality of papers, or flag.

# CLVIII.

Cape Coast Castle, West Coast op Africa, *March 18, 1860.*

On our departure from Sierra Leone, we proceeded down the coast of Liberia, and landed at Harper, Cape Palmas. I found the Rev. Mr. Ramba in charge of the Missionary Establishment. There were two young ladies who had recently arrived from the United States. One of them had not recovered from the African fever. I found there, in the little town, many manumitted slaves from Kentucky, Virginia, and Maryland, with whom I conversed; also, some of the recaptured slaves from the brig Echo, which were sent out by the frigate Niagara. The United States Government pay one year's schooling, and those unable to take care of themselves are apprenticed. I was invited to dine by the family who occupy the Asylum buildings, erected by the Protestant Episcopal Society of the United States. The position is most commanding and elevated, on a promontory bathed by the rolling surf, with tropical fruits and flowers in the background. But notwithstanding its advantageous location, the malignant fever of Africa finds its way. Being in a country where no distinction is made in color, I find myself at table with white and black missionaries and their wives, reminding me of my peregrinations in the island of Hayti, where my table companions in some outside villages were only of the sable hue. You are aware that the English and French are unlike the Americans in their prejudices in this particular. On board our steamer, we have had in the first cabin, and at table, practical amalgamation. Foreigners have native wives, and you find children running about of every dye. It goes even further, in the marriage of white women with black men.

Liberia, you are aware, is a republic, having its President, Senators, and Representatives. The towns are mostly occupied by the native population, whose wants are quite limited, as is the case with the black race generally in this country, whose dress consists at most of a small handkerchief or a string of pearls about the loins. The incentive to labor is slight, and the efforts of the missionaries meet with little success; and unless through some special providence, this benighted coast can make but little progress. An intelligent mulatto woman came down with us to Cape Coast Castle, in the cabin. She was from Savannah, Georgia. She had come over with her husband, to visit her father and mother, who had emigrated to Liberia, and died with fever. She had lost her husband by the same disease, and wished herself back again. She remarked, that at times she had hopes for the Colony, and then again felt discouraged, as many of the manumitted slaves, instead of showing an example to the heathen, fell into their vices. The trade of Liberia is very limited; and, were it not for the Colonization Society, their case now might be hopeless. They have a small war schooner, presented by the British Government; one schooner, called the Monrovia, was in port, which trades with the United States. I must here mention a circumstance which occurred in sending over a parcel of manumitted negroes from New Orleans. A philanthropic captain offered to bring over the party for a nominal sum; he supplied himself with water casks well filled, and abundant provisions for a long voyage, and returning with ample berth accommodations. Of course he obtained his clearance for such a benevolent object without difficulty, landed the released blacks, ran down the coast, filled up with slaves, and landed his cargo of human flesh on the island of Cuba!

We proceed along, down to the Dutch town and fort of Elmina, and the English fort and town of Cape Coast Castle, on the Gold Coast. The surf and breakers along this coast at times are frightful; but the naked natives, in boats dug out of the trunks of trees, containing from ten to fifteen persons, with side oars or paddles, not unlike huge wooden shovels, swarm around the ship, and carry you ashore through the foaming billows. Once the beach struck, they jump in the water to draw the boat up, and then carry you on their backs to dry land. The Dutch Governor, six miles above here, has just visited the English Governor, and held what is termed a Palaver with the Queen of Assin, who was escorted by bands of nearly naked negro troops or subjects, with the most wild and discordant music from tom-toms or kettle-drums, reed flutes, frightful sounding gongs, ringing of small bells, etc., amid the yells and shouts of this maddened crew. Another body of Bushmen, who were going to war with a neighboring tribe, were congregating with their muskets, which they are all provided with; they had been parading with a white umbrella over the captain's head, under a vertical sun, with as much veneration as the carrying of the Host over the head of the Pope, in the church ceremonies of Rome. At length they bivouacked under the shade of a wide-spread mango tree, where rum, the usual beverage of the natives, was passed around, amid the shouts, laughter, and war songs of these half savages, much to the edification of a half dozen slave girls, who were peeping over a wall adjoining.

Ships come down to the coast of Guinea from Boston and New York, loaded with the two staples of negro luxury, rum and tobacco; but I am sorry to learn that some of those people who cry out so strongly against our domestic institution of the South, and would willingly sacrifice our beloved Union, lend themselves to the slave trade, in furnishing empty rum casks to slavers, which are filled with water, and get a clearance from the Custom House, as if engaged in legitimate traffic; thereby enabling them to run along the coast for the sale of articles without suspicion, when they fill up with slaves and start for Cuba.

The soil here abounds with particles of gold, which the natives wash when their daily wants require small means, but they are destitute of the merit of perseverance unless forced to it. The white population consists here of only a few officers in the fort, supported by native or apprenticed soldiers. The native houses or huts are of wicker or reed work, plastered with mud and covered with palm leaves or branches. The Wesleyan missionaries have a fine, eligible establishment. I found three of their number here present, as also some native preachers and teachers. One of the number is the nephew to the king of the Ashantees. He had been sent to England for an education. They were well provided with the good things of this life in eating and drinking, which they are entitled to in this barbarous country.

I saw sheep and goats on the grounds—some monkeys chattering about; large numbers are found in the woods; the natives are fond of them, and their skins are an article of exportation, for ladies' muffs.

We have had a melancholy duty to perform: one of our fellow passengers, who-occupied a state room opposite to me, died night before last. He was a physician, who could not heal himself according to the command in Scripture. Our number of passengers was now reduced to four. He had supped with us, and two hours after was a corpse. I felt it a duty to assist in performing the last rites of a Christian burial, not knowing but others might be called upon to perform a similar service for one seven thousand miles from home. The ship carpenter made a rude pine coffin, which was covered with the English union jack. We solicited the offices of a missionary, but whether from the sudden shock, or fear of fever, I know not, but I found myself the only passenger among the group following his mortal remains to the white man's little graveyard, carried upon the shoulders of negroes. The captain, purser, first engineer, and myself, stood with white umbrellas under a broiling sun, the parched earth almost blistering our feet, until the burial service was read by the officiating Episcopal clergyman in his white robes. It was the mournful sight of a Christian burial in strong contrast with the listless, idle, and gazing groups of dark, naked figures, which curiosity had attracted to the spot. A civil engineer in the Government employ, was the only resident who joined us in the funeral, and to whose house we adjourned after the ceremonies were over; we were provided with refreshments, which we stood in need of.

Many forts along the coast, which once amounted to thirty, have fallen into decay; they were used for slave factories, and were in the possession of the Portuguese, the Dutch, the Danes, and the English, to provide the Colonies with slaves.

We proceed to Acra, further along the coast, in possession of the Dutch and English, and thence to the territory of the king of Dahomy, who is now waging war to procure slaves for the annual sacrifice, and I may be able to give you some of these barbarous statistics.

# CLIX.

Steamer Athenien, off Lagos, West Coast of Africa, *March 23, 1860.*

After visiting the Grain, Ivory, and Gold Coasts, and the territory of the king of Dahomy, we now find ourselves off the formidable breakers of Lagos. The mail bags we headed up in a puncheon, in the event of capsizing the native boat. The landing is so unsafe, and being probably the worst on the coast of Africa, none of us are allowed to make the attempt. Two passengers from Acra go on board of vessels lying outside, at anchor, until a more favorable opportunity offers. Sometimes no landing is effected for weeks. The sharks are so abundant that they upset crews of natives, and strangers are often lost.

Acra, our next landing-place after Cape Coast Castle, is one-half occupied by the English fort and native town, and the other half by a Dutch fort and settlement. The resident traders complain of the want of commerce, as the king of the country, whom the English had punished and laid under tribute of ten thousand pounds, payable in palm oil, at fixed prices, would not execute the payment. I there found two merchants from Cape Coast, who had bought the contract, &c., which the king now rejects. It remains to be seen if the British will enforce it.

The Danes were in possession of a large fort at Christianborg, a few miles from Acra, which they have sold to the English for the nominal sum of five thousand pounds. The Commandant of the English fort politely offered me his horse, and a recommendation to the officer in command, which I accepted, and found, in the absence of the Governor, only one officer and the doctor of the station. Five officers had died of the African fever, and the soldiery consisted of one hundred and thirteen negroes. The town looked abandoned, and in part battered down, as the native tribes had attacked the fort, which is well mounted with small brass guns. They were soon put to flight, and the broken walls of the village indicated the result.

The fort is eligibly situated; the sand was scorching hot, but the sea breeze in the shade was cool and refreshing; the surf was rolling in strongly, and hundreds of negroes were in it bathing. The little cemetery, as I passed, showed the new-made graves; the African ants had thrown up, hastily, pyramids of a conical form, ten feet in height.

Notwithstanding the curious scenes to occupy the mind, and the white umbrellas as a protection from heat, I felt the blood boiling in my veins, and if I had given way to my emotions, would have fancied the fever was upon me.

In Acra, I met with a Yankee trader, whose house was situated among and surrounded by the huts of the natives. The walls of the court inclosed his cooperage and his buildings for palm-oil casks, and supplies of rum, tobacco, and notions.

A group of nearly naked boys and girls were counting cowrie shells from Zanzibar, which furnishes small currency, and which are separated in little parcels with great alacrity. They are there worth forty to the cent, or four thousand to the dollar. They are also strung as beads, and worn about the neck and loins by both sexes.

The Yankee looked sallow, as if the African climate was doing its work; but the desire of gain is an incentive sufficient for the white man to try to live in a climate which nature designed only for the black race.

The king of Dahomy, whose capital is about ninety miles from the coast, permits no forts in his dominions. Whydah and Badagry have been famous for the slave trade. When the late king died some six hundred slaves were buried alive with him. They were made drunk and then driven into an excavated grotto or prison house, which was then walled up. I here give you a list of the articles and objects deposited on the occasion of the funeral from an eye-witness:

Ten pieces of silk, five dozen country cloths, twenty guns, eight bags of cowrie shells, two boxes soap, male and female slave, as present from the Yavogah of Whydah, scarfs, table cloths, satin, silk handkerchiefs, velvets, carpets, packages of unbleached shirting, a present from the great slaver Domingo, a cocked hat and plume, gold chains, slippers, ten puncheons of rum, forty kegs of powder, another male and female slave, with letter to the deceased king, in addition to the six or eight hundred already mentioned.

The king of Dahomy is now at war with his neighbors to procure prisoners and slaves for the anniversary custom of sacrifices and consecration to the memory of the late king. All the whites within his territory on the coast are invited and commanded to be present at the sacrifices. All resident traders and vessels are compelled to pay tonnage dues for the privilege of trade, or make presents to the king. A Portuguese whom we landed from the steamer, and who had delivered a cargo of negroes in Havana, for which he obtained one thousand dollars per head, and which had cost from twenty-five to forty dollars, had four trunks of valuable goods, comprising rich crimson velvets, and other articles, as presents for the king.

He is said to have some twenty-five thousand warriors, and a body-guard of eight thousand Amazons, with a vast number of wives in addition. He also possesses extensive buildings and palaces, all of which have been contributed without doubt by the whites in the way of trade, or for the purchase of slaves.

If a vessel is wrecked, or goes ashore, the whole property belongs to the king, and the officers and crew are sent up to his capital. A Hamburg brig just wrecked lost everything, and the captain and crew would have been sent up, had not the king been absent making war for slaves. We found three of the crew on board of an American brig now in the offing.

The captain of the brig Jehosse has just come on board of us from the American trading barque Baron de Castine, whose supercargo we brought down from Acra. The former captain had died and been replaced; the present captain was also sick, but under the care of the doctor of the British steamer Viper. He represents that he came out with lumber and provisions from Charleston, S. C., and was on a legitimate trading voyage, when he was boarded by Captain Fitzroy, of the British steamer Falcon, who demanded his register and list of crew, which were given up, who declared him to be a slaver, and ordered him to haul down his flag, which he refused; he was then ordered to open his box of private papers, which he also refused. A prize crew was ordered on board, and himself and crew sent as prisoners on board the steamer. The men were stripped and examined, the captain's box broken open and papers examined. The clearances, &c., were all found legal, and the captain and crew released. He protested against a release, but was put on his vessel, where he found his liquors all drunk, cigars smoked, prize crew drunk, and the vessel in danger of beaching in the kingdom of Dahomy. The officer in command of the prize crew begged of him to come to his relief, and gave a certificate to that effect. The brig has waited fifty or sixty days for an American cruiser, but not finding one to take up the case, the captain sends his vessel to the United States as abandoned, and takes our steamer to catch an American man-of-war before which to bring his case.

It will be a serious matter for Captain Fitzroy, who is represented as a dissipated commander, of aristocratic family, but will now probably lose his commission, and the British government will pay heavy damages.

A singular custom prevails among the natives of the coast. I asked particularly the details of a black missionary. Every man has a lien upon his nephews and nieces, and can pawn them for debt, or sell them into slavery, but this right he cannot exercise over his own children. In the event of the death of a person, his property goes to his sister, as next of kin. She or her husband takes care of the children, and if occasion demand, they are made slaves, or pawned.

# CLX.

BONNY RIVER, GULF OF GUINEA, *March 27, 1860.*

From Lagos, our steamer proceeded to the river Benin, landed some cargo, and received forty-two puncheons of palm oil. We there found a Hamburg ship, just in from Zanzibar, on the coast of Africa, with a full cargo of cowrie shells, used for currency and ornaments. The shores are here monotonous; the vegetation is rank, as well as at the mouth of the Niger, which we passed on our way to this place.

A project is on foot for a new expedition up the Niger, the former expedition on the part of the British government having met with disaster. We have a disabled steward now on board, who accompanied these adventurers; he is as yellow as a marigold, and the seeds of fever in him will probably never be eradicated.

The entrance to Bonny river is difficult, and requires watchful navigation. We brought on deck a huge iron riveted air-tight boiler, to be used as a buoy or guide to mariners passing the bar, and came near losing it, as well as our vessel.

Sunday morning, May 25th, according to usual custom on board of British vessels, the Church of England service was read in the presence of crew and passengers; and I was quite interested in noticing some blacks from Monrovia, who were present, and seemed to take some interest in the ceremonies. At five P. M., just at the close of dinner, the ship some seven miles from the mouth of the river, under full sail and heavy head of steam, the captain on the bridge, struck a sand-bar, jumped twice, and we rushed on deck and found her in a perilous condition. We got out hawsers astern, furled all sail, and worked the machine and windlass back, to haul off, but without success. Night was approaching, and the breakers increasing, the ship at times keeling over, and then jumping as if the masts would come out of her. The ports and skylights of cabin closed, with the sea breaking over the stern, made it look dreary enough. Being on a barbarous coast, where no white man lives, the prospects were not very flattering. The boats were all got in condition, with buckets for bailing. Rockets were sent up for relief, hoping they might be seen some five miles up from the mouth of the river, where lay a small steamer, used as a tender, and for the continuation of the voyage to Fernando Po. Our own steamer being at the end of her line in the Gulf of Guinea, usually takes in her coal from a hulk moored in the stream, brushes up, and waits the return of the tender, with freight picked up in the Old Calabar and Camaroon rivers. A little time after the accident occurred, one of our passengers, an old sea captain, came to me, and said softly, "If you have anything valuable which you wish to save, you had better get it out, as

I would not give fifty pounds for the vessel." I was hurriedly packing up a few articles, when the purser came to me and said, "I have been securing the ship's papers and valuables, and I would advise your taking a few articles in your valise, as we may have to take the ship's boats outside the breakers, and wait for the tide." You can imagine we passed a wretched and sleepless night. The engines were soon choked up with sand, and all began to think the ship must be lost, although strongly built. Morning brought us more quiet weather. We sent the second mate with a boat's crew up the river for relief. He had twelve miles to make, with sails and oars. At mid-day the little steamer came. We threw overboard coal, and palm oil in puncheons, to lighten the ship, took advantage of the wind, steam, &c., and succeeded in forcing her over the sandbars by nightfall. We had taken refuge on board of the small steamer, in the distance, as she could not approach us for the shoals; and I got off with a portion of my effects, in wet condition.

The Bonny is a broad and navigable river. The New Calibar River comes in a short distance from this place. The trade of the two rivers is in palm oil. Vessels of large size come out from England with a variety of goods, that can be used by the natives in the interior, such as waistcloths, beads, rum, tobacco, guns, powder, &c.

The vessels are anchored, sails put away, the ship is housed in, with peaked roof, covered with palm leaf, making it cool; and here they remain for two years, or until they get full. They have their cooperage on board, the casks being brought in shooks [bundles of staves]. The natives come alongside in canoes, with the oil made from the berry of the palm tree, boiled and skimmed, and enter the ship, fitted up like a country store for barter and trade. Some want brass stair rods as currency, which treasure can, in emergencies, be buried, and not injured by rust. Some want a portion of most articles named. The native chiefs and traders buy largely, and some on credit, which is paid for in oil in quantities.

The small currency here is not the cowrie-shell, but small horseshoe-formed brass articles called manillas.

At this enlightened age of the world we hear so little of cannibalism, that were I not an eye-witness, I also should be doubtful. I lauded with a party here on the shore, proceeded through the bush, was carried on the shoulders of our Kroomen sailors, through the pools of water, and came to the village of Bonny, composed of huts of reed, plastered with mud, covered with palm leaves, without any attempt at ornament or architecture in construction on lines of alleys or streets. A party of girls and boys, of some ten years of age, whose dress consisted of a string of beads about the loins, and with long poles in hand, were trying to drive out a "guana" [a species of lizard] into the marsh, and he persisted in not going voluntarily. This brute was five feet in length, harmless, and one of their fetisches [idols]. They would punch him along, and turn him with their poles, at which he would bite, but they dared not lay hands on the holy animal. Woe to the man who inadvertently or wilfully kills one! We were then told that the heads of the two prisoners who were killed, and whose bodies were eaten the day previous, were in front of the Joujou House, or heathen temple, to which we repaired. We found the head of a female, some eighteen years of age, having good teeth and features, but little distorted, notwithstanding the beheading with a dull axe. The man appeared to have been forty years of age. A party of men were dancing like wild Indians around the heads, and in front of the mud temple, to the sounds of tom-toms, or kettle-drums, reed flutes, &c.; the Joujou men, or priests, were singing monotonous and discordant songs. The heads of the victims began to smell, rendering the feast, perhaps, more acceptable to the priests' wives, whose privilege it is to have soup made from the heads, after which the whitened skulls will be placed upon a rude platform, standing in front of the temple, which now contains the craniums and bones of the last victims; and these ghastly relics will add further trophies to the paved floor of the building, whose walls are also provided with scores of others. I have often gazed upon the beautiful and variegated mosaic floors of marble in the churches of Italy, but it had never occurred to me that I should ever see a heathen temple with a mosaic floor of the skulls and bones of prisoners who had been killed and eaten. When I reflected upon the narrow escape we had just made upon this barbarous coast, within a few miles of such wretches, who might now be feasting upon our remains, if thrown helpless in their hands, I could only express my gratitude to heaven for my protection.

# CLXI.

MAYUMBA, SOUTH AFRICA, *April 3, 1860.*

I abandoned the good staunch ship, which barely escaped leaving her wreck upon the bar. I there found a little steamer called the Rainbow, which formed a part of the Niger Expedition, but she was not in running order at present. I came down with the Retriever, a small steamer acting as tender for the old one I had left, and we proceeded to the island of Fernando Po, about forty miles from the main land, after getting out of the Gulf of Guinea. The island is fertile, with high mountainous country, and is very gratifying to the eye after the monotonous scenery already passed through. It is occupied by a different race of negroes from those of the African coast, called Boobies, and whose habits and manner are milder and more harmless. They daub their bodies, faces, and wool with red clay, and one of their belles squatted on the ground before a small mirror, adorning herself, her only garment being a strip of a handkerchief, would certainly be considered a droll sight in a civilized country. They differ from all the negro races of the African coast, whose reputation for chastity is not remarkable. The crime of adultery is punished there with the loss of the right arm, and in some cases is enforced.

Tornadoes are not infrequent in the Gulf of Guinea. We experienced one on our way down from Bonny. I was awakened past midnight by terrific peals of thunder and forked lightning, the howling of the winds, and the cry of officers upon deck. Looking out, I perceived amid the vivid flashes of lightning, the naked stalwart figures of the Kroomen, or African sailors. I could only compare the reality of what occurred with the faint efforts of some dark and wild demoniacal scene upon the stage. Our ship did her duty, and we came out safe.

On the African coast one sees many strange phenomena. One evening the whole sea seemed a sheet of phosphorescent brightness, lighting up the night, so that one could almost read. The crest of the waves was tinged with silvery light, and the vessel seemed ploughing through quicksilver. On another occasion, one hundred miles from land, the fine dust and reddish sand covered the deck, the wind bringing these particles from the parched and burning south.

The Spaniards are in possession of the island of Fernando Po, for the second time, having once abandoned it. They are now attempting the re-occupation of the country. The insidious fever is making sad work, and a large part of the colonists have already died. The Governor's family is on board of a war vessel, and will go back to Spain. It is a singular fact that white females cannot live there. The only lady is the wife of the English Consul, who suffers much from ill health. Quinine is the most valuable article here as an antidote and cure for fever. One of our commanders paid ninety dollars for twenty-nine ounces. When I arrived at Fernando Po, I had reached the terminus of communication by English steamers, and unless I could fall in with some man-of-war, I must retrace my steps. I fortunately found the United States war steamer Mystic, Capt. Leroy, whose brother I had made voyages with in California and Oregon, and his first Lieutenant, Haxton, whom I had known intimately years since. When we met at the English Consul's house, they expressed their great surprise at meeting one whom they had spoken of recently, in this barbarous part of the world. My desire being to continue down to St. Paul de Loando, and all along the cruising ground of the American squadron, Capt. Leroy kindly offered me the half of his cabin.

We proceeded to Princess Island, one of the group of several, including Fernando Po, which are of volcanic origin. There we made a connexion with the sloop-of-war Portsmouth, to put on board three officers recently from the United States by the war steamer Mohican.

We paid Capt. Calhoun and his ship and officers a visit. They are bound to Madeira, to communicate with the flag officer, Commodore Inman of the Constellation. A day spent in taking in wood and water, and getting supplies of chickens, oranges, limes, bananas, alligator pears, and other fruits, and looking at and admiring the freaks of nature in the formation of peaks, pyramids, domes, cones, and every conceivable feature in scenery, with the richest and most exuberant growth of tropical forests and fruits, we then left for this point, to meet the United States steamer Sumpter, and transfer the correspondence for the vessels on the station below. The discipline and order on board of the Mystic are of a high character, perfect unity and good feeling existing between officers and men, which is so desirable, especially on stations so much exposed and so remote. The Sabbath is strictly observed, with religious exercises. The health of those on board of the ship was remarkably good, which is much to say on this fiery coast, with upwards of one hundred and fifty men.

We have just spoken the British war vessel Archer. This is the fourth English ship cruising for slavers that we have met on the coast thus far. We expect soon to see the Sumpter, when I shall be transferred to her, to proceed down to the Congo River—a great point for the shipping of slaves, and from thence by a schooner to the Portuguese city of St. Paul de Loanda, in latitude eight deg. south. It is the most important settlement of the coast south of Sierra Leone.

We have now crossed the equator, and proceed south. You can imagine the heat, as this is the height of summer. Awnings, umbrellas, fruits, and refreshing drinks, would at times be abandoned willingly for a pound of ice. The African station is the hardest and most wearing upon the constitution of our naval officers. It is withering and weakening, and were it not that they are almost constantly on shipboard it would make sad work with them. Those of the men who are imprudent enough to sleep ashore and expose themselves, suffer the penalty of fever. The crew never have the privilege granted in these latitudes, but occasionally a sailor on shore duty gets astray, and has to suffer the consequences. During a two years' cruise, if a vessel goes to Saint Helena or Madeira, then the captain avails himself of these healthy points to give his men, in rotation, such hours of liberty as may be deemed prudent.

The British steamer Pluto captured, not long since, the American bark Orion, with seven hundred and fifteen slaves on board, composed of men, women, and children; one hundred and fifty-two had died on the passage, as she started with eight hundred and seventy-one. She was taken to St. Helena, and condemned—the negroes apprenticed as usual. The officers having hauled down their colors and thrown their papers overboard, would have escaped, but this steamer went in pursuit and secured the officers, and sent them to the United States; whether they will be convicted or not, remains to be seen.

# CLXII.

ON BOARD U. S. WAR STEAMER SUMPTER, ST. PAUL DE LOANDO, *April 14, 1860.*

I was transferred from the war steamer Mystic, and presented to the officers of the Sumpter, from whom I have received the kindest evidences of hospitality. Captain McDonough offered me his table and cabin, and Lieutenant Stewart, and his brother officers, of the wardroom mess, always make me a welcome guest. A tourist is scarcely ever found on this benighted coast, and for that reason I am well treated. It is only when I find myself out of the way of all civilized lines of communication, that I am willing to trouble either our own officers, or those of foreign governments; but necessity has obliged me to sail under the flags of several.

We met the British war steamer Falmouth, which took the American brig Jehosse, and afterwards released her, the captain abandoned her, as I wrote you, and came in pursuit of an American man-of-war. Lieutenant Stewart came on board to verify the certificates which Captain Fitzroy gave Captain Vincent, who is now with us. He and his officers admitted their signatures. The documents will be sent to the United States, copies having already been forwarded for diplomatic action.

We met the sloop-of-war Marion, Captain Brent, and passed a few hours on board of her, as pleasantly as circumstances would permit, after the disappointment the officers had experienced in not receiving instructions to return home after a two years' cruise. They expected confidently such orders by the mail we brought down. Fortunately for me, instead of being transferred to a small schooner at the Congo River for this port, the Sumpter was ordered here for supplies at the naval station.

At the Gaboon, a French settlement, they have their barracoons for free labor, which is slavery under another form, and which the English and Americans dare not interfere with. The negroes are enlisted for a term of years, under the payment of a certain sum for service, in the islands of Martinique and Guadaloupe. They are shipped legitimately, and not packed as with slavers, who are forced to watch their opportunity, and escape with as many as possible, without regard to breathing space or supplies of water. The negroes shipped are either slaves already, or pawned for debt, and made to say they are willing—and probably escape much worse bondage than they would in their native country. They certainly do, if they are treated as our negroes in the southern states.

Our ship overhauled recently an American brig, with slave deck laid; but her papers were in order. The captain at first sent a lieutenant and men on board of her, and was going to send her to the United States as a prize, no doubt being entertained of the intention of running off a cargo; but upon reflection and advice, he abandoned the project. If she was not condemned at home, the owners would come upon the captain for all the damages, and his private funds would be taken to pay for it. The government does not assume the responsibility. If commanders do their duty, they must put their property out of their hands, and have nothing to lose. They can then take suspicious vessels and send them to the United States—but they may have judgments hanging over them all their lives. It is an undisputed fact, that the slave trade is carried on by American vessels mostly, and to the shame of our northern and New England states, whence come the constant cries against the South. A ship which I once made a passage in to Havre, has been fitted out as a whaler, with all the appliances, for the purpose, without doubt, as a decoy, and instead of catching the black whales, they intend to capture another kind of animal of the same color. Her papers are all in order. Captain Goudon, of the new war steamer Mohican, whom I visited on this station, boarded her. She is just out from the United States, and is in suspicious waters, where there are no whales. His excuse is, they wanted some fresh water. She can take a thousand negroes, and is here under the garb of a whaler; but no American officer dare take her without the negroes on board, unless he is made liable for personal damages. The whole thing is a farce. If our government was honest in the suppression of the slave trade, and would take the responsibility of loss in case of failure of confiscation, the trade would soon be lessened.

We have a squadron of four vessels now on the African coast, and three are off active duty. The flag ship is at Madeira, the Portsmouth has just started for that place, and I met the San Jacinto at Teneriffe, going to Cadiz for repairs.

We are expending large sums to keep up a squadron of eighty guns, according to the Ashburton Treaty, and are hunting up the game for the English to bag. They watch and wait, and have their spies; and when the vessels are filled they seize them. The captain, under threat of being handed over to an American man-of-war, and tried for piracy, makes a bargain for his life and the lives of his crew, probably saving some property, hauls down his flag and throws his papers overboard. The Englishman gets his bounty money, and turns over the negroes for colonists for seven years, which probably often means life.

The bay of Loando is deep and tolerably broad; the water close to town is shallow from the washing of the high clay banks, which extend along the coast, and form the upper town. This is the oldest settlement (Portuguese) along the coast, and I notice some old dates, of the year 1600. The slave trade built it up. The Brazil markets were supplied from here. Some fifty thousand were supplied annually. That has ceased, and the town and country become commercial. The soil in the interior is fertile, and produces excellent coffee, which rivals the Mocha in quality. There is a Governor-General, a custom-house, police and military force. The lower town is very sandy and hot. The negro population is large. Slavery continues, but will expire by limitation in ten years. Fever prevails to a considerable extent; the only safeguard is, to sleep on shipboard. No hotels or restaurants are to be found. The merchants who have vessels trading with the United States, Portugal, and other countries, have as large and comfortable houses as possible, and frequently invite friends to their table. The English have a consul and adjudicator for condemned vessels.

The American Consul is connected with a business firm in Salem, who have trading vessels and factories on the coast. At Quecimbo, a bartering point along shore, we found four factories, or bungalows, English, Dutch, and American. They are constructed of reed and palm, large, light, and airy, inclosing courts or yards by picket-worked fences, and there they are without protection from the natives, other than a few fire-arms. An important event occurred there a few days before our visit. A Congo prince, who had been educated in Portugal, wishing to make some reform in the negro administration of matters, was pursued, and took refuge in the English factory. He was demanded by the natives, who surrounded the establishment in thousands. Finding that the building would be sacrificed and given up to pillage, he gave himself up, and was killed within thirty feet, his body cut in pieces, and scattered about. We were surrounded by a group of these black, dirty, and naked subjects—two were called princes, but the only distinction was they wore a sort of cap, while others disdain every covering but the wool.

# CLXIII.

ON BOARD PORTUGUESE STEAMER ESTAPHANIA, PROVINCE OF
ANGOLA, *April 24, 1860.*

Being so far down on the south-west coast of Africa, my full intention had been to proceed to the Cape of Good Hope, if by any possible conveyance I could get there; but it appears I have run out the end of the chain, and no opportunity offering, I must get back by the best possible means. This steamer is my only chance, direct to Portugal, and, if nothing presents itself, I must turn my face again towards Europe, with the prospect of a thirty-five days' passage, touching along the African coast at Ambriz and the Island of San Tomé, and thence up to the Cape de Verdes.

The captain of the English gunboat Lynx, now bound to the island of Ascension, has kindly offered to take me, through the recommendation of the English consul, but the chance being less of getting away from there I declined.

This is the province where the African traveller, Livingstone, came out when he returned to England. The captain of the Lynx met him recently, on the east coast of Africa.

The colonial government here is in trouble. I noticed Portuguese and black soldiers going on board of a brig moored near us. The negroes rose near Ambriz in large numbers, attacked the troops, and succeeded in killing and driving into the river some one hundred and forty men. One of the officers, who dined with a government employé where I was invited the other day, narrowly escaped with his life.

The heat is now most oppressive and overpowering. We have frequent thunderstorms with vivid lightning, which tends to purify the atmosphere. It is far the safest to sleep on shipboard, as the fever is prevailing ashore.

Maxillas are used for moving about the town of Loanda, as the least exertion produces violent perspiration, and exposure to the sun brings disastrous results. The mode of conveyance is somewhat like the palanquin in the East Indies, but not so spacious or convenient. You are carried by two negroes, instead of four or six, as are used there. Here a sort of sofa bottom of cane work is suspended by cords from a light roof, attached to a strong pole, resting upon the shoulders of the bearers. A cushion supports the back, and curtains are floating on each side, which keep off the sun, and the motion produces a gentle breeze. In this manner you make your visits and excursions in the town and suburbs.

There are no American or English men-of-war in port. We have three persons on board waiting for a passage; one a purser of an American man-of-war going home invalided; a Portuguese from Benguela who has exposed himself and got the fever; and myself, afflicted with "Job's comforters," which keep off the same disease. Our numbers will be augmented in a day or two.

The English are making great efforts to introduce the culture of cotton in Africa, so as to render them less dependent upon the United States. I heard at Acra, on the Gold Coast, that a few bales had been shipped to Liverpool. In Liberia I learned that the Manchester Cotton Association had sent medals and fifty pounds sterling as premiums, for the encouragement of the growth of the plant in that district. I learned also at Bonny that two bales, purchased at Rabba on the Niger, had been brought down by the Rainbow, attached to the Niger expedition, which is the first from that country. The captain reports he could have filled his ship with uncleaned cotton. The price of the cleaned was from three to four cents per pound, our currency, uncleaned about one cent. Another report said one hundred and fifteen pounds of cotton in the seed were bought for five and-a-half yards of cotton velvet and eight pounds of salt. There is plenty of raw cotton, and gins and presses are all that is required to produce a merchantable article. If the English persevere and the natives turn their attention to cotton, there is no calculating what the production might in time amount to; but there is this satisfaction for the American planter, the consumption is rapidly increasing, and there is not much fear of a surplus for years to come. The culture of the plant, as I have seen it in Algeria and the East Indies, cannot come in competition with the negro labor at the South; but we may rest assured that the British are using every means possible to have it produced, and make themselves less subject to our Southern King Cotton.

I must say something of a peculiar race of negroes on the African coast, who seem far superior to their fellows. They are the Kroomen, who make invaluable sailors for men of-war-and merchant vessels, and indeed are indispensable for all labor on shipboard, saving the white mariners from service and consequent fever. They are generally large, stalwart, well-formed men, obedient and industrious. They are shipped in Monrovia by vessels of war for the cruise, and receive from five to eight dollars per month, the chief as much as twelve dollars. In Sierra Leone, merchant vessels procure them for five dollars per month. Many of them understand a little English, and they could not be made slaves of without great difficulty. They rather look down with contempt upon common negroes. On shipboard they answer to the call of the roll. Some names given them are so ludicrous one can scarcely refrain from laughing when he hears them. Some bear the names of ships upon which they have sailed, and feel highly flattered in consequence, such as Constitution, Congress, Vincennes, Dale, &c., but the others, Up Side Down, Tom Bottle, Sunbeam, Main Mast, Main Hatch, Joe Propeller, Inside

Out, Tar Bucket, Ash Bucket, Last One, Nothing New, and so on, display the extraordinary nomenclature conceived by the Jack Tars. When on duty ashore from men-of-war they wear blue woollen shirts and pants, but always on shipboard they have the privilege of the native waistcloth. They choose their chief, who is at the head of the gang, and whom they obey most rigidly. The Marion will land sixty or more at Monrovia before she leaves the coast for the United States, being the complement of two vessels. They save their money to increase the number of their wives.

The process of coaling here is of the slowest kind, and that of ballasting ships the same. The distance from the shore is considerable, and the manner of doing things is, as the Portuguese language describes it, poco-a-poco, little by little. The coal or ballast is put in at the rate of thirty-six tons per day, with baskets like good-sized soup dishes, passed from hand to hand, not unlike the old-fashioned system of handing buckets at a fire.

No freight of consequence is offering, as the disturbance in the country has checked the movement. Ordinarily elephants' tusks, palm oil, gum, coffee, etc., are coming forward.

We are now in the height of midsummer, with the thermometer over a hundred. There is no such thing as restraining perspiration, except by the fever. What would one give for a cooling draught of ice water, and the other luxuries and comforts of a northern clime, which are not obtainable even at an advance of two hundred or three hundred per cent. We are looking forward to our deliverance from this heated atmosphere in a few days at least, and to be under motion, when some circulation will be produced.

The slow, backward Portuguese colony even requires strangers, as well as its own citizens, on leaving it to procure a passport, with all the formalities attending the same, at an expense of five dollars, without recognising the passport of one's own country. This may be in part caused from apprehension of the escape of felons and soldiers, who are sent to this convict colony to expiate their crimes. I should think no worse punishment could be inflicted than a residence in such a climate.

# CLXIV.

Island of San Miguel, Azores, *June 8, 1860.*

In my last I informed you that I was on the eve of leaving the Portuguese province of Angola, on the south-west of Africa. I expected to reach the Cape de Verde Island in time to catch the English steamer for Lisbon, but arrived two days too late.

We stopped at the town of Ambriz, in the Congo territory, now the seat of war between the Portuguese and the blacks, and found the residents in great consternation from the recent successes of the negroes. A war vessel had just arrived with fresh troops.

We then proceeded to the island of San Tomé, one of the volcanic group consisting of that, Prince's and Fernando Po, which for fertility, magnificent mountain scenery, and beautiful tropical forests can scarcely be surpassed, producing the choicest coffee and fruits in abundance, but occupied mostly by the dark race, with small numbers of Portuguese colonists, the former indolent as usual unless force is exercised, and the latter lethargic from the oppressive heat and afflicted with fevers—otherwise, these islands might be considered perfect gems of the ocean.

On the ninth day we left San Tomé for Porto Praya, Cape de Verdes. Our complement of passengers had now reached fifteen, including one white lady. Our ship reminded me of Noah's ark, as we had such a variety of animals and birds on board, either as supplies, or belonging to passengers bound to Portugal and carrying specimens of the brute creation occupying the countries they came from, not forgetting a few negro boys and girls, from six to seven years old, as presents to friends, which seem to be classed in the same category, as they cost from ten dollars to fifteen dollars each. For a voyage of twenty to thirty days in a large screw steamer of only fifty horse power, relying upon wind as well as steam, the auxiliary force being only four or five miles per hour, it was necessary to provide abundantly, and we had oxen, sheep, goats, chickens, turkeys and guinea fowls. The rigging and chain about the boats suspended on the sides were hung with green bananas to ripen, and vegetables of different kinds. A full supply of limes, oranges, and other tropical fruit was also laid in. A part of our upper deck or promenade was monopolized with bird cages containing hundreds of every color and variety. The main deck had its share of baboons, gazelles, monkeys, and parrots. It was a menagerie in itself, and it required at first strong nerves to accustom one's self to the chattering, chirping, singing, and other vocal sounds of such a mixed tribe. Little by little they, like passengers at the outset of a voyage, got quieted down, and were rather a source of amusement than an annoyance.

I was fortunate in obtaining a large and airy cabin, or state-room, to myself, which made the long passage more supportable, as most of our passengers were suffering from debility on account of the climate, or from the effects of fever. I was still a martyr to the African boils, but recovered from them as soon as we reached cooler latitudes. One of our passengers, whom we took in at San Tomé, died before reaching here, and his remains were thrown overboard. It was the result of prostration caused by long residence in an enervating climate.

Our supplies of all kinds were abundant, but a bad Portuguese cook was a source of vexation to all; for in no position is the exercise of the culinary art more desirable than on shipboard, where travellers are deprived of their usual exercise, and the stomach and digestive organs are most sensitive.

Our passage to Porto Praya, one of the Cape de Verdes, was a fair one, say nineteen days, but a delay of five days, taking in coffee and sugar, caused me the loss of the English steamer, which would have taken me direct to Portugal in seven days. The disappointment was great, as the strong trade winds from the north-east were blowing, making a prospect of another twenty days' sailing; it must be submitted to, however, as in these parts of the world we cannot choose our conveyance and embark when we please, as in the United States.

Porto Praya has hitherto been the naval station for the American cruisers; and although a small town, situated upon a high, arid bluff, with bleak and dreary mountains in the background, it has its redeeming qualities in fruitful palm, banana, and coffee groves in the valleys, which induced the American officers, after a long cruise in the scorching climate of the coast, to call it the paradise of the African station.

Porto Grande, or St. Vincent, our next island, possesses an excellent harbor, of great size. Here we found a steamer coaling for China, and another for Java. The English have large coal yards here, and the iron launches and little tug steamers give every dispatch, quite like England. The contrast between the energy of the races could be seen at a glance.

As I apprehended, the strong head winds, which we could not resist, have carried us to the west, and we found ourselves short of coal, and our supplies so much reduced that we made for the Azores. It is, however, worth the delay of a few days to visit this beautiful and highly cultivated island. Its population is dense, and exceedingly industrious. The town of Punta Delgada contains twelve thousand inhabitants, is well built of stone, its streets well paved, is favorably situated in a rainy latitude, and produces most exuberantly. The exportation of oranges to England keeps a large number of vessels employed during the fruit season. The Quintas, or estates of the nobility which I have visited, are magnificent, and would not disgrace the parks and gardens of some of the small princes of Europe. The immense variety of flowers in bloom, the fountains of water, the close cultivation to the very summit of the hills upon this isolated spot, and the general amount of production rather took us by surprise, particularly as our last port, St. Vincent, was entirely barren, with scarcely a sign of vegetation; and the time before, when we touched there on our way to Brazil, some years since, we landed famine supplies, as half the population had died from starvation.

Our prospects now are for an early arrival in Lisbon, and I hope in the course of five or six days to be in direct correspondence with Europe and America, and shall rejoice in having accomplished a long and perilous African trip, without any desire to repeat the same.

## THE END.

Milton Keynes UK
Ingram Content Group UK Ltd.
UKHW041921151124
451262UK00007B/1129